NORTH AFRICAN PRELUDE

1550 - A MAP OF AFRICA

NORTH AFRICAN PRELUDE

THE FIRST

SEVEN THOUSAND YEARS

BY GALBRAITH WELCH

Member of La Société de Géographie

Author of THE UNVEILING OF TIMBUCTOO

GREENWOOD PRESS, PUBLISHERS
WESTPORT, CONNECTICUT

The Library of Congress has catalogued this publication as follows:

Library of Congress Cataloging in Publication Data

Welch, Galbraith.
    North African prelude, the first seven thousand years.

    Includes bibliographical references.
    1. Africa, North--History.   I. Title.
DT167.W4 1972   961   76-143313
ISBN 0-8371-5969-5

To *JAMES FRANCIS DWYER*

In whose good company I have traveled from Morocco to Egypt,
and from the Mediterranean to the Niger

CONTENTS

MAPS

The map facing the title page is from the 1550 edition of Sebastian Münster's "Cosmographia," and is used by courtesy of the New York Public Library.

FOREWORD

NOTWITHSTANDING ALL THE BOOKS WE POSSESS THERE IS AN AS-
tonishing gap which this book is intended to fill. Odd though
it seems there exists no other book either in English or French
dealing with the past of all North Africa through the years.

North Africa is therefore at once one of the oldest subjects in
the world and one that is entirely new. History was born in
North Africa. Her traditions are as ancient as man's memory.
She lies at the doorstep of Europe and—as the airplane flies—in
America's front yard. Her future promises to be involved vitally
with our own. Yet there has been no book available giving a compact idea of the interwoven history of Africa from the Atlantic
to the Red Sea, from the Mediterranean down across the Sahara
to the Niger.

This peculiar deficiency troubled me some twenty years ago
when first I started to travel deeply into Africa. Since then I
have covered many thousands of miles across the country with
which this book deals, crossed the Sahara and ridden by the
Niger and the Nile. No one in these uncertain days could dupli-
cate my African wanderings. For my own satisfaction I collected
a mass of literature on Africa—some of it exceedingly rare and
hard to find—classical; medieval Arabic, Hebrew, French and
Portuguese; and modern, and spent the intervals between African journeys in African study.

Often I dreamed of attempting such a book as this one, but
hesitated before a formidable piece of writing about a subject
unfamiliar to the general public.

Then came a morning in the autumn of 1942 when we read

an astounding announcement: American and Allied troops had landed in Africa. Africa suddenly became news, world news, the scene of a great universal conflict as she had not been since the Punic Wars. A few days later I began this book. It has taken me nearly six years.

Whatever its defects it has at any rate no competitor. And I have in addition to long familiarity with the subject one other qualification in that, as an American citizen, I belong to a country which has not dealt in African colonies. Thus I see Africa without prejudice, as a European could not do.

No one can doubt that Africa's future, perhaps more than that of any other part of the world, is aquiver with uncertainty. A knowledge of her past will help us to understand whatever may happen. I have thought of my book as the story of her *Prelude*. To what? . . .

*   *   *

Since I have no predecessor to emulate I have had myself to invent the pattern, a responsibility and a privilege not that of the historian of other parts of the world. It has been for me to decide what to include in my space limits and what to emphasize.

Seven thousand years and a stretch of country big enough for all Europe to rattle about in is a large subject. The mass of material at my disposal—Egyptian inscriptions; Greek and Roman writings; medieval Arabic, Hebrew, Portuguese, French; modern English, French, German, Spanish; American and English and French war records—is immense.

A pageant, romantic, gorgeous, bloody and bloodcurdling, exalted and tender, fantastic, exotic, comical, lustful, from the past of some seventy centuries crosses a vast strange land to crowd and push for place upon my pages:

Antique Egypt's solemn majesty and humiliations. The wonder tales of mythical Africa when pagan gods hunted across its wastes and made love, and rumors came from the hinterland of monstrous men and weird animals.

The gold and greed and greatness of Carthage. The Greek colonists with their mysterious silphium. The pomp and downfall of Rome. The coming of Jewish refugees to proselytize. The tribulations and triumphs of early Christianity. The garish Vandals.

The drive of Mohammedan conquest from Egypt to the Atlantic and over to Spain. The envenomed mad heroism of intersectarian Moslem strife. The glitter and cruelty and lechery of medieval Africa under its shifting despots.

The Sahara's terrors, golden trade and hidden cities in the old days when the desert (except for the Nile) was the only road to the South.

The fierce years of Christianity's attacks, when Roger of Sicily, St. Louis, Charles V and Don John of Austria ripped at Africa's shores. Henry the Navigator's sailors creeping along the Atlantic coasts, peering into the desert and up rivers, and fetching home natives to save their souls and wreck their happiness.

The wide-flung Negro empires by the Niger. The pitifully marooned Christians up the Nile. The fanatical leaders who swept across the land with sword and Koran.

The courage and hideous cruelty of Corsair days. The modern return of the Christians: Napoleon's venture in Egypt, Gordon at Khartoum, the French adventures with Abd-el-Kader. The struggle of brave colonists seeking to domesticate a harsh and hostile country. Modern international diplomacy's tricks and travail on the African terrain: "Incidents" at Fashoda, Tangier, Agadir.

The conquest of the Sudan—East and West—and the last terrific native struggles of The Mahdi, El Hadj Omar, Samory. The exploration and subjugation of the Sahara, the pacification of its Veiled Men and the start of modern travel across its wastes.

And finally the tremendous arrival of the United States and Allied troops on Africa's coasts in 1942 and what they did there.

I could fill a work as large as the Encyclopaedia Britannica with Africa's past. But I remind myself that everybody is not so much interested in Africa as I am! So reluctantly, as I planned this book, I drowned many of my litter of beloved historical kittens. The choice of survivors has been my hardest task. As for the method of presentation, I have thought that—given the novelty of the subject—it would be preferable to tell fully about the best rather than to attempt to tell a little about everything. By "the best" I mean those passages which carry forward the narrative of Africa's past and give a vision of her peoples.

Furthermore I have devoted less space to phases of Africa's history about which an ample literature already exists, such, for instance, as antique Egypt and modern Egypt, the Punic Wars, the highly creditable civilizing work of France, England, Spain and lately Italy, and the events of the Second Great War. On the other hand I have given space to aspects about which it would be difficult, almost impossible, for the average student to inform himself. I have dwelt on the Middle Ages both for this reason and because that period was Africa's Golden Age. I have given space to the history of the Sahara and the Sudan. To read of the culture and civilization of the African Negro in the Niger region in medieval times will be astonishing to most people.

Another effort which has been made is to explain geography more fully than does the historian who deals with territory familiar to his readers. In fact I have thought of my work as being of necessity one of Geo-History, if I may invent the term.

*   *   *

OFTEN WHILE WRITING I HAVE RECALLED THE STATEMENT OF THE learned Sir Arthur Helps, "I generally find that I gain most from those books which presume the reader to be most ignorant." There is no shame, let me insist, in being ignorant about the history of North Africa. It is the common state of almost all of us. Probably the average well-educated person would be hard put to mention the names of a bare dozen historic figures of North African birth, even given the easy start of Cleopatra and Moses.

Being aware that the story I have to tell must introduce many unfamiliar personal and place names and many novel customs and points of view, I have simplified whenever possible, and have often used a typical authentic anecdote to forward the tale. These I have culled from the best sources available, contemporary in most cases: from the classics, from Arabic authors, from native traditions and from the records of explorers.

In the use of anecdote to forward the tale I take as model and justification glorious Herodotus (toward whom I look as an ant blinking at the sun) who first invented a way of making far places vital and clear to his readers, and who did not forbear—all in maintaining his historic scheme—to grasp attention at the start by choosing the experiences of a naked woman as subject for the first big episode of his opening chapter, to tell good tales throughout, and to finish with an incident of wild and fiendishly cruel sex jealousy.

*   *   *

LET ME CONCLUDE THIS LITTLE NOTE WITH A FEW WORDS ABOUT spelling and about the borrowing of books.

There are in use a great variety of English spellings to render the Egyptian, Greek, Arabic and other proper names which I shall be mentioning. I have chosen in each case that form of spelling which seems likely to be the easiest upon the eye and the ear of the reader. Obviously it would be inconsiderate to use in a book of this kind such erudite forms as Qoran for Koran, Kleopatra for Cleopatra, or al-Qayrawan for the holy city of Kairouan. I have followed no rule or system, except to try for easy reading. My aim has been to smooth the reader's way amongst Africa's many odd names rather than to display what knowledge I may have by being complex or rigid.

I have also sought to keep the wanderings and alterations of place names as clear as I can. An odd complexity in African geography is that during the ages many names have completely changed their associations. A perennial name like Libya, for instance, once applied to all Africa except Egypt (which in the very old days was regarded as a part of Asia). Even as late as the seventeenth century you can find Libya used as synonymous with Africa. Lately Italy seized on the name for its Mediterranean colony. The name Africa, on the other hand, meant only what we call Tunisia. Mauritania which is now applied to a section of the western Sahara was once what we call Morocco and western Algeria. And so on. Ethiopia is a name which has been a veritable tramp, cropping up all across Africa and in Asia too.

*   *   *

AS TO THE BORROWING OF BOOKS, I EXPRESS MY HUMBLE APPRECIATION of the generosity of the American reference library system. Long an expatriate from my country I found myself during the years of World War II at home again and temporarily separated from my own large collection of African material just when I wished to start writing this book. The readiness of American reference libraries to confide valuable and rare books to a student astonished me. The words of the librarian of one southern university are worth writing in gold: "It is better to risk the occasional loss of books than not to have them read." I wish to thank for special courtesy the Library of Congress, Duke University Library, the University of North Carolina Library and the Sondley Reference Library of Asheville (whose collection of classical material was surprisingly full, given the relative smallness of the city in question). In Europe I have at times read at the British Museum and the Bibliothèque nationale reading rooms, but only by my own friends, La Société de géographie of Paris, have I ever in Europe been entrusted with books to read at my own home. The American reference library system, as I have benefited by it, is typical of a generous and confiding nation.

Another word of thanks I owe to the devoted neighbors at our home in Pau, France, who voluntarily cared for my large collection of rare books and manuscripts on Africa during the wartime enemy occupation of the country and returned everything to me safe when I returned after the war's end. In secreting in their houses American property of this delicate sort they took considerable personal risk. But for their act of courage I should not have felt competent to complete my work.

G. W.

BOOK ONE

WHEN OUR WORLD WAS YOUNG

GEOGRAPHY AND HISTORY

NORTH AFRICA'S CONTOUR HAS SHAPED HER DESTINY. GEOGRAPHY has been her master. The country from the Red Sea to the Atlantic, from the Mediterranean to the Niger is an oblong of territory such as does not exist elsewhere in the world. It contains the world's greatest desert—bigger than the whole United States—and this desert has been no mere negligible tract of wasteland. The Sahara has been a mighty constructive influence.

Between the Mediterranean and the Sahara runs a thin ribbon of green. From west to east this strip makes up the habitable portions of the countries of Morocco, Algeria, Tunisia, Tripolitania and Cyrenaica (these last two lately retitled Libya by the Italians). It is a jagged strip some twenty times as long as it is broad which runs between sea and sand. The politics, trade and all the development of its inhabitants have been affected by this peculiar geographical shape.

To the east lies Egypt, "the most splendid of the Sahara's oases," stretching along the Nile, and sand framed on both sides. Here was the hothouse of history.

Beyond the Sahara to the south is Negroland, the western Sudan. Up the Nile, another Negroland, the eastern Sudan to which in recent years was given the name of the Anglo-Egyptian Sudan.

The Great Desert has been North Africa's protector and her

jailer. When humanity was young the Sahara was the white race's belt of chastity. But for its impassable stretches vigorous, fecund Negroes could have swept up from the tropics and swarmed over Mediterranean white Africa, crossed to Europe perhaps. But for the Sahara we might all be mulattoes today. The Sahara enclosed Egypt in an incubator where infant civilization could grow up in safety. The Sahara shoved Mediterranean Africa almost into the sea and hampered normal development. The Sahara has been one of the greatest impresarios of history.

*   *   *

IN NORTH AFRICA HISTORY WAS BORN. FOR SOME SEVEN THOUSAND years it has sheltered people sufficiently civilized to leave records behind them. During this time North Africa has experienced every sort of adventure which has been offered and inflicted on man.

The novel horror of a horse-drawn vehicle wrecked Egypt in the days of the Hyksos; Sherman tanks chased Rommel's Afrika Korps across the sands.

Fighting foreigners—North Africa has known them in uncountable numbers from the Shepherd kings to Eisenhower. Invaders, conquerors, men who used Africa impersonally as a ground to fight upon, even some few of benevolent intention whose fight was to save Africa's soul. The pillaging Assyrian, the heat-maddened epileptic from Persia. Alexander the Great, Caesar, Augustus. Zenobia who put her lovely face on Egypt's coins. Lame Genseric with his Bible aloft, the eunuch general, Solomon. Sidi Okba and his magic horse. Noble Saladin whom even the Christians loved. St. Louis to whom the Africa for which he hankered spelt tragedy: first chains; twenty years afterward, death. Barbarossa of the scarlet beard and the silver false arm. Visionary Henry the Navigator, ambitious Charles V, Napoleon, Decatur.

The black tyrant from the south, Samory, so arrogant that his name—like that of a mystic god—must never be spoken aloud. Père de Foucauld, the martyred hermit of the Sahara, Faidherbe of Senegal, Joffre of Timbuctoo, Lyautey of Morocco. Eccentric Gordon and grimly efficient Kitchener. Montgomery with his familiar beret and Patton with his famous pistols.

They all came to North Africa to fight in their different ways, came from the Near East, from all South Europe, from England

and America, from Australia and India and little Pacific Islands, from Germany. . . .

To only one other place have so many foreigners flocked. North Africa has been an Ellis Island through the ages—a grim Ellis Island. North African ground holds many foreign bones.

Foreign faiths too are buried there. Egypt's own mighty and grotesque gods and the primitive idols of her African neighbors were supplanted by a procession of imported gods. Phoenicians brought the god who delighted to sniff at the burning flesh of sacrificed infants. Greece and Rome brought sleek-limbed suave gods to beauteous temples. Doul Karnein (a manifestation of Alexander the Great) was venerated. Jealous Jehovah came. The compassionate Christ. Finally Allah, in the name of whose various sects how many million Africans have given their lives! Allah survives.

*   *   *

THROUGH ALL THIS AND MUCH MORE OF WHICH THIS BOOK WILL try to give some notion North Africa has passed. Yet of all the lands on earth her future seems likely to show us the greatest surprises.

Anything could happen in Africa. Africa despite her immensely long historic past is still young and capable of all the caprices and unpredictable behavior of youth. Unlike the other continents her possibilities are still before her. This again is a matter of geography, of that great desert which—if transformed by science— could revolutionize everything. Her people too seem fresh and untired for all their mighty history. The future of the other continents seems clearer and more certain: their lands and their peoples have shown us their potentialities. It is not hard to foresee what lies ahead of brilliant, strong, precocious youth, or of bravely struggling middle age, or of that time-ridden old woman who now and then—corseted and painted—darts out of her disordered house to recapture for a little while the conquests of her girlhood. By this last I mean Asia; that the other metaphors refer to America and Australia, and to Europe is evident. But for Africa I can find no figure of speech. We have seen only her Prelude.

OLD EGYPT'S LITTLE WORLD APART

THE HISTORY OF ALL NORTH AFRICA IS INTERTWINED IN THE fashion in which a hammock is woven. As we look back across the ages we see that at times its various sections were tied closely together. Then comes a period where we see great gaps in the fabric, Africa's peoples like folk on widely separated islands, islands remote from one another both in physical contacts and in degree of civilization.

The most striking of all the many gaps in the weaving is that which separated Egypt from the rest of the continent in remote antiquity. Egypt's culture was not shared with Mediterranean Africa. But Egypt's records have something to tell us of the vigor of these savage neighbors when at times they struggled across the hard road between sea and sand to crash at Egypt's gates.

On the whole Egypt was a miniature world apart, saved from interference by its sand stretches. Its climate was good, yet not so perfect as to make for lethargy. It was fertile and lovely to the eye. It was the most propitious nursery Nature could offer to any people. The ancient Egyptians took enthusiastic and competent advantage of Nature's offer.

Thus "the development of Egypt is the longest and most informative of all the panoramas of the past of man," as Sir Flinders Petrie has said, adding a rider—very natural from a man who had spent more than seventy years on the subject—that this panorama is the most fitting subject imaginable for general study. That many have thought as Petrie did is proven by the mass of our literature about ancient Egypt. It is outstanding among the few phases of North Africa's history about which plentiful material exists at the hand of all. On the rest of North Africa's history one must hunt for information in dispersed and remote corners.

It is pleasant to read of ancient Egypt and to picture these wonderful folk rocking civilization's cradle so neatly and so graciously. It is pleasant to imagine their proprietorial satisfaction in the sleek, dark Nile which each year swelled into a benevolent flood and gave them food. One can envy their blissful ignorance of any troubled world beyond their paradise, the tube of the Nile Valley, hemmed between sand dunes.

They were an engaging people, elflike but strong. The average Egyptian of those days, it has been discovered, was a slim person under five feet five, the average woman barely five feet tall, but their limb bones "possessed certain characteristics commonly supposed to indicate great muscular strength." They were deft with their hands and craved to have nice and beautiful things. They wove linen, made pretty blue glass beads and the like back at a time when the ancestors of most of us were living in clumsy and sodden ugliness. They were clever and inventive in larger ways, thinking out such devices as the building of portable wooden houses which at flood times were moved into the dry desert, and back again into the green plain when the floods subsided. They designed excellent boats. A gay little picture, which we are informed is the earliest known painting in the world—it was done in water colors on the wall of a tomb at Hieraconpolis—represents a fleet of half a dozen of these tidy ships, with cabin amidships and rudder.

Perhaps most significant of the racial mood are those whimsicalities of the ancient Egyptian. He performed those comical little acts that indicate an untroubled life, such as the ceremonial burying—its grave has been unearthed—of a pet duck in a coffin large enough for a man.

Life was joyful and so it was ultraprecious. It was natural that, as their civilization grew and they became more thoughtful, they should have sought to convince themselves of immortality and should have shored up their hopes with elaborate ritual. To die with complete finality and leave Egypt forever would have been too tragic. Therefore the Egyptians, as Herodotus says, "were the first to teach that the human soul is immortal."

So in a triple way the wonder story of Egypt is a gift from the Sahara. The desert protected Egypt's infant civilization from attack. Its dry climate and its packing of sand saved ancient records for us. And the realization that they lived in such a preservative climate presently inspired in the ancient Egyptians a peculiar longing to gain posterity's good opinion, with its associated benefits in the afterworld, by a painstaking setting down of all that happened.

EGYPT'S FIRST GREAT HERO

THE FIRST KING OF EGYPT'S THIRTY DYNASTIES WAS MENA, alternately spelt Menes. There were kings in Egypt before him, but his name heads the official dynastic list which has become the basic arrangement for Egyptian history.

The First Dynasty opened at a date which has been variously placed from about 5500 B.C. to about 3300 B.C. (Detail upon the divergent opinions on the dating of events in very early Egyptian history will be found on a later page.) It corresponded in a general way with the consolidation of Upper and Lower Egypt into a single nation, destined to endure uninterruptedly from then till now. Egypt has been often conquered and occupied, but never truly destroyed, never unimportant in the world. Egypt's prestige seems to be deathless.

Possibly the accomplishments of several kings were put to the sole credit of Mena, the traditional first king, in order to give national history a good send-off. Certain relics from the dawn of the First Dynasty have been discovered. One of these is an ebony tablet which shows Mena himself. He is represented as offering libation and holds a basin or tray in his two outstretched hands. Above and below and beside him are animals, boats and a quantity of hieroglyphic symbols. As a portrait capable of giving one any notion of what the great king looked like it is useless. Another relic of this general period shows a king ceremonially turning up the first hoeful of dirt for a new canal. An especially treasured item is the famous green slate palette (a sort of tray) whereon is carved the kingly figure, arm upraised to smite a kneeling victim, plus a row of already executed persons, each with his severed head between his feet. Another treasure is the macehead upon which is shown the king on an elevated platform surveying the results of a mighty victory. There had been taken 120,000 men, 400,000 oxen and 1,422,000 goats. The macehead gives sample men, oxen and goats together with symbols indicative of the respective numbers.

The last two royal portraits are attributed to one Narmer, who was perhaps the immediate predecessor of, or perhaps identical with, one side of the personality of the traditional Mena.

Mena is said to have founded the capital, called "The City of the White Wall," later named Memphis. The great adventure of pyramid building was not his, but came some centuries after his time. The opening experiment was what is called a step pyramid. Then came the first true pyramid which was erected some forty miles south of modern Cairo.

Mena is said to have reigned for sixty-two years and to have been an athlete to the very end. His adventures come down to us: how he went hunting with savage dogs who turned on him and might have killed him, but Mena plunged into a lake and rode safely across to the other side on the back of a crocodile. His final hunting exploit was fatal. He was killed by a hippopotamus. Since he reigned for sixty-two years he must have been a very old man to be out on a wild animal hunt. It is suggested that the story may be interpreted not as proof of Mena's prowess in old age, but as conveying a criticism of him. The hippopotamus of the legend may have been an avenger sent by the gods to destroy Mena.

One charming item in the Mena legends is that it was he who invented that mode of eating dinner in a reclining position which became one of the most luxurious elements of the antique social scene.

Mena is the very earliest secular personage known to us in intimate detail. (Adam in some computations goes back two hundred years before the earliest date that could be assigned to Mena.) Mena is genially known too, and his name is still in everyday use close to the capital he founded, for it was adopted by Mena House, the renowned hotel beside the Sphinx and the Pyramids of Gizeh.

It is a favorite diversion to wish that the famous folk of old could see the happenings of today. It would unquestionably have been a delight to King Mena if he could have seen the hotel bearing his name in the autumn and winter of 1943 when an American president, a British premier, a great Chinese, a prominent Turk and others met there for war talks, and Mena House was mentioned in newspapers all over a vast round world that Mena himself had never dreamed of. Mena, with the ancient Egyptian's intense longing for posthumous fame, would have been deeply gratified.

This imaginary reconstruction of Mena's psychology is not frivolous. It is intended to illustrate the miracle of Egypt. These people craved immortality far more wholeheartedly than did any other race. The craving animated their lives. Their palaces and homes were ephemeral, their tombs of far greater moment. Their performances and virtues were to be recorded so that men to come would know of them and speak well of them in prayer, which would work to their advantage in the afterworld. Memorial constructions—monuments uncountable, temple inscriptions, statues, etc.—having for motive to court the good will of posterity, appear to have been a main, perhaps the main royal preoccupation. Unquestionably it was done to gain the high opinion of people yet unborn.

One king who came to the throne late, the aged son of a near-centenarian father, Ramses II, was in such a panic lest he die without adequate monumental work in his own honor that, in order to get building material in a hurry, he demolished the lovely temple of a predecessor of his, but a century and a half dead. Down came "a temple which was one of the most magnificent things on which the sun ever shone," whose floors were inlaid with silver, whose statues were encrusted with gold and jewels, whose very flagpoles were adorned with electrum (silver and gold mixed). Such vandalism, given the motive, did not intolerably shock contemporary opinion. The old king could not risk going to the afterworld without suitable monumental advertisement. The fabric of ancient Egyptian life had as a constant pattern the wish to consolidate, by boasting and explanation, the individual's standing in the hereafter.

Now it is beyond us to say how the Egyptian fared in the afterworld. But in the matter of gaining posterity's interest and sympathy his success has been prodigious, almost miraculous.

Here we see a busy world thousands of years later studying the minute details of Egypt's past with an avidity rarely given to the more recent and more closely related pasts of other nations, nations which are our neighbors. You have only to go to the ordinary town library to prove this.

THE ROSETTA STONE

SOME NOTION OF THE DEEDS OF MENA AND HIS SUCCESSORS HAS come down to us in the hieroglyphic, or sacred writing which

Egypt developed for monumental purposes. The Egyptian desire to tell posterity what she had accomplished in more detail than would have been possible by mere carved or painted pictures bred the science of writing. Egypt's autobiographical urge fathered the alphabet. In old Egyptian the letter *A* was a bird, *B* was a leg up to the knee, and so on. Presently a simplified system called "hieratic" was developed. This could be written with facility and was used for the ordinary business of life. Much later a form of writing which could be used with rapidity was worked out. It rendered the language of the times and was called "demotic," the people's writing. Hieroglyphic writing continued in use for ceremonial purposes and still employed the archaic Egyptian tongue of the old days.

Much of what Egypt wrote in her various scripts survived, but it would have taught us nothing except for a lucky find and a lot of ensuing hard work. The find was made by members of the party which accompanied Napoleon into Egypt. In itself it was not an impressive or handsome object, being a block of syenitic basalt, three feet one inch high, by two feet five inches broad, and of irregular thickness, varying from six inches to a foot. It was the famed Rosetta Stone, one of the treasure discoveries of all times, the most valuable single document in existence. Upon this stone was carved the same statement in hieroglyphs, in the "people's writing," and in Greek. Thus by comparison the secret of hieroglyphic writing was solved.

It took twenty-odd years of study to penetrate the hieroglyphic code as displayed upon the Rosetta Stone. But when the work had been accomplished the translation of Egypt's many inscriptions— till then a complete puzzle—was possible and the scientific study of Egypt's past began. Its very difficulty lured men on: the tremendous effort of digging out the various objects on which inscriptions were recorded, the tremendous effort of deciphering them. Had Egyptology been easy, it might have been neglected.

As to the message inscribed upon the Rosetta Stone itself it contained nothing of dramatic interest. Its words vaunt with the usual sycophantic reiteration the pseudo greatness of a boy king, not one of the Pharaohs of old, but a Ptolemy reigning about 200 B.C. It goes into relative trivialities such as mention of the remitting of certain debts, an announcement that the duty on

linen cloth was reduced by two thirds, and that forced service in
the navy was to be discontinued. The stone itself passed into the
hands of the English and was deposited in the British Museum.
Its decoding was a joint job, in which stand out two names:
one English, Dr. Thomas Young, one French, Jean François
Champollion. Thanks to their work and that of their successors,
there has been opened to us man's long record as a civilized,
historically conscious person.

The finding and decoding of the Rosetta Stone was in itself a
part of the near-miraculous fashion by which ancient Egypt attained her desire to be known and remembered.

THE UNKNOWN WEST

THE HISTORY OF NORTH AFRICA IS LOPSIDED. WITH REGARD TO
the Nile Valley our knowledge dips far into the past. As for the
rest of North Africa all is silence and mystery. The people who
lived between the Nile and the Atlantic had neither the talent nor
the inherent self-consciousness of the ancient Egyptians. They left
us no memorials about themselves. Thus, at one and the same
period of time, the definitely historic and the vaguely prehistoric
are side by side. By the Nile was a race of men who had been
fascinated by their own story ever since their earliest mental
awakening and had "devoted themselves to the memory of their
past actions" to such an extent as to become—as Herodotus discovered thousands of years after that awakening—"the best skilled
in history of any men I ever met." The remainder of North
Africa had lived through these years as non-autobiographical as
oysters.

Only through mentions of them in Egyptian inscriptions can
we find out anything definite about the peoples living between
the Nile and the Atlantic during the period previous to that of
the early classical authors. Then at last we have some fragments
of Hecataeus, an invaluable mass of material by Herodotus, etc.

To the Egyptians these people were enemies. They were a great
and recurrent trouble to Egypt and for a time even Egypt's
masters. Naturally Egyptian records give us no gossipy vision of
their home history. The Egyptians' attitude would have been like

that of the colonists who considered that the only good Indian was a dead Indian.

Peacetime contacts between Egypt and the lands lying between the Nile and the Atlantic were almost impossible. For this the Sahara was responsible. We would have to peer back through the fog of prehistory—into those days when the Sahara had not yet become a complete desert—to discern any indication of relationship, other than frontier wars between Egypt and the lands to the westward.

To the Egyptians the peoples to the westward were known as Tehenu, Lebu, Rebu, Meshwesh. They were later known by classical writers as Libyans. They were the ancestors of what we now call the Berbers, the same stock which—broken down by Arab invasions, European and other immigrations and a little Negro blood—now populates Morocco, Algeria, Tunisia and Tripolitania. They were of the white race, resembling South Europeans.

An uncertain quantity of these Libyans are thought to have entered the Delta country of Egypt in remote antiquity, mixing with the Egyptian stock. Some historians believe that the victory celebrated on the famous macehead (see page 8), where 120,000 men plus immense booty in live stock were taken, told about a victory over the Libyans. As to this there is controversy. Professor Breasted says that they were. Mr. Oric Bates, historian of the early Libyans, says that they were not.[1] The colossal figures of their herds as recorded in the booty list—400,000 oxen and 1,422,000 goats—rouses uncertainty in the mind of anyone who knows the desert; one wonders how, if the enemy were Libyans, such a vast animal group got across the sands into or near Egypt.

At all events we have later Egyptian representations of persons who were unquestionably Libyans. For instance Fifth Dynasty captives. These are neat-looking folk, the men wearing short trimmed beards, and a girdle for costume, while the women wear girdles, little drawers and what we might call brassières. A much later representation of Libyans from the Twentieth Dynasty shows both sexes in knee-length kilts and with a cloak draped across one shoulder.

*   *   *

[1] James Henry Breasted, *A History of Egypt,* p. 47; Oric Bates, *The Eastern Libyans,* p. 210 footnote.

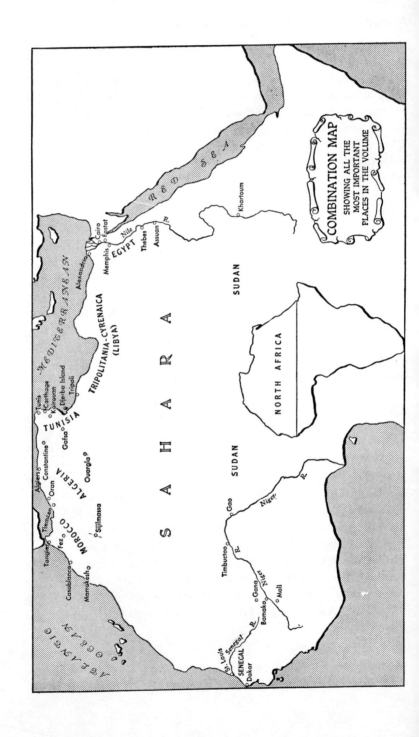

COMBINATION MAP

SHOWING ALL THE
MOST IMPORTANT
PLACES IN THE VOLUME

IN ADDITION TO EGYPT'S RECORDS THERE EXIST TRACES OF PRE-
historic life across North Africa west of the Nile. Notable, for
instance, is the proud position in the vocabulary of prehistory
which Gafsa has won for itself. Gafsa, the Tunisian town, under
its old-style spelling of Capsa, has had a "culture," a stage in the
development of prehistoric man, named after it because—evidently
something of a metropolis in the old, old days—the Gafsa region
contains a treasury of tools and weapons from which students
have formed a typical picture. This distinctive Capsian type of
culture is identified elsewhere in North Africa and "passes into
Spain and southern France and extends into Syria." It is, writes
Professor John L. Myers in *The Cambridge Ancient History*,
"best and earliest represented near Gafsa." The very old and the
very new met when Allied troops fought at Gafsa in the spring
of 1943.

Also notable is the wealth of prehistoric art—engravings and
paintings on stone—which has been found in the Sahara. These
designs represent animals, many of them tropic beasts, and sometimes grotesque humans. The drawing is excellent, though to
modern taste sometimes marred by the emphasized maleness of
the animals and the exaggerated prominence given to the sexual
parts of the humans. Some of these drawings were perhaps made
five thousand years before Christ.

In the Gafsa remains there are indications that the place was
then less arid than now. The Saharan drawings give further and
stronger proof of how completely the climate has changed. Anyone
who has traveled into certain sections of the deep Sahara knows
that it was not always a desert. Its petrified trees are common
landmarks. I recall one big tree prone in a waste of sand between
In Salah and Aoulef; one of its hefty chips is at my hand as I
write.

Whether the modern Sahara is progressively becoming worse
and worse has been a much discussed question. We have not yet
had the opportunity to study the desert over a long enough period
to come to scientifically exact knowledge about this. The general
aspect of the Sahara is no worse today—could be no worse—than
the earliest written reports which have come down to us. The
awesome silence, emptiness and ferociously blazing heat are the
same as when Herodotus told of them. The Sahara as a whole

corresponds with the descriptions of medieval Arabic geographers.

We do know however that certain specific localities have deteriorated. The scientific explorer, Captain Cortier, reported the drying up of so many wells along one of the important trans-Saharan caravan routes to Timbuctoo toward the end of the nineteenth century that the road in question had to be abandoned by camel traffic. And the wonderful medieval city of Gana, of which I shall speak later in these pages, died partly from enemy attack and partly from the attack of the remorseless desert. Where it once flourished is now uninhabitable.

*   *   *

AFRICA'S CLIMATE ALONG THE MEDITERRANEAN HAS CHANGED definitely. Morocco, Algeria and Tunisia were evidently once semijungle. Well into historic times elephants lived in North Africa; and in Morocco there grew those giant trees which supplied wealthy Romans with the so-called "panther tables" carved from a single piece of wood. The biggest of these tables is still famous in furniture annals and so is one of the earliest "antiques" on record. It was known in Rome as "The Nomiana" after its owner, Nomius. It measured three quarters of an inch less than four feet across and was the color of wine splashed with spots, some honey colored, some vivid and darker. The fertility of the country was fabulous in classical days. Strabo tells of grapevines whose girth two men could scarcely compass on which grew "bunches of grapes a cubit (about one foot, nine inches) in size."

THE GODS IN AFRICA

THOSE PICTURESQUE DETAILS OF WHICH WE FEEL THE LACK WERE supplied with enthusiastic generosity as soon as classical authors sensed the suitability of this strip of country as a setting for myth and romance. They turned it into a Land of Legend. The most imaginative of their stories, those they dared not place nearer home or in better known sections, they located in this Shangri-La of antiquity. Across that green coastal strip of Mediterranean Africa tramped gods and mythical heroes.

Here Hercules went a-hunting. At Cape Bon near modern Tunis he struggled with Antaeus, or near Tangier, as some would have it. The body of Antaeus, 60 cubits in length (105 feet) was allegedly dug up near Tangier by a Roman general, who very prudently "offered sacrifices and closed up the tomb again." This from Plutarch's *Life of Sertorius.* The widow of this splendid giant was Tinga, and she became the sweetheart of Hercules. Their son founded Tangier and named it after his mother, a woman of such vigor she had not feared the embraces of two supermen. Across the gap of uncountable centuries we perpetuate the fame of this legendary heroine in our fruit shops. The tangerine orange is named after Tangier, and Tangier was named after her.

Hercules opened the strait between Europe and Africa, but considerately made the passage "so narrow that the great whales could not pass out of the ocean into the Mediterranean." He then set up the hills to either side—one was Gibraltar—"as lasting monuments to his expedition." No one in antiquity called the strait other than his "Pillars" or "Columns." Similarly, desiring to see the desert in a hurry, Hercules opened with a single casual kick the gorges now called El Kantara which lead from the fertile land into the Sahara along the route toward Biskra.

He visited Atlas who held on his shoulders the vault of Heaven and whose name is still worn by the mountains that cross part of the top of Africa. Hercules founded Gafsa and Tèbessa, giving the latter so many gates that its earliest name was translatable as "Of-the-Hundred-Doors." Friends of his founded a city upon the site of modern Algiers. At the Garden of the Hesperides he performed his twelfth and last "labor" by fetching away the golden apples after he had killed the dragon on guard. This garden was reputedly in North Africa. Perhaps it was in what is now Cyrenaica. Perhaps near Tangier. One must not demand exact geography from myths.

But of all the exploits which Hercules performed in this territory the oddest, least creditable and least gallant concerned the legendary Amazons of Africa. We read of them in the history written by Diodorus of Sicily. Their kingdom is vaguely set "in the West," presumably what is now Morocco. Perhaps the thirty thousand female soldiers of Queen Merina in their war dress made from "the skins of vast serpents" trod across much the same country as that of the first American landings in North Africa in the autumn of 1942. These women after a youth of warrior virginity took mates and had children, condemning their husbands to do the housework, whilst—their soldiering days over—they saw to the affairs of state. Hercules, hearing of this unnatural state of society, foamed with rage and forthwith wiped them out, "for it was a thing intolerable to him," as Diodorus writes, "to suffer any nation to be governed by women."

SOME INTERESTING EGYPTIAN PERSONAGES

WHILE THE REST OF NORTH AFRICA WAS FLOUNDERING THROUGH the centuries in unrecorded barbarism with never a defined historic person nor detailed and dated fact to contribute to history Egypt piled dynasty upon dynasty and inscribed her story with care in tombs and temples.

In a book like this one which attempts to give an idea of the whole past of half a continent it is obviously impossible to offer even a skeleton résumé of Egypt's vast history. Rather I shall concentrate upon the careers of a few remarkable personages who seem typical of her ancient glory and grandeur, of her high intelligence and her special way of behavior. Let me tell of the very first famous woman of history, a queen endowed with extraordinary character and brains as well as with that beauty which was a commonplace amongst the royal women of her country. And let me tell of that spectacular king who possessed the peculiar glamor attaching sometimes to a historic figure and making him stand forth to posterity when better men are forgotten. Of his son who perhaps saw Moses and of a few other ancient folk of note.

THE FIRST GREAT WOMAN IN HISTORY

THE QUEEN IN QUESTION WAS HATSHEPSUT, THE WOMAN PHARAOH. She lived about 1500 B.C. and was of the Eighteenth Dynasty, at which period in Egyptian history one can for the first time start to assign even approximate dates with safety.

When I say "with safety" I use the words advisedly. The Egyptian dating dispute is a bitter conflict. Some great authorities have believed in the "long," some in the "short," and some in the "medium" systems as they are formally described. Between certain of the longest and certain of the shortest there is a variation of more than two thousand years as to the fixing, for instance, of the date of King Mena of the First Dynasty.

Nothing could give a more instant and thrilling notion of the immensity of Egypt's past than the fact that there is space across its vastness to put in or leave out at will a term of more than two thousand years, a longer term than the whole span of the Christian Era. It is a solemn thought.

The facts and theories upon which long, short and medium date historians base their beliefs are discussed in *The Cambridge Ancient History*, Vol. I, and in simpler fashion in Dr. James Baikie's *A History of Egypt*. Much detail is presented in highly argumentative fashion in Arthur Weigall's *A History of the Pharaohs*. I recommend study of the question to the scholarly reader who will find it to possess the charm of a novel and erudite detective tale.

As we reach the period of Hatshepsut's immediate forebears we begin to tread, so far as dating is concerned, upon sure ground.

*　　*　　*

HATSHEPSUT WAS BORN INTO THE MOST INVIGORATING TIME OF THE country's whole history, and—as will be indicated presently—of the most exalted parentage imaginable.

Egypt was just on the rebound after a prolonged national humiliation. The country had just expulsed the detested Hyksos invaders. This had been the spirited work of Hatshepsut's great-grandfather. Egypt was still in a mood which mingled exultation at new freedom with fury toward the memory of the despicable enemy. Hatshepsut's own scandalized abhorrence shows in the words of one of her temple inscriptions: "the foreign hordes ignorant of the god Re" (Re, the great sun-god).

The significance of the racial name of Hyksos and where they came from are alike uncertain. Manetho, the famous historian of old Egypt to whom we owe the thirty-dynasty system by which Egyptian history is handled—and hampered!—says that Hyksos derives from *Hyk*, a prince, and *Sos*, a shepherd (a form of derivation which some modern scholars do not fancy). Consequently the Hyksos have been popularly and rather confusingly known by the gentle and romantic name of "The Shepherd Kings," not at all in accord with their ferocious behavior.

"They burnt down our cities and demolished the temples of the gods," in Manetho's words, which come to us via Josephus, Manetho's original text lacking, "and used all the inhabitants after a most barbarous manner; nay, some they slew and led their children into slavery."

As to who they were and where they came from, there are several theories and no proof at all. Perhaps Arabs. Or Mongols. Or folk sweeping down from North Syria. Recently a supposed home town of the Hyksos has been dug up by students of the British School of Archaeology at Ajjul in southern Palestine.

The manner of their invasion horrified and demoralized Egypt. Manetho says the Egyptians were afraid to try battle. The reason was that the invaders had a terrifying new weapon—the familiar story of war! The new weapon, when you consider the circumstances, can be described as the most shocking novelty that ever surprised an army. It meant a complete revolution in fighting. It was the horse-drawn chariot. Both the beast and the vehicle were then unknown in Egypt. Egypt had never seen a wheel of any kind. Men on foot could not compete against such speed and power.

For a long stretch Egypt suffered Hyksos domination. How long the stretch was is a matter of much argument. Sir Flinders Petrie, a confirmed "long date" man, set the period at over five hundred years. Professor Breasted believed it to be but a century. The fact that Egypt during their dominion retained her national pride and will to revolt against the forces of occupation would seem to suggest that the Hyksos period cannot have been so immensely long as half a millennium. But one cannot apply the same standard of psychology to ancient Egyptians which one might use in considering modern peoples. Egyptians had preternatural racial self-confidence and long memory.

At all events the Hyksos period was a dark passage for Egypt of which history knows little.

*   *   *

THEN CAME THE GLORIOUS DAYS OF HATSHEPSUT'S GREAT-GRAND-father, Aahmes, who consolidated Egypt's loathing into a mighty effort and threw the Hyksos out.

Aahmes founded the brilliant Eighteenth Dynasty. The second king after him tore across Asia Minor and put Egypt's frontier on the Euphrates, or—as he himself picturesquely phrased it—"as far as the circuit of the sun." He spoke sincerely according to his lights for Egyptians then believed that the world ended in the marshes beyond the Euphrates, these marshes being bounded by the "Great Circle," the ocean. The name of this conqueror was Thutmose I. He was Hatshepsut's father.

TRIUMPHANT INCEST

HATSHEPUT WAS A WONDERFUL WOMAN. BY THE LAWS OF ANTIQUE Egyptian eugenics she had every right to be for she was completely inbred for three generations from that great pair: Aahmes, "The Liberator" and his wife and half sister, Nefertari. Nefertari, by the way, may have been a partly black woman, born of a Sudanese father. Aahmes was white. The parti-colored couple—if indeed she was a mulattress, which some doubt,[2] were afterward religiously adored in Egypt, most especially the wife who grew to be the most venerated person in all the history of the country. Hatshepsut, therefore, came of glorious stock, and she was able to claim that only through her father's mother was it possible that a drop of blood, other than that descending to her from this revered pair, could have got into her veins. She maintained furthermore that this single dilution had been miraculously averted.

This miracle was the work of Amon, the local god of Thebes, lately promoted to especial prominence because the Eighteenth Dynasty was Theban.

Upon the night when Hatshepsut was conceived Amon, the story runs, substituted for Hatshepsut's father. It was not the usual symbolic divine fathering claimed by Egyptian royalty, but an alleged physical seduction of the most romantic sort. Amon en-

[2] Nefertari, "as the ancestress of the world famous XVIIIth dynasty, was given divine honor, and is sometimes represented with her flesh colored blue-black, like the gods of the Underworld," Baikie's *History of Egypt* II, p. 13. Petrie, *History of Egypt* II, pp. 4 and 9, insists that she "was black," and in one of his last works, *The Making of Egypt* (1939) still sticks to his opinion. A portrait statuette of her shows what might well be a Negro cast of countenance. The Negro strain, if there was one, had vanished by the day of Hatshepsut.

tered the queen mother's chamber on his two feet like an earthly lover, wearing the guise of the queen's husband, the Pharaoh, Thutmose I. She saw the god "in a flood of perfume and light," was fascinated and gave herself in ecstasy to his embrace. Hatshepsut was conceived. The love scene in detail was recorded later by Hatshepsut in her autobiographical inscriptions.

Amon had thus intervened to the end that Hatshepsut's lineage should be undilutedly noble. She possessed but a single pair of earthly great-grandparents instead of the usual eight. And even that pair had been half brother and sister. A series of incestuous marriages, plus Amon's opportune assistance, had kept her family tree as simple as a bean pole.

Incest in ancient Egypt was a virtue. In royal circles it was during a certain period obligatory. Thus was the sacred blood kept pure. The results were not such as we are nowadays led to believe must follow inbreeding. Take, for instance, the Eighteenth Dynasty to which Hatshepsut belonged, and part of whose incestuous processes we have just studied. This dynasty was one of particular brilliance and vigor, and physically seems to have been of good standard. Indeed in the complete sweep of ancient Egypt's history we see "only one solitary example of a deformed Pharaoh" (Thutmose IV, see Baikie, *The Amarna Age*) and we meet only one notoriously eccentric or ill-balanced Pharaoh (Ikhnaton).

The cynical suspicion that Egypt's queens may have operated against the effects of inbreeding by being unfaithful to their husbands can probably be ruled out: supervision of the heir producer would have been strict. The reason why Egypt's inbreeding escaped the penalties we consider likely and which even primitive savages appear to dread seems to be unfathomable. Perhaps because all sense of moral turpitude and social obloquy was absent. When a Pharaoh married his sister he felt and the public felt that he had done a pleasant, desirable and inevitable thing.

*   *   *

GIVEN HER INCESTUOUS ANCESTRY THERE WOULD SEEM TO OUR IDEAS reasonableness in what happened to Hatshepsut. She had a great deal of trouble with her relatives. Trouble such as would be inconceivably complex to the modern understanding. I beg the reader's patience for the passage which follows, wherein I offer a summary of her confused and contentious family life. Although a veritable snarl, the story is not without humor.

It was Hatshepsut's half brother who became this masterful lady's dissatisfied husband, and her stepson and nephew (or according to some historians, another half brother) who became her even more dissatisfied son-in-law (an alternate theory being that when widowed Hatshepsut herself was married to this young man). She and these two men reigned off and on together in a tangled fashion, and some historians would have it that her father may have survived into a part of the joint reign. Certainly no woman ever suffered greater domestic trouble.

But Hatshepsut weaved and beat her way through it all, being a woman of exceptional strength of character. In later life she recorded her own romantic version of how she, a female, came to the throne. This was to the effect that in her girlhood, her father, Thutmose I, the conqueror who had put Egypt's frontier "as far as the circuit of the sun," felt that his end was near, called a solemn meeting of the nobles and went through what was practically an abdication in her favor.

His choice of his daughter as heritor was a snub to his son (later Thutmose II) justified by the fact that the youth had been mothered by a lesser wife, while Hatshepsut's breeding, as we have seen, was pluperfect. The intention was that Hatshepsut and this son should marry and enjoy a sort of joint rulership.

But Queen Hatshepsut ignored her husband, except in that she bore him two daughters. Literally she wore the trousers, in such fashion as Egyptian royal costume offered an equivalent. On festive occasions she appeared in male dress. On monuments she would cause herself to be represented as flat breasted and wearing the short loincloth of a man, with cropped hair and the ceremonial false beard shown on Egyptian kingly chins from back in the days of Narmer.

Yet this official hermaphrodite was a truly feminine person. She kept her country in peace over a long reign like Victoria.

Her husband, Thutmose II, presently died and it has been suggested that Hatshepsut may have procured his death. "His body, as may be seen at the present day. is covered with small tubercules or eruptions. . . . Personally I feel rather disposed to regard his death as due to poison," writes Arthur Weigall. Others, basing opinion upon the gruesome 3500-year-old corpse, consider his death was due to some virulent disease.

Another Thutmose survived, a child who had been born of a concubine, either to Hatshepsut's late husband or to her father. Hatshepsut, as a convention, associated this youth with herself upon the throne as Thutmose III, and—as has been mentioned—caused him to be married in due time with her own daughter (his half sister or niece). Alternately it is suggested (Breasted) that Hatshepsut may have gone through a form of marriage with the child herself.

However it may have been, it was Hatshepsut, and Hatshepsut alone, who reigned, while Thutmose III bit his fingers. His frustration must have been almost unbearable, for he was a soldier born, boiling to lead men to battle. When, after years of waiting, he succeeded to sole power, he plunged Egypt into war and never halted in his career of spectacular conquest until he died. Another expression of his frustration is to be seen in an odd act of vandalism. He ordered the mutilation of many autobiographical inscriptions recording the overshadowing greatness of the late Hatshepsut. This has embarrassed students and muddled our understanding of some of the details of Hatshepsut's career. Its broad outlines, however, are preserved in many inscriptions which escaped or have been salvaged.

THE "LAND OF CINNAMON"

THE MOST INTERESTING EVENT IN HATSHEPSUT'S CAREER COMES TO us in detailed form upon the walls of the temple of Der-el-Bahri (Thebes). This event was an effort typical of a female sovereign given to peace, national development and beauty. It was also one of the most romantic episodes in all Egypt's ancient history, being an elaborate naval expedition to go direct to Punt, the "Land of Cinnamon," to fetch perfumes and exotic objects for the embellishment of the sacred premises of Amon.

Punt (Somaliland) is the native country of the trees that yield the bulk of the frankincense used in modern commerce. It was the *regio romataica* of the Latins, because it produced such a profusion of aromatic plants. It was a land reputedly so delicious that sailors could steer toward it by the sense of smell alone—literally follow their noses. To the perfume-adoring Egyptians Punt was a place of mystic wonder. Its other name to them was "God's Country": it was the place from whence in the old, old days they thought their ancestors had come.

Its distance was truly terrific, taking into consideration the travel limitations of antiquity. Nor were the great distance and the tangible dangers of the journey the only difficulties. There was an intangible hazard. Punt was regarded as a boundary strip between the world of the living and that of the gods and the dead.

All this had not prevented Egyptians from procuring the incense which the gods loved. There is record of a land, a cross-country, expedition to Punt as early as the Fifth Dynasty. From such expeditions were brought back not only sweet-smelling things but odd trophies of which the most exciting were certain "dwarfs" (pygmies) which poor little captives were regarded as treasures and taught to take part in festival dances.

Egypt's land route to Punt passed through the country which we now call the eastern Sudan. That part of the Sudan just south of the First Cataract of the Nile had originally been populated by folk similar to the Egyptians. Farther south lived black savages. To the westward desert Libyans. Off and on Egypt had controlled the top part of the Sudan and maintained trade routes across the savage lands. But at those times when Egypt herself was in a weak position the Sudanese country slipped from under her thumb. At such times the Egyptianized population living near the frontier of Egypt proper would, very naturally, drift into closer touch with their dark neighbors to the south. The result was a dusky race, which, however, still had Egyptian ways, dressed like Egyptians and worshiped Egypt's gods. Mention has just been made (see page 21) of how the famous and revered great-grandmother of Hatshepsut perhaps had a strain of this dark Sudanese blood.

The trade gate between Egypt and the southland was Assuan, a market place from the days when men first learned to swap their home wares for strange things from beyond. Its modern name is a variant of what was merely the word meaning market (*Suan*). It became the focus of trade to which came the produce of Wawat (North Sudan) and of Kush beyond. Via Assuan there entered Egypt gold, ostrich feathers, panther skins and ivory, plus the sweet-smelling stuffs from far-off Punt.

To facilitate her southern trade and for military purposes Egypt opened up a channel so that the First Cataract would not stop her ships. This she did as long ago as 2500 B.C. or 4000 B.C., according to whether we take the opinion of short or long date history. A few centuries later these prodigious people had the ability and energy to cut a canal in the rock for this same purpose. The canal was two hundred sixty feet long by thirty-four wide and twenty-six deep. The name of this fine enterprise is a poem. The canal was called "Beautiful-Are-the-Ways-of-Khekure" (Khekure or Sesostris III in whose reign the work was done).

During the black years of the Hyksos occupation the Sudan slipped apart from Egypt, but Hatshepsut's grandfather had invaded its nearer reaches and taken back partial control, which eventually Thutmose III and his son carried deep into the Nile land to the Fourth Cataract.

*   *   *

THE RECORD OF HATSHEPSUT'S NAVAL EXPEDITION TO PUNT IS authentic and beyond dispute. (I mention this because I have referred to a certain muddle in the surviving records of her family relationships.) The carvings telling of the expedition's adventures are detailed and realistic. Even the great variety of fishes shown swimming near the ships of her fleet were correctly observed and have been identified with Red Sea fishes of today.

Five large sailing ships which could also be propelled by oars made up the fleet. Their route was northward down the Nile as far as the ancient canal running east to the Bitter Lakes. The canal left the Nile at a point considerably to the north of where Cairo now stands. Thence the fleet proceeded to the Red Sea and then south and east to the "Land of Cinnamon." It seems to be the first important all-water expedition of which we have detailed knowledge. It is an odd coincidence that the date of its return to Hatshepsut's capital was 1492 *before* Christ, thus matching to a year the date *after* Christ of that brave peacetime expedition which gained the world two continents.

Hatshepsut's delight at the safe return of her adventurers is evident from the record graven in the temple. She attributed the whole project to Amon, her supposed father, saying that the god had asked her to procure aromatic gums and plants for perfuming the temple service. He had wished this done by direct expedition of pious Egyptians instead of by importation via trade routes, in which latter case the objects in question were handled by impure foreigners and also so delayed that the essence was stale. There can be no doubt that when Amon communicated his whim to his earthly daughter his idea fell on willing ears. Hatshepsut was a counterpart of Henry the Navigator who loved to send adventurous men to explore Africa's far shores while waiting at home all a-drool with impatience and curiosity to behold the strange souvenirs they would bring back, to hear the wonder stories they would have to tell.

Hatshepsut's souvenirs were many: growing trees in baskets so that in future Egypt might produce her own incense, living animals of exotic kinds—a giraffe, baboons, panthers—piles of green *ana* incense. These things the queen offered to Amon.

The stories too were many. She heard of folk who lived in conical houses raised on piles and reached by ladders. And of the wife of the chief of Punt, a woman named Aly, who was so fat that the shape of her was quite unrecognizable, and of her young daughter built to scale.

To the lean Egyptian queen and her subjects news of this type of womanhood was amazing. Yet such steatopygous women were, and are still the delight of their mates in some parts of Africa. (Steatopygia, from two Greek words, fat and rump.) "Their thighs are often as large as a man's chest," writes a nineteenth century explorer, and adds that the usual woman would weigh twenty stone (280 pounds). The local conception of feminine charm was jokingly called, and is shown in old prints as "The Hottentot Venus." Evidently a racial characteristic.

Elsewhere in Africa, where this characteristic did not occur, artificial fatness of monstrous dimensions was sometimes produced. A woman who needed two slaves to help her walk was observed by one of the earliest Europeans to write about the territory now known as Mauritania in the western Sahara. He added that one who could not even walk at all was considered to represent "perfect beauty." Such loveliness is the result of forcible feeding when young. Travelers tell of screaming girls rolling on the ground in agony while their nurses oblige them by pinching, whipping and other tortures to swallow quart after quart of milk. Mlle du Puigaudeau had the experience of seeing a once-slim

ten-year-old of her acquaintance turn within a few months into
"a monstrous maggot, milk stuffed and brutalized by fat, who
could scarcely—when she wanted to sit down in the native fashion
—cross her fat little legs beneath her hanging belly."

The "Fatting House" to which girls go for a stay of several
months before marriage is an institution in some parts of Africa.
What in the Victorian age was delicately called post-tuberance was
especially valued, both at home and for export. Slave girls possessing this characteristic were eagerly snapped up for Turkish
harems and a slave trader making his purchases would choose his
human merchandise from the back—lining up the girls and,
irrespective of facial charms, buying the ones "whose persons most
projected beyond that of their companions."

The admiration for very fat women appears to have been one
of man's oldest sexual whims. Amongst the very oldest objects
found in Egypt are small carved figures of immensely large-hipped
and big-bottomed females dating back to about 7500 B.C. They
are thought to represent women of an aboriginal Negro race imported into Egypt as slaves. (By the way, similar little figures have
been discovered in the caves of southern France.) During one
reign sometime following that of Hatshepsut's the steatopygous
form became the local mode. This was, it has been presumed,
because the king himself suffered from such obesity as the result
of an obscure malady, and his family and court tried to imitate
him, or at any rate caused themselves to be so shown in portraiture.

But speaking generally, Egyptians liked their women svelte and
one of the lithest of them all was Hatshepsut herself. She and her
subjects heard with astonishment about the mountainous chief-
tainess of "The Land of Cinnamon."

THE LADY PHARAOH HERSELF

OF THE PRECIOUS THINGS BROUGHT BACK FROM THE EXPEDITION
Queen Hatshepsut evidently withheld some portion from her
divine father, Amon. For the temple story records that, "Her
Majesty prepared with her own hands a perfumed unguent for
her limbs; she gave forth the smell of divine dew, her perfume
reached even to Punt. Her skin became like wrought gold and her

countenance shone like the stars in the great festival hall in sight
of the whole people."

The lush description, approved of course by Hatshepsut herself,
might suggest that Hatshepsut was abnormally conceited. It was,
however, mere official boasting, the usual type of extravagant
phraseology employed by Egyptian royalty. Scarabs mentioned by
Mr. Winlock, who made excavations at Der-el-Bahri, give some
of the titles and tags which Hatshepsut assumed: "Mighty of
Souls," "The Favorite of Two Goddesses," "Fresh in Years," "The
Beautiful God," etc. In records she caused herself to be described
as of her youth in these words: "more beautiful than anything,
her form . . . divine . . . a maiden beautiful and blooming."

As a matter of fact, Hatshepsut had reason to take pride in her
appearance. When not officially masquerading in male guise, she
was a handsome, even a lovely woman, and a very appealing one,
although not ultraseductive and sensuous of face, as were so many
Egyptian queens. Representations of her show a delightful, slight
body, small breasted, graceful, poised with dignity and very feminine. Her face is powerful yet sensitive, lively and intelligent, and
very "taking." She looks to have been just what her career proves
she was: a woman of brains and charm, able to win devoted
friends and to hold her position against incessant intrigue. Out-
maneuvering the males of her family, she held the power which
she asserted her kingly father had bestowed upon her and reigned
from girlhood till her death when she was nearly sixty.

Hers would have been a phenomenal performance for any
woman in any age and in any land, and is especially noteworthy
when we consider that she lived fifteen hundred years before
Christ and in Egypt. I have wondered why the general public is
not familiar with her name. Perhaps she has failed to become
famous because, as yet, no details on her love life have come to
light; and so the world, which dearly loves its historic women to
be lovers, has not been intrigued by her personality. Yet Hatshepsut's greatness is all the greater in that she upheld herself without
being a siren. She was the first important woman recorded in all
the world's history.

LITTLE MAN: BIG TOMB

GRANTING THAT THE LADY PHARAOH HAS NOT ENJOYED FAME equal to her merits, we presently find by compensating contrast two other Pharaohs—males—whose extraordinary renown has been quite above their deserts. These two came close on her heels: that is, within two centuries of her day—and two centuries are but a moment in the mighty stretch of ancient Egypt's history. One of them was Ramses II. The other, Tutankhamen.

Tutankhamen came recently into sudden notoriety quite disproportionate to any accomplishments during his lifetime, because his tomb was discovered almost intact. This discovery, made in 1922 and naturally of immense interest to students, seized the public fancy in a fashion new to the experience of archaeology, a form of scientific activity which works usually without the slightest popular applause. Tutankhamen gained instant and wide celebrity—a half-joking celebrity. You remember the cheap jewelry and ornaments named after him and rushed out by the shops, and how "King Tut" figured in comic drawings. You might wonder what vile element in the man's career caused him to become ridiculous in far foreign lands when more than three millenniums dead and forgotten. That is more to think about than the supposed curse on those who trouble his tomb.

So far as we know, however, Tutankhamen was no villain, not much of a personality at all. History books written before the tomb discovery (for instance, Breasted, 1912 edition) practically ignore Tutankhamen, and his parents-in-law were regarded as the only interesting thing about him.

Tutankhamen had perhaps the most beautiful mother-in-law ever vouchsafed to a man. She was the glorious Nefertiti (meaning "The-Beautiful-One-Has-Come") whose bust is so often reproduced, that long-throated creature with the mysterious smile. Tutankhamen's father-in-law was the outstanding "crank" of antiquity, the eccentric Ikhnaton who attempted to change Egypt's religion and her capital, discarding Amon for a new god, Aton, and abandoning Thebes to build a new royal city at Amarna about three hundred miles to the north, which he called by a name translated as "The horizon of Aton."

In discarding Amon, Ikhnaton snubbed his alleged grandfather, for a second case of Amon's actual physical intrusion into the royal bedchamber had supposedly occurred when Ikhnaton's father was conceived. A snub of more actual danger to himself lay in the fact that he offended Amon's powerful followers.

Neither his new religion nor his new capital lasted much beyond his own short reign. But long after his capital became a deserted ruin it acquired fame because it was there that in 1887 was made a find of vast historic importance: that is, of the so-called Amarna letters.

A peasant woman found them by chance and having, naturally, no notion of their value, sold them for the equivalent of fifty cents, probably considering herself overpaid, for they were merely a number of little clay oblongs with marks scratched on them, and "looked like nothing so much as a lot of stale dog-biscuits." But upon learned study these things were found to be the international correspondence of the Egyptian court of Ikhnaton's period. They told of Egypt's dealings with the kings and rulers of Asia. They were written in cuneiform.

The cuneiform system of writing has been even more difficult for moderns to decipher than were hieroglyphs. Cuneiform consists of little wedge-shaped or arrow-shaped marks which, as Maspero has said, "have the appearance of nails scattered about haphazard." It is difficult to believe, but such is said to be the proved case, that cuneiform was a bastardized form of the quaint and pretty hieroglyphs, the entertaining little hieroglyphic figures of birds and human limbs and so on, having been reduced to straight line images to suit the cuneiform method of scratching upon clay. Cuneiform did have the advantage, however, of producing an easily transportable written message which could stand a lot more knocking about than could papyrus manuscripts. Witness the famous Amarna letters which survived over three thousand years in a ruined and deserted city.

The discovery of the Amarna letters had a value for students far greater than the finding of Tutankhamen's tomb, but the romantic general public was fascinated by the tomb's glittering magnificence.

Tutankhamen was second successor to his father-in-law, the eccentric Ikhnaton, whose innovations were already antipathetic to Egypt. Tutankhamen was obliged to move the royal residence up river to Thebes again, and to change his own name, which had been the equivalent of "Living-Image-of-*Aton*" (the new god) to the equivalent of "Living-Image-of-*Amon*" (the old established god whom Ikhnaton had put aside). His reign was feeble and short. He was verily the little man with the big tomb.

THE COLOSSUS KING

RAMSES II WAS ANOTHER ADMITTEDLY OVERRATED PERSONAGE. No king in all Egypt's thirty dynasties is so familiar to us today. He was "the Pharaoh of Pharaohs." (The word "pharaoh," by the way, is from the Egyptian *Per'o*, the Great-house or royal palace, which got to mean the King's Majesty, the King himself, as in America "the White House" is used synonymously with the President.)

The modern man in the street who knows so few Africans by name has heard of this Ramses. His high repute over three thousand years after his death is because of a rather surprising circumstance. It is because Ramses II possessed a remarkable ability to dramatize himself. No other Pharaoh seemed to understand so well how to build up an exciting and grandiose personality, both in his own times and for posterity. He was a self-advertiser of the first order. Other kings—now forgotten by all but the student—accomplished more than he did in conquest and in administration. But none left so plentiful a supply of gigantic statue portraits, none made such a fuss of his own exploits. Egypt reacted with enthusiasm. A string of ensuing Pharaohs were named Ramses until the word was no longer regarded as a personal name, but was worn as a sort of title. Ramses II had sold his trademark well.

He had glamorous, though not first-class material to work on.

Ramses II was the handsomest man of his day. Pomp came to him early. "From the time that I was in the egg," he boasted in a record of his reign, "the great ones sniffed the earth before me." (This phrase was the customary manner of designating the prostration, nose in the sands.) His father, the narrative goes on to claim, carried the little boy Ramses in his arms to show to the people, announcing his intention of having the child made king immediately, so that he "might see Ramses in all his splendor

while still on this earth." The boy, the story continues, attended
state councils at the age of ten, commanded armies and administered justice in his boyhood—such is the tale of his glorious pre-
cocity which Ramses characteristically caused to be recorded in
the temple of his father at Abydos. It is interesting to learn that
the whole statement was an invention and that Ramses II, instead
of receiving the throne in this gracious and romantic manner,
really grabbed it away from his elder brother, the rightful heir.

Early in his reign this ardent young Pharaoh went into Syria
to battle with the Hittites and their associates. Then occurred the
great adventure of Ramses II's life, the adventure he loved to
remember and gave others no chance to forget, for he caused a
sort of moving picture of his exploit with an explanatory poem
of praise to be graven on the walls of temples, even into the far-off
Sudan.

By a trick of the enemy it so happened that the Egyptian army
was split and of a sudden Ramses found himself isolated and
surrounded.

> He alone by himself; no other with him.
> When His Majesty turned to look behind him
> He found around him 2500 chariots

Not strictly alone: Ramses in his chariot had his faithful shield-
bearer, and at the chariot's side his tame lion clawing loyally for
his master's life. Against the crowding enemy the young king
fought with inspired dash and courage. Chariots overturned before
him. He overrode men and horses. His arrows slew right and left.
At the spectacle the tricked and separated army took heart and
held till reinforcements came. The battle was won. It was the
Battle of Kadesh fought on the Orontes not far from Beyrouth.

Ramses was full of artless joy at his own heroism. And grateful
too. The lion's work was celebrated along with that of his master.
The shield-bearer was rewarded with high honor. And to the two
steeds in the chariot came lasting fame beyond that of all other
horses. "Victory-in-Thebes" and "Nurit-the-Satisfied" they were
called. Said Ramses, "I shall cause them to take their food before
me each day." Their names are still remembered.

*   *   *

BY RAMSES' TIME THE HORSE, WHICH WHEN THE HYKSOS CHARIOT-eers used it in the invasion literally paralyzed the Egyptians by its novelty, was a regular element in their warfare, used with wondrous skill. Egyptians did not ride horseback. They used chariots with pair, chariots built of light material so that a man—if need be—could carry his chariot on his shoulder. Splendid drivers they were, and had to be, for the light chariot bounced always and would tip readily. The charioteer drove standing with one foot on the pole, reins tied round his body and directing the horse by the movements of his loins, so that his arms were free for the management of bow and arrow. Clinging to him with one hand, protecting him with the other, rode his shield-bearer. It was an art learnt from childhood, in which Ramses was evidently highly competent.

*   *   *

BUILDING—OUTSTANDINGLY SUCH BUILDING AS GLORIFIED HIS OWN self—and the gentle arts of love occupied much of Ramses' attention.

He erected remarkable statues of himself. One, the monolithic, granite, 900-ton colossus of Tanis stood approximately 92 feet high. (The figure part of the Statue of Liberty is 111 feet high. The Ramses colossus and its mates are said to be the biggest monolithic statues ever set up.) If the Tanis statue stood on its feet today—it is now in fragments—one could probably catch sight of it from the Cairo to Ismailia railway trains. In Ramses' day it must have been an invigorating sight, a lighthouse of majesty and power giving Egyptians confidence in their government.

As for the tenderer side of his life, Ramses when he died—at perhaps eighty-five or perhaps nigh onto a hundred, authorities differ—had fathered a family of grand proportions. Maspero says, "one of the lists of his children which has come down to us enumerates, although mutilated at the end, one hundred eleven sons, while of the daughters we know of fifty-five." Petrie makes the number of his daughters fifty-nine—of whom three at least were also his wives!—and is of opinion that he probably had a total family of one hundred seventy-six.

Many of these children were survived by the grand old egoist. It was his thirteenth son, Merneptah, who succeeded him.

This prince, by the way, became the hero who first figured in the racy folk tale which is still so familiar in various forms. Herodotus tells how Pheros (Pharaoh) who followed Ramses II to the throne became blind and, being told he would be cured by the use of "the issue of a woman who had never had intercourse with any man but her husband," confidently made trial at home—alas in vain! Finally, after prolonged search, he found a woman who met the standard, recovered his eyesight, married her and burned all the others alive.

* * *

THE DEATH OF RAMSES II MUST HAVE BEEN A PROFOUND SHOCK TO his people. They had known no Pharaoh but him back to the memory of their grandfathers and great-grandfathers. They had lost not *a* king, but *the* king.

His death must also have jolted the already aged Merneptah, who had seen his dozen brothers die off one by one while Ramses still lived on, and probably had fallen into the apathetic belief that the wonderful old man would outlive him too. The elderly prince found himself confronted by a critical period in national affairs, in addition to the worry of having to get his mortuary monument ready in frantic haste, lest he die tombless. (See page 10.)

EXODUS

A CRISIS WHICH IT IS SUGGESTED FELL TO MERNEPTAH TO HANDLE was the escape of the Jews which we call the Exodus. Many students have placed the Exodus in his reign, though the fact that Merneptah's body was buried and has been found on dry land at Thebes does not match the Old Testament as of the pursuing Pharaoh who perished in the Red Sea. However, neither would the circumstance of a drowned Pharaoh seem to match with the death of any other Egyptian king, except the obviously-out-of-the question young brother of Cleopatra, drowned just a few years before Christ. And much else of the Bible story does seem to match with events in the reigns of Ramses II and Merneptah. Egyptian records about the Exodus, as we view it, are lacking.

A discovery made by Sir Flinders Petrie in 1896 contains the earliest known reference to the Jews. This is a triumphant statement wherein Merneptah tells of the accomplishments of his reign and lists amongst these that "Israel is laid waste without seed." This would seem in opposition to the notion that the Exodus took place in Merneptah's reign. His boast of a victory over Israel might seem to presuppose that the Jews had already established themselves in a country of their own outside Egypt. However Petrie himself interprets his discovery, which in his autobiography he calls the greatest he ever made, as supporting the theory that the Exodus Pharaoh was Merneptah.

There are at least three other opinions as to when the Exodus happened. One of these opinions is that the expulsion of the Hyksos invaders (see pages 19 and 20) and the Exodus are one and the same episode viewed from two points of view: that of those who hated a group of foreigners and saw them go, and that of those same foreigners telling how they got away.

Who was the Pharaoh of the Exodus remains one of the most discussed puzzles of antiquity, interesting, as it does, two types of students. A historian of Egypt who is also a man of religion, James Baikie, D.D., suggests that the Exodus narrative of the Bible should not be taken as referring to a single specific event, but rather to a process which "went on at intervals during a considerable period of time." The culminating success of the Jewish escape might have been dramatically rendered in the Old Testament. See Exodus 12:37, 40, 41; 14:7, 10, 16, 23, 28, 30; 15:4, 19, whose penultimate passage tells that "Pharaoh's chariots and his host hath he cast into the sea: his chosen captains also are drowned in the Red sea." (A passage in Judges 11:16 on the same subject is variously translated as Red Sea or the sea of reeds.) Stanley A. Cook, one of the editors of *The Cambridge Ancient History*, makes the very significant remark that it was not until the sixth century B.C. that "the Old Testament began to assume its present form." In other words some five hundred years had elapsed from the latest of the several dates suggested as that of the Exodus. The latest generally suggested date is sometime during the Twentieth Dynasty, 1200 to 1096 B.C., wherein reigned a series of ten Ramseses.

Egypt took no notice of what was so important to the Hebrews and which still forms a part of Christian teaching. It was not until the time of the Ptolemies, a thousand years after Merneptah, that a translation of the Pentateuch came to Egypt and its people read with astonishment about the adventurous departure from their midst of this long-forgotten foreign group.

DEFEAT OF THE WESTERNERS

ANOTHER CRISIS INDUBITABLY CAME IN MERNEPTAH'S REIGN. EGYPT was seriously menaced by invasion from the west. Ever since the early dynasties the desert folk and the Egyptians had bickered. Desert people had even occupied lands near the Nile's triangular mouth, "called Delta," said Strabo, "from its resemblance to the letter of that name." This time it was very serious. A veritable attempt to rob Egypt of her northland threatened. To the familiar neighboring enemy there had joined a horde of others coming from afar "to seek the necessities of their mouths," as Merneptah's record says. Once started on the drive upon Egypt, starvation chased them. They struggled across North Africa's stretches of arid sands. They must take over North Egypt or perish. They had brought along their women and children and herds. It was—or it sought to be—an immigration. Along the road babies were born and women died dreaming of Egypt's green comfort—water, corn. Thirsty cattle smelt the Nile.

Egypt must have sensed that she had grown flabby under the senile rule of the complacent Ramses II who dwelt exclusively on the prowess of his youth, and that she now faced desperate danger under the leadership of another old man who might well have lost his self-confidence through long dull years of waiting for his heritage. Egypt was frightened.

But this new old king, Merneptah, proved a surprise. He blazed with long-suppressed ardor. He led Egypt like a warrior in his prime. He was "furious against the invader as a lion that fascinates its victim." His army was inspired.

The battle was fought on April 15, 1221 B.C., about fifty miles to the southeast of modern Alexandria. Merneptah had planned well. His bowmen slew the enemy for six hours from a distance, possessed evidently of superior weapons and technique, then closed in on them with the sword. The enemy chief, King Meryey, fled so fast that "arrows remained behind him." This picturesque phrase and that describing Merneptah's courage are quoted from contemporary accounts.

The booty was immense. Enemy dead considerable. Here is a part of the tally, also from an Egyptian official statement: (The detail is of especial interest and will be analyzed as offering our best early information about the peoples of North Africa to the west of Egypt.)

Slain
King's children and brothers	6
Lebu	6,395
Shakalsha	242
Tursha	750
Shairdana } Aqayuasha }	1,124

Captives
Total (including Harem of the Chief, 12)	9,376

Booty
Bronze swords	9,111
Weapons	120,214
Horses of the Lebu	115
Cattle	1,308
Goats	x
Metal vases	54
Silver drinking bowls, vases, swords	104
Breastplates, bronze razors, bronze vases: total	3,174[3]

It will be noted that the killed are listed very particularly, both as to races and as to numbers. The numbers were calculated, as was the custom, from adding up bundles of right hands and phalli which had been brought in by the soldiers after the battle and submitted to "the royal reporter" for checking up. Upon the number of such proofs of military prowess men gained advancement in the Egyptian army.

DEDUCTIONS FROM THE BATTLE TALLY

NOW TO CONSIDER THE LISTS WITH AN IDEA OF TRYING TO GET FROM them, plus a few scraps of other available information, some

[3] Taken from Sir Flinders Petrie, *A History of Egypt,* Vol. III.

notion what North Africans of the West were like some three thousand years ago.

First to take the identifying names of the dead. The Lebu, who start the list are the Libyans, the familiar enemy-neighbors of the Egyptians. Theirs is one of the well-known names of ancient geography. You will find it mentioned in two of our oldest books: Genesis 10:13 (spelt Lehabim) and the *Odyssey*. Herodotus claims that the name Libya was taken from that of a local woman—just a slave, some say. Unlikely. So also is the Arabic legend that makes Libya a great Egyptian queen, the granddaughter of the founder of Memphis. Probably we shall never trace the first "Libya."

The changes in geographical significance of the term Libya have been great. In the beginning Libya was a name associated by the Egyptians with the desert marauders who plagued them, and so a name vaguely applied to the unknown westland. Then it became definitely the name of all North Africa except Egypt. Then the name of the whole continent. The word Libya is used as an alternate for Africa as late as the seventeenth century. Recently the name Libya was grandiloquently given by the Italians to their colony, made up of Tripolitania and Cyrenaica and the adjoining desert.

The identification of the other names which follow on the list of slain is harder. These allies of the Libyans are believed by some historians to have been non-African peoples from overseas: Sardinians, Sicilians, Etruscans. Others believe that they were Africans from lands to the west. If the latter theory be true it would represent the debut on the stage of history of the people of what we now call Algeria and Tunisia.

       *   *   *

THAT PART OF THE LIST WHICH DEALS WITH THE BOOTY IS ESPE-cially instructive. Note the mention of Libyan horses. The once-novel Oriental animal had moved farther on its way into the Occident. Not so very long ago the people of Asia Minor had looked with amazement at what they called "the ass-from-the-East." It was only a few centuries since the horse had been the surprise element which conquered Egypt for the Hyksos. Now the horse has already found a home for itself in the semidesert top of Africa just west of the Nile. Presently we shall be hearing of the brilliant accomplishments of the Numidian cavalry yet farther westward.

The "silver drinking bowls, bronze razors" and so on are significant items. Western North Africa was clearly no longer a place of uncouth savagery. Its people possessed sophisticated and elegant trappings.

Mention has already been made of their neat style of dress. A striking additional detail of which we find representation both in the Egyptians' monuments and in their own very old local carvings was a headdress of ostrich plumes. Chiefs liked to wear this headdress. It was evidently the popular habit to paint or tattoo the body. Sometimes these tattooings or paintings showed the symbol of Nit. Nit was the goddess of the Delta country of Egypt and possibly may have been borrowed by the Egyptians from the Libyans, but, as we know of her, she seems a typical product of the wonderful Egyptian religious imagination. She was one of the very old goddesses, mother of Re, the sun-god, and of other offspring—notably two crocodiles and a lion whelp, the latter fathered by Osiris. Yet she was to the gallant Egyptian notion ever virginal!

*   *   *

THE NUMBER OF CAPTIVES TAKEN BY THE EGYPTIANS FROM THE would-be invaders included an item: "Harem of the Chief—12." In this we see an indication of the enthusiastic male sex life of North Africa which later on so impressed the classical writers of Greece and Rome.

This feature of North Africa's social picture greatly interested Herodotus, the first Greek to tell in detail about the people of the West. In fact the Father of History reveled in tales of North African passion and promiscuity. His studies were made on or near the spot—he was for a certainty in Egypt, and may have traveled to the westward—and although his observations were made centuries later than the period we are speaking about they probably give a fair general running notion of local morals.

Herodotus tells that certain of the tribes inhabiting the Tunisian-Tripolitanian region, as we now call it, held their women in common, not troubling to marry, and mingling "like cattle." Another tribe delighted in their sex prowess. (Herodotus names severally the various tribes about which he tells, but it would be of no value to the reader to rehearse these now-forgotten group names. The passages occur in Book IV, called *Melpomene* —pages 176 and 180.) The women of this tribe would wear with pride the record of their sex generosity, "adding a leather ring to their ankle after each love episode." In another and more inland section of North Africa a custom was maintained which one would think might have been useful throughout this free and easy land. This was that when a youth came to puberty the men of the community should assemble, look him over and declare him to be the son of whomsoever he seemed most to resemble.

Herodotus perhaps overcolored his African picture, but there is no question that sex throbbed in the more torrid and less intellectual lands west of the Nile and that extensive polygamy was the custom. To this testify many other classical writers less picturesque and romantic of pen than Herodotus.

THE COMING OF THE COLONISTS

CLOSE UPON THE DEFEAT OF THE LIBYANS ON EGYPT'S FRONTIER a great change came to the lands of the West. Colonists arrived from foreign lands and for the first time we hear of African cities outside Egypt other than fabled Tangier and the cities of supposed Herculean foundation.

It was the Phoenicians who started the colonizing considerably over a thousand years before Christ. The Phoenicians were an old people, though they were children compared to the Egyptians, in so far as available historic record is concerned. But the Phoenicians had something which Egypt lacked: a genius for handling ships. They said, "Our gods taught us navigation," and that the island city of Tyre was in the beginning like a ship and rose and fell with the waves. Phoenicia was a sort of prolonged dry dock, only twenty-five hundred square miles in extent, just a strip of towns and gardens on the sea front to shelter and feed sailors and traders and their families.

Their first colony or trading and reoutfitting post was established on the island of Cyprus. Presently they peppered the Mediterranean coasts with their settlements and even ventured into "the circumfluous ocean," the Atlantic, where they founded that city which has maintained its vigor and identity under a substantially unchanged name longer than any other town in Europe. It was Cádiz which the Phoenicians called Gadir (Castle), varied to Gades by Roman, to Kades by Arabs and Cádiz by Spaniards. It was close to and presently replaced as a trading post—the romantic Tarshish of Old Testament renown, about whose location scholars till recently argued so vehemently, some even thinking Tarshish was a mythical spot like the Garden of the Hesperides.

PURPLE

ONE OF THE PHOENICIAN LURES TO VOYAGE AND COLONIZATION WAS the purple industry. Tyrian purple was one of the glories of antiquity. A mystic value was attributed to the color throughout at least two thousand years. In the tenth century A.D. Constantinople had such confidence in its influence that pregnant empresses —it puts modern teeth on edge!—were expected to reside and bear their children in the so-called Imperial Purple Chamber. "To wear the purple" is still today a phrase connoting majesty.

Phoenicians discovered the process and the first purple gown ever made was given to the goddess Astarte by her suitor Melkarth (the Phoenician equivalent of Hercules) as the price of her favors. The purple dye was found in the head of a little Mediterranean shellfish—just a drop "no bigger than a single tear" in each mollusc. A system which included long boiling produced vivid and beautiful dyes that ran from dark crimson through all the shades of violet and amethyst. No wonder Astarte's head was turned by such a gift. However, Strabo says realistically that the smell of the dye works of Tyre rendered the city very horrid "as a place of residence."

The search for the purple mollusc probably prompted the founding of Phoenicia's first African trading posts. To get the molluscs at their best it was necessary to collect them in autumn and winter. This was too stormy a period for navigation in the days of old. So permanent fisheries were established at which Phoenician ships could call in the summer season.

A NEST FOR HISTORY

THE EARLIEST REAL COLONY IN AFRICA FOR OTHER THAN FISHER-folk was Utica (between the site of modern Tunis and Bizerte). Utica was allegedly founded in 1101 B.C., and well and strongly founded too, for Pliny, who lived in the first century after Christ, states in his *Natural History* that the cedar beams in Utica's great temple were "as whole and entire as at the first day when they were set up 1178 years ago." For some reason which it would be interesting to have explained, the name of the old Phoenician city (said to have meant "the ancient" or "the magnificent") has proved very popular in the United States. One out of every three states possesses a Utica!

The few square miles round ancient Utica became one of those nests which history provides here and there in the world. Things happened there. Vast stretches across the earth never know any events but those of local importance, while to certain little sections, such as the few square miles near Utica in Africa, come piling in through the centuries occurrences that shake the world. Near Utica was Carthage. Near Utica was Tunis. Through the ages of antiquity, through classical days and the times of early Christianity, in the Middle Ages, and now in World War II, these few square miles—scarcely greater in extent than some western farm—have been a focus for truly tremendous movement. A center of power that reached across the world, of wealth and luxurious living that lured the greed of every neighboring nation. The site of scores of immensely important battles. Despite the obvious geographic advantage of the place all this constitutes a fact which provokes some wonder.

THE TYRIAN PRINCESS OF CARTHAGE

CARTHAGE, WHICH FIRST DREW GREAT EVENTS THIS WAY, WAS Phoenicia's most spectacular colony. It was founded in the ninth century B.C. And it was founded by the people of Tyre. This much is undisputed. It is worth telling the legend of Carthage's beginnings in some detail. Let the romantic believe it all, encouraged by the fact that sober modern historians do not invariably scoff at the dramatic story. In its earliest form we derive it from the Greek of Timaeus. Of his narrative only a fragment remains. Justin, the Roman historian, gives the same story at second or third hand, but fully (XVIII, chaps. iv, v). The famous Virgil story in the *Aeneid* is a variation. Here is the basic Timaeus-Justin version:

The King of Tyre, whose name was Mutto (sometimes spelt Mutton and in other ways; it meant Gift, i.e. "The Gift of God") died, leaving his realm to a son Pygmalion and a daughter Elissa, "a virgin of great beauty," later destined to wear the descriptive name of Dido. Pygmalion grabbed the throne. Elissa consoled herself by a love union with her uncle who was the high priest of Melkarth and a man of immense wealth. Pygmalion coveted his money and caused his death. But his crime was vain; he could not find the hidden fortune. Elissa, twice bitterly injured by her brother and heartbroken, prudently concealed her fury while in secret she prepared to leave Tyre forever. Many Tyrians hated Pygmalion and agreed to go with her. Elissa, carrying the treasure and accompanied by these people, left one night.

Their ships stopped at Cyprus and there Elissa, evidently a woman of executive brain, strengthened her group in a pleasant and useful manner. It was an old and honored custom at Cyprus that maidens should at certain festivals give themselves for the night in a form of religious prostitution. Elissa's party arrived at one of these interesting dates. Elissa ordered the amicable kidnaping of some eighty of these maidens ere the sacrifice of their purity had been made and carried the girls away on her ships. Thus children would be assured to her new city.

Then Elissa's fleet sailed on. The legend does not describe her ships. Undoubtedly they were boats with two banks of rowers. The trireme with its three banks was not invented till about a hundred years after Elissa's day. Elissa's ships would have had single masts and sails of linen cloth. They traveled very slowly, making only two and a half or three nautical miles an hour. The Phoenicians had discovered the trick of doubling their progress by navigating at night instead of beaching their ships every sundown as was the old-fashioned way. This was a revolutionary discovery. The polestar by which they steered was called through antiquity by the name "Phoenice" (the Phoenician star).

What was Elissa's route after leaving Cyprus is something else which the legend does not tell. Presumably along the top of the Mediterranean, which according to Stéphane Gsell, the distinguished student of ancient Tunisia, was probably the route followed regularly by the Phoenicians when making for Africa.

We may picture her standing like a figurehead at the prow of the leading ship, a beautiful, determined and very angry young woman, gowned in the eastern manner which she brought from Phoenicia and which was ever the mode at Carthage. Over her head was a long veil held at the shoulders by implements rather like our safety pins (such objects have been found in the ruins at Carthage). She may even have worn a nose ring! And she was sure to have been heavily jeweled and heavily perfumed.

A princess of the Orient going west. As Venus told Aeneas afterward it was a good voyage—"with prosperous winds; for a woman leads the way."

*   *   *

AT LAST ELISSA'S EYES GLIMPSED THE LAND OF HER DESIRES, THE spot chosen for her city of refuge. However exalted her dreams she could never have guessed the destiny which awaited her city. It would have been beyond any sane ambition to have fancied that the city she proposed to found would eventually become so important that the name of the immediate surrounding territory would be given to the second largest of the world's continents!

Elissa looked into the wooded point of land where—except at Gibraltar—the Mediterranean is at its narrowest. It was to her mind Libya, if indeed she gave it a name at all. Six hundred years afterward the Carthaginian home empire was for the first time formally known as "Africa." The name was stretched gradually to include the whole continent. Today one hundred fifty million men and women are known as Africans. A startling vision to Elissa and her companions could they have seen into the future. To make a comparison: Suppose that the country adjacent to St. Augustine had become so world important that the whole continent of North America (the United States, Canada, Mexico) got gradually to be included under the name of St. John's (St. Augustine's county designation). Well, there you have what happened to the city which Elissa went ashore that day to frame in a strip of oxhide!

THE NAME OF AFRICA

AFRICA IS A MAGICAL, SONOROUS AND SUGGESTIVE NAME. IT WOULD be satisfying to be able to attribute to it a sure and worthy derivation—especially since Africa is the subject of this book. Satisfying to be able to state that it meant, let us say, Lion or Elephant in some old tongue, or was the equivalent of Vastness and Mystery. But the fact is that Africa is a name unexplained. As to its origin there are many, many theories: Did it derive from a Phoenician word having the general significance of a separation, i.e. those who had left home, a colony? Or did it come from the name of one of the local tribes which is of a similar sound? Did it come from one Afer, a son of Hercules? Or from Africos (or Ifricos) a legendary son of Abraham, who was supposedly one of Hercules' companions? (The rather similar name of Epher *does* appear in Genesis as one of the descendants of Abraham.) Or does it derive from another personage by the name of Afer, or Ber, who was a forebear of the giant Goliath? Goliath's family allegedly fled from the Asiatic continent after his disaster to establish themselves in what we now call Africa and might have brought Afer's name along with them. There seems no biblical confirmation for this. Or did Africa derive from Aphrodite? . . .

At first Latin writers wrote the name as "Afri." It got to be the Roman province of Africa. Ifrikia (a variant of the word, Africa) is still the Arabic name for Tunisia alone. At a certain period in the Middle Ages the name Africa meant to Europeans just one single town of the Tunisian coast which they designated as "The City Africa." This was the now unimportant place, Mahdia.

In antiquity the continent, which they called Libya, was not supposed to include Egypt. Egypt was a part of Asia. Not unreasonable, since it was accessible only on the Asiatic side. The uncertainty as to whether Egypt was or was not in Africa seems to have lasted into nearly modern times. A book of geography published in Paris in 1667 found it necessary to offer the theory that in bounding Africa we "should include up to the most easterly arm of the Nile" (from the French translation of Marmol). This indicates a still wobbly frontier and a continued controversy.

The extension of the term Africa to include anything beyond

Tunisia was gradual. It was some time before even Algeria and Morocco were counted as part of Africa. As late as the fourth century A.D. a message from the emperor, Constantine, quoted by Gibbon, lists separately, "Africa *and* Numidia (roughly Algeria) *and* Mauretania (roughly Morocco)."

PUNIC FAITH

Now LET US FOLLOW ELISSA ASHORE, RESUMING THE TIMAEUS-Justin legend. The colonists debarked near modern Tunis, somewhat to the eastward. Digging commenced and a distressing incident shocked everybody. A cow's head was turned up. This was "the presage of a city which would meet much sorrow and be destined to live always in slavery." They went elsewhere, dug again and uncovered the head of a horse. That was the symbol of a warlike and powerful people. This was the place for Elissa's city. It would be called Qart Hadasht, meaning in Phoenician the same as our New Town. This name was deformed by the Greeks and in turn by the Romans and by moderns until it became Carthage. The resemblance in sound can still be noted.

The natives were friendly. Elissa entered into a deal with them which has become famous as the first example of that trickery that made "Punic faith" a byword for bad faith amongst Carthage's enemies. (As to the word Punic, as meaning Carthaginian, it is interesting to note that it appears to associate with the name of the mystic land of Punt, "The Land of Cinnamon," whose people were supposedly the ancestors not only of the Egyptians, but of the people of Phoenicia, who in turn fathered Carthage.)

Elissa's display of "Punic faith" was as follows: She suggested that she would be ready to pay a small fee for as much ground as an oxskin could cover, just so she and a few friends could "rest a moment" before going on. The guileless Libyans agreed. Elissa caused the oxskin to be cut into ribbons and secured enough ground on which to build a citadel, the Byrsa.

The Libyans were unresentful of her double dealing. The reason was soon manifest.

A friendly agreement was made for the annual rental price of the additional ground. The Libyans admiringly gave Elissa a new name. They called her Dido "on account of her numerous perigrenations"—the word probably meaning "wanderer." Some students however translate it as "Woman-Strong-as-a-Man."

Then came out the reason for Libyan cordiality to the newcomers. Hiarbas, king of the Maxitani, called ten of the leading colonists aside and made a communication. He had fallen in love with the beautiful widow and, if he did not get her in marriage, he would make war against feeble little New Town.

The ten men employed a truly Punic trick. They told Elissa that Hiarbas had demanded as the price of his friendship that some Phoenician individual should go and live amongst his people and teach them civilized ways, but, they complained, nobody wanted the assignment. Elissa, now Dido, tossed her head and reproached them for seeking to dodge a patriotic duty. Then they told her Hiarbas' real demand. Elissa-Dido was caught. After her exhortation to others she could not in decency refuse. Yet she could not bring herself to accept, for love of her murdered uncle-husband was still in her heart, and Hiarbas, the untutored Libyan, was distasteful to her.

After three months of procrastination she announced that she would burn an offering to the memory of her dead husband ere going to new ties. A funeral pyre was built. Then suddenly Dido, the wanderer, the woman strong as a man, plunged a sword into her bosom and fell dying into the flames with the words to her people, "I go to a husband as you wished!"

Remorseful now, the people revered her. As long as Carthage endured as a Punic city they worshiped her memory.

So, tradition says, was Carthage founded. Founded because of crime in the homeland of Phoenicia, founded by a woman boiling with rage, and associated from the start with duplicity and tragedy.

It is odd that in the legend of the very beginning of the colony a woman should have played the leading part, for in all the rest of Carthage's career only one single other woman was ever to stand out as a definite personality. Carthage was unlike Egypt, Greece and Rome. Its women were ignored. Dido and the other unlucky and romantic woman, of whom I shall tell later, were the only female characters mentioned with any emphasis in all Carthage's seven hundred years of history.

*   *   *

CARTHAGE, THOUGH CUSTOMARILY DESCRIBED AS A COLONY OF Phoenician Tyre, was never a colony in our present-day sense. She was free of the home country. The only thing resembling tribute was the sending from Carthage, at times, of rich gifts to the temples of the Phoenician gods. Relations between Carthage and Tyre were friendly. For instance, Carthage took in Tyrian refugees when Tyre was overrun by a conqueror. Tyre had at a previous time of crisis refused another triumphant tyrant use of her fleet with which to attack Carthage. But Carthage received no governor from Tyre. Carthage governed herself.

Other Punic colonies, either sent out from Phoenicia or founded by Carthage, grew up on the African shores. Some are cities that still survive under new names. We met them in the news of World War II. There was, for example, Hippo Regius, close to modern Bône. There was the other Hippo, which was called Hippo Diarrhythus. This was the old name for Bizerte. The second half of the name was because the getaway of the lake rushed through it. There was Sousse, called in antiquity Hadrumetum which meant "The Circle of Death."

THE STAMMERING KING

PRESENTLY GREEK COLONIES CAME TO NORTH AFRICA. THE MOST important was Cyrene. The story of Cyrene's foundation is unique. Also humorous. Herodotus tells it.

In the seventh century B.C. there lived a Greek bastard of royal descent named Battus. Battus had a grave impediment in his speech. He consulted the Delphic oracle, asking how he might be cured. The oracle replied—and we shall see how good the advice eventually turned out to be—that he should "go as an oecist to Libya." (An oecist was a colonizer.)

But Battus could find no one who knew anything about Libya. A pathetic picture presents itself of this afflicted young man stammering the question, "Where is Libya?" to hundreds of ignorant and indifferent persons. Finally he discovered a man who had voyaged widely as a fisher of the purple shellfish and who said he had once been driven onto the shores of Libya by a storm.

Thus aided, Battus and some companion oecists set out in two penteconters, fifty-oared galleys. They reached the African coast, mistaking an island for the mainland. On this island they attempted to set up a colony. But the most miserable hardships fell on them. And Battus' speech was not a whit improved.

After two years the bitterly disappointed man consulted the oracle again. "But," the oracle protested, "you didn't do what I told you to! You have never seen Libya at all!"

Battus bravely made a new start. He returned to Africa and after a preliminary sojourn on the coast—of the mainland this time—he and his party were led by friendly natives to the interior site where he founded the city of Cyrene (seventh century B.C.). It was a place exceptionally favored, above which, as the native guides boasted, "the sky was perforated," meaning that it often rained. Cyrene on a plateau some eighteen hundred feet above sea level looked out toward the Mediterranean from a scene of green and flowered beauty.

Cyrene became rich and powerful under Battus and his descendants. She was progressive enough to have a coinage system almost from the start, which made her unique in Africa, for—though this is surprising—Egypt and Carthage did their trading almost entirely by barter and without the help of any government guaranteed monetary arrangements. (It was centuries thereafter before Egypt acquired a real coinage, though she had developed way back in her early days a form of "ring money," said to be the oldest thing in any way resembling currency. This was used for big transactions only and consisted of rings of gold or of copper of a fixed weight.)

Cyrene's name as Cyrenaica is one of the oldest territorial names on the African map. Morocco and Algeria are relatively modern, Tripolitania came after the Christian Era. Egypt was not the name by which its own people called their country in antiquity. (That name was Kem—or Qimit—black, from the dark Nile Valley soil.) Cyrenaica and Tunisia are truly old names.

A highly satisfactory item of Cyrene's early story is that the Delphic oracle's promise was fulfilled. One day as plucky and afflicted Battus was wandering about alone a lion sprang toward him. Battus in his terror found his voice and let out so mighty a yell that the lion fled. Battus was cured. It was another triumph for the Delphic oracle, a deserved reward to Battus for his persistent effort to get well. So was a city founded.

THE WONDERS OF SILPHIUM

CYRENE WAS BORN WITH A SILVER SPOON IN HER MOUTH. SILPHIUM, of which in its grade A quality Cyrene had the monopoly, made the city's fortunes. It was so valuable that the representation of one of its stalks appeared upon Cyrene's coins, and the city's third king was called Battus the Fortunate because Cyrene's silphium brought wealth.

Now, by a miraculous circumstance silphium, according to Pliny, began to grow for the first time in the neighborhood just seven years before the first Battus founded his colony. On land where silphium had never been seen before it appeared suddenly after a drenching rain which was "as black as pitch." There it was waiting when Battus and his friends arrived.

It was an ordinary enough looking plant, somewhat resembling celery as to stem and root, and with a leaf like that of parsley. But its properties and powers were extraordinary, and although an inferior quality was to be found in other parts of the antique world,[4] the silphium of Cyrene was what the men and the women of the day craved, and were ready to pay for.

Here is just part of what Pliny says silphium could do, either in the form of an extract called laser or by the steeping of its leaves:

Taken as a drink it "allays accidents and griefs of the nerves" and "extinguishes the venom left in the body either by poisoned darts or serpents' stings," whilst if a serpent itself drinks it, mingled with wine, of which Pliny claims serpents are "most greedy," it will "cause the serpents to burst." As an ointment it cures scorpion stings, carbuncles and the bite of dogs (presumably mad dogs), and applied externally it removes corns and callosities. "Tempered with wine and saffron and pepper and mice dung and vinegar it heals ulcers."

[4] It seems to be incorrect to say, as do some learned authors—*The Cambridge Ancient History*, IV, p. 110 and Prof. Rostovtzeff, *History of the Ancient World*, text with Plate LXV—that silphium grew only in Cyrene. It must also have been grown in Asia for it was mentioned on the menu in Persia in the time of Alexander the Great.

It is efficacious against maladies produced by drinking bad water and against the contagion of pestilence, and sovereign for coughs, jaundice and dropsy. And recommended as an agent for bringing on abortions.[5]

*   *   *

BUT THIS WONDER DRUG HAD ONE DEFECT. BEWARE OF USING IT FOR toothache. Pliny speaks to having himself seen "the fearful sequel to such an experiment in a man who, having put silphium extract mixed with honey in a hollow tooth and stopped·the cavity with wax threw himself headlong from a high loft and broke his neck so horrible were pains he sustained."

Silphium was so greatly prized at Rome that even in the relatively sophisticated times of Julius Caesar Rome's supply was kept in the treasury along with the national gold and silver. In later years, when enemies had practically exterminated the plant in the effort to injure Cyrene, a single stalk of silphium was counted important enough to be sent formally as a present to the emperor, Nero.

In a wild state silphium was found growing up to fairly recent days. No longer is it valued. On the contrary, it was said to be fatal to camels and shunned. An early nineteenth century explorer (Captain Smyth, 1819) brought a specimen of silphium back to England alive and for a time at least it flourished in a Devonshire garden, the gentle and innocuous daffodils and primroses all unaware presumably of the spectacular past of the new arrival.

THE ALTARS OF THE PHILAENI

BETWEEN GREEK˙ CYRENE AND PHOENICIAN CARTHAGE LAY A GAP of some thousand miles, much of it semidesert. Notwithstanding, as the two colonies grew strong, jealousy rose between them. Where did Cathage's dominion or sphere of influence end and that of Cyrene begin?

A novel method was invented for settling the dispute. It was agreed, according to Sallust, that on a fixed day and hour people

---

[5] Pliny, *Natural History* Book XXII, chap. xiii: . . . "makes a drink for to cleanse and purify the matrice and expell the dead infant therein." Second Tombe of the 1634 edition translated by Philemon Holland.

should leave each city and proceed along the beach, and that the place where they met should be regarded as the frontier.

Two brothers called the Philaeni left Carthage and went forward as fast as they could. Men left Cyrene.

Naturally the reader will wonder what form of control can have existed to insure that the departure times corresponded. This same question bothered the Cyrene representatives when they met the Philaeni from Carthage unexpectedly close to Cyrene.

A quarrel broke. The Cyrenians accused the Philaeni of Carthage of trickery, charging that they must have started before the agreed time. The Philaeni retorted that it was the Cyrenians' own fault for dawdling. So a new test was decided on, the cruel conditions to be the same for each group. The Cyrenians agreed that, if permitted to go forward to what they regarded as a fair frontier point, they would submit to be buried alive. On their side the Philaeni of Carthage agreed that, if the present meeting place be accepted as the frontier, they would submit to the same death.

The first choice was for the Philaeni. With grand patriotism they grimly asked for their awful fate. And where the two young men were buried alive in the sands were built two altars marking the frontier, which were called the Altars of the Philaeni.

It may be but a fable. At any rate there is no question that the frontier was called the Altars of the Philaeni. The place was near El Agheila, a locality prominent in the Montgomery-Rommel campaign in December, 1943.

SALE OF BARBARISM'S
BIRTHRIGHT

As THE YEARS PASSED THE NATIVE POPULATION, THE LIBYANS FROM Cyrene to Carthage and beyond, came to realize that they had sold their birthright of easygoing barbarism for a pottage of uncongenial civilization.

These foreigners—these people from Asia and Europe—gradually took over their best fishing places and fields. These people gradually persuaded or forced them to irksome labor and enrolled them in their armies. The old free days were gone. It was the beginning of the foreign intrusion in North Africa, destined to be carried on by one alien group after another from then till now: after the Phoenicians and Greeks, Persians, Romans, Vandals, Arabs, then medieval and modern Europeans—Americans even.

When the first colonists came to Africa the Libyans of the West —farther from Egypt's influence and example—had been very close to savagery. They worshiped sun and moon, held certain animals in mystic reverence. In some places to kill a monkey was a major crime. They were gay folk, loved a lot, danced a lot, adored music. It has been claimed that they invented the flute.

In upon these primitive, erstwhile happy people had moved the self-seeking representatives of two superior races: Phoenicians and Greeks.

In the former the Libyans encountered men of a peculiarly slick type, men who knew all the tricks of profitable colonization. The Phoenicians had mopped up many of the most promising colonial sites of the then known world. They had presumably perfected all the methods for cajoling, scaring and outtrading simple natives.

In the Greeks, Libyans dealt with a more gracious race than the dour Phoenicians, it is true. But it was not long before the natives discovered that these Greek newcomers, whom they had guided to an ideal city site at Cyrene with such childlike and unsuspecting cordiality, were in process of absorbing their homeland.

An instance of the woe which alien occupation of their lands was eventually to bring to the brave barbarians of Libya is to be found in the coincidence that on the very same day, according to Herodotus—the year was 480 B.C.—Libyans died fighting for their foreign masters in far lands and for a cause they cannot have understood in two of the greatest battles of antiquity: at Himera and at Salamis.

A LIBYAN PHARAOH OVER EGYPT

THEREFORE IT IS A COINCIDENCE RATHER SATISFYING TO ONE'S SENSE of poetic justice that at the same general period when the Libyans of the West were beginning to writhe under adversity, their racial brothers, the Libyans of the East, should have been enjoying triumphant success.

In the year 945 B.C. an age-old Libyan dream was realized. For centuries the Libyans living near Egypt's frontier had hankered for Egypt's green pastures. Like poor children outside a sweet-shop they had pressed their noses against the windowpane. Now at long last a Libyan chieftain had become Pharaoh and founded a dynasty, the Twenty-second. His name was Sheshonk. His dynasty endured for two hundred years.

This must have shocked profoundly the native Egyptian population who knew Libyans through tradition and through their "history books" (graven inscriptions) as an inferior race. Records going back to the earliest dynasties showed Libyans in subservient poses, as conquered people or captives. It was but two centuries since Ramses III had given the Libyans two mighty beatings, which followed hard on the defeat which Merneptah administered.

The story of these Libyan reverses, plus accounts of other crushing Libyan humiliations, were inscribed across the length of Egypt. In Dr. Baikie's *Egyptian Antiquities in the Nile Valley* I pick up reference after reference to representations of one Pharaoh or another dragging a Libyan captive by the hair, or holding a Libyan chieftain beneath his bow, or slaying Libyan captives, or telling a conquered Libyan chief, "Thy name is blotted out forever and ever!" One scene shows a royal sphinx trampling down Libyans, this being used as the decorative motif in a chair. Libyans were easily recognizable because they were customarily shown with a characteristic feature, like personages in modern cartoons. Libyans wore a feather in the hair.

The fact that a member of the inferior and oft-chastised race was able to take over the country without a fight proves that Egypt was slipping. The previous dynasty had been a weak caricature of pharaohdom. Libyans had infiltrated into the country. Libyans formed a large element in the mercenary army. Then Sheshonk, strongest of the resident Libyan chiefs, grabbed power and said baldly, "I am Pharaoh!"

SHESHONK AND SOLOMON

THE LIBYAN UPSTART, SHESHONK, MAY WELL HAVE BEEN THAT Pharaoh before whom Solomon was but a vassal, protected and patronized. If so it would have been a Libyan girl, the Pharaoh's daughter, who had a place in Solomon's harem (I Kings 9:16). To this we cannot speak with certainty, so far as biblical testimony goes, since the passage in question does not give the Pharaoh's name, merely calling him by his title. Authorities differ as to whether he was Sheshonk or another Egyptian king.[6]

But there is no question at all that it was Sheshonk whose troops entered Jerusalem and despoiled it in the days of Solomon's successor. The Book of Kings names him specifically (I Kings 14:25, 26) spelling the word "Shishak." He is the first Pharaoh to be named by name in the Bible. Eleven Pharaohs are referred to in the Old Testament, but only three are mentioned by their names, and Sheshonk was the first.

It is a striking thought that one of the racial family of Libyans—who are the same as the Berbers, a simple and often rag-tailed lot in the modern North African scene—should have played so pompous a role in high biblical society.

PIANKHI FROM THE SOUTH

THE NILE HAD HER WAY WITH THE LIBYAN PHARAOHS AS SHE HAS had her way with so many foreigners. They became Egyptianized.

Also, as other Libyan kings succeeded the vigorous Sheshonk, royal power weakened and disorder grew so that, after two centuries, there were opposition kinglets and local chieftains sprinkled almost all over the country.

Then, at the other end of the "tube" that is Egypt, a new intruder pushed his way in. It was the somewhat mysterious Piankhi. He conquered Egypt right up to Memphis and into the Delta and opened the road to another dynasty of outsiders.

We know all about his exploits, his military genius, his religious ardor—he was a pious worshiper of Egypt's gods—his chivalry to women and his love of horses. All this from inscrip-

---

6 Maspero thought it possible that the Pharaoh who regarded "Solomon as merely a crowned vassal of Egypt" was the weakling who preceded the Libyan Pharaoh, and this view is often tentatively advanced in Bible comment. But there seems much reason to agree with Breasted that a Pharaoh vigorous enough to deal with Solomon *de haut en bas* and to perform the military acts described in the Book of Kings (1-9:16) is unlikely to have been the weakling who went before Sheshonk, and is more probably Sheshonk himself. The "degenerate king" (Pesibkhenno II, last of the failing dynasty before Sheshonk) cannot have done the important deeds in question, Breasted argues, adding, "we know of no king of this time who answers the description save Sheshonk I." Breasted, *A History of Egypt*, p. 529.

tions he left behind and from his "horse cemetery" which has been found.

But Piankhi's racial background does not seem sure. The dynasty which, thanks to his conquests, took over Egypt came later to be called by Greek historians "the Ethiopian dynasty." This does not convey a right idea of Piankhi himself. This energetic and gifted person, who—so his inscription explains—went into Egypt to put in order the house of "his father, the god Amon" can certainly not have been the typical black man that the name "Ethiopian" would suggest.

* * *

THE WORD ETHIOPIAN IS ANOTHER OF THE CONFUSING ITEMS IN African nomenclature. The word had two meanings. One as of skin color. One as of geography.

The word derived from the Greek, meaning burnt skins. In that connection it was applied indiscriminately to any Negro and sometimes to folk who were merely swarthy. For instance, Herodotus tells about straight-haired Ethiopians.

Used geographically the word meant, primarily to Greek writers, the country up the Nile south of Egypt, the Sudan. But— here comes an added bit of confusion!—Ethiopia was a geographical term which was also used about other lands where people had dark skins. For example, Strabo tells about "Western Ethiopia," where, so he says, great serpents grew grass on their backs. From the rest of his context it would seem that he meant what we now know as southern Morocco. There was an Asiatic Ethiopia, said to have been evangelized by St. Matthew. And even into relatively modern times the name Ethiopia was applied to what we know as French Sudan and the Guinea coast of West Africa. Today's maps give the name Ethiopia exclusively to Abyssinia.

* * *

PIANKHI WHO CAME FROM THE SOUTH TO CONQUER EGYPT WAS AN Ethiopian in the geographical rather than the complexional sense. He was already the king of a newly established kingdom whose capital was at Napata near the Fourth Cataract. In the days of Egypt's vigor this territory had belonged to Egypt and been influenced by Egypt's religion and culture. As Egypt grew weak Ethiopia-up-the-Nile had broken away. The organizing heads who had molded this new kingdom may have been persons of Egyptian origin. They may have been Libyans. They certainly were not Negroes.

"*SPOTS ON THE PANTHER'S SKIN*"

ONE THING IS ACCEPTED AS HIGHLY PROBABLE ABOUT PIANKHI'S forebears: whether they were Egyptian refugees who had been thrown out of Thebes, or whether they were Libyan adventurers, they are believed in either case to have approached the up-Nile country where they carved themselves out a kingdom via the oases. If refugees banished from Egypt, one of the oases west of the Nile had been their place of exile whence they moved in upon the Sudan. If ambitious Libyans, the oases similarly had been their base.

One of those so-called "Spots on the Panther's Skin" had almost certainly been the place where Piankhi's ancestors hatched plans to capture the lands up the Nile and nurtured ambitions which eventually led to Piankhi's conquest of Egypt.

Till now there has been no opportunity to speak about those oases beyond the Nile which so excited the imagination of ancient Egypt. Perhaps no human being can ever have received a more startling shock than did the first Egyptian who, wandering or lost in the desert, came suddenly upon an oasis and saw floating on the surface of the burning yellow sands an island of green. To the ancient Egyptian oases were supernatural. Not unreasonable. Even we dull moderns, who cannot truly thrill to any natural marvel because we have heard all about it beforehand, must tremble with amazement when for the first time we see that almost incredible thing which is an oasis. I shall not forget the first oasis I ever saw, that of the Figuig in southern Algeria, and now, after many thousands of miles of Saharan travel no oasis ever seems a commonplace.

Early Egyptians believed that this miracle country was the place where went the dead. In a word it was Heaven. Yet at the same time common sense and experience had shown them that this same oasis country served as a dangerous base for the attacking Libyans. It must have been with mixed sentiments that the Egyptians at last undertook the military conquest of the oases, at once enemy territory and the "Land of the Mummies."

The sprinkle of oases west of the Nile is almost as nothing compared to the vastness of the surrounding sand stretches: the Great Oasis (Kharga), the Western Oasis (Dakhla), the Lesser Oasis and a few more minor oases. It scarce justified the oft-quoted classical statement that the desert resembled a panther skin splashed with spots. And the classical comparison seems even less applicable now that we have seen what the ancients did not see— that is, the sparse distribution of oases over the Sahara as a whole— and can appreciate that the panther of the classical simile would have been a very inadequately spotted beast indeed. The term "oasis," by the way, was first used in a comprehensive sense by Strabo. Herodotus had referred to "the city of Oasis," meaning Kharga, but had no notion of the word oasis as a geographical designation. Strabo said oases were "like islands in the sea."

The Great Oasis (Kharga) was some one hundred fifty miles southwest of ancient Abydos and about dead west of Thebes. At Abydos there was a gorge in the desert hills whose mouth was the opening of the road oasisward. Through this mouth the souls of the dead were thought to travel to the happy land and so it was a sacred spot. Egyptians longed to be buried near by. Such a luxury was not possible to all so a custom arose of depositing "a votive pot" there in token of the beloved dead, and there can still be seen two mounds composed of broken pottery. Locally the place is called today "The Mother of Pots," and so—after perhaps six or seven thousand years—is still marked the start of the road toward what Greek historians called "The Island of the Blest."

* * *

FROM THE TIME OF THUTMOSE III THE OASIS COUNTRY BECAME OF practical value. The Great Oasis was highly cultivated; its farmers raised three crops of millet a year; it was renowned for its wines. You will find it mentioned repeatedly in classical history. Darius caused it to be fortified and built a temple there. The Romans were there defeated by desert fighters. Even Gibbon has something to say of what he quaintly calls merely "Oasis" with no "the" or specific name, as if there was only one and as if "Oasis" was a place name like Rome or Alexandria. Gibbon speaks of it as a place of exile, which it evidently was off and on through the ages.

BLOODY ASSYRIAN VISIT

THE SO-CALLED ETHIOPIAN DYNASTY DID BECOME MORE ETHIOPIAN, complexionally speaking, as it progressed. Its last Pharaoh, born of a dusky mother, shows a Negroid appearance in contemporary sculpture. Shortly after his death the Ethiopians were driven back to the southland.

The terrifying Assyrians had come, having seen that old Egypt was grown feeble and smelling an easy victory. They were professional conquerors, a people who had brought the art of war to new heights and had perfected a useful system of terrorization. "Massacres of the whole population in conquered towns and villages and horrible tortures inflicted upon the leading victims became the policy of the Assyrian," says Professor Rostovtzeff, adding that it was the invariable habit "after each victory to flay men alive, to impale them by hundreds, to cut off legs, arms, noses and ears, and then to keep their mutilated rivals shut up in cages." By such well-advertised frightfulness Assyrians made other nations quiver at their approach and oftentimes yield without a fight.

Egypt held them off for a little. But presently the Assyrian, Ashurbanipal, would record a boast of his treatment of Egypt in the seventh century B.C. that might almost have been written as of Europe in the early 1940's. Said Ashurbanipal, "My hands took the whole of Thebes, silver, gold, precious stones and the furniture of the palace—all that there was—costly and beautiful garments, great horses, men and women . . . I brought to Assyria. I carried off spoils unnumbered." It is recorded elsewhere that the young children of Thebes "were dashed to pieces at the top of all the streets . . . and all her great men were bound in chains" (Old Testament, Nahum 3:10). In this passage Thebes is called by its biblical name of No, short for No-Amon, meaning the city of Amon. The Douay Version translated No in Nahum's lyrical passage as meaning Alexandria. This is impossible, for Nahum lived about three centuries before Alexandria was founded. It was the children of Thebes whom the Assyrians tortured.

Some fifty years later Assyria paid for her aggression and four centuries afterward under one of the Ptolemies the most sacred of the spoil, the trappings of the Egyptian gods, was recovered and brought back.

RESULT OF THE CYRENE LAND BOOM

A FEW YEARS AFTER THE ASSYRIAN RAPE OF THEBES EGYPT, THANKS to a big leader and to its inherent resilience, was able to "come back" for a little while. The leader was Psamtek (663-609 B.C.) whose name in the Libyan language meant "The Lion's Son." His dynasty endured for over a century and marked Egypt's last period of true, prolonged independence.

It was in the reign of the third Pharaoh following "The Lion's Son" that the Libyans of the West again caused disturbance. The natives near Cyrene sent out a cry for help. In the process of answering this call Egypt's king lost his throne.

It was Cyrene's land boom which started the trouble. The infant colony, which had not yet passed her seventieth birthday, felt herself to possess great potentialities and desired to increase population by getting over more colonists from Greece. She made the offer that to each settler arriving before a certain date a lot of land would be given free. An announcement was made through the Delphic oracle that "whosoever shall reach the place too late for the land division shall have reason to repent it." Settlers came flocking.

Then arose an awkward contretemps. In order to fulfill her promise Cyrene had to dispossess some of her Libyan neighbors.

The Libyan chief was indignant and begged Egypt for help. The Pharaoh Apries fancied that he would have an easy win and get Cyrene for himself. He was disappointed. The Greeks of Cyrene wore armor. They were "brazen men," invulnerable when combating with the scantily dressed Libyan soldiers and the Egyptians who had come to help them. (Apries had Greek mercenaries, but had not dared send them on an expedition against their fellow Greeks at Cyrene.) The Egyptian army was mauled along the way of its retreat and few got home. Egypt blamed Apries, rebelled and eventually killed him.

CAMBYSES

AND NOW DOOM FROM ASIA AGAIN CAME TRAMPING UPON EGYPT.
Doom in the shape of Cambyses, the mighty madman from Persia.
Egypt fought him and lost. Persian domination started, to last for
one hundred twenty years (525-405 B.C.).

Cambyses began his rule of Egypt with tact. He put on the dress
of a Pharaoh and practiced the religion of the country, just as
Napoleon, twenty-three centuries later flattered Egyptians by
toying with Mohammedanism. Then began Cambyses' much-
advertised excesses and disasters—for Cambyses in Egypt was a
veritable Job.

He hankered for Carthage; Cyrene had already volunteered her
submission. He demanded that the Phoenicians, whom Persia had
subjugated, should give their fleet to be used against Carthage.
The Phoenicians pluckily refused to fight against their own
kinfolk.

Cambyses then determined that he would penetrate into the
Sahara and perhaps take Carthage by the back door. He would
send an army overdesert. An advance guard of fifty thousand men
went forward to establish posts for the main force. Between two
oases the fifty thousand disappeared. Just vanished between the
Great Oasis (or one of the other oases west of the Nile) and the
oasis of Siwa, far to the northwest.

Admitting that Cambyses chose an impossibly difficult route,
the complete disappearance of every soul was, and remains, one
of history's puzzles. Swallowed by a sandstorm? Such was the
explanation offered to Cambyses. Did he believe it? Can we? A
sandstorm in the Sahara I know to be an ordeal beyond description. There have been stories of big parties lost in these Saharan
sand blizzards; for example, two thousand caravanners allegedly
disappeared on the route northward from Timbuctoo in 1805,
and a military expedition of twenty thousand is said to have
vanished when going southward from Morocco in the sixteenth
century. Of course a sandstorm could not have buried Cambyses'
fifty thousand in a mass, but it might conceivably have produced
panic and revolt, and a dispersal and flight of the soldiers. Leader-
less in the unknown they might all have perished of thirst. Their

bodies would soon have been covered by shifting sand. Someday a Saharan explorer may find some of their gear. The terrible fifty-day wind of the desert, khamsin, was at one time believed to have been named for Cambyses.

* * *

HOPES OF CARTHAGE LOST, CAMBYSES SET HIMSELF TO ANOTHER piece of conquering. He would master the up-Nile country.

These people had kept to the south of the cataract since the last of the Ethiopian-Egyptian Pharaohs fled from the Assyrians two centuries before. Their faces, which grew duskier as times passed, were definitely turned southward toward Negroland. They were strong and self-confident and they jeered at Cambyses' spies who came bearing gifts. They were, they said, the "Long-Lived Race," not passing on till they were 120 years old, their longevity being due to their repugnance to "eating dung" (Herodotus III:22), i.e. grain from fertilized ground. Under their king, Nestesen, they inflicted upon the foolhardy Persian one of the most complete reverses ever suffered by an invading army. This king's inscription survives with its contemptuous reference to his victory over "that man Kambasauden" (Cambyses). The Persian army—what was left of it—starved on its retreat through what is called "The Belly of Stone," so desolate is it. They ate each tenth man.

MURDER OF THE SACRED BULL

REELING FROM THE AFTEREFFECTS OF SUNSTROKE AND BOILING WITH disappointed ambition, Cambyses, who had personally led the expedition up-Nile, came back to Egypt. He was near to madness and sore ill with "the sacred sickness" (epilepsy).

At Memphis a scandalous incident befell the unlucky tyrant. He had reached the city just at the moment of a local religious celebration when the folk, momentarily forgetful of their Persian master, were gay in their best. To Cambyses, preoccupied with his own fiasco, this meant but one thing. It meant that Memphis was staging a taunt against himself.

Useless to tell him that the festival was for an appearance of Apis, the sacred bull, the god of Memphis. His anger merely switched to the animal-god. He plunged his dagger into its flank and Apis died. The story of this sacrilege is told by Herodotus and sometimes doubted because the records of the Apises' careers have come down to us and there is no mention of the death of one of them during Cambyses' period in Egypt. However the Herodotus story states that the bull for a while after the murderous assault "lay and languished in the temple," which may explain the inconsistency.

Egypt, the story goes on, shuddered. And upon Cambyses punishment fell instantly. He was stricken with madness so violent that he kicked his pregnant sister-wife to death, sought to murder Croesus, once the richest of the rich, and committed uncounted other senseless cruelties. His own people revolted. Soon he was dead, dying of a wound in the hip at the same part of the body where he had wounded the Apis. All this consoled Egypt for a shocking occurrence.

*   *   *

TRULY TO GRASP THE MYSTIC VALUES OF ANOTHER RELIGION IS impossible. In estimating Cambyses' outrage we must try to understand that the institution of the sacred bull was a heritage from the remote days of the second king of the Second Dynasty, whose own name meant "Bull of Bulls," and that the heritage possibly went back to an even earlier period. Through all these centuries Apises had been buried like kings and worshiped like gods. The sacred bull calf was conceived by a ray of lightning. He was known at a glance from all other calves. He was black and had a square white spot on his forehead, upon his back the figure of an eagle, and on his tongue a mark resembling a beetle. As each Apis died search was made for a suitably marked successor. When found the new sacred animal would undergo four months of education to fit him for his exalted and delicate position, for henceforth he was to be not only god but oracle to the people, foretelling the future in special fashions of his own.

PUNISHMENT OF A CRUEL QUEEN

THE HATED CAMBYSES WAS SUCCEEDED BY DARIUS I, AND IN HIS reign there came another cry for help from Cyrene. This time it was a woman's voice. Cyrene had fallen out with her new neighbor, the city of Barca (the place name still exists, a little northwest of Benghazi). Barca had slain Cyrene's king and his mother begged for Egypt's aid. Her name was Pheretima and her cruelty and terrible death are reported by Herodotus, who was in Egypt a generation after her time and presumably heard her story in the way of local gossip. It was the sort of thing Herodotus would have pounced on, for it was a dramatic tale of wickedness, swiftly and hideously punished.

The Persian masters of Egypt sent Pheretima the help she craved, being glad of the occasion to spy out the land. Barca fell. Pheretima took her revenge. She impaled the chief men amongst her son's enemies, sticking their bodies up all around the city's walls, and to the outside of the walls she hung the bloody breasts of their wives: "studded the wall with breasts," as Herodotus puts it. The lesser fry went into slavery.

Pheretima, exultant, traveled to Egypt with the returning Persian army. But "odious to the gods are the excesses of human vengeance," and immediately that Pheretima reached Egypt she sickened of a loathsome disease, of which she died: she was consumed by worms, "even while alive she swarmed with maggots." (Variations of this strange malady were reported frequently in antiquity. Herod, the New Testament tells us, "was eaten of worms, and gave up the ghost." Plutarch mentions a great Roman whose flesh "turned all into lice, so that he had many persons employed both by day and night to clean him," and names for us a poet, a divine and a lawyer who all died of this same sickness.)

THE RISE OF CARTHAGE

CARTHAGE, WHICH ONCE COULD BE GIRDLED IN STRIPS CUT FROM A single oxhide, grew while Egypt staggered from the clutches of one conqueror after another. Carthage was on the way to becoming the richest city in the world. Her name applied not to a single city but to an empire. The western Mediterranean was called the Tyrian Sea because Carthage of Tyrian stock practically controlled it.

As to the steps by which Carthage attained such wealth and power we are pretty well without information. When Carthage was destroyed by Rome her books passed into the hands of the native princes of Africa. What was in them we shall never know, for abstracts made by two learned African kings have been lost. Only one Carthaginian work did Rome think it worth while to keep for herself: a set of manuals on farming, wine making and the like.

Thus Carthage is unique amongst the major ancient powers in having hardly a scrap of fair-minded, friendly history. Just about all we know of Carthage is the spiteful accounts given by her enemies, the Greeks and Romans who hated her.

Why did everybody hate Carthage? It is true that she balked her contemporaries. But there was more to it than normal rivalry. More to it than the prejudiced antagonism which precedes and follows wars. Carthage was hated in an instinctive sort of way because she was queer.

Her people were misfits from Asia on that doorstep of Europe which was Tunisia. They looked queer; their manners were queer; their religion was queer; they even smelt queer. Those long loose gowns hiding them from feet to finger tips—what a dress for a bearded man! And their groveling prostrations at the feet of distinguished foreigners—disgusting orientalism to Europe's idea. Garlic—they reeked of it (and you really have to reek to offend Mediterranean noses!). And simultaneously they overperfumed themselves in the Asiatic manner. Terrible rumors came from Carthage too of human burnt offerings—little children sacrificed to their horrid gods. Carthage in every way put the contemporary world's teeth on edge. They were too different from the rest of mankind as Greece and Rome knew it. And yet they were not to be viewed with easy contempt as mere barbarians. Carthaginians were clever, awfully clever.

As traders they were diabolically shrewd. Money was their god. They had a genius for colonizing and commerce, and they worked like beavers. They went everywhere, selling and buying not only Carthage's products and monopolies and what Carthage needed, but chaffering locally. They dealt not only in goods but in their own inspired services as jobbers. Some Carthaginians stayed years in foreign parts trading and building up fortunes, and, "knowing that foreigners resented them, they would sometimes," Professor Gsell writes, "join or substitute a Greek name to their own."

PERIPLI

IT WAS CARTHAGE'S EAGERNESS FOR TRADE AND YET MORE TRADE, for new markets and new sources of raw material which led to one of the most—perhaps *the* most—daring effort of expansion ever undertaken by any people. It is the only episode in her early history of which we know by her own records. It was that adventure which is called the Periplus of Hanno (periplus, a sailing around).

The story of this adventure was carved by Hanno's orders upon a bronze tablet set into the wall of the temple of Cronus at Carthage. The temple was destroyed like the rest of Carthage. But a translation into Greek has survived, and—put into French—I have it before me to the extent of several printed pages. It is the detailed account of the first journey to the southern Atlantic of which there is authentic proof. Not for nearly two thousand years would men go that way again and come home to tell of it.

Hanno's motive, having been colonization and the opening up of trade, he sailed with a considerable fleet and carried a stock of goods. There were sixty vessels of fifty oars each, men and women colonists. He sailed through Gibraltar and south along the Moroccan coast. His first stop and first colony was at a place he called Thymiaterion, meaning "the Censer," so named because there was incense burnt in consecrating the new town. This same place was the scene of an American landing in November, 1942. The place Hanno called piously The Censer was no other than Mehdia to the north of Casablanca.

From the Censer Hanno's fleet sailed south. A brave voyage. Here and there they would stop and trade perfumes and crockery for lion and panther skins. Sometimes they saw the shores lit up as if the whole world was ablaze. This frightened them. Perhaps it was only the annual burning off, which, carried on with exuberant recklessness, is still the dangerous custom in the lands beyond the Senegal's mouth. Perhaps, had Hanno reached these shores at another season than that of the burning off, he would have been emboldened to go even farther.

As it was he went far. Just how far we cannot be sure. Perhaps as far as Fernando Po, a few degrees off the Equator, the loveliest island I ever looked at. So keen have some folk been to identify in the light of modern geography the various stages of Hanno's voyage as described on the temple tablet, that a modern sea captain actually tried to reconstruct and repeat the periplus. He wrote a book about it, published in Paris in 1885, *Mémoire sur le periple d'Hannon* by Captain Auguste Mer.

Hanno's culminating exploit was the capture of three of what he described as the women of his last stopping place. Very ungallantly Hanno's men skinned these females. It was their only way of carrying back to Carthage a sample of what they believed to be tropic Africa's womanhood, for these females fought like demons and could not have been brought back alive. The three female skins went back to the homeland and were fastened to the walls of a temple and remained there for centuries. They provoked much wonder at Carthage because they were so hairy. For the females which Hanno's men had captured were not, as he supposed, the women of Fernando Po—or whatever was his ultimate point—but gorillas.

The date of the Hanno Periplus we do not know. The earliest suggested date is between six hundred and five hundred years before Christ.

*   *   *

THERE MAY HAVE BEEN AN AFRICAN PERIPLUS PERFORMED AT A yet earlier date. If it was indeed made, this earlier voyage was far less valuable as a piece of geographic exploration, being indefinite and almost without detail. Herodotus tells about it with reservations. Some modern historians believe the story. Others do not. The voyage was allegedly performed by Phoenician mercenaries who went out of Egypt in the days of Pharaoh Necho about 600 B.C. and made a tour right round Africa. It took three years; each year the sailors landed, planted seed and raised a crop for their needs. One striking detail of the story almost gives solidity to the claim that they really did double the Cape of Good Hope. After they had gone a long way, says the narrator, the sun to their amazement shifted: "they had the sun on their right hand."

Whatever was the truth of the Necho Periplus, it certainly did not accomplish what the Egyptian Pharaoh had in mind which, we are told, was to secure a quick and easy water communication between the Red Sea and the Mediterranean!

The Periplus of Hanno on the contrary had practical results. The trading posts Hanno founded were useful elements in building up Carthage's power, in framing into what was practically a private Carthaginian lake all the western part of what we call the Mediterranean, then known simply as "the inner sea." (It was not until the sixth century of our era that the imaginative name of Middle-of-the-Earth Sea, Mediterranean, was invented by St. Isidore of Seville.)

Carthage held the monopoly of business from what was known in classical times as "Merchants' Bay," the indented Atlantic coast of Morocco from Rabat to Gibraltar, into the Mediterranean as far as "The Emporia." The Emporia (plural of emporium—a name oddly chosen for a single city in Kansas) was the designation for a string of market cities on the Tunisian coast and near reaches of Tripolitania.

LOTUS-EATERS

THE EMPORIA WAS A STRETCH OF COUNTRY REGARDED BY THE ancients as possessing a marvelous value. Not only was it fertile and commercially desirable. It also was blessed by a pair of miraculous adjacent islands.

One was Cyranis where "the maidens of the country draw up gold dust out of the mud with feathers smeared with pitch" (Herodotus IV:195). The other was that supremely romantic place, the Land of the Lotus-Eaters, usually identified with the Island of Djerba, which from the days of Homer gained such renown that even now "a lotus-eater" means to us one who lives in idle luxury.

Homer's lines:

> They eat, they drink, Nature gives the feast:
> The trees about them all their food produce;
> Lotus the name, divine, nectareous juice!

together with the ensuing passage, to the effect that those who visit Lotus Land and eat the lotus never again think of leaving to go home, made up the most effective bit of travel advertising ever written. For nearly three thousand years it has dragged our dreams toward Africa. It is a pity to have to admit that the lotus was in reality a poor thing. Just a little brownish wild berry with an insipid taste. But the classical writers did not know this.

So in antiquity the Land of the Lotus and all the other fabulous and real possessions of Carthage were a magnet to the greedy. But Carthage's empire was for long impregnable. She had a great fleet and a mercenary army as large as she desired to recruit, for she had all the men of the northwest corner of Africa to call upon. Carthage's own first citizens, as time passed, did not willingly become warriors. They were an aristocracy of traders. To risk money-producing genius on the battlefield did not suit the national policy.

QUEEN OF THE WESTERN SEA

CARTHAGE WAS THE TRAFFIC POLICEMAN OF THE WESTERN MEDI-terranean and ruled the sea lanes, though there were a few infringements of her rule, notably Marseilles.

Rome obeyed her traffic laws. A treaty made before the year 500 B.C. was graven on bronze and kept in the Capitol. It stated that the Romans were not to navigate to the west of the Gulf of Carthage unless obliged by storm or enemies. If a Roman ship master was driven there against his will he must not buy or take anything except what might be vitally needed to repair his vessel, and must go away in five days. This stern rule was repeated in a subsequent treaty a century and a half later.

But Alexander the Great gave Carthage a scare. With typical cunning Carthage dispatched a spy to the conqueror's side to find out whether he planned to include a Carthaginian grab amongst his adventures. This spy obtained an audience under the pretense that he had been badly used at home and wanted to enlist with Alexander. The information he managed to worm out of Alexander and his entourage was reassuring and he transmitted it to Carthage written on wooden tablets which were hidden under a layer of wax. Justin recounts this twenty-two-hundred-year-old secret-service episode. Later on, Alexander formed plans to construct a great fleet of a thousand vessels to take over the western Mediterranean. His death saved Carthage. Diodorus of Sicily tells how a scheme for the campaign against Carthage was found in what he calls Alexander's "Book of Remembrance" after he died.

*   *   *

FOR CENTURIES CARTHAGE WAS ABLE TO SEE THAT NO ENEMY FOOT touched her home soil. She did all her fighting in other people's countries—largely in Sicily.

That afflicted island, stuck in the cross fire between Africa and Europe, was really a pathetic victim of geography. Greeks, Carthaginians, Romans came there. It was a blood-soaked squared ring.

The Sicilian contests often went against Carthage. In 480 B.C. she met at Himera one of the meanest disasters in all history. She came to Sicily with three hundred thousand men. Just one small boatload got home. Their leader, Hamilcar, had thrown himself into the great fire at which he had been offering sacrificial prayer for victory. Carthage cursed his memory and exiled his family.

Seventy years later his grandson, reinstated in Carthage's confidence, went to Sicily with an army. His name was Hannibal.

He was not, of course, *the* Hannibal. Nor, of course, was his defeated grandfather *the* Hamilcar. A parsimony of proper names existed in Carthage and they did not use family names. We meet a repetition of Hannos, Hamilcars, Hasdrubals, Magos, Hannibals and a few others. These names had a religious significance, on the order of certain old Puritan names. Hanno, for instance, meant "[God has] Favored Him"; Hannibal, "[He who enjoys] the Protection of Baal." (Baal was a general word for god.)

Hannibal carried black fury in his heart to Sicily and avenged the family honor in hideous style. His victorious soldiers mutilated the dead; some were seen with amputated hands strung together and fastened round their girdles. On the precise spot of his grandfather's death he sacrificed three thousand prisoners.

Such were some of the ups and downs of the Carthaginian battle scene in Sicily. New arms came into use. There was that great projectile machine for stones and darts called the catapult—an astounding novelty invented by Carthage's enemies. There was new armor adopted by the Carthaginians and worn to their own doom. Their army had been equipped with outside shields, iron breastplates and bronze helmets. The battle was fought on a river (Battle of Crimissus, 340 B.C.) and in a terrible storm. Hail rattled

on their armor and they could not hear their officers. They slipped
in the mud and were so heavily weighed down by their proud new
hardware that they could not get up again. The river rose and
they wallowed about to their death. It was a great victory for the
Greeks. A comeback battle followed. Thereafter Sicily enjoyed a
whole generation of peace!

SACRIFICE OF THE CHILDREN

THEN, IN THE YEAR 310 B.C., CARTHAGE HAD A SHOCKING SURPRISE.
It began with the usual variations of fortune of a Sicilian campaign. A remarkable figure had pushed into power in Sicily. He
was Agathocles, son of a maker of earthen cook pots, who had
himself started life as a potter. He was a man of gigantic strength,
very handsome and very, very slick. He made himself dictator of
Syracuse. He and Carthage had fallen out. We have first a Carthaginian disaster at sea so terrible that, when the news reached
Carthage, "the city walls were hung with black serge," and then
a battle where Agathocles was defeated. In this latter, Carthage
used a group of one thousand slingsmen who hurled stones of a
pound weight which pierced holes in the body armor of the
enemy.

After this defeat Agathocles was in a very deep hole. He showed
imagination. He did something no one had yet dreamed of doing.
He slipped through the blockade and invaded Africa. By the
lucky circumstance of an eclipse of the sun he dodged pursuit.

Landing a few miles to the southwest of Cape Bon the first
thing he did was to burn his ships. Trumpets blared. The soldiers
shouted. It was a bold spectacular gesture.

To Carthage an enemy appearance on the home soil was a
thunderclap. The citizens were stupefied. A minority of them
were so psychologically shaken that they were inclined toward an
immediate capitulation without a fight. They braced themselves,
met Agathocles and were driven back. Carthage quivered inside
her walls.

A wave of mass superstitious terror swept over the people. This
was their punishment because they had cheated their gods. In a
frenzy of remorse they set about making reparation.

*   *   *

THE PHOENICIAN RELIGION WHICH CARTHAGE HAD BROUGHT WITH her from her fatherland was peculiarly hideous even in an age when cruel practices were common. Carthage revolted the world. This was not because she sacrified human beings. Human sacrifices were not then a horror. Rome, for instance, sacrificed helpless foreigners at a moment of panic during the Second Punic War, and even later the Celts used to sacrifice prisoners and malfactors *en masse*. What disgusted the contemporary world in the case of Carthage was that she cold-bloodedly sacrificed her own children —the children of her leading families—and that this sacrifice was voluntary.

In normal times two children, two little boys, were chosen by lot every year, or else were brought forward by such parents as were exceptionally devout. These little boys were destroyed in the worship of Cronus (sometimes locally known as Moloch). They were placed upon the great hands of his brazen statue. The hands were manipulated by machinery and the pitiful little pair—it was forbidden to ease their terror and their pain by cutting their throats—were dropped into the fiery furnace below. Their parents were present at this heart-rending scene, it being their pious duty to endeavor to keep their children from shrieking which would not have been agreeable to the god.

This annual sacrifice had been scamped in the years that preceded Agathocles' attack on Carthage. Cronus had got his yearly victims, it is true, but certain parents had secretly provided themselves with slave children of suitable age and appearance which they had substituted for their own little dear ones if the lot fell upon them. In other words they had paid their tithes in counterfeit coinage.

Now that the city's life was threatened they knew that Cronus had seen their deception. Frightened Carthage paid up her back debts to the god. Paid up with interest. Five hundred little boys were burnt in the Cronus furnace. (See Diodorus, Book XX, for a description of the sickening mechanism of the brazen god.) At first two hundred, chosen by lot from the first families. Then three hundred more, given of their own accord by families who had dodged their pious responsibilities in the past.

To the European world of her day it seemed obscene and nearly insane, as well as a despicably selfish and cowardly attempt to save

their own skins at the expense of innocent children. But Carthage
had such notions in her blood. Her tradition was that Cronus
himself in the days of the Phoenicians' origin, "being lord of the
land and having an only begotten son called Jeoud, dressed him
in royal robes and sacrificed him upon an altar when the country
was in great danger."

*   *   *

CARTHAGE, WE PRESUME, CONGRATULATED HERSELF THAT HER
religious orgy had been her salvation, for Agathocles' attack
eventually failed though only after many and varied thrusts and
maneuvers.

He established a base at Tunis, at Carthage's door. He took
some two hundred smaller places along the Tunisian coast. The
Libyan population, resentful of Carthage's tyranny, joined with
him. He again defeated Carthage's army. But two years had passed
and he realized he was not strong enough to conquer the city.

He then conceived the idea of getting outside help. In Cyrene
one Ophelas was then master. Agathocles invited him to come to
his aid with the understanding that they would divide Carthage's
empire between them. Ophelas, enticed by the prospect, set off
with more than ten thousand soldiers. So confident was he that
he also brought along civilians with their ten thousand women
and children.

Their journey from Cyrene across semidesert was hard enough
for the army, quite demoralizing to the noncombatants. His
band arrived at the meeting place exhausted and half starved.
Agathocles met him with all cordial sympathy, but with tricks in
his heart. He caused Ophelas' death and by glib talk took over
his forces.

Thus reinforced he slaughtered Utica with a clean sweep and
went on to Bizerte. His army ravaged as far as the present Algerian
border. But still Carthage baffled him. And to the end she baffled
him. Finally after four years he fled the African shores one night
in a rowboat, abandoning his sons and what remained of his army.

Carthage years afterward must have snickered when she heard
what had happened to the adventurer who had caused their first
humiliation on home soil. Agathocles, now a hoary old despot in
his home, Syracuse, rose from table one night and called for his

"toothpicker," as Diodorus tells the grim story; received the implement from his secretly disgruntled servant and "plied all his teeth and gums with care and earnestness." Presently Agathocles fell ill and suffered excruciating torment, for the disgruntled servant, instigated by the despot's greedy grandson, had dipped "the toothpicker" in poison. Agathocles' inflamed gums stopped his speech. Still alive he was thrown onto his funeral pyre.

START OF THE PUNIC WARS

THE PUNIC WARS HAD TO COME. "WELL WOULD IT HAVE BEEN," said Hannibal the Great, "if the Romans had not coveted anything beyond the extent of Italy, nor the Carthaginians anything beyond that of Africa!" (Polybius, who was present at the final destruction of Carthage and whose *History* is the best source available for the Punic Wars as a whole, reports Hannibal's speech in full.) Under the geographical circumstances covetousness was inevitable. Probably, however, the trouble broke a little sooner than it otherwise would have done because Rome noted Carthage's panicky and inept defense against Agathocles.

The First Punic War lasted nearly twenty-four years (264 to 241 B.C.). The Second Punic War came on its heels. Thus in a period of sixty years Carthage and Rome spent about two thirds of their time savagely fighting one another. It constituted a lump of human misery which Livy called "the greatest and most memorable war that was ever carried on."

*　　*　　*

IT WAS MOSTLY IN SICILIAN WATERS AND ON AFRICAN GROUND THAT the First Punic War was fought. Rome used a new sea weapon, "the crow's bill," a grappling spike. She gained control at sea and the famous Regulus went to Africa.

At first he did well, capturing Tunis and many other towns. In the spring he would take Carthage, he told himself. He did not do it.

There may have been something intentionally symbolic in the story of his encounter, in those days of his glowing confidence, with the giant serpent. This mighty creature met and opposed Regulus' army on the banks of the Medjerda River. He was 120 feet long and killed the Roman soldiers with his bad breath. It was needful to "lay siege to him like a fortress." Rome overcame him only by the use of her artillery—the big ballista, an outside catapult which shot heavy bolts and stones and from whose name we have the word ballistics.

The serpent fable, which is reported by an early war correspondent, the poet Naevius, who himself took part in the campaign, may have been invented, I suggest, in the light of what happened to Regulus afterward, as a supposed warning to him from the gods that he should watch his step in Africa. When Regulus tackled Carthage in all optimism he came against a reorganized army. The Romans were practically annihilated. Regulus himself was taken prisoner.

His subsequent career is one of Rome's noble legends, subject of one of Horace's odes and of a long passage of Cicero's. At a time when it suited Carthage's purpose Regulus was sent on parole to Rome to give counsel on the question of an exchange of prisoners and a possible peace. Regulus sniffed the air of his beloved Rome, looked into the eyes of his dear wife, and then refused to recommend the prisoner exchange and the peace which would have let him stay. Regulus went back to Carthage. "Yet well he knew that there the savage torturer for him was planning," what "exquisite torments he was going to"—to quote Horace and Cicero. Legends say that one of the torments was to be shut up in a small stable with an elephant where he dared not sleep lest the animal tread upon him. Legends say too that Regulus was avenged by his widow who—getting possession of two Carthaginian prisoners—shut them in a cask to die: one died quickly; the other lingered long beside his rotting companion.

*   *   *

AT LAST BY A NOSE, AND A VERY TIRED NOSE, ROME WON. The young Carthaginian general, Hamilcar, nicknamed Barca, which meant Lightning, negotiated a peace. Carthage was to keep out of Sicily. She was to pay an indemnity. But it was a Pyrrhic victory for Rome. Her exertions and sacrifices had been awful: seven hundred galleys lost, one hundred thousand men at sea, and an incomparably larger number of men on shore.

"THE PITILESS WAR"

THE DETAIL OF CARTHAGE'S LOSSES I DO NOT KNOW, INSIDE RECORDS of her history being so skimpy. Polybius believes she must have lost about five hundred ships. But she was not crippled. Of this we have proof. This proof is that, during the twenty-three years between Punic Wars I and II, Carthage could stand up to a pair of gigantic efforts. She won through the horrors of a peculiarly hideous local war. She engaged in a tremendous conquest scheme in Spain. And yet, when Rome hinted at a repeat war, Carthage felt herself quite strong enough to accept the challenge almost nonchalantly, and conducted herself with such ferocious vigor as nearly to shake out Rome's teeth.

The local war, known as the Mercenaries War, was called in classical times "The Pitiless," "The Truceless," or "The Unforgivable." Polybius said, "Never was any other war to my knowledge soiled by so many cruelties and infamies."

It came about in this fashion. Carthage by the terms of peace had to evacuate Sicily. Twenty thousand mercenary troops—a mixed gang of Libyans, Spaniards, Gauls and Greek half-breeds—were tossed into North Africa in a fury of ill temper at the defeat which had robbed their hopes of reward and pillage, and in a fury because their wages were long unpaid. They camped alongside Tunis howling for their rights.

Carthage could not pay, parleyed with them, and by fatal bad judgment failed to disperse them. They remained in an angry group, to which soon joined some seventy thousand of the ever-uncertain Libyan population.

The fighting which followed was the *ne plus ultra* of wickedness and misery. Both sides starved. At times the mercenaries ate their prisoners. At other times they cut off the hands of captured Carthaginians, broke their legs and threw them still alive into a ditch. Eventually Hamilcar Barca by a trick took forty thousand of the rebels alive and slew them all. These horrors lasted over three years.

The famous novel, *Salammbô,* deals with the Mercenaries War. Flaubert lived and studied at the site of old Carthage in about 1860. Certain of its characters are historic. The heroine—a fancy

picture—was Hamilcar Barca's daughter. One incident is a supposed action of Hamilcar Barca's in saving his little son from
sacrifice to Cronus by substituting a slave child in disguise. The
little son who was saved was Hannibal the Great.

HAMILCAR

NO SOONER WAS THE MERCENARIES' REVOLT CRUSHED THAN HAMIL-
car Barca, who had become Carthage's dictator, prepared an
expedition to reclaim those rich holdings in Spain which had
slipped out of Carthaginian control during the period of the war
with Rome, hoping thus to raise his country's fortunes and set her
on her feet for a revenge match.

As he was about to leave he led his little son before the statue of
Cronus (in whose furnace Flaubert would have us believe the
child had barely escaped perishing) and made him swear undying
enmity to Rome. Hamilcar Barca then tramped his army across
the top of Africa from Tunisia to the Strait of Gibraltar—a far
more difficult route than by sea which he had chosen so as to
display Carthage's might before the eyes of the Libyans along the
road.

Hamilcar Barca's Spanish adventures and those of his son-in-
law, Hasdrubal, and of young Hannibal were splendidly successful.
They live still in Spain's finest city which, known in earlier times
as Laie, took its present name of Barcelona (Barca-town, Lightning City) from the Carthaginian, Hamilcar Barca. Hasdrubal
founded Cartagena—new Carthage—a stronghold in antiquity.
Hannibal trained in Spain for his great destiny as the almost
conqueror of Rome, and married a Spanish wife. Spain became,
in fact, the tail that wagged the Carthaginian dog. But the dog
prospered.

It was more than jealous Rome could bear. She sought war
again, demanding as the only price of peace the surrender of
Hannibal. Carthage was indignant and self-confident. *"You
choose!"* was her insolent reply when the old Roman ambassador
offered the two tails of his toga, saying, "This side is peace; this
side war. Which will you pick?"

HANNIBAL

THE SON OF THE MAN WHO HAD WON THE NICKNAME OF LIGHTNING loved lightning war. While Rome dawdled Hannibal shot out of Spain, through the Pyrenean foothills, across France, over the Alps and into Italy. Rome had never dreamed he would attack their home territory. She wobbled.

Hannibal had History in his hands. He might have turned Europe into a Phoenician province. Those early days of the Second Punic War made a lot of difference to you and me—a difference beyond our conception. The language and notions of life which were to go from Rome into the European continent and across the Channel and the Atlantic might have been lost and something quite different substituted had Hannibal's drive possessed a little—a very little—more power.

"In five days' time," his officers gloated after the Cannae victory, "we shall be dining in Rome!" Rome thought so too. Old men and boys were drafted to the walls. The signs and prodigies were terrifying: shields sweated blood, corn bled when cut in the fields, red-hot stones fell from the sky. Rome quaked. But Hannibal hesitated. They say that afterward when he was old and broken and suicidal—a refugee in Asia Minor—he would sometimes cry out in anguish, "O Cannae! Cannae!" [7] bemoaning the lost chance which wrecked his destiny, and very possibly profoundly altered yours and mine.

NUMIDIAN HORSE AND AFRICAN ELEPHANT

HANNIBAL BROUGHT A NEW WAR ELEMENT INTO ITALY. No, NOT elephants. I mean his African cavalry, the Numidian horsemen of whom he had five thousand when he left for Rome. They were demons. They adored war. Their horses adored war. The conventional Roman army was shocked by their frenzy. "A great line

---

[7] Plutarch's *Life of Fabius Maximus, Savior of Rome,* and *Life of Titus Quinctius Flaminus,* in the latter of which Hannibal's tragic last days are described.

of dust would suddenly rise on the horizon; there would be a galloping upon them, and a rain of darts from a cloud filled with flaming eyes" (*Salammbô*).

The Numidian horses were as ugly as sin. We can see their likeness on Carthaginian coinage of the day: short-legged and small, graceless, with thick heads thrust forth on stiff necks. We can read about them in contemporary authors: creatures that were tireless and of extraordinary speed, seeming to thrive on nothing but grass scraps and to need no care at all. They were fearless in war, and in peace gentle to the point of weeping with joy at the music of the native flute. (This last is seriously told us by a classical writer who presumably found the statement in one of the lost books of the learned Numidian king, Juba II.)

The war would have gone quite otherwise if Hannibal could have procured reinforcements of Numidian horsemen—or indeed substantial reinforcements of any kind, except such help as he got from disaffected Italian cities. Or if he could have got siege guns to use against Rome. But Carthage did little for Hannibal. There was an excuse. The Carthaginian fleet was not what it had been, and Rome made the land passage via Spain difficult. It is said that he did receive forty additional elephants.

Hannibal had thirty-seven elephants when he set out on his lightning war. Their sufferings on the slippery cold Alpine passes are something to weep about. But some survived to fight in the Italian plains. The last of them carried Hannibal across the Tuscan marshes.

Their aspect horrified the mountain peasants. To the Roman soldiery they were alarming enough, but not a complete novelty. Romans had already fought against elephant-equipped armies.

*   *   *

THE KNOWLEDGE OF THE ELEPHANT AS A WAR MACHINE CAME FROM the East in the time of Alexander the Great. An antagonist of Alexander's—an Indian king "four cubits and a palm high" (well over seven feet) rode an elephant trained to be a sort of primitive Florence Nightingale. In the height of battle "he knelt down in the softest manner and with his proboscis gently drew every dart out of the king's body."

It was via Pyrrhus of Epirus, a miniature Alexander, who attacked Rome around the year 280 B.C. that Rome gained her first experience of war elephants. It is easy to imagine the amazement and terror these charging monsters must have caused to men who had never seen an elephant before. It is hard to overpraise the courage of those who stood and fought them. "The Bulls of Pyrrhus" the soldiers called them in their ignorance, speaking of their "hand in the form of a serpent." Roman horses bolted. Many Romans were crushed beneath the elephants' feet.

Pyrrhus and his irresistible "bulls" drove to within thirty-seven miles of Rome. Then occurred an incident of rare courage. A Roman ambassador went to Pyrrhus, a man who had never seen an elephant. Pyrrhus had caused the biggest of his elephant corps to be put into its battle dress and concealed behind a curtain in the audience room. Suddenly, by arrangement, the curtain dropped and the elephant "raised its trunk over the Roman's head and made a horrid and frightful noise." The Roman never quivered. "As we were saying, Pyrrhus . . ." he went on. It is an anecdote told by Plutarch in his biography of Pyrrhus, who was rated important enough to be ranked as a very great general. Hannibal put Pyrrhus into his own class. I cannot forbear to tell of his remarkable personal peculiarity— or so it seems to me, though there is at least one other such case mentioned in antiquity—: Pyrrhus "had an air of majesty rather terrible than august; instead of teeth in his upper jaw he had one continual bone, marked with small lines resembling the divisions in a row of teeth."

Rome eventually proved too strong for Pyrrhus despite his elephants. At one stage of his career he proceeded with them to Sicily where he fought Carthaginians and planned to invade Africa. This he did not do. But his elephants were an eye opener to Carthage. She snapped at the new idea.

Carthage had a source of supply of elephants in her back yard, in the wild country of southern Tunisia, and presently had them there literally in the great elephant stable which was erected behind the city's ramparts with room for three hundred beasts.

Elephants were common game in those days in Mediterranean Africa from Morocco to Tunisia, though Egypt's prehistoric elephant race was no more, and Egypt, after experimenting with

imported Asiatic animals and with Sudanese animals, had decided that the Asiatic elephant was the better war machine. By
the days of late antiquity Mediterranean Africa's elephants had
died out. In the fourth century A.D. there were none left, and as
the years passed the elephant was quite forgotten. At the end
of the sixteenth century a specimen elephant which had been
dragged across the western Sahara as a gift to the Sultan of
Morocco so amazed the people of a country, where once elephants
had roamed wild and ivory been so common it was used as door-
posts and fence stakes, that Fez turned upside down with astonishment. Afterward people used to designate the date of its
arrival (1599) as "The Year when the Elephant Came."

Carthage found this hitherto unexploited animal of vast ad-
vantage, especially at first. She beat Regulus in the First Punic
War, thanks to them, and used them in the conquest of Spain.
She very justly honored them on her coinage.

But like all new war implements elephants were beatable by
new tricks. The first and simplest trick was employed by the
Romans against Pyrrhus. It was to turn loose a herd of wild
swine in their path. Later a machine was invented to shoot burning firebrands at them, and a technique was thought out by
which open corridors were left in the ranks through which the
elephants were induced to plunge to their doom.

A disadvantage to the use of elephants was that, when frightened, a contagious madness would sweep through the elephant
corps and they would turn on their own army. Each driver
therefore was equipped with an iron spike and mallet so that
he could instantly destroy a crazed beast by a blow in the neck.
Furthermore the transportation of elephants overseas was immensely difficult. Special rafts were needed and in storms the
losses were great. Some said that the floor of the Mediterranean
was covered with elephants' bones! Pyrrhus lost ninety per cent
of his on his first voyage to Italy.

All in all, once the fleeting element of surprise was lost, the
elephant was not of great military value. And Rome had early
and shrewdly seen to it that the surprise element was destroyed.
Some of "Pyrrhus's Bulls" which Rome was able to capture were
sent to the city's circus. Rome saw elephants slain by men with

mere javelins and learnt that these monsters were just beasts like any others.

Hannibal's elephants therefore did not panic the Roman army.

THE HOME FRONT

FOR FOURTEEN YEARS CARTHAGE WAITED ON HANNIBAL. THE WAR did not come close to them in a vital way, although Rome made certain minor attacks in Africa—at Djerba Island, the supposed Lotus-Eaters' Land, and elsewhere—and although the work of Rome's secret agents amongst the Libyans caused some worry, Carthage's blood and heart were not involved. Carthage's citizens, her sons and husbands, were not fighting. With the exception of a few officers Hannibal used an exclusively mercenary army.

News came slowly and was puzzling and contradictory. Carthage would hear that Rome seemed doomed. Then silence and they felt they had been fooled by overoptimism. Bad news came. Hannibal sick and disfigured—he had lost an eye through some infection—a bad omen.. Superstition aside, this misfortune may explain why it was that Hannibal faltered when Rome seemed in his grasp. Such a loss and mutilation, coming not from a battle wound in which an ardent young general might take pride, but from some nasty poisoning of the system, would have been demoralizing. It would have reduced his personal self-confidence, his belief in his Star.

Then the news glowed again. Hannibal had ridden right up to Rome's great gates, tauntingly thrown his spear into the city and ridden away again unharmed. Surely that must mean that the Romans were cowed. But again disappointing silence followed.

More bad news: Rome's successes in Spain, the death of Hannibal's brother who had made a rush into Italy, the capture of certain Carthaginian citizens on his staff, Hannibal's withdrawal into the sole of the Italian boot.

Then of a sudden a rumor shocked them. Scipio who had beaten their army in Spain was clamoring to invade Africa. Scipio protested that it was absurd to wait indefinitely while Hannibal wove back and forth in Italy. Scipio wanted to attack the heart of Carthage. Despite opposition at Rome which Scipio described as "senile," and despite the charge that Scipio's real reason for wanting to go to Africa was to by-pass the dangerous Hannibal, Scipio had his way. In 204 B.C. he landed on a promontory between the site of modern Tunis and Bizerte.

He landed in the middle of a tangle of Rome's fifth column activities. Rome had been seeking to seduce local native notables —Libyans being often ready to plot against Carthage. Rome's emissaries had flattered King Syphax, had given him "a toga, a purple tunic, an ivory throne and a gold cup weighing five pounds," and Syphax seemed to be their man.

BEAUTIFUL SAPHONISBA

BUT SUDDENLY EVERYTHING WAS OVERTURNED BY ROMANCE—THE sole and only bit of romance in Carthage's grim and grasping annals. Syphax, no longer young, fell in love with a Carthaginian girl of the ruling family. He received her in marriage, and henceforth Syphax and Rome were enemies. For this girl, Saphonisba, was not only beautiful but dominant and persuasive. Syphax, a weak man, was her tool. He became the tool of her Carthaginian father.

Rome had however another native prince on her list of seducibles. He was the young man destined to become the great African king, Massinissa. He was a dashing and adventurous person, whom Syphax hated. The lovely and brainy Saphonisba is said to have been betrothed to him before Syphax won her hand. When Scipio landed in Africa Massinissa, who was only potentially valuable at that time, joined him with a small following, but big vigor.

Scipio, aided by Massinissa, beat a Carthaginian force, aided by Syphax. Saphonisba was furious and pushed her husband to a revenge battle against her old fiancé. Syphax lost again, was wounded and dragged back in chains to his own palace in Cirta (modern Constantine in northeastern Algeria, Eisenhower's advanced command post in 1943). Saphonisba suddenly shifted her allegiance. She looked into the eyes of the conquering Massinissa, then threw herself down before him, begging his protection. Massinissa was of a notably amorous nature. (He died leaving forty-four sons and uncounted girl children.) Saphonisba had glamorous associations in his mind. Ignoring her husband, standing near in chains, Massinissa instantly went through a marriage ceremony with her. Syphax's comment was biting: "I am glad that my greatest enemy has fallen into the hands of the woman who caused my ruin!"

But Saphonisba's days of political power were over. Scipio showed anger at the marriage. This woman was to have been the star of his Roman triumph. Massinissa's marriage spoiled his plan. Also Scipio felt that she would be a bad influence on his ally. Massinissa was amorous, but he was very ambitious. Perhaps too his will had soon clashed with that of this fair, firm girl. At all events Massinissa sent his bride a poisoned drink. Saphonisba, whose name meant "She-Whom-Baal-(god)-Protects" accepted the cup and died. She was, except for Dido-Elissa, Carthage's only recorded heroine.

AGAIN, PUNIC FAITH

THIRTY MEN CAME FROM CARTHAGE IN A BODY TO SCIPIO, prostrated themselves and kissed his feet in their oriental way. It turned Scipio's Roman stomach. But he stated his terms and there was a truce pending the final formalities. The bootlickers knew that Hannibal was on his way home. They were trying to gain time. Rome called it an instance of Punic (bad) faith.

Hannibal came and was conquered. The famous Battle of Zama (202 B.C.) ended the Second Punic War. Again noble Carthaginians licked the dust at the feet of the nauseated Scipio. The peace terms were harder than before. Carthage had made a fool of Scipio and Rome was angry, Carthage's fleet was solemnly burned in her harbor, all her elephants were turned over, hostages given, and a huge money indemnity exacted. Carthage was left a ruined vassal, subject to Rome's nod.

To Massinissa was handed over ceremoniously, and before the army, title to the city of Cirta and other territory which had belonged to the first husband of the wife he had murdered. He became King of all Numidia.

* * *

NUMIDIA—THERE IS NO SUCH PLACE TODAY—WAS ONE OF THOSE geographical words with a vague and shifting meaning which are so common in old-time Africa. As first used it was not a geographical term at all. It just meant nomad, a wandering shepherd, and was used by early Greek writers like Herodotus to describe one of the two varieties of persons inhabiting the wild stretches of the interior and between coastal towns. The others were described as farmers. The term with a capital *N* was not used until some four hundred years before Christ, when it was applied as a general title to all the peoples of North Africa from Carthage to the Atlantic. Later the folk living in what is now Morocco and the folk of the desert ceased to be regarded as Numidians. Numidia then corresponded roughly with modern Algeria and was split into two native kingdoms. Massinissa's father had been king of the smaller of these.

The nomads who had given the country a name had in part settled in towns by this time. But some continued wandering. Pliny tells about their custom of "carrying their houses upon waggons"—forerunner of the trailer. The house was mounted on a two-wheeled, square chariot and was perhaps ox drawn, perhaps dragged along by the family.

THE CAREER OF MASSINISSA

MASSINISSA, THE NEW KING OF ALL NUMIDIA, SEEMS TO BE THE FIRST man in all North African history of whom we have a clear human picture. We have his portrait on coins. We have his life story, as told by Polybius, who knew him personally, and by others.

Massinissa helped bury Carthage. As a young adventurer he witnessed the beginnings of her downfall. In his maturity he despoiled her as she lay weak after the Second Punic War. In the rising ambition of his old age he seemed about to grab the city altogether. Furthermore it has been suggested that it was this ambition of Massinissa's which produced Carthage's final and complete destruction. It seems probable that his evident plans of conquest startled Rome. Rome would not have wanted the great strategic port to fall into the control of this vigorous man who might have founded a powerful native dynasty with Carthage as capital. A fear of Massinissa presumably combined with a fear of Carthage's gradual recrudescence to motivate Rome toward the Third Punic War. So it would seem that Massinissa played a major part in the ruin of Carthage, albeit he died just before her hour of agony. His career was native Africa's vengeance on the interloper.

* * *

MASSINISSA LIVED TO BE NINETY YEARS OLD, A HEARTY MAN WHO till almost the last jumped unaided upon his barebacked horse (Numidians scorned saddles). He commanded in battle at eighty-eight, and left behind him a toddling son of four.

He had both vigor and vision, the latter a heritance from his mother, an exceptional woman known as seeress and prophetess. He saw the possibilities of his country and felt that, if he could "form its nomads to husbandry and its brigands into soldiers," as Strabo said, he could lift Numidia out of the barbarian class and make her one of the important powers, and in this he succeeded.

It is true that Massinissa sometimes consented to send his fleet into the Mediterranean pirating. That in those days was no reproach. "Pirates" were mentioned respectfully along with "traders" in the old Rome-Carthage sea treaties. Massinissa's pirating did not injure the prestige of the rising Numidia.

Massinissa learned Latin and Greek, whilst Punic, rather than the vulgar native tongue, was the court language of his capital Cirta. In that city of eerie drops and precipices he lived in regal style. He could give banquets with silver and gold plate. He could give concerts where imported Greek musicians entertained his guests. He loved great wild dogs, and adored his little children and grandchildren, who must have made a mighty flock around his knees.

In middle life, as shown upon his coinage, he was handsome with a pointed beard and wide wise eyes. Except for the packs of great wild dogs one might envy Polybius who visited and told about his palace at the crossroads of barbarism and civilization.

Gradually he became master of the provincial cities which had been Carthage's. To move his headquarters there—what a fine end for his career! But Rome was planning otherwise. Massinissa fell ill, and—always friends with Rome, although it is to be supposed that Rome at times wondered whether her erstwhile protégé

was not becoming too big for his boots—he called in Roman advice
on the disposal of his heritage.

Scipio, the adopted grandson of the Scipio who had beaten
Hannibal, favored the splitting up of the kingdom between
Massinissa's sons. One need not be of unduly cynical nature to
guess at Scipio's motive in recommending a breaking up of Numidian power. The results on Massinissa's death (148 B.C.) were
as the Romans had hoped.

THE VICTOR WEPT

THE THIRD PUNIC WAR (149-146 B.C.) WAS IN FULL SWING. CATO
had made that sinister voyage of his to look into the quarreling
between Massinissa and Carthage and returned to report that
Carthage was again strong enough to be dangerous. He tagged
that familiar sentence of his, *"Delenda est Carthago"* (Carthage
should be destroyed) to every Senate speech he made on whatsoever subject. It was a "gag" that wrecked an empire. It consolidated Rome's fear of a Carthaginian comeback and her secret
jealousy of a Massinissa dynasty across the Mediterranean Nar-
rows from Italy.

Carthage defended herself with the fury of a wounded scorpion, which I know of my own knowledge can put up a grander
battle for its size than any other beast. Had Carthage shown half
such spirit before, she would not have been in this extremity.
Every gram of metal went for weapons, women gave their long
hair for catapults. This despite bad leadership, for Hasdrubal
put on weight while Carthage starved, and gave up at the end
like a craven, while his wife—too proud to crawl at Scipio's feet
—shamed him by throwing herself and her two children into the
flames.

*   *   *

THE DESTRUCTION OF CARTHAGE WAS A GRIEVOUS BUSINESS. MEN
and women rushed for refuge to the central town and fought
through streets and over roofs for six days. Carthage had tall
buildings—six stories high if you measure them European style,
seven by American reckoning. It was a custom brought from
island Tyre where space was precious. The people barricaded
themselves—each house a fortress. The Romans broke into the

houses, one after another, swarmed up to the roofs, killing as they went, and bridged the gaps across the streets or else broke through the walls from one house to another. Carthaginian men, women and children and Roman soldiers fell from the roofs and windows. The streets were an omelet of blood and broken bodies. Then the Romans set fire to the place.

On the seventh day fifty thousand survivors gave themselves up. Carthage's population at the time was estimated—perhaps overestimated—at seven hundred thousand, which, if correct, would make Carthage bigger than any North African city of today except Cairo. The city burned for ten days. Then orders came from Rome to Scipio that he should completely destroy every bit of Carthage. It was done with cold thoroughness and Scipio pronounced the famous curse which forbade men ever to live upon the site.

* * *

THEN SCIPIO LOOKED AT WHAT HE HAD DONE AND WEPT. "WHY DO you cry?" asked Polybius, the historian, who was there. Scipio then quoted the words of Homer: " 'A day will come when Ilium will perish' " and added, "I do not know why, but I am afraid that some other will stand as I stand now and repeat those words about my country!" Could he, in his mood of foreboding, have looked forward six centuries into the future, he would have seen Carthage, rebuilt, used as a Vandal base for the sack of Rome.

ALEXANDRIA

NORTH AFRICA HAD LOST A GREAT CITY. BUT SHE HAD ALREADY gained another: Alexandria. Carthage had been an introvert. Alexandria, quite the reverse. With cordial self-confidence Alexandria raised the first important lighthouse the world had ever seen to beckon ships into her harbor, and she treated foreign brains so generously that the intelligentsia of the day came flocking.

Alexandria's lighthouse on Pharos Island gave a name to its imitators which still survives in many languages (French *phare,* Spanish *faro,* Portuguese *farol,* etc.). Its light could be seen 300 stadia (33 miles) to sea. A conjectural restoration from ancient data looks surprisingly like a New York skyscraper of the most beautiful type.

As for the lights of learning—Alexandria sheltered marvels. To Alexandria came the geographer who about 250 years before Christ was able to calculate the world's belt measurement within relatively few miles of the correct figure. (Eratosthenes' mileage was 28,000; modern figuring makes it 24,899.) There Euclid, who survives today as Public Enemy Number One of many youngsters, tartly informed the puzzled king of Egypt that there was "no royal road to Geometry." And at Alexandria were made those early anatomical investigations, so valuable to the science of surgery and so shocking to antique sentiments, for these investigations and experiments were allegedly carried out upon living prisoners from the Alexandria jail.

The city's collection of books was enormous: 532,800 volumes, perhaps more. The vastness of the Alexandrian library inspired the familiar story to the effect that the Arabs when they arrived in the Middle Ages regarded the classical works as heretical and used the papyrus rolls as fuel for the city's public baths. There were hundreds of bath establishments, but "such was the incredible multitude of the books," so the story runs, "that six, months was barely sufficient for their consumption." Sober history discounts the tale, not so much for the reason that there could not have been enough volumes to do the work as because the library had probably been dissipated before the Arabs arrived.

*   *   *

ALEXANDRIA IN ANTIQUITY WITH ITS BOULEVARDS 150 FEET WIDE, running from gate to gate, and its shady colonnades to either side must have been a delightful place—and quite different from the Alexandria of today.

It had been created as a new capital for Egypt in 331 B.C. by Alexander the Great, an outstandingly useful performance in a turbulent and bloody career.

Alexander took Egypt with a prestidigitator's ease, a wave of the hand and the country was his. Inside five months his restless mind had done with Egypt and he plunged away again, destined to go on and on till he burned himself out. A tribute written three centuries later: "Thus died Alexander, when he had reigned twelve years and seven months, having performed such mighty acts as no king ever did before him, nor any since his day." An Athenian contemporary of Alexander's saw his career from another angle, "It cannot be true!" he cried in incredulous ecstasy when the report came of the conqueror's sudden demise. "For, if Alexander were really dead the whole world would have stunk of his carcass!" Another contemporary, a minor king, expressed his opinion of the departed by a simple physical reaction that spoke louder than any words. He fainted away with joy when he heard the news.

THE ALEXANDER PUZZLE

THE WHY OF ALEXANDER—IT HAS BEEN ONE OF THE QUESTIONS OF the ages. Was this man who did so much damage and gained so much glory merely one—though probably the greatest one—of the men born mad to conquer their fellows? Or was he a man really different from others, a person moved and strengthened by some mysterious force? Did he sincerely believe that he was not human but a god—"the Lord of the whole world," as he called himself? Or was it perhaps the itch of intolerable curiosity that dragged him from country to country, the longing to see new places, new trees and animals and birds, men of new tints and forms of face, women with new ways and morals? In a man of Alexander's fierce energy and conscienceless courage, in a man hampered by royal prohibitions as he was, the travel passion necessarily would have torn the world to tatters. To conquer the earth was his only way to see it. Alexander could not wander the globe from Greece to India like a private citizen. He must first butcher the lands he longed to see. So he swept on, sailing a sea of blood, and dreaming always of further lands beyond the then known world. He died prattling of a periplus around Arabia and Africa. A short life (he was only thirty-two when he died) but from his own point of view a good one, for, though he had been hacked by terrible wounds and harassed by superstitious fears, he had seen and killed men of nearly every sort then known. His diversion, says Plutarch, was "hunting—or rather war—for his game were men."

His wounds were inevitable, given the hand-to-hand fighting

and direct leadership of the day. And so were his superstitions. Alexander seems to have believed himself to be superhuman. This belief automatically made all the world supernatural to him. He saw omens in every incident of the day and his court swarmed with odd gentry who catered to his weakness.

The road to India before him, he learned that a sheep in the camp flocks had "yeaned a lamb with the perfect form and color of a tiara upon its head on either side of which were testicles." Alexander considered this animal with horror because he saw in it proof that his empire would fall into the hands of an obscure and weak man. As he went on, a joyous omen came to cheer him. Men were digging in the ground near the Oxus River to put up his tent posts when suddenly "a spring of oily liquor" welled up in the holes. This liquid did not differ from real oil, "though there were no olives in that country." Alexander was delighted and pronounced it "one of the happiest presages the gods had ever granted."

These two omens are recounted in Plutarch's *Alexander*. The explanation that Alexander's find on the Oxus was a misplaced supply of olive oil was on reflection discarded. Strabo, centuries after Alexander's time, says learnedly, "It is probable that certain nitrous, astringent, bituminous and sulphurous fluids permeate the earth; greasy fluids may be found, but the rarity of their occurrence makes their existence almost doubtful." It is curious to read about this early bewilderment as to the oil which makes the world go round.

THE SIWA ORACLE

It was, however, in Africa that Alexander's appetite for the supernatural was especially well fed. In Africa Alexander found a new father.

His beloved mother had been divorced by her husband, Philip, on suspicion that Alexander was not his child. A strange, visionary woman, she had confessed to infidelity and had named tauntingly "a serpent of extraordinary size" as her lover. Her husband "had lost one of his eyes when he applied it to the chink of the door" at a moment when he believed his queen was entertaining the great snake. Just before Alexander set forth on his conquests his mother, it is said, told him the secret of his birth. Presumably her story was that the god Amon had come to her in serpent guise. And presumably Alexander then guessed the reason for that surge of more than human self-confidence which he had always felt within him and also for certain minor personal peculiarities such as the sweet odor which came from his breath and person so that his undergarments were perfumed from contact with his body. He saw promise of a wondrous destiny if he could but prove his mother's claim by inquiry addressed direct to Amon himself.

The above is the romantic explanation of Alexander's motive for his expedition to the oracle of Amon situated in the oasis of Siwa. It was recounted by classical writers, notably Plutarch and Justin, and accepted literally in classical times. Why not? In the days of old it was no mark of an unsound mind to believe men's boasts that they descended from gods and mythical heroes. A further reason for Alexander's pilgrimage was the practical consideration that Amon's recognition would be valuable politically now that Alexander had occupied Egypt, and would also be an interesting piece of self-advertisement likely to startle his enemies.

The oracle at Siwa, an oasis in the northwest corner of Egypt, was accounted to be one of the seven great oracles of the period, and it was the only one of the seven situated outside of Greece. Siwa also possessed a natural wonder in "The Fountain of the Sun," a spring which ran daily hot and cold water: cool at noon, boiling at midnight.

To reach Siwa would then have meant in normal circumstances a hard journey, but Alexander is said to have been helped forward by heavenly aid. Showers fell when his party was in the extremity of thirst, crows led them on their way when lost. At Amon's temple in the oasis Alexander confronted the image of the god "adorned in every part with emeralds and precious stones," and the god, through his priests, greeted him as a son. Maybe the priests had received instructions in advance, or knew the conqueror's hopes and spoke tactfully. To Alexander's entourage the god, through his priests, gave orders that in future they "should reverence Alexander as a god and not as a king."

Henceforth, says Justin, Alexander's whole personality changed.

He became haughty and arrogant. His charm of demeanor was lost.

Alexander never again saw the homeland of his new father. A decade later he was brought back to Egypt a corpse—the empire he had conquered already in disorder, his family under dangers soon to be fatal to the three persons he would most have wished to protect. All three were murdered—his beloved mother, his posthumous son, his wife Roxana, the girl captive who had roused both his passion and his respect, so that, as Plutarch tells us, he would not offer her a caress before the marriage ceremony.

Apropos of Roxana, I diverge for a moment to glance back at Alexander's intimate character in the light of our modern notions. His continence in the matter of women, given his uncontrolled, hard-drinking and passionate nature and given the unlimited opportunity he had to claim for his pleasure any lovely woman in all the Near and Middle East, is notable. Statistical information on his sex behavior is naturally lacking and confused, Alexander being over 2000 years dead and there having survived no complete contemporary biography. Here is the general picture: His failure to maintain a harem was regarded as an eccentricity, and the sparseness of his love experiences was notorious; his matrimonial alliances, aside from the union with Roxana, appear to have been motivated by political reasons, and to have been limited to two, and to have been entered into only shortly before his death. (Roxana is said to have killed one of these women. There was an old stage play about their rivalry, in which Peg Woffington used to act.) The paucity of Alexander's progeny is additional proof of his frigidity. Roxana, his wife for some four years, he left pregnant when he died. There is mention that another child had been born to one of his politically dictated marriages. Diodorus states as a fact that, after Roxana's child was killed, "the seed royal was extinct." Alexander's peculiar emotional nature included intense mother reverence and adoration, and he was rocked to despair at the death of one of his man friends, Hephaestion. (He crucified the doctor who had failed to save his favorite!) These things combine to make what at first glance might seem a surprising temperament for a ferocious and superbly courageous warrior—such a temperament as might, in our more sexually self-conscious day, cause a man to be the subject for psychological anxiety. (And yet the supposed sex peculiarities of another spectacular conqueror of recent fame have been common gossip. At the start of World War II a British "Blue Book" emphasized their ambassador's opinion as to Hitler's abnormality and throughout and after the War the alleged oddities and gaps in his love life have inspired countless newspaper columns.)

ALEXANDER'S RETURN TO EGYPT

THE WIPING OUT OF ALEXANDER'S ONLY BELOVED, OF HER CHILD and of his adored mother were a heartless insult to his memory. It was a pitiful finish to all his brilliant effort and godlike pride. And yet they gave Alexander the most gorgeous funeral of all time. Two years it had taken to prepare the chariot which carried the dead conqueror toward the Amon Oasis where it was planned to lay him within sight of his "father's" oracle.

All the way from Babylon to Egypt sixty-four mules dragged the great glittering car, which must have been shaped like a carnival floaʒ. Each mule was "adorned with a crown of gold and with bells of gold to either side of its head, and its neck was fitted into a collar set and beautified with precious stones." I quote from Diodorus. A company of men went on ahead to clear a way across country flat and wide enough for its passage.

People came flocking from adjoining lands to wait and watch —and in some cases to gloat. In the Gaza neighborhood, for instance, near the edge of Egypt there must have been satisfaction mixed with the local awe as folk considered the passing of this young man who had chopped his way through them ten years before, and contrived "a novel punishment" for that leader of theirs who had dared to oppose his passage. Alexander had "directed that the feet of this man be bored and a brazen ring passed through them" and, while the man was still alive, Alexander had driven his chariot at full speed with him tied to its tail.

Now dead Alexander rode by in a coffin. It was a coffin of beaten gold and he lay in a bed of aromatic spices "which served as well to delight the sense as to preserve the body from putrefication." Over the coffin rested a purple robe embroidered with gold, and the funeral car was surmounted by a golden arch twelve cubits (twenty feet) long. From the arch flapped a network fringe to which hung large bells which could be heard at a great distance. Everything was made of gold. Every object was studded with jewels.

But Alexander did not go to his "father" at Siwa. Alexander was dead and powerless, and it suited the policy and ambition of Egypt's ruler to lay him in due course in a fine tomb at the new capital, Alexandria, a city which its founder had never seen, so short had been his stay in the land of Amon.

THE SCANDALOUS PTOLEMIES

FOR THE THREE CENTURIES WHICH FOLLOWED ALEXANDER'S DEATH the Ptolemies ruled over Egypt. Ptolemy was merely a man's name transformed into a royal title: it meant literally "Mighty-in-War" and was well deserved by the first of the dynasty who bore it—a trusted officer in Alexander's army. (He was also believed by many to be Alexander's bastard half brother.) For a time he took charge as satrap (word derived from the Persian, meaning governor) on behalf of Alexander's estate. Then he slipped under the crown, called himself king of Egypt and started a royal line.

The tale of the Ptolemies when, as soon happened, the dynasty got into its downhill slide, makes sad reading. You would have to hunt History for a succession of kings so wicked or worthless or both as the last dozen of the Ptolemies—to my count there were sixteen of them in all,[8] some of whom barely got a chance

[8] There is no established way of saying how many there were. The Ptolemies were not known at the time by numbers, and are not listed clearly like the Louises of France and the Georges of England. The careers of several of them shot with such swiftness from the proclamation of kingship to the grave that opinion is confused as to whether they count at all. Some students of history have ignored these Ptolemies-who-died-young altogether in numbering the dynasty. (On this see a learned discussion in the preface of Bevan's work on the Ptolemies.) Some have chosen to ignore certain of them while including others, nor do various authorities ignore and include the same ones! If we are to count all possible Ptolemies the list totals sixteen, and I have preferred to include all of them as a trifling retroactive tribute to those unlucky boys thrown without fault of their own into such dangerous greatness and dying before their crowns were warm.

to reign at all in the swift and perilous Ptolemaic kaleidoscope.

As for their womenfolk, let me quote an authority on the period, J. P. Mahaffy, who, in summing up the careers and characters of the Ptolemaic queens and princesses, says that they offer "such pictures of depravity as make any reasonable man pause and ask whether human nature had deserted these women."

Egypt watched patiently for the most part, observed the progressive deterioration of the Ptolemies and their queens, whose crimes in many cases were more against one another than against the population, even laughed and gave the more corrupt or foolish of them comic nicknames.

*   *   *

PTOLEMY I IN HIS FAIRLY HONORABLE OLD AGE GAVE OVER THE power to his son. As a tribute to the old man's memory was held the most gorgeous festival of history—match it if you can! It is described by Callixenus of Rhodes with enthusiastic detail to the length of eleven closely printed pages which have been preserved in *The Deipnosophists,* or "Banquet of the Learned," a sort of classical Book of Quotations, collected by Athenaeus of Alexandria.

The procession which passed through Alexandria on that day took from torchlight before dawn till torchlight after sunset. It was an orgy. It was a circus. It was an exhibition of golden glory that blinded the crowd. I pluck bits from Callixenus' pages:

There was a great float drawn by three hundred men, upon it a wine press with sixty satyrs tramping the grapes, the new wine running out across the whole roadway. Followed another yet bigger float carrying a giant sack which held three thousand measures of matured wine. The sack was made of leopard skins so sewed together that it allowed the liquor to escape gradually and flow into the street in rivulets.

The city's whole air was perfumed with myrrh and frankincense, saffron, cassia, cinnamon, iris and two hundred other spices borne on golden dishes by boys in purple tunics.

Curious, lovely and lewd things were to be seen. The forms of forty dancing satyrs, their naked skins painted in gay colors. Sixteen hundred pretty boys skipping along in golden crowns, and little else. Two dozen chariots drawn by four elephants each, and eight carts pulled by teams of ostriches. Zebras harnessed in

pairs. Camels piled high with rare spices. An immense white bear
sweltering under Egypt's sun. A rhinoceros from Ethiopia.

After the big animal parade came one hundred fifty men carrying exotic trees on the branches of which were tied strange
small animals and cages holding birds from the far southland:
pistache-green parrots, gleaming feathered creatures that were
scarlet and metallic blue and snow white and pink like the meat
of watermelons.

There were seven palm trees that had been plated completely
in gold, and huge golden figures of animals. One figure was that
of an eagle thirty feet in height. There were all sorts of other
golden objects: thrones and incense burners, lamps and so on.
One article displayed puzzles me. It was a *stove* twenty feet in
circumference and having a golden top—odd, indeed, but so
described by Callixenus.

All this was done "at the expense of 2239 talents and 50
minae." What terrific labor and loss of life it cost, none can
guess. How many, for instance, suffered cruel hardships and
how many died in the job of capturing and transporting that
immense white bear from its lair to Alexandria? Or in the job of
fetching those "two hundred other spices" from the remote lands
of their origin?

*   *   *

EGYPT REMEMBERED THIS SHOW WITH SATISFACTION FOR A LONG
time. She remembered too the fine deeds of Ptolemy III, surnamed Euergetes, "Benefactor," a freak among the Ptolemies in
that he lived a morally pure life.

This efficient ruler pushed down farther into the south than
any Egyptian king had ever invaded. Some two thousand years
afterward his name was found graven upon a stone which was
used as a footstool before the Abyssinian throne.

This Ptolemaic revival of interest in the lands to the south
was a novelty. For centuries Egypt seems to have pretty much
ignored the up-Nile country and historic records of contacts with
the region are rare. A long line of Ethiopian rulers had held isolated sway with headquarters at Napata near the Fourth Cataract
and at Meroë. The explanation of the revived Egyptian interest
in the up-Nile country was that it was elephant land and the war
potentiality of the elephant had been realized. When, after ex-

periments, the African elephant had been recognized as a poor warrior compared with his Asiatic cousins, Ethiopia again dropped from Egyptian notice.

Ptolemy Euergetes, "The Benefactor," furthermore drove into Asia Minor and came back in triumph with a prize of great senti-mental value. This was a collection of the holy things which the Assyrians had stolen when they violated Egypt's temples in the long ago. So the images of Egypt's gods were restored by a for-eign master whose interest in Egypt's religion must have been a mere matter of outward show for policy's sake, for this Ptolemy was so indifferent to local matters that he did not even bother to learn the language of the country. It was a happy day for Egypt when those homesick and humiliated gods which had been more than four hundred years in exile came back to their devotees.

* * *

THE SUCCESSOR TO THIS PTOLEMY WAS A DEBAUCHEE. TO HIM WAS attributed with grim whimsicality the surname of Philopator, meaning "Father-Loving," although he is charged with procur-ing the deaths of both of his parents. This presumed parricide set himself to become famous as the builder of the largest ships ever launched. His Nile river yacht which he called "The-Car-rier-of-the-Bed-Chamber" was three hundred thirty feet long. His warship had forty banks of oars and a length of two hundred eighty cubits (equaling four hundred ninety feet, if the cubit be taken as one foot nine inches). It took four thousand men to row this monster. A third ship which he gave to a Sicilian king was large enough to carry eight turrets capable of shooting arrows eighteen feet long. From a distance such a ship looked like "a huge castle in the midst of the waves." These vessels were diffi-cult to handle and very dangerous. The jeering world of the day commonly nicknamed them after some island or mountain: Etna, for instance.

The next Ptolemy was the boy king of the Rosetta Stone dur-ing whose reign Egypt lost much territory. He married the first of the royal Egyptian Cleopatras. Cleopatra I was remarkable amongst the line of queens so named, in that she appears to have died a natural death. The next queen of that name, Cleopatra II, was the victim of that hideous story wherein her second husband, who was also her born brother *and* her brother-in-law, served her, at a banquet, pieces of her own son. Later she was presumably murdered by her daughter, and this daughter, Cleopatra III, was in turn killed by her son just when, according to Justin, she was planning to murder him.

*   *   *

THE PHENOMENAL BITTERNESS OF THE FAMILY HATRED OF THE royal house may have been due in part to their habit of incest, a practice which—whatever its perverse secret appeal upon occasions —might well be nauseating when obligatory. In the case of the Ptolemies, who were but imitation Egyptians, incestuous marriages did not produce normal children as had been the case in the days of the old Pharaohs (see page 22). To ancient Egypt it had been a natural and sweet thing for royal brother and sister to marry and their love life was without shame or self-conscious-ness. To the Greek idea the antique royal marriage system which they undertook to imitate must have seemed unnatural and nasty. Ptolemies and Cleopatras, persons of Greek culture, who went to the marriage chamber as brother and sister, uncle and niece, etc., would have felt abhorrence to the act they were consummating. Or else their intercourse would have been marked by the naughty excitement of a forbidden sin. Neither mood would have made for good offspring. Often they bred physical monsters and moral irresponsibles.

*   *   *

EGYPT KNEW THE CLEOPATRAS OF WHOM WE HAVE TOLD AND OTHERS whose lives were a rosary of infamies and tragedies, and a series of Ptolemies whose careers repeated wickedness and weakness.

Run them through: the Seventh Ptolemy, not bad perhaps but slack (I refer to Philometor, who in some listings is called Ptolemy VI). The Eighth who was murdered by his uncle as a child. The Ninth (alternately called Ptolemy VII in some lists; a footnote on page 96 deals with the confused numbering of the Ptolemies) was the same who is accused of having served to his wife "the head, hands and feet of her baby" at a feast; in later days he was nicknamed Physcon, "Big Belly," and was noted for the delight he took in exposing that which gave him his soubriquet through a robe of transparent muslin. So feared and unpopular was this pervert that the Alexandrians quit the city in a body and he found himself "a king not of men, but of empty houses." And so it went.

The thirteenth and last adult Ptolemy to figure in Egypt's history was sternly classed by Strabo as "one of the three worst of all." His "throne name" translates as follows: "Heir of the god that saves, chosen of Ptah, doing the rule of Amon, living image of Re." It contrasts with the nickname given him by his subjects which was Auletes, meaning "The Fluter." Playing the flute was his one accomplishment, and he took so little pride in his position that it was his habit to enter himself in public band competitions.

The Egyptians revolted against him. Rome rooked and restored him. He reigned another four years. He was undignified and incompetent. But he was the father of the most famous female personage in all History.

BOOK TWO

CLEOPATRA TO MOHAMMED

THE MOST FAMOUS AFRICAN
OF ALL TIMES

BETWEEN THE PERIODS OF THOSE TWO CONTRASTING PERSONAGES, Cleopatra and Mohammed, is framed a specific section of North Africa's history. At Cleopatra's death all of then known Africa became Roman. One of her lovers projected the rebuilding of Carthage as a Roman city. One of her children became consort to a Roman protected king in the Far West. Just as Mohammed's death marked the end of Roman Africa, Cleopatra's death marked its beginning. The intervening six hundred-odd years were—with some local interruptions—a time of Roman domination.

* * *

CLEOPATRA'S FAME—AND IT IS UNDOUBTEDLY GREATER THAN THAT of any other African—was a triumph of unaided personality. Her origin and early years were, for a princess, squalid. The shaping of her career was full of peril and uncertainty.

She was in the Egyptian sense illegitimate, for her mother was not the official queen. The meaning of the name Cleopatra was in her case pathetically inept. It means "She-Who-Has-a-Glorious-Father." Ptolemy, "The Fluter," was a shabby adventurer, despised in Egypt and cheated and snubbed at Rome. His kingdom, though still rich, was a faded relic, far other than the gorgeous Nile kingdom of old. Everybody knew that Egypt's days of independence were running short.

Cleopatra's girlhood was passed in a setting of intrigue, disorder and crime, and under the shadow of oncoming tragedy, moral irresponsibility and soulless greed. Yet Cleopatra so lived, ruled and loved that we have never forgotten her. Her name is one of the very few we use descriptively. "You are a Cleopatra!" men still say to women they seek to flatter. There are scarcely any other women whose names have so entered into modern speech.

We can study Cleopatra's face upon a coin—winning and wise, mouth faintly smiling at the corners, wavy hair drawn back into a knot at the nape: such a woman as you might see and like today.

Says Plutarch, whose *Life of Antony* is our best and a relatively contemporary account of Cleopatra (He lived within a century of her time and heard about her from his grandfather whose friend and gossip knew Cleopatra's cook and visited her kitchens): —"Her actual beauty, it is said, was not in itself so remarkable that none could be compared to her . . . but the contact of her presence was irresistible, the attraction of her person, joining with the charm of her conversation and the character that attended all she said and did was something bewitching. It was a pleasure merely to hear the sound of her voice, with which—like an instrument of many strings—she could pass from one language to another, so that there were few of the barbarian nations that she answered by an interpreter; to most of them she spoke herself, as to the Ethiopians, troglodytes (meaning those special cave dwellers who lived by the Red Sea), Hebrews, Arabians, Syrians, Medes, Parthians, and many others whose language she had learnt."

Cleopatra was born about 69 B.C. When she was seventeen or eighteen Ptolemy, "The Fluter," died; he had been "expelled from Alexandria for his vices"—a striking statement since Alexandria had then the reputation of containing the most licentious population of all times, who wallowed in a stew of artfully mixed wickedness that "combined the vices of the East with those of the West."

During his years of exile and upon his death "The Fluter" provided the elements for a series of those bloody brawls in which Ptolemaic families seemed to revel. While he was away a legitimate daughter some seven years older than Cleopatra took charge. Less successful in love than Cleopatra was destined to be she mar-

ried a Syrian who was allegedly involved in the scandalous steal-
ing of Alexander the Great's golden coffin,[1] and who was strangled
at his wife's request, she being "unable to endure his coarseness
and vulgarity," as Strabo delicately puts it. She then married
another Syrian. Upon her father's return from exile both she and
her second husband were killed.

When Ptolemy, "The Fluter," died Cleopatra and her little
brother—and appointed husband—of ten inherited the throne.
According to family psychology each hoped to do away with the
other, the little boy, a tool of his elders, of course. While the
situation was boiling up Cleopatra met and presumably gave herself to the son of Pompey the Great, then on a mission in Egypt.
Shakespeare represents this early romance as a bitter annoyance
to the jealous Antony who once sneers, "You were a fragment (a
leftover) of Gnaeus Pompey's!"

It was Pompey the Great, her supposed sweetheart's father,
who led Cleopatra indirectly into the arms of Julius Caesar.
Pompey had suffered complete defeat in battle, was in flight and
sought refuge in Egypt, remembering that in the old days he had
aided the exiled "Fluter," father of the present two joint rulers.
Pompey blundered. He was murdered as he stepped onto the
Egyptian beach. Great Pompey was then fifty-nine. Long past
was the pride of the boy general who had subdued "all Africa"
(meaning the region of Carthage's former empire) in forty days
and had time over to hunt lions and elephants—still easily found
game in Tunisia—before he returned to his triumph at Rome.

In pursuit of Pompey and unaware of what had happened came

---

[1] The disappearance of this massive gold coffin is one of the minor mysteries
of history. Strabo, who was in Egypt shortly after the Ptolemaic dynasty ended,
reports (XVII:8) that it was no longer in the *Sema*, the temple tomb at
Alexandria, and that Alexander the Great's body then lay in a coffin made of
hyalus (alabaster?). Strabo attributes the theft not to the Syrian husband of
Cleopatra's elder sister, but to one whom he indicates as "Cocce's son." Strabo
refers to that unsightly and unnatural child of the Ptolemy who was known
as "Big Belly" (see pp. 100-01) by the lady who was both his niece and his
stepdaughter, Cleopatra Cocce or III. This child grew up to murder his
mother and to become a much-hated king. He may have grabbed the gold
coffin to pay foreign troops brought in to re-establish his power. It is recorded
of him that, like his father, he was a monster of fat and that he could not
walk unaided, but that when drunk he found the strength to leap down off
his high banqueting couch and shake the folds of his huge body in violent,
indecent dancing (Posidonius, quoted in *The Deipnosophists* of Athenaeus).

Caesar, then well over fifty. Cleopatra was just over twenty. Plutarch tells how, eager to gain Caesar's help in her quarrel with her brother, Cleopatra caused herself to be rolled lengthwise in a coverlet, tied up in a bundle and smuggled into Caesar's quarters—bold beauty this that dared court a cagey old warrior with charms so disheveled! All the world knows that she succeeded, that Caesar became her lover, gave her back her royal rights, and that her greedy young brother perished in the Nile. His frail body—he would have been not over fourteen—was dragged up from the Nile mud in a suit of pure gold. He was almost the last Egyptian Ptolemy to die murdered—only two more victims were to follow him.

A still younger brother was placed on the throne with Cleopatra as her titular husband, and busy Caesar marched forth again to combat—to the famous "Veni, vidi, vici!" combat, as it happened.

WHERE CARTHAGE HAD BEEN

WHILE CLEOPATRA CARRIED AND NURSED CAESAR'S CHILD, THE BOY Caesarion, Caesar, amongst other adventures, proceeded to Tunisia to chase dead Pompey's friends.

By a very odd coincidence Caesar's Tunisian campaign occurred exactly one hundred years after the destruction of Carthage (46 B.C. and 146 B.C. were the respective years). During the intervening century this region of Africa had suffered from shock following the amputation of a great city which had been its heart and brains. Nor had a native king risen to replace the grand old man, Massinissa, although—like good wine turned to vinegar—a grandson of his, the tricky Jugurtha, had made trouble in plenty.

For twenty-three years the site where once Carthage had stood was a gaping wound. Then came an aborted attempt to rebuild the city. This was sponsored by one of the Gracchi, son of that famous Roman matron who said of her children, "These are my jewels!" and who was by some monstrous incongruity sought in marriage by the horrid wretch "Big Belly" Ptolemy when he was on a visit to Rome. The matron, Cornelia, declined.

The new city of Carthage which her son proposed to establish would have been Rome's first colony outside the Italian peninsula. Some six thousand colonists were persuaded to join the enterprise, no doubt feeling a bit squeamish at the prospect of crossing the water to live in a locality accursed by Scipio's malediction. In political circles there was opposition. A colony in a spot so favored for trade and war might grow up to overshadow the mother city.

The city was in process of dedication—Gaius Gracchus called it Junonia after the goddess, and indicated a site exactly the same as that of old Carthage—when dread events happened. The staff of the leading standard in the procession was broken by violent wind. The sacrificial materials were blown from the altars, and wolves (or jackals) came and seized the boundary marks and "carried them to a great distance." This is the classical story. Professor Gsell suggests that the omens were worked up by Gracchus' political opponents. In all events Junonia died unborn, and the site of accursed Carthage remained a waste for a while longer.

JUGURTHA

A DECADE LATER THE ROMANTIC VILLAIN, JUGURTHA, BECAME THE nightmare of Rome. He was child of a concubine of one of Massinissa's sons. He had known the old warrior king and had a wide streak of Massinissa in his nature and in his body. He was handsome, very athletic, brave to rashness. But there was another wide streak in him from some other source. A sober old historian (Niebuhr) said in so many words this streak was from Satan! Jugurtha was absolutely perfidious and he firmly believed everybody else was as false as himself. In his earlier dealings with Rome he sought to prove his opinion—and was fairly successful. As he rode from the city after a performance of bribery which had profoundly shaken Rome's belief in her own integrity he wagged his thumb over his shoulder and sneered, "A city for sale!"

In war his cunning was diabolic. He trapped and fooled lumbering Roman armies. He was an artist in guerrilla, "little war," fighting go-as-you-please style and ignoring the established rules of Mars. In the end Rome too turned tricky, inducing Jugurtha's father-in-law to betray him into their hands. It had taken seven years to beat him. Rome hooted when the conquered villain who had shaken their faith in their armies and in their honor was led along in the triumph. His end was hideous. Half mad (he had always been subject to nervous crises) he went smiling and jeering and making jokes into the terrible underground prison beneath the Capitol. They stripped him of his tunic, tore off the tips of his ears to get the valuable pendant rings he wore. They left him six days to starve and then strangled him. Comprehensible cruelty from a great power which had been badly and prolongedly scared by a petty enemy—a barbarian bastard, not even a proper kinglet, for he had stolen power by the murder of his three cousins.

*   *   *

JUGURTHA—WHAT A FINE ROLLING NAME IT IS!—STANDS A PECULIARLY tragic and intriguing figure of antiquity, a character for drama —true Shakespeare meat. Two generations after his day he inspired what is called "one of the best pieces of all classic literature": Sallust's work of art, the *Bellum Jugurthinum.*

One of its passages describes the Roman capture of Gafsa, a town which adored the dashing Jugurtha. The Roman general had marched his men secretly by night for three nights. On the fourth dawn he watched the unsuspecting populace go out as was their custom to work in the gardens in the oasis beyond the town walls. Then his cavalry rushed the gates. The unarmed men outside, the helpless women and old folk within were Rome's victims. The Romans did not lose a man. Gafsa was burnt, the partisans of Jugurtha slain or sold as slaves. This was Gafsa's first important appearance in history. Its prehistoric importance has been mentioned. Gafsa was prominent again in World War II— a long career.

CAESAR IN TUNISIA

FROM THE TIME OF JUGURTHA TUNISIA AND ADJOINING PARTS OF Africa were quiet and without known history for many years. Then again it was a Roman battleground—for Pompey and then for Caesar.

Caesar landed at what is now Sousse, and as he landed upon the Tunisian shores he stumbled. It was an evil omen. Like a flash

Caesar saved the situation, threw himself down as if on purpose, clutched up a handful of sand and kissed it, crying, "I hold you in my grasp, O Africa!"

At first it looked as if the language of the omen, as unamended by Caesar's quick-wittedness, had spoken truth, for Caesar had bad luck. He found himself in so poor a fix that, as Plutarch tells us, he had to "feed the army's horses on sea weed which he caused to be washed thoroughly to take off the saltiness and mixed with a little grass to give it an agreeable taste."

The Roman enemies he had come to Africa to fight were strong, and they had furthermore induced the native king, Juba of the Massinissa blood, to join them on the promise, it is said, that all Rome's holdings in Africa should be his if he would help them to defeat Caesar. Juba had a big army and sixty war elephants. He was sufficient of a potential danger for Rome, under Caesar's direction, to proclaim him "a public enemy." Caesar prepared for battle, working his war industries on the very spot, making arrows and javelins with machines and material—iron, lead and wood—imported from Sicily. One spring morning in the year 46 B.C. he fought the surprise Battle of Thapsus, a bit down the coast from Sousse, and "in the small part of a single day . . . killed fifty thousand of the enemy with the loss of only fifty of his own." Plutarch says this. The figures on Caesar's losses are probably accurate; enemy losses, some say, much exaggerated.

Juba's elephants did more harm than good, and Juba himself fled toward his capital in inland Tunisia at Zama, now called Jama. There Juba had, before leaving for war, done that which might be interpreted either as a proof of confidence or of fear. He had built up a big pyre, swearing that if he did not conquer Caesar he, his wealth, his family and the whole population should be burnt up. When Juba, defeated, returned and knocked at Zama's gates, Zama which had taken his bravado seriously would not let him in. He and a companion in flight decided to make a gallant end of things. They ate a fine supper, then joined in a duel to the death, the understanding being that the victor should then kill himself. And so it was.

CATO AND THE PSYLLI

NOR WERE THESE THE ONLY SUICIDES TO FOLLOW CAESAR'S VICTORY. To the north of Tunisia at Utica the Roman, Cato, great-grandson of the Cato who cried out so insistently for the destruction of Carthage, did away with himself in circumstances so impressive that his suicide simultaneously made his own reputation and that of the place where he committed it. "Utica is ennobled by the death of Cato!" cried Pliny. Literally the suicide of Cato was regarded by classical opinion as the very most important event of all Utica's thousand years of history. Cato's self-destruction was not artistic. He stabbed himself clumsily, was found "weltering in his blood with his bowels fallen out," and when an attempt had been made to sew up the wound, "he tore it open again, plucked out his bowels and immediately expired" (Plutarch's *Life of Cato, the Younger*). What outstandingly won the admiration of the contemporary world for an action which we might call that of a "quitter" was apparently that Cato passed the evening hours previous to his suicide in reading Plato on the immortality of the soul.

Nothing could more quickly illustrate the difference between the modern and the old Roman point of view than the true reverence with which classical opinion regarded Cato's hari-kari, motivated by a natural enough, but to our idea rather cowardly wish to dodge facing the conquering Caesar. He could not bear a patronizing forgiveness from his old enemy.

Far, far more praiseworthy to the modern notion was Cato's last great deed before his death—that agonizing march of his across the top of Africa to join in the war against Caesar. That march *was* something to brag about.

Cato led ten thousand men through the sands from Cyrenaica to Tunisia. Their sufferings were fearful and Cato showed splendid courage. He was not young, as ages counted in those days, being about forty-eight, but he would not ride while his men had to walk. He was always first in the march and last to accept drink at the water holes. A noble leader of men at a period when democratic sharing of hardship was not usual.

*   *   *

A CURIOUS FEATURE RECORDED ABOUT THE MARCH IS THAT CATO had provided his army with a detachment of "the people called Psylli who obviate the effect of the bite of serpents (meaning in this case the dread horned viper of the desert) by sucking out the poison, and who deprive the serpents themselves of their ferocity by their charms."

These odd folk, the Psylli, are one of the marvel stories of antiquity. I have collected quite a dossier about them: from Herodotus, Pliny, Plutarch, from the learned Professor Gsell and many others:

The tribe of the Psylli lived in the desert of Tripolitania. As an independent nation they were wiped out by their neighbors, the Nasamonians, after they themselves had been weakened by making a "war against the South Wind" because it dried up their water holes (Herodotus). In the bodies of the Psylli was "a certain poison which was fatal to serpents" (Pliny, *Natural History*). The very smell of a member of the tribe would put a serpent to sleep! This innate poison was common to all the tribe from birth, and adulterous women were detected by the exposure of their babies to fierce snakes. Bastardy through a father outside the tribe carried a passport to the grave.

In latter years the Psylli commercialized this talent not only as paid aids to desert travelers but as entertainers, going even as far as Italy. Pliny claims to have seen exhibitions where Psylli resisted the bites of a creature "more swiftly fatal than even the asp": it was the "bramble frog." In order to irritate these bramble frogs to give a good show the performing Psylli placed them on "flat vessels made red hot." Furthermore these enterprising Psylli brought along with them pests from Africa—scorpions and so on—which they scattered about in Italy as they traveled so as to create demand for their services as wound suckers!

CAESAR'S TRIUMPH

CAESAR LEFT AFRICA IN GLORY AND WITH SOME PICTURESQUE BAGgage. For the embellishment of his triumphs—he had a triple triumph, one for his victory in Egypt, one for Pontus in Asia Minor, and one for Tunisia—he brought to Rome a zoo of animals: four hundred lions, forty elephants and a giraffe, probably the first ever seen in Europe. He brought also two interesting young humans: Arsinöe, a sister, so naturally an enemy of Cleopatra's, and Juba Junior, a frolic of four who misconstrued the whole affair and, instead of seeing it as the humiliating celebration of his late father's defeat, thought it a fine show got up for his amusement. He was carried in the procession and "was the happiest little captive ever seen."

CLEOPATRA AND ANTONY

CLEOPATRA SAW CAESAR IN HIS GREATNESS AT ROME. SHE HAD taken little Caesarion to show to his father; she had been Caesar's guest. When he died assassinated she fled back to Egypt. It had been a distressing trip. She had lost her lover-protector and her reputation, so far as Rome was concerned. She also seems to have lost her little brother-husband, her associate as joint ruler of Egypt. It is said that the boy died by her connivance, Cleopatra wishing to make the young Caesarion her throne partner in his stead. Cleopatra, true to the family tradition, saw many of her family die after she had nudged death's elbow. Presently Arsinöe, her sister, was to go—her murder a love token to Cleopatra from Antony.

It was three years after her return from Rome that Cleopatra, seeking to weave her way through Rome's snarled politics, set out to become Antony's beloved.

Antony was then in the early forties, Cleopatra in the late twenties. He had been the playboy of Rome, accustomed to drive a team of lions and to picnic off golden dishes with singing girls and actresses. Now he was a triumvir—one of the Big Three of Rome. But in so far as his taste for pleasure went he had changed little, rioting his way through the Near East in a whirl of "license and buffoonery," escorted by "a set of harpers and pipers . . . by the dancing man, Metrodorus, and a whole Bacchic rout of the like Asiatic exhibitors." He was a handsome fellow, claiming to descend from Hercules, and in his bold masculinity resembling the statues of his supposed ancestor. He delighted to dress like the statued Hercules, wearing a tunic belted low on the hips, a broadsword clapping against his thigh and a great mantle tossed back from his shoulders. He was, in short, a bounder. But sympathetic —one of the most human and lovable males of classic days.

Cleopatra was his ruin. He was hers. But their love glows across time. It was the first *modern* romance of which we have knowledge, passionate and full of character. It inspired a splendid bit of biographical writing, Plutarch's *Life of Antony,* which in turn inspired the play, *Antony and Cleopatra*—the most famed of the three big items of poetic literature founded upon North African womanhood. (The other two are a section of the *Aeneid,* dealing with Dido, and *Salammbô*—more poem than prose—which deals with Hamilcar Barca's daughter.)

I shall quote a few passages from *The Life of Antony.* It would be impertinent for me to paraphrase what is our only source on their intimacy.

Here we see Cleopatra as she went forth to entice Antony:

. . . she came sailing up the River Cydnus (which flows into the Mediterranean in the eastern part of modern Turkey) in a barge with gilded stern and outspread sails of purple while oars of silver beat time to the music of flutes and fifes and harpers. She herself lay under a canopy of cloth of gold dressed as Venus in a picture, and beautiful young boys like painted Cupids stood on each side to fan her. Her maids were dressed like Sea Nymphs and Graces, some steering at the rudder, some working at the ropes. The perfumes diffused themselves from the vessel to the shore, which was covered with multitudes, part following the galley up the river on either bank, part running out of the city (the city was Tarsus) to see the sight.

Six years later Antony, still crazy with love for Cleopatra, despite separations, despite his marriage in the interim to the sister of Octavianus, the embryonic great Caesar Augustus:

He sent a messenger to bring Cleopatra into Syria. To whom on her arrival he made no small or trifling present: Phoenicia, Coele-Syria, Cyprus, a great part of Cilicia, that side of Judea which produces balm, part of Arabia—profuse gifts which much displeased the Romans. . . . Their dissatisfaction was augmented also by his acknowledgment as his own of the twin children he had by her, giving them the names of Alexander and Cleopatra, and adding as their surnames the titles of Sun and Moon.

Now fatal Actium where Cleopatra fled the battle, Antony abandoning his men to follow her. He overtook and got aboard her ship:

> But he would not see her or let himself be seen by her. He went forward by himself and sat alone without a word at the ship's prow, covering his face with his two hands. . . . He thus remained for three days either in anger with Cleopatra or not wishing to upbraid her, then the women of their company succeeded first in bringing them to speak and afterwards to eat and sleep together.

The defeated lovers in Alexandria: doom oncoming, Antony despairing and ashamed, Cleopatra sometimes confident and full of plans for some bold new enterprise that might save them, sometimes heartsick. Between festivals and banquets—for both loved joy to the last—she studied a sinister new art. She experimented with poisons, trying them out upon prisoners condemned to die, and discovered that "the bite of the asp caused death without convulsion or groaning, the patient in appearance being sensible of no pain."

Then the end: The invading Octavianus master at Alexandria; Antony dead by his own hand; Cleopatra so desolate "that in the extremity of her grief she had inflamed her breasts by beating them." She feared for her children, feared she herself might be dragged to Rome to face a howling crowd at Octavianus' triumph. Clever to the last, she fooled Octavianus who for this purpose wished to keep her alive, and gained a few hours of liberty and solitude that she might make oblations to the departed Antony. She wept before his tomb.

> Having made these lamentations, crowning the tomb with garlands and kissing it she gave orders to prepare her a bath, and coming out of the bath she lay down and made a sumptuous meal . . . (they found her) . . . stone dead upon a bed of gold set in all her royal ornaments . . . (the maid) was adjusting her mistress's diadem.

Cleopatra was buried beside Antony. Caesarion, her son by Julius Caesar, and the last of the royal Egyptian Ptolemies, died true to pattern, for he was murdered by the order of Octavianus, his father's adopted son and grandnephew. Her twins by Antony whom he had named Alexander, the Sun, and Cleopatra, the

Moon, were shown in chains to the people of Rome. The young Cleopatra we shall meet again. Octavianus (Augustus) became Egypt's master and in his honor and in celebration of his victory the month of Sextilus took the new name of "Augustus," it being the month when the war against Cleopatra had been won.

Thus we still carry in our calendars a memento of Cleopatra's tragedy.

THE STALLED-OX POLICY

HAVING CONQUERED EGYPT ROME OWNED ALL NORTH AFRICA—IN fact all Africa so far as she knew, for the vast continent up the Nile and beyond the Saharan fringes was still nebulous. From the Red Sea to the Atlantic was Rome's: some already, some presently, branded by name as Roman provinces.

It was an altered North Africa. It now had a new *raison d'être*. Its mission in life was now primarily to feed Rome. North Africa was Rome's nose bag. It became a country castrated. In Rome's eyes—the eyes of its efficient master—its function was to produce grain, not History.

North Africa's importance as a world center was in a sense therefore suspended during the centuries of Roman domination. Previous to this domination North Africa had been the scene of a big share of the vital events of history. It had not been North Africa *then* which was a Dark Continent. The dark spots were northern and western Europe, eastern Asia—to say nothing of the Americas and Australia. With Rome's arrival as master, North Africa's predominance in the annals of the day decreased, both because it was no longer free to shape any historic destiny, and because simultaneously the known world was growing larger. North Africa was but a subject land, one of several.

The Roman period is a passage in African history about which we possess relatively little in the classics or in modern literature. As Professor Gautier says, "the average cultivated man has never heard about what happened in the Orient (in which he includes North Africa) between Alexander and Mohammed," and our ignorance is particularly noticeable as of the period after Cleopatra's death.

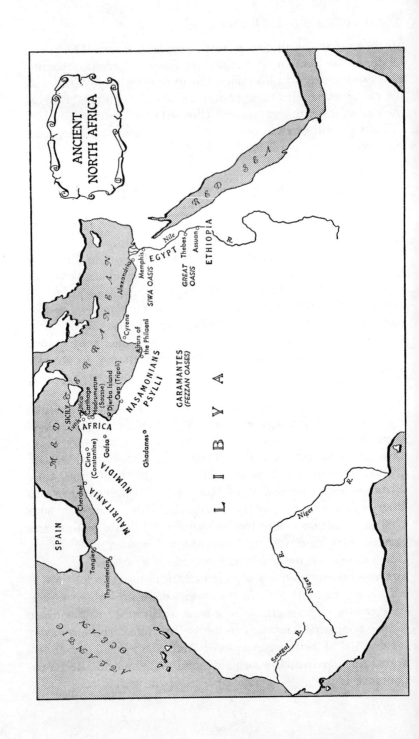

The utilitarian possibilities of Egypt and of Carthage's former empire delighted the Roman master: oil, wool, grain. The region became an area of intensive cultivation. From Egypt could be brought each year enough grain to feed Rome for four months (twenty million modii, or pecks). From the Carthaginian section enough for six months.

Besides food Africa supplied fun to Rome. She catered to the luxury trade. She provided wild animals for the Roman circus, often accompanied by African humans, for the Roman audiences were more difficult in the matter of thrills than ours of today, who are satisfied by a trainer with whip and pistol. Rome liked to watch from behind a wire grating plus a trench of water a fighting melee of strange beasts and outlandish men. Pliny tells us with dates and all exactitude of a hundred lions fighting against spearmen from Mauritania; of a hundred bears reputedly brought from Numidia opposing a hundred specially imported Ethiopian blacks; of elephants matched against bulls. Pliny does not indicate the result of this last combat. Circus animals in general were often called in Rome by the general name of "Africaners."

So Rome consumed African produce, munching or marveling, as the case might be, and in a wider sense pretty well ignored the great continent which had come into her possession.

JUBA II AND CLEOPATRA'S DAUGHTER

ROME'S PRACTICAL WISDOM IN THE HANDLING OF HER AFRICAN colonies, however, was great. It was shown, for instance, in her use of the junior Juba, that baby captive who made something of a farce of Caesar's triumph.

After causing young Juba to receive his education at Rome, the Empire sent him to Mauritania as king under Rome's protection—doubtless a pleasing appointment to native Africa. Mauritania then corresponded to modern Morocco plus the western side of Algeria. Juba II's capital was at Cherchel near the present city of Algiers. Rome further showed tact in the picking of his consort: a compliment to Egyptian pride and a flattering choice to young Juba. Rome, in fact, offered him what ought to have been a peculiarly delightful and glamorous wife.

Juba II's marriage is one of the oddest on record. He, who as a child had figured in a triumph as symbol of Rome's conquest in the Tunisian regions, married a princess, who as a child, had figured in a subsequent triumph as symbol of Rome's conquest of Egypt. The princess was that daughter of Cleopatra and Antony called Cleopatra Silene (The Moon). I have said that she should have been a very glamorous girl. But it is a remarkable circumstance that this daughter, born of the passionate mating of the most famous charmer of all history and a notably handsome and virile man, was not even of reasonably pleasing appearance. I have studied the photograph of a coin which shows her profile. Hers was a heavy face, far from pretty. Professor Gsell describes a marble head believed to be her portrait as follows: "a woman of energetic, hard face, with hooked nose and a disdainful expression of the lips. The general impression is rather masculine . . . without charm, and cross." This eugenic surprise died in early middle life, leaving a son called after her mother's family: Ptolemy. It turned out a name of ill omen, as we shall see.

*   *   *

KING JUBA II WAS AN EXTRAORDINARY AND FAMOUS MAN. HE WAS maybe the most prolific royal author of all times. He wrote poetry, also prose works on the history of all the then known world, on geography, on natural history, on the arts, on music, on the drama, on grammar—in short, on about every subject then open to an author. Unfortunately these books in their complete form have been lost, but fragments from them are quoted in Pliny and elsewhere. To judge by certain items which Pliny culled from Juba and copied into his encyclopedia, the *Natural History,* Juba's outstanding quality was credulity. Evidently he read everything he could lay hands on and listened to every story he heard, believed them all, and recapitulated them in his works. Had Jules Verne, "Superman" and the like existed in his day Juba II would have noted down piously all their fantasy in his history books and his manuals of natural history and geography.

However at times he supplemented his credulity with serious investigation. He himself went on a voyage of study to the Near East. He also sent out exploring parties, notably to the Canaries, and to a certain pond in southern Morocco whence was brought back to him the crocodile which was proof enough to Juba that his emissaries had found the source of the Nile—for did not the Nile have crocodiles too?

This odd notion that the Nile came from Morocco running *under* the sands of the Sahara to some spot south of Egypt was common in Juba's day, and before—and after. That Juba believed it is no reflection on his judgment. A wiser man than he—to wit, Alexander—is said by a certain classical author to have been impelled to go to the Siwa Oasis in the desert, not as supposed to consult the oracle about his fatherhood, but "to discover the source of the Nile"! The unreasonable notion that one of the world's greatest rivers sprang from and ran for an immense distance underneath the world's driest territory is something to make you wonder, but was widely held up till relatively recent times.

A further enterprise of Juba's was the establishment of a purple dyeing works near what we now know as Mogador on the Atlantic coast of Morocco. This purple dyeing works indirectly produced tragedy and the extinction of a fine family of African kings—first coming to our notice with grand old Massinissa (Juba II's great-great-great-grandfather) and including Rome's famous *bête noire*, Jugurtha (Juba's great-great-uncle) and Rome's "public enemy," Juba I, who was his father. It was a vigorous and spectacular line to be destroyed by the produce of the little shellfish from whose head came a dye drop "no bigger than a single tear." But that is how it was.

When Juba II had died in his seventies Ptolemy, his son, had succeeded him. Ptolemy was a vain young man by nature, made additionally haughty by the knowledge of a splendid ancestry. Good enough on his father's side. On his mother's, glorious to the extreme. Fancy being able to say, "Cleopatra was my grandmother"! It is no wonder that Ptolemy, king of Mauritania, put on airs.

For some seventeen years he reigned in luxury, wearing fine clothes, proud of his fine palace furniture, and on excellent terms with Rome, where the new emperor, the wicked and irresponsible Caligula, was a cousin of his on the side of his maternal grandfather, Antony. (Ptolemy was Antony's grandson, Caligula was Antony's great-grandson.) One day when on a visit to Rome Caligula invited Ptolemy to be his guest at a public show. Ptolemy wore a purple cloak from the Mogador dye works. It gleamed in all its rich color and the Roman crowd stared approvingly. Caligula was furious with jealousy that this kinglet, holding power only by Rome's protection, had dared wear imperial purple and steal imperial thunder. So another Ptolemy, far from old Egypt, died to pattern by the order of a relative.

*   *   *

MAURITANIA NOW BECAME A ROMAN PROVINCE, OR RATHER TWO Roman provinces: Tingitana and Caesariensis. The name Mauritania, from Latin *Mauri,* and a similar Greek word, which we translate Moor, has a confusing history. What it came from or originally meant is unknown. It may have meant "brunette" from the skin color of the people. It may have meant "western" from the part of Africa where they lived. Or it may simply have been the name of some tribe stretched to include a nation.

Presently the name stretched yet farther. The folk of all North Africa nearly as far as Egypt were often called Moors. Later yet a mistaken idea arose that the Moors were Negroes. The old term, "blackamoor," speaks for itself. The subtitle of *Othello—The Moor of Venice*—certainly conveyed the indication that Othello was a Negro. "Haply, for I am black," says Othello himself (Act III: scene 3) and the curtain is hardly up on the start of the play before he is jeeringly referred to as "Thick-Lips." But the Moor, the native Moroccan, was never a Negro, though Negroes and persons of mixed blood live in the country.

The name Moor and the name Morocco, by the way, have quite different derivations. Morocco is the European deformation of Marrakesh, the city. The name Mauritania has lately been given to an especially wild Saharan stretch along the Atlantic. Juba II, despite all the explorations he sponsored, never dreamed of the existence of the Mauritania which has now appropriated the name of his kingdom.

NEW CARTHAGE

AT APPROXIMATELY THE SAME MOMENT JUBA II WAS STARTING HIS reign in Mauritania a great new city was rising in Tunisia. Caesar had had a dream. Camped near the ruins of Carthage he had seen in his sleep "a great army in tears." The meaning was clear to him and in the morning he jotted down upon his tablets, "Colonize

Carthage"—witness to the number and the grandeur of his plans that he must needs make a memorandum to remind him of so vast a scheme.

Caesar died too soon, but Octavianus—later Augustus, the emperor—his heir and adopted son, took over the dream responsibility along with the rest of Caesar's inheritance, and presently Carthage rose again, this time untroubled by the bad omens and attacks of mysteriously sinister animal enemies which had arrested a previous effort.

Inside fifty years Carthage, new-built by Augustus, became very populous. Its civic life was destined to be almost exactly as long as that of the original city—about seven centuries—and it too was destined to cruel tragedy. During the early years of its rebirth it was an opulent and learned city—the "Rome of Africa."

THE CANDACE

It was in the far eastern corner of her new African empire that Rome met the first important disturbance of her stalled-ox policy. Oddly, this disturbance—like the last previous serious trouble in the East—was caused by a woman. Less than a decade has passed since the end of Cleopatra's career and one wonders whether the second woman was inspired by the hope that she might be able to pick up where Cleopatra had laid down and become herself a great and spectacular queen in Egypt.

If such was her ambition she must have realized that physically, at any rate, she was most ill fitted to replace that flower of the Nile who had been so lovely that she received most of Asia Minor as a second honeymoon gift from her Roman sweetheart. For the second lady was "a woman of masculine bearing who had lost one eye," according to Strabo who traveled in Egypt with the Roman general who opposed her efforts.

She was a Candace: the queens of the upper Nile wore as a general title that word we are accustomed to employ as a given name. The dynasty of dowager queens, called the Candaces, continued for several centuries—for four centuries it would seem, since one of them, so legend says, had dealings with Alexander the Great and the treasurer of another figures in the New Testament. Sculptured representations of certain Candaces show them

as very fat women with pronounced Negro features and loaded
with lumpy savage jewelry.

Assuming that the one-eyed Candace who pictured herself in
fancy on Egypt's throne was of this same bulging physique, she
would indeed have cut a queer figure there to those who remembered the last svelte lady to sit upon it. And for a time the
Candace's hopes looked rather rosy.

She invaded Upper Egypt, took Assuan and, Strabo says, "threw
down the statues of Caesar"—i.e. Augustus, whose statues were the
symbol of Roman sovereignty. It was a triumph. But her fine
hopes were disappointed. Rome's army, though outnumbered
three to one, put her hordes to flight with ease—for the most part
of her men were armed but with hatchets. They razed her capital
and turned back to Alexandria. The Candace was a game fighter.
She attacked again, and was again defeated. In her humiliation
this one-eyed, harsh-faced queen received more chivalrous treatment than had the beautiful Cleopatra. Perhaps for just this
reason, because to prim Augustus a seductress was a creature
peculiarly detestable. Augustus granted pardon to the ambassadors
of the Candace's army and "even remitted the tribute which he
had imposed."

A CANDACE'S TREASURER

It was over a half century later that the treasurer of one
of the warrior queen's successors, a man described as "a eunuch of
great authority under Candace, queen of the Ethiopians," was
riding in his chariot along a route in Palestine, met Philip, the
Evangelist, invited him to have a ride, and—as the two drove along
together—listened to the story of Jesus. Presently the Candace's
treasurer spied a spring of water, asked for and obtained Christian
baptism, and then "went on his way rejoicing" (Acts 8:26-39).

The supposed exact spot of this romantic religious episode
became sacred to early Christians. A sixth century pilgrim lists
it among the important sites of the Holy Land, naming it along
with "Joppa where the whale threw up Jonah," and was evidently
very sure he had seen the very spring in question. It would have
been, according to the Bible account, somewhere between Gaza
and Jerusalem.

It is notable that this "eunuch of great authority" should be one of the very few individuals in North Africa, except Egypt, to figure importantly and personally in the Bible: so far as I know, the only one.

The respectful fashion in which he is described must have surprised many Bible readers who think of a eunuch as a mere harem slave to be despised. So also may Philip's readiness to deal so intimately with such a person. We are told that Philip's friendliness showed that "in Christ's Church disabilities of physical condition have no place," thus differing from the harsh law of the old Jews whereby such unfortunates—even though their misfortune resulted from accident—were forbidden to "enter into the congregation of the Lord" (Deuteronomy 23:1). Jesus's own generous and compassionate statement on the subject is to be found in St. Matthew 19:12.

Some traditions, not confirmed historically, would have it that, in his enthusiastic gratitude for Philip's goodness, this "eunuch of great authority" traveled far into inner Africa to spread the gentle and democratic faith of Jesus in his own old homeland. A map made in an Italian monastery in the fifteenth century shows the exact place in what we now call Abyssinia which was supposedly visited on his missionary travels by this *"eunucho che fo batiza da Santo Phylippo."*

However, without discounting the eunuch's undoubted joy in his conversion, we can assume that he did not appreciate Philip's kindness at its modern value. To his mind there would have been no especial condescension on Philip's part. The obloquy of the eunuch was something the convert would not have understood.

SOME HISTORIC EUNUCHS

IN THE OLD DAYS EUNUCHS WERE OFTEN TO BE FOUND IN HIGH places, certain of them possessing fine courage. It is inspiring to read through the names of a few of these men who distinguished themselves despite so great a handicap.

The most famous of them all was Narses, "who rescued the unhappy name of eunuch from the contempt and hatred of mankind," in the words of Gibbon. Narses, who in his youth worked at the distaff, became a formidable general, fighting and defeating Goths and Franks in the sixth century A.D.

Another eunuch general was his contemporary, Solomon, who fought against the Vandals in Africa—not an ex-slave like Narses, but one maimed by an accident in childhood. Batis in the days of Alexander the Great was a most gallant eunuch. His bravery got for him that cruel and "novel" punishment (see page 95). He had been chosen, though a Negro and a eunuch, to captain the defense of Gaza, and to be brave in Gaza was to be brave indeed. Its ferocity when attacked made the city a byword in antiquity (Polybius, Book XVI).

Later in these pages will be found an account of Kafur, the Negro eunuch and ex-slave, who reigned for many years over Egypt (see page 265). The Arabic histories of medieval Africa repeatedly refer to eunuch generals and admirals. The ex-Christian renegade who conquered Timbuctoo for the Sultan of Morocco was a eunuch (see page 412). So were many recklessly brave corsair captains of the pirate days.

One reason why such persons were chosen for positions of especial trust was expressed by Cyrus in the long ago. Cyrus picked none but eunuchs "from doorkeepers upward" to be his body guards, for only this class of humanity, he thought, could be relied upon never to betray him through greater love for some other person—the eunuch being "destitute of all ties" to wife or child. Xenophon tells Cyrus' shrewd philosophy on the subject in much detail (*Cyropaedia* VII:5,65-68).

So we may quote with conviction the Old Testament exhortation, "Neither let the eunuch say, Behold I am a dry tree" (Isaiah 56:3). History has disproved the usual and cruel notion which considers only the eunuch of commerce, the bloated slave boss of the harem, an individual who probably would have been an objectionable character even if he had not been tampered with.

The manufacture and export of castrated slaves was for centuries a tragic and leading business in North Africa, notwithstanding the Mohammedan tenets forbid such mutilation. It was a very old form of cruelty. Gibbon says that "the first practise of castration is imputed by Ammianus to the cruel ingenuity of Semiramis." However, much perverse behavior is offhandedly imputed to that semilegendary lady, one such item being the contribution of our friend, Juba II, the author-king, who is quoted by Pliny as saying she "was so greatly enamored of a horse that she had connection with it" (*Natural History* VIII: p. 65).

Medieval and relatively modern geographers report on the specific disgusting places where this luxury item of the slave trade was produced. In the Middle Ages a place called Waslu, not identified on modern maps, but located somewhere near the Abyssinian border, was a center for the performance of the operation. Boys were taken afterward to another locality, Hadya, where alone postoperative care was understood. More than half died, but the value of the surviving slaves was vastly increased. This, from the fourteenth century Arabic work called the *Masalik*. In later years other places became infamous as eunuch manufactories. Burckhardt, in the first quarter of the last century, writes of a section which was "the only country in eastern Sudan where slaves are thus mutilated for exportation." Thence they were carried to Egypt or sent as presents to the great mosques of Mecca and Medina. He tells of another such spot, a village near Asyut in Egypt, "which supplies all European and the greater part of Asiatic Turkey . . . the operators are two Coptic (Christian) monks." A boy's value in consequence rose from three hundred piasters to a thousand. Browne a few years earlier (1799) commented on a similar spot in Upper Egypt and added the gruesome words, "Some families there resident have the hereditary exercise of this ancient practice."

There were reports from travelers that roads leading away from these places were lined with the skeletons of young victims. Such horrible stories as these did much to inspire the attempts of the last century to put down the slave trade, and incidentally led to the opening up of Africa. So the sacrifice of these pitiable boys played its part in the development of the Dark Continent. And consolingly we can be assured that those boys who survived, having become a rich article of merchandise were better treated than other slaves and settled into cosy comfort in cushioned harems while their normal brothers worked under the courbash.

*   *   *

SLAVERY IS A DARK PASSAGE IN AFRICA'S HISTORY. NOT DOMESTIC slavery, but slavery for export. Let us not forget that, though the supply was African, the demand came from all the world.

TALL TALES FROM INNER AFRICA

THE SAHARA CHALLENGED ROME. NO SOONER WERE THE ROMANS masters of all of then known Africa than they sought to invade the desert, to conquer whatever men they might find there, set up garrisons and colonies in oases. It was a brave venture. And a battle with geography itself. Could the venture have succeeded and the top of the Sahara been permanently endowed with a system of roads, wells and forts in the Roman manner, the destiny of North Africa might have been different. For the trouble with North Africa is that the useful part of it is too thin. It is corseted between the Mediterranean and the Sahara. Viewed as a habitable place it is a long lank worm of a country wriggling along the coast, at times even disappearing altogether when the sands of the desert merge with the sands of the sea. So it has been hard to unify and govern, and has been easily conquered by outsiders.

The first big Roman invasion of the Sahara was in 19 B.C. To plunge into the empty desert needed a Columbus' courage—perhaps more than his. Not only were the hardships of the great desert before them, that country which Herodotus described: "without water, without animals, without rain, without wood, without any kind of moisture." There was worse than that. In inner Africa, reports said, were weird terrors, indescribably revolting and horrid things.

Of a night in the desert these soldiers of Rome who had tramped all over Europe and the Near East with their crested helmets and their greaved shanks lay and quivered in the dark and told one another scraps of dreadful gossip—those legends which made up classical geography so far as the Sahara was concerned. There was in those days an ample fund of legends. Pliny had not yet composed his famous *Natural History* nor had Mela told of Africa's marvels, but much of Pliny's original sources, especially Cornelius Nepos, were already available. Also, of course, Herodotus. All this curious stuff must have drifted to the ears of common men.

In bated whispers they discussed, no doubt, the Himantopodes, wondering when they might expect to meet that hideous "race of people whose feet were like thongs"—like snowshoes, I fancy from Pliny's words—so that "they moved with a crawling gait like serpents." Or with those mouthless humans who sucked their food into their nostrils through a reed. Or with the monster men without heads who had eyes in their breasts, or those with dogs' heads, of both of which Herodotus heard when in Africa.

To the more imaginative amongst them even more shuddery must have been the picture of those men and women they might expect to meet in inner Africa who were without souls and without identity. The Atlantes, they were, who had "no mode of distinguishing amongst each other by names, *nor were they ever visited by dreams like other mortals.*" To think of meeting, here in this boundless desert forgotten by the gods, the blank stare of a man like that, who did not know who he was from other men any more than a grain of sand can know itself from another, a man whose nights were bereft of the consolation and counsel of dreams —it made the Romans squalmy.

But they went on—brave Romans in those days.

After a march which must have taken them nearly a month into the sands, they approached the oasis group which we now know as Fezzan (after the old Roman name of Phasania). It was the country of the Garamantes, and promised well to a body of vigorous soldiery, for these Garamantes were a race whose womenfolk were reputedly quite without inhibitions, there being "no institution of marriage whatsoever, the people living in promiscuous concubinage." Innocent fun there would be as well in watching the eccentric feeding process of the Garamantes' cattle of which Herodotus spoke as follows: "they feed backwards for the reason that they have horns that are bent forward, therefore they draw back as they feed, because their horns would stick in the ground." Many centuries later this gymnastic feeder was still the subject of wonder in another guise. The Saharan ox had moved to North Europe and wore a new hide. He was the German mule, described by Solinus, the fabulous world geographer whose *Collectanea* was a standard work of reference in the Middle Ages. The German mule had such a long upper lip that he could not eat "except walking backwards."

The Garamantes, though it was their loose morals and trick cattle which particularly attracted the attention of classical writers, were a people of some consequence. They bossed the sparse desert population scattered about their own oasis group. They sometimes streamed northward and bothered Roman peace on the Mediterranean coast. They procured slave labor by capturing the near-by wild troglodytes, who spoke in a manner all their own "like the screeching of bats." The Garamantes went on these slave-hunting trips in four-horse chariots, the troglodytes in question being "the swiftest of all men." And with the help of pack oxen— those oxen with the troublesome horns—they went deeper into the Sahara. None can say how far.

Fezzan, the Garamantes' country, was farthest into the Sahara, so far as the rest of the world had any real knowledge until a great miracle happened. This was the coming of the camel.

SAHARA WITHOUT CAMELS

It is startling, but incontestably true that the camel, which we always associate with the desert scene, was not used in the Sahara until well into the Christian Era.

The camel was imported into North Africa from the East and came tardily and gradually. Or rather came back. In prehistoric days it had existed in the coastal regions that are now called Tunisia, Algeria and Morocco. Its bones have been dug up. But the wild camel died off before man learnt to use it.

The slowness of the process by which the camel—the much-needed camel—moved westward from Asia Minor toward and into the Sahara is a puzzle. One would have thought that this seemingly heaven-sent desert vehicle of transport would have swept into popularity in a few years. But it took centuries. The reader may like to follow with me the camel's leisurely progress westward, to whose detail I have given considerable study, and will certainly marvel with me that it took North Africa so long to adopt the ship of the desert.

In early historic days even Egypt, so close to the East, had no camels. The father of Ramses II was obliged to have a cistern built in the desert east of the Nile so that his men could reach the gold mines without risking death by thirst, they having had no transport but asses to carry water for their journey. By the seventh century B.C. there is noted the limited use of camels in Egypt.

Did Alexander the Great enjoy the benefit of camels for that pilgrimage of his to the oasis of Siwa in search of a father? Some historians say, no. Some say, yes. It appears that there is no mention of camels in contemporary accounts of the expedition—strong indication that Alexander did not use them, and strong suggestion that there were none to use at the coastal point whence Alexander plunged into the desert. But Curtius, a Latin writer of about four hundred years after Alexander's time, gives us a purple passage about Alexander's hardships in the course of which he says (chapter vii): "Here the water failed which had been brought in bottles *on camels* and there were no springs in the fervid ground." I am inclined to suspect that Curtius put the camels in out of his imagination, like a greater writer than he, as I shall presently mention. Curtius was notoriously irresponsible in the matter of local color. It was he who lightheartedly committed the "howler" of causing the Persian king, Darius, to ride in a processional car dedicated to the Roman god, Jupiter. However, some historians take Curtius' word for it that by Alexander's period camels had got as far west as Siwa.

A small but significant circumstance which I have noted is that at Alexandria, which was far closer to the East whence camels came, and at a considerably later date than that of Alexander the Great's pilgrimage, the celebrated procession (described on pages 97 and 98), included camels along with exotic and unfamiliar beasts like zebras, a white bear, a rhinoceros. It seems obvious that camels must still have been much of a rarity, else they would not have been given a place in this great show.

Similarly if we proceed westward and into later times we find that camels appear to be treasured curios. There is mention of Julius Caesar's capture of a few camels from the king, Juba I, as if they were an outstanding item of remarkable booty (Chapter lxviii of *The African War* from Caesar's *Commentaries*).

Carthage in the days of Punic greatness had no camels despite Flaubert's colorful account of them in *Salammbô*. It is doubtful that camels progressed westward in quantities before the third or fourth centuries A.D. and it is worth remarking that to the horses of Tunisia they were still an outlandish, stinking terror as late as the sixth century.

In short, at least a thousand years elapsed between the first introduction of the camel into North Africa, in Egypt, and its adoption as a regular means of transport. Yet it was the camel alone that was capable of, and eventually did open up that immense trans-Saharan trade which made Mediterranean Africa rich and brilliant in the Middle Ages and gave splendor and culture to the Negro empires by the Niger. Here is an instance of the great volume of camel-borne trade: In one year and along only one of the several South-North desert routes there passed an estimated six million pounds of luxury goods—light stuff of very high money value for its weight. (Ibn-Khaldoun in his history of the Berbers gives a firsthand report as of the year 1353 that twelve thousand laden camels went through Takedda annually; a camel carries about a quarter of a ton.)

Antique man's thousand-year delay in recognizing the potentiality of the camel amazes us. Perhaps, however, ages to come may look back with similar amazement upon our deafness to some equally interesting opportunity now knocking at *our* door. . . .

*   *   *

BEFORE CAMELS CAME SUCH DESERT TRAVEL AS THERE WAS USED horses specially trained to go two days without a drink. Pack oxen, also so trained, carried waterskins. Asses helped too. Camels were needed to make the complete Saharan crossing practicable. Camels can go up to fourteen days without a drink, can carry four hundred- to six hundred-pound loads of water for their masters. Until they came to man's help the inner Sahara and places beyond were almost a complete mystery.

Specific mention of any extended Saharan travel is just about nonexistent in classical literature. So far as I can trace them such mentions are but four in number. Let me tell of them in their chronological order:

THE FIVE NASAMONIAN YOUTHS

THE FIRST IS THE ADVENTURE OF THE FAMOUS FIVE NASAMONIAN youths told of by Herodotus. The five Nasamonians came of a nomad people whose headquarters were along the Great Syrtis Gulf where the Mediterranean bites deep into Africa east of the Tunisian rump. These five were chosen by lot to explore the desert, according to Herodotus' picturesque story which he passes on at third hand. Pluckily they plunged into the heart of the unknown, bearing to the south and west. They passed "the region infested by wild beasts" and then plodded over the "utterly desolate" desert. At length they saw trees, were captured by diminutive men of less than middle stature who drove them along through vast morasses to a city where Negro pygmies lived and by which flowed a great river running from the west where crocodiles swam.

The story has been taken very seriously and much studied, for it was one of the few items about inner Africa available to European geography previous to the days of modern exploration.

Some students of the pre-exploration days were persuaded that the city visited by the five adventurers must have been the much talked about and long secret town of Timbuctoo. This supposition was subsequently recognized as an absurdity, since Timbuctoo—so modern investigation has shown—was not founded until some fifteen hundred or two thousand years afterward.

The crocodiles suggest the notion that the five adventurers got to the Niger. It is quite true, as I have seen for myself, that the Niger possesses an ample crocodile population. But the fact that they saw crocodiles does not prove that they got anywhere near as far south as the Niger. In antiquity crocodiles existed in North African waters. King Juba II's searchers found a crocodile in southern Morocco. And even in our own times the truly amazing discovery of living crocodiles has been made in Saharan underground waters. Lest this may seem incredible to the reader I mention that the distinguished explorer, Duveyrier, heard about Saharan crocodiles in the 1860's, and that fifty years later Captain Nieger and others saw and actually captured crocodiles in the desert's subterranean pools. Another crocodile survived till 1924, and there may be some alive in the Sahara today.

So the fact that the Nasamonian adventurers saw crocodiles does not indicate that they got to the other side of the desert. It seems improbable that a party of youths could have performed such a difficult and hazardous journey in an impromptu fashion. More likely that they pushed into the Sahara as far as one of those *oueds,* or gulches, which after a storm can momentarily resemble a great river.

Their exploit is interesting because they were the first men of whom we have knowledge ever to attempt African exploration for its own sake. They were the first of a line of heroes. And luckier than so many of their successors, the five Nasamonians got home safe to tell their tale.

THE DUBIOUS CASE OF MAGO

THE SECOND SPECIFIC HINT OF ANY TRANS-SAHARAN TRAVELING before camel days deals with Mago of Carthage and is something of a joke. It would not be worth noting but for the reason that— our literature on the Sahara in classical times being so sparse —historians have mentioned it. Stéphane Gsell, to whom all students of North Africa's past owe so much, seemed to take Mago seriously, though in one of his later volumes Professor Gsell reconsidered Mago and sneered at him.

This is what Athenaeus has to tell us about Mago in a chapter (xxii) consisting of a quantity of stories and quotations from various classical writers on drunkenness and abstemiousness: "Mago, the Carthaginian, passed three times through the African desert, eating dry meal and never drinking."

Considering that the trans-Saharan crossing would have taken Mago several months the anecdote is laughable. Possibly we should understand from Athenaeus' passage that Mago went, not across, but merely a certain short distance through the desert. It would have had to be short. In the Sahara a man cannot live four days without water.

FLACCUS

NUMBER THREE OF THE AVAILABLE MENTIONS OF DEEP SAHARAN adventure is from Ptolemy, the geographer, who lived in Egypt in the second century A.D. It concerns Flaccus, a Roman military leader who went from Fezzan, the Garamantes' country, southward for three months and reached a place where there were Ethiopians (i.e. Negroes) and that is all. Where Flaccus got to we do not know. The mention of Ethiopians does not in itself tell us anything, for there were Negroes even in coastal North Africa. If Flaccus did indeed go steadily south from Fezzan for three months he would have got into the green country beyond the desert, and surely there would have been mention of that dramatic fact in the report rather than the mere remark that he met Negroes. So we may suspect that Flaccus dawdled, or else that he rambled about the Fezzan oases rather than going due south.

A further thought, which is also a possibility in connection with the fourth instance of early Saharan penetration. Flaccus may have come just at the start of the camel era, and his not be a pre-camel exploit at all. His date is uncertain. The scene of his exploration was in the eastern Sahara, and it was from the East that the camels came.

AGISYMBA: WHERE?

THE FOURTH STORY OF A FAR-FLUNG SAHARAN JOURNEY IS A puzzling one. It too is from Ptolemy. Its hero, like Flaccus, may have had the benefit of camels. We do not know his date, but it was later than that of Flaccus.

It concerns a man named Julius Maternus. He lived at Leptis, one of the three towns—the others were Sabratha and Oea, on the site of modern Tripoli—which made up in later Roman days the province of Tripolitania, the "Three-Cities" (*polis*, Greek for city). He may have been a merchant rather than a military man. Whatever he was, he was a remarkable adventurer. He used Fezzan as a springboard, dived into the desert waste and after marching for four months toward the south, arrived at a country inhabited by Ethiopians (Negroes) called Agisymba, "in which rhinoceroses abounded."

Again that is all. But no sentence in geography has been more discussed. Where was Agisymba? There is no place so named. It has been tentatively identified with a variety of places. The best modern opinion appears to be that it corresponded with the oasis of Aïr in the southern Sahara or with Lake Chad beyond the Sahara's southern borders. In the former case the presence of rhinoceroses would be odd, only explainable by the assumption that the Aïr region has grown immensely drier since the time of Maternus' journey.

Anyone would be rich who had a dollar for every page which has been published in speculation about the mysterious lost land of Agisymba. In the days before African exploration the Agis-

ymba story plus Herodotus' rather fantastic tale about the five
Nasamonian youths constituted pretty well all the information
about the Sahara and mid-Africa which Christian geography possessed. Or, I should say, which they cared to consider. Christian
Europe did not like to accept information about Africa from
Arabic sources. The students of Europe made an exception in the
case of Leo Africanus; he had been converted to Christ. But no
follower of Mohammed was going to teach them anything! Nor,
to be fair, did they have much opportunity to read Arabic geographic works. So Ptolemy's scrap was revered through the later
Middle Ages and beyond.[2] And the site of Agisymba was a matter
of vital interest.

After all—and this is rather a startling fact—"Agisymba," discovered by a Latin-speaking explorer and recorded in Greek,
constituted the only published contact of Europe with inner
Africa for many, many hundreds of years. No European Christian
would cross the Sahara and give the world an account of his
accomplishment until the start of the nineteenth century. Certain renegades in the service of Morocco crossed the desert. So
did a Christian captive (French, seventeenth century) and perhaps a Christian free traveler (Italian, fifteenth century). But
none of these experiences were known to the contemporary
world. Maternus of Agisymba was the only known explorer of
inner Africa whom Europe could claim as their own for about
seventeen hundred years!

*   *   *

IF MATERNUS WAS INDEED A MERCHANT HIS JOURNEY FROM A TRADE
point of view can be assumed to have been a disappointment

[2] As to the queer way in which Europe, especially England, chose the long
dead and scantily informed Ptolemy as their prime authority on Africa
Beazley says, "In the history of human knowledge there are few stranger
chapters than that which records the influence of the Ptolemaic revival in
delaying the formation of an accurate world map in the 15th, 16th and 17th
centuries" (C. Raymond Beazley, *The Dawn of Modern Geography*, Vol. III

I own a map of a part of Africa based upon Ptolemy's information and
printed in 1540. This was not issued as a quaint curio. It was issued because
it was regarded as the best Europe could do. The peculiar belief in Ptolemy
endured not only through the 17th century, as suggested by Beazley, but into
the 18th and 19th. See D'Anville and Rennel, also an extremely careful
reconstruction of Ptolemy's African geography read before the Royal Geographical Society in 1832, and even the tone of the extended discussion of
Ptolemy by Bunbury in his *History of Ancient Geography*, Vol. II (1879

For there is no evidence that other merchants imitated his venture, or that any attempts at trans-Saharan trading were made until the age of the camel was in full and indubitable swing.

The Sahara was in another world. Except for what may have been seen of it by the four expeditions I have mentioned, and except for such glimpses of the country as may have come to Hanno and his Carthaginian sailors, or to the navigators who allegedly doubled Africa in the days of the Pharaoh Necho (see pages 67 to 69), or to the members of a Nile exploring party in Nero's time, no outside individual—so far as we know—had sight of, or claimed to have sight of Africa's mysterious interior until the camel came.

There may have been some movement across the Sahara in prehistoric days when, though already a desert, it was presumably a less terrible desert. The finding, for example, of objects of antique Egyptian type in Africa south of the Sahara suggests this. But it is safe to affirm that, from the period when the Sahara first took on the dread aspect it now wears, anything like transdesert traffic had to wait for the camel.

In considering the puzzle of why the use of the camel spread so slowly we must bear in mind that its evident usefulness was overweighed by the difficulties of handling this novel beast. The camel is a complicated creature, quite unlike the ass to which North Africa was accustomed. The ass was an adaptable commoner; the camel an aristocrat come down in the world. The camel showed a truly noble gallantry combined with a faddy irritability about details. It took hard-earned experience to learn how to raise and handle the newcomer, and many a native in those long-ago days must have been driven to fury and despair: this animal that had the courage to travel day after day without a drink over burning sands like a highborn hero, this animal that screamed till the desert echoed if an extra feather was added to its burden; this animal that could eat with benefit plants hard as splintered rocks, and become sick unto death at certain succulent green stuffs—the camel was very exasperating, and maybe that is why North Africa took to it so slowly despite its pre-eminent appropriateness to the terrain.

But no animal ever played so decisive a role in history. The

camel created a continent—or rather gave a continent to the rest
of the world.

For more than one thousand years until at last ships again
ventured down Africa's Atlantic coasts it was the camel alone
which made possible any contact with inner Africa beyond the
Sahara.

ROME FORGOT THE DESERT

ONCE ROME'S CURIOSITY ABOUT THE DESERT WAS SATISFIED SHE
decided that this far and ill-favored part of her empire was diffi
cult beyond its value. She did not have the imagination to avail
herself of the means of transport, almost within her hand, which
would have opened to her the gold and exotic treasures of the
Sudan on the desert's other rim. She decided to ignore the
Sahara and whatever might be to the southward beyond.

Classical history complains of the trouble Rome had in "keeping open the road that leads to the country of the Garamantes
because predatory bands of that nation fill up the wells with
sand," and adds that, to the Roman idea, the locality was "very
near uninhabitable from the intensity of the heat."

Rome's milestones and monuments remained to mark the road
to the land Rome had forgotten. Native travelers came, after a
while, to view these pillars and archways and statues, standing in
lone desolation alongside desert paths as something supernatural.
They did not class these stone human figures as statues made
by man, but thought them actual people who had been turned to
stone. Thus Rome's statuary in the desert was not repugnant to
Mohammedan feeling and did not meet the fate of such monuments in some regions of North Africa where—regarded as idols
—statuary was loathed and, as an old time traveler says, you could
often see a native "spoiling a good lance or dagger to pick out the
eyes of what he called a god made by some vile pagan."

Natives told a story about a petrified city to be seen at a point
along the road to Fezzan. This city, they said, was all of bluish
stone. You could see there stone palm trees, stone men at their
various trades and occupations, stone women suckling their stone
babies, and even stone dogs, cats and mice. In the seventeenth
and eighteenth centuries its fame was wide amongst the few ven-

turesome Europeans who visited North Africa. Could it be some ancient Roman garrison town preserved in some phenomenal fashion? At that time it was impossible to get into the interior to find out. Dr. Thomas Shaw, eighteenth century traveler, tells of the experience of the French consul at Tripoli who had been instructed by the royal government to find out about the Saharan stone city, and to send back some concrete proof. The consul delegated the investigation to certain natives who agreed that, for a price, they would go to the supposed locality—some seven days into the wilds—and bring him back, not a petrified adult—that would be too heavy—but a stone child. After delays and stories of dangers encountered they produced a small figure. But their "stone child" never went to Paris. To the consul's disgust it turned out to be no human baby stricken to stone at its mother's breast by a desert catastrophe of the long ago, but just a statue of Cupid which the enterprising natives had procured from temple ruins near Tripoli and from which they had broken off the bow and quiver.

POGROM IN REVERSE

RELIGIONS DISTURBED ROME'S DOMINATION OF AFRICA MORE THAN any other factor.

Native rebellion was made ineffectual by Rome's might and by the geographical layout of the country. Its people, dispersed along a narrow strip, were unaccustomed to and incapable of co-operative wars.

Attacks from outsiders were damaging, it is true, and included some startling incidents, such as the adventures in Egypt of a determined and beautiful woman of great ambition, the frontier skirmishing of an enemy so ferocious that a supernatural quality was attributed to him, and the century-long occupation of a part of Africa by a wild race from Europe on the rampage.

But, viewing the period of Rome's African tenure as a mass, it is indisputable that religions were the greatest danger to her power, and in the end it was the exaltation of a new religion which drove Rome out of Africa altogether.

*   *   *

THE FIRST OF ROME'S MISADVENTURES WITH ALIEN FAITHS WAS A dramatic and very bloody episode with the Jews which occurred in the Cyrene neighborhood and elsewhere in the second century A.D.

The Exodus from Egypt of long ago had not left Africa a permanently Jewless continent. In the days of Cambyses there was again a Jewish community in Upper Egypt. The Ptolemies encouraged Jews to live in Alexandria and permitted them to translate the Old Testament, though it is true that Ptolemy IV obliged them "to have their bodies marked with pricks in the form of an ivy leaf." By the time that Rome took over Egypt from Cleopatra there were about a million Jews in the country, doing well as a whole.

Oddly, the world's unkindness to Jews appears to be a habit which has increased with civilization. So does the peculiar Jewish character appear to have been something noted in relatively recent years. In old times Jews were not regarded as a people given to sedentary pursuits and the handling of money. It was not they who started the banking business. That was a Babylonian invention. They were not even a commercial people, for which their early writer, Josephus, apologized. The Jews of old were known as farmers and fine soldiers. North Africa considered them to be a dangerous and extremely violent race.

When Jerusalem was destroyed its Roman conqueror, Titus, made slaves of nearly one hundred thousand of its inhabitants, many of whom he drove into Egypt, some to work in the mines. The penal mines of Egypt were a horror. They were near what was known as the Golden Berenice by the Red Sea. Who went into these mines to work never came out. Even children were driven into those galleries to live the rest of their lives in the dark. The guards were chosen as foreign to the prisoners and thus unable to understand or be moved by their plaints. Naked, almost unnourished, flogged to their work, they stumbled by torchlight farther and farther into the winding tunnels of the mines "having their bodies appearing sometimes one color and sometimes another, according to the nature of the soil in which they worked." This terrible picture of the mines is by Diodorus, who was in Egypt something over a century before the arrival of the Jewish slaves.

From these mines Ramses II had taken thirty-five million dollars' worth of gold every year, and to reach them his father had caused to be drawn out the very earliest map which has come down to us. It is done in two colors, red and yellow, on papyrus and on it are shown marks intended to represent the soles of a man's foot as indications of the way which a traveler should follow toward the mines.

In the time of the Jewish slaves the mines were wearing thin and the work of picking gold from their bare bones, far into the caverns, was hard beyond bearing. Soon "overworn with the weight of their misery," just as in Diodorus' day, they fell dead—pitiful corpses, their naked bodies harlequined by the varicolored clay.

*   *   *

FORTY-FIVE YEARS AFTER THE FALL OF JERUSALEM JEWRY REvolted. It was the culmination of years of humiliation and homesickness and sorrow for lost glory, inflamed by rumors that a conquering Messiah might soon come to lead them. In the uprising in Palestine this pseudo Messiah presently did appear. He was the prodigious Bar-Kokba who was reputedly so strong that he could catch on his knees and kick back against the enemy the great stones fired from the Roman *ballistae* (catapults).

In the fiery debut of the Jewish revolt it was nip and tuck but that the Jews might win all the eastern side of North Africa and establish a Jewish African empire.

It was well prepared. On an appointed day the Jews rose together. They killed in North Africa alone hundreds of thousands. Cyrene and Egypt and the island of Cyprus ran blood.

Modern Jewish authorities themselves give credence to the account of the Cyrene reign of terror and the associated events of the revolt as given by Dio Cassius, a Roman historian who was born a generation afterward. I quote his story of this pogrom in reverse:

> The Jews of the region of Cyrene had put one Andreas at their head and were destroying both the Romans and the Greeks. They would cook their flesh, make belts for themselves of their entrails, and wear their skins for clothing. Many they sawed in two from the heads downwards. Others they would give to wild beasts and force still others to fight as gladiators.

In all, consequently, two hundred and twenty thousand perished. In Egypt also they performed many similar deeds and in Cyprus under the leadership of Artemio. There likewise two hundred and forty thousand perished. For that reason no Jew may set foot in that land, but even if one of them is driven upon that island by force of the wind he is put to death. Various persons took part in subduing these Jews, one being Lusius, who was sent by Trajan.

Some Jews escaped Roman vengeance. Some fled westward. Some fled into the desert, ever the refuge of the defeated, oppressed or persecuted. There is a theory, much discussed by historians, of which I shall speak again later on (see page 256) that Jews by degrees moved across the Sahara to the Niger and that an early Sudanese native kingdom had a Jewish origin.

ZENOBIA

SO, AFTER A HIDEOUS ACCOUCHEMENT, THE JEWISH DREAM OF AN African empire died stillborn. In the next century another dream threatened Rome's domination. Zenobia, the famous warrior queen, decided to grab Egypt. Her home, Palmyra, was in inland Syria, but Zenobia was, or believed herself to be descended from the Ptolemies, and—like the Candace—she saw herself in fancy on Cleopatra's throne. But with far better right, in so far as appearance went, for Zenobia was one of the famous beauties of history.

See her as she appeared before her people: "She went in state to the assemblies in a helmet with a purple band fringed with jewels. Her robe. was clasped with a diamond buckle and she often wore her arms bare. Her complexion was a dark brown and her eyes black and sparkling and of uncommon fire. Her countenance was divinely expressive . . . her teeth white as pearls and her voice strong and harmonious." Zenobia was very learned, and "of a manly understanding." Her valor was beyond that of woman: she hunted lions, panthers and bears and she loved war. Sometimes she would march at the head of her army, and it was her habit to sit and "drink deeply with her officers, but ever with sobriety." (This account is from translations of Pollio, an historian of about her period.)

Zenobia, born seemingly so long before her time, occupied Egypt in 270 A.D. The country was presumably rather easy to invade at the moment, and it is even said that Zenobia was invited in by certain of the people, for Egypt was in a state of disorder and discontent. Alexandria remembered with hatred Caracalla's cruel revenge when on a visit to Egypt he became angered by a joke about himself in a local theater, tricked all the fighting men outside the walls on the pretext of a military census, slaughtered them and then massacred the population in their homes. Alexandria shuddered at the recollection of a plague, born within her precincts, and so virulent and wide spreading that Gibbon would have it that during its fifteen years' run (250 to 265 A.D.) "war, pestilence and famine consumed the moiety of the human species."

For these and other reasons Egypt was in a bad way when Zenobia sent in her seventy thousand soldiers to take charge. And Rome was preoccupied with troubles in places outside Africa. Zenobia, who had been under Rome's patronage during the earlier part of her career and had pretended that she undertook her military operations in Egypt as a policing measure on Rome's behalf, artfully sought to bite off Egypt for herself.

That Egypt required policing was indisputable. The country's peace was threatened simultaneously by two other forces, besides those of Zenobia: by the followers of one Firmus, a nationalist leader who wanted to make himself emperor, and by the hordes of the Blemmyes, a terrifying crowd of alleged human monsters in the South. Firmus' dreams of empire came to a swift end. The ravages of the peculiar Blemmyes lasted over several centuries and we shall meet them again.

As for Zenobia she was able for a few months to call herself Egypt's queen. Aurelian expressed bitter resentment that he should have such difficulty in "a war I am waging with a woman." Zenobia fought personally in bloody battles, but eventually was taken prisoner and met that fate which her alleged relative of the house of the Ptolemies had escaped by suicide.

Zenobia was carried to Rome to endure the nightmare of the defeated, a Roman triumph. That in which she figured is said to have been the most magnificent and interesting display the city ever saw. It showed two hundred of the most curious breeds of wild animals brought from every part of the Empire. It showed ten woman soldiers in full armor, Gothic women who had been captured fighting. It gave Romans a preview of a sartorial novelty: namely trousers, then considered by the togaed Roman to be a horrid barbarism. They stared contemptuously upon the costume worn by a vanquished ruler from the land we now know as France, who marched "in Gallic trousers, a saffron tunic and a robe of purple." But Zenobia was the best of the show. Preceded by her portable wealth, her rich gold tablewear and her gorgeous and exotic wardrobe, walked the beautiful woman who for just a little while had been queen of Egypt. She wore fetters of gold. A slave supported the dragging gold chains which were locked round her throat. She almost fainted under the weight of jewels which had been piled upon her and hung against her bosom and from her shoulders and arms.

There are conflicting stories as to what happened to Zenobia. One is that after the triumph she refused all food and so killed herself. The other that she settled down and lived out the rest of her life as a Roman matron. Purely on the probability of character I would favor the latter. Had Zenobia been of such a temper that to appear in a Roman triumph would be an intolerable humiliation to her she would have suicided before the torment, as did Cleopatra. Zenobia, it seems to me, was one of those who fought, failed, and was ready to take her punishment. A very gentlemanly lady.

THE "HEADLESS" BLEMMYES

ROME HAD RID HER EGYPTIAN COLONY OF A WOULD-BE QUEEN AND a would-be emperor, but the odd Blemmyes remained a continuing danger, so great a danger that a monstrous quality was attributed to them, perhaps as a sort of excuse for Rome's failure to handle them.

The Blemmyes were the ancestors of the modern Bisharin and racial relatives of the famed Fuzzy-Wuzzies. They were probably queer looking, as are these two modern groups. To their enemies of the period they were classed, not as human beings, but as monsters. They were soberly described in classical literature as a race who "had no heads, their mouths and eyes being seated in their breasts" (Pliny V:8).

This was not one of those wonder stories about the mysterious inhabitants of some remote, unknown quarter of Africa, but a report seriously given about an enemy with whom the people of Egypt and their Roman masters had actual and prolonged contact on the Egyptian frontier. The Blemmye myth survived for a long time. In that tourists' item, the thirteenth century world map in Hereford Cathedral, there is shown a pair of headless Blemmyes with eyeholes and mouth holes in their torsoes. Shakespeare knew about the Blemmyes and caused Othello, in telling his adventures, to describe such people, though not by name (Act I: scene 3). Hard to guess what can have been behind the original and perhaps sincere impression. One classical writer says that the Blemmyes "were in the habit of falling on one knee and bowing the head to the breast, by which means—without injuring themselves—they afforded a passage to the horses of the enemy." It is suggested that this certainly difficult maneuver gave them the effect of headlessness. Or it can have been that the Blemmyes wore some form of *litham,* or face veil of dark material like the modern Tuareg, who when seen from a distance in the glare of the African sun do sometimes seem to be men without heads.

At any rate the Blemmyes dominated the Thebes region for a time and attacked Upper Egypt with such recurrent ferocity that the Romans felt obliged to draw back their frontier almost a hundred miles. Their attacks so frightened and disturbed Egypt that Rome imported and subsidized a group of fiery Negroes, called the Nobatae, to guard the border, which the Nobatae did in competent style.

CHRISTIANITY

BUT A FAR BIGGER TROUBLE THAN HUMAN ENEMIES OR MONSTROUS Blemmyes plagued Rome. It was a new mystic force. It was Christianity. The new religion swept early into the part of Africa adjacent to Christ's own home country. Local peace was disturbed, Roman control weakened. But more important than this, Rome's own self-confidence was shaken by Christianity.

"I believe," said Gibbon in his autobiography, "that the propagation of the Gospel and the triumph of the Church are inseparably connected with the decline of the Roman monarchy."

THE NEW FAITH WENT WEST

NORTH AFRICA SNAPPED WITH AVIDITY AT THE NEW FAITH. EGYPtians were attracted toward the teaching of Jesus. His democratic philosophy delighted a people living in subjugation to a haughty master race. The rest of North Africa was moved by the same sentiment.

Furthermore it was characteristic of the North African temperament that, outside Egypt, its natives assimilated imported religions with enthusiasm.

North Africans, ancient Egyptians excepted, had seldom invented religions of their own. In the dim years of antiquity they had, even while fighting against Egypt, respectfully borrowed one of Egypt's deities, the ram-headed god, and advertised him across the whole Sahara. What is believed to be his image has been found recently some seventeen hundred miles from the Nile as the crow flies—which, of course, he does not in the Sahara, nor do men travel in a direct line, so the Egyptian god's fame may well have made its way over several thousands of miles of sand. I speak of the idol of Tamentit, that ancient settlement near Adrar, a stage on the west trans-Saharan route.

Later they worshiped the cruel gods of Carthage and later yet the gods of Rome. And the Sahara even said its prayers to Alexander the Great, whose dramatic deification at the oasis of Siwa had, naturally, become a matter of excited Saharan gossip. They got to calling Alexander by the name of Doul-Karnein "The Man-with-the-Two-Horns" and took the Koran's word for it that he had traveled across their country to "the place where the sun setteth in a spring of black mud."

Alexander on this mythical journey westward to the Atlantic performed alleged miracles of monster killing and geographical rearrangement, recalling the exploits which the people of antiquity attributed to Hercules. Alexander freed the people of an island adjacent to Morocco from the depredations of a dragon. He placed at the entrance to its lair two bulls stuffed with "a mixture of resin, sulphur, chalk and arsenic" intermingled with iron hooks so that it could not, after snatching at its prey, vomit the mess out of its insides. He also caused his engineers to separate Europe and Africa, which were then Siamese twins, by digging a canal which we now call the Strait of Gibraltar. Indeed, North African legend worked Alexander's personality shamelessly.

The North African natives' sole important invention in the matter of worship was the hybrid deity, Gurzil, and even Gurzil was a foreign importation on his father's side, for he was believed to have sprung from the mating of the ram-headed adoptee from Egypt with a local cow! Gurzil was worshiped in Tripolitania, retaining his prestige well into Moslem times. In the eleventh century the Arabic geographer, El-Bekri, was scandalized to find people making sacrifices to a Gurzil idol and praying to it for health and wealth.

*   *   *

THIS INHERENT READINESS TO FOLLOW A FOREIGN SPIRITUAL LEAD, combined with a racial tendency to be "agin the government" caused the western side of North Africa to adopt Christianity. The revered names of early martyrs come down to us: St. Cyprian, St. Felix. Other heroes: the centurion of Tangier who threw down his arms crying that he would no longer obey any general but Jesus Christ; another local youth, an early instance of the conscientious objector who believed so sincerely in a gentle Jesus that he refused to be drafted into the Roman army. Both he and the Tangier centurion died for their convictions, as did the two saints.

THE NEW FAITH WENT SOUTH

EVEN THE PRIMITIVE POPULATION OF THE COUNTRY UP THE NILE to the south of Egypt was presently converted to Christianity by missionaries from Alexandria. Silko, the king of the Nobatae, adopted the new faith and told his people to do likewise. His was the buffer state which had been subsidized to hold back the "headless" Blemmyes. Silko was faithful to the task and upon a temple wall at Kalabshah there has been found and translated his graven boast that, with God's help, he had conquered the

Blemmyes "once and for all" and caused them to swear an oath to him on the images of their pagan gods.

The land of the Nobatae was to show itself persistent in its Christianity at a time when most of the rest of North Africa shifted to Mohammedanism. A substratum of old paganism evidently remained, however, for a Moslem account of conditions in the up-Nile country (Selim el-Assouani, via Macrizi) reports local belief in demons, friendly demons. These were accustomed to sow seed, cut corn and stack it for the local farmers in return for gifts of *booza* which would be left in the fields for the demons' entertainment. *Booza* was one of the names of the beer of the country. This beer was made by cooking leavened bread slowly for hours in water and leaving it to ferment. There were three qualities. *Booza* was the medium grade; the first quality was called "Nightingale's Mother" because it made men sing. This tasted "like champagne turned sour," according to Burckhardt, an early explorer of this part of the world.

However, despite such incidental vestiges of paganism as belief in demons, the natives of the country up the Nile were tenaciously Christian well into the Moslem Era, being surpassed only by the Abyssinians, who—as everyone knows—still cling to Christ's faith in a section of the world which has turned almost entirely to Mohammedanism.

CHRISTIANITY IN EGYPT

MEANWHILE IN EGYPT CHRISTIANITY HAD BECOME VERY STRONG. The faith of Jesus was traditionally first taught there by St. Mark, whose tomb at Alexandria was—again traditionally—opened up by the Venetians eight hundred years afterward so that they might possess the bones of the patron saint who had stood upon the then uninhabited island, where Venice later rose, and had prophesied that it would be the site of a great city.

A century after Egypt's conversion the life of Jesus was rendered into the Egyptian language. Some leaves of this manuscript were taken in 1896 to the British Museum. There survives also a fourth century Egyptian portrait of Jesus "worked in white on a purple background, showing a young man with curly hair and beardless" who holds aloft a cross in His left hand whilst with His right "He spears a snake-like crocodile."

Egypt's Christianity in those days was in some cases a frenzied affair. Folk were very close not only in time but in place to the life of their Lord on earth. They had a childish, a pathetic longing to excel one another in the uncouth sacrifices which they fancied would be sweet to Him, as if to please a human master who might repass at any moment to note and praise their devotion.

From the behavior of certain of these Egyptians—saintly eccentrics, hermits and monks—was born the monastic system of medieval Europe. The monastic idea was already in the Egyptian air; some time before the followers of St. Anthony established their institutions there had been a non-Christian monastic order in Egypt. This was the Jewish Therapeutai.

Christian men and women by the thousands withdrew into the desert to live monastically. Usually they forswore marriage. Often they performed, it is said, shocking penances and submitted to shocking punishments. You may read how women who had brought their children with them would on occasion obey the order to cast them into pools to drown, or how men caused rigid iron greaves to be soldered for life upon their legs, and rigid gauntlets upon their hands, of existences panted out in the burning air alongside salt lakes, of bloody whippings accepted with pious joy, and fastings almost beyond belief.

Such accounts of self-torture have been among the familiar wonder stories since the days of Gibbon. Modern research is of the opinion that, although "Egyptian monks practised austerities of the severest kind, they were what might be called natural, as prolonged abstinence from food and sleep, exposure to heat . . ." and that it was in Syria that "austerities of a highly artificial character were in vogue." I quote from Dom E. C. Butler, Abbot of Downside Abbey, writing in *The Cambridge Medieval History*. Let us at any rate look back with tenderness upon these auto-martyrs of the dim ages of Christianity. Their behavior was based on sincere adoration of a new-found Saviour.

ROME VACILLATED

THE TEMPORAL MASTER, ROME, LOOKED UPON AFRICA'S SPIRITUAL adventures with a vacillating policy, her own attitude toward Christianity being uncertain. On occasions Rome sniffed longingly at the new faith. We hear, for instance, how during one reign the Roman court placed Christ's statue along with those of the familiar pagan gods in the royal chapel, and how one of the emperors, Philippus (244-249), during whose reign was celebrated the one thousandth anniversary of the founding of Rome, was suspected of having forsworn the old, old gods completely to give his sole allegiance to Jesus.

But at other times Rome viewed Christians with loathing, blamed them for her mounting troubles and considered them guilty of the vilest infamies, charging that they ate newborn babies alive—first dredging them in flour—and completed their secret meetings by incestuous orgies. At such periods of anti-Christian agitation there would occur both in Rome and in her colonial possessions the horrors of persecutions—physical, moral and mental: martyrs burned and beheaded, virgins officially raped, Venus' statue tauntingly set up, it is alleged, in the holy spot of the Crucifixion.

At any moment Christians would be in danger, a likely butt for public ill humor. If crops failed or there was some local calamity the mob would be incited to blame the Christians. The amphitheaters of North African cities saw many a poor gentle Christian dragged in after a chase through alleys and cellars and heard popular yells of delight when Numidian lions pounced on the pretended cause of the community's troubles. It interested the crowd to observe the technique of lions when devouring humans: "if the victim was a man it was the genital organs which were first eaten, if a woman, the breasts."

*   *   *

THEN BY WHAT SEEMED A MIRACLE TO CHRISTIAN HEARTS THEIR faith came suddenly into its own a mere decade after the very worst period of their persecutions. To the emperor, Constantine (313-337), appeared visions and dreams of the Cross combined with the slogan "By This Sign Conquer!" He himself died Christian, and within that same century all men of the Roman Empire were commanded by law to adopt the new faith. Paganism was legally forbidden.

FALL OF THE GODS

SO DIED THE GODS. THE PATHOS OF IT! AN IDOL, MADE HOLY AND fearsome by the self-hypnosis of its worshipers, the workman's vulgar tool forgotten as men groveled at its stone feet, or its brass pedestal, suddenly thrown down from its honored shrine—a mere lump of rock again, or a scrap of metal. It was the death of an abstract idea, a stab at pagan man's own very heart, for his gods he had invented in his own image. The moral shock to the devout pagans of the day must have been very cruel, very tragic, very frightening.

The story of the destruction of the colossal Serapis at Alexandria is typical of what happened across the stretches of Africa. It has the drama of the sudden downfall of some old dynasty. The god Serapis was a mystic blend of Osiris with the antique sacred Apis bull. Serapis' statue in the temple was made of a great number of plates of different metals joined together and was a thing to which mysterious power was attributed. If violated the heavens and the earth would instantly return to their original chaos.

Upon the issuing of the decree that all men must henceforth be Christians, battle raged in Alexandria's streets round the temple. The die-hard pagans fortified themselves within its precincts; soldiers attacked. From his heights Serapis, glittering in his dress of silver and gold and brass, and wrapped in the aura of a prestige that went back over thousands of years to the origin of Apis worship and the adoration of Osiris, looked down on waves of blood and saw that his end was near. But so strong was superstition that it is said even the Christians trembled when a soldier climbed up and crashed a mighty blow into the god's shining cheek.

Would the world immediately curdle into a chaotic mass? The crowd counted the seconds. Nothing happened. So Serapis fell.

And so across the top of Africa old idols bit the dust, old temples began to work for Christ. The huge temple of the Celestial Venus at Carthage became a church. The temple by the Nile on whose walls Hatshepsut, the great woman Pharaoh, recorded the expedition to seek incense for a god of Egypt became a monastic building, Der-el-Bahri. At Der-el-Bahri have been dug up the bodies of early Christians buried in the shadow of Amon's erstwhile greatness and wearing on the left shoulder the swastika which was then used in Egypt, as elsewhere, as a Christian emblem. (The swastika, of course, has been a widely used emblem: it has been found on "button-badges" dating back to the Seventh and Eighth Egyptian dynasties; its origin, Petrie says, is unknown; it first appeared in Babylonia and was known in Italy in 1100 B.C.) Pagan premises were taken over by Christians far up the Nile. At Sebua there has survived a comic indication of the hurried eviction of the old gods. Peter with his key was painted hastily on top of the representation of a pagan deity. Alongside him still stands the effigy of Ramses II, seemingly presenting a sort of floral offering to the Christian saint.

HYPATIA

CHRISTIANITY HAVING NOW GAINED OFFICIAL SUPPORT ACROSS ALL North Africa the formerly persecuted could be the persecutors, and naturally, though regrettably, they sometimes took the opportunity. The fate of famous Hypatia, beautiful pagan "bluestocking" whom the Christians of Alexandria martyred is typical. A Christian mob, after rioting in the Jewish quarter of the city, turned their fury toward such pagans as still persisted in their ways, spied this prominent pagan woman, dragged her from her chariot, stripped her, stoned her to death with crockery and broken oyster shells, tore her corpse to bits and burnt it. All this they performed inside a Christian church.

Hypatia is a chastening memory to Christian pride.

THE CIRCUMCELLIONES

CONSIDERING THAT PRACTICALLY EVERY NORTH AFRICAN IS TODAY a Mohammedan it is startling to recall that in the early centuries of our era the ancestors of these same people made North Africa Christianity's hottest hothouse. However, it is typical of the regional character to take religion very hard. It was so in ancient Egypt. It is so today in all North Africa. It was the same when North Africa was Christian. It is a part of the world which always throws itself headlong into religious experiences.

One manifestation of exaggerated fervor in early Christian days is worth recording. It concerns the wild behavior of a sect called the Circumcelliones. This sect was a breakaway or subdivision of the Donatists, themselves a breakaway from the orthodox Catholic church as upheld by the famous contemporary bishop, St. Augustine. These technicalities would be out of place were it not that the Circumcelliones in the Tunisian and Algerian region took so prominent and turbulent a part in the life of the times (fourth century).

They were gangs of runaway slaves, disgruntled laborers and peasants who had abandoned work, and they roamed the country pillaging and burning in accordance with their special understanding of the rules of Christianity, and cried out "Praise be to God!" with each new act of sabotage. Their idea was to establish equality, as they considered it had been preached by Jesus. Wealth was a crime. Slavery was a crime. Did they meet a rich man driving in his chariot with his slaves trotting behind on foot, they would drag him off his perch, put slaves in his place and force *him* to run behind. To such whimsicalities they added wholesale murder and destruction. They burnt farms, ruined irrigation canals, defiled wells. It was a veritable and very long-continued revolution. Its effect on Rome's intensive local cultivation was disastrous.

The Circumcelliones were sincere. They were ready—eager even —to give up life for their religion. They would sometimes, as they wandered the countryside, be seized with a mass longing for martyrdom, would pull up any stranger they met and order him to kill them all, suicide being accounted by them to be wrong. If the stranger refused they killed him!

Fanaticism such as this has been typical of the North African temperament. We shall meet its like again.

THE VISITATION OF THE
VANDALS

SOMETIMES YOU FEEL AS IF HISTORY WERE HOLDING A REHEARSAL.
Only a few years after the vandalism of the Circumcelliones North
Africa experienced the visitation of the real Vandals.

In the whole sweep of Africa's immensely long story there was
never an odder episode. These blond giants from the north darted
into Africa with a sudden rush, used Carthage as a base to sack
Rome, were demoralized by the soft climate and were thrown
out again, leaving scarcely a trace behind, all inside a hundred
and six years.

It was in 429 that the king of the Vandals in Spain embarked
for Morocco. What was the past story of the Vandals does not
concern this volume. Their reputation is known to us all, for
their name is one of the very few national or tribal names which
we have come to spell with a small letter and use as a descriptive
term. Another such name is assassin. As to the employment of the
word, vandal, in a general and derogatory sense, I chanced during the days of World War II when the world was shuddering
over Teutonic destructiveness, to read a curious plaint from a
German pen. This plaint had been uttered by Dr. Ludwig
Schmidt, writing about the original Vandals in *The Cambridge
Medieval History*. Said he, "It is unjust to brand these people with
the word 'vandalism.'" Comment would be superfluous.

Another bit of defense of the Vandals comes from the always
ingenious pen of the French authority, Professor Gautier, who
says that the fact that many of the great Roman cities of the
Tunisian-Algerian region were destroyed willfully during the
Vandal period is the reason why certain magnificent ruins survive for the enlightenment of today's antiquarians. "Timgad,"
says he, "rivals Pompeii. A volcanic eruption or the sack and
burning of a band of pillagers are phenomena infinitely less destructive (to a town) than the continuance of life there."

*   *   *

AT THE TIME WHEN THE VANDALS INVADED AFRICA THEY WERE
Christians, and ardently pious. They marched into battle carrying

a Bible before their army like a standard. It was presumably the same expurgated version of the Bible which Ulphilas, the Goth, had recently translated, inventing an alphabet perforce since they had none, and omitting the more bellicose Old Testament passages because to his shrewd notion those Teutonic peoples were blood-thirsty enough already!

The Vandals, after devastating southern Spain and giving it the name it still wears (Vandalusia, shortened to Andalusia; an alternate derivation takes the names from the Arabic, "Western-Land"), had met with reverses and wanted a change of pillaging ground. Rumors of African grain fields had come to them, and by a piece of tragic folly a sort of fifth column in Africa had invited their intervention.

They tore across the open country from Tangier to Tripoli. Big towns held them off for a while. St. Augustine died during their siege of Bône; Carthage fell last of all. The city, as rebuilt by Rome, had by then become the finest town in all North Africa. It was beautiful with shady parks and magnificent buildings, suave, learned and luxurious. The Vandals stripped the people of everything—jewelry, clothes, furniture—and settled in their homes. Roman attempts to protect or recapture the region failed. Rome's belly suffered; no more grain was shipped to Italy.

*   *   *

PRESENTLY ROME WAS TO SUFFER YET MORE ACUTELY, FOR SIXTEEN years later the terrible hoppy-legged Genseric (or Gaiseric), the Vandal king, sailed forth from the port of Carthage with a horde of his own countrymen and native African recruits, all of them drooling for plunder.

And plunder they got. Rome could not stand against them. From mid-June of 455 they sacked Rome for a fortnight, raped women and pillaged everything. They tore the gilt bronze roof off the Capitol, they clawed all the gold plate from the imperial palace, they pried off every scrap of brass or copper to be found anywhere. They stole the seven-branched golden holy candlestick which Rome herself had stolen from Jerusalem, and they snatched the sacred treasure of the Christian churches. Finally they stripped the jewels from the empress and her daughters and bundled them, along with thousands of other Romans, onto their ships and sailed back to Carthage.

Did any at Rome during that harrowing fortnight recall Scipio's words of foreboding when he destroyed old Carthage six hundred years before? Did any regret that at Caesar's behest they had set aside the curse upon the site of old Carthage and permitted the refounding of a base port to be used for Rome's plundering and humiliation?

EFFEMINATE VANDALS

THINGS BECAME TOO EASY FOR THE VANDALS IN AFRICA. WICKED-ness, like an art or avocation, needs exercise. The Vandals loafed about innocuously and grew flabby. No longer terrible warriors without fear or mercy, they put off their armor and slipped into loose silken robes, bathed daily, overate and overloved, and lounged their days away. They had become, says Procopius, historian of the period, "the most effeminate of all known nations."

The so-called Romans, with headquarters now at Constantinople, saw their chance. The famous general Belisarius recaptured Carthage in 535. These fierce Vandals, whose name has remained to us today as a synonym for greedy ruthlessness, had become so feeble of temper that the job of conquering them required only three months.

The Vandal king appeared in Constantinople at his conqueror's triumph, wearing a gorgeous purple gown and muttering continuously as he walked—so the story goes—those words which are ever true and never truer than in his case: "Vanity of vanities . . . all is vanity!"

The Roman church and city treasure was returned. The holy Jewish candlestick also went back eventually to its home town. It was a cunning Jew who brought about its return to Jerusalem. Procopius (*De Bello Vandalico,* Book II, chapter 6) tells how this Jew exclaimed when the thrice-stolen candlestick was carried in the Constantinople triumph, "It is unlucky. Where it goes conquerors come and take it. Witness Rome's sacking and the capture of Vandal Carthage. It is not good that it should stay in Constantinople!" So back to Jerusalem went the candlestick that beckoned to bad luck, albeit it was lodged in a Christian church.

DARKEST AFRICA

A PERIOD OF GLOOM AND DISORDER FELL ON ALL NORTH AFRICA, A hurrying, swift-mounting desolation. To the west bloody rebellions, for now that the Vandals had been thrown out the natives wanted no return of the former Roman master. They wanted to be free barbarians again, unexploited by a hungry Europe. To the east, in Egypt, a foreign invader came into a country already in anarchy. The Persians returned.

It would be interesting to have the considered opinion of some wise man living about the year 600 A.D. on the then worth and on the future prospects of Africa. It would, however, have been impossible to get such an opinion because in the year 600 there would have been no competent wise man to express it. World knowledge, and most particularly knowledge about the African portion of the world, was then at its lowest ebb since the days of savagery. Classical geography, except for its wonder stories, had been forgotten—not that it had ever amounted to much so far as Africa was concerned.

Nobody in the year 600 knew anything definite about Africa beyond the rim along the Mediterranean and the banks of the lower Nile. It was, the intelligentsia of Europe thought, just a little place—less than half as big as Europe—and such territory as it possessed was mostly made up of impassable desert. This desert ended well to the north of the Equator. That was all the Africa there was. Thus the continent was egg shaped—an egg lying on its side. The Equator, some believed—of course nobody had yet reported on it—was a stream of boiling water girdling the world. Naturally untraversable.

To the other side of this boiling gap geographical theory placed a mysterious imaginary continent, which, of course, nobody had visited. It, like Africa, was oval. It was about the same size as the Afric-egg, and to it was given the name of "Australia." This was a thousand years or more before any explorer ever saw the real Australia.

It is pleasant to think that the gracious syllables of the name Australia were thus earmarked so long in advance for the youngest of the earth's continents, like a name picked hopefully for a long-

awaited baby. The "Australia" of early medieval fancy was imagination's playground. Some peopled it with shocking and distorted
freaks. Others, yet more morbid, suggested "Australia" was a
place of weird horror, bereft of stars, uninhabitable, just a blank.

And Africa, once you turned your back upon the coasts or the
Nile Valley, was believed to be little better. The fact was that
Africa was regarded as dangerously remote from the World's
navel, that spot near the place of Calvary which pious Christians
thought that Jesus had indicated with His own hands as the
earth's central point.[3] Africa—if the average citizen of the year
600 gave it any consideration at all—probably seemed to be
practically slipping off the world altogether.

*   *   *

HOWEVER, FOR ARGUMENT'S SAKE, LET US INVENT A WISE MAN OF
the year 600 who possessed more knowledge of Africa than his
fellows. There can be no doubt that, viewing African conditions
as they were—shortly after a rebellion in the West which allegedly
led to the death of five million persons, and just at a time of
anarchy in Egypt—our wise man would have said that the future
of the continent never looked worse: Darkest Africa indeed!

How wrong our wise man would have been! North Africa in
the year 600 was about to break from the long lethargy which
had afflicted her during Rome's control. The stable door was to
burst open and instead of that plodding stalled ox, there would
come forth a curvetting steed.

Just when Europe was destined to slip into a time of bleak
gloom, of dull and sodden inhibition, there was to flash across
Africa a period of self-confidence and brilliant accomplishment.
Africa's coastal strip was to be the boulevard of adventure, its
sands a crisscross of caravans, its harbors the departure points for
triumphant conquest.

Of all the times and places of the past, North Africa in the early
years of the Middle Ages, would, to my notion, have been the best.

[3] A Christian pilgrim reported that he saw at Jerusalem at this period a
column which marked "the umbilical spot" of the world. A somewhat later
pilgrim told that the spot had been chosen by Our Lord, Himself. It was
sometimes called "Compas" and the belief that it was the world's "middle"
lasted for nearly a thousand years. (See passages in Beazley's, *The Dawn of
Modern Geography*, Vol. I, p. 338; II, pp. 149 and 150, as of Arculf and
Seawuld, the pilgrims, and as of "Compas" on maps as late as 1400.)

BOOK THREE

THE BLOOD AND GLORY OF ISLAM

PART ONE

The Rise of the Crescent

THE BATTLE OF THE
ELEPHANT

IN THE SIXTH CENTURY WAS FOUGHT NEAR MECCA ONE OF THE
decisive battles of the world, though you may not find it on any
of the lists. It was the so-called Battle of the Elephant. It determined the religion and way of life of a large part of the earth's
population. It led to the founding of the Mohammedan faith.
"By it the field was cleared for the birth of a giant." Or, as Gibbon
has it, but for the result of this battle "Mohammed must have
been crushed and a revolution would have been prevented which
changed the civil and religious state of the world." Thanks to the
outcome of this battle one of the most important babies of all
times was born in safety. On the career of the baby thus saved
depends a pageant of grand conquests, depends all the romance
and miseries of the Crusades. On his career depends all the
subsequent history of North Africa.

Mohammed was born two months after the battle. But for the
Miracle of the Elephant he would have perished. So in the Arab
tradition the date of his birth is called the "Year of the Elephant."

Near the end of the Koran stands a chapter entitled "The
Elephant" which tells the story of the most influential individual
animal of all the beasts which have been immortalized in fact or
fable, excepting only the snake of Eden. To most of us in America
and Europe the Koranic elephant must seem fable. But to countless millions of Mohammedans during the past thirteen centuries

he has been revered as the instrument of a glorious miracle, and more than two hundred twenty millions venerate that elephant today (World Almanac figure; Professor Hitti of Princeton in his *History of the Arabs* claims that "every sixth or seventh person in our world today is a follower of Muhammed").

*   *   *

THE ARABIAN PENINSULA WAS THEN A RELIGIOUS PIEBALD, SPOTTED with communities of Jews, of Zoroastrians, of Christians and of pagans. Mecca was pagan and contained that ancient idol house, the Kaaba, said to have been first constructed by Adam on a celestial model erected by Allah's orders long before the creation which possessed pillars of jasper and a roof of rubies. Adam's Kaaba was believed to have been destroyed in the Flood and rebuilt by Abraham with the help of Ismael, the legendary ancestor of the Arabs. The Kaaba was in its seventh form just previous to Mohammed's birth. (These traditions are set down by Dinet, a French Moslem, and by Burton, both of whom made the Mecca pilgrimage.) It was a much-frequented shrine and contained many idols, as well as the "Black Stone" supposed once to have been of a dazzling white, darkened through the stroking and kissing of its pagan adorers.

To the south of Mecca lived Christians who had received Christianity from Abyssinia just over the Red Sea gap. An Arabic Christian church had been indecently defiled by a pagan from Mecca and a mighty avenging band marched against the little city under the leadership of one Abraha, surnamed Slit-Nose. Slit-Nose rode upon an imported Abyssinian elephant, traditionally named Mahmud, which is a variation of Mohammed. The Christian army had sworn to destroy the Kaaba; Mahmud—mystically protective of the unborn babe—had a different plan.

The Meccans, amongst them the family and pregnant mother of the Prophet-to-be, were in despair at the approach of the overwhelming force. Slit-Nose led his army forward, confident of easy victory. Suddenly Mahmud, the elephant, saw the Kaaba and knelt down. Urged to his feet he would not go forward. The advancing army faltered in bewilderment. And at that moment, when the halted men milled round their leader, there came all of a sudden "a flock of birds like swallows, every one of which carried three stones, one in each foot and one in its bill, and these stones they dropped upon the heads of the invaders, certainly killing every one they struck." These magic stones were "no bigger than vetches" (a sort of bean) but fell with such force as to pierce the helmet and right through its wearer, "passing out at his fundament." It is said that *on each stone was written the name of the man who was slain by it*. Mecca was saved. Mohammed was born.

CAREER OF MECCA'S CHILD

SOME FORTY YEARS LATER MOHAMMED BEGAN PUBLICATION TO A small secret group of the first chapters (suras) of what was destined to become the most widely read book in the world, the Koran. (It is curious that the three most familiar of all religious books— the Old Testament, the New Testament, and the Koran—should have been originally associated with a small area in the Near East; the Koran, which has been used not only as a holy manual but also universally amongst Moslems as a school textbook, has had —we are assured—more students than either of the other two.)

Till this moment of spiritual inspiration Mohammed, like all the best people of Mecca, had been a pagan. He was in his pagan days a competent businessman, managing the affairs of his elderly rich wife and living with her for over a score of years in faithful marriage—a striking example of devotion and control, given the amplitude of his love life in his later and presumably less passionate days.

Mohammed's outburst of prophecy, his capture of the hearts and minds of his fellows, his power to enter into them like yeast in a batch of bread, raising them to a national stature hitherto undreamed of—these things might make any of us hesitate to repudiate what Moslems claim for him. When Mohammed was born the Arabs were an incoherent group of tribes, romantic, high-spirited, poetical, but politically insignificant and much dominated by the foreign patronage of Romans and Persians. As a nation they were practically nonexistent. When he died the Arabs were ready to flash their eyes proudly across the Menu of the World, ordering what pleased them.

His career as Prophet lasted some twenty years: the secret group who knew of his revelations—this group included his elderly wife

—increased; there were opponents to fight and blood flowed, and all the while the Koran grew, sura by sura, and racial self-confidence augmented. The unexpressed slogan, "Arabia for the Arabs," gave place to the haughty hope, "The World for the Arabs! The world for the followers of Allah!" It was all Mohammed's doing. Even Allah, as now understood, was his invention. The name, Allah—an old, old name—had been that of a pagan god. Mohammed disinfected the name of its pagan associations and gave it to the mystic Power from Whom he received his revelations. And yet this extraordinary accomplishment—the creation of a grand new religion, the inspiration of a puny nation to glorious conquest—seems to have been almost accidental, something which budded and blossomed as simply as a flower.

Few nowadays are so narrow as to name Mohammed a faker. Gone are the centuries of prejudice when, jagged by the sudden rise and continued brilliance of the Mohammedan rival, the outside world railed at what they called "The False Prophet," when the word "mummery" was commonly supposed to derive from his name, and Christians would have it that Mohammed was a madman who had arrogated the Godhead to himself; when a learned American prattled of Islam's "blood-stained altars," a Spanish historian termed Mohammedanism "an absurb sect," and a high-class English publication described the major part of the Koran as "rubbish." We are now told that Allah was but another name for the Jewish and Christian universal God, and there are few thoughtful men who would speak of His Prophet with disrespect or suggest that his revelations were based on calculation or duplicity.

During his early prophetic career Mohammed appears to have had no notion of using his genius to acquire political control. Then ambition came. He left to his people a priceless heritage: they were perfectly sure they were right! His name, which in Arabic signifies "The Praised" and in Hebrew, "The Desired," surely merits in his case the latter translation: probably no man who ever lived so closely and so immediately corresponded to the unrealized potentialities of his fellows. He was the key which opened the Arab door to a great destiny.

THE ARABS RIDE FAR

INSPIRED BY THEIR NEW FAITH ARAB EXPEDITIONS OF CONVERSION and conquest were of an extent and a speed that was nearly miraculous. From the borders of China to just south of Paris, in a swift sweep that took in all the known part of one of the continents and a big slice of the other two (there were but three recognized continents then) Arabs subdued men's bodies and convinced men's minds. No people before nor since have performed such a feat. The Arabs of those days were genuine supermen. They possessed exceptional animal beauty and strength. They were adorned with romantic chivalry, fortified by a religious fervor that was like a potent drug. They rode across the world in superb self-confidence of body and soul, one with their horses, high and proud on their camels.

Like a crowd of splendid wild things let loose they plunged westward across the top of Africa and down into the Sahara. They were everywhere. They reached Fezzan and the borders of the eastern Sudan. North Africa quivered to the pound of galloping horses and the swish of trotting camels. An Arab army reached the Atlantic and its leader rode his horse into the waves and roared out a shout of anger because his charger was not amphibious and could not carry him across the seas to kill more men in Allah's name. North Africa watched with a mixture of fascinated awe and indignation these odd, onrushing foreigners with their sudden pauses for prayer and prostration.

ARABS AND "SOI-DISANT" ARABS

MOST OF NORTH AFRICA FOUGHT THEM BACK VALIANTLY. THE detail of the long struggle will be told presently. For the moment I diverge to meet the inevitable comment of anybody who has been in western North Africa or read the news of World War II: namely that these splendid Arabs of old seem to have altered a lot since the magnificent days of the conquest. They have, even in their home, Arabia. But the fact is that many a so-styled Arab in North Africa has little or no Arab blood.

Of course the name Arab has lately come to be applied to any

Mohammedan. But I am speaking here of a racial, not a religious distinction.

The heroic blood of the original conquerors is today diluted almost out of existence. The conquerors came in comparatively small numbers and they came a very long time ago, and most of them were males. The Arabic blood in modern North Africa (Tripolitania, Tunisia, Algeria, Morocco) proceeds from certain riffraff Arabic tribes who invaded the country long afterward (eleventh century) and from Moslem refugees from Spain. We have no right to expect to find in North Africa's Arab of today a reincarnation of the high-riding conqueror of the grand old days.

Furthermore all who call themselves "Arabs" are not of Arabic blood at all. That he is an Arab is the invariable native claim. He speaks Arabic, it is true, but is far more likely to come of the indigenous stock—Libyan now called Berber—or to represent a mixture of the two races of Arab and Berber. In Morocco the Berber element makes up almost all the population. The farther eastward you go, the larger is the Arabic strain, for it was from the east that the riffraff eleventh century invasions came.

Behind the popular desire to be regarded as Arabs lies natural vanity, a wish to belong to the conquering race of the Prophet. In fact Berber intelligentsia felt this desire so strongly in medieval days that they worked out many quaint theories by which they attempted to show that their people had once lived in Arabia. Goliath and others figure in these traditions, which are soberly discussed by Edrisi, Ibn-Khaldoun and other medieval Moslem writers.

But there was another reason for trying to avoid the racial name of Berber. The word has humiliating associations.

It was in the days of the Arab invasion that the name, originally an adjective with a contemptuous significance, was forced upon the native race of North Africa as a general title. It happened in this way: The Romans had borrowed a word translatable as "barbarous" from the Greeks, who used it to designate anybody who was not Greek. To the Greeks it expressed an insular and rather childish contempt for foreign languages. To the Greeks all foreign talking was just "Bar! Bar!" Just meaningless animal barking. Hence the Greek word from which was derived "barbarous." The Greeks so described every alien. They so described the Romans.

The Romans copied Greek snobbery and applied the word to all inferior races. When they took over western North Africa they applied it in a general sense to the natives. It was a term of disdain. Nobody liked it. The North Africans did not like it. Presumably it was as distasteful to them as such modern terms as "coon," "Dago," "Wop," "Chink," "Yid," "Frogeater," "Limey," and so on.

When the Arabs arrived in western North Africa they found two classes of population. There were persons of European stock in Carthage and other cities and on the big estates. To these the Arabs gave the name of "Roums." And there were those other people whom the Roums designated as "those barbarians." The Arabs heard the descriptive adjective and took it for a proper name. They considered it a very suitable name too, since it resembled an Arabic word meaning "a mixture of unintelligible yelling": a roaring lion, for instance, "berbers."

So for a double reason the Arabs knew the North African native race as the Braber (singular, Berber). And so it came about that these people who in antiquity wore the melodious and dignified name of Libyans were tagged with a most discriminatory title.

The modern Berber does not so describe himself. Even when he does not claim to be an Arab, he never says, "I am a Berber."

The name of Barbary States which we at one time applied to all North Africa except Egypt must have riled the people. No group could be expected to like being called by a name which originally meant something like "The Grunt-Grunts"; no group could have cared to wear a general title associated with derogatory words like "barbarous" and "barbarity."

FROM EGYPT TO FRANCE

Now to return to the Arab sweep to the west, destined eventually to move from Egypt across the whole top of Africa and into Europe.

Naturally, being adjacent territory, Egypt was the opening point of the African conquest. The taking of Egypt was fairly easy. Mohammed himself had opened the way. When the new religion was in its toddling infancy, in about the sixth year of the Hegira, Mohammed had been seized with the ambitious notion of converting the world by correspondence. He dispatched terse letters to the leading nations near Arabia inviting them to become Moslem. One government we know to have snorted. Another probably sneered. But Egypt responded politely.

Christian Egypt sent presents to Mohammed. One of the gift items was of a dynamic character. It was a Christian girl named Mary. I think that the full story of Mary's career would make interesting reading. I picture her frightened journey from her Christian homeland to the country of this queer new Prophet, and her amorous and tragic adventures as a hated outsider in his harem—hated, that is, by the women. Mohammed fell in love with her. This was natural. Mohammed's susceptibility was well known and well advertised—perhaps overadvertised—by Arabic legend, for to these romantic people it seemed quite suitable that a fierce light should beat upon the bedchamber of their venerated hero. To them his love of women was a source of pride. ("The three things he loved best in this world were prayer, perfumes and women," boasts a pious Moslem biographer.) The sensuous side of his nature was however a useful peg to which Christian Europe later hung much of their virulent abuse of the Islam they feared. Europe cried out that Islam's leader had been a fellow of disgusting morals and in their sober history books used to call him by such names as "the Old Lecher."

Christian Mary became Mohammed's sweetheart and the center of a scandal which endangered Mohammed's prestige. He had indiscreetly chosen as the scene for their love-making the residence of one of his wives—he lived with his wives in a row of cottages "separated from one another by palm branches cemented together with mud." The wife in question interrupted. Such a disturbance ensued as caused Mohammed to make a vow of celibacy—not kept. A chapter of the Koran (LXVI, entitled "Prohibition") is given to the affair. Therein Mohammed nonchalantly refers to the scandalous discovery of his rendezvous with Mary as "a certain accident."

Mary was the mother of a son, to Mohammed's joy, for the Prophet was often a bridegroom but seldom a father. The babe died under suspicious circumstances, possibly destroyed by childess and envious wives of the harem. This web of passion and jealousy woven about Egyptian Mary strikes oddly on Western minds as a page in the career of the founder of a great religion, but is recounted in Moslem tradition with sober care.

*   *   *

THE SAME OFFICIAL IN EGYPT WHO HAD SENT GIFTS TO MOHAMMED aided in the Arab conquest of the land. Eight years after Mohammed's death the Arab general, Amr-ibn-Asi, had occupied a good part of the country. Egypt's resistance can be described as midway between the "token" and what is usually called feeble. The Roman Empire there expired with the ceding of Alexandria on September 17, 642. It was 672 years since the death of Cleopatra which marked the start of Roman domination.

Alexandria ceased to be Egypt's capital. A new one was founded near ancient Memphis, near modern Cairo. It was called Fostat, which meant "Tent," its site being around the spot where the Arab general, Amr, had set up his military camp.

The Christians of Egypt were treated with fairness. Some accepted Islam. The reason may be cynically diagnosed: by so doing they dodged tribute payment to their conquerors. It is a credit to the sincerity of the faith of the country as a whole that a century later there were still five million Christians left in the land.

*   *   *

IN AFRICA TO THE WEST THE ARAB CONQUEST WAS VERY MUCH MORE difficult and very much slower. Its ups and downs will form a chapter by itself (see page 171 and following). In 732, one hundred years after Mohammed's death, the Arabs—having converted, if not conquered, the Berbers—had reached via Spain their farthest point in Europe, near Tours in France. Italy and Sicily were repeatedly attacked.

Europe cringed and sulked under the onslaught and scarcely attempted to strike back across the Mediterranean.

This period of the Mohammedan outburst coincides with the very dingiest and dullest passage of Europe's Dark Ages. Never were our forebears so stupid, so lethargic. Christian Europe wallowed in a gloomy inhibition while Moslem lands—North Africa, the East, and Mohammedan Spain—blazed with physical and mental energy.

HAD MOHAMMED LEFT A WILL!

BUT FOR ONE CIRCUMSTANCE IT SEEMS AS IF ISLAM MIGHT HAVE mastered the world. That circumstance was that Mohammed did not leave a will. He did not appoint his successor. He had no surviving son. Discord and bickering diminished the Moslem drive. Had this drive been consolidated into a firm dynasty all men might be today openly polygamous, all women wearers of the veil!

Some little résumé of the quarreling amongst the chiefs of Islam and especially of the trouble about Ali, Mohammed's son-in-law, is needed if we are to understand North Africa's medieval history.

Upon the Prophet's death his followers, lacking instruction from him, chose first one and then another of his fathers-in-law as caliph. (The word originally meant merely "successor," later becoming a title of splendid associations.) The first caliph was the father of Ayesha, the celebrated child bride with whom Mohammed consummated marriage when she was only nine. The second was the father of that wife who so bitterly resented Mohammed's entertainment of the Egyptian Mary in her premises.

After these two caliphs, whose combined reigns were short, open trouble started. The third caliph was murdered by rebels. Then the affair of Ali came to a boil.

Ali was the widower of Fatima, the Prophet's beloved daughter. Mohammed had pronounced her to be one of the four perfect women who had lived in the world. Classed with her were the Virgin Mary, "Asia, the wife of Pharaoh" (who was tortured to death because she believed in Moses) and the Prophet's first wife, the elderly rich widow who befriended him in his early career. When Mohammed died Fatima is said to have been disgusted to find herself and her husband cheated of what she considered their natural inheritance and to have died in consequence of a broken heart. The traditions and early writings on Fatima's grief and death have been collected by D. S. Margoliouth.[1]

Ali still seemed to many a proper choice for caliph. To many

---

[1] *The Last Days of Fatimah,* forming a part of the *Mélanges Hartwig Derenbourg,* a collection of works of erudition dedicated to Derenbourg's memory.

others he did not. One of the others was the influential Ayesha who had a long-standing grudge against him based upon his having urged Mohammed to divorce her for alleged infidelity.

There are various versions of the Ayesha scandal. One is that while traveling she had been "compelled by a pressing need" to descend from the curtained litter carried upon her camel's back. Soldiers passed while she was hidden modestly behind rocks, and —supposing she was inside the litter of the halted camel—drove the animal along. The stranded Ayesha was saved by one of the rear guards and rejoined the rest of her party after riding on his camel and after suspicious delay. Another explanation of her jaunt in the company of this young man has to do with a lost necklace. Such behavior did not accord with the Moslem code of manners. However, Mohammed received divine guidance (Koran: XXIV) leading him to believe her guiltless.

Out of the quarrel between Ali's friends and his enemies issued factions destined to rip holes in the Moslem fabric. In fact the Ali dispute developed into one of the longest and bloodiest and most complicated disagreements of all history. Ali himself was assassinated by one of a dissenting group which had broken away from his own party. A new caliph grabbed power and moved the capital to Damascus where he and his successors reigned for about a century.

Those who were loyal to Ali's memory and to his descendants became a dangerous underground from which have spurted vigorous dynasties and fanatical wars across all North Africa.

The group which carried out Ali's assassination formed a third party.

Almost uncountable side parties and sects of Mohammedans formed. They fought bitterly amongst themselves. Much of the vigor of a new spiritual enthusiasm was dissipated. Mohammed's failure to arrange for his successor was therefore a most important circumstance.

THE ARAB-BERBER STRUGGLE

THE ARAB CONQUEST IN THE WEST, in TRIPOLITANIA, TUNISIA, Algeria and Morocco, to use their modern names—if indeed it can

be called a conquest at all—was slow and merged into the subse
quent general history of the land in such a fashion that I have
reserved the passage to recount as a whole.

The dubious conquest took some seventy years and was at no
period a tidy and complete job. Dissension in the supreme control
which produced confusion in the field, made the successive inva
sions of the West a series of fumbling and expensive efforts. There
were frequent changes in military and civil leadership, jealousy
between generals. All resultant from uncertainty at home. What
might have become a strong Moslem empire in Africa was shaken
into little pieces—but such colorful and romantic pieces.

Only Egypt and the adjoining coastal flatlands and deserts were
quickly subdued. The country to the west—from Tripoli to
Morocco—abounded in those hills which breed free spirits. The
distance from the caliphs' troubled capitals increased the diffi
culties. The Berbers fought well. It does not appear that the
Christian-European element, the Roums, did. Arab losses were
immense.

Gradually a religious conquest, as apart from a political con
quest, made progress. But even in the matter of spiritual submis
sion the natives were reluctant. Twelve times, so Arabic tradition
tells us, did the Berbers agree to become Moslems, and then break
faith and turn back to the various religions of their tribes and
regions: some back to either primitive paganism or formal idol
atry, relic of the old Carthaginian masters; some to Christianity
and some to the Jewish faith, learned from Jewish refugees.

The second of the caliphs understood Berber character and
foresaw the disappointment which his people would have to en
dure in their efforts to convert the West. He embodied his senti
ments in a stern command to leave the country alone. Said he—
quote from Ibn-'Abd-el-Hakem, a very early historian of the con
quest—"As long as my eyelids are moist (i.e. during my lifetime)
I forbid any expedition to go to that land. It deserves to be called
'The Far-Off-Place-of-Perfidy.' "

The disheartened cry of one Arab general was "To conquer this
country will be an impossible thing!"

However there was a persistent sentiment in the Arab mind
that the conversion through conquest of western North Africa
was a peculiarly holy duty, something especially commanded by

the Prophet. There were many traditions to this effect: Mohammed had said that the Arabs who went there in Allah's service
would suffer greatly from the cold (as indeed all who have experienced winter weather in the North African high altitudes can
testify) but that their reward would be great. These statements of
Mohammed's may be read at great length in the work of El-Bekri.

So strong was this sentiment that it became a popular saying
amongst Arabs that "the man who has sinned a lot should put the
East behind him," meaning that he should go to convert the
infidels of western North Africa and so gain Allah's pardon. In
short, the war in the West was a sort of Moslem Crusade.

THE ARABS' OWN STORY OF THE
STRUGGLE

THE ARAB STRUGGLES IN WESTERN NORTH AFRICA BECAME A FRAME
to which their own writers hung many romantic stories. We have,
for instance, the rape of the prefect's daughter (Tunisia, 647); the
adventures and final so-called martyrdom of Sidi Okba, in which
figures the fable of the foundation of Kairouan (670); the exploits
of the Berber wonder-woman called "The Cahena" concluding
with her death in battle (probable date 693) and the renowned
trick of Tarik, the Berber, apropos of Solomon's table leg (711).

All these are to be found in those Arab histories which are our
sole sources, for there exist upon this exciting period no non-
Arabic records. We must be content with Arabic history, sometimes more picturesque than convincing. Professor Hitti says that
someone has listed 590 Arabic historians during the first thousand
years of Islam. I venture that there are few general readers who
could name one of them! Upon the period of the Arab conquest
I have consulted notably these three: Ibn-'Abd-el-Hakem, who
wrote sometime before the year 817; En-Noweiri, an Egyptian
writer of the fourteenth century who includes in his history
alleged reminiscences of one who took part in one of the campaigns; and outstandingly the tremendous Ibn-Khaldoun, also a
fourteenth century figure, whose personal life will be mentioned
later on in connection with his quick-witted "kidding" (no other
word would do) of the ferocious Tamerlane (see page 390).

Since Ibn-Khaldoun's accomplishments as a historian are pre-

sumably not familiar to the average reader I will justify the
adjective I applied to him by quoting from modern authority.
Professor Hitti calls Ibn-Khaldoun "one of the greatest historical
philosophers of all time." Professor E. F. Gautier describes him as
"an Oriental of genius, perhaps the only historian in Arabic
literature in the sense that we understand history." Ibn-Khaldoun's
story of western North Africa was based upon "an immense
quantity of historic documents and other writings, the major part
of which is now lost," according to the Baron de Slane by whom
it was translated into French (*Histoire des Berbères*). Its many
volumes are fine reading, despite its amazing mass of detail. Ibn
Khaldoun had a democratic desire to mention the name of every
single person who had, up to his time, played any part at all in the
history of the land. And, as was the Arabic custom, these names
are expressed as "So-and-So-Son-of Such-and-Such-Son-of Some
body-Else." In certain special cases one man's name can take up
as much as four printed lines. Ibn-Khaldoun's own full name is
made up of thirty-five words. This, plus the fact that a specific
episode is often treated from various aspects in widely separated
places, demands careful reading and rereading.

One remark of Ibn-Khaldoun's (not in the history of the
Berbers) is worth quoting, and worth the attention not only of
writers, but of every literate human being. He says: "Nothing is
more common than to see the annalists, commentators and writers
who merely copy what others have recounted, make grave mis
takes in the recital of events, because they have accepted with
blind confidence what others pass along, without judging it by
sane criticism and without purging the recital by deep and ripe
reflection." It is a warning especially to be kept in mind by one
who attempts, as I am doing, to tell about Africa, whose history is
poorly documented in the serious sense, and a land which has been
—from the days of Herodotus to the days of the Sunday supple
ment—the subject of the tallest of tall tales.

THE RAPE OF THE PREFECT'S DAUGHTER

A NEW CALIPH HAD SUCCEEDED TO THAT PESSIMIST WHO FORBADE
all further adventures in western North Africa, and who had died

assassinated. This new caliph had quite different ideas and called upon his people to go on just such an expedition as his predecessor had repudiated. The bravest of Arabia's nobles gathered under Abd-Allah-ibn-Sad. An army of twenty thousand, says En-Noweiri, was assembled in Egypt with their faces turned toward the west.

Tripoli fell and the Arabs rushed forward. They came to what we now know as Tunisia, where governed the Roum whom Arabic historians call Djoredjir. We would write it Gregory. This man appears to have revolted against European control and set himself up as an independent ruler, issuing money with his effigy upon it. The Arabs of the period regarded him not as prefect, but as the "King of the Roums in Africa."

Gregory had an army of one hundred twenty thousand. The Arabs, notwithstanding he outnumbered them six to one, ordered him to become a Moslem or else to pay them an annual tribute. "Not one dirhem!" was Gregory's answer. A dirhem would have been in modern values about eighteen cents.

There followed a long campaign, fighting being done "every day until noon when the armies would retire to their respective camps and stop the combat." This humane arrangement because of the heat. Gregory possessed a gorgeously lovely daughter, whose practice it was to ride into battle with the army, "dressed in the richest garments and wearing over her head a parasol of peacock feathers."

This lovely girl became the carrot of the campaign, so to speak. Her father promised her hand in marriage to whosoever would kill Abd-Allah-ibn-Sad, the Arab leader. The Arab leader's response was to promise the beauty's hand and person (no mention of marriage) to whosoever would kill Gregory. Her prize value had great military importance, and she subsequently became one of the famed characters in Arab history and poetry. The beautiful Roumish amazon figures in the *Kitab-el-Aghani*, the Book of Songs, "which more than any other work gives a complete picture of the Arabs" up to the time when it was collected (tenth century).

One of the invaders, inspired by a wish to bring the tedious combat to a swift end and to win the girl, thought up a simple trick which settled everything. One noontime the Roums, overcome with fatigue after a morning's fighting, punched their time clock as usual and retired from the fray. So seemingly did the Arabs. But certain of Islam's best had been held in reserve. These charged from the tents where they had been hiding and killed a vast number of the Roums who had already dismounted and shucked off their armor. Gregory himself was killed and his fair daughter fell prize to the clever Arab who had performed the killing and thought out the very simple trick of surprising the Roumish army.

The story has a pathetic finish. The clever Arab placed the girl upon his camel and, turning, taunted her. No more fine garments and peacock feather parasols; she was destined, he told her, to become a slave and a water carrier in far off Araby.

"Hearing his words," says Ibn-'Abd-el-Hakem, "she asked, 'What did the dog say?' and when their meaning was translated she threw herself off the camel and broke her neck."

*   *   *

THESE THINGS HAPPENED IN THE YEAR 647 AT SBEITLA IN TUNISIA, a town mentioned in the newspapers in the winter of 1943. It lies a few miles away from the famous Kasserine Pass.

*   *   *

THE SURVIVING ROUMS WERE "STRUCK WITH TERROR AND OFFERED Abd-Allah-ibn-Sad 300 kintars of gold if he would cease hostilities and evacuate the country." This he did. It was a great sum. Just how much is not certain, but it is estimated as equaling nearly a million current United States dollars.

Each soldier received a share—cavalry men getting three times as much as the infantry for themselves and horse. One of the foot soldiers having died later, his family—one of our historians reports —subsequently was paid his share—evidently an efficiently run army.

The Arabs retired with their booty and for a while almost forgot their ambition to master and convert the western side of Africa. Egypt they held as a Moslem province without much effort. They were too much preoccupied at home for further African conquest. Yet another caliph had been assassinated and civil war followed; except for purposes of raiding there were no more expeditions into the West.

THE ROMANTIC AND MYTHICAL
EXPLOITS OF SIDI OKBA

SIDI OKBA WAS THE FIRST ARAB LEADER TO ATTEMPT PERMANENT occupation of the territory we now know as Tunisia, Algeria and Morocco. He was the hero of that rush across Africa's top as far as the Atlantic and it was he who uttered that oft-quoted cry of defiance as he rode his charger into the waves. But despite his many adventures Sidi Okba's memory enjoys high fame far above the value of his accomplishments. (Sidi means something like "His Excellency," a general title of respect; the same title supplied the nickname for the renowned champion of Spain, The Cid.)

Sidi Okba is another of history's whims, a man like Ramses II, gaining a reputation seemingly far beyond his deserts. Indeed Sidi Okba's fame went farther across Africa and endured in a more intimate fashion than did that of the Pharaoh.

Sidi Okba's tomb near Biskra on the border of the Algerian desert is today one of the shrines of Islam. It bears his name and an appeal to Allah's good will in what is said to be the oldest Moslem inscription in Algeria. His Koran is one of the treasures of Islam. There is a record that it was used to swear in the sultan of Morocco in 1584, nine centuries after Okba's death.

A whole section of mythology has grown up around his personality. For instance, there is the legend of how Okba was "elected by Allah to conquer from Tunisia to the Niger (I substitute modern geographic designations for clarity) and as far as the confines of the inhabited world," and how he married a desert woman and founded that celebrated family, later known as the Bekkays. These were a dynasty of religious sovereigns, wielding incalculable power on into the nineteenth century. We shall meet them again.

During its first nine hundred years this nobly begotten family was so keen to concentrate the precious Okba strain that it was their practice "to murder all the male children except one." Sheikh Omar el Bekkay, who died in 1553, put an end to this custom, according to information in a pedigree of the Bekkays which was supplied to Dr. Barth at Timbuctoo.

Another chapter of the Okba myth is set much farther into

Africa's depths and deals with his alleged fathering of the whole
race of Fulas, those copper-colored people beyond the desert whose
women are called—very rightfully, I think—"the Parisiennes of
West Africa." According to this legend Okba converted a country
called Toro and married the chief's daughter, Tadjimaou, from
which union descended the whole Fula race (from the *Tarikh* of
Tierno Mamadou Samba, found by Guebhard and published in
the *Revue des études ethnographiques*). The country of Toro was
in the original legend Tor, or Sinai, of the Bible, and a very long
way from the Fula lands. But the Fulas, desirous like so many of
us to grow their family tree out of a fine pot, claimed the place of
Tor as being in their own West Africa and claimed Okba as their
progenitor.

The fact that such genealogical pretensions as these have been
hung upon the peg of a mythical "Okba" and carried along all
these centuries by nomads or semisavage peoples, much of the
time by word of mouth, indicates that some intense value attached
itself to the figure of Sidi Okba.

He seems to have been put almost on a footing with "The Man-
with-the-Two-Horns," the supernatural manifestation of Alexander the Great (see page 146) and to have possessed furthermore a
class of prestige not claimed for Alexander, in that Okba was
regarded as a highly sainted figure.

*   *   *

YET NEITHER AS A SAINT NOR AS A CONQUEROR WOULD THE REAL
Okba seem to us to merit such a reputation. His tactics as a missionary were ferocious, rather than saintly. And his military accomplishments as an Arab general in charge of expeditions into
western North Africa seem to have been of uncertain value.

Okba's plan for the conquest appears to have been to rush from
place to place and away again. One is reminded of the good old
Duke of York in the song who marched his ten thousand men up
a hill and "marched them down again." Even the foundation of
Kairouan is sometimes attributed to another and the city—if
Okba did found it—was wrested from the Arabs by the defeat
which the imprudent Okba suffered in that last tragic battle
where, to the Arab notion, he died a martyr.

Sidi Okba appealed to the Moslem mentality, however, in three ways. He was a tremendous traveler, a space eater par excellence. He uttered fine speeches. He was fervently religious.

*   *   *

LET US FOLLOW OKBA'S CAREER AS ARABIC HISTORIANS RECORD IT. In what they have chosen to tell about a favorite hero in North Africa we can glimpse something of the psychology of the time and place. So, even those parts of Okba's biography which we cannot believe have a general historic value.

Okba was sent to the West as Arabian governor of the country, although it was as yet unconquered. His journey started in the year 666. On his way Okba broke his westward drive to swing south on a missionary venture. I shall give a résumé of his five-months' adventure in Allah's name, as it is recorded by Ibn-'Abd-el-Hakem. It will be noted that Okba was of the opinion that his duty to his God required that he treat with cruelty all who did not worship as he did.

Having reached the Tripoli region he learned that certain peoples to the south were recalcitrant. Okba then plunged into the desert with "400 cavaliers, 400 camels and a provision of 800 sacks filled with water." He arrived at Oueddan, a little way into the Sahara, and crushed its rebellious population. Okba then "cut off the ear of the king of the country. This personage cried, 'Why do you treat me thus when I have already made peace with you?' Okba's answer was, 'It is a warning I am giving you. Every time you raise your hand toward where your ear used to be you will remember!' "

Having thus implanted a reminder of the God of the Arabs in the local mind, Okba asked what countries lay beyond and learned that there was Djerma (a city named after the Garamantes near modern Murzuk in Fezzan). He pressed on and after eight nights of travel reached the city's environs.

Okba "invited the inhabitants of Djerma to embrace Islamism." They sent—very wisely—a favorable reply and Okba halted several miles outside the town. The king of the place then came out to greet Okba. Okba's officers dragged him from his horse and forced him to walk across the desert toward the conqueror. "As he had a delicate constitution he arrived broken with fatigue and spitting blood. 'Why do you treat me thus?' he demanded in his turn and Okba replied, 'To teach you a lesson.' " Okba then went through all the oasis group of Fezzan subduing one town after another.

Was there any inhabited place yet farther into the Sahara, he asked, and was informed that there was, so he marched into the sand for yet another fifteen nights. There he laid siege to a certain strong place, but gave up the siege after a time, marching on yet farther and taking other strong places, one after another. "At the last stronghold he found the king and cut off his finger. 'Why do you treat me thus?' demanded the king like his predecessors, and Okba answered as usual, 'Every time you cast your eyes toward your hand you will remember the Arabs!' "

Okba was now presumably almost to Lake Chad, and still anxious to go on and on, but there were no paths, no guides. Wily Okba then gave out he was going back to the Mediterranean coast and marched northward. The people of the largest stronghold whose siege he had abandoned opened the gates of their town.

Okba, marching north, was meantime in great distress. He and his men, prostrated by thirst awaited death. "In his extremity Okba prayed for Allah's help. While he prayed Okba's horse had scratched a hole with its forefoot and laid bare a rock, whence suddenly water oozed. Okba, seeing the thread of moisture called his men, who dug and from seventy holes came water. Henceforth this place was called Ma-el-Fares, "the Water (place) of the Horse."

To be truthful a lot of places were henceforth called by that name and rivaled amongst themselves as the site of saintly Sidi Okba's first miracle. Amongst the claimants: Ghadames, two Ma-el-Fares' in the deep Sahara, one near the modern Morocco-Algeria border, one in western Algeria. . . . The performance attributed to Okba's horse deeply stirred the North African imagination as is comprehensible in a land where water and its lack mean life or death.

After the miracle Okba, as he had planned all along, swung back toward the stronghold which had withstood him. Its inhabitants were asleep, all unsuspecting. "Okba cut the throats of all the men of fighting age and carried away the children and wealth of the place." On his ensuing march toward the coast he took other places, including Ghadames, and then invaded Tunisia and took Gafsa. It had been a wondrous tour: he must have covered at least two thousand miles of wild desert. The usefulness of it from a military point of view was nil. He had made no attempt to establish governors. Even the mutilated kings would forget Allah.

KAIROUAN

Perhaps Okba himself sensed the wastefulness of his procedure. After capturing Gafsa he announced a policy.

"Said Okba to his troops," according to En-Noweiri, " 'Whenever we come to this country, the population put themselves out of danger by making profession of Moslemism, but no sooner do we go away than these folk fall back into their faithless ways. I am of the opinion, O Moslems! that I should found a city which can serve as a camp of support for Islam until the end of time.' His advice was followed. Okba founded Kairouan." (Although a previous Arab leader has been mentioned as founder of the city, the main tradition attributes the job to Okba.)

Kairouan came by its name in unpretentious fashion. The word was merely a common noun with the general meaning of a storage place for material and arms—a base, let us say. Okba, having chosen the site which pleased him, "planted his lance in the ground and cried, 'Here is your *kairouan!*' "

It might seem to us that Okba was easily contented in the matter of sites. But the place he picked had advantages in his mind, amongst which was that it was well inland and so free from surprise attacks by the Roums's fleet. The situation chosen was flat, poor ground with salt marshes near by. At that time it was even somewhat of a jungle with impenetrable scrub woods, crawling with snakes and reptiles and alive with wild animals. (There were many wild beasts in North Africa's coastal strip up to recent times. Sir Harry Johnston states that in 1880 he "knew an eastern Algeria of lions, chitas, hyenas, leopards. . . ."

Okba performed another miracle. On this many Arabic historians are of accord. "He called together the holiest men in the army and cried out in a loud voice, 'Serpents and ferocious animals, we are the people of the blessed Prophet and we are going to settle here and we shall kill any of you who remain after this warning!' At this were to be seen the wild beasts and snakes leading away their young, and at the spectacle many Berbers were converted to Islam." And so it came about "that for the next forty

years you could not have found either a serpent or a scorpion in
the land; even if you had offered a thousand dinars (about three
thousand current United States dollars) you could not have procured one single one."

*   *   *

THUS WAS BORN THE OLDEST CITY OF MOSLEM FOUNDATION IN
North Africa. Fostat in Egypt was founded a few years earlier, but
did not survive. Kairouan was regarded as the Moslem capital of
western North Africa and held its political power almost continuously for some two and a half centuries. Then its temporal
importance waned. But it still holds place as a sacred city, the
fourth of Islam, ranking after Mecca, Medina and Jerusalem.
There is a prophecy from old times that—if ever Mecca falls to
the infidels—Kairouan will take its honored place.

Old Kairouan was a distinguished town, sheltering a group of
great scholars, possessing a mosque whose columns of red marble
flecked with yellow had been removed from some Roman ruin
and had, when in their original place, been regarded as having
"a beauty that was incomparable . . . it being recounted that the
sovereign of Constantinople had wished to buy them for their
weight in gold." Such was the story of El-Bekri, the geographer,
who wrote of Kairouan in its days of glory. Furthermore Kairouan,
according to another medieval geographer, Edrisi, possessed three
hundreds baths "mostly in private homes," which was a considerable installation for the Middle Ages, even for a town then so
populous that on a festival day it slaughtered nine hundred fifty
beeves alone, plus uncounted numbers of the local favorite,
mutton.

Kairouan during its early period had a wild and bloody career,
the wildest and bloodiest of any city in all North Africa's history,
I should estimate. During its first three hundred years Kairouan
saw a battle after which one hundred eighty thousand men were
counted dead. It also saw a besieging army of three hundred fifty
thousand outside those brick walls that were "ten forearms lengths
in thickness" and it suffered from heretical insurrections so em-
bittered that the rebels stabled their horses in Kairouan's mosque.
Kairouan watched the degradation of the great revivalist, "The
Man on the Donkey," whose skin, stuffed with straw, was carried through the city, a plaything for a pair of trained monkeys.

Kairouan's civic childhood was ferocious. I find a phrase in Ibn-Khaldoun which is pathetic proof of its agitated youth. Speaking as if it were something noteworthy he says, "Kairouan now enjoyed the advantages of peace for two years!"

When Kairouan was about four centuries old it was ravaged by hordes of Arabs recently come from the East. Just after its twelve hundredth birthday it was occupied by the French. In its last phase to date it was a big airport and scene of fighting in World War II.

We shall be meeting Kairouan again and again as we weave our way through the history of North Africa.

OKBA TO THE ATLANTIC

OKBA, WHOM WE LEFT SUPERVISING THE ANIMAL EVACUATION OF the site he had chosen for the building of Kairouan, reverted after a time to his old wandering ways. He again became a space eater and performed his second and more famous rush across Africa. This time (681-2) he went westward, traversing what we call Algeria and Morocco and then swinging southwestward to the Atlantic.

It was a strange expedition. Along with him Okba took a pair of very odd mascots: two enemies in chains. These were his Arab rival, Abou-l-Mohadjer, known as Dinar, and the Berber chief, Koceila. Dinar had during several years superseded Okba as governor of the Arab holdings in the West. Okba had succeeded in getting back the governorship. During his degradation Dinar, then triumphant, had made a friend of the local Berber chief, Koceila, and persuaded him to renounce Christianity and turn Moslem. Okba hated his rival and he hated his rival's protégé. So when he set forth on his expedition it seemed best to him to take both men along as prisoners in chains.

Dinar, he probably thought, was capable of plotting against him if left out of his sight. As for Koceila, Okba considered that the Berber ex-Christian was an unreliable opportunist. We have heard of "rice Christians" who in the East profess Christianity for their bellies' sakes. Okba suspected that the converted Berber chief was a "sword-Mohammedan" who had taken to Moslemism to save his skin.

Okba was right in his mistrust of Koceila. But Okba's lack of tact in treating the powerful native prince as a servant made Koceila his savage enemy and led to Okba's eventual downfall.

*   *   *

OKBA DROVE HIS BLOODY WAY WESTWARD. HE CAME TO TANGIER, at the point where the Mediterranean meets the ocean. Here he is reported to have made friends with a personage destined to be very useful to the Arab cause. I say personage rather than person, because the man in question is a rather misty character in the view of modern students. This friend of Okba's was the Count Julian, Christian governor of the regions to both sides of the strait we now call Gibraltar. Okba picked his brains, or thought he did.

Into Okba's restless mind there had popped the notion of invading Spain. He consulted his new friend. Count Julian told him that the Spanish shores were well guarded and made a counter-suggestion. To the southward, Julian said, was a strange wild land. He described it in detail calculated to fascinate the boyish imagination of Okba. Possibly by so doing Julian postponed for a time Spain's downfall to the Moslems.

Said Julian, "The people who live to the south are without religion, they eat corpses, they drink the blood of their flocks, they live like brutes, do not believe in God and do not even dream of His existence." Hearing this Okba cried, as might have been expected from one of his fiery temperament and bellicose piety, "Forward in Allah's name!" (En-Noweiri).

So to the south and westward he fought his way into the Sous, which is the region beyond the Atlas Mountains on the desert's top.

At a point beyond Taroudant was a terrible battle with the Berbers, whose numbers were so great as to merit the favorite Arabic phrase that "Allah alone could count them." Okba massacred many and took among the captives one of the local girls so lovely that she "sold later in the East for a thousand *mithkals.*" A mithkal was the Arabic weight widely used in Africa for gold. It was the equivalent of a number—varying according to period and locality—of the seeds of the carob tree (from which we take the word, carat).

*   *   *

THEN CAME THE GREAT MOMENT THAT MADE OKBA IMMORTAL. The scene has become one of the familiar legends, along with such things as the Cherry Tree, the Burnt Cakes, the Roman Geese and Cleopatra's Pearls.

Okba reached the Atlantic and looked westward into the empty horizon. He rode into the waves until their waters broke against the breast of his horse. Raising his hand to Heaven he cried, "Seigneur! If this sea did not stop me I would go into far countries to the land of Doul Karnein (meaning where the sun slips into 'a spring of black mud') fighting always for Your religion and killing all who did not believe in You or who adored other gods but You!"

* * *

HAD OKBA BEEN ABLE TO TRANSPORT HIS ARMY WESTWARD FROM that southern Moroccan beach where he uttered his challenge he would have had a very, very long journey before reaching a place where he could convert or kill.

This place would have been the coast we know as Florida. Somewhere in the neighborhood of St. Augustine. And what outlet for his bloodthirsty missionary talents would Okba have found when he got there? It is a rather startling thought that we, so short is our history, have absolutely no knowledge. We do not know the name of a single person or settlement existent then in all the three million square miles of the United States.

There stood Okba on the western edge of the African continent where History was born. He took his orders from the Arab headquarters at Fostat, a few miles from Memphis which was a beautiful and civilized city some five thousand years before his time. In his march westward he had dodged around Carthage, which had been a place of organized commercial enterprise a thousand and more years before. He had just been flirting with the notion of Spanish conquest at Tangier—and Tangier was so old that it claimed to have taken its name from the sweetheart of Hercules.

Okba looked yearningly toward the land which something over a thousand years later would become the United States. All *its* history was before it. Absolutely all. It is a somewhat humiliating comparison. But encouraging. A long history is a heavy load.

It is interesting to consider that what was at the moment de-

scribed as "the greatest armada in world's history" chose for one
of its landing points a spot not far from where Okba stood that
day. United States troops came ashore on Moroccan beaches in
November, 1942.

*   *   *

OKBA AND HIS ARAB COMPANIONS SAW THE WIDE STRETCHES OF THE
Atlantic that day for the first time. They did not like its looks.
The Arab was a desert man. He had in those days a cat's dislike
of water. The second caliph having heard reports of the sea asked
what it was really like. Amr, who had invaded Egypt and thus
had seen this novel geographical element—the Mediterranean, not
the savage Atlantic—replied that the sea was a wild beast. To
cross it, he said, men must "ride like worms on logs."

Presently the Arabs of North Africa grew skillful in handling
ships in relatively short Mediterranean voyages. But the Atlantic
always frightened and disgusted them. Such exploits as those of
Columbus and Vasco da Gama were not for them. They never
emulated the Periplus of Hanno, the Carthaginian. For many
centuries a little fishing was practically the limit of their ocean
ventures.

A remark about the world's great waters made some centuries
after Okba's time reflects Arab awe of the ocean. Ibn-Khaldoun
said, "It is to be noted that in general mountains are more numerous near the sea than anywhere else: the divine power which
created the world adopted this arrangement so as to put a strong
obstacle against the invasion of the waves." In Ibn-Khaldoun's
opinion the ocean off Africa's west coast was "the receptacle of
all the waters of the world," presumably draining the excess from
the Mediterranean, and was thus peculiarly dangerous.

THE GREEN SEA OF GLOOM

THE NAME GIVEN TO THE ATLANTIC IN ARABIC IS SIGNIFICANT.
It is translatable as "The Green Sea of Gloom." Sometime after
Alexander the Great's mythical visit to the western shores of
Africa "shadows came and covered the surface of the waters" and
the ocean became a place of horror. Medieval Arabs believed
that it was impossible to navigate beyond the "Strait of the
Copper Idols" (Gibraltar), which idols bore a warning inscrip-

tion, "No vessel sails on that sea. It is without cultivation or inhabitant, and its end like its depth is unknown."

In all the medieval period, during which the Moslems controlled the Atlantic coasts both of Africa and of part of Europe, there seem to be records of only three attempts to explore the ocean, two of which at least are dubious. They are these:

Sometime in the days when Lisbon was in Moslem hands eight men set forth from there and sailed to the west, meeting varied unpleasant adventures, including the discovery of a stretch where "the waves had a nasty smell and there was scarcely any light." Having landed on some Atlantic island they were deported blindfolded and with tied hands and abandoned on the African coast at a place then uninhabited, and now known as Safi, Morocco, its name coming from the Arabic word for "Alas!" which they uttered at this stage of their unlucky voyage. Eventually they got back to Lisbon and were thereafter known by a name which may be rendered as "The Eight Loons," indicative of what their contemporaries thought of the wisdom of Atlantic exploration. Edrisi, the Moslem twelfth century geographer, tells us about them and adds that in his day there was in Lisbon the Street-of-the-Adventurers, named after them. Perhaps they had reached Madeira. On the other hand perhaps they never existed at all.

Another legend of Atlantic adventure deals with "The Young Man of Cordova" who sailed away and was gone for a long time and came back with a rich cargo to be famous in all Spain. This vague tale is from Masudi of Bagdad, the celebrated tenth century geographer and encyclopedist, who wrote a book about all the world as he knew it—and he knew a great deal, for he had traveled from India to Spain and knew Africa well. He wrote thirty volumes of which part survives under the charming title—who but a man of Bagdad would have thought to give an encyclopedia so sweet a name?—*Meadows of Gold and Mines of Precious Stones*.

A third Moslem whose Atlantic travels are recorded is Ibn-Fatima, who is said to have sighted "a glittering headland" on the African coast. This is conjectured to have been Cape Blanco, which is some seven hundred miles below the South Moroccan frontier. His voyage was perhaps during the thirteenth century.

Besides these three intentional Atlantic voyages performed by Moslems in the Middle Ages I have picked up a reference to a shipwrecked vizier of Andalusia of the thirteenth century who was driven into the Atlantic by storm when trying to make the Moroccan coast.

Presently, said the shipwrecked vizier, it became so dark upon "The Sea of Gloom" that "when one of us held out his hand before him he could scarcely see it." They were driven ashore in Negroland where the natives, thinking them to be painted white, rubbed them with palm husks. Eventually the vizier got to his destination by overland travel. His name was Abu-'Abd-Allah-Mohammed-ben-Ragano and his story is told in the *Masalik-el-Absar-fi-Mamalik-el-Amsar,* a sort of encyclopedia composed by a writer usually known for short as al-Omari.

In this same work there is the verbatim story as told by a fourteenth century Mohammedan Negro emperor, Kankan-Musa, of how his own father went out into the Atlantic with two thousand ships and was never seen again. Obviously the story was not intended to be taken seriously.

From the sparseness of Arab records about Atlantic adventures and by the fabulous character of what they do have to tell, it is quite evident that for many centuries after the day when Okba rode his horse into the Atlantic waves his coreligionists got little farther into the ocean than he did.

"SHAKE FOR THE HEAD OF SIDI OKBA!"

Okba turned away from the Atlantic with the words, "Let us return with Allah's blessing!"

But Allah withheld the blessing. Trouble fell on Okba. The people of "The Far-off Place of Perfidy" rose against him. Koceila, the Berber chief, whom Okba had dragged along as an ignominious prisoner, seized a chance and got away to lead his people. Okba had grown careless. He split up his forces.

At a spot a little outside Biskra Okba and a small band made their last stand. Dinar, the Arab enemy whom Okba had kept with him in chains during his expedition, begged to be set free so that he could die fighting. Okba struck off his irons and both men prayed. Then drew their swords and symbolically broke the scabbards. Side by side they fought to the death.

As a result of the debacle the twelve-year-old city of Kairouan, which Okba had so proudly proclaimed would "serve Islam until the end of time," was lost, and the remnants of the Moslem army fled almost to the Egyptian border.

Near the spot of Okba's last battle there is today a pilgrimage place, for Okba who ripped across Africa with so much bloodshed is now regarded as a martyr by the descendants of those who fought and killed him. The tower of the mosque of Sidi Okba Village where his body lies will, so the natives tell you in awe, tremble visibly when a true believer standing before it calls out in Arabic the words, "Shake for the head of Sidi Okba!"

* * *

OKBA'S STORY IS THE CLIMAX AND THE END OF THE HEROIC PERIOD of the Arab conquest in North Africa. The end of a wonderfully romantic passage when men flung themselves across space in the name of an adored new faith and died joyously in Allah's service. Okba had accomplished nothing definite in the way of conquest. The realism of intelligent military operations was to come. But Okba spread a vision of bravery and devotion to his God which was deathless.

The native of Algeria will tell you today stories of those battles of Okba's "when blood flowed across the earth like the waves of the sea," and of how the Arab heroes as they fell in combat were found to measure "from head to foot three metres and a half (eleven feet, three inches), such being the height of those men in those days" (from a popular Algerian fable).

A study of the Okba legend, as recorded by Arabic historians and as affectionately believed by so many native Africans, is worth while. It gives us a compact notion of North Africa's mentality: of what it thought in the past and of how it thinks today.

WOMAN GENERAL

AFTER THE ARAB DEFEAT THE PEOPLE OF THE WEST THOUGHT THAT they saw freedom from these obnoxious intruders who wished not only to master their bodies, but to boss their souls. At first Koceila ruled them. Then they took guidance from quite the oddest character in all the history of this land.

This latter was the woman general known as The Cahena. Okba had died a failure, but Allah had spared him the culmina-

tion of shame which was to fall upon another Arab leader. He
was not beaten by a female.

A woman general—remarkable anywhere and at any time—was
a true phenomenon in medieval North Africa, for women there
were, and still are held of small account outside their animal
functions.

The rise of Daia, The Cahena, to leadership is a unique romance. Arabic historians revel in The Cahena's career. They
have festooned it with quaint episodes and to deduce the truth
in all the mass of curious, grand and startling detail is difficult.

However, there is no question that The Cahena was a real
person. Modern history takes her seriously. It is probable that it
was she who dislodged Okba's would-be avenger. This was the
Arab, Zoheir, who had returned to the lost city of Kairouan and
beaten the Berbers. The Cahena is presumed to have animated
the brilliant effort which drove him away and again threw the
Arabs out of the West. It is certain that it was she who defeated a
succeeding Arab invasion under Hassan-ibn-en-Noman. Hassan
was the best military man as yet sent by the Arabs. The Cahena,
leading her own troops, beat him in battle. She beat him so badly
that he had to flee back almost to Egypt. His state of mind at being worsted by a woman warrior is beyond description.

*   *   *

AN ENTHUSIASTIC MODERN WRITER HAS STATED THAT THE CAHENA
seems "the greatest woman in history." This is a rather large
claim to make on behalf of any woman. One may in all events say
without reserve that The Cahena stands out in the medieval history of all lands as one of the very few women to attain greatness
on her own account. The Cahena did not owe her power to husband or sweetheart or inheritance. She was self-made.

Her career in this respect, and also because she freed her people,
prompts obvious comparison with that of Joan of Arc. But The
Cahena was a more remarkable person in that she was able to
make herself a great leader while under a handicap from which
Joan did not suffer. The Cahena was a woman in Africa. Joan was
a woman in France. The difference is enormous.

The Cahena was probably a Jewess, though this has been questioned. Her surname, Cahena, meant prophetess in Arabic. But
its resemblance to the Hebrew word cohen (priest) is suggestive.

Her tribe, all Jewish, according to Ibn-Khaldoun, lived in the Aurès Mountains. Some say that they were relatively newcomers; others that they descended from Jews who had fled into the region to escape Roman vengeance five centuries before at the time of the hideous Cyrene massacres (see page 139 about a "pogrom in reverse"). The Cahena, if she was Jewish, shines a splendid jewel in the racial diadem. She was a wonder lady who—had a Virgil or a Plutarch or a Shakespeare chosen her for heroine—might be as universally famous as Africa's other two popular heroines, Dido and Cleopatra.

Historically The Cahena's career begins when, as a mature woman—perhaps an incredibly old woman—she took charge of the Berber army. It is told by Ibn-Khaldoun, En-Noweiri and other Arabic historians, and by the geographer, El-Bekri. Legend supplies the item that as a maiden she freed her people of a local tyrant of cruel character and vile habits. She agreed to marry him, went to his arms on the marriage night, dagger in hand, and killed him. This legend is supplied by a Jewish writer who recently collected material on The Cahena—the same admirer whom I quoted above as being of the opinion that The Cahena was "the greatest woman in history." I refer to Nahum Slouschz. The authentic story of her love life after this alleged tragic debut is not known. She had three sons. One at least was Berber. One was of Roumish fathering.

She possessed the gift of prophecy. "She could foretell the future and what she announced never failed to happen," says Ibn-Khaldoun. We may guess that her prophecies were not whispered in her ear by her pet demon, as Arabic records wish us to believe, but resulted from her ability to think clearly and talk persuasively. Because of her gift she became queen of the tribe, and then of all the Berbers of the region. And she became a terror to the Arabs.

She was a woman of imagination and expedients. In her early military career she conceived the idea of using an ancient Roman amphitheater as an armed camp. This was the still surviving ruin at El-Djem, often visited by tourists and called by Baedeker "the grandest Roman structure in Barbary." Modern visitors do not see it as it was when The Cahena adapted it to her uses. A piece has been knocked out on one side. Arabs henceforth called the place Cahena's Castle, and presently got to believe that it was The Cahena who built it.

In the end it was The Cahena's imagination that was her downfall. She realized that her people were too weak to fight off Arab aggression indefinitely. To one of her grand courage and savage love of freedom there seemed only one thing to do: to make the whole countryside so poor and hideous that the Arabs would not covet it and would go home and leave the Berbers alone. While farmers and townsfolk watched in helpless horror, The Cahena's men burned and sacked. Her own immediate followers, who in their wild mountains had neither rich towns nor fertile gardens, suffered little by her destructiveness. The rest of the population was indignant. Her power waned. So, this desperate move of hers, instead of discouraging further Arab attack, hastened it. Hassan heard of her people's unrest and pushed westward by forced marches. The Cahena met him and was defeated. Hassan "massacred 100,000 individuals during the campaign," according to Ibn-Khaldoun. The Cahena fell back into her mountains and died fighting, sword in hand.

The probable date of her death was 693. The place was afterward called after her, Bir-el-Cahena (Cahena's Well) and was, like the spot where she had previously inflicted crushing defeat on Hassan, in the mountainous country on the Algerian-Tunisian frontier. The names of the Meskiana and Nini rivers appear in the Arabic accounts of her victory over Hassan. These streams some 1250 years later muddied the boots of many an American soldier. About sixty miles to the westward lies the famous Kasserine.

When she fought her last battle The Cahena was allegedly 127 years old. Ibn-Khaldoun quotes this from an earlier chronicler, being too wise to make so startling a statement without the hedging of quote marks. It is probably to be taken as a gallant tribute to the undoubted fact that The Cahena showed splendid courage and vigor to a great age, rather than as literal statement of fact. Romance claims that she was beautiful and amorous to the end!

As to her beauty the caliph himself was given the chance to form his own judgment. Hassan, of whom this woman had made a fool and a laughingstock, cut off her head and shipped it home to his master.

THE FALL OF CHRISTIANITY

THE FALL OF THE BERBER PROPHETESS, THE CAHENA, WAS THE rise of the Arab prophet, Mohammed. The Cahena's culminating act of prophecy was to the effect that her people would forego their old religions and become Moslems. "She had learnt what was to be from her familiar demon," says Ibn-Khaldoun soberly. Presently the Berbers did indeed decide to embrace Islam—as the odd phrase goes—and this time the embrace, unlike previous temporary conversions—was sincere. After a long and a very rough courtship Islam had really won their hearts. This clearly was the religion they craved. Their previous history had been a mere matter of religious flirtations and some fleeting passions. The Berbers, group after group, became Moslems, and have been so ever since, though intensely given to sectarian disputes.

*   *   *

BUT THOUGH THE BERBERS ACCEPTED THE ARABS' RELIGION THEY did not lie down for long under the Arabs' physical mastery. The first heroic period of their national defense died when The Cahena died, but they struggled on with bloody violence and often with success.

This contrasted with the situation at the other side of North Africa. In Egypt the Arabs were able to control men's bodies with relative ease, but their souls remained free: it was a long time before the Coptic (Christian) church went down before Islam. The variation between western North Africa and Egypt may have rested in the fact that the Berber was a primitive fighting type to whom physical control was more painful than moral or mental direction, while the Egyptian had become slack in war, but was strong in intellect and could bear more readily physical than spiritual dictation.

CARTHAGE DIED AGAIN

CARTHAGE, THAT CAT-OF-NINE-LIVES AMONG CITIES, DIED YET AGAIN at the hands of the Arab conqueror. During the earlier invasion efforts the Arabs had left Carthage pretty much alone. It was Hassan, The Cahena's enemy, who took the city by assault. The date is uncertain, but it was at the very end of the seventh century. Hassan, known to Arabic history by the title of "The Honest Old Man" pillaged, killed and made prisoners, and gave orders for the city to be put in ruins, which orders were carried out after a fashion. Some of Carthage's buildings survived. Carthage had lived fifteen hundred years with a gap just about midway following the Roman destruction. Always it had been an important capital of the world of the day. It had been a striking case of civic longevity.

The Carthage booty taken by the Arabs must have been vast. Hassan won his nickname because of the care he took that the best of the treasure should not be intercepted by the governor of Egypt as he made his way home to deliver it up to the caliph. Hassan "hid the precious gems, pearls and gold in leather water skins and left these skins out in plain view" when the rapacious governor sought to interfere. Arriving home before the caliph, Hassan tipped up the water sacks and poured out their glittering contents before his dumfounded master.

Hassan also brought back thirty-five thousand captives: some Berbers, some Roums from Carthage. The major part of the Carthaginians had been able to slip away by ship to Sicily or to Spain before the city fell. Hassan had found only the poorer Roums when he entered the city—that is those unable to buy their way aboard ships. The familiar sad story of the refugee!

*   *   *

OF THESE POORER ROUMS WHO FAILED TO GET AWAY FROM CARthage some must have escaped Hassan's soldiery. And to these joined a few Christians from other cities and a few Berbers of especially deep conviction who persistently declined to turn Moslem at the Arab command. These made up a Christian minority which after the first excitement of the conquest was not persecuted though probably its members knew hard days, particularly after the Crusades started. Marmol, the sixteenth century geographer, tells of seeing a Christian settlement still clinging to its faith in a suburb of Tunis some eight hundred years after the defeat of the Roums.

Gradually quaint beliefs grew up about the Christian population which had lived in the land before its Moslem conversion and about the supposed continued secret residence there of great numbers of their descendants. Legend told how the Christians in spite had found means to dry up certain rivers before their flight. About how they had hidden immense wealth inside the cut stones of their great buildings and carried away the keys "which they transmit to their children, planning to return sometime and recover the treasure."

One such supposed treasure house especially roused native cupidity. It was the so-called Tomb of the Christian Woman (*Kbour er Roumia*) about thirty miles out of Algiers, and originally some 120 feet high. Its construction had nothing to do with any Christian woman. It was built before Christ's time in honor of a native Moroccan king. But to the native notion it was a Roumia's burial place and she herself in spirit guarded the place. It was reported to be literally stuffed with gold and silver coins, and in relatively modern times a pasha of Algiers dragged cannon to the spot to blow tunnels into it. There was no gold and silver stuffing.

As to secret Christian communities: "The inhabitants of the Sahara say that the Christians . . . have not ceased to live here, but have gone into subterranean cities, taking with them the waters, rivers and brooks which formerly fertilized the land." Sometimes—especially in a certain spot indicated in the legend— one can by night hear queer noises coming from underground. "It is the Christians who are making a row in the subterranean city."

TARIK AND THE TABLE LEG

THE ARAB IN THE FIRST ENTHUSIASM OF HIS CONVERSION-*cum*-CONquest effort was disposed to order everything on the world's menu, often grabbing more than he could absorb. As a conqueror he had the fault suggested by the French saying, that his eyes were bigger than his belly, meaning that he was inclined to conquer more and more without assimilating the conquests already made.

Now that North Africa was started toward Islam, he turned his appetite to Spain, and used for his Spanish expedition many native North African soldiers.

The expedition was aided, according to the romantic legend, by that same Count Julian who waved a carrot before Okba's nose and sent him adventuring into southern Morocco. Almost

thirty years had passed since then, and in the interim Julian had
turned against Spain because of a bitter grievance. The king had
violated Julian's daughter, so goes the story. If it is true it is a
striking thought that a girl's dishonor facilitated, perhaps alone
made possible, the Mohammedanization of Spain which lasted
seven centuries and had considerable to do with provoking the
Crusades.

As to the importance of Julian's aid, he is said to have provided
the ships which carried the invaders and to have given local
information and advice to the Moslem army after it landed. He
was present at the battle where his daughter's ravisher lost his
life, the king (according to el-Hakem) having gone into the fray
"on the throne of the realm, slung between two mules, and wearing his diadem, gloves and other royal ornaments." He fled after
the Spanish defeat and was believed to have been drowned in a
river. All that was found were his muddy boots. So was Julian's
grievance avenged.

The story of Julian and his daughter for whose sake he turned
traitor is one of those incidents which sober historians have found
too improbable to believe and too good to ignore. So it is mentioned hesitantly, with a sort of "I do not take this seriously, but
you will like to read about it" manner by authorities, old and
new. Gibbon doubts it, but tells it. Hallam goes into it with great
critical detail. Moderns like Lane Poole, Hitti, *The Cambridge
Medieval History* refer to it. Some call the daughter Florinda,
some Cava. The so-called Tomb of the Christian Woman was
allegedly her burial place. Sometimes Julian is Ilyan, Urban,
Olban. He is perhaps to be regarded as a picturesque symbol of
the disunion in Spain which made possible the astonishingly easy
and swift victory of the Moslems.

The swift Moslem victory was also helped by disgruntled Jews.
The Jews had good reason to be disgruntled: their people in Spain
had been reduced to slavery and their children torn from Israel
and raised as Christians. The Jews in Morocco were also thought
to have conspired to aid the Arab invaders. Jewish help was rewarded. It is significant that Arabic accounts of the invasion mention the installation of Jews in high posts in various cities of Spain
as soon as the conquest was accomplished.

*　　　*　　　*

It was the celebrated Tarik who led the way into Spain. He was a Berber and was the lieutenant of the Arab governor of western North Africa, Musa-ibn-Noseir.

Musa had secured the caliph's permission for this oversea venture by advancing the argument that "there was only a narrow sea to cross." Tarik and his men landed behind the rock which is called after him, the Hill (*Jebel*) of Tarik—Gibraltar. So after twelve hundred years Tarik's fame is kept alive by geography. No mention in the history books can give a man the lasting popular renown he gains through association with some important geographical landmark. People who do not know the name of any other Moslem who ever lived, except perhaps Omar Khayyám and Harun al-Rashid, have some vague knowledge about a man named Tarik after whom Gibraltar was named. To the Arabs its alternate name was "The Hill of Victory," and it was accounted to be "one of the glorious landmarks of Islam where sorrow was forced down the necks of the idolaters" (meaning the Christians!).

Tarik, the Berber, had the bad luck which sometimes befalls a brilliant underling. He did too well. He mopped up many of Spain's important cities and captured the most valuable of Spain's booty before his master got there. Musa, following, was jealous. He was a vain old man who, we read, used red powder on his white beard to conceal his age. Meeting Tarik at the head of his troops he struck the too-successful lieutenant in the face with his whip and reproached him for having gone beyond his orders.

Forthwith Musa took charge of Tarik's booty so that it should be he who would have the glory of presenting all this fine stuff to the delighted caliph at home.

The booty was reported to be something stupendous. That was to be expected for Spain still conserved some of her old repute as a land of fabulous wealth—a reputation gained in the far back days of Tarshish. Arabic authors fairly wallow in the listing of the spoil. Let me quote:

"The Moslems found in Toledo incalculable riches, amongst other things 170 gold crowns encrusted with pearls and precious stones, 1000 royal sabres garnished with jewels, pearls and rubies by the bushel measure, a quantity of vases of gold and silver and"—here Edrisi describes the prize item of the lot—"the table of

Solomon, son of David, which they say was made of a single emerald." En-Noweiri's account of the table: "It was made of green
emerald, having its edges decorated with pearls, coral, rubies and
other precious stones, as well as its feet which were 360 in number" (*sic*—very puzzling).

But it is Leo Africanus, the Moslem converted to Christianity,
who sets the crowning glory upon this wonder table which Tarik
captured in Spain. Says Leo Africanus: "It was covered with fine
gold and enriched at the extremities with jewels. *And* it was the
table on which Jesus Christ made the Last Supper with his
disciples" (*la table sur laquelle Jesuchrist feit la Cene avec ses
disciples*—the odd spelling is that of the Temporal Translation,
reissued about fifty years ago by M. Charles Schefer).

Leo Africanus also states that the table's value was estimated
at 500,000 ducats. Taking the value of the ducat of his day and
the current value of the United States dollar, this sum would
work out at $1,875,000, which—considering the intrinsic value
of the table and its sacred associations—seems a modest figure.
I suggest that it was the most vaunted single trophy ever brought
back from any war.

No wonder that Musa resented the fact that it was his lieutenant
and not himself who had captured it and that he tried to sneak
away the glory by demoting his lieutenant. His meanness was his
ruin. The trick of Tarik led to Musa's downfall.

The shrewd Tarik had foreseen trouble with his chief and desired to ensure that he should get right credit for himself. So,
before Musa could lay hands on the treasure, Tarik had removed
and hidden away one of the table's legs. Musa asked an explanation for its mutilation. Tarik answered that so had he found it.
Musa then replaced the missing leg with a new one of gold, all
unaware that Tarik retained the true table leg to be used later
as proof that it had been he, not Musa, who had captured the
glorious souvenir.

But in the beginning Musa enjoyed his triumph without
qualms. Across the top of Africa he marched in pride toward
the caliph's capital, taking with him thirty thousand young virgins, daughters of the princes and notables of Spain, and a group
of male nobles wearing coronets and golden belts. Plus, of course,
the table. All unaware was Musa of the sad surprise which awaited

him at his journey's end when Tarik produced the missing leg and proved him a liar and a cheat.

The procession must have been a gorgeous, strange sight for Africa to see. It must have taken days to go by any given spot.

Undoubtedly the spectacle of some of Christendom's best in slavery had much to do with consolidating Berber confidence in their new religion. And the display of such rich booty was vastly invigorating. Their men had shared in this conquest. One of their men was its veritable hero. They foresaw, rightly, profitable opportunities for Berbers in the newly conquered land of Spain.

ARAB PROFIT AND LOSS IN AFRICA

THE PHRASE, "THE ARAB CONQUEST" IS SO FAMILIAR THAT ONE might infer that the Arabs operated the stretch of North Africa as a colony or set of colonies. They did not.

The administration of North Africa by the caliphs was a painfully difficult matter. If some early caliph had chanced to cast up a reckoning of his people's dealings with North Africa as a whole he would have found that the balance was very unsatisfactory. Here is a résumé of what his books would have shown:

Egypt: profitable.

Country up the Nile to the south of Egypt: no business of any real value, despite considerable expensive effort.

Sahara and western Sudan: practically no business.

The West (what we call Tripolitania, Tunisia, Algeria and Morocco): allegedly in his possession, but so troublesome to control that the caliph must have carried it at a loss. The grand days when the Roums gave up huge sums to earn respite from attack and when captured cities disgorged gold and jeweled treasure had not lasted long. Soon it had become a matter of costly and dangerous expeditions of reconquest for the reward of primitive, insignificant tribute.

Let us go into detail concerning the four regions listed, which in their ensemble make up all North Africa.

*   *   *

EGYPT WAS THE IDEAL COLONY. IT WAS CLOSE ENOUGH TO THE caliphs' capitals (Damascus from 661 till 750; afterward Bagdad) to be controlled and exploited. Its geographical position was marvelous. Alexandria was "the market of all nations," from which great profit came. Egypt was a fertile land with a population that on the whole was obedient and industrious. During the two and a quarter centuries which followed the Arab capture of the country Egypt bowed to a series of some one hundred of the caliphs' governors. The fact that such revolts as there were came from excessive taxation proves how much the Arabs were getting out of the country. The place was a treasure chest. There is a fabulous tale that Amr-ibn-Asi, its conqueror, left an estate of seventy sacks of gold dinars. Each sack held ten bushels. Impossible, but the yarn shows what the home folk thought about Egypt's potentialities as a colony.

*   *   *

THE COUNTRY UP THE NILE TO THE SOUTH OF EGYPT WAS INVADED by an Arab army shortly after Egypt was conquered. The Christian population defended themselves with ferocity and appalled the invaders by their sharpshooting with lances. The Arabs gave them a name, "the-shooters-at-the-eyeball."

A native army collected in the Southeast to help the Nile Valley Christians. Legend says that fifty thousand savages came and that "they had with them thirteen hundred elephants, each bearing upon its back a vaulted house made of leather in which ten men took their post in the battle." Also in the horde was a group of men from the Red Sea region who wore tiger skins and had copper rings in their upper lips.

The Arabs won the day, but made no attempt to occupy the country. A tribute arrangement was come to. It was of a trifling character, evidently symbolic in intent. And so little weight did the symbol carry that the up-Nile Christians attacked the frontier of Arab-held Egypt within a decade. Another Arab expedition was required. This time the Arabs got better results in a military sense, besieging Dongola, the capital, with slinging machines which threw rocks into the town and shattered the Christian church. The king came out humbly and asked for peace. The Arabs received his request with affability, from which we may be sure that they had found the campaign up the Nile hard and the country unpromising. Otherwise they would certainly have pursued the conquest attempt.

The Arabs made a treaty with the Christians: they, "in the name of Allah and his Prophet"; the Christians pledging themselves "by the Messiah and the Apostles and all those we venerate." The text of the document I have before me in the report of Selim-el-Assouani. It is dated "in the month of Ramadan, in the year 31" (31 A.H., or after the Hegira, equivalent to 651 A.D.). The agreement provides for the annual payment of tribute: "360 head of slaves of the middle sort of slaves of your country, none with any bodily defects, male and female, but no old men and women, and no children."

But, as it worked out, the arrangement between the Arabs and the up-Nile Christians was really a matter of the exchange of gifts: slaves and occasional local souvenirs, such as a giraffe, against shipments from Arab-held Egypt of wheat, barley, wine, blooded mares, linen and other cloth.

Therefore the caliph's dealings with this part of Africa—which had cost two military expeditions—were not profitable.

It did involve, however, one item of glamorous business—for the female slave from the up-Nile region was a veritable *objet de luxe*. I venture to quote a lush passage about these women from the usually prim pen of the geographer, Edrisi, omitting certain intimate technicalities: "They possess," says Edrisi, "a ravishing beauty, and have been excised. They come of a race having no relationship with ordinary Negroes and have perfect faces: thin lips, small mouth, white teeth and soft smooth hair, not crinkly. There is no hair to compare with theirs. . . . No women are better than they for marriage and that is why they fetch up to 500 dinars . . . the nobles of Egypt buy them for the delight of their embraces." Edrisi concludes by listing some special, individual up-Nile women whom he knew to be treasures in Spanish and Egyptian harems. It is evident that the Nubian slave woman classed across Moslem lands as the show girl of her day.

*   *   *

ONE FURTHER ELEMENT OF THE RELATIONS BETWEEN THE ARABS and the up-Nile Christian folk is that the Arabs gave them a new name. The country had been vaguely known in antiquity as a part of Ethiopia, but by the time that the Arabs arrived this name

had been appropriated by Abyssinia alone. The Arabs heard o
the Nobatae, that tribe Rome had put in as a buffer against the
"headless" Blemmyes, and called the country Nouba, whence
Nubia. The name went into medieval geography and still sticks
though its exact boundaries are vague. The Arabs with their passion for genealogy and lofty lineage vamped up a noble explanation for the country's name. The Nubians, they would have it
descended from an individual named Nuba, who was "the son
of Couch, the son of Canaan, the son of Ham" (Masudi, as quoted
by Ibn-Khaldoun).

*   *   *

THE SAHARA, NEXT ITEM ON THE CALIPH'S BOOKS, MOST ASSUREDLY
produced no profit for the Arabs during the early years of the
conquest. It will be remembered that Sidi Okba and his contemporaries pushed into the central part of the Sahara's depths
and promptly pushed out again, also attacking Fezzan, Ghadames,
etc., and that Okba died on the desert's fringe at Biskra. A later
Arab general, Musa, the victim of the table-leg trick, sent troops
as far as Tafilelt on the borders of the desert to the westward,
but evidently did not occupy the region, for we are told that he
took hostages away. A still later Arabic expedition, dated about
736, allegedly went farther yet into the sands and "brought back
immense booty"—such being the usual complimentary sentence
to Arabic reports of far-flung expeditions, resembling the inevitable phrase at the end of fairy stories . . . "and they lived hap-
pily ever after." This supposedly profitable venture into the
Saharan wastes is vague. Mayhap the Arabs reached the desert's
other shore and saw the Niger, or even settled down there and
bred a "white" colony in Negroland, as El-Bekri claims. Mayhap
they did not. In any case there was no Arabic ownership established. And beyond the above incursions into the Sahara I have
traced no other attempt to harness the sands to Arab profit during the period of the conquest.

We can be certain that there was no exploitation of the desert
on a scale to repay the hardships, loss of life and expense of these
expeditions. Indeed there would have been almost nothing then
to exploit.

The oases of the inner Sahara, as they are now operated with
their wealth of date palms, had with a few exceptions only just

started to get into action. "The date palm appeared in the Sahara with the camel, shortly before the time of the Arab invasion," writes Professor Gautier, great Saharan authority. (In this wide statement he is referring to the French Sahara, not to the eastern desert.) The reason why oasis development in a large way had to wait for the camel is clear. The date must have water, and—in the Sahara—water must be dug for. In a few localities only, there is water near enough to the surface so that date roots bathe in moisture, or so that primitive gardeners could irrigate. Elsewhere the effort of getting water for the date crop has been tremendous, almost fantastic. And naturally it waited, as Professor Gautier says, for the coming of the camel which first made Saharan travel in a large sense possible.

Those dates which grew in North Africa in antiquity—Herodotus mentions dates—grew near the Mediterranean and in the relatively well-watered region of Fezzan. Evidently not of good quality, for the Romans—ever seeking to get food out of their African colonies—thought little of them.

When he attacked Tafilelt, the Arab Musa would have found none of those superb dates which in the later Middle Ages made Tafilelt the subject of proverbs. In Musa's day it was a barren plain, its gardening prowess a thing of the future. There is an anecdote of later times that a sheikh of Tafilelt, being asked by a friend to ship him a sample of each of the various breeds of dates of the place, discovered that the collection made the loads for two camels. This anecdote is current across the date-conscious Sahara and was told to, and repeated by, Captain Charlet, who made a specialty of collecting legends about the date palm.

Nor would Musa have found at Tafilelt any hint of the industry in fine leather which was later to make the region famous when *lali* (from Tafilelt) fathered the Moroccan leather business. The tanners of Tafilelt discovered methods by which they could produce leathers which—according to an early English traveler—"surpassed anything in Europe." He adds that the "lion and tiger skins they prepare are white as snow and soft as silk. Shoes of the thinnest leather are impervious to water."

Tafilelt—in Musa's day a wilderness—would become generations later a caravan crossroads that dripped golden profits, and its capital, Sijilmassa would be called "one of the most illustrious cities of the universe."

But to the caliph of conquest days the Sahara and the western Sudan beyond the desert seemed negligible, and so were almost completely neglected.

THE FINAL ITEM ON THE CALIPH'S BOOKS

THERE REMAINS—IN CONSIDERING THE VALUE OF THE CALIPH'S North African holdings—that part we now know as Morocco, Algeria, Tunisia and Tripolitania.

To the Arabs this was a particularly exasperating piece of property. During the eighth century, that is the century following the Berber conversion to Islam, the caliphs appointed a series of twenty-nine governors. These governors had a very hard time of it. It is stated that 375 battles were fought between their troops and the rebellious native population.

The new religion which the Arabs had taught them, instead of making them subservient to their teachers, seemed to have given them increased self-confidence and irritability.

The list of Berber grievances was long. Some items are prosaic: such as the Berber complaint that they did not get their fair share of the Spanish booty, and the fact that excessive taxes were exacted from them by threats and torture. Some of their grievances are unusual and of a touching simplicity and pathos:

For instance, Governor Mohammed-ibn-Yezid organized a personal native guard and conceived the haughty notion of tattooing on each man's left hand the words, "Yezid's Guard." Humiliated and furious, these men assassinated Yezid.

Under Governor Obeid-Allah-ibn-el-Habbab the Berbers were roused by joint injuries, both directed to their tenderest interests home and the flock. They were obliged to cede their prettiest girls into slavery. And they were obliged to supply yellow baby lamb skins as tribute. "Often," says Ibn-Khaldoun, "they would have to kill a whole flock of ewes to have a foetus or two of which the fleece was of the required color." These things led to the assassination of a subgovernor at Tangier.

Governor Kolthoum came into a country in complete revolt. The caliph had supplied him with troops in such numbers as should, he thought, teach the Berbers a lesson. The caliph's boast was that it was "an army such as they had never seen in their country: the head of the column will be in their land while still its tail is with me here" (at Damascus).

The new governor met the folk he had been sent to govern in a battle near Tangier (741). The Berbers beat him by a trick. They tied waterskins full of stones to the tails of a number of horses and sent them off at a gallop into the Arab lines. A stampede followed, Governor Kolthoum was killed. Some of his troops crossed into Spain. The rest fled back toward Tunisia. When Kairouan saw the Arab army in defeat, its people revolted.

Then under Governor Handala with a reorganized Arab army followed war on a full scale. Near Kairouan occurred one of the bloodiest battles in African history. Yet, though one hundred eighty thousand Berbers perished, it was not decisive.

      *   *   *

THE CRESCENT HAD RISEN AS A RELIGIOUS EMBLEM. BUT THE CALIPH'S control of the lands in the West seemed likely to be impossible. Attempting to discipline Berbers was like trying to keep a cupful of fleas in order. Berbers were a very volatile people.

PART TWO

The Crescent Flashes in Secret

THE MEDIEVAL PAGEANT IN AFRICA

THE EARLY CENTURIES OF ISLAM IN AFRICA WERE SECRET FROM the rest of the world. They are still secret from us today, revealed almost alone through the pages of Arabic chroniclers. Yet those years were the belly of Africa's history. I propose to give space to this unfamiliar passage and to show, if I can, a picture of this hidden period of brilliance, high culture, fantasy and horror.

It was a medieval pageant alongside which our Christian Middle Ages seem demure and drab. It was an age of barbaric splendor, nauseating cruelty, uplifted spiritual sacrifice, desperate adventures and vast opportunities.

Men rose from nothing to the throne, slaves became great leaders: once even a woman slave became an independent ruler, and so again did a Negro rise from slavery. Kings died tortured to death by their brothers and rivalries made palaces run blood Incredibly adroit religious tricksters played on popular fanaticism. Mystic foreign personages, swathed in the prestige of real or pretended sacred lineage, swayed multitudes and urged millions to their deaths. Some of these personages were holy men of sincere conviction, most were impostors of unbelievable impudence. The people, exalted by their new faith, were pathetically gullible.

Pilgrims traced spider-web patterns to and fro across the burning sands. Black emperors marched toward Mecca in a blaze of golden panoply. Gold streamed into the cities' markets: Guinea gold, Wangara gold, gold of Gana and Mali. Traders of great courage shuttled gold, ivory and Negro slaves; damasks, satins and trinkets back and forth across the Sahara, risking at every mile a hideous fate. Thirst killed its thousands and the desert was strewn with the bones of men and camels.

There were tigerish fights over sectarian differences, seemingly of no more import than the placing of a comma. Cruel and perverse despots tortured their subjects whimsically and wiped out their kinsfolk with a flick of the finger. Bold Saracen raiders sailed forth to harry Europe's shores and brought back blond Christian girls to languish in African harems.

Kings rode beneath jeweled umbrellas, gorgeous in robes of fabulously extravagant fabrics, glittering with gold and precious stones. In a single day in a single town ten thousand died of the plague.

There were famines that drove men and women to cannibalism. There were periods of fat plenty when you could buy a whole beef for the value of sixty cents, or a camel load of grain for thirty.

New cities were born: Fez, Cairo, Marrakesh, Mali the Golden, impregnable Mahdia which they called "The City Africa," Timbuctoo. . . . Kairouan was the abode of studious wisdom. Alexandria, gateway between the East and the West, traded in every exotic luxury the world knew.

In those days Africa was the world's wonderland. It had everything. Gallant fighters. Hot lust and beautiful women of every tint; captured or imported from every clime. Frantic hero-worshipers, door mats to some idealized fellow man and tossing their lives away without stint. Always the limitless love of Allah for which men died gladly; across every bloody scene was the cry to prayer.

*   *   *

THROUGH THE PERTURBATIONS OF NORTH AFRICAN HISTORY THERE ran almost invariably in those days a religious motif. Varieties of Moslemism caused the death of millions. We have no counterpart for this excessive religious preoccupation in Christian history.

Such sectarian disputes particularly excited the populations of the West (Morocco, Algeria, Tunisia, Tripolitania). The Berbers for the first time in their racial career had developed an intellectual interest. They were in their mental springtime, as happy as a puppy with his first slipper, and equally destructive.

Some notion of the distinctions of Mohammedanism is necessary if we are to follow the convulsive fanaticism which molded history. But—since it has seemed to me that the history of Moslem lands has been made burdensome to the reader because he has been called upon to wind his way through a maze of Mohammedan technicalities and to keep in mind the many different and difficult names of sects, religion-inspired dynasties and fighting groups—I shall make this element of my story as simple as possible.

The total of Moslem sects has run into hundreds, and between certain of these sects there has existed a hatred greater than any Mohammedan feels for Christian or Jew.

A list of the most important sects with a phrase about each takes up three and a half columns of fine print in the *Encyclopaedia Britannica*. Mohammed himself expected splits and brawls in the family of Islam, but foresaw only seventy-three parties. He is said to have remarked—perhaps as a bit of sarcasm and as a warning to the cocksure and the intolerant—"Seventy-two of these parties will be pernicious, and only one of them right!"

ALI THE PIVOT

TWO MAIN PARTIES (EACH DIVIDED INTO SEVERAL SECTS) CONCERN us at this moment: the Kharijites and the Shiites. Kharijite disputes soaked the Morocco-to-Tripoli corner of Africa in blood. Shiite hero worship was the cornerstone of kingdoms.

Put in the simplest way, the origin of the Kharijite party was as follows: A group who had backed Ali, Mohammed's son-in-law, for caliph, left him. The word Kharijite comes from an Arabic word we would render vulgarly as "to walk out." This group "walked out" on Ali because they thought him weak and sinful not to push his claim to the caliphate with force. The Kharijites since then have had no belief in caliphs.

Similarly to explain the origin of the Shiite party in the simplest way: The Shiites revered Ali and considered that he should have been the founder of a line of caliphs, controlling all Islam. They revered his descendants and in various localities have accepted certain of them as leaders, the notion of different groups of Shiites varying during the ages as to which of Ali's descendants they preferred to accept. This naturally has produced a great many different Shiite sects.

* * *

THE PIVOTAL POINT OF BOTH PARTIES WAS THEREFORE THE PERsonality of Ali. The Kharijites hated his memory. The Shiites adored it.

Ali possessed almost unique power to arouse controversy. Through the centuries he has been a veritable and continuous battlefield. He was one of the most influential individuals who ever lived. Indeed, I suggest that he produced more bloodshed, battles, dynasties, revolts and fanatical movements over a longer period of time than any man in history.

It is hard to see justification for this in Ali's own character. It is evident that Ali's continuing importance has been solely because he was his wife's husband.

Ali was Mohammed's admiring little cousin, converted to Islam as a boy of ten. He married Fatima, the only child of Mohammed's who survived. Fatima was pronounced by Mohammed to be one of the four perfect women of all times, and the only one of her own times. It would appear therefore that Ali passed his life as a hero- and heroine-worshiper. Even his own followers found him feeble and turned against him because he consented to arbitrate his claims to the caliphate instead of continuing the fight, and we know that he had previously let slip three chances to secure the caliphate to which he would have seemed to have an obvious right. At times admittedly he showed courage, both moral and physical. He dared to oppose Ayesha, Mohammed's pet girl wife, so violently that years afterward Ayesha said, "I wish that he was sewn up in a bag; I would carry him myself and throw him into the sea!" And it is reported that he was a mighty warrior. Once in battle, having lost his shield, he tore away one of the doors from a city gate and used it instead "until Allah gave him victory. . . . Seven of us tried to pick up the door afterwards and could not move it." [2]

* * *

[2] From Aboulfeda's chapter on the expedition of Khaibar, quoted in the Chronicle of Abou Zakaria, see page 221.

ALI, WHATEVER HIS DESERTS MAY HAVE BEEN, ROUSED PASSIONATE posthumous loyalty. Some went so far as to say that Allah had planned to use Ali, not Mohammed, as Prophet and that the angel Gabriel made a mistake. Ali's supposed grave, Ibn-Batuta tells us, was a pilgrimage place where people went to be cured of their infirmities and where on the annual "night of revival" miracles happened.

Extremists among Ali's adorers still refer to the first of the caliphs, who--to their notion—robbed their hero of the caliphate, by the name of "The Old Hyena." And they carry their hatred of those, who they believe cheated Ali, to the point of boasting it as a glorious deed of piety that they have defiled in an indecent manner the graves of "The Old Hyena" and the ensuing two caliphs who successively pushed Ali aside.

The assassination of Ali to such as these is accounted a crime hideous beyond compare. They blame the Kharijite party as a whole, for it was a Kharijite individual, Ibn-Modjem, who cleft Ali's head open between the eyes "with a poisoned sabre." (The insistence upon the poisoning of the weapon seems a naïve superfluity!)

Ali's descendants have possessed prestige which is astounding. It is now running toward thirteen hundred years since North Africa was converted to Islam. During this period some dynasty claiming descent from Ali has been in power over some section of North Africa almost the whole time, and uncountable leaders and mahdis have gained a following by boasting to possess Ali's blood.

"THE FAR-OFF PLACE OF PERFIDY"

AS ISLAM SPLIT INTO SECTS AFRICA WAS FOUND TO BE A MOST profitable ground for proselytizing. Those who brought sectarian arguments to the Berbers often made fame and fortune thereby. Berbers were ready to listen with all their ears. Furthermore, being a people who had been oppressed by a series of foreign masters since the days of Carthage, they instinctively craved a strong battle cry which might bring them independence from this latest conqueror of all—the Arab. They sensed that if they were to unite for a religious idea, or in support of a religious hero, it would give their rebellion dignity and emotional appeal. Some sections opted for the theory of the Kharijites; some for the glory of the Ali strain (the theory of the Shiites).

So, thanks to the varieties of that Mohammedanism which the Arabs had forced upon North Africa, the Arabic caliphs soon found their vaguely consummated conquests in the west corner of Africa were becoming impossible to hold.

One great difficulty was that of distance. The West was far from the caliphs' capitals. The delay in getting reports and sending orders, let alone the time required to send armies, must have been appalling.

As to the exact time it would have taken a postal messenger to cover the distance in those disordered days of Berber rebellion I can but offer a few items as of normal caravan travel from old geographers: from far western Morocco to Tripoli, ninety days (Leo Africanus); Tripoli to Sört, and Barca to Alexandria, eleven days and twenty-one days respectively (Edrisi). The gap between Sört and Barca, on which I have no data, might have taken ten days or more. The total time, therefore, merely to get across the top of Africa in the plodding days of old would have been almost four months, to which add further time for the journey in Asia Minor. This was at the rate of caravan travel. A special messenger would have gone faster. Leo Africanus tells that letter messengers over flat country made sixty miles a day on foot.

Wonder stories are told of the swiftness and endurance of African messengers. For instance: "In 1846 the Arab named El-Thouamy of Laghouat was sent to Berrian. In fourteen hours he had covered 168 kilometres, travelling at the rate of twelve kilometres (seven and a half miles) the hour." This is from a report by the messenger's contemporary, a French investigator of Saharan ways, the well-known General Daumas. This astonishing run was made over a rocky path, as the character of the present road testifies—I have bumped over it often by car.

Desert messengers, according to General Daumas, went "at a pace which the French call the *pas gymnastique* (which is quicker than the English 'double') and which they themselves call 'a dog-trot.' " Their endurance seems incredible. "A special messenger travels night and day and sleeps only two hours in the twenty-four. When he lies down he fastens to his foot a piece of cord of a certain length to which he sets fire."

The carrier of good news proverbially travels fast. We are told that when the Arabs won their spectacular victory in Tunisia in the early days of the conquest an elated messenger, riding on the wings of victory, got the word to Medina (the then seat of the caliph) in twenty days, or perhaps twenty-four, historian En-Noweiri adds prudently. It was not a performance to be duplicated in the ordinary routine of government correspondence.

And, alas, there was little in the way of triumphant good news to speed a messenger's heels during the period of Berber rebellion against their would-be Arab overlords.

THE WEST BREAKS WITH THE ARABS

WITH WHAT EXASPERATION THE SERIES OF CALIPHS WHO REIGNED during the latter part of the eighth century must have received belated reports of one disaster after another. Disasters that got worse and worse. There came news of the capture of Tripoli by members of one of the Kharijite sects (the Abadites). Of the hideous circumstances of the capture of Kairouan by members of another Kharijite sect (the Sofrites) who carried their fanatical hatred of orthodox Mohammedans to such a point that they stabled their horses in Kairouan's mosque and dragged Kairouan's women into its sacred precincts for the double infamy of rape and profanation. Then came news that Kairouan had been the scene of a battle between sect number one and sect number two, sect number one massacring the fanatics, and that a rebel government had been set up under the leadership of the winning sect across all the land from Tripoli to Tunisia.

With what difficulty did the home government inspire the prolonged series of costly efforts by which Kairouan was won back from the rebels!

And with what dismay did the caliphs hear that members of three dissenting sects (two Kharijite and one Shiite) were attempting to set up independently. And that a further bite into the African Empire was to be expected on the part of the Arab governor of Kairouan. This man had become so powerful that he reigned as a king—accepting the caliph as patron rather than master—and planned to set up a dynasty.

Thus four separate states were in the making: two in Morocco, one in Algeria, one in Tunisia. The debuts of these states were typical of various phases of African sentiment. One sprang to life round the personality of a hero of sacred lineage; one round a saintly religious leader; one had bloody fanaticism for its background; one—the Kairouan dynasty—resembled the usual temporal despotism of medieval times anywhere. Presently I shall tell how each state got its start.

In the face of such widespread revolting the Arab central government lost heart. Caliph after caliph had listened to tales of turmoil from the west and asked himself, "Is it worth the trouble?"

One day a caliph uttered the realistic answer, "No!"

It must have been a relief to the caliph to face the definite loss of this territorial possession which, in its restive rudeness, as much resembled the usual notion of a tax-paying, governor-respecting colony as a half-grown Newfoundland resembles a lady's lap dog.

It was certainly a relief to the caliph's home subjects when they learned that western North Africa had been written off their national books as a piece of nonprofitable business, and that no more live men were to be thrown after the dead ones.

The West had indeed proved to be "a Far-Off Place of Perfidy," and the caliph of the day angrily accepted facts. The caliph of the day was the famous Harun al-Rashid. That he was very angry at the fiasco in the West is evident from his vengeful conduct toward Idris, that kinglet of whom I shall speak first, as I give an account of the rise of independent rulers which eventually caused Harun to abandon the West.

HOW IDRIS CAME TO AFRICA

THE RISE AND THE MURDER OF IDRIS MAKE A ROMANCE OF THE REAL Oriental type. However, in the Idris story Harun al-Rashid plays the part of villain rather than that of hero, as in the *Arabian Nights*.

Idris was the great-great-grandson of Ali. His family fought the Abbasid dynasty, of which Harun al-Rashid was the fifth caliph.

At a battle near Mecca in 786 many of Idris' relatives were killed.

Idris himself escaped and went into hiding, Harun hunting for him in vain. Now, Idris had a servitor, a man of courage and expedients, by name Rached. This man dressed Idris in common garb, wrapped a rough turban round his head, and caused his master to pass as his servant. The two joined a caravan of pilgrims that was leaving Mecca and got safely as far as the Egyptian capital, Fostat. At Fostat the two men—the real and the make-believe servant—paused before a handsome residence and sat down upon a bench to rest. The master of the house came out and questioned them. Rached shrewdly sized him up and, after some preliminary talk back and forth, invited the householder "to protect the blood of your Prophet" (meaning Idris, a direct descendant of Mohammed through Fatima's marriage to Ali).

No doubt Rached had guessed the man to be, as he indeed was, a secret Shiite, or member of the Ali party. That the man kept his religion secret was natural. He held an official position under the orthodox caliph.

The secret Shiite listened sympathetically to Rached's plan to conduct his master "to the country of the Berbers, in which far land he might find a safe refuge where his enemy would not be able to reach him." The exact speeches and other detail of Idris' flight are recorded in the picturesque narrative of one Abou'l Hacen en-Naufeli who had the story from his father at a time when it must have been relatively fresh. En-Naufeli's history is now lost, but was available to the eleventh century author, El-Bekri, who copied into his book a long chapter dealing with the adventures of Idris.

The secret Shiite agreed to help Idris, who was his master, Harun al-Rashid's enemy, for which act of disloyalty he was subsequently crucified and beheaded. He smuggled Idris across the Egyptian frontier and arranged for both men to join a caravan. Riding on the same camel, Idris and his loyal servitor set out for the Far West. They reached Tunisia and dared not attempt to pass across it by the main road, knowing Harun al-Rashid's hatred. By a roundabout route they attained at last the northwestern coast of Morocco. The journey, plus Idris' period of hiding, had taken two years.

Idris told his story to the Berbers of the region. They were fascinated. Ibn-Khaldoun lists eight tribes who rallied to his cause. The sudden and mysterious arrival of this noble stranger from the East captured their imagination. They made him king. Idris led them forth and by force or persuasion induced the neighboring tribes to join him.

THE POISON PLOT OF SOLEIMAN, THE ZAIDITE

MEANTIME HARUN AL-RASHID FOAMED WITH FURY. HIS ENEMY had slipped through his fingers. His enemy had founded a kingdom in lands still traditionally part of his caliphate. Harun al-Rashid's vizier spoke comforting words. "Prince of True Believers, I will free you from this man!" he promised.

The vizier sought out a person of high religious standing in Idris' own special Shiite sect (the Zaidites). This man our narrator describes as "softy-sweet in his ways, brave when occasion demanded and a demon in human form." His name was Soleiman-ibn-Horeiz-el-Djezari. The vizier promised him a magnificent reward if he would go to the Far West, worm his way into the confidence of Idris and destroy him. Soleiman accepted.

Soleiman reached Morocco in due course and presented himself before Idris who already knew of him as one who supposedly should be his friend and supporter. Soleiman told a tale of loyal admiration, of how he had managed to escape from the caliph and had come to seek refuge with Idris. Idris was "charmed by his words" and received Soleiman as an intimate.

After a time Soleiman saw his chance. He had been provided by the vizier with "a flacon containing poisoned musk perfume." When alone one day with Idris he offered him this flacon with a pretty speech. Idris sniffed. The poison "mounted to his brain so that he fainted and remained senseless." His servants and his loyal servitor, Rached, could not guess what was wrong. Idris' pulse continued to throb, but he never regained consciousness and died toward evening.

That Idris should have accepted the perfumed flacon and put its contents to instant and greedy use was natural. Musk was a precious item to the Oriental and an especial love of perfume ran in the blood of Idris, for did not his ancestor, the Prophet, count

perfume only second in importance to prayer, and a greater
pleasure than women, forswearing the use of onions or garlic lest,
when he spoke with angels, they might be offended? Idris in the
wild Berber lands of Morocco had been long deprived of musk's
sweet delights.

*   *   *

IN DUE COURSE THE MUSK OF THE CIVET CAT WAS TO BECOME AN
important item in North Africa's export trade. The civet cat was
a wild thing and a living perfume container. Those of its family
which were trapped and caged lived the most tragic life of any
animal in Nature. They were teased and beaten to the state of
fury which caused musk excretion, after which the substance was
removed from them. Three days later whipped again to fury. A
life of routine torment. "Each time affords about a drachm and
a half" and "a savage old cat will produce about ten or twelve
dollars' worth in three heats." In medieval days it was worth "sixty
ducats a pound, and the cat itself was worth 200 ducats." A civet
cat fetched the price of four camels or ten male slaves! As late as
1912 I find respectful mention of a certain civet cat breeder whose
stable of forty cats put him in the class of a man of outstanding
wealth and consequence.[3]

*   *   *

ALTHOUGH THE REASON FOR IDRIS' DEATH WAS AT FIRST NOT GUESSED,
there was no doubt who was responsible. Soleiman gave indication
of guilt by flight. On a horse "trained down thin so it would run
very fast" he had covered a great distance before the avenging
servitor, Rached, overtook him. The two fought. Rached slashed
Soleiman's head and face and crippled one of his hands, but
Soleiman escaped and got back to the East where, says En-Naufeli,
"a man has told me that the traitor is still to be seen with a
mutilated arm."

Thus did Morocco lose her first king of the line of Ali. Or such,
at any rate, is one of the methods by which Harun al-Rashid is

[3] These items on the North African primitive perfume industry are from
Gov. Durand's *Voyage to Senegal* (1806); Capt. Lyon's *Travels in Northern
Africa* (1821); Leo Africanus; and the Cheik Mohammed-ben-Otsmane-el
Hachaichi's *Voyage aux Pays des Senoussia* (1912). In the chronicles of
Portuguese Navigators in the 15th and 16th centuries one notes that "Fernao
Gomes received permission to buy one musk cat per year, a thing much
appreciated. This in the neighborhood now called the Gold Coast.

said to have procured the death of Idris. But a mass of other murder tales attached themselves to Idris' name. One is to effect that a certain Es-Chemmakh, who is no other than Soleiman under a pseudonym, arrived in Morocco pretending to be a physician and prescribed for Idris when he had a swollen jaw. He gave Idris a powder (poisoned of course) "to be used on a toothpick next morning." The fake doctor then bolted eastward, making good his escape before the crime was consummated. Another version of the Idris murder mystery tells of a truly ingenious method, albeit requiring a very delicate hand and steady nerves. The assassin— always our friend Soleiman—allegedly offered Idris a slice of watermelon. "To cut the fruit he used a knife which he had poisoned on one side of the blade only. He gave Idris the slice which the poison had touched and to disarm any suspicion ate the other slice himself."

IDRIS, THE SAINT

IDRIS HAD REIGNED BUT THREE AND A HALF YEARS IN THE MOROCCAN kingdom he founded and he died childless. Yet Harun al-Rashid's scheme had failed. He had not wiped out the Ali line in the Far West. The dynasty of Idris survived and reigned for some two hundred years.

The mysterious murder of Idris turned out from Harun's point of view to have been a grave mistake. It inflamed the loyalty of the Berbers. At the time of Idris' death one of his concubines was pregnant. The ever-faithful and ultracompetent servitor, Rached, held his dead master's kingdom together for the child.

The boy grew up to be Idris II, the famed and sainted Moulay Idris (Moulay, master or my lord, originally used as a title of great deference and attributed only to persons of the Mohammed-Fatima-Ali blood). His mother, the woman Kenza, though a lowly pagan slave woman whose name derived from a word meaning rottenness or filth, became one of the few female figures mentioned in North African medieval history. Her renown rested primarily upon the animal devotion with which she protected the interests of the baby whom her master had bred to her before his tragic death. She was the instrument by which the Idrisite dynasty survived.

The child Idris at eleven appeared before his father's subjects and received their oath of allegiance. At seventeen he founded, according to tradition, what was to become and still remains one of the world's famous cities—Fez. He is today a figure of incomparable holiness, so holy that, in the words of the Messieurs Tharaud, "in the popular imagination he is almost equal to Allah." Moulay Idris is a tremendous name in modern Morocco. No man so far back in European history (very early ninth century) is held in such affection and reverence by his people, or seems so real to them as Moulay Idris does to the folk of Fez.

THE FOUNDATION OF FEZ

FEZ WAS A CITY OF SPLENDID DESTINY. IN A COUNTRY WHERE countless cities were founded and sank into oblivion Fez was, by contrast, born to survive. She was born also with—not a silver spoon—but a golden pickax in her mouth. The tradition is that a golden pickax, *fas,* was dug up in the excavation and that from this the city took its name. Another tradition takes the name from Sef, turned back to front, Sef being the name of a former city which may have existed on the same site. And there are various other explanations suggested for the name of Fez, some of them very fantastic.[4]

The fact remains that the name of Fez, so simple and vigorous, so easy to say and to remember, has been an asset to the city. It is noticeable, by the way, that Fez—like Paris—has been advertised by its hats. The familiar red "fez" cap was originally an exclusive specialty of Fez, where grew the berries used to dye its felt. The "fez" of picture and fancy dress carried Fez's name round the world.

The other great asset of Fez was water. Fez had a natural water system running through the city. Every rich man's house had a garden with little canals running through it. There were 360 water-turned mills—"one for every day in the year!" in the language of amazed visitors from scorched neighboring places. Not only did these houses have private baths, they had also what Ibn-Said says he never saw anywhere else in his life—and probably

---

[4] See *La Geographie,* organ of La Société de Géographie (April, 1939): "Notes de toponymie Marocaine," by Paul Odinot.

few of us have either—that is, baths fed by private springs in the owners' grounds. North Africa in those days was even drier as a whole than it is today and the average medieval city was as dry as the inside of an earthen casserole. Fez in comparison is geography's favored child. Once in the days before the railroad crossed Morocco I rode toward Fez in the primitive *drassine* (military motor train on miniature tracks) with a little boy from the arid country. I told him that Fez was known as "a green city." He repeated my words in awe, *"A green city!"* He had never seen natural verdure in his life.

The outstanding desirability of the site where Fez was built had been obvious to the men of old. Two groups who already had some primitive settlements there were bought off. They received respectively about 2500 and 3000 dirhems; these sums would be about 375 and 450 current United States dollars and, considering the period—over 1100 years ago—and the nature of the country, the price shows that the superiority of the spot was well understood.

As time passed another advantage appeared. Fez was the hub of Morocco. It was situated at "ten days (caravaning) from Marrakesh, from Ceuta (at the strait of Gibraltar) from Sijilmassa (the gate of the Sahara) and from Tlemcen."

So Fez, the water blessed, wriggled its way through history. Wriggled is correct; Fez has always been a disheveled city, made up of incoherent and disjointed sections. It began in a disconnected manner. Two cities were built at about the same year side by side each with a separate wall. It was more than 250 years before the two Fezes were combined. Later three new Fezes were added. Even in the time since I first traveled that way another Fez has been added—the French city near the station of the railway.

* * *

THE TWO ORIGINAL FEZES WHICH SAT SIDE BY SIDE, CLOSE TOGETHER yet with separate identities, like Siamese twins, were both founded supposedly by Moulay Idris II. Certainly one of them was. It is suggested by some Arabic writers that the other had already been established by his father, and the date of Fez coins which have been found bears out the latter theory. Fez people will have none of this idea. Moulay Idris II is their first, sole founder, their patron. His name belongs, they are sure, on the list of the heroic, the more than human, city builders of Africa, along with the name

of Mena of Memphis, Dido of Carthage, Alexander of Alexandria,
and Sidi Okba of Kairouan.

Moulay Idris is revered as a superman. He was wise and mature
at eleven. He was brave in war and affectionate at home. In battle
"he spat often for his mouth was never dry with fear." He died at
thirty-three (or possibly thirty-six, or thirty-eight, sources varying)
leaving at least twelve sons, of whom one inherited, and seven
others were old enough to become local governors of various parts
of his realm: certainly a case of precocious paternity. The manner
of his death departs from the heroic pattern. He choked to death
on a grape seed. Many years after Moulay Idris II's death his body
was dug up and found to be intact and with flesh still on its bones.
Moulay Idris waked up and spoke!

Such is the debut of the Idrisites of Morocco, the first North
African dynasty to base its prestige upon the memory of Ali.

*   *   *

AT ABOUT THE SAME TIME TWO DYNASTIES SET UP IN NORTH AFRICA,
both of the religious group which detested the memory of Ali.
Of these two dynasties—both so-called Kharijites—one was of a
singularly intense but contemplative type, the other fanatical and
violent.

A PIOUS KINGDOM

THE DYNASTY FOUNDED BY THE GENTLER OF THESE TWO SECTS HAD
a romantic background.

Five wise, pious and ambitious men came to North Africa from
the East in the middle of the eighth century with the motive of
converting the people to their form of Kharijism and, of course,
with the hope of exploiting the country. Their leader, or Imam,
was named Abou el-Khottab and after he had gained a following
in the region of Tripoli he determined to take the town. Tripoli
was then still under the control of a caliphic governor.

Abou el-Khottab played a neat trick. Certain of his followers,
each with his weapons, were put into sacks, which were tied tightly
and slung across camels—the opening at the bottom, two camou-
flaged men to each camel. Then the camel train was driven into
the city like any ordinary trade caravan. When it reached the

center of town each man emerged from his sack and, arms in hand, they all cried, "There is no master but Allah and none to be obeyed but Abou el-Khòttab!" The populace was stupefied. It was a very successful commando raid. The caliph's governor gave up the treasury key and was permitted to run back to his caliph.

Abou el-Khottab's success attracted many converts to his form of Kharijism. Descendants of his converts still practice his doctrine and it is from their collected traditions that I take the story of how Tripoli was captured. This collection is the Chronicle of Abou Zakaria, dating from the eleventh century, which the learned men of Melika permitted a French savant, Emile Masqueray, to see and to copy back in the days of the French conquest of the Sahara. Melika is a little city on a Saharan hilltop, one of the seven cities of the Mzab confederation, all of whose people cling to the religion taught to their forebears by the man who took Tripoli in a commando raid nearly twelve hundred years ago. (The full and correct name of the sect is Ouahbite-Abadite, the latter word sometimes given as Ibadite.) I shall speak of these people again, as they appear today, an extraordinary community which is a living museum from the Middle Ages.

The Chronicle of Abou Zakaria, published in a French translation in 1879, is our best and one of our few sources on the dynasty which sprang from the efforts of Abou el-Khottab and his companions. The frail browned pages of the copy, which I procured after years of searching in Paris, Algiers and in the Mzab itself, are full of curious and quaint tales.

*   *   *

POSSESSED NOW OF A FOLLOWING AND A CITY, ABOU EL-KHOTTAB looked farther westward. His attention was called toward Kairouan where Kharijites of another and of a fanatically bloodthirsty and irresponsible type had seized the city, violated the mosque and ill used the people. "A woman wronged cried to him, 'O Abou el-Khottab, come to my aid!' Allah prolonged her voice and Abou el-Khottab heard her at Tripoli (hundreds of miles away). He answered, 'I am with you, my sister,' and immediately gave the order to proclaim war."

His people were "priests by night and lions by day," very pious and ascetic, and very brave. They cleared Kairouan of the enemy and Abou el-Khottab installed as its governor one of the five original companions from the East.

This was Rostem, destined to be the first of a dynasty of rulers with a capital in the highlands of western Algeria. Rostem was of Persian origin. We are assured that he was the direct descendant of that king of Persia who was reigning at the birth of Mohammed. The Chronicle states that upon that birth night the Persian king's castle shook and fourteen casements fell, and that next morning there came galloping to the king a man crying out that the sacred fire of Persia which had burned for one thousand years had gone out. Rostem's ancestors had become Moslems and Rostem himself had adopted this special Kharijite sect.

Rostem is described as a glamorous person. When as a young man he was receiving his religious instruction he was of such great beauty that his teacher "was obliged to stretch a veil between him and his fellow students so that the latter should not be distracted from their studies." He was equally admired by women, the Chronicle reporting at length the farewell scene on his departure for North Africa, on which occasion a group of elderly women compared him to the sun, to salt, etc.

In repeating the quaintness and hyperbole of the Chronicle I am not seeking to be whimsical. Such items can indirectly give a truer idea of history than a list of sober facts. When a chronicle is written by the people with whom it deals, or by those closely associated with them in time and sentiment, even its obvious absurdities and childish boasting tell much. Primitive history of this sort is national autobiography. Very revealing.

*   *   *

ROSTEM DID NOT LAST LONG AS GOVERNOR OF KAIROUAN (758-761). The caliph's representative drove him out and Kairouan became again for a little while an orthodox Moslem capital under the caliph. Rostem fled farther to the westward, now the sole leader, for the original head, Abou el-Khottab, had been killed in battle.

Escaping pursuit, Rostem and his followers set about choosing a place where they might build a city which would be "a boulevard of Islamism" (a bulwark). They picked a site in the high mountains of inner Algeria. It was nineteen days by caravan to the west of Kairouan. In the same general location there had been a city prominent in antiquity. There is a prosperous small town in about the same spot today. All three cities, the ancient, the modern, and Rostem's—used the same name: Tiaret, alternately spelt Tahert. Of the city Rostem built, nothing remains.

Rostem's city was laid out in a square. The ground chosen was semijungle. The colonists fired the trees and, finding that "the roots and the lower parts of the trunks remained, they went and got lettuces and hid them in the ground under the trees. When night fell the wild boars came and, attracted by the smell of the lettuces, dug them up, and the next morning all the roots were exposed and could be pulled out easily." Tiaret became a handsome and prosperous city. It was the capital of the Rostemid Imams for 150 years. Their power was considerable, not only in the Tiaret region, but in Tripolitania.

The folk of Tiaret were a peculiar people. Their descendants who live in the Mzab were described as "the Puritans of the desert" by the first French writer to tell about them, General Daumas in 1845. The citizens of Tiaret like those of today's Mzab were mystic, contemplative, ascetic, and of an extraordinary religious obstinacy. With these qualities a pleasant strain of cunning, as I have suggested by a few anecdotes.

Their simplicity of life was proverbial. Distinguished foreign visitors who came to visit the Imam Rostem found him, the Chronicle says, building his house with his own hands, a slave passing up mortar to him. The succeeding Imams were of similar nature. A descendant of Rostem's, the Imam Yagoub, was so insistently unworldly a person that "if he had to touch a piece of money he would push it with a stick." This item is from Ibn-Saghir, who lived at Tiaret. Another Imam, he tells us, had at his death an estate of only seventeen dinars (around fifty current United States dollars). The Imam who handled his money with a stick was of marvelous abstemiousness. "He would drink a full goblet of milk and thereafter remain three days without taking further food nor drink, nor going to the toilet."

Tiaret, though well placed for trading, was in itself an incentive to the sober life. It was a bleak, chill spot, often foggy or snowbound. Said one of its citizens who visited the glowing and cheerful desert, "Blaze as much as you like, O Sun! I have seen you a miserable little figure of scorn at Tiaret!" Its population resembled the climate: solemn folk. Tiaret was the place of their choice, an expression of group temperament.

NEW CAPITAL ON THE
SAHARAN BORDER

SIJILMASSA WHICH WAS THE CAPITAL ESTABLISHED AT ALMOST THE same moment as Tiaret by the other and rougher Kharijite sect was a completely different city, just as its founders were a completely different sort of people. To them their special form of religion appears to have been a pretext for unrestrained violence. It had been others of this same sect (Sofrites) who violated Kairouan's mosque and women.

Yet Sijilmassa, a city built by rough and cruel men, flourished long as one of the richest and most famous capitals of Africa, while Tiaret, conceived in piety and asceticism, lived in genteel and modest prosperity for a relatively short period.

*   *   *

SIJILMASSA WAS ON THE DESERT'S BORDER IN THE TAFILELT OASIS of South Morocco (see pages 203, 204). It was a spot of unique trade potentiality. In later medieval days it did so well that it developed lofty notions about itself, and forgot its true origin. It laid claim to a noble legendary past: it had, so its citizens said, been founded by Alexander the Great. An attempt at verisimilitude was given to the yarn by the local boasters. Alexander, they said, founded Sijilmassa "as a rest station for the sick and wounded of his army." As neither Alexander nor any of his army ever came within two thousand miles of the place, Sijilmassa's claim was nonsense.

Sijilmassa and the Tafilelt Oasis will appear often in these pages. The town is now a ruin. The region was subdued by the French only recently. The penultimate historic appearance of Tafilelt—that is the last mention of it before its French capture—is strangely pathetic, and lest, when its time comes, it may be overlooked, I venture to mention it here. Rohlfs, the German explorer, reported it—he being one of the first Europeans to penetrate into this remote part of Morocco.

Rohlfs reported that this spot of erstwhile wealth, battle and intrigue had become "the great harem where were shut up all the women of the deceased Moroccan sultans." They were shut up in a fortress and guarded by eunuchs. Rohlfs got into the place on an invitation to give medical advice to one of the woman inmates, and says, "The harem probably holds about 300 women, old and young, all surviving companions of the late sultan. No woman who crosses the threshold of this fortress can ever go out again; she is in prison." This was in 1864.

*　　*　　*

SIJILMASSA WAS FOUNDED IN 757 BY ONE EISA, SURNAMED "THE Black." He was a Berber of the great Miknasa tribe, whose name survives in that of the Moroccan city of Meknes.

Sijilmassa was the capital of the first medieval African kingdom, north of the Sahara, to set up under native leadership. Previous attempts had been ephemeral; we must go back to antiquity to find a lasting native state. Sijilmassa's contemporaries: Fez, Tiaret, Kairouan, were ruled by persons of foreign descent, and Egypt—as always since the fall of the Pharaohs—was governed by foreigners.

The founding of Sijilmassa was evidently of a rather slipshod order. It was not until some fifty or more years later that it was walled. In the interim its bloodthirsty Sofrite population had taken a dislike to Eisa. Their discontent was inflamed by the Imam Abou el-Khottab of Tripoli fame who had come to Morocco on a visit. "Dark men," said the Imam, pointing to Black Eisa, "are always thieves, and I don't except him!" At this Eisa's subjects seized him, "tied him to a tree on top of a hill and left him there exposed to the bites of mosquitoes until he died."

Sijilmassa's construction was completed by Elisa, a despotic man, hard and violent who crushed the pride of every Berber who dared to resist him. He conquered the neighboring oases and taxed the mines of the near-by Dra region at one fifth of their production.

The Dra mine grab was regarded as very profitable to Sijilmassa's treasury. The mines of this section were fabulous—literally fabulous. Modern searchers have not yet reported traces of their wealth and odd products. But early medieval writers mention not only the usual mineral riches: gold, silver, copper and iron masses "that will not melt in fire," but also—I am quoting from El-Bekri—tell of a mountain near by "where they find precious stones of all sorts, as remarkable for their high quality as for the brilliance of their colors." These stones, he adds, "are as rough to the touch as the skin of a sea-dog. They cannot be cut, even emery will not bite into them." Finally he dilates upon a strange substance to be found near the Dra River: "a sort of stone called *tamatghost* in the Berber language. When anyone rubs it between his hands it gets soft to such a point that it takes on the consistency of flax. It is used to make ropes and halters which are quite unburnable."

El-Bekri continues, "A man of proven veracity once told me how a trader had imported for King Ferdilend (*sic*, Bekri means Ferdinand I of Castile and Leon) a napkin made of this material. He offered it for sale to the King, declaring that it had been the property of one of the disciples of Jesus and that fire would make no impression on it. He put this to test beneath the King's eyes. The King, amazed by such a prodigy, spent all his wealth to buy the relic." (The Moslem narrator's malicious satisfaction at the duping of a Christian is manifest. El-Bekri was a contemporary of "King Ferdilend's" and a fellow Spaniard at a time—the early eleventh century—when Moslem-Christian hatred was very bitter.) Bekri says that cloth made of this mineral substance had the appearance of fine linen and that when put into the fire it became whiter than ever, that is how one cleaned it.

Sijilmassa's one-fifth share of all the produce from this unique mine section was an enviable element. Elisa, the ruler who had accomplished the coup, showed furthermore good diplomatic sense in that he married his son to a princess of Tiaret. So the two Kharijite kingdoms of the West joined hands.

KAIROUAN FREE

Meantime, forty-six days' march to the northeast, Kairouan which had with certain breaks been the caliph's headquarters in Tunisia since the days of Sidi Okba was setting up as the capital of an independent state.

This was accomplished in a businesslike manner and without the romantic detail attendant on the foundation of the kingdoms of Fez and Tiaret and, to a certain extent, Sijilmassa. No mystic figure came from the East to found a city. No novel religious sect was involved. The city of Kairouan was already there. So was the man who took charge. The orthodox religion continued.

This was how the Aghlabite dynasty started in Kairouan in the year 800. Ibrahim-ibn-el-Aghlab, son of a former Arab governor, wrote to the caliph, Harun al-Rashid, offering to take over at his own risk and expense the management of Kairouan and as much of the surrounding territory as might be possible to control. To his offer he coupled interesting conditions. He would forego the subsidy of one hundred thousand dinars (estimated as equaling three hundred thousand current United States dollars) attributed annually and would furthermore give the caliph forty thousand dinars a year for what you might call the concession.

Ibrahim-ibn-el-Aghlab was accounted a responsible man. And—like his father before him—a warrior of high repute. He, the son, was the subject of a simple bit of contemporary verse: . . . "a hero who leaps into the melee, death at his elbow, upholding on his lance the pennant of inherited glory." His offer came at a time when Kairouan was—as so often happened—in an uproar of revolts, intrigues and assassinations. The caliph accepted with alacrity, he being, as I have said, very tired of western North Africa.

The original idea was presumably that Ibrahim-ibn-el-Aghlab would take charge as the caliph's man. But caliphic control lapsed. Aghlab and his family after him reigned over Tunisia for more than a century.

*   *   *

So ended forever the Bagdad caliphs' hold on North Africa to the west of Egypt.

The wide stretch from the Atlantic almost to the Nile had a chance to work out its own destiny. On the whole it started off well. The interrelationship of the four kingdoms was a model of politeness and tact for the whole of the ninth century. Being human they scrapped at times, but there was nothing like the blood baths of the preceding century. Or of our own days. It was the Victorian era of North Africa.

*   *   *

It was also the Golden Age of Arabic culture. Civilization is a bird which shifts its nest from time to time. At present the bird—for what it is worth!—resides with Christians. In the middle of the Middle Ages civilization nested with the Moslems. The

culture of Christian Europe was in comparison so slim a thing as
to be almost invisible. I offer the following supporting opinions
for the benefit of those who are unfamiliar with Islam's past and
may find my statement astonishing:

In his *History of the Arabs* Professor Hitti remarks drily that at
a time when Harun al-Rashid's subjects "were delving into Greek
and Persian philosophy, their contemporaries, Charlemagne and
his lords, were dabbling in the art of writing their names."
Professor Gautier in a long résumé of Moslem contributions to
the world's knowledge (*La Civilisation sarrasine,* a chapter on
"Moeurs et coutumes des Musulmans") reminds us that Harun
al-Rashid sent an ambassador to Charlemagne with gifts including
a clock, and adds, "We do not realize perhaps that in order to get
the true atmosphere of this presentation scene we ought to compare it with the moment when a modern explorer works a phono-
graph for the amazement of a Negro king." (Clocks did not come
into use in Europe until the thirteenth century—that is not for
four hundred years thereafter. The clock which astounded Charlemagne was, Gibbon says, a water clock.)

The western corner of North Africa enjoyed a share of this
Moslem culture, especially in that region now called Tunisia
where the Aghlabites reigned in an old established Arab setting
at Kairouan and had close relationship with the court of the
orthodox caliphs.

                    *   *   *

KAIROUAN BECAME A PLACE OF LEARNING AND BEAUTIFUL BUILDINGS.
A delectable pleasure capital was built near by. Tunis was embellished, and restored to the number of important cities after a
long period of obscurity. The Aghlabites were of sufficient consequence to have ambassadorial dealings with Charlemagne, as is
vouched for by Charlemagne's secretary in the *Annales Fran-
corum.* They were so sure of themselves at home that, in order
to enjoy adventure, they must go abroad. They attacked that part
of the world which in World War II we heard blithely described
as "The Soft Underbelly of Europe," and seemingly found the
Belly softer than we did. Aghlabites conquered all Sicily and successfully attacked the Italian mainland.

PORTRAIT OF A DESPOT

THE MOST FAMOUS AND THE MOST INFAMOUS OF THE ELEVEN Aghlabites, the one who accomplished the most of them all, yet led his dynasty to the edge of disaster, the one who was quite the most abnormal, vicious and fanatical of a family, almost all of whom were picturesque villains, was Abou-Ishac-Ibrahim (875-902). He was the great-great-grandson of the founder of the dynasty. We shall call him Ibrahim II and trace his life story, as typical of the rest and of the North African despot as a class—for through the centuries there have been many somewhat like Ibrahim II. As source for our story we take En-Noweiri who gives us the full, and sometimes filthy, detail of each reign of the Aghlabite line, but to Ibrahim II devotes especially long space, discussing his character and quoting the opinions of other Arabic writers.

Ibrahim II clearly fascinated the psychological student of his day. We would probably call him a notable sex maniac, a religious fanatic and a sadist. But we would have to admit that he was no fool. Ibrahim II was a competent ruler and got things done.

He became ruler at twenty-five, successor to a brother who was a renowned toper, like many of the Aghlabites. In the story of Ibrahim II's life there occurs mention of his mother to an extent that would be surprising in any biography and is positively astonishing in the case of the life history of a Moslem living in Africa. We hear of his quarrels with The Sida (The Mistress, so called). We hear how The Sida repeatedly interfered in his love life. Of how the two—mother and son—were so associated in people's minds that, when a plot was formed to assassinate him, she was included. And of how she cursed him for a certain act of satanic whimsicality.

Ibrahim II had evidently a horror of women, although he had relations with them and bred sons and daughters. The girl children born to him were put in charge of his mother, The Sida. One day, having raised a flock of sixteen of them to girlhood and, "seeing him in a good humor," she proudly exhibited them to him in a group. Ibrahim II pronounced them pretty, went

away and called a Negro slave. "Go," said Ibrahim, "and bring
me the heads of those young girls!"

He was not more pitiful toward the young of his own sex.
Suspecting perversion amongst themselves on the part of a group
of sixty boys of his service, he executed them either by roasting
them in batches of five or six in the great ovens of his castle, or
by cooking them to death in the hottest room of the royal baths.

He destroyed his concubines by various ingenious cruelties and
finally, "he had left not a single woman in his entourage. Lonely,
he went to his mother's apartments. 'I want to eat with you,' said
he. Enchanted by his mark of favor and seeing him in a good
humor (I interject into En-Noweiri's narrative the reflection that
she was a poor judge of her son's moods) she said, 'I have brought
up a pair of slave girls for you and reserved them for your pleasure,
for since the death of your concubines it is a long time since you
have had any distractions.' "

Ibrahim II agreed to receive the maidens, listened to their lute
and guitar playing and to their recital of verses from the Koran.
The Sida suggested that the girls should accompany him when he
left her apartments, "it being a long time that you have been
without companionship!" Ibrahim went off, followed by the girls.

"Less than an hour afterwards a slave came to the mother
carrying on his head a tray covered with a napkin. The mother
imagined that it was a gift from her son. When the slave put
down the tray before her and lifted the napkin, what did she see?
The heads of those two young girls. Struck with horror she
fainted. Sometime afterward when she had come to herself her
first words were imprecations against her son."

Unlimited power in the hands of a sex maniac—oriental annals often give us hints of such types. In the case of Ibrahim II
we happen to possess a very intimate study.

Yet the other and so different phase of his character, his professional side as ruler, is an extraordinary contrast. We know of
his ability as prince and general, of his fairness toward his subjects: "the most equitable of princes, never did he repulse one
who asked justice . . . he was severe on the misdemeanors of the
powerful and the rich."

*   *   *

IT IS PARTICULARLY INTERESTING TO FIND THAT IBRAHIM II'S DOCTOR attempted to treat his mentally deranged royal patient in something of the modern manner. He used suggestion upon the unhappy prince. He was a Jewish doctor, Ishac-ibn-Soleiman of Kairouan who died in 932, and some of whose treatises have survived.

Ibrahim II could not sleep. Dr. Ishac advised him to walk out into the country. He came to a certain place where the zephyrs were soft. It was four miles from Kairouan. There the troubled Ibrahim II lay down and slept.

Doubtless at the advice of Dr. Ishac he moved there to live. A city was founded called Raccada (The Sleeper)—a pleasure city, a garden city, a city where "should one visit it, one would never cease from smiling and one felt gay without cause." What the reason was I cannot tell. Such atmospheric miracles were recorded in the days of old. In the upland country beyond Kairouan lived a group of men called "The Sleepers" who fell sometimes into a profound sleep lasting for two or three days. Coming to himself again a "Sleeper" would be like one drunken and on the next day the gift of prophecy would come to him and "he would predict what was going to happen during the year; abundant crops, famines, wars or other remarkable events." This is set down by El-Bekri.

*   *   *

IBRAHIM II'S CITY OF RACCADA, ASIDE FROM ANY MYSTIC ATMOSphere or artful suggestions of Dr. Ishac, possessed one tangible reason for seeming gay to the visitor. The sale of *nebid* (wine) was permitted at Raccada, though regularly forbidden at Kairouan since some thirty years. This demarcation between dry and wet territory is a modern thing such as we might look for in the United States of today. Ibrahim II loved his *nebid*. It was a fermented wine made from grapes or dates. The usual name for date wine was *lagmi*. It is procured by tapping the date palms. A tree can be milked of four gallons a day over a period of two or more months. The syrup soon turns into an intoxicant sold locally very cheaply. Within my time you could get a quart of it in the oases for about three United States cents. A disadvantage is, however, that little worms breed in *lagmi* and you can see them swimming in your glass.

Indifferent to this disadvantage—perhaps drinking from a golden goblet and so unaware—Ibrahim II lived and drank deep at Raccada until a whim seized him to move his capital again.

Raccada has now completely disappeared. Perhaps the latest use made of the site whose mystic atmosphere made men "never to cease from smiling and feel gay without cause" was as an airfield in the Tunisian campaign of World War II.

ATTACK FROM EGYPT

Three years after Ibrahim II's reign began a startling attack came from the east. From Egypt arrived an angry young man who had revolted against his father and had sought to set up on his own account. He was Abbas, the son of Talun. Talun had turned himself from caliph's governor into the independent ruler of Egypt. Abbas, the son, got as far as Tripoli before the Aghlabite army stopped him in a bloody defeat.

The insult rankled with Ibrahim II. Affairs in Sicily and elsewhere kept him busy but he did not forget.

His armies captured Syracuse that same year "with such boot as never had been taken in any city of the Polytheists."

This name of Polytheists was sometimes applied to Christians because of the three parts of the Trinity: "the Father, the Son and the uncle," in the unconscious blasphemy of a certain learned Moslem. The English explorer, victim of his sneer, complained afterward, "Thus do Mohammedans ridicule the purest dogma of Christianity." In fairness we must admit that it is in such hoodlum fashion that all of us at times ridicule the details of another faith of which we have only superficial and prejudiced knowledge. Many might assure you that the *houri* is a leading element in Moslem religious thought!

Some years after capturing the "city of the Polytheists" Ibrahim II retook Palermo which, already Moslem, had revolted, took Taormina, and occupied Messina.

All these things—city building, victory in war, foreign conquests—cannot have been inspired by a madman. Ibrahim II had evidently a double personality.

Tunis revolted against his authority. His troops carried the town by assault, pillaged, raped and reduced the survivors to slavery. News of the victory came to Ibrahim by carrier pigeon. He sent an order back to his general not to decapitate the dead and to await a train of carts which were proceeding from Kairouan to collect the corpses. These gruesome and odoriferous trophies were subsequently paraded through Kairouan's streets. (It was a two or three days' march from Kairouan to Tunis; the dead at the triumphant display must have been at least a week old.)

Shortly thereafter Ibrahim II decided to quit his pleasure city where one never ceased from smiling and to establish his capital at Tunis, which certainly cannot have been a gay resort at the moment.

COUNTERATTACK

THEN CAME THE DAY HE HAD BEEN WAITING FOR. HE FELT READY to avenge himself on Egypt. How extensive a plan was in his kinkish brain we do not know. Sixteen years had passed since an Egyptian army had dared to invade his sand stretches and besiege Tripoli. The insult had festered in him. It was following the Egyptian attack that his character and conduct—till then described as excellent—had completely changed. It would seem that Egypt had become an obsession with him. He may have dreamed of getting his vengeance on the Nile.

Marching eastward with his army Ibrahim II met a check at Tripoli. The city was his, but the surrounding open country by an old agreement belonged to associated members of the Kharijite sect of Tiaret. These people tried to stop his passage Egyptward. It was a bloody battle. Ibrahim II won and pursued his enemies into the sea "his sword at their kidneys" in the picturesque Arabic phrase, and "the waves were dyed with their blood."

This pained Ibrahim II who was a sincerely religious man. He deplored having killed fellow Moslems—Polytheists were a different matter. He was however soon consoled. He questioned prisoners amongst the defeated Kharijites, asking them a test question: what did they think of Ali, who to the orthodox Ibrahim II was a figure to be respected. Bravely the Kharijite prisoners spoke up. "Ali," said they, "is now in the fire of Hell!"

Ibrahim II declared, "Now it is a pleasant duty to kill you all!"

So, seated on his throne he killed personally five hundred b
striking each in the heart neatly with his javelin. The Chronicl
of Abou Zakaria gives even more rude detail of Ibrahim's cruelty
including how one of the Kharijite leaders was cut to pieces gradu
ally, "starting with the thumb. When they got to the shoulde
he entered into Allah's pity" (died).

DESPOT'S END

Despite all this, Ibrahim was destined to die with *Egyp*
written on his heart. His expedition was a fiasco. Just as he swun
into the dip of the Syrtis Bay his army deserted him in a body an
fled back to Tunisia. An Arabic historian has said that somethin
happened there by which his followers finally and at last knew
him for a madman. He had killed fifteen of the enemy and "give
orders to cook their heads, letting it be understood that he an
his officers proposed to eat them."

Back in Tunisia Ibrahim II presently received a message from
the caliph at Bagdad. The caliph invited Ibrahim to resign i
favor of his son. How the invitation could have been enforce
had Ibrahim II been recalcitrant I cannot guess. But Ibrahim
had come to the end of his energies. He obeyed. Again his char
acter changed. He became a penitent. He dressed himself in rough
clothing, forgave all the prisoners in his jails, went to Tripol
and gave away largess to the poor, departed to join in the Hol
War against the Christians, set right all injustices of which the
conquered people of Sicily complained and crossed to the main
land of Italy to subdue further lands in Allah's name.

At a place in Calabria called by the name of "Kasna" i
Noweiri's pages "the internal malady from which he suffere
took on suddenly great intensity." He died in the autumn of 902
Kasna simultaneously gave up. Kasna—we call it Cosenza—sur
vived to give up in another autumn 1041 years later to the Allie
armies.

*   *   *

Ibrahim II's story has been told fully as illustrative of th
career of many a North African despot. Frequent North Africa
rulers have been on his model: monsters of perverse cruelty i
the harem and palace—killing off woman companions and mal

relatives like flies—wise in the judgment hall, brave on the battle-field, and intensely religious after their own fashion. He was a fair example of the run-of-the-basket royal bad man, and here you have had his portrait.

Before I leave him let me say a word of excuse as to one side of his behavior: his multiple murders of brothers, sons and other male relatives. Such crimes were common in North African royal circles. They are described as unnatural. Really they were the most comprehensible of the royal wickednesses. Brothers—half brothers, rather—raised in the intrigue and rivalry of the harem knew what to fear when they mounted the throne. So did fathers with grown-up, ambitious sons. No palace was safe to a ruler with adult males in his family. Where public opinion was negligible and power absolute it was often mere self-protection to kill and to keep on killing the potential usurpers.

Ibrahim II, for instance, felt it to be in his interests to kill eight brothers in a batch, plus a son, or perhaps two.

Ibrahim II of Tunisia can stand in the reader's memory as a type. His like will occur again in later dynasties from Morocco to Egypt, but I shall not distress or thrill the reader with a rehearsal of their detailed naughtiness.

SARACENS

SICILY HAD BECOME AN AFRICAN ISLAND. ATTACKS ON SOUTH EUROPE by Mohammedans from North Africa and elsewhere made life a nightmare. The word Saracen was "a name which every Christian mouth has been taught to pronounce with terror and abhorrence," in the words of Gibbon.

"Saracen" carried a grim feeling like Vandal, Tartar, the modern term Hun. There was nothing villainous in its derivation, which is merely from a word meaning eastern, or alternately from the name of a tribe mentioned in classical geography. But historians of old, writing when the Saracen danger was a close terror, said unhesitatingly, *"Saracen* comes from *sarak,* which means thief."* Their etymology was based on the opinion that if it did not so derive, it ought to, anyhow!

Besides the feeling of abhorrence which it carried, the word

Saracen held dark mystery, especially when it applied to the
people of North Africa, for Europe had no vision of the raiders
homeland. The Mediterranean was a one-way sea. There was no
traffic, or very little, originating on its European side.

There was as yet practically no retaliation for Moslem injuries.
One exception is noted, a raid on Tunisia's coast in the early
days of the Arab conquest. This supine attitude astonished the
Moslems. They expected revenge and were on their guard against
the attack which did not come. There existed a system of inter-
communicating lights along the whole North African coast, legend
tells us, whose motive was to report invasion. The supernaturally
powerful Alexandria observatory could pick up "the sails of the
Roums" far out at sea and the danger could be flashed from tower
to tower. News could have been flashed from Egypt to Gibraltar
in a single night, or such was the incredible claim. But "the ships
of the Roums" did not come.

A FEW WHO SAW AFRICA THEN

THOSE FEW EUROPEANS WHO VISITED AFRICA DURING THE EARLY
Saracen period came in peace, and fell roughly into three classes:
captives, pilgrims and traders.

The captives—men, women and children dragged away after
raids—were an army of lost souls who vanished into Africa's maw.
We hear, for example, of nine thousand Christian slaves taken
at one time in the ninth century out of Tarentum, of which
number two shiploads were despatched to Tunisia, two shiploads
to Tripoli and two to Alexandria. No word from such as these
ever got back to inform Europe what Saracen Africa was like.

The pilgrims who caught a glimpse of Africa on their way to
the Holy Land were on the other hand a very articulate group.
Their records about Africa are much trimmed with fantasy, but
do not as a whole suggest that the African Moslems ill used the
brave religious adventurers.

Incidentally the sentiment existing between Moslems and Christians at this period—before the Crusade preliminaries crystallized
mutual hatreds—is rather hard to grasp. The Saracens raided
Europe's coasts. Yet there was trading back and forth. And the
relations between the caliph and Charlemagne were cordial.

Their friendliness moreover was advertised across Europe in a spectacular way. The caliph sent Charlemagne not only the clock already mentioned but also a gift which attracted vast attention —as well it might, for it was an elephant!

The caliph's gift animal, by name Abou Labaz, made the trip via North Africa, was brought by ship to Port Vendres in southern France, and crossed the Alps just as its remote cousins had done a thousand years before in the days of Hannibal.

The elephant was a complete and startling novelty to the Franks. Charlemagne made it his pet and it accompanied him on all his expeditions and journeys until its death eight years later when Charlemagne was marching against the Danes. Those two striding across Europe—the giant man (Charlemagne was six feet four inches tall) and his giant mascot were pro-Moslem propaganda of obvious value. Less showy, but more precious was another gift of the caliph's: facilities for the safe passage of pilgrims, to which, it is said, was added symbolically the Key to the Holy Sepulcher.

Resident Christians in Moslem Africa however felt increased disfavor. In the ninth century a special dress was imposed on such as lived in Egypt, a sort of primitive form of alien registration. Christians must wear yellow clothes and put images of an ape or dog over their house doors. Crosses must not be shown.

*   *   *

UNDISMAYED MEN CONTINUED TO MAKE THE PILGRIMAGE. As A RULE they touched North Africa only at Egypt. But there is record of a pious Breton who prayed at the tomb of St. Cyprian in Tunisia. This would have been just before Ibrahim II's reign.

Egypt's wonders and antiquities delighted the pilgrims. They especially reveled in the Alexandria lighthouse and in the mystery of Joseph's Barns.

The lighthouse had stood for a thousand years and was then classed as one of the Seven Wonders of the World. If we were to believe what was then said of it and if it were still working in its miraculous fashion of old, it still would be a world's wonder, even in our proud days of scientific marvels. Here are some of the medieval claims made for the lighthouse: Its mirror could "reflect all that happened in Constantinople" (a good seven hundred miles away). Again "its fire could be seen in Acre, in Africa

(meaning Tunisia) and in Provence (France)"—three continents
Its watchman "could perceive in its mirror the approach of enem
ships at a distance of fifty days' sailing."

Its destruction, legend says, was brought about by a *saboteu*
working for the Christian enemy who induced the Moslem rule
of Egypt to dig too energetically for treasure under the tower
the foreign agent having planted and pretended to discover pearl
and gold in the neighborhood. The *saboteur* is variously de
scribed as a Greek or a Jew.

As for Joseph's Barns, such was the name Christians gave to
the pyramids. These had allegedly been erected in Bible day
to serve as granaries. They were described as being as big a
mountains and the belief was that they were so lofty that "the
passed beyond the measure of shadows and cast no shadow at all."

Such notions continued and you will find that a traveler recen
enough to be included in Hakluyt reported on Joseph's house
Laurence Aldersey, having embarked at Bristol in 1586, eventu
ally reached Egypt and states, "The house of Joseph is yet stand
ing in Cayro, which is a sumptuous thing, having a place to wall
in of fifty-six mighty pillars, all gilt with gold, but I saw it not
being then lame." Aldersey's landmark cannot have been Joseph'
house. For this there are several reasons, one being that Cair
was not founded till nearly 1000 A.D.

*   *   *

CHRISTIAN TRADERS IN THE EARLY SARACEN PERIOD DID NOT GE
beyond the ports, notably Alexandria. One class of trader from
Europe did however push deep into Africa and across country
Driven by the frenzied commercial energy of their race intrepic
Jews marched over North Africa from the Atlantic to Egypt.

The oldest Arabic geographical work which we possess tell
of them in romantic terms. "These merchants," wrote Ibn-Khor
dadbeh in about the year 900, "speak Arabic, Persian, Roman
the French, Spanish and Slav languages. They journey from Wes
to East, from East to West, partly on land, partly by sea. The
transport from the West eunuchs, female slaves, boys, brocade
castor, marten, and other furs, and swords. They take ship from
Firanja (France) on the Western Sea and make for Farama"
(Pelusium at the mouth of the Nile near modern Damietta).

Others, the old geographer reports, cross from Spain or Franc to Morocco; "from Tangier they walk to Kairouan and to the capital of Egypt." After peddling their wares across Africa they proceeded, striding across space like Martians, over Asia Minor and Persia to China. Then back again with musk, aloes, camphor, cinnamon and other products of the East "to sell their goods to the Romans, or to go to the palace of the King of the Franks to place their wares."

*   *   *

IN MAKING UP THE BRIEF LIST OF THE VARIOUS SORTS OF PERSONS from Europe who glimpsed North Africa during the centuries when traffic between the two continents was almost exclusively a one-way affair, we must remember the Norsemen.

Norsemen passed through Gibraltar as early as the eighth century and the wildness of their attack on what is now Spanish Morocco horrified the natives. They visited Morocco's Atlantic coasts just before the middle of the ninth century, where a port called Arzila was named after them by the local inhabitants. It was named Bab-el-Madjous, the Port of the Pagans.

The Norsemen were charmed by North Africa, so warm and fruitful, and attempted to gain a permanent foothold, alongside where Arzila now stands, by a childish trick. They hid alleged treasure in the ground—the same being only rotten millet seeds —and, on a return visit, begged the natives for permission to land and dig it up. Watching them, the local folk saw the yellow gleam of the grain, took it for gold, and rushed the Norsemen. So the Norse hope of being allowed to settle down on the promise of sharing the spoil was ruined, and the Norse robbed of their dream of lolling on the sunny beaches and of colonizing what they pronounced to be "the richest country on earth." To the Norsemen it was "The Great Land of the Blue Men," it being the odd impression of these platinum-haired, rosy-skinned men that the swarthy Berbers and Arabs of Africa, and such Negroes as they saw, were *blue*.

THE FAMOUS FATIMITES

ALL IN ALL THE NUMBER OF VISITORS FROM WITHOUT WAS INFINITES-imal. North Africa enjoyed such freedom from foreign interference and such mutual tolerance between her own states as is rare in history. This, oddly, when her Saracens were the terror of Europe.

This ideal situation was not to last. A tornado was sweeping in from the East. Unsuspecting their danger, the rulers of all North Africa's states were blown suddenly off their thrones. We cannot blame them for being caught napping. Who could have guessed that a mystic personage would come along and would be so expertly pushed upon their people—"sold" to them, we might say in our modern argot—as to rock a continent?

The dynasty of the Fatimites constitutes one of the few passages in North African medieval history familiar, at least by name, to the average person. It was a spectacular period. Within sixty years the Fatimites had made themselves masters of an empire stretching from the Atlantic to Egypt. It was the most brilliant conquest ever accomplished in Africa, before or since. That of the Romans was more prolonged and less penetrating; that of the Arabs slow and spotty.

To this add that the Fatimites had during this sixty years built two capitals—one important enough in its days to be called in foreign parts by the pompous name of Africa City, the other a place destined to become and to remain the greatest town in Africa, and one of the oldest of the big world capitals of today. I mean, of course, Cairo.

*   *   *

THE FATIMITE DYNASTY WAS FOUNDED UPON THE MYSTIC AND ROmantic personality of a mahdi. Its first ruler claimed to be one of that series whose glamor has captured African loyalty through the centuries.

The word "mahdi" means, literally translated, "directed" or "guided." A Mahdi, One Directed, would appear to lead the Moslem world on the right path. He would be a direct descendant of Ali. A sort of Messiah of Islam.

The particular Mahdi who founded the Fatimite dynasty claimed to descend from a mysterious lineage which for three generations had been in hiding. Now, as Mahdi, he planned to "show himself" and on consideration chose the western side of North Africa as a suitable display ground. His name was Obeid-Allah. The sect supporting his claim was known as the Ismailian branch of the Shiites. They took this name from that of the Mahdi's ancestor, Ismail, the first of the three who had gone into hiding. The Ismailian sect is still powerful. *Who's Who* (British edition) mentioned that the Aga Khan, that well-known sportsman, was "head of the Ismaili Mohammedans." One branch of the Ismailians founded the startling group called the Assassins.

* * *

THE MAHDI OBEID-ALLAH'S APPEARANCE WAS MAGNIFICENTLY prepared in advance by a propaganda campaign covering some twenty years and starting back in the days of the Mahdi's father, the third of the "hidden Imams."

This preparatory campaign was the work of a man of genius, a sleek schemer, a fascinating preacher, a brilliant military general, a man of tenacity and courage who drove his teeth into a job of work—the establishment of the Mahdi on the throne—and never let go. He was Abou-Abdallah, the so-called Dai (missionary).

The *bona fides* of the Mahdi was naturally subject to attack. Both self-interest and sincere doubt prompted his enemies to question whether this man was, as he pretended, a descendant of Fatima and Ali, mystically chosen to lead his fellows. Some suggested that he was not even a Moslem, let alone a Moslem of noble ancestry and special destiny. He was, they charged, of a Jewish or even of a Christian family. Arabic historians have held opposing views. Ibn-Khaldoun believed in him.

As for his propagandist, the Dai, Abou-Abdallah, there can be no two opinions. The Dai was an opportunist and a confidence man. Many details have come down to us to indicate this. Ibn-Khaldoun refers to him as an adventurer. Yet, considering him, I am reminded of the tone of the rejoinder made by a United States president when told that one of his generals was a heavy drinker. Many an ambitious man today would be lucky could he find a manager like the crook, Abou-Abdallah, to push him along.

THE DAI

THE DAI, ABOU-ABDALLAH, OPENED THE WAY FOR THE FATIMITE conquest of North Africa by a series of artful and brave maneuvers.

His first move was to worm his way into the confidence of a party of Berber pilgrims at Mecca. He made great play of piety and self-denial, then told them about his form of Mohammedanism, hinting much, keeping much back. They listened eagerly. Then the Dai pried into their secrets, learning of their dissatisfaction with their ruler at home. This ruler was no other than the despot, Ibrahim II, whose portrait was sketched in some detail in previous pages.

The pilgrims invited the Dai to go with them when they returned home. They were men of the great Ketama tribe, Berbers of a wild and independent type, living in the region where modern Algeria adjoins Tunisia, that is, the Constantine section. They were an ideal group for his purpose, headlong and unsophisticated. It was the Ketamas who won the cause for the Fatimites.

In 893 the Ketama group which had become the victims of his spellbinding arrived back in the Ketama land with their guest. He gained new followers by the thousands. Then began the gradual undermining of the Aghlabite power, the ruler, Ibrahim II, unaware how great was his peril. Ibrahim II was busy with his futile expedition toward Egypt, with penitential Holy Wars in Sicily—fiddling away his energies while his kingdom burned from within.

After years of minor fighting the Dai was able to advance against the Aghlabites with an army of two hundred thousand. By now Ibrahim II was dead, his son and successor had been assassinated and his grandson was upon the wobbly Aghlabite throne. He was Ziadet-Allah, a chip off the old block, who had found it desirable to instigate the death of his father and to kill twenty-nine of his brothers and cousins. He was a weak opponent to the Dai.

At Laribus, a place in the mountains of northwestern Tunisia, the Dai won a mighty and horrible victory. "The inhabitants," says El-Bekri, "had taken refuge with the survivors of the soldiery inside the great mosque where they crowded in, standing upon one another's shoulders. Blood came rushing out of the doors of the edifice and ran down the streets like brooks after a heavy storm. We are assured that 30,000 individuals died in the mosque's interior and that the carnage lasted from the hour of the evening prayer till the end of the night."

Three days' journey away at Raccada, near Kairouan, Ziadet-

Allah knew all was lost and planned flight. To gain time for his preparations he announced to the population that his army had won a great victory, and to make them believe his story he killed all the people in the prisons and caused their heads to be carried through the streets as if at a triumph. He meantime was packing up his treasure, dressing each of a thousand slaves in a belt stuffed with a thousand gold pieces and mounting on horse or muleback the most pleasing of his womenfolk.

He fled to the east and the last that we hear of him—the last of the Aghlabites—is that "having lost all of his hair and his beard following an illness caused by poisoned food served him by a Negro slave," he died at Jerusalem.

* * *

KAIROUAN WAS IN THE HANDS OF THE DAI AND HIS BRAVE KETAMAS. Still the inspired salesman for the mysterious figure on whose behalf he had been struggling for all these years, he contrived to maintain provocative silence when his followers asked him who was to be their king now that the fighting was over.

Then he set out to fetch the Mahdi.

THE MAHDI

WHEN MILITARY SUCCESS HAD BEGUN TO LOOK ASSURED THE DAI had sent messages to the Mahdi inviting his presence in Africa. The Mahdi, Obeid-Allah, his young son and certain trusted followers forthwith proceeded secretly toward the west. The caliph at Bagdad, recognizing in the Mahdi a potential danger, gave orders for his arrest en route. The Mahdi and his party, disguised as merchants, tricked the pursuers and passed safely across Egypt. At Tripoli the Mahdi again escaped arrest and went on westward, passing close to the Dai near Constantine, but not daring to make contact with him, and so continuing yet further right into Morocco. In fact the Mahdi found it prudent to keep on until there was no further road before him—merely the vast emptiness of the western Sahara. At Sijilmassa on the desert's rim he stopped perforce.

He was received with courtesy by the king of Sijilmassa, ruler of the line that had founded the city a century and a half before. But presently there came word to Sijilmassa that they were entertaining a very dangerous guest, and the Mahdi was thrown into prison.

There the Mahdi remained until one great day in August, 909, when the Dai arrived at the gates of the city, demanded that the Mahdi be turned over to him, was refused, and won an easy victory, put Sijilmassa's king to flight, burst into the city and flung open the Mahdi's prison. "Then he paid homage to his master, placed him upon horseback and walked on foot before him, tears of joy running down his cheeks. 'Here he is!' he cried to his Ketamas, 'Here is your King!' "

After forty happy days at Sijilmassa the Mahdi and his Dai turned back toward Kairouan. The famous dynasty of the Fatimites—later to spread across all Africa—was born. "The Sun of their Glory had risen on the western horizon and astounded a startled humanity!" according to the author of the *Masalik-el-Absar,* and for once we can admit that the characteristically high-flown Arabic text is justified.

THE MAHDI AND THE DAI

LIKE EVERY GREAT ACCOMPLISHMENT THE ESTABLISHMENT OF FATI-mite power appears upon study to have been more a matter of stern effort and less of a miracle.

The Mahdi's part of the effort commenced at once. He saw that he and the Dai had come to the parting of the ways. A man as competent as the Dai must inevitably have planned it that he would be setting up a mystic nincompoop and that he himself would be the master. He may even have planned to get rid of the Mahdi altogether, once his usefulness as a rallying point was over.

The Mahdi sensed this, saw that the Dai would be at best a nuisance, at worst a danger, and—just one year after his arrival at Kairouan—the Mahdi caused the Dai to be killed.

Some of those who had been the Dai's followers during the fight which put the Mahdi on the throne were indignant. They rioted in Kairouan and the Mahdi—evidently physically as well as morally brave—rode into the mob on horseback and ordered them to disperse. The trouble spread into the Ketama country where the Dai had started his campaign and certain naïve Ketamas conceived the droll notion of setting up an impromptu competitive mahdi. They picked a child for the position and were—child and all—forthwith cut to pieces by the troops of the Mahdi's young son.

The Mahdi was a big enough man to fill the place so carefully prepared for him. And he was to the common idea a true king. He was like the princess in the fairy story who was recognized for what she was because she sensed a lump under the mattress made by a single dry pea. This royal fussiness delighted the Mahdi's subjects. Long after his death they remembered and repeated with pride such items as these:

At Biskra the whole crop of the special white date, *liari*, "was set aside for Obeid-Allah, the Mahdi," and "he must always have his food seasoned with salt from the salt mines near Biskra." He "would drink no water except that of the Ain-Djocar (which formerly supplied water to Carthage) which he caused to be brought to him daily, charged upon pack animals." Finally, from way across country (nine days caravaning from Kairouan) "a fish called *bouri,* or mullet, to which nothing comparable existed in any other place was habitually sent to Obeid-Allah, after being varnished all over with honey to keep it fresh" (El-Bekri).

THE BUILDING OF AFRICA CITY

Foreseeing days of fierce fighting for himself and succeeding Fatimites, the Mahdi felt the need for a stronger capital than Kairouan. He set about the construction of the celebrated fortress which he called Mahdia after himself, and which the Christian world got to know in later years as Africa City.

Its site was a headland on the Tunisian coast south of Sousse. It was described as a city sticking out into the sea like a wrist with a clenched fist, and its military strength was regarded as prodigious. As an instance: "Mahdia had two great iron gates into whose construction there had gone not a sliver of wood. Each gate weighs one thousand quintals and is thirty empans high." This according to El-Bekri; Ibn-Khaldoun claims only two hundred quintals. A quintal was about a hundred pounds; an empan was the space between a man's thumb tip and little finger when the hand was spread wide—say nine or ten inches. "Each nail used in these gates," El-Bekri adds, "weighs six pounds."

Part of Mahdia's ruins have survived to modern days and saw something of the fighting in 1943. In the days of the Mahdi and his successors it was a mighty port in peace and war. Ships came trading from the Moslem countries round the Mediterranean: Egypt, Sicily, Spain, Asia Minor. It could hold thirty ships at once and its channel could be closed in time of war by a great chain between two towers.

In the Mahdi's day such danger as might be to the port was not Christian. The Christians were still supinely accepting Saracen injuries. Retaliation had not yet started.

The Mahdi's men and those of his son and successor harried Calabria and other parts of "the country of the Franks." In the latter reign a Fatimite army beseiged Genoa and took it "by the special favor of Allah," in the words of Ibn-Khaldoun.

*   *   *

MAHDIA TOOK YEARS TO BUILD. WHEN ALL WAS FINISHED—WALLS, gates, silos, cisterns by the hundreds, hewn-out caves for the arsenal and for the storage of ships and gear—the Mahdi made an inspection and cried out, "Now I am happy for the fate of the Fatimites!"

His prophetic words were wise. The whirlwind subjugation of a continent which the Fatimites planned was destined to include certain dangerous passages when the Mahdi's successors would be glad to slam the great gates of Mahdia, and when they blessed the forethought of their ancestor who had built them.

DEFEAT OF THE PIOUS KINGDOM

THE FATIMITES MET PROLONGED DIFFICULTY IN THE CONQUEST OF the West as a whole, but none whatever in subjugating the pious Abadites. Their capital, Tiaret, fell in the days of the Mahdi's debut. The Abadites did not show fight. Nor good judgment either. They believed in a promise of general amnesty and gave up.

It was to be expected, and the Abadites should have known, that an army inspired by reverence for a leader claiming descent from Fatima and Ali would deal harshly with a group like them-

selves who based their religion on the hatred of Ali's memory.
Indeed their own records boast that members of the Abadite sect
spat in the face of the Mahdi when he was scuttling across Africa
before his rise to power. Naturally, despite the supposed amnesty,
Tiaret was destroyed. Many were massacred and their heads
conveyed to Kairouan as trophies. The Imam Yagoub, that ruler
of Tiaret who carried spirituality to the extreme of living upon
a cup of milk every three days, managed to get away with a few
friends. They fled into the desert. Their first refuge was at
Ouargla. They had lost everything except their own peculiar
religion. To this they clung fanatically and made a fresh start.
Near Ouargla they built a new Abadite capital.

OUARGLA

THE SAHARAN CITY OF OUARGLA STOOD AND STILL STANDS IN A
favored position, if one may so describe any town in the terrible
desert. Its oasis possessed ample water. It was only eight days by
caravan to the south of Biskra, that is to say from the Sahara's
edge. Along the intervening stretch were a series of habitable
places and water points so that the journey to Ouargla was relatively easy even in precamel days, and Ouargla had developed
early. It claimed to be the oldest important settlement in the
desert, though probably Ghadames, the great oasis of Egypt and
others were older. It has been suggested that it was a town on the
site of Ouargla that was visited by the first of all recorded Saharan
explorers, the five Nasamonian youths of the Herodotus story. I
have heard that there is a local legend that Ouargla was founded
upon the order of King Solomon!

Modern Ouargla is outstandingly the show place of the Sahara
(I have seen most of the well-known Saharan settlements). It has
everything which an exotic novelist, painter or cinema creator
could ask for. Rolling dunes of golden sand. One million date
palms by official count. A walled medieval city with a moat.
Shining white, Moorish-style buildings outside the wall to house
French administrative and military activities which have gathered
at this important center and constructed for themselves facsimiles
of Oriental palaces. To these add a salt lake, the harder parts of
which might be made of glass bricks. The human element is par-

ticularly picturesque: Spahis sweeping red cloaks. Foreign Legionnaires, Ouled Naïl dancers, specialists in those dances of the quivering muscle from throat to crotch which some find shocking, dressed in bright-tinted brocades with fluffy muslin overdrapes and a numismatist's dream of antique gold coins tinkling against their beige throats. Negresses—Ouargla is largely populated by colored stock born of its centuries as a clearing house for Sudanese slaves—trail their court trains in the sand. They usually wear garments of Irish green. Their hair is molded very high upon a formation said to contain sand and is garnished with visible and smellable oddities: squashed dates, butter, beads, buttons and other souvenirs.

Ouargla for centuries profited by being at the crossroads of the trans-Saharan trade between certain Mediterranean ports and Negroland by the Niger.

A LOOK TOWARD THE SOUTH

BY FATIMITE TIMES TRANS-SAHARAN TRADE WAS DEVELOPING INTO something very important, a business full of unique risks and offering colossal rewards. Let us look into the south, consider the circumstances of medieval desert travel, and glance at some of the strange and—to most of us—quite unknown capitals beyond the great sands whose exotic treasures made trans-Saharan commerce so immensely valuable. This digression will eventually lead us back to the Fatimites, for it was from one of these lands beyond the desert that came the greatest danger which the Fatimites were destined to encounter in their climb to the mastery of all North Africa.

Measured by Arabic terms the great desert was "seven months wide by four months deep." Trans-Saharan trade crisscrossed over this stupendous waste and in every mind as one torturing day succeeded another during the long journey to the south was the same dream: a dream of the Land of Gold in the Sudan.

WHERE GOLD GREW

PROVIDENCE TEMPTED MEN TO THE TERRIBLE RISK AND HARDSHIP OF Saharan travel by a miraculous trade opportunity, an opportunity the like of which was never elsewhere offered to the greedy.

It was the opportunity to swap something of practically no value for something vastly desirable—salt for gold. In inland western Sudan there was no salt. In western Sudan gold abounded. A trader carrying salt from the land where it was cheap might make an immense fortune in a round trip over the desert. Provided that he survived!

There were regions in the Sudan where "salt can be sold for its weight in gold," said El-Bekri, whose geographical information was collected during the period of the Fatimites. Other medieval authorities agreed. A surviving fifteenth century map shows the famous kingdom of Mali with an inscription indicating that its people would make this same bargain: *"un carech de sall evem un carech d'or."* A Jew of Avignon in the sixteenth century tells—gloating at the profit and shuddering at the journey's hardships—of the exchange possible in the Sudanese back country: "a measure of salt for a measure of gold." Similarly "a heap of salt for a heap of gold," says the author of the *Masalik*. It seems so preposterous that I have offered several supporting statements.

* * *

As traders learned that gold was held of such small account in the lands beyond the Sahara fantastic stories of inner Africa sprang up and were believed, not only in the Middle Ages but into relatively modern times.

The idea early became current that gold grew like a plant in that part of the world. "They make gold gardens in their sands as one might plant carrots," says a tenth century Moslem writer. The gold plant came up in midsummer. In the autumn the plants were pulled out and gold clung to their roots, says a later writer, the author of the *Masalik*.

"The Negroes from all around flock to the gold fields. Each gathers the quantity of gold—big or little—which Allah accords as his share. None is left without some gold. . . . The greater part of this gold is sold to the people of Ouargla and of the western Maghreb (Morocco). . . . This happens every year. It is the principal industry of the land of the Negroes." Edrisi, who gives this account, means the Negroes of the western Sudan.

The Gold of Africa: Stories like the above gradually reached Europe and produced an intolerable itch for exploration. These stories eventually brought about the end of Africa's darkness.

A fourteenth century map of Africa's west coast displayed to Europe the River of Gold, which was "a league wide" with wording to the effect that "the majority of the inhabitants of these parts are employed in collecting gold from this stream." There was in the western Sudan, according to a French geographer of the late eighteenth century, a treasure-stuffed hill "3000 paces in circumference and 300 feet high . . . composed of gold." Even as recently as the start of the last century an English diplomatic agent and serious, though sometimes credulous, investigator, Mr. James Grey Jackson, passed along a story from the Sudan about a certain locality where hunters were accustomed to go out at night and mark places which glittered. Next morning they would collect the surface earth, of which "a bushel has produced the value of three pounds sterling of pure gold." As for the alleged "gold roofs of Timbuctoo"—these launched a thousand explorations.

Mariners, such as Richard Jobson (*The Golden Trade,* 1623), for instance, came back from the African coast and repeated native boasting about "a great Towne (four Moones' journey into the interior) the houses whereof are covered with gold," or again "of houses covered with gold . . . further up the river." It was tantalizing.

         *   *   *

WE SHOULD NOT SCOFF AT THESE STORIES MERELY BECAUSE THEY ARE unbelievable. The important thing is not whether they were true or not. The important thing is the effect they produced. They lured men as nothing else could have done into one of the most awkward sections of the world, the great desert and the Sudan beyond. In the days before sea travel down the west coast of Africa—that is during almost all the medieval period—the only approach to the fabled gold of inner Africa was across the Sahara. These tall stories affected history. They opened a continent. They made North Africa's world fame. And—a point to remember— trans-Saharan trading was Africa's school for character.

"May Allah ever add to the prosperity of Ouargla," sang a medieval poet-trader.[5] "It is the paradise of the world, the open door

[5] Abou Yakoub Youcef ben Brahim ben Mennad of thirteenth century Ouargla, quoted by Motylinski in *Guerara* (Algiers, 1885).

to the mines of gold powder. . . . True riches are never acquired save by the intrepid man who crosses the spaces and fears neither the pathless desert, nor fatigue, nor the sun, nor the dark of sandstorms. By him who scorns the soft couch and flees contact with the women of the long veils who make men languid. By him who can brave all hardship."

SAHARAN HORRORS

THE SAHARAN CROSSING TOOK THREE MONTHS OR MORE IN EACH direction by caravan. These were months of such moral and bodily strain as men never elsewhere have undertaken voluntarily.

The complete, unearthly emptiness worked on men's minds. No one can be normal in mid-Sahara. The physical hardships hardly need talking about. The terrain was all bad. The worst was what is locally called *hamada,* a sort of chaos of rocky masses, gulches and loose stones. Crossing it on camel or on foot might be compared to traveling back and forth all day over the surface of a bombed city. But even the *erg,* the soft sand stretches of the picture books, were bad; up to the ankles at every step. The vertiginous Saharan mountain passes, dangerous with loose small stones, were much dreaded.

As a matter of course the caravan accepted the pangs of thirst. Water was often almost undrinkable, or even near-poisonous. Such as it was was always short. No caravan ever carried enough for its members to drink their fill. It would have been a mathematical impossibility when wells were many days apart, and often scanty. Food was insufficient and usually eaten cold, fuel lacking. Sand storms were a hideous ordeal. Eyes became half blinded with the glare. Lips and skin cracked. One might have seen men at resting places sewing up the cracks in their feet.

But of the dread features of Saharan travel the most feared was to be lost. Food and water supplies being at the minimum, a day's delay between oases or wells meant suffering, two or three days' delay meant death for everyone in the caravan. A very horrible death with a bestial prelude: the drinking of vile water from the stomachs of slaughtered camels, the drinking of urine of camels and humans, the sucking of blood drops from their own bitten finger tips.

The guide held their lives in his hand. The ability of guides was—and had to be—prodigious. They had developed the power to find their way across a pathless emptiness which seemingly possessed no recognizable features whatsoever. Some were said even to know the route by a sense of smell, by "smelling the sands." The very reliable reporter, Ibn-Batuta, tells of being guided by a man blind of one eye and not able to see well with the other. Another guide, made famous by Leo Africanus, was able, when struck blind en route, to lead his caravan for three days to safety. Furthermore desert guides possessed the art, called *kyafat el ater,* that is of recognizing varieties of men and animals by the traces they left upon the sand. Every footprint was potentially a personal or tribal autograph. An expert guide, after studying the depth and arrangement of camel prints and the character of their droppings, could announce, "These are the marks of harmless traders," or, "These are the tracks of bandits of the So-and-So tribe."

The truth of the above is vouched for. Other claims made for the detective ability of desert guides are farfetched. One questions, for instance, the statement that the footprints of a walking slave woman indicated whether she was or was not virginal. Also the anecdote about the two guides who quarreled over the sex of a camel whose marks they had noted, and subsequently discovered it was hermaphroditic. Burton said the last word when he told of a desert man who lost a pregnant camel and four years later recognized the footprints of its offspring!

*   *   *

WHEN A GUIDE RECOGNIZED RECENT BANDIT TRACKS—A QUITE POSsible feat to differentiate these from tracks made by a plodding caravan, because of indications of speed and light load—his caravan shuddered. Camels' mouths were tied lest their noise betray their owners. No fire was allowed. No smoking. In that brilliant emptiness visibility is very great. Small things seem magnified. "A bone seen from afar looks like a tower, a camel's dropping would seem to be a man," says El-Bekri.

If a caravan actually saw a group of men, supposedly dangerous, mad terror seized them. And with good reason. Especially if they were traveling northward and gold laden. Some swallowed their gold. Leo Africanus tells how the shrewder bandits learned of this trick, administered hot camel milk and shook the suspected traders pitilessly so that they were "constrained to vomit all they had in their stomachs to the point of ejecting their very entrails." Another traders' method of burying their treasure led to yet more painful consequences. Before starting the journey some men would cut holes in the fleshy parts of their bodies and insert gold lumps. This practice became known and led to unmerciful hackings and slashings of suspected persons.

*   *   *

BUT TO BE LOST WAS THE WORST OF ALL. THERE IS THE FAMILIAR story of the tombstone in the Azaouad section of the southern Sahara, on which is graven the tale of the rich man who bought for 10,000 ducats his poor companion's last cup of water. After the exchange both men died. The poor man presumably with a less prolonged agony and with the final satisfaction of being rich, if only for a little while. The place of their death was 200 miles from a well.

The record camel journey between wells, by the way, was performed in 1937 by an explorer traveling light. The distance was 489 miles. When I crossed the Sahara by automobile we traversed what is called "The Desert within a Desert" (Tanezrouft), a waterless stretch which took us a total of nearly twenty-four hours to cover. Camel caravans never attempted to cross the great oblong of the Tanezrouft. Caravans plod at the rate of fifteen miles a day or thereabouts. Swift camels, unloaded, can do four times as much at a pinch. To caravans a section of the route involving a week or more between wells was something to be attacked with the solemn formality of special prayer.

The trans-Saharan journey was martyrdom for trade's sake. And yet, despite its physical and mental torments, men pursued this business with increasing avidity. Ibn-Khaldoun (fourteenth century) has told us that twelve thousand loaded camels passed through one single desert crossroads town in one season. This, of course, represented only a fraction of the total desert trade by all routes. I have no figures on this total, nor any at all upon the period of which we are speaking, that is, the tenth century, when first the gorgeous possibilities of the gold trade gripped the adventurous spirits of North Africa in a big way.

THE KINGS OF THE GOLD LAND

IT IS SURPRISING TO FIND THAT IN THOSE DAYS THERE EXISTED A civilization, an old and elegant civilization, in that remote pocket of the world—the far shores of the Sahara.

The city which controlled the gold fields, the city of Gana, is described by Ibn-Khaldoun as having been "one of the greatest and most populous cities of the world." Presently I will tell something of its glittering beauty.

This capital was an eight days' march from the borders of the region where gold grew in crops "like carrots." This preposterous story, by the way, should not discount our belief in the general account of the place. It and similar incredible yarns were very probably deliberate protective inventions on the part of the inhabitants of the gold-producing country. It was no doubt the intention to build up a supernatural atmosphere which would be like a guard to their rich land and prevent depredations from their superstitious neighbors.

The place of the gold fields was known as Wangara. There is no Wangara now, and no one could indicate the boundaries of the Wangara that was. Strictly speaking it was a section three hundred by one hundred fifty miles in extent. But sometimes the name was applied to all the western Sudan gold lands. And sometimes it was taken to include the coastal Guinea country which gave its name to that old-time English coin. Wangara was, in effect, "the gold coast" long before Europeans dared sail down Africa's shores and give the name to the modern Gold Coast where they were literally made giddy by its blaze of gold. (Bowdich, 1817, complained of "the insupportable glare of the massive gold ornaments which glistened in every direction" under the tropic sun when he was received by the king at Ashanti.)

Wangara's gold drained into Gana. The king of Gana used a single immense nugget of pure gold as a hitching post for his horse. This lump of gold had a long career in Sudanese annals, nor—naturally—did it grow smaller with the years! El-Bekri calls it "as big as an enormous stone"; Edrisi claims it weighed thirty pounds. Centuries later its weight had reached the colossal figure of fifteen hundred pounds, according to the account of "a man of proven veracity," quoted by Ibn-Khaldoun.

Gana exists no longer. Its site has recently been fairly satisfactorily identified after preliminary guessing which covered half across inner Africa. Gana was in the western corner of the Sahara's lower shores, almost dead north of Bamako, modern capital of the French Sudan. The region was then less desertlike than it is now, according to indications given by medieval writers (Edrisi says Gana was "situated on both sides of a river") and according to the theory of modern geography.

Gana was at her peak in the days of which we are speaking. Her first kings had established themselves in the early part of the Christian Era: the assigned date is the fourth century. A dynasty had already reigned at Gana before the Hegira whose kings numbered either twenty-two or twenty.

Our knowledge of these rulers, called Kayamaga, meaning Kings of Gold, and the estimated number of them come to us respectively from two old histories of the Sudan: the *Tarikh es-Soudan* and the *Tarikh el-Fettach* (usually called "the *Fettassi*"). Both these tarikh, histories, were written by native Sudanese in Arabic. Each gives a résumé of Gana's origin based upon data now lost to us, and upon legends. Legend in the Sudan is not a historic prop to be taken lightly. A guild of court storytellers (*griots*) carried on the tale of the past with remarkable accuracy, and have been described by an outstanding authority, Maurice Delafosse, as "veritable living encyclopaedias."

*   *   *

THE KINGS OF GOLD AT GANA WERE NO GILDED SAVAGE NEGRO potentates, as the era, the place and the flamboyance of their gold hitching post might lead one to think.

In the first place they were not Negroes. They were men "of the white race, but we do not know whence they took their origin," as the *Tarikh es-Soudan* says. "What is very certain," says the *Fettassi*, "is that they were not Negroes."

THE JEWS OF THE SAHARA

THE NATURAL ASSUMPTION WOULD BE THAT THEY WERE OF THE indigenous Berber race of North Africa. In such case they could have been pagans, Jewish converts or Christians.

But there is an alternate and widely argued theory that Gana's white kings were of true Jewish blood descended from the Jews of Palestine.

It is undisputed that the Sahara sheltered many Jews. Nearly every large oasis had its Jewish colony. Some were refugees from European lands. Others had lived in the Sahara since shortly after the flight from Cyrene. The Jews' Saharan capital was at Tamentit, "The Perfection of the Eye," in the top part of the Sahara some five hundred miles dead south of Oran. The locality was a desert crossroads and they prospered exceedingly until their alien presence roused Moslem hatred to such a pitch that they were wiped out with the usual cruel thoroughness of all pogroms. Jewish heads fetched seven mithkals apiece (at that time and place the price can be estimated at equaling about $5.25 in current United States values). Their synagogue was squashed into the sands. This was back in the familiar date: 1492. The Jewish colony of Tamentit was then some twelve centuries old.

Tamentit was on the so-called "Palm Tree Road," an archipelago of oases stretching for nearly eight hundred miles across the western Sahara. Its name, I can assure the reader, is overkind. There is a lot of sand between those palms. But, compared to the Sahara's desolation, it is a wonder stretch.

Furthermore Tamentit was in the favored *foggara* region. The Saharan *foggaras* are a miracle—a twelve-hundred-mile-long system of underground canals by which water is collected and distributed through the oases. The canals are large enough for a small man to move about in them. Often they run along two hundred feet below the surface. As you travel across the *foggara* country you can see lines of little chimney-like vents marking the route of the canals. The human moles who did this colossal job of engineering with primitive tools and in a terrible climate performed a feat which has been compared to that of the pyramid builders.

Tamentit, the old-time Jewish capital, possessed alone a *foggara* system—main canal and branches—of about twenty-five miles.

In the South Sahara as well as at Tamentit there were Jewish colonists. The *Fettassi* notes that there had been a great Jewish settlement upon the Niger. At this settlement "seven princes, descending from the kings of the Jews" (the *Fettassi* gives the princes' names) operated big agricultural estates. They sank wells, some as much as a hundred yards deep (two hundred forearms in the text) by a special method of their own where through a process of firing clay with stone and ash and vegetable butter they attained a well lining having "the appearance of cast iron." I understand that traces of this colony have been recognized by archaeologists.

Jewish industry was a byword. It was forbidden to sell, and thus to lose from the locality, a Jewish slave. "The sale of Negro Jews is rigorously forbidden by the Sultan (at Katsena) because all are jewelers or tailors or useful workmen, or else brokers indispensable to commercial transactions; for black skin or white, the Jews have the same instincts and talent for languages and trade." This, from a manual about the slave trade published just a century ago.

They were especially sought after as builders and masons. El-Bekri, describing Sijilmassa, says ". . . the business of masons is reserved specially to the Jews." Examples of Jewish century-old masonry still stand and students have found at least one Hebrew inscription, a pathetic few words recording the death of a Saharan Jewess, by name Monispa, who died in childbirth "in the year of the Creation 5086" (1329 A.D.).

* * *

ARCHAEOLOGISTS, HOWEVER, ARE UNLIKELY TO WASTE TIME IN THE search for traces of that great Jewish empire in Africa which thrilled Jews in the Middle Ages. It was Eldad the Danite who told about it. He visited Kairouan with his story in the ninth century—a very early travelogist—and for hundreds of years thereafter Jews and others heatedly discussed his fantastic tale of inner Africa. He has been called "a faithless swindler." Perhaps he rather deserves the name of the first African novelist. The authors of *She* and *Atlantide* are his disciples.

His story is at any rate the earliest detailed account of deep

Africa, and a few of its elements match facts. Eldad was shipwrecked and after adventures found himself in "the land where
the gold is," an empire "seven months' journey across," and
owned by Hebrews. Eldad's narrative glows with wealthy circumstances: "glorious houses and castles," and with pleasant items:
"no flies, no fleas, no lice" . . . "no son dies in his father's lifetime, and they live to be 120" . . . "they are all equal" . . .
"they do not need to shut their doors at night." He mentions also
that whimsical and pious river of which other old writers also
tell, the Sembation, which runs six days a week and rests upon the
Sabbath.

"His words were sweeter than honey and the honeycomb" to
Jewish ears, and bitter to the Christians. It is the Jewish belief
that it was Eldad's boast about Hebrew greatness in inner Africa
which prompted the Christian counter-legend about Prester John.

GANA

THE WHITE KINGS OF GANA—WHETHER THEY WERE ORIGINALLY OF
Jewish blood or no—were an historical curiosity, and there is no
doubt that they *were* historic. They ruled in their black empire
for a total of forty-two or forty-four reigns: the original dynasty
which preceded the Hegira plus a second dynasty of twenty-two
more white kings.

The two Sudanese histories and the early Arabic geographers
tell us of the pompous elegance of their court. The palace possessed "apartments adorned with sculptures, paintings and glass
windows," according to Edrisi. When the king went forth on a
promenade his sumptuous procession was led by a troop of elephants and giraffes.

I excuse myself for quoting a droll item from the *Fettassi,*
indicating Gana's high standard of equine hygiene. It deals with
the royal stables of King Kanissa'ai who reigned at the end of
the seventh century. "He had 1000 horses. . . . None of these
animals slept except upon a carpet, nor was he tied except by a
silken rope round his neck and to his foot. Each of them had a
copper pot into which he urinated. (It is to be noted that copper
classed as a precious metal in that gold rich land; copper exchanged for two-thirds its weight in gold.) No drop of urine

should fall except into the receptacle, were it night or day. One would never see beneath these horses the slightest droppings. Each horse had three persons attached to his service and seated near him. One took charge of his food, the second of his drink, and the third took charge of his urine and droppings. Such is the recital made to me by the Sheikh Mohammed Tokado."

At nightfall every night the king of Gana served supper by torchlight to ten thousand of his subjects, he watching from a seat of red gold and the torch flames "lighting up all the space between sky and earth and illuminating the city."

* * *

IT IS SAD TO READ OF THE DOWNFALL OF THE WHITE KINGS OF GOLD. Certain of their Negro subjects rebelled and were victorious. They "decimated the aristocracy and put to death the king's children, even going so far as to open the stomachs of their women to take out and kill the foetus."

But Gana went on under its new black masters and under succeeding conquerors and was for long the controlling center of the western Sudan gold trade. As an idea, Gana—white Gana—was a long time dying. It figured on maps long after Gana itself was in ruins. And it probably was the inspiration for most of those legends about mysterious white groups in inner Africa which keep recurring. As late as the start of the last century an English map showed a section marked WHITE PEOPLE in the Sudan. Early European explorers were keen to find the lost brother race. Horneman in his farewell letter written in 1799, just as he was about to plunge into an African expedition from which he never returned, expressed a wistful longing to find "Christians and tailed men."

A TENTH CENTURY REVIVALIST

THE MOST IMPORTANT EXPORT FROM THE SUDAN DURING THE TENTH century was not gold, however, but a certain mulatto infant.

This mulatto infant was the child of a Tunisian trader and a Sudanese Negress. His father brought him back across the desert, little suspecting that his tawny half-breed offspring would turn into one of the most startling persons in North Africa's medieval history, would set the countryside aflame, and bring the brilliant Fatimite dynasty within a tissue paper of extinction.

The child grown to maturity became famous as "The Man on the Donkey." (His real name was Abou Yezid Moghith.) He was one of the greatest revivalists of all time. He roused the western part of North Africa to religious frenzy. His career as agitator against the Fatimites spread across three reigns: that of the original Mahdi, that of his son, and that of his grandson. During his last five years (942-947) he had become so powerful as a military leader that he made fools of the Fatimites and reduced their empire to one sole city, the strong place Mahdia.

His revolutionaries held all the rest. The Fatimites had sunk to such depths of discouragement that they had to cling to superstition: Had not the Mahdi prophesied, when he shot an arrow from Mahdia's walls many years before, that an enemy would one day advance as far as his arrow had landed, and then turn back? Poor comfort.

All this rebellious fury was roused by religious differences within the frame of Mohammedanism. Such pious exaltation was in the Berber character. The dispute again involved the memory of Ali, the revered ancestor of the Fatimites. The revivalist from the Sudan, half pagan by birth, became a fanatical Moslem of the type which believed that Ali was the worst of villains. His especial sect was that of the Noukkars, a particularly bloodthirsty variety of Kharijism. "Hate Ali!" was its motto. To kill all who disagreed was regarded as a duty and a privilege.

*   *   *

THE REVIVALIST WAS A PICTURESQUE LEADER. HE PREACHED A STERN morality, dressed in poor clothing and went about mounted, not like other great men, but upon a gray ass. Hence his soubriquet, "The Man on the Donkey." He called himself "The Sheikh of True Believers." One contemporary name for him was "Allah's Enemy." He was described as "a black and furious savage" by a Tunisian poet of the period.

District after district fell to him. Thirty thousand villages and hamlets were ruined. There were such massacres as to "fill the land with corpses." That fertile region, then called "The Granary of Ifrikia" (Tunisia) where a camel load of grain fetched only two dirhems (about thirty cents) was desolated. Its leading place, Béja, was ruined. The Man on the Donkey drove out its people, destroyed its bazaar and fine houses, pillaged the dwellings and even the tombs, according to the poet.

Tunis, Kairouan, Sousse gave up. At Sousse "but a few escaped either death or shocking mutilation." The Fatimite army was cut to pieces. The second Fatimite ruler, El Caim, fled with a few survivors and shut himself up behind Mahdia's great gates. Inside the besieged city El Caim, himself, died. Its people ate the corpses of fallen soldiers.

DEATH OF THE MAN ON THE DONKEY

BUT WITH SUCCESS THE EFFORT OF THE REVIVALIST SLACKENED. HE grew luxurious and lax, proudly mounted a prancing horse and put on silk raiment. And, in the words of the Chronicle of Abou Zakaria, "Allah's Enemy did not pass a night without having near him four virgin girls." His army disintegrated, preferring expeditions of pillage to the dull business of besieging the Fatimites in Mahdia.

So the third Fatimite ruler, Ismail, won the surname of el-Mansur, the Victorious, by ridding the land of the bugbear. The rebel army was defeated, "the number of their heads brought back to Kairouan for the children to use as toys and footballs mounted to 10,000," Ibn-Khaldoun assures us.

The Man on the Donkey was captured, badly wounded. The Fatimite, Ismail-el-Mansur, very naturally longed to enjoy the spectacle of the death of his ancestral enemy by some prolonged process of torture. To this end doctors tended the prisoner and then an attempt was made to skin him alive. "But," says the Chronicle of Abou Zakaria, "when they arrived at his navel Allah's Enemy expired." The Fatimite then conceived a form of posthumous torture, the degradation of his enemy's dignity after death. The skin of the great revivalist was stuffed with straw, put in a cage along with two monkeys trained to play with it, and paraded through the streets of Kairouan.

LIVE FISH

THE GRANDIOSE PLAN OF THE FATIMITES HAD BEEN DELAYED BY THE Man on the Donkey, but was not abandoned.

The subjugation of all western North Africa was the necessary first step in the conquest of the continent's top, from the Atlantic to the Red Sea. The early days of the first Fatimite had seen the disintegration of two of the four little kingdoms of the West: that of the Aghlabites of Tunisia, and that of the pious folk of Tiaret. The two which remained, that of Sijilmassa and that of the Idrisites of Fez, were slower to extinguish.

Sijilmassa was repeatedly conquered, and repeatedly members of the old royal family replaced themselves in power. Finally in 958 the brilliant Fatimite general, Jauhar, removed the Sijilmassa king from his throne and shipped him to Kairouan.

The Idrisites of Fez had already been wobbly before the arrival of the Fatimites. The sixth of the line named Yahya had created a damaging scandal. He became love crazy for a Jewish girl, Hannah, and committed the unforgivable indiscretion— from the Moslem point of view—of chasing her into the woman's part of the public baths. This shocked the whole population of Fez. He was driven away and died that same night, presumably by violence. His aggrieved father-in-law, also of the Idris family which was enormous—their family tree being a veritable jungle— took over power.

Another Yahya of the Idris family was ruler of Fez when the Fatimites came upon the scene. He abdicated. Years later this unfortunate—of the third generation in direct line from the sainted Moulay Idris, founder of Fez—died of starvation while trying to make his way to throw in his lot with the Fatimites, then besieged in Mahdia by the Man on the Donkey, that bitter enemy of Ali, the mutual ancestor of both Idrisites and Fatimites.

Other Idrisites however carried on the struggle against the Fatimites in Fez and elsewhere. General Jauhar sent back to Kairouan as part of his rebel "bag" the children of brave Hamza, the Idrisite.

Along with the royal prisoners from Sijilmassa and Fez another souvenir also reached the Fatimite ruler. It was a fish from the

Atlantic Ocean, packed in a jar of water and still living. It was intended to show the Fatimite in a picturesque manner the extent of his empire.

Now a live fish is notoriously a slippery object and difficult to hold on to. There was unintentional symbolism in the gift. The Fatimite and his representatives and assignees had continuous difficulty in keeping possession of the alleged conquests in the West.

A decade later another Fatimite general, Bologguin, son of Ziri, had to fight a hard campaign against further revolts and fought with such brilliance that he won the title of "Father of Victories," plus a reward of extraordinary importance, as we shall see.

ON TO EGYPT*

THE GREAT MOMENT of which the FATIMITES HAD DREAMED FOR four generations was very close. Soon Fatimite majesty would move to a noble setting. The Fatimites were at last the conquerors of Egypt. A new capital waited by the Nile.

The Mahdi, the first of the Fatimites, had passed across Egypt on his way to establish himself in the West. He had longed to possess this lush country and had bequeathed the longing to his descendants.

Egypt when the Mahdi saw it was at the climax of a period of special and short-lived gorgeousness. The brief dynasty of the Talunids had just been wiped out. Smoke was still rising from the marvelous Talunid residential city of Kitai, alongside the then capital of Fostat, burnt to the ground when the Talunids fell. Kitai had been a place of magic wonder, with its gardens of cunningly laid out flower beds which spelt words and formed pictures, with its golden palace, and its sleeping place where the royal bed, moored with silken cords, floated upon a lake of quicksilver, and a tame *blue-eyed* lion guarded the king while he slept.

So should a king live! the Mahdi must have thought, as he slunk through Egypt, a disguised fugitive with no kingly baggage but his dreams.

As Fatimite power strengthened in the West the sensuous side

of the Mahdi hankered for the Nile's green loveliness, his orien-
tal greed thrilled at the thought of Egypt's riches, he contrasted
Egypt with the semi-barbarism and sun-baked discomfort of his
Tunisian hills and deserts, with the bleak fortress-capital of
Mahdia. The ambitious side of him, moreover, recognized Egypt
as the potential center of the Moslem world, whereas he, in the
West, was on the world's outskirts.

*   *   *

EXPEDITION AFTER EXPEDITION CROSSED THE TOP OF AFRICA IN THE
Fatimite effort to capture Egypt (913-915; 919-920; 935-936).
Alexandria fell into Fatimite hands and was wrenched away
again. Repeatedly the caliph's men pushed back Fatimite armies
and ships. Egypt's traditional defender, "General Plague," helped
protect the country from the invader. The Mahdi died disappointed, but his dream lived on.

At last Jauhar, having accomplished those conquests in the
West which he symbolized by the gift of live fish, spoke to his
master, the fourth of the Fatimite line, El-Moizz Li-Din Allah
(meaning He who Exalts Allah's Religion).

Said Jauhar in a long speech, rehearsed word for word by
Leo Africanus, "Master, I swear and promise that I . . . will
perform the same (in the East) and give you Egypt, Syria and
Arabia . . . and put you back upon the antique throne of your
magnanimous ancestors and the noble progenitors of your illustrious blood!" (meaning Ali, the alleged forefather of the Fatimite line). Thus did the Fatimites justify a series of unprovoked
attacks and a final conquest of a harmless neighbor.

*   *   *

BOTH MEN KNEW EGYPT TO BE THEN ESPECIALLY FEEBLE.

Her people, a mixed population, demoralized by repeated conquests, had formed the national habit of passing unprotestingl
from one master to another like some lovely, lethargic loos
woman. Following the Mahdi's passage through the country sixty
five years before, she had accepted an assortment of rulers. After
the Talunids she had endured a series of about a dozen governor
Then had come the short independent dynasty of the Ikshid
When its founder died his sons, a pair of weak fellows, succeede
him—in name only. Egypt was in reality ruled by one of the odde
personages ever recorded.

For twenty-two years (946-968) a black eunuch Abyssinian ex-lave ran the country. He was Abu-al-Misk-Kafur (Musky Camphor). He deserves a chapter to himself in any book about The Famous Negroes of History. He appears as the dusky major-domo's ideal. He worked into the control of the household of a king. When his master died he completely dominated the two young masters, atrophied into inertia by their own laziness and his competence. Upon the death of the second, "Camphor" became in name what he had been all along in fact. He became virtual king of Egypt (965-968)—regent, so called.

Now that "Camphor" was dead the country was at a loose end under the supposed rulership of a little boy of the feeble royal family. Secret messages reached the Fatimites which indicated that Egypt was practically waiting to be conquered and exploited. In this latter respect the prospect was enticing. It was known that old tombs had recently been dug out which contained "marvellously wrought figures of men, women and children, having eyes of precious stones and faces of gold and silver." The wealth of the Pharaohs was ready to be tapped.

Moizz and his general, Jauhar, decided that the great—and fourth Fatimite expedition against Egypt was due. Jauhar left Tunisia in 969.

* * *

JAUHAR'S NAME MEANT "JEWEL." IT HAD BEEN A FRIVOLOUS NAME patronizingly hung to a good slave boy. General Jauhar deserved it in all earnestness. His racial origin is disputed. Some call him Greek or Roman; Leo Africanus thought him Slavonic; Ibn-Khaldoun, a Sicilian. Jauhar, himself, is reported to have described himself as "Jauhar-el-Kateb (Jewel, the Penman or Secretary), coming from Sicily," in the original inscription of the Cairo great mosque, which he erected—El-Azhar (The Resplendent), now the home of the largest Moslem university in the world.

Whatever Jauhar's race, there is no doubt he was born a slave. Such careers as his and that of "Camphor," plus those of many other noted old-time slaves, force us to reconsider our usual notion of slavery. In that place and period neither slavery nor castration were an insuperable obstacle. (Jauhar was not a eunuch; many generals and admirals of the period, however, were; "Camphor" was.)

Jauhar, the ex-slave, was one of the great world figures of his
times. He subdued all North Africa from the Atlantic to the Red
Sea, plus part of Asia, and he founded a great capital, Cairo.

THE BIRTH OF CAIRO

JAUHAR'S VICTORY IN EGYPT WAS A MATTER OF DAYS—HOURS EVEN
Jauhar, after marching triumphantly into Fostat, the capital, set
himself the immediate task of building a new royal city for the
reception of his master, Moizz, who was expected to move into
Egypt as soon as he could wind up his affairs in the West. Jauhar
chose a site a little to the north of Fostat. His choice was accord
ing to tradition. That stretch of country by the Nile had at
tracted the great ones of the earth for thousands of years. Within
a few miles' radius had stood Heliopolis, Memphis, Babylon-in
Egypt (so called), Fostat, Kitai, the beautiful and short lived; and
now came Cairo. Cairo was called by its founder after the Arabic
name for Mars, "Kahir," from which by mispronunciation we
derived Cairo.

Cairo endured and grew great. Presently it possessed twenty
thousand skyscrapers five or six stories tall. By the fifteenth cen
tury it had got so enormous that a certain German enthusias
felt justified in reporting that it had twelve thousand streets with
twelve thousand houses in each street! The more reliable Leo
Africanus in the sixteenth century calls it "the great and marvel
lous city" and asserts that "in all the parts of the earth there is no
to be found a city which is equal to this one in grandeur." Today
Cairo is the biggest Moslem city in the world, and the biggest
town of any kind in all the African continent.

THE GREAT AFRICAN ROAD

MOIZZ WAS IMPATIENT TO GO TO HIS NEW LAND—NOT ON A VISIT OF
triumphant inspection, but to live there for the rest of his life and
his descendants after him.

But before he went he had a great present to give away. The
whole west corner of North Africa, no less. His choice fell upon
Bolloguin, the Berber, the fighting son of a fighting father. Ziri
the father, had been a man among men, so handsome that he

became the subject of a local proverb, so strong that at ten he was like a grown man of twenty. He had been a useful fighter for the Fatimites. Bologguin, his son, had just performed feats of war which won him the title, Father of Victories.

Moizz called him to Kairouan and placed the country from the Atlantic to beyond Tunisia in his hands. It was a fine royal gesture, only marred in its complete munificence by the fact that Moizz carried away with him the palace furniture.

It was the start of the Zirite dynasty (972-1148), at first ruling under Fatimite authority, later quite independent.

A little distance south of Kairouan, at Sfax, Moizz bade his beneficiary good-by, dressed him in "a magnificent garment of honor," gave him "the handsomest of his own horses" and bade him go back to Kairouan and install himself in the former Fatimite palace. It must have been a wonderful moment for Bologguin, the Zirite, and it is a pity to have to note that later on his progeny were disloyal to the Fatimites.

* * *

It took six months for Moizz, traveling in leisurely luxury, to get from his old home in Tunisia to his new home in Egypt. His caravan followed the great West-East Road across the top of Africa, the longest and oldest road of the continent (if we except the Nile Valley). It was a road over which, or parts of which, History's personages passed from the days of Hercules to the days of Rommel and Montgomery.

Moizz appears to have been the first individual actually to survey it as an artery of a country which he personally owned in its entirety. His ancestor, the Mahdi, rode over it going west to make the family fortunes. Now the fortunes were made after four generations of struggle, and all that Moizz looked upon en route was his.

* * *

Tripoli, the first important station on the journey, was entrusted by Moizz to a Berber governor. It was a fair city, famed in those days for its dazzling whiteness. It was one of the few beauty spots along a route as a whole so arid, bleak and desert-like that it had been necessary to sink wells in advance of the Fatimite drive upon Egypt.

The whole stretch beyond Tripoli was then often called Barca,

after the name of the ancient city. Barca, the city, was described
as a horrid place by medieval geographers. It had the nickname
of "The Red" and you could recognize a traveling Barca man
anywhere because his clothes and even his skin were dyed from
contact with Barca's red earth and ruddy winds. At Barca the
joy of Moizz's triumphant journey was clouded by sorrow. "He
lost his favorite poet, Mohammed-ibn-Hani, the Andalusian,'
says Ibn-Khaldoun, "he being found assassinated upon the sea
shore." After a thousand years we wonder, picture how perhaps
an indignant courtier, lampooned by the Andalusian, got his
revenge.

Passing towns where the soldiers of his ancestors, fighting to
ward Egypt, had built fortresses, towns they had angrily sacked
when driven back during their several retreats, Moizz must have
rejoiced that—in so far as was possible—he had arranged that
these ancestors should participate in the final victory. He piously
carried all the corpses of the direct Fatimite line along with him
as he moved into the land they had longed for and failed to con
quer. Three generations came with him in coffins.

*   *   *

MOIZZ REACHED ALEXANDRIA IN MAY 973. HE HAD TRAVELED OVER
pretty much the same route as that of which we heard so much
nearly a millennium later during World War II and had seen
the sites of many familiar wartime places: El-Agheila, Agedabia
Tobruk, Sidi Barrani, Alamein and the rest. Many of these are
mentioned in medieval Arabic geography. "Toburg" (Tobruk)
Es-Solloum (Salum) and others appear in an account given by
El-Bekri, who wrote very shortly after the day of Moizz, of the
sea route from Mahdia to Alexandria. Along with these recog
nizable names he lists some fancily designated localities, such a
"The Port of the Olive Tree," "The Island of the Tamarisk,"
"The Jewry," "The Port of Glass."

*   *   *

A MONTH LATER ON JUNE 10, MOIZZ WAS AT CAIRO, HIS NEW RESI
dence. He kissed the ground and thanked Allah. The dead in
their coffins—his father, grandfather and great-grandfather, the
Mahdi—led the procession into the city.

THE MYSTIC CHARM OF THE FATIMITES

THE FATIMITE CONQUEST OF EGYPT WAS SUCCESSFUL, WHICH MANY are not. Perhaps the Fatimite success was because it had been a conquest motivated by love and respect for the place conquered. The Fatimites moved into Egypt with whole-souled enthusiasm. They lived there as kings for two hundred years. They had already reigned in the West for sixty-odd years. It was therefore a dynasty of exceptional strength and tenacity. It is true that under the luxury of Egypt its kings petered out into feebleness or eccentricity, but as a whole the Fatimites stand out in medieval—or any other—history as a tremendous family. They were a notable exception to the rule set up by Ibn-Khaldoun that the average dynasty fades out after three generations.

There was moreover a mystic potency about the Fatimites. They were not only a dynasty but also a cult. After their temporal power had faded enthusiastic admirers looked for their return and kept looking for centuries. There were several Fatimite pretenders in Egypt. A *soi-disant* Fatimite mahdi set up in Morocco in the thirteenth century, another in the seventeenth. As far as the Atlantic and in the deep Sahara men remembered the Fatimites and talked and fought about the so-called "Awaited Fatimite."

It is odd that this remarkable royal house, the only dynasty to master the whole of Mediterranean Africa under a single individual with headquarters in Africa, should have carried the name of a woman—women playing so small a part in African affairs. To contemporaries they were sometimes known as Obeidites (after the Mahdi's given name) or Shiites (after their religious classification) or as Alids, after Ali, but usage has firmly named them Fatimites, giving them the exclusive claim to Fatima's name, albeit her descendants and alleged descendants pepper the pages of African history. This last fact—the wide distribution of her descendants—is odd in view of the solemn conviction in Moslem circles that Fatima was "a perpetual virgin." Burton in his account of the pilgrimage to Mecca tells of the prayer at Fatima's tomb, adding "she is called Al-Batul, the Virgin, a title given by Eastern Christians to the Mother of our Lord.

The perpetual virginity of Fatima even after motherhood is a
point of orthodoxy in Islam." In the case of Fatima I suppose that
the phrase merely infers a pretty oriental compliment to her
continued feminine charms.

THE DAYS OF PLENTY

IN THE EARLY DAYS AFTER THE FATIMITE ARRIVAL IN EGYPT ALL
North Africa did very well. Egypt had not been so brilliant since
the days of the Pharaohs and Ptolemies. Western North Africa
under the Zirites prospered amazingly.

In the West trade boomed. The ports dependent upon Kairouan
took in eight thousand mithkals (equaling some quarter of a million United States dollars) a year in customs, plus heavy local
dues on goods handled incoming and outgoing. At Sousse they
made gold thread which fetched double its weight in gold money.
Agriculture flourished. Camels staggered across Tunisia in thousands, loaded with grain. Zirite military operations were victorious. Fez and all Morocco were subdued—for a little while.

The city of Algiers made its historic debut so far as the Middle
Ages were concerned, using the site of a town of antiquity whose
"images of various animals perfectly fashioned" (i.e. Roman sculpture) still survived and shocked Moslem eyes which did not favor
such representations. The city's name was El-Jezair, The Islands,
later corrupted to Algiers.

A fairy tale splendor maintained. The fourth Zirite, whose
name, Moizz, is confusingly repetitive of that of the Fatimite conqueror of Egypt, gave festivals and held funeral ceremonies that
make one blink. His sister's marriage and trousseau cost a million
gold pieces. His mother's funeral a hundred thousand. Royal
coffins were made of wood imported from India and carpentered
with gold nails. The father of Moizz gave away a single present
consisting of "thirty loads (camel or donkey not stated) of silver,
and eighty bales of rich cloth."

TWELVE THOUSAND DRESSES

AT A TIME WHEN THE RELATIVELY UNSOPHISTICATED WEST COULD
and did display such glittering pomp it is obvious that rich Egypt

would show magnificence and prancing luxury. The Fatimites in the early days after their removal to Egypt were on top of the Moslem world, and the Moslem world in those days was so vast that a traveler might march for ten months from west to east without setting foot outside the land of Allah. All the North African part of this stretch—plus a considerable section of the Asiatic part—was under Fatimite patronage.

The royal Fatimite was something to see when he went forth on a great Mohammedan religious fete day, or at the Nile festival.

His family had from the days of the Mahdi understood the king business. It was the Mahdi's son who introduced the famous royal umbrella—a complete novelty to western Africa. It became the special mark and insignia of Fatimite majesty and has been imitated by Moslem kings into modern days. Arabic records describe the Fatimite umbrella in lengthy detail. I should say umbrellas, for the Fatimite umbrella obligatorily matched the Fatimite costume, and the Fatimite had different costumes for various occasions. For the grandest festivals white—the particular Fatimite color, the color of their personal standard for war and for the Pilgrimage. For other ceremonies, the costume was sometimes red, sometimes gold tinted.

This presentation of the royal person in an ensemble setting was an impressive bit of showmanship. A rebel brought before Moizz, the conqueror of Egypt, said, "I thought I was a lost man: the whole world was red!" Moizz had received the man in "a room hung with red tapestry, himself seated upon a couch whose ivory feet had been dyed red, he dressed in a red costume with a red cap on his head."

The great and gorgeous umbrella with a top like a golden, jewel-studded pomegranate took four men to raise. It was held over the royal head by a prince of high rank, Fatimite and prince both on horseback. When he rode forth beneath its shadow the Fatimite was a symbol to his people. Our parades and processions of today—bunting and painted wood and bits of cut-up paper— seem poor in comparison to the Fatimites' gold and brocade and real jewels.

*   *   *

FROM THE CROWDING DETAIL OF FATIMITE MAGNIFICENCE: EMER- alds by the bushel, literally, gold and silver furnishings, palace banquets where a single sweet course weighed nearly two thousand pounds, horses with "collars of gold and garlands of amber and gold, and silver rings above their fetlocks"; I choose one item which—like some single bone of a prehistoric beast—reveals the whole. The item in question shows the wealth and extravagance of the Fatimite court better than a page-long list. It is that one of the daughters of Moizz left at her death twelve thousand dresses!

THE MARKET OF TWO WORLDS

SUCH POMP COST A GREAT DEAL OF MONEY. BUT EGYPT WAS TRADITIONALLY rich. A glance at the map tells one of the main reasons why. The plan of the continents made her a highway bridging the gap between two worlds. In those days there was no long sea route to India round the Cape of Good Hope, nor anything corresponding with the modern Suez Canal. Alexandria was a hyphen between West and East where goods from Europe and goods from India and Arabia and the African east coast changed hands.

From Alexandria eastward it was a rude journey. According to Macrizi it was customary to go up the Nile as far as Kous, near Luxor. There, travelers—traders or Mecca pilgrims—mounted camels for a seventeen days' journey to Aidab on the Red Sea, along a road where "no water is to be found for three, and once for four days." Aidab is not on modern maps. It is said to be the same as antique Berenice. At this port pilgrims embarked for Jidda in Arabia. To this port came merchant ships from India, Arabia and Abyssinia. Aidab itself was wealthy but desolate. It was a region devoid of vegetation. All provisions, even water, were imported. But its people grew immensely rich by renting camels to merchants and selling passages on ships to pilgrims.

The hospitality of Aidab was a disgrace. The local people, Bejas, gouged strangers mercilessly. They packed travelers into their ships "loaded one above the other" so that many were literally squashed to death. They sneaked after persons to whom they had rented camels, watched them die of thirst and grabbed their property. They were, in short, in Macrizi's words, "brutes . . .

with no religion and no understanding"—except how to exploit men far from home in a barren desert.

They disgusted the famed Jewish traveler of the Fatimite period, Benjamin of Tudela (Spain), who came to Egypt from the east, after shipping from Aden (which sun-baked spot, boasting a single tree as a landmark, he oddly confused with Eden!) Benjamin went to Assuan on the Nile after a twenty-day journey across the desert from the Red Sea. He reports "people like animals who have not the intelligence of ordinary men, go about naked and cohabit with their sisters and anyone they can find." He tells how the men of Assuan would raid their land, trapping them by the bait of dried grapes and figs and catching them to sell into slavery in Egypt.

Yet, despite its uncouth dangers, the desert tracks between the Nile and the Red Sea were "peopled by caravans of merchants going and coming with loads of spices and drugs, pepper and cinnamon. . . ."

*   *   *

To Egypt the profit from this trade and traffic was enormous—transit fees, personal taxes, incidental expenditure of travelers. Alexandria was a bustling Babel. Traders from all Christendom were there, traders from the east, traders from eastern and inner Africa. A traveler of the Fatimite period listed twenty-eight different Christian states represented in Alexandria. These several Christian traders had premises of their own (*fondouks*) with warehouses, residential quarters, and even church or chapel.

The markets of Alexandria and Cairo offered everything which the medieval world possessed from raw material to exotic marvels, from wood and iron, English tin and copper to Circassian boy and girl slaves—a luxury item. At Cairo there were for sale "3,300 different kinds of goods, mostly spices and medicines," reported a Jewish traveler. "There is nothing in the world that you do not find in the *fondouks* of Cairo, even the smallest things."

A little passage by Leo Africanus, written sometime after the Fatimite period but in all probability applying equally well to that luxurious age, has a sting in its tail, which shows that competitive exporters long ago learned their arts and tricks: "There are shops in Cairo where they sell the richest and noblest cloth that is made in Italy—such as cloth of gold, velvet, damask, satin,

taffeta and others—and I can affirm never having seen—*there,
where they are made* (meaning in Italy)—anything to approach
them in perfection and *naïveté."* By this last word, so given in the
old French version of Leo, we must understand, I think, grace and
purity.

THE PRANKS OF TWO DESPOTS—HAKIM

SOME PASSAGES IN HISTORY, LIKE SOME PASSAGES IN AN INDIVIDUAL
life, entail unpredictably mighty consequences. In Egypt in the
days of the sixth Fatimite (the third to rule in Egypt) there began a period of about a third of a century during which despots'
pranks were to cost not only North Africa but the world very
dear. Rarely has royal insouciance produced such widespread
property damage and led directly or indirectly to so many deaths
and so much misery as did the two carelessly spiteful actions
performed by two Fatimite rulers in the first half of the eleventh
century.

*   *   *

HAKIM WAS THE GRANDSON OF MOIZZ, CONQUEROR OF EGYPT. HE
was the son of a wise father and a Christian (Russian) mother.
He was one of the world's notable madmen. His follies ranged
from bits of local tyranny—the killing of all dogs in the street,
the complete imprisonment of all women in their homes, even
forbidding them to take air on the roofs, humiliations of Christians and Jews, the imposition of a dry law and the destruction
of all grapevines, the stopping of all public amusements—to vaster
crimes, such as setting fire to the old city of Fostat adjacent to
Cairo. Fostat was a densely packed place with very large houses
of seven to fourteen stories, what we would call apartment houses.
Some were the homes of as many as three hundred fifty persons.
There is no need to insist upon the horrors attendant on Hakim's
act.

Also excessively disgusting to the major part of his people was
the notion promulgated by Hakim that he was the incarnation of
God. The notion was, however, taken up by a new Moslem sect,
the Druses. The Druses still survive in Lebanon, and are said
still to cherish and revere Hakim.

*   *   *

But all this cruel or mad behavior did only local damage. Hakim's great coup of villainy, in so far as world-wide reaction was concerned, was the deliberate defilement of Christendom's most holy spot on earth, the supposed site of Christ's tomb at Jerusalem. Hakim not only ordered the demolition of the Church of the Holy Sepulcher, but caused the very rock tomb itself to be broken up into rubble. After his vandalism only a few projecting angles of rock remained and still remain as a tragic souvenir for the pious.

Hakim's act supplied a war cry for the Crusades. It is true that after his death the Christian buildings were rebuilt. But the Christians had seen that this sacred locality could be defiled at a Moslem whim and feared that it might be defiled again. To prevent repetition of such defilement became a Crusading slogan. Hakim's prank was an instrument in producing the deaths of uncountable Christians.

A peculiarly disgusting element in the affair was that Hakim at the moment had a Christian vizier and that it was this Christian who was obliged to sign the decree for the demolition of his Saviour's tomb and the edifice which marked the spot. Nor did this craven conduct save the poor man. A year later he was killed. Such employment of Christian functionaries at the Egyptian court was not unusual. In the reign of Hakim's father another Christian, by name Jesus, was vizier. And, as has been mentioned, Hakim's mother was a Christian.

THE PRANKS OF TWO DESPOTS— MOSTANSIR

A third of a century after Hakim's act of bigotry the next Fatimite ruler but one, by name Mostansir, gave vent to his spite in such fashion as almost to ruin the western side of North Africa.

His spite was justified. The West had hurt his feelings most bitterly. He desired to get even. He did.

It will be remembered that when Moizz moved his headquarters from Tunisia to Egypt he practically made a free gift of the western lands from the Atlantic to near Tripoli to his loyal servitor, Bologguin, son of Ziri, who became the first of the Zirite dynasty.

The Fatimite control over their Zirite protégés had been largely a mystic and a religious matter. The name of the Fatimite of the day was to be regularly mentioned in prayers, that form of Mohammedanism which the Fatimites represented (Shiism) was to be the state religion.

The arrangement was a generous one to the Zirites. But nevertheless it did not continue to appeal to them. A man seldom gives loyalty to another for the mere reason that his ancestor received benefits from a long-dead member of the other man's family.

By the time of Moizz, the Zirite, that munificent spender who buried his mother so expensively, there was grave disloyalty in the Zirite heart. At an even earlier date an offshoot of the Zirite family had broken away not only from Zirite control but also from the spiritual authority of the Fatimite overlords, setting up for himself as the founder of a new and anti-Shiite dynasty, whose capital eventually was at Bougie (Algeria). It was from the name of Bougie, by the way, that the French word for "candle" derives, grease being shipped from that port to Europe in the Middle Ages.

When the Zirites rudely repudiated his religious ascendancy Mostansir, the Fatimite, was pained in his tenderest spot. His noble descent from Ali, his own function as a sort of Moslem pope, was scorned by the heritor of a man whose fortunes the Fatimites had made. And he seemed powerless to get even. Between Mostansir and the Zirites lay wastes and deserts. A military campaign to resubdue the West was out of the question. The reverse, it was true, had been accomplished. But it was one thing to capture a squashy Egypt with a fighting Berber army; quite another to send the motley and disunited gang of Egypt's troops against the Berbers.

The Egyptian army was at the moment conducting a sort of battle royal amongst itself. Its various elements: Berbers, Turks and Sudanese Negroes fought one another and killed one another by the thousands. The black troops had become strong and dangerous. The use of Negro soldiers, who, being of foreign slave origin, were presumed to be less likely to form cliques against their royal master than free soldiers locally born, was an old Fatimite habit, dating back to the days when they fought The Man on the Donkey. Apparently this habit had been carried to excess. The black guards in Egypt had grown from a group of docile fighting animals into a haughty unit.

It was comprehensible. The Fatimite ruler, Mostansir, was himself mothered by a black ex-slave. During his minority this competent Negress, aided by the Jew who had been her original master before she passed into the royal harem, ran Egypt. Naturally the other Negroes of the country and, outstandingly the Sudanese guard, had gained confidence and power.

Mostansir, grown to manhood, was confronted with a very vexing problem. An insolent protégé in the West. A home army in turmoil. He could not reconquer the West; he could only punish it cruelly.

It was his vizier who showed him the way. It happened that Egypt was at the time plagued by the turbulent misbehavior of a great body of Arab nomads whose ancestors an earlier Fatimite had very injudiciously imported into the country and attempted to intern there. The undisciplined ways of these Arabs spread devastation in their "location" up river, on the east bank of the Nile. Said the vizier to Mostansir (Ibn-Khaldoun quotes his speech at length; I give a résumé), "Let us ship these people to the west. We shall thus get rid of a nuisance at home and they will gravely damage and probably ruin the rebellious Zirite."

Mostansir was tickled by the suggestion. He sent his vizier to broach the matter to the nomads with the message, "I make you a present of western North Africa and of the kingdom of Moizz, the Zirite, a slave who has rebelled. From now on you will live there in plenty!" Simultaneously he dispatched a sinister letter to the Zirite: "I send you swift riders and intrepid men. Let Fate decide!"

A body of Arabs were off with a bound. They took and plundered Barca near the Egyptian borders. So attractive was the account which they sent back to the rest of their tribesmen on the Nile that "the slothful ones hastened to buy permission to cross the river and, since each favor (passport) cost a gold piece per head, the Egyptian government made a good profit."

THE SECOND ARAB INVASION

THE EPISODE HAD STARTED IN A JOCULAR MANNER. ITS FINISH WAS tragic. The misery which so soon came upon Mostansir's homeland might seem poetic justice. A few years after Mostansir had so cynically ordered this ruffianly gang into the West, into the country where his family fortunes had been built up, and had heard how they fell upon it "like a cloud of locusts, spoiling or destroying all that was in their path," Egypt knew such famine as this hungry world of ours seldom experiences. Starving Cairo lost all decency. People fished with hook and line from high house windows, caught up men and women from the street, hauled them up, killed, cooked and ate them. Human flesh was sold openly like butcher's meat. Seven years of famine. Then pestilence came. Apartment houses, homes of hundreds, were emptied of life in a night. When plague came to Egypt in those days of primitive hygiene royalty had no safeguard. Mostansir's predecessor had died of an earlier plague. Mostansir escaped and lived to accomplish a phenomenally long reign—fifty-nine years, said to be the longest of any Moslem ruler.

*   *   *

THE RABBLE WHICH IN HIS SPITE AND WEAKNESS HE HAD SENT TO DO his avenging for him swept westward. Doom rode across Africa. The Arabs rode ten deep "half the former inhabitants of Arabia Deserta," Leo Africanus would have it. More conservatively estimated at forty thousand warriors with women and children by countless thousands.

They were Arabs of a far different sort from the exaltedly pious knights of the days of Sidi Okba. Though Moslems, they had no more true piety than a column of driver ants, and no more respect for property. Even after the heat of fighting was over, they wantonly destroyed crops, chopped down trees and burnt off fields. Agriculture was unknown to them, outside their nomad mentality. The plow was a shameful implement to their eyes. When they had eaten their full off someone else's labors they destroyed the rest with irresponsible cruelty. Man, to their idea, was made to wander with his flock. Never to settle in houses. Never to plant gardens and fruit trees.

The results were heartbreaking. The work of generations of husbandmen was lost. The magnificent olive forests which covered much of Tunisia hacked down. Figs and vines and dates destroyed.

The population was not organized for defense. Moizz, the extravagant Zirite, had spent too much thought on luxurious living and was soft and a poor leader. He tried at first to make friends with the invaders, using a favorite Oriental method and offering his daughter in marriage to one of the Arab chiefs. It did no good. A battle followed near Gabès. Moizz was badly beaten. He shut himself up inside Kairouan and the frightened folk of the countryside piled in after him.

The Arabs ravaged the open country, captured minor cities, and shared amongst themselves the pillaging of the whole stretch from the Egyptian borders through Tunisia and eastern Algeria. Moizz, still intriguing with the enemy and still believing in his old scheme of placating the invaders with girls, married three more daughters to Arab chiefs. In exchange he got a safe conduct to the seacoast and fled by ship to Tunis. Kairouan, abandoned by its king, gave up to the Arabs. They pillaged the shops, tore down the public edifices, ruined the private houses. Fair Kairouan was a ruin.

*   *   *

FOR A TIME EVERYTHING BELONGED TO THE ARAB INVADERS, TOWN and country alike. But they had no notion of government. The townsfolk, having got back their wind, were able to rise and put the Arabs out of their cities. The open country could not be protected. There was a situation recalling the early colonist days in America when the redskins plagued and pounced and made farming a dangerous and almost impossible adventure. The farmers of Africa, victims of Arab surprise attacks, finished by paying tribute to be allowed to work their fields. The exploitation of isolated country at a distance from cities was altogether abandoned.

*   *   *

THE ABOVE PITIABLE STORY IS FROM THE PAGES OF IBN-KHALDOUN, writing some centuries later. There exists also an almost contemporaneous account of the situation in the reports of Edrisi, the geographer. Edrisi gives a list of towns "deserted because of the devastations committed by the Arabs. . . . There exists no trace of former habitations, the good things of the earth and the population have all disappeared." Such was the report of Edrisi, born a generation after the Arab invasion.

The Arabs were like vermin, spreading everywhere. Or so they seemed to the property holders whom they injured. In their own minds they were brave adventurers opposing the dull *bourgeoisie,* the slaves of the plow who were too timid to wander as men were meant to do. You can still hear Arab native songs exalting the exploits of the invaders of nine hundred years ago.

Gradually the Arab fury subsided. He became again a foot-loose, easy-going nomad, mingling his blood to some extent with that of the native Berber, leading his flocks about to graze in a countryside which once had been a network of rich farms, pitching his tents in the ruins of prosperous villages. Eventually Arabs penetrated into all the West, going as far as Morocco and into the Sahara. But their greatest numbers and their greatest damage was in the region lying between Egypt's borders and the eastern side of Algeria. Here they changed everything. Here they put government out of joint.

The population of some of the larger cities formed into little kingdoms; little dynasties and local kinglets sprang up. The Zirites went on after a fashion, but we hear no more about glittering funerals and rich wedding parties. The Zirites did not have the force to repel the next foreign invasion; it was Edrisi's patron, the Christian king of Sicily, who pushed the last Zirite from his throne.

*   *   *

THE EVENTUAL RESULT OF THE SECOND ARAB INVASION WAS TO KILL any possibility of a Berber nation in the West. A prosperous autonomous Berbery had looked to be in the making. The bastardizing of the race by the injection of Arab blood destroyed Berbery, as such. Whatever happened thereafter, and whatever may happen there in future, western North Africa could never be the pure Berber place that it was, a territory inhabited by a cousin race to South Europeans.

Before the second Arab invasion Berber blood was practically pure. The first Arab invaders had come without womenfolk. The presence of Punic, Greek, Roman and Vandal had not appreciably altered the Berber race.

The second Arab invaders were mixers and they brought their women.

ALMORAVIDES

DURING THE SAME DECADE THAT THE WEST WAS IN PROCESS OF SUCH profound alteration by the second coming of the Arabs a most surprising movement was shaping in another section of North Africa. It was the place of its origin which was particularly surprising. None would ever have thought to see the sands of the desert breed a body of conquerors.

Saharan peoples have never played a great part in the general history of North Africa. Any notion that the Sahara could rise and invade Mediterranean Africa seems absurd. Yet this is what the Almoravides of the southwestern Sahara did. Not only did they invade the West. They also captured Moslem Spain and governed it for half a century (1090-1147). These Saharans, regarded heretofore and since as amongst the world's poor relations, were masters of the greater part of the western Moslem world from the Niger almost to the Pyrenees, from the Atlantic coast of Portugal to mid-Algeria. The tail wagged the dog.

*　　*　　*

THE ALMORAVIDES' PLACE OF ORIGIN IN THE SOUTHWESTERN PART of the desert was typical nomad country. The semidesert stretch offered intermittent, seasonal pasturage for flocks. The flocks wandered and their masters learned to wander with them. Settled homes were impossible. Farming impossible. Folk did not know the taste of bread, says El-Bekri, except such of them as received a sample of it by the charity of a passing caravan. They lived on meat and milk alone. Dried meat was crushed and mixed with its own grease or with butter. Milk was their only drink. They thought little of water.

VEILED MEN

THESE NOMADS, LIKE THE REST OF THE SAHARA'S WANDERING POPUlation, were veiled men. They amazed travelers in medieval days just as the veiled Tuareg of the desert startles travelers of today. I have never seen an odder looking human being than the veiled Tuareg.

Let El-Bekri, who was a contemporary of the Almoravide early period, describe the male veil wearers: "All the men of the desert tribes constantly wear the *nicab* (veil on the forehead) above the *litham* (veil covering the lower part of the face) so that one can only see the part across their eyes. Never in any circumstances do they remove this lower veil and a man who took it off would be unrecognizable to his family and friends. If one of their warriors is killed in battle and his veil displaced no one can tell who he is until it is replaced. They call other men who do not dress as they do 'fly-mouths'" (i.e. fly trappers).

I have no information on how the females of that century dressed. The modern Tuareg woman goes with uncovered face. It combines into a topsy-turvy version of the usual Moslem veil custom. The motive in the two cases is antithetical. The usual Moslem woman wears a veil to conceal those charms which might endanger her chastity. Saharan men wear veils to avoid what they regard as disgusting exposure. They have persuaded themselves that the male mouth is a part of the person which it is indecent to display. Even eating should be done in such a way that the mouth is hidden. "They have alleged as the reason for this strange novelty," says Leo Africanus, "that, just as it is a great shame for a man to eject food from his body in the sight of anybody, so it is an offense to permit anyone to see him put food into his body."

THE RIBAT ON THE ISLAND

THE VEILED MEN OF THE SAHARA WERE ORIGINALLY HEATHEN. THE passage of Moslem traders across the desert brought them Mohammedanism of a vague sort. Naturally travelers did not arrest their forced marches across that arid region to go into religious intricacies with wandering nomad groups.

Certain amongst the nomads were fascinated. The dignity of a formal religion with high-sounding ritual and the noble novelty of *A Book* delighted a people whose forebears had known only the haphazardry of idol and fetish worship. By great effort—the detail of which is given at length by Ibn-Khaldoun—a teacher was imported "to teach them the Koran and the practices of religion." He was Ibn-Yasin.

The teacher proved too stern to be popular. With a few of his devoted pupils he retired to live apart from the world. The setting chosen for their hermitage was an island on an unspecified river beyond the desert. This river was probably the Senegal, but could have been the upper Niger. Their hermitage—colony, or "ribat," gave the Almoravides their name. Almoravides is a Spanish distortion of the words, El-Morabetin, meaning "The People of the Ribat." We further distort the name by putting a double definite article to it, the al-Moravides. The word "marabout," a holy man, so widely used in Africa derives also from "ribat."

THE FANATICS AND THEIR TEACHER

THE NUMBER OF IBN-YASIN'S DISCIPLES INCREASED. THEY BECAME a thousand strong. Ibn-Yasin cried, "Let us go from here and fulfill the appointed task!" He made Yahya-ibn-Omar, one of his original followers, military chief. They set off northward across the desert, most of them on foot, armed only with picks and javelins, plus "a gallantry and fearlessness that they alone possessed," as their disapproving contemporary, El-Bekri, admits.

They attacked and captured Sijilmassa, lured in the first instance by the prospect of getting its fifty thousand camels.

Abou-Bekr, brother to the original military chief, succeeded as commander and called upon the Almoravides to conquer Maghreb (Morocco). Though robbed of the inspiration of Ibn-Yasin, their teacher, who had died in battle, they went on with undiminished fanatical enthusiasm.

* * *

IBN-YASIN HAD DONE HIS WORK. A REMARKABLE MAN. HE NOT ONLY inspired his people, but disciplined them like a jailer, whipping them personally for their faults—even the general himself because he had risked his life unwisely in battle. Beatings were prescribed by rule: for drinking intoxicants, eighty blows; for fornication, one hundred. . . . He laid down a stern moral standard: four wives only, no sodomy.

His was a case however which puts us in mind of the old saying, "Always do as the parson says, not as the parson does!" For Ibn-Yasin himself "had such a passion for women that he married and repudiated several each month. No sooner would he hear of a beautiful woman than he demanded her in marriage and would not give more than four mithkals (say twelve current United States dollars) in marriage price" (El-Bekri).

THE WIFE OF TWO COUSINS

DISSENSION AT HOME IN THE DESERT'S DEPTHS REQUIRED ABOU-Bekr's presence. He passed the command of the Moroccan campaign to his cousin, the great Tashfin—Yusuf-ibn-Tashfin—and transferred to him simultaneously the hand of his wife, Zeineb, whom he divorced for the purpose.

Zeineb was the insignia of leadership. Possessing her was the marshal's baton. She had been concubine to a great sheikh, then wife of a South Moroccan king, then wife of his conqueror, who now turned her over to his cousin. She was one of the very few famed ladies of Moslem North Africa, a woman of beauty and political skill. Ibn-Khaldoun says that it was by the benefit of her advice that Ibn-Tashfin rose to supreme authority. From a Moslem historian this tribute to a woman is startling. Zeineb was a phenomenon. In addition to her other gifts she had humor. When her former Almoravide husband, Cousin Number One, returned to Morocco and seemed inclined to get under foot, she suggested to her new husband, Cousin Number Two, that he make the pointed gesture of handing the lingerer a farewell gift of desert equipment—a hint that he be on his way.

It was the Almoravide acceptance of such forceful females as Zeineb and also, it is hinted, the looseness of their ladies which got the Almoravides a coarse pseudonym in latter years. The Moslem world was used to females as quiescent in their public relations as so much package goods on a shelf. Enemies of the Almoravides spitefully called them by the title, *El-Djichem,* meaning "The-Husbands-of-Whores."

INNER AFRICA

ALMORAVIDE TEMPORAL GREATNESS WENT WITH IBN-TASHFIN WHEN the cousins split company. To Abou-Bekr went the pious glory of mass conversions of the heathen, plus the thrill of conquest that was measurable by the quantity rather than the quality of the territory captured.

Abou-Bekr came of a line of desert chiefs. We have his pedigree going back through five generations of Saharan nobility. He reorganized the Veiled Men and gave them congenial work to do. Inner Africa was to be subdued and converted. It was a wild, far-flung adventure. Abou-Bekr's hordes "carried their victorious arms as far as ninety days' distance." Islam was forcibly thrust down countless thousands of dusky throats.

Nor was all the profit Allah's. By Abou-Bekr's campaigns the Almoravide Empire gained control over the complete length of the western gold shuttle from the place in the Sudan where the gold "grew like carrots," and was sold to traders by the quaintest business system ever invented, to Sijilmassa where the gold was distributed to the world.

The quaint business system in question was usually called "Dumb Commerce." It seems scarcely credible, but is recorded by sober chroniclers from Herodotus to Ca' Da Mosto.[6] This is how it was operated: The savages who had collected the gold were too cautious to approach the traders who wanted it, fearing capture and enslavement. The traders therefore left their goods in heaps at recognized spots—salt, trinkets, etc.—and went away. In the night the gold sellers came, examined the stock and placed

[6] Ca' Da Mosto (mid-fifteenth century) is the latest travelers' report of Dumb Commerce I have found (*Relations des voyages d'Alvise de Ca' Da Mosto, publiés par* M. Charles Schefer (1895, pp. 57, 58). There are hearsay stories that the system was used as late as the 17th century. Herodotus (IV:196) tells how the Carthaginians traded in this fashion with coastal Africans, adding "Neither party deals unfairly with the other." There is a considerable literature on the variations of this strange custom. For a list of the classical items see *Textes relatifs à l'histoire de l'Afrique du nord: Herodote* by Stéphane Gsell (Algiers, 1916), footnote to p. 239. For a list of Arabic items see Gaudefroy-Demombynes' footnote to p. 83 of the *Masalik* of Ibn-Fadl-Allah al-Omari.

the amount of gold they estimated fair in front of each heap. In the morning the traders—if contented with the bargain—removed the gold and left the salt and other stuff. If the gold offer seemed niggardly they left their goods for yet another night so that the savages might increase the offer. The whole transaction was carried out without either party seeing or speaking to the other. The system indicates wonderful honesty on both sides. It is impossible to imagine an analogous process in modern business life —that is to say the entrusting of one's fortune absolutely without check to strangers and foreigners. The practicers of Dumb Commerce had learned honesty was the best policy; the whole profitable trade would have collapsed had either side been tricky.

*   *   *

As for Sijilmassa at the other end of the gold shuttle which the Almoravides controlled, this city, situated where the Sahara met Morocco, was "the brains of the desert" where brilliant executives did their planning. "From Sijilmassa," writes an Arab gloatingly, "merchants pass across the immense desert to Gana and to it they bring back *nothing but red gold!*" Out of Sijilmassa via the Triq-es-Soltan, the Royal Road into Morocco, gold went forth to all the Moslem world. It was reputedly the purest gold in the world and held in particular esteem. Sijilmassa was the center of the gold web, the hub of a wheel, very prosperous, a place of beautiful houses, magnificent public buildings, and many gardens. So much did its splendor impress El-Bekri that he lost his head a little and reported it to be "without flies." This—to those of us who have sojourned in date oases—was carrying enthusiasm beyond reason.

AOUDAGHOST

Along the terrifying desert road which connected the two extremities of the western gold shuttle the most important and one of the very few intermediate settlements was the once-famous town of Aoudaghost, two months from Sijilmassa and fifteen days from Gana. This point, previously part of Gana's empire, had fallen to the Almoravides in the early days of their career of conquest.

There is no Aoudaghost on modern maps. It sat upon a sandy

plain in southwestern Sahara; its natural setting was "absolutely sterile and without vegetation." It seems madness to have established a city in such a locality. It was the triumph of greed over humanity's inherent right to live decently. What a place to bring women to; what a place in which to raise children! All for the love of gold.

The detail of its glittering, fantastic and uncomfortable civic life comes to us in Arabic geography. It was very busy, rich, gluttonous and lustful. Some individuals owned a thousand slaves or more. Its market, in which all purchases were paid for in gold dust—a haughty touch indeed—were so crowded all day long that "one could scarcely hear the words of the person who was squatting at one's side."

Its prosperity came from the very horror of its setting. Alone in a wilderness of arid sand it broke the desert crossing and catered to tired wealthy travelers. Its rewards were immense. So were its sufferings. "All the inhabitants have a jaundiced skin; you can hardly find anybody who is not victim of either fever or affections of the spleen." Grain and dried fruits were imported. Such small cultivation as was done by painstaking handwatering was insignificant.

The fame of Aoudaghost's cooking, oddly enough, comes down to us across nine centuries (I have been quoting from El-Bekri). The cooks were Negresses, slaves of course, and so talented that they fetched one hundred gold pieces each. They could make nut cakes (*djouzincat*) and macaroni with honey (*cataif*) that made caravanners' mouths water.

Also much appreciated by travelers were the girls and women of Aoudaghost. They had the reputation of having lovely figures, given the tastes of the day and place: svelte waists, big shoulders, breasts and hips. An elderly and especially pious Moslem of Fez is authority for the report that a woman had been noted at Aoudaghost lying on the ground and that, so small was her waist and so ample the rest of her body, "she amused herself by passing her child under the tunnel of her body and pulling it out at the other side." These ladies of Aoudaghost, the reporter continues, were so proud of their charms that they habitually either stood or lay down, seldom sitting and thus risking to compress the most beautifully rounded part of their forms. Such ampleness was greatly admired in the Sahara. The modern Tuareg, whose males are lean as a whip, say *tebulloden*—a word which seems to carry its meaning across the language barrier—when describing the sort of feminine figure which is the national ideal. To attain *tebulloden* Tuareg women have been known to experiment with a deadly poisonous local plant, *falezlez,* having noted that it caused certain animals to distend in their last agonies. (The explorer, Duveyrier's horse puffed up like a full water sack after eating *falezlez* leaves.) Eaten in small quantities and with special precautions, Tuareg women found it a fattening if dangerous drug.

Behind this male adoration of superfluous feminine flesh, which women risk their lives to gratify, was presumably the hungry nomad's craving for the symbol of well-fed plenty.

             *   *   *

THIS RICH, VOLUPTUOUS AND UNHEALTHY CITY, AOUDAGHOST, BE-came the capital of Abou-Bekr and his Almoravides. Gana fell to their attack. Then the Veiled Men drove south. Negroes who previously lived on the desert's fringe fled before them. Almoravide exploits of conquest were wide and successful, but to translate their extent into the terms of modern geography is difficult.

Tekrour figures as a stage in Abou-Bekr's triumph. In western Africa we still speak of the Tucouleur people, which word is the same as Tekrour, and has nothing to do with the English words, Two-Colors, as was suggested by lighthearted early travelers.

Tekrour is one of those elastic geographical names of Africa. It could mean a city on the Senegal River in the neighborhood of modern Podor. It could mean all of the western Sudan. It is so used in the *Fettassi.* It could mean even more. The great Sultan Bello in the manuscript history which he gave the English explorer, Clapperton, at the start of the last century called the whole stretch from the borders of the Anglo-Egyptian Sudan to the Atlantic, Tekrour. Eventually the words, Tekrour-man, came to be applied to all Negro African pilgrims at Mecca; and in Africa was the Arabs' name for any Negro who was a Moslem.

Tekrour fell to Abou-Bekr in 1080. Seven years thereafter the fighting missionary of Islam who had spent his whole life forcibly interfering with other peoples' beliefs, succumbed to a poisoned pagan arrow.

TASHFIN, THE GRAND OLD MAN
OF MOROCCO

BY THEN HIS COUSIN, YUSUF-IBN-TASHFIN, HAD ACCOMPLISHED TWO very big things. He had founded the gorgeous red city of Marrakesh, called "the Bagdad of the West." He had gained a glorious victory in Spain and was on the way to make Spain an African province. Two rather extraordinary feats to have been performed by a desert nomad whose mother probably never saw the inside of a house.

Ibn-Tashfin was a man of great vigor and great simplicity. It was he who turned the Almoravides from wild raiders to true conquerors. In the days of his debut it appeared to the outside world that Almoravide fanatical zeal had spent itself. Of this we have a firsthand contemporary witness. El-Bekri writes, "Today in the year 460 (1067-68 A.D.) the Almoravide . . . empire is split apart and their power divided." This was written in the year when he finished his remarkable geography book. El-Bekri had clearly no notion of the great things ahead for the Almoravides under Ibn-Tashfin's leadership.

Ibn-Tashfin governed his people for forty-five years. He lived to be a centenarian, as centenarians are measured by the Mohammedan calendar; we would give him ninety-seven years. That is to say he lived from the year 400, counting from the Hegira, to the year 500. By the Christian calendar, wherein the year is a little longer, his lifetime ran from 1009 to 1106.

The old towns of Morocco and western Algeria fell to him: Fez, Tlemcen, Oran. Marrakesh he built in part with his own hands. He was a muscular, dark-skinned man with a soft voice and the kinky hair of a Negro. Though he conquered all the western Moslem world it is said that he never learned the language of the Koran, content to speak throughout his near century of life the Saharan Berber tongue of his childhood. Yet, like many Berbers, Ibn-Tashfin was pleased to think that he came of Arabic stock. He cherished the belief that he descended from a certain personage who traditionally reigned in Arabia many centuries before the days of Alexander the Great.

THE "CITY OF MOROCCO"

MARRAKESH WAS ADDED TO THE NUMBER OF AFRICAN CITIES IN THE year 1062. It is the youngest surviving big city from Morocco to Egypt, excepting always the infant prodigy, Casablanca. When Ibn-Tashfin built Marrakesh he had no idea at all of its potentialities. He sought only to make a walled camp where he could keep his treasure and arms in safety and in whose neighborhood there would be pasturage for camels. Its swift growth was amazing. His immediate successor saw a Marrakesh with a population of nearly a million—"a hundred thousand hearth fires" in the old-fashioned phrase.

An authentic and curious indication of its rapid growth is supplied by Edrisi, whose geography was prepared during the century which followed the foundation of Marrakesh. Says he, "The inhabitants of Marrakesh eat thirty loads (camel loads presumably) of locusts a day." This argues a very big population, considering that the grilled locust would probably have been an occasional item of the appetizer class of Marrakesh's menus rather than the main part of its food. However "a person may eat a plateful of them, containing two or three hundreds, without ill effects," remarked a tolerant early English visitor to Morocco, who said that their taste resembled that of shrimps. Mohammed himself ate locusts, tradition states, and was at first of the opinion that their wholesale destruction was improper. Later the Prophet, examining the wings of a captured locust, found words written thereupon "in Hebrew characters": "We are God's troops. We lay each one of us ninety-nine eggs and we are so numerous that— if we should lay a hundred—we would devastate the world." Mohammed was alarmed and altered his command, crying, "Kill them all!" This quaint bit of natural history was extracted from a book by Sheikh Kimal al-Din and passed along by that great collector of curious lore, General Daumas.

*   *   *

MARRAKESH IN THE RAPIDITY OF ITS GROWTH FROM A CAMP TO ONE of the largest cities in the medieval world lived up to its name, which was in the Berber language the equivalent of "Go quickly!" —or as we might say "Step lively!" The reason for it was that the site of Marrakesh had been a place where caravans often were attacked and across which it was the habit for travelers to urge one another to speed their pace. It was a brisk name for a new town. Europe in later years deformed it into Morocco (Marocco, in old English; Maroc, French, etc.) and took to calling the whole country by that name. Such was the prestige of Marrakesh, which —though shrunk from its early medieval size—is still the biggest city in its land.

Marrakesh delighted the men of old. Its setting astounded them: a glowing red city, fringed with palms and backed by the dazzling wall of the snowy Atlas Mountains. That snow was a cocktail to the eye of hot and tired travelers, a thrill to parched caravans.

The city itself was full of beauties and luxuries new to the North African scene. The Koutoubia was the skyscraper of old Morocco. From its tower "men of the tallest stature on the ground below looked like little children" and, Leo Africanus adds, "you could see the country for fifty miles round about." Strangers craned their necks to see the celebrated three golden balls which surmounted the tower. These balls were allegedly made from a royal lady's boiled-down jewelry. They were so large that the mosque door below had to be cut away to permit them to pass through. They were not solid gold, let it be admitted, but it was stated that the gilding of the foundation base metal cost one hundred thousand dinars (three hundred thousand current United States dollars). The tower was partially coated with an ornamentation of breath-taking loveliness: turquoise blue tiles. At its base were the stalls of two hundred merchants of Arabic manuscripts, which gave the Koutoubia its name, "The Mosque of the Booksellers," and which would indicate a remarkable local interest in literature. How many towns have two hundred stores selling only books?

The marvels of Marrakesh were the gossip of Africa. Folk talked of its guesthouse so thronged with distinguished travelers from far lands that a medieval poet says it sheltered "the world of all the Seven Climates . . . I did not know that such a reunion would be seen until the Day of Resurrection."

Folk told too about the palace of the vizier with a courtyard so large that five hundred women could play therein on wooden horses and have mock fights with lances—which, by the way, gives an athletic vision of harem life not at all in accord with our usual notions.

But the one aspect of Marrakesh about which modern visitors would be most likely to gossip was in the days of old a very different place. The great square called Djemaa-el-Fna, so gay today with its snake charmers, droll dancers, native music and storytellers, was once a spot where were exhibited the severed heads of executed men, a locality of desolation and vultures.

The original walled camp which Ibn-Tashfin established was near where the Koutoubia now stands. "When the ramparts were being raised Yusuf-ibn-Tashfin pulled back his sleeves and set about making mortar and placing the rubble and rough stones along with the workmen, acting thus," says the Arab chronicler, "so as to show his humility before All-High-God."

AFRICANS TO SPAIN

MOSLEM SPAIN WAS ENFEEBLED. THE KING OF SEVILLE CAME PERsonally to Yusuf-ibn-Tashfin at Fez and implored his help against the Christians. Ibn-Tashfin, whose delight was a Holy War, proceeded to Spain and that same year (1086) met and defeated Alfonso VI of Castille near Badajoz. Christian losses were high. Ibn-Tashfin's army also is said to have lost heavily. Ibn-Tashfin was proud to be able to ship back to Morocco the heads of forty thousand enemy dead.

Presently Ibn-Tashfin moved into Spain, not as one intervening to give help to fellow Moslems but as a master. Spain was added to the Almoravide Empire, Ibn-Tashfin becoming the king of the so-called Adouatein, the two coast lines, African and Spanish. The detail of the conquest is outside the scope of this book, as also it is to give an account of the impression which the civilized luxury of Spain made upon Ibn-Tashfin and his rude followers and of the impression which his uncouth gang, which included Negroes, made on suave Spain.

Eventually Spain's amenities were the ruin of the fundamental fierce fanaticism which had been the making of the Almoravide movement. It had been one thing to live ascetic lives and plan missionary conquest on a sun-baked, crocodile-infested, mosquito-tortured island beside the Sahara; it became quite another thing to maintain religious fighting spirit in sweet, soft Spain which generations of sophisticated Moslem rule had made into a dream of beauty. So Spain had her revenge by demoralizing her conquerors.

*   *   *

THERE HAD BEEN SUITABILITY IN THE FACT THAT MEN FROM NORTH Africa should master Spain in her feebleness. When Spain had been strong she had interfered continuously in Africa, and often it had been Spain which had controlled the Adouatein, the two coast lines. Spain's intrigues in Africa in the days of the all-powerful vizier, Almanzor, are described in detail by Ibn-Khaldoun. Spain's effort had culminated (991) in the triumph of an African pro-Spanish general, Ziri-ibn-Atia, who on Spain's behalf had conquered a great stretch in Morocco and Algeria. He celebrated his success and his resultant appointment as Spanish governor of the captured ground by sending his Spanish overlord a rich and exotic gift. The items of the gift are worth listing, not merely because they are picturesque, but also because they supply a picture of the time and the place.

A PRESENT FROM AFRICA

THE PRESENT WAS COMPOSED AS FOLLOWS:

> 200 blood horses
> 50 racing camels (*mehari*) of extraordinary speed
> 1000 shields of *lamt* skin
> several bundles of bows made of *zan* wood (a sort of African oak)
> several civet cats
> a giraffe
> several *lamts* and other wild animals of the desert
> 1000 loads of dates
> several loads of fine woolen cloth

The *lamt* was an animal of the antelope type. Its hide had great repute from the Mediterranean to Negroland because it was both very light and very strong and thus could be made into the ideal warrior's shield. A single *lamt* shield fetched at Fez the price of eight ducats at a period when a handsome slave girl was worth only fifteen. Leo Africanus says that a *lamt* hide shield "could not be pierced by a fire *pistolet*." The living *lamt* which was sent to the vizier of Spain, whether male or female, was equipped with very long thin horns; if an old animal these would have been four empans (about one yard) long, so long—El-Bekri assures us—that the male and the older female could not have relations.

The giraffe which was the *lamt's* companion in the gift to Spain was the first of its breed to visit Europe in the Middle Ages (giraffes went to the Roman circus). It is agreeable to pause for a moment in the study of African humans to consider the adventures of certain individual African animals which gained notoriety by their travels in foreign lands. There is the record of several giraffes which left Africa to astonish Europe in olden days: one was sent to Frederick II by an Egyptian sultan in the early thirteenth century, another was noted in Florence in 1524. Then, so far as I note, giraffe emigration to Europe seemed to suspend until the middle of the last century. I find a passage in the learned *Proceedings of the Association for Promoting the Discovery of the Interior Parts of Africa* (1790) indicating complete unfamiliarity with giraffes. It refers in a puzzled way to "a large and singular animal called *Zarapah*" of which an explorer had given a hearsay account, "which is described as respectively a camel in the head and body, as having a long and slender neck like an ostrich and as being much taller in the shoulders than the haunches." A Monsieur Thibaut, merchant in the Egyptian Sudan, is stated to have sent the first giraffe to London to the zoo. This would have been about the middle of the nineteenth century.

In the case of the giraffe sent from Morocco to the Spanish vizier a miracle of transportation must have been performed. Unlike the others mentioned which came via the Nile Valley, the vizier's giraffe came across the Sahara. A test of skill and patience hard to parallel. That such a mighty effort was for the entertainment of Spain's vizier shows in what awe North Africa then held her neighbor across Gibraltar.

Now all that was changed. A Saharan ex-nomad, Ibn-Tashfin, occupied Spain as master, and when the power of his heritors declined Spain would know yet another line of African overlords.

THE INCIDENT OF THE
SCOLDED PRINCESS

ONE DAY IN THE EARLY YEARS OF THE TWELFTH CENTURY THE PRIN-
cess, Soura, daughter of the deceased Ibn-Tashfin and sister of
his successor, Ali, was insulted in the streets of Marrakesh by an
ill-favored and ragged little man. She was veilless as was the
habit of Almoravide women, for the use of the veil has not been
a universal habit with Mohammedans and the Koran's rule on
the subject is not definite. There are two Koranic passages about
veils: that the daughters and wives of the Faithful should "let
their veils fall low" so as to cover the split between their breasts,
and that women should "throw their veils over their bosoms"
(suras XXXIII and XXIV respectively). Many Saharan and Sudanese women of good character go unveiled. But the little man
who accosted the princess professed to be shocked. He reproached
her for indecent exposure—he had a wonderful flow of language.
He and his companions struck her donkey and the princess fell
off. She made her way home in tears.

It appeared to be just one of those incidents usual enough in the
Orient where religious eccentricities are permitted much license
by a pious public. But this scrubby little man was no ordinary
street ranter. His tackling of a member of the reigning family
was no mere crankish accident. This street preacher was to be
one of the great religious figures of Islam. And his handsome
young companion who helped beat the princess' donkey would
be called "the greatest of all the Berbers."

This queer incident, in fact, marked the beginning of Almoravide downfall. Born of fanaticism, they were to fall before the
hysteria inspired by a yet more high-flown and brilliant fanatic.

*   *   *

MOHAMMED IBN-TOUMERT LEFT MARRAKESH THAT NIGHT. His
reprimand of the princess had been the culmination of a campaign. He had trudged across North Africa "reforming morals,"
breaking wine jars, destroying musical instruments, insulting persons in high places, lecturing people on their loose habits and
producing a series of riots. At Alexandria he had nearly been

lynched. At sea en route to Tunisia they wanted to toss him overboard. At Bougie in Algeria his rage against "young boys dressed up like women with false plaits of long hair, ear-rings and eyelids painted with antimony" was so violent as to provoke a street battle. His various exploits are a matter of general record; the last item is from an ancient and anonymous manuscript recently discovered in an old Arab bookseller's shop in Casablanca by Levi-Provençal.

But this troublemaker was no vulgar, mouthing crank. Ibn-Toumert was a person of great learning and a traveled man who knew most of the Moslem world: Spain, the East, Bagdad, Egypt, Tripoli, Tunisia. He was also a man of destiny. He had fixed his mind on ruining the Almoravides. He succeeded. The instrument of his posthumous success was that handsome young man, his companion.

Ibn-Toumert hid himself in the high Atlas Mountains in which wild region he had been born. The mountaineers became his devoted disciples. The Almoravide ruler woke to the danger but could not procure the assassination of the agitator. Ibn-Toumert's influence increased.

The dramatic moment came. Ibn-Toumert called together the mountaineers—all members of the great tribal group, the Masmoudian Berbers—and swore them to support his form of Mohammedanism. He then made a startling announcement. He told them that he was the Mahdi of the holy blood of Mohammed and Ali, mysteriously sent to lead them. His followers thrilled with joy and pride.

They believed in him with childish confidence. They were a rude people isolated in their high hills. They were also, as a tribal family, notoriously gullible. They had a record of credulity. A cousin tribe, members of the Masmoudia group of the lowlands, had accepted with enthusiasm one Saleh, a *soi-disant* mahdi whose appearance, he claimed, marked the end of the world. Jesus, said he, would eventually give over to him the leadership of the Christians! His religious and political power was great and passed on to his family. Another religious hoax by which another section of this tribal group had been victimized was played by one Hamim, "the false prophet of Tetuan," who got up a Koran of his own and gained large influence. There had been yet another instance.

TRICKS OF THE MAHDI

THE NEW MAHDI, IBN-TOUMERT, WAS A NOTABLE PERFORMER OF fake miracles. He secretly trained a clever individual, unknown to the locality, to imitate a froth-mouthed idiot. This person then appeared suddenly one day "well dressed and perfumed" and able to recite passages from the Koran. It had all been done in a moment by an angel who had visited him the previous night, the ex-idiot claimed. Furthermore the angel had given him the power to distinguish men destined for Paradise from those who would go to Hell. The latter, his angel had told him, ought to be killed. Several angels would back up his story. They were waiting in a certain well, ready to give their testimony.

Ibn-Toumert, himself, questioned the hidden angels who cried from their hiding place, "He tells the truth!"

Ventriloquism? Not at all. Ibn-Toumert had concealed certain persons there in advance. And now we see proof of the Mahdi's real ability. He cried, "The well is sanctified as the abode of these angels. Let us cover it over lest impurities fall into it." So the crowd covered over the Mahdi's accomplices with rocks and earth and there was none left except the ex-idiot to betray the Mahdi's trickery.

It had all been done with an important purpose. The ex-idiot now became the Mahdi's instrument for a purge of his followers. The deaths of seven thousand whom he distrusted was called in the annals of his disciples "The Day of the Sorting Out."

Another miracle: After a battle which had gone against his people and disheartened them, Ibn-Toumert caused supposedly dead men to cry out from their graves that they were the souls of those who had died in the good fight, were in Paradise and could assure their surviving comrades of victory if they would but persevere.

It is hard to understand how such great and surviving prestige could have been secured by conspiracies so tricky and so cynical. Clearly Ibn-Toumert was immensely clever. Equally marvelous must have been his oratory. Into the heads of these simple folk

he put somehow enough understanding to inspire them to frantic
effort. This was his teaching: "The principal obligation of his
doctrine was to reject anthropomorphism, the heresy toward
which the people of the West were drifting under Almoravide
leadership in avoiding deliberately the use of allegorical interpre
tations to explain equivocal passages in the Koran." How this
was explained to a set of primitive mountaineers is a problem
Ibn-Toumert called his doctrine "The Profession of God's Unity."
He named his followers Unitarians, or Al-Mowahhedin, a name
deformed to Almohades.

ALMOHADES

THIS NAME, ALMOHADES, BECAME THE DESIGNATION OF A GREAT
dynasty (1130-1269), one of the greatest in all the history of North
Africa. The Almohades mastered a great stretch "ninety days by
fifteen," from the Atlantic to Tripoli, and they controlled Mos
lem Spain. Their offshoot, the Hafside dynasty, reigned in Tu
nisia into the sixteenth century. It is peculiar to see such tempora
power wielded by a group named after an abstruse religious doc
trine. Thirteen kings were called Unitarians (Almohades) and
the list of the Almohade-Hafsides is immense. The first Almohade
king of them all was that pleasant-faced young man who aided
Ibn-Toumert to discipline the unveiled princess. He was Abd-el
Moumen, the brave, "the greatest of all the Berbers."

The name of the dynasty has been, from the standpoint of the
student, a hardship. The fact that the word Almohades and that
designating the opposing dynasty, the Almoravides, are almost
identical—only four letters different, almost an anagram—has
made the reading of this period of history difficult and has led
to much blundering. During the ensuing passage where both
dynasties figure I shall help the reader by putting "Unitarians"
in parentheses in mentioning the Almohades.

BACK TO THEIR DESERT

THE MAHDI ENCOURAGED HIS MOUNTAINEERS TO BELIEVE IN THEIR
invincibility. The semihypnotic gift of dictators was his. His
mountaineers, he told them, would capture Marrakesh and over

throw their traditional enemies, the Almoravides, now nicknamed insultingly "The Husbands of Whores": This came about. But not until the Mahdi had been nearly twenty years dead. The glory of crashing through Marrakesh's walls and cutting off the head of the last of the Almoravides, a pitiful child king, crying for his mother—this fell to Abd-el-Moumen, the one-time gay young companion of the Mahdi.

All these years, war between the Almoravides and the Almohades (Unitarians) had slashed back and forth across Maghreb. The Mahdi's death had been hidden from his mountaineers lest it discourage their effort, hidden for three years, a seemingly miraculous bit of trickery. Then, sure of his hold on the people, Abd-el-Moumen had let out the news and assumed open leadership. He had fought brilliantly. The last adult king of the Almoravides, grandson and namesake of the grand old man, Ibn-Tashfin, hopelessly besieged in Oran, had died dramatically, perhaps suicided by riding his horse over a cliff. The Almoravides were lost. Two children had reigned for a few months. In the spring of 1147 Marrakesh fell. All Maghreb belonged to the Almohades (Unitarians). It was as the Mahdi had prophesied.

*   *   *

So ENDED THE ALMORAVIDE EMPIRE, THE ODD AND UNIQUE ATTEMPT of the Sahara to master Mediterranean Africa. Few of the Veiled Men whose ancestors had set out on the adventure of conquest a century earlier got back to their desert. But their less ambitious fellows lived on there, and still live there. One Almoravide survivor we shall meet later in the shape of a certain Ibn-Ghania whose escapades, Professor Gautier says, constitute "the most extraordinary epic of brigandage that ever was."

Of the Almoravides as a dynasty here is Ibn-Khaldoun's epitaph: "They perished worn out by trying to dominate, used up by far-flung expeditions, and ruined by luxury."

EXPANSION IN AFRICA

THE ALMOHADES (UNITARIANS) HAVING WON A GREAT VICTORY found, as often happens, that their problems were just beginning. Spain was one of their greatest problems. Its taking was easy.

Certain Moslems in Spain had indicated a desire to go over to Almohade control even before Marrakesh fell. Its holding was harder. Many Africans crossed to Spain never to return during the century of Almohade rule. Amongst them was the second Almohade king himself who was killed in Portugal by a Christian arrow which pierced his navel. The most interesting item of all the effort seems to me to concern the preparations for the great campaign when all Morocco went into armament work. There is a modern touch in the passage from an Arabic chronicler reporting that Abd-el-Moumen ordered all his subjects to set themselves to making arrows, and that the people, working at top speed, delivered ten quintals a day (over eleven hundred pounds). These sacrifices were eventually rewarded by the victory of Alarcos (1195) "on which famous day 30,000 Christians were cut to pieces and the rest took to flight."

*   *   *

ON THE AFRICAN CONTINENT THE ALMOHADES SHOWED THEMSELVES wild-riding and brilliant warriors. They succeeded in time in consolidating firmly all the country from Morocco to Tripoli—something new, for the Fatimite Empire in the West, it will be recalled, was a slippery affair very correctly symbolized by a live fish (see page 263).

Five years after the final defeat of the Almoravides Abd-el-Moumen set off on his first African expedition. It was a surprise attack cunningly timed when there was disunion in the coveted land. Leaving Marrakesh with the announcement that he was on his way to Spain to fight the Christians, Abd-el-Moumen went to the coast opposite Gibraltar, then gave out that the Spanish situation was so good that he could abandon the campaign and would return home. Then by forced marches he cut eastward across the top of Africa.

He surprised and captured Algiers and hurried on toward the far more important place of Bougie, for it is notable that Algiers—probably now the most familiar city name in Africa, except that of Cairo—designated in the Middle Ages a spot of very little consequence. Bougie, insignificant today, was then incomparably more important. Bougie was the capital of a local kingdom. At Abd-el-Moumen's attack the ruler ran away with his treasures.

The hardest test of Almohade fighting came from the Arab

nomads. These, the offspring of the hordes of the second Arab
invasion, felt that there was no room in eastern Algeria for themselves and the newcomer. It must be a fight to the death. To prove
it the Arabs, it is said, hamstrung their own horses and camels
on the eve of battle so that flight would be impossible. For three
days they stood and fought a cruelly losing battle, with dead
mounting high around them and their women and children and
flocks packed in behind them. This happened near Sétif in northeastern Algeria. At last they ran away after all, not stopping till
they got to Tébessa.

To have defeated these people, these human locusts who had
run their undisciplined way for about a century was an accomplishment. And the Almohades furthermore even succeeded in
taming them temporarily and making them into useful citizens.
Abd-el-Moumen was able to use certain of them in his armies
in Spain. As a whole these erstwhile Arab gangsters were relatively harmless for the next thirty years.

*   *   *

ABD-EL-MOUMEN ON HIS VICTORIOUS WAY BACK TO MOROCCO MUST
have contrasted his present fine situation with the circumstances
of his poverty-stricken tramp across the same stretch with the
Mahdi thirty years before, when he was the adoring young
disciple, "gay, generous-hearted and handsome" and his fanatic
master was ranting at the frivolous, breaking up wine jars and
smashing every *rhaita, guezba* or *darbooka,* whose giddy music
annoyed him. Now he was caliph, one of the greatest of all
caliphs.

Perhaps it was during that journey that he planned the visit
to his home village which he actually performed a few years
later. Into the mountain village of Tagrart near Tlemcen he
marched with two hundred enormous drums beating. (What
would the Mahdi have thought!) There the caliph, Abd-el-Moumen, had been born, his father a poor porter. The caliph was
almost sixty, but a few remembered him and one old lady cried
out jovially, "That's how anybody ought to come home!" Then
Abd-el-Moumen made a pious pilgrimage to his mother's burial
place.

TURN OF THE CHRISTIAN WORM

DURING HIS FIRST TRIUMPHANT EXPEDITION EASTWARD THERE WAS one thing which Abd-el-Moumen had not accomplished; he had not ejected the Christians.

The European worm had lately turned on its African persecutors. For centuries the Christian side of the Mediterranean had sulked supinely under Saracen attacks, making no attempt to cross the sea and get even. North Africa had sneered, "The Christians aren't able to make even a plank float!" At last retaliation had started. At first by raids only, notably the Christian attack back in 1087 when three hundred ships fell on the Mahdia neighborhood and had to be bought off by the payment of one hundred thousand pieces of gold. Later attacks had been more serious and led to permanent occupation. When Sicily fell into Christian hands it was a blow to Moslem Africa. When the control of Sicily was taken up by the very brilliant and vigorous king, Roger II, it was from Moslem Africa's point of view a disaster. In fact, had Roger II given his full attention to the project, Tunisia and the Tripoli region might have been lost to Islam forever. As it was, Christian interference lasted only twenty-six years.

HE LOVED AFRICA

ROGER II, CALLED REDDJAR OR SOMETIMES LODJAR IN ARABIC chronicles, was the greatest king of all medieval Christendom in the eyes of North Africa. He deserved to be so regarded by them not only for his conquests on their soil, but because his was the first respectful approach Christian Europe ever made to the African continent. Roger took a sober intellectual interest in Africa, which from the days of Herodotus through Pliny and Solinus had been regarded by Europe (except Moslem Spain) as a sort of freak museum. Roger sponsored the first serious European effort to study inner Africa realistically. So he merits a little space in this book.

Roger had "a passion for geography." Geography in those days when so much of the world was an unknown mystery was really something to get passionate about. We today who know the shape of the world's lands and waters cannot imagine the thrilled curiosity felt by a man like Roger. He was responsible for the greatest medieval study of African geography, that of his Moslem protégé, Edrisi. It was called, and rightly called, by Arabic scholars the *Kitab-Rodjari,* the "Book of Roger," or sometimes just *al-Rojari.* Its author, Edrisi, gave to his book a title which, translated, would read *The Entertainment of Those who Long to Traverse the Divers Countries of the World.* It was completed in the year 1154.

Edrisi had himself traveled in Spain and North Africa and he had the benefit of information procured by a set of reporters who had been specially sent by Roger to investigate far lands. Also Edrisi availed himself of previous geographical study he had undertaken when he engraved at Roger's order a beautiful disc-shaped map of the world made in silver and weighing four hundred fifty pounds.

Roger literally loved the geography book he had inspired, is said to have given his pet geographer nine hundred pounds' weight of silver along with other treasure as a reward, and to have had the book "always in his hands so that he might study it."

*　　*　　*

BUT THE CHRISTIAN WORLD, ASIDE FROM ROGER, STERNLY REFRAINED from any interest in this Moslem account of God's world. Hundreds of years passed before even extracts from it were translated into Latin.[7]

Today the reading of Edrisi is necessary to anyone who studies medieval Africa. He is awkward reading because he follows the "Climates" system, which consists of slicing the world across arbitrarily in stripes without regard to frontiers or racial groups. You will, for example, find part of the information about some country at the start of the "First Climate"; it breaks off abruptly; the rest of what Edrisi has to tell you about the country in ques-

[7] *Geographica Nubiensis* (Paris, 1619). Edrisi—though born of a Spanish-Moroccan family—was supposed by Christian Europe to have been a Nubian (see Rennell in the *Proceedings of the Association for Promoting the Discovery of the Interior Parts of Africa,* Vol. II, ft. to p. 56). A manuscript of Edrisi's work was acquired by the Bibliothèque Nationale and translated into French in 1836-40. A better translation was published in 1866, *Déscription de l'Afrique et de l'Espagne,* Dozy and de Goeje, Leyden.

tion must be hunted for many pages farther along in the "Second Climate." But for all that, Edrisi's geography with its careful account of African towns and countries and its painstaking touristic information—all intercity routes given by days of march, sailing time, etc.—constitutes a wonderful Baedeker to have been prepared eight hundred years ago.

It makes us realize how recent is our knowledge of the Dark Continent when we hear that *only a century ago* a great authority on Africa stated, "today there are still portions of the continent where the historian and the geographer would be without guide if the patronage of Roger had not been given to Edrisi."

ROGER AS CONQUEROR

ROGER'S PASSIONATE INTEREST IN AFRICAN GEOGRAPHY DID NOT GO to the chivalrous lengths of stopping his ambition to conquer Africa's coasts. From early manhood to his death he coveted, as was but natural, the African shores opposite to Sicily. After certain false starts, some intrigue and bickering with local chiefs, the capture of less important towns, Roger took up his African project on a full scale.

The moment was favorable. The country was miserable. Five years of famine had beat the people down. Roger hastened to mount his big attack. His admiral, George of Antioch, was put in charge. George possessed "a perfect knowledge of arithmetic and of the Arabic language," as Ibn-Khaldoun says rather quaintly, and he had the tact to put the latter accomplishment to good use. He visited Tunisia and wormed his way into the confidence of local notables. He was able to take the fortress, Mahdia, with scarcely an effort. The seventh direct descendant of the first Zirite, Bologguin, "Father of Victories," was pushed off his throne. The Christians held the coast from Tripoli to the neighborhood of Tunis. Presently they took Bône in Algeria.

*   *   *

ROGER WAS TOLERANT WITH HIS NEW MOSLEM SUBJECTS. HIS AT-tack on the African coasts had been a war of conquest, not a Holy War or Crusade. Ibn-Khaldoun says, "when he conquered African places he authorized the people to stay on, gave them their fellow citizens as chiefs, and in his dealings with them always followed the rules of justice." This tribute from a Mohammedan to a Christian is startling, and is really not diminished by the fact that Ibn-Khaldoun sometimes adds a perfunctory, "May Allah curse him!" to the mention of Roger's name. Another Arabic chronicler, however, records that Roger burnt alive one of his servitors who had been indulgent with the Moslems of Bône and who was suspected of being a secret Mohammedan. "For this action," says Ibn-el-Athir, "Allah did not let Roger go unpunished, and soon afterward he died." Christian critics thought that Roger, who wore Moslem dress like his Sicilian subjects, and was on the whole so sympathetic toward them, was little better than a heathen.

"THE GREATEST OF ALL THE BERBERS"

ROGER'S SUCCESSOR WAS OF ANOTHER TYPE, GLOOMY AND TYRANnical. The Moslems of Africa whom his father had treated fairly rose in revolt. A distinguished Moslem hostage was crucified in reprisal. The Christians of Tripoli were massacred; Mahdia and its neighborhood were the scene of Christian retaliation: Moslem women and children were butchered.

Certain Moslems escaped and made their way to Morocco to beg the help of Abd-el-Moumen. "In all of Islam you alone are powerful enough to save Tunisia," they pleaded. Abd-el-Moumen wept. He also gave orders for a great military expedition: water sacks for the march, new wells along the route, and at intervals from Morocco to Tunisia grain to be stored in great heaps covered with clay. Three years were spent in preparations.

Then with one hundred thousand warriors and as many more valets and servitors Abd-el-Moumen took the road eastward again.

Four months on the march and then—coincidental with the appearance of his fleet—Abd-el-Moumen arrived at the city of Tunis. Tunis, weakened at the moment by internal disorder and badly shaken by the Christian conquest of sister towns in the neighborhood, gave up without much fight. Abd-el-Moumen made a generous deal with the place, according to his lights: he spared everybody, asking only half of their money and possessions; no pillaging allowed; any Jewish residents or odd Christian leftovers could acknowledge Islam or die. Some opted for Islam, some for death.

The capture of Mahdia, that fortress built to be impregnable, was far harder and longer. There was a great sea and land battle, "during the whole of which action Abd-el-Moumen remained prostrated, his forehead pressed against the ground, weeping and imploring Allah to uphold the Moslems." It was as he had prayed, though Mahdia did withstand the besiegers for six months.

Abd-el-Moumen announced that he would listen to no surrender proposal unless the defenders first turned Moslems, but later he permitted himself to be blackmailed into kindness and sent the survivors back to Sicily in his own ships. A threat had been made that, if he treated Mahdia's defeated Christians harshly, all the male Moslems on Sicily would be killed, their women and children made slaves.

Eleven months after the start of his expedition from Morocco Abd-el-Moumen entered Mahdia (January 22, 1160). The Christians had been pushed out of Africa. He turned back toward the west. He had made the Almohades masters from Tripoli to the Atlantic. It was a notable accomplishment for the son of a porter in a little Berber hill village. He was indeed "the greatest of all the Berbers."

SEESAW OF AFRICAN DYNASTIES

IT IS A COINCIDENCE THAT JUST AS THE ALMOHADES CAME UP IN the West the only other really great medieval dynasty of North Africa, the Fatimites, faded. The unhappy child who was to be the last of the Fatimite rulers in Egypt came to the throne in the same year that Abd-el-Moumen completed that series of victories which consolidated the great new Almohade Empire.

Since the reign of Mostansir who whimsically sent the Arab "locusts" into the West the government of Egypt had been in turmoil. Of the six Fatimites who had followed Mostansir two were murdered, one died at eleven of epilepsy, having spent all his reign in terror and being literally frightened to death, two who escaped violent deaths had reigns full of intrigue and personal tragedy, and the sixth died in seclusion before he was twenty-one, probably unaware that he had been deposed.

The story of those seventy-odd years is a tangle of crime and conspiracies and helpless royal writhing. The Fatimites had fallen except in name long before the deposition of their last caliph. The story is the typical hideous sunset of an oriental dynasty: assassinations, scheming viziers, harem plots, helpless child kings victimized and thrown aside, interfamily murders. In 1171 the last Fatimite caliph was no more. Egypt's next ruler was the great Saladin.

WAR OF BROKEN PLEDGES

EGYPT MUDDLED THROUGH THE EARLY PART OF THE CRUSADES, LOS-ing Jerusalem in the glorious First Crusade, seeing an attempted Christian invasion of Egypt stopped by the death of its leader nineteen years thereafter, and escaping Christian capture yet a half century later through no merit of her own.

This last, the attack of Almaric, Christian king of Jerusalem, was a nearly fatal disaster to Moslem Egypt, during whose confusion the poor country never knew her enemies from her friends and was in her feebleness a mere tilting ground for Christians, Kurds and plotting would-be viziers. Fostat, like the Moscow of Napoleon's day, was fired to prevent it from falling to an enemy. Egyptian *amour-propre* was scarified by the knowledge that their caliph (not only ruler, but revered leader of their religion) had been obliged to receive Christian dogs in audience, even to shake the hand of Almaric's Christian ambassador as a pledge of amity, bought at the price of two hundred thousand gold pieces. This amity did not endure.

Indeed no five years of history could contain more broken pledges and shifting loyalties than this polygon of a campaign (1163-68). The expressive phrase, *double-cross*, forces itself from one's pen. The barest résumé: Its start, an exiled would-be vizier ousted his rival and regained office by Kurdish aid, broke with them and called the Christians into Egypt. From this came a kaleidoscope of changing alliances and broken friendships. The end was a Christian withdrawal in face of a combination of Egyptians and Turks which caught them by surprise.

*   *   *

IN THIS UNSAVORY GARDEN BLOSSOMED A FINE FLOWER OF MOSLEM chivalry, that most famous and universally beloved of all Mohammedans, saintly figure to Moslems, beloved hero to Christians—Saladin.

Saladin was nephew and successor to the Kurdish general during the campaign. He became virtual ruler soon after the Christian flight from Egypt. The death of the last Fatimite, and later the death of his own master, Nur-ed-Din, left Saladin eventually the sovereign of Egypt. He was the first of a new dynasty, the Ayyubites.

*   *   *

SALADIN'S EARLY YEARS IN EGYPT WERE FULL OF WORRY. IN ATtempting to take over control on his own account of the country which he had conquered in Nur-ed-Din's employ he had bitten his master's hand and, until his master's death (1174) he was in constant fear of a punishing slap.

With this fear in mind Saladin set about preparing not only one, but a choice of retreats against the expedition of revenge he dreaded from Nur-ed-Din. Both of these refuge places were sought in Africa, one to the south, the other to the west of Egypt.

This prudent and foresighted episode in Saladin's career is far less familiar than his dashing adventures in the Holy Land, his chivalrous dealings with Richard Coeur de Lion and the many glorious actions which so amply justified his name, translatable as "Honor of the Faith." Therefore I quote two nearly contemporary Arabic sources. Commenting on Saladin's motive for his expedition into the Sudan, the author of the *Masalik* says that Saladin "feared that Nur-ed-Din would come to attack him in Cairo and remove from him the power he had taken into his hands." Commenting on Saladin's motive for the expedition sent westward at the same period Ibn-Khaldoun says that Saladin desired "to secure places of retreat in case of a war with Nur-ed-Din, sovereign of Syria. Saladin was then Nur-ed-Din's vizier and since he had succeeded in setting himself up independently in Egypt he expected to be attacked by his former master."

THE PERSISTENT BLACK CHRISTIANS

SALADIN IN ATTACKING THE SUDAN SOUTH OF EGYPT WAS DOING NOT only a prudent but a pleasant thing. He was both studying out a possible refuge and chastening Christians. The expedition had the elements of a Holy War.

The Negroes up the Nile were persistently Christian. Their tenacity can be attributed both to conviction and to geography. Like the Abyssinians they lived in places so hard to reach that Islam had dodged the effort of converting them. Eventually the Negroes of the Sudan were destined to slip into the arms of Islam. In Saladin's time they were Christians of the Jacobite church.

Till recently they had been kept in place by Egyptian troops stationed at the frontier, Assuan. With the decline of the Fatimites this frontier protection, like other matters, had been neglected. The king of the Nubians took the opportunity to invade the Assuan region and carry away its Moslem population in slavery. This insult to Islam demanded punishment.

A brother of Saladin's invaded the homeland of the black Christians and plundered the capital "where the house of the king was the only one built of stone, the rest being huts." Their poor little church was pillaged, their bishop tortured, and seven hundred pigs—unclean to the Moslem invader—were destroyed. Aside from the religious satisfaction it afforded, the expedition was a failure. Saladin was informed that the region up the Nile was a desolate place, burning hot, dry, and without resources, in short "uninhabitable" and "quite unsuited to people like ourselves." So here was no possible hiding place if Nur-ed-Din should come.

* * *

THE NUBIAN BISHOP AND THE CHRISTIAN-OWNED PORKERS WERE avenged, quite unintentionally, a decade later when a Crusaders' raiding party crossed the Red Sea and fell on Aidab, the port of Moslem pilgrims, took a shipload of the Faithful who had just reached Africa on their return from Mecca, annihilated a caravan of pilgrims in the desert between the Red Sea and the Nile, and caused Macrizi, the Egyptian historian, to exclaim that never such a misfortune had been heard of in all the time of Islam and that never before had the Roums (Christians) come to these parts. The Christian raiders—bravest of the brave, surely, to venture into such remote unknown desert lands—were captured at sea and two of them were taken to Muna, the place of sacrifice near Mecca, and "slaughtered there in the same manner that a ram is immolated." The rest were beheaded at Cairo.

SALADIN'S SEARCH FOR A WESTERN REFUGE

AT ABOUT THE SAME MOMENT THAT SALADIN SENT HIS BROTHER southward to investigate the potentialities of the Sudan as a place of retreat should Nur-ed-Din come, he dispatched his nephew westward, along the Mediterranean shores. The nephew turned back, perhaps because this country also failed to appeal as a refuge place. But one of his generals, Caracoch, went on and on. His name translated meant "Black Bird of Prey." He deserved it. He called himself the Chargé d'affaires of True Believers. This latter was less justified.

The motive which had been behind the expedition into the west was forgotten. The master whom Saladin feared was long since dead. But Caracoch plunged on across Africa with the remnants of his original troops to whom were added a rabble of Arabs of the "locust" invasion whom he had picked up and a powerful rebel chieftain of the old Almoravide party with whom he had struck up an alliance. Among Caracoch's exploits was the capture of the Fezzan Oases far south of Tripoli, and the taking of Gabès and other places in southern Tunisia.

Presently Caracoch and his friend, the rebel, had occupied almost the whole of Tunisia. The Almohade ruler came hurrying from Morocco to try to regain the lost territory, and at the first encounter was badly beaten by the two adventurers, though later he was able to discipline them temporarily. The rebel friend died and Caracoch found a new comrade in the notorious Yahya ibn-Ghania of the erstwhile kingly family of Almoravides. He is a personage of whom I shall speak again.

Caracoch, the Black Bird of Prey, who had been harrying Africa for eighteen years, suddenly reformed and made his submission to the government. It may be that his shift was due to the diplomatic foresight of Saladin.

However, Caracoch's nuisance career was merely suspended. He broke away from the Almohades and once more fought them bitterly. Finally Destiny caught up with the Black Bird. His comrade, Yahya ibn-Ghania, a yet wilder fellow than himself, took a dislike to him, chased him into the desert, caught him and crucified him. A son of Caracoch's, evidently a feather off the old bird, is to be heard of half a century later as meeting a violent death in the Far South. After a career of raiding he was assassinated by emissaries of a Negro king.

All this activity, originally launched by Saladin's wish to investigate possible places of refuge to the west of Egypt, had been divorced from its motive. It had not helped Saladin except in the matter of prestige. In the beginning Caracoch took Saladin's orders and celebrated Friday prayers in Saladin's name. Thus Saladin's might was advertised in far mosques.

But by far the most important result of the expedition had been to disturb Almohade tranquillity. It is therefore astonishing to find that at the very moment when the adventurer whom Saladin had shot into the Almohade Empire was capturing and sacking erstwhile Almohade towns and conspiring with rebel chiefs, Saladin should have thought it suitable to ask the Almohades to do him an important service.

A LETTER FROM SALADIN

SALADIN IN 1189 WAS VERY MUCH WORRIED BY HIS CHRISTIAN ENEmies. He was ill, dispirited and knew himself to possess a most inadequate fleet. He knew that the Almohades had a strong navy. It was the moment for Saladin to eat humble pie and to suggest that bygones be bygones. Saladin sent a letter of appeal to El-Mansur, begging for the loan of his fleet to help blockade the Christians in the Holy Land.

Saladin's ambassador carried especially beautiful gifts for El-Mansur, from which we may infer Saladin was nervous as to how his request would be received by the monarch he had injured. The list of these gifts comes down to us: two Korans written in the special writing called *mensoub,* a hundred drams (a little more than one pound) of balm, twenty *ratls* (pounds) of aloe-

wood, six hundred mithkals (over six pounds) of musk and ambergris, fifty Arabian bows with cords, twenty Indian lances, and
several saddles embossed in gold.

The most interesting item is the balm. It was presumably the
famous honey-colored balm of Gilead "for which kings warred,"
the subject of considerable biblical mention and of uncountable
traditions. One tradition was that the shrub which produces the
balm had been presented to Solomon by the Queen of Sheba. Another was that it sprang up at the prayer of Mohammed. Another
that it grew by the miraculous well not far from the site of Cairo
where Mary washed the coat of the Baby Jesus, taking its roots in
the sweat which ran down from the garment, one little bush
springing up from each drop that fell. The spot where the balm
shrub grew, as of this last tradition, was a place of peculiar mystery. A very old legend caused the well where the Child's coat was
washed to be the pool in which "the Sun-god bathed his face
when he arose upon the world for the first time." Modern tourists
go there, as did old Christian pilgrims. By its associations it was
a suitable place for the culture of a balm so famed and so treasured through the ages, both for its curative properties—it was
supposed to cure blindness, dry up wounds, and prevent dead
bodies from decaying—and for its supposed sacred value.

*   *   *

SALADIN'S AMBASSADOR ARRIVED IN MOROCCO WITH THESE GIFTS
when El-Mansur was absent in Spain. Morocco astonished the
man from Egypt and he wrote down his impressions. In the gardens of the lush, green city of Fez he paced off the circumference
of a basin and found it to be 864 *coudées* (about 1300 feet).
Morocco in the reign of El-Mansur was in its zenith, in so far as
the Almohade period was concerned. It was then that the Koutoubia in Marrakesh was garnished with the three immense golden
balls made, according to the popular story, from the boiled-down
jewelry of El-Mansur's wife. It was El-Mansur who erected the
famed Hassan Tower at Rabat, one of the "Three daughters," so
called, the other two being the Koutoubia Tower and the Giralda
in Seville.

*   *   *

EL-MANSUR RETURNED FROM SPAIN, READ SALADIN'S LETTER AND
begged to be excused from collaboration in the Holy War against

the Crusaders. Probably—questions of spite aside—El-Mansur very wisely preferred that the Crusades should stay in the East and not involve Morocco.

Saladin pleaded. Further correspondence has lately been discovered,[8] also an almost comical set of private instructions that were sent by Saladin to his ambassador at the Almohade court. The ambassador was to apologize for the dirty doings of Caracoch, the Black Bird of Prey, and to disown him entirely, insisting that he had been a mere "good-for-nothing, such as always trails along after an army" who had troubled the Almohades quite on his own initiative. In short, diplomatic lies.

El-Mansur, the Almohade, was able no doubt to recognize the trickiness and insincerity of these protestations. The relations between his people and Saladin seem to have been consistently scratchy. There had even been an expectation at one time that the Almohades would try to take Egypt away from Saladin. Notwithstanding El-Mansur perhaps softened toward his rival. It is suggested by Ibn-Khaldoun that eventually 180 vessels were sent to Saladin and that "this fleet prevented the Christian landing."

THE MOHAMMEDAN VIEW OF CRUSADERS

IBN-KHALDOUN'S VAGUE TONE IN REPORTING THIS ALLEGED PARTICIpation of western North Africa in those anti-Crusade wars which so vitally preoccupied eastern North Africa is part of the general position. Western North Africa was relatively indifferent to the Crusades. The whole Crusade movement, except for one late episode, was outside their territory, and in those happy days people were not agonized over, or obligatorily involved in events in far places. Ibn-Khaldoun in his history of the West refers in a casual manner to the fact that "the Franks had subjugated the maritime regions of Syria and taken possession of Jerusalem," and has no more to say on a matter which so agitated Europe. A modern writer in an interesting little book, *The Arab Heritage,* sums up the Mohammedan sentiment toward the Crusades in a fashion which is particularly true as concerns the West: "The Crusades

[8] *Une Lettre de Saladin au Calife Almohade,* Gaudefroy-Demombynes, Publications des hautes-études marocaines (1925).

were but distressing incidents in the long history of the struggle in Syria" and were "never the vital affairs that western (i.e. European) writers would make them appear."

*   *   *

To Moslems as a whole the Crusading impulse was a puzzle. Naturally they could have no sympathetic understanding of a Holy War wherein the element of holiness was not contributed by Islam. Of course, fanaticism and pious devotion are but two names for one and the same emotion, according to one's point of view, and few of us can take an alien religion seriously and respectfully.

The Moslem official opinion of the Christian religion, as laid down in the Koran in the sura called "The Table" was that "The Messiah, Son of Mary, is but an Apostle: other apostles have flourished before him; and his mother was a just person (meaning that she did not give herself out to be a goddess). They both ate food." (That is, they were merely human beings.) A later passage in the same sura classes Christians as somewhat less inimical to Islam then the Jews.

The popular Moslem sentiment was that Christians were polytheists and idolaters, a natural enough error when we have in mind the Moslem bewilderment at the Trinity and their dislike of representations of the human form, so that the images of Jesus, the Virgin and the saints made a very evil and confusing impression on them. "These rigid unitarians were scandalized," says Gibbon, "by a worship which represents the birth, death and resurrection of a God."

The Crusaders, since they fought for a faith toward which the Moslems felt contempt, were regarded as maniacs—brave, of course, but madmen all the same. Professor Hitti quotes from an Arabic source that they were "animals possessing the virtues of fighting and courage, but nothing else."

DISASTER IN SPAIN

Then in a single day, the black Monday of July 17, 1212,[9] the Crusaders taught the Moslems of Morocco a grim lesson. This

---

[9] 15th Safer, 609 A.H., is the Moslem date for this great battle, called Las Navas de Tolosa by Christians and Hisn-el-Ocab, "Castle of the Eagles," by

happened in Spain where the warriors of Christendom had gathered at the Pope's preaching to oppose Almohade attack: troops
of two Alfonsos—the VIIIth of Castille and the IInd of Portugal
—troops from France and Germany and Italy. Inflamed by the
words of their several archbishops, Cross in hand, who urged
them "to fight for their altars," these Christians slaughtered Moslems in one of the worst defeats of Islam's history at Navas de
Tolosa in the rocky, bitter borderland country between Andalusia
and Castille.

The defeat was a merited punishment for slackness. The Almohade sovereign, En-Nacer-li-Din-Allah, whose name translated
means "The Champion of Allah's Religion," was a feeble fighter
and a procrastinator who—having opened a campaign to capture
Christian Spain—wasted time in prolonged futilities. Moslems
themselves sneered that he dawdled so long that swallows built
nests and raised their chicks under his tent while he waited
inactive.

Winter overtook him, still dawdling. The Almohades from the
gentler African climate suffered terribly. There is a set of Arabic
verses scarifying Spain's weather, in which the poet says that
Moslems neglect their prayers in that country and drink forbidden wine so that they may find refuge in Hell: "When the north
wind blows here what felicity is his at his ease beside Hell's fires!"

Soldiers' pay was overdue. The vizier in whose hands En-Nacer
left everything had stolen it. The army, that splendid army which
had "spread across the plains and hills like a cloud of locusts,"
was demoralized by inaction, hungry, almost in mutiny, and
ready to let itself be beaten from hatred of its leadership.

En-Nacer watched the disaster from a distance. They say that
he sat upon his shield in front of the scarlet royal tent with the
Koran in one hand and a sword in the other, muttering over and
over, "Allah is just and powerful; the devil is false and perfidious."
His special guard of ten thousand Negroes died in hand-to-hand
fighting to protect him, and En-Nacer in a sort of stupor of
misery went on reciting his text. Finally he was shoved upon a
horse and persuaded to take flight and save himself.

En-Nacer, the pitiable "Champion of Allah's Religion," re-

Moslems. This date would correspond with July 17, 1212. Christian history
makes the date July 16.

turned to Morocco, shut himself up in his harem and would have drunk himself to death but that one of his concubines slipped poison into his wine and shortened his sufferings.

*   *   *

SPAIN WAS LOST TO THE ALMOHADES. IT WAS LESS THAN A CENTURY since the shabby little Mahdi, their founder, had pushed an unveiled princess off her donkey in the streets of Marrakesh. The death rattle was in the Almohade throat. There were the usual wretched circumstances of an African dynasty's decline.

A series of ten rulers, mostly weaklings, staggered through short reigns under pretentious names and met for the most part violent, even ridiculous deaths. Here is a résumé of their tragedies—I omit one only, who died naturally, but whose career was peculiarly unfortunate to his family's fortunes; of him I shall speak separately.

Mostansir (whose full name meant "Who Counts on God's Help") was killed by the blow from a cow's horn. His successor was strangled. So was the next ruler. The next fled to the mountains and eventually was assassinated. The next but one, surnamed The Prudent, was drowned in one of the palace cisterns. His successor (whose throne title meant "Upheld by God's Favor") was killed by rebels. The next ruler was murdered by a usurper.

The usurper, calling himself "He who Has Confidence in God" —all these names seem to jeer at their unlucky wearers—was the last Almohade to rule. He fell before a powerful new dynasty. After him came only the Almohade prince who reigned for five days and whose title was "The Virtuous of God's Grace."

HIGH PRICE OF CHRISTIAN AID

IN THE LIST OF THE ALMOHADES IN THE PERIOD OF THEIR DECLINE one was omitted. He was El-Mamoun (1228-32), a vigorous man and an extreme oddity.

El-Mamoun at his accession imported twelve thousand Christian soldiers from Spain to subdue his rebellious subjects. These mercenaries were bought at a high price. The price of their services included an agreement to build a Christian church in Marrakesh with permission to ring bells—an infamy to Mohammedan ears.

Aided by these trained soldiers El-Mamoun established order, executing allegedly forty-six hundred Moroccans and planting their heads on lance tips around his palace. Said a courtier, "They stink." Said El-Mamoun, who had the reputation of a bloody man even in that frankly bloody age and place, "The odor of a dead traitor stinks only to the noses of other traitors. Faithful subjects find the smell good!"

El-Mamoun then did a thing very startling to national sentiment. He repudiated the holy memory of the Mahdi on whose teachings the Almohades had been founded. Perhaps this was from a sincere and just re-estimate of the old humbug, some of whose tricks have been mentioned (see page 297). Or perhaps El-Mamoun's Christian wife and efficient Christian soldiers had shaken his faith. Or again he may have felt that it was politic to suggest to his puzzled subjects a criticism of the sect as an excuse for the courtesy he had been obliged to show the Christians in exchange for their services.

This last is suggested by the fact that not only did he repudiate the Mahdi but even went so far as to praise Christ, saying, "There is no Mahdi, except it be Jesus, Son of Mary." Naturally the Moslem world was shocked. The moment was badly chosen. The leader, a bloody tyrant, was scarcely the man to preach tolerance successfully. His eccentricity cost him dear. Yet it is a curious and interesting episode, unique in the annals of the long Moslem-Christian quarrel.

THE HAFS FAMILY

THIS INSULT TO THE MAHDI'S SACRED MEMORY ANTAGONIZED AMONG others the great family which had been the Almohades' most precious support throughout the dynasty's career. This was the family of the Hafs.

One of the Hafs, a mountain chief, had been the Mahdi's dearest friend, excepting always the handsome young disciple who was to become the Almohades' first ruler. There had always been a Hafs in every Almohade effort, triumph and trial. One of the Hafs had advised against the ill-fated expedition which culminated in the Navas de Tolosa defeat. Hafs were always at the Almohade elbow.

One of the Hafs had been persuaded to undertake the governorship of disordered Tunisia. This man's son, the viceroy, Abou
Zakaria, grandson of the mountain chief of old who had been the
Mahdi's dear friend, was indignant when his overlord repudiated
the sacred memory of the supposedly "Impeccable Mahdi," crying
out publicly, "Call him not impeccable, but rather a misled and
guilty wretch!"

The viceroy's indignation culminated in a declaration of independence. The Tunisian declaration of independence was the
start of the Hafside dynasty (1228-1534, or later, the situation at
the end of the dynasty's career being very tangled). Again an attempt to unite the western corner of North Africa (what we call
Morocco, Algeria and Tunisia) had failed. It was in this case
inevitable that there should have been a breakaway. The least
observant of rats would have recognized that the Almohade Empire was a sinking ship.

BRIGAND WITH A GRIEVANCE

Symptom of the general state of feebleness was the bizarre
career of Yahya-ibn-Ghania whom his enemies called a brigand,
but who was a brigand with a certain legitimate excuse. He was
the last wild scion of the old Almoravides. His family had been
deposed and he was hungry for revenge. For fifty years he pillaged his way back and forth across the top of Africa from the
region of Sijilmassa to the Egyptian border. He blackmailed
frightened communities out of huge payments. Tunis gave him
one hundred thousand dinars; the Tripoli countryside two million (about six million current United States dollars). When he
was defeated his booty was recaptured and consisted of "18,000
camel loads of gold, silver, precious stuffs and furniture." Undis-
couraged, this valiant villain started again. At one time he attacked Algiers and crucified a local prince on the city walls. In
another exploit he besieged Tunis with catapults. I have already
quoted Gautier—that his was "the most extraordinary epic of
brigandage that ever was."

Ibn-Ghania's ultimate wickedness, from the Moslem point of
view, was the unnatural act of condemning his daughters to
celibacy, giving them this command as his last solemn wish.

For a Moslem to live an old maid was practically unheard of. These daughters of the famous and highborn brigand are, so far as I have noted, the only spinsters in all North African history. The first of the Hafsides magnanimously gave them protection despite all the trouble caused by their father. A palace was built for them, known as "the Chateau of the Girls." Their virginal lives were long. The father of the historian, Ibn-Khaldoun, saw one of them in 1310 (that is, seventy-three years after her father's death) and reported her "the most virtuous in conduct of all the women of the world."

THE RISE OF THE TRIBE OF MERIN

ANOTHER SYMPTOM OF ALMOHADE FEEBLENESS WAS THE UNARrested rise of the tribe of Merin, destined eventually to take Marrakesh and to extinguish the Almohades altogether. During all the series of fumbling reigns which I rehearsed a few pages back, the Merins were gnawing into Almohade country. They made their debut in the time of the ruler who was killed by a cow. They were nomads in all their fresh vigor. Unlike so many great movements in Morocco theirs had no element of religious hysteria for its impetus. They merely craved land and power. They harried Morocco, captured Fez (1249) and reduced the Almohade holdings to no more than the suburbs of Marrakesh. A dozen years later they fought at the very gates of Marrakesh and the Almohades agreed to pay them yearly tribute if they would go away. In 1269 they took Marrakesh.

It was the end of the Almohades. Ibn-Khaldoun's epitaph: "God alone is eternal."

AFTER SALADIN DIED

A COUNTRY WITH AN EXCEPTIONALLY BRILLIANT RULER IS OFTEN to be pitied. Its advertising is out of proportion to its ability. Egypt was in that case after the death of Saladin (1193). His citadel, made from pyramid stones and built in part by the labor of Christian prisoners he had captured, stood on the hills beside Cairo with its proud inscription about the great king who had made Egypt powerful, "The strong-to-aid Saladin, conquest-laden, the restorer of the Empire of the Caliph." But Saladin's fighting vigor which had called Crusading attention to Egypt was no more. Egypt had become a main target for Christian hatred and was twice invaded within thirty years, while Saladin's relatives quarreled amongst themselves and finally, in the middle of the thirteenth century, slid off the throne altogether.

Aside from war and politics Egypt suffered in a more poignant manner. Eight years after Saladin's death the Nile ran low and crops failed. Next year the same. According to a Bagdad physician who lived in Cairo at the time and whose account is quoted by Lane-Poole, things happened which surpass even modern hunger horrors. People openly and frankly went cannibal. Parents killed and cooked their children and "a wife was found eating her husband raw." After famine, pestilence. After pestilence, earthquake.

*   *   *

SOON THEREAFTER EGYPT SAW A MOST PUZZLING MANIFESTATION OF the Crusading impulse. Cairo's slave markets were suddenly filled with Christian children, and when purchasers asked, why this glut of young blond slaves, they were told an almost unbelievable story about how a band of "infidel" youngsters had been permitted to set off on a Holy War, had been lured onto slavers' ships and brought to Egypt's markets. It was the culmination of the queerest and saddest juvenile mass movement in history—perhaps the only organized mass movement of children the world ever saw. But to Egypt it was merely an indication of the enemy's contemptible madness, it was merely something to laugh about.

Then came the Crusading invasion led by the romantic old man, John of Brienne. This was war on a big scale fought against a hampering background of Egyptian royal family quarrels. The Nile was blocked with a great chain. The chain was cut by the Crusaders. Then the sultan sank ships to obstruct the river and the Crusaders cut a by-passing canal to besiege Damietta. When the place was near yielding, says Macrizi, wind rose and drove the Crusaders' ships against its walls where they were overcome by the defenders. These ships were allegedly five hundred forearms in length (say two hundred fifty yards) and protected by plates of iron fastened to them with nails each of which weighed twenty-five *ratls* (a *ratl* was a pound more or less, varying as to time and place).

Had it not been for a domestic dispute which dragged Saladin's nephew, Sultan El-Kamil, back to Cairo, the danger would have been over. As it was, the Crusaders were able to take Damietta. But Moslem engineers cut dikes and flooded the Christian camp. Peace came after three years of struggle and hostages were exchanged, one being the sultan's son. A cemetery near Damietta—then in a different site from the modern town—still bears the name of the "Sea of Blood" because of the Mohammedans who perished there in defense of their faith.

THE TOLERANT SULTAN

AN ODD EPISODE INJECTED INTO THE MIDDLE OF THE CAMPAIGN WAS the visit of St. Francis of Assisi to the Egyptian court. St. Francis arrived during the Damietta siege, was taken prisoner, led before the sultan and preached the Gospel to him. The sultan bore the saint with politeness, which is surprising, given that the doctrine was abhorrent to him and that St. Francis' coreligionists were at the moment attacking the country.

Sultan El-Kamil was evidently cosmopolitan and tolerant. Presently he even entered into a friendly deal with Frederick II, king of Sicily and Holy Roman Emperor, exchanging territory in the Holy Land against Christian help in his family quarrels, and cementing the understanding by the gift to Frederick of a giraffe.

But the family rows were not arrested and seethed to fresh heat at El-Kamil's death. One of his sons reigned briefly and gave place to another, the latter being the prince who in his younger days had been hostage to the Christians after the aborted Crusade.

* * *

THIS SULTAN, LAST REALLY TO RULE OF THE DYNASTY FOUNDED BY Saladin, was associated with two famed and very unusual personalities: the Christians' saint-king, Louis IX, and the ex-slave girl who became Egypt's reigning queen and was the only Moslem woman ever to rule in North Africa. This sultan's name was Es-Salih.

Es-Salih was ill and absent from Egypt when news reached him that Louis was going to invade Egypt, such news having been sent him privately by one described by Arabic chroniclers as "El-Melek-el-Franghi-el-Almanieh" (the Frankish king of the Germans). The sultan caused himself to be rushed home in a litter, only to die while the enemy was still preparing his big attack (1249).

What then happened would have been vanity shattering, could he have foreseen it. The sultan of the line of the mighty Saladin was replaced at this critical moment by a woman. And replaced with brilliant success. An ex-slave girl who had been his favorite caused him to be buried secretly. She called in the commander in chief of the army and gave orders to conceal his death. For the next three months, until the sultan's eldest son could be notified and brought back from afar, this woman was Egypt's ruler. Thus was kept from the army, the people and the enemy knowledge that the throne was vacant at this time of grave danger.

PEARL-SPRAY

THIS WOMAN WAS ONE OF EGYPT'S TWO GREAT ROMANTIC FEMALES. The other was Cleopatra. Her career like that of Cleopatra concerned all three of the continents that then made up the known world: Europe, Asia and Africa. Her life, though less well known to most readers, was even stranger, wilder and more tragic than Cleopatra's. Her name was Shajar-al-Durr, translatable as Pearl-Spray. She was of Turkish or Armenian origin and had made her debut in high circles as a member of the harem of the caliph of Bagdad. She was beautiful, clever and spirited. Presently she passed into another royal harem, that of Sultan Es-Salih.

To Salih, Pearl-Spray bore a son. Automatically this made the slave girl a free woman, for it was the Moslem practice that "a slave whose master had made her a mother should take the title of 'Mother of a Child' and enjoy all the rights of a legitimate wife. Her son is not a bastard."

Pearl-Spray proved herself a brilliant executive. She saved Egypt which—kingless and invaded—would presumably have collapsed but for her. It would have been an honor to any woman and doubly so to one of her religious and social background.

A curious feature of her life story is that she was associated with two dynasties at the moment of their expiration. She was a sort of political "Typhoid Mary." Her first royal master, the caliph, Mustasim, of Bagdad, was the last of a line which had endured for 524 years. Her second lord, Sultan Es-Salih, was for all practical purposes the last of the dynasty founded by Saladin. She herself became the first of the succeeding dynasty, that called the Mamluks, a word meaning "owned," and being the term applied to a slave when the slave was white, not Negro. Es-Salih had purchased great numbers of mamluks to man his army. Now they took charge and Mamluk sultans were to govern Egypt for the next two and a half centuries and to remain a powerful force almost into our own days.

Pearl-Spray took on responsibility at a time when just for a little while it looked as if Louis of France might conquer Egypt. Damietta had fallen to him. He had at great loss pushed forward so far that he was "on the threshold of the palace of the queen." Pearl-Spray within the palace was carrying on her patriotic deception, pretending that the sultan still lived, though ill, causing his meals to be sent to his supposed sickroom, producing forged state papers, while she herself consulted with officials and generals and planned the defense of the country.

The tide turned. Louis was cut off from his supplies. Egypt's faithful ally, a relative of "General Plague," intervened. The Christians—it being Lent and more suitable food lacking—had eaten Nile fish fattened on corpses and they fell sick in a mass.

In a night of horror (April 5-6, 1250) Louis and what remained of his army tried to fight their way back to the Damietta base. The whole Christian force was lost, either killed or taken captive, in a defeat so cruel that the natives for long afterward claimed that the earth was permanently stained crimson. Louis himself was captured and carried away prisoner, lodged in the house of one Ibn-Locman under the guard of a eunuch, and—Arabic history states—chained up.

It was a notable victory for Pearl-Spray, who had almost to the climax operated as sole ruler. At the return of the sultan's son she resigned. He held power for a few weeks only. His own folly and Pearl-Spray's natural resentment ended his reign by a complex and horrid assassination. At a banquet given on the battlefield a month after the victory the generals of the army fell upon him. He fled and they set fire to his refuge place. He fled again and what was left of his burnt and bleeding body perished in the river, one of the generals tearing out his heart as he expired.

*   *   *

AGAIN PEARL-SPRAY TOOK CHARGE, THIS TIME OPENLY. A SOUVENIR of her reign has come down to us, a coin bearing mention of her in words which signify, "The former slave of the Caliph Mustasim and afterward of Salih, now Queen of the Moslems." [10]

It is evident that Pearl-Spray was proud of her humble beginnings in life, proud of being a self-made queen. But after all in this new Mamluk court where most persons of consequence were of slave origin her start as a harem slave was nothing to blink at.

Her dealings with the vanquished enemy were both practical and humane. She promptly collected ransom money from Louis and saw that he and what remained of his men got safely away. The amount actually paid is variously reported and, whatever its figure, would be difficult to turn into current values (variously given as 167,103 livres of Tours, as 400,000 besants, etc.). The money was paid over by Louis' queen, who accompanied the Crusade and who—in addition to her other troubles during the tragic period—had been with child and given birth to a boy of the melancholy name of Jean Tristan, a true Crusader for he was both born and died during Crusades. (He died in St. Louis' second Crusading fiasco in Tunisia.) Did the two queens meet, I wonder, she who had pushed her way to the throne after being slave in two harems and she who was the pitiable victim of a saintly crank?

FIRE IN WARFARE

ONE OF THE CAUSES ASSIGNED FOR THE COMPLETE FAILURE OF LOUIS' Egyptian Crusade was the use by the defenders of what was called in medieval warfare "Greek Fire." The employment of this fierce flame which nothing could extinguish save "sand, urine (*sic*) or vinegar," which shot through the air with lightning speed and whose composition was a secret Louis' army did not share, was regarded as shabby and unchivalrous.

[10] Stanley Lane-Poole, *A History of Egypt in the Middle Ages:* the only surviving example of this coin, so far as he knew, was at the British Museum.

Nevertheless the use of fire in war was not really a new thing. It had been used since remote antiquity. I have chanced to find in a Fragment of Polybius (who was born about 204 B.C.) an account of "the engine for throwing fire." Says he, "On each side of the ship's prow noosed ropes were run along the inner side of the hull into which were fixed poles stretching out seaward. From the extremity of each hung by an iron chain the funnel shaped vessel full of fire so that, in charging or passing, the fire was shot out of it into the enemy's ship, but was a long way from one's own ship owing to the inclination."

Even specially produced chemical flame was nothing new, though knowledge of it appears to have been spotty and irregularly distributed. It was, for instance, used when the Fatimites first attacked Egypt over three centuries before it horrified Louis' Crusaders. Again in Tunisia "a fleet of ten *merakeb harbia* (war ships) equipped with naphtha" awaited the arrival of Roger II on one of his invasion attempts.

Chemical flame had been originally invented in Syria, according to Professor Gautier, and imported to Constantinople where it got to be regarded as a special Christian holy treasure. It was looked on as a mystic possession, angel revealed, and protected from non-Christian use by Heavenly taboo.

Notwithstanding, the secret shifted its religious affiliations. It became, as already noted, a Moslem property. And we hear of it as used by Tartars—a horseman carrying "wild fire" in a copper container, a man with bellows mounted behind. The *sang-froid* of the horse is admirable! The so-called Northern Barbarians who lived in a country now included in Russia "used to ask for the secret of Greek fire" back in the days when its ownership was exclusively Christian.

THE TRAGEDY OF PEARL-SPRAY

AFTER ST. LOUIS AND HIS ARMY HAD LIMPED OUT OF EGYPT PEARL-Spray reigned there for seven years. At first she reigned alone. This could not last. To live under the rule of a woman was too strange a thing for Moslem taste. Mohammed had declared, according to tradition, that "no nation would ever prosper which put its affairs in a woman's hands." The caliph of Bagdad was

shocked to hear that his former slave girl was a queen and sent a
sneering message to Egypt: "Had they no men?" Furthermore
there was opposition from the die-hard supporters of Saladin's
dynasty to the complete usurpation of power by the White-slave
(Mamluk) group of which Pearl-Spray was the directress.

So Pearl-Spray found it politic to share her throne not with
one only, but with a pair of male associates. One of these was a
leading Mamluk general, Aybek, with whom she also shared her
bed, it having been decided that a joint reign of a married couple
would overcome the public prejudice against female rule. The
other associate was a lad of six of the Saladin strain, added to the
royal party to satisfy the old-fashioned. Of this triangular group
Pearl-Spray was the real control.

After two years the lad was dropped. Pearl-Spray and her consort, Aybek, did not get on. At length Aybek proposed to take
another wife, both for pleasure and policy, she being influential
as a Near Eastern princess of rank. Pearl-Spray murdered him in
his bath. The Mamluks of the court were indignant and abandoned her. Pearl-Spray's end was terrible. She was battered to
death by a gang of slave women who fell upon her with their
wooden clogs and threw her broken body into the citadel ditch.

In her last moment it would have gratified the wild temper of
the queen had she known that her death would be followed less
than a year afterward by the death, very nearly as terrible, of
her ex-master and sneering enemy, the caliph. Bagdad fell to a
grandson of the great Genghis Khan in 1258. Eight hundred
thousand were massacred, amongst them the caliph, last of the
Abbasids, who, according to Marco Polo, was a secret Christian!
After that a shadowy impotent caliphate set up in Cairo. But its
prestige was finished.

Pearl-Spray by a peculiar fatality had shared the intimate
moments of the last of two dynasties, and furthermore had procured the deaths of two other rulers: the stepson who temporarily
deposed her and the husband who shared her throne.

There still stands in Cairo a little mausoleum bearing her name
and presumably containing what was left of the beautiful body
of Pearl-Spray (Shajar-al-Durr) one of the most daring, clever and
ruthless women who ever lived.

WHY DID ST. LOUIS ATTACK TUNIS?

ONE MORE FIASCO WAS NEEDED TO DESTROY CRUSADING HOPES OF the conquest of Moslem Africa. This last attempt, twenty years later in a new place, again had St. Louis as its leader.

What reason prompted St. Louis to direct his Crusade to Tunisia, so remote from the Holy Land, is a matter of much assorted theorizing.

For one thing St. Louis unquestionably had the pious hope of Christianizing the country. Looking back at it his hope seems absurd. Louis, however, had received reports which—given that he was what Julius Caesar had in mind when he declared that men readily believe what they desire—made him imagine that the Hafside sultan of Tunis, El-Mostansir, might turn to Christ.

Amongst the supporting reasons that led St. Louis to Tunis is that he may have been influenced by the ill will which his brother, Charles of Anjou, king of Sicily, felt toward the Tunis government. Another possible reason is that Tunisia seemed to Louis a good base from which to reattack Egypt. Considering the terrain which separated the two countries, the idea was poor, but St. Louis knew less of the geographical difficulties than we do. There are other motives suggested. It remains one of history's puzzles.

*   *   *

ONE EXPLANATION WHICH CHRISTIAN HISTORIANS HAVE NOT NOTED is interesting. It shows how inimical nations misunderstand one another. Ibn-Khaldoun writes, "It is said that the motive for the expedition against Tunis on the part of the Chief of the Franks was as follows: merchants of his country had lent money to Luliani (Luliani was a financial wizard who had been discredited and killed). After the catastrophe which closed the career of this official the merchants asked the sultan of Tunis to repay the sums lent, which amounted to 300,000 dinars (about 900,000 current United States dollars). As they had no proof to support their demand the sultan refused. Then they went to complain to their own king (Louis). This ruler took their part and permitted himself to be persuaded to undertake an expedition against Tunis, 'a city,' so they told him, 'very easy to capture.' "

Such, in the opinion of a very wise Moslem, was the ignoble reason animating a Christian saint when he started a Crusade!

Having invited other Christian kings to help him, Ibn-Khaldoun goes on, and having secured the approval of "the Pope, a personage who the Christians regard as the vicar of the Messiah," Louis made his preparations.

DIPLOMACY'S FAILURE

THE SULTAN OF TUNIS VIEWED THESE PREPARATIONS WITH DISMAY and sent an ambassador to Louis to propose such a deal between them as might induce Louis to leave Tunis in peace. To grease the way these ambassadors, Ibn-Khaldoun says, took with them twenty-four thousand gold pieces. "The king (Louis) accepted the money and then declared that the expedition would go on as planned."

Another Arabic source represents the Tunisian attitude toward Louis' proposed attack in a much less placatory light. According to this alternate story, a letter was sent to Louis from Tunisia as follows:

FRENCHMAN,
   Tunis is the sister of Cairo. Be ready for the fate which waits for you here. At Tunis the house of Ibn-Locman (alluding to the prison where Louis was confined after his dire Egyptian defeat) will be your tomb, and, for the guardian eunuch, you will have instead the two angels of judgment.

*   *   *

IN JULY, 1270, LOUIS SAILED AWAY FROM FRANCE ON THE SHIP so well named *Paradise,* for it carried the saintly warrior to the threshold of Heaven; he died a month later. It is said that the *Paradise* on this tragic voyage had aid of the first *sea* map of which we have knowledge.

Into the midsummer heat of Tunisia debarked Louis and his men, it having seemed best to the sultan not to attempt to prevent the landing but to fight it out on shore. Ibn-Khaldoun's grandfather watched the landing and saw how Louis installed a fortress in the ruins of Carthage. At first things went badly for the Moslems. The Sultan feared that he must give up the town of Tunis and flee to Kairouan.

DEATH OF A SAINT

THEN CAME THE END PROPHESIED IN THE WARNING LETTER, Louis IX died. The Christian story of his end represents him as having been a sick man before he left France, so weak he could not sit his horse, and attributes his death, whispering, "Jerusalem! Jerusalem!" to fever and dysentery.

His Moslem enemies record something quite different. The sultan of Tunis had the opinion that it was nothing but greed which led Louis to attack his shores, and he plotted to use this greed to destroy him. Naturally the sultan had no appreciation of the disinterested fighting piety of the man who "more than any other who had ever lived was impressed with a belief in the duty of exterminating all enemies of his own faith," as Hallam says. The sultan's analysis of St. Louis was that he must be madly avid for gain to have come back again to a Moslem country after his wretched first adventure in Egypt. The sultan therefore, so the story goes, prepared an extravagantly jeweled sword with poison so cunningly concealed that only he who unsheathed it would come in contact with the liquid. This rich object he caused to be presented to Louis by an agent. The trick worked. Louis accepted the gift from the pretended admirer. "The poison infiltrated into him and he died at once. All High Allah had saved the Moslems!"

The contrasting ideas about St. Louis' last Crusade are interesting. Both are sincere attempts to tell history: from the sympathetic Christian point of view, and from the inimical Moslem one.[11]

*   *   *

THOUGH HIS CAREER SO CHARMED THE POPULAR IMAGINATION THAT his name through the centuries has been chosen for a vast number

---

[11] In addition to the seriously recorded historic view of St. Louis in Arabic literature there are curious local legends about him. For instance, Cardinal Lavigerie was told by Moslems living in the Tunis region that St. Louis had turned Mohammedan on his deathbed, following a special apparition before him of the Prophet. Lavigerie's informants claimed that the famous mosque of Sidi Bou Said near Carthage really commemorates St. Louis: the Moslem saint, Bou Said, was in short, no other than St. Louis under another name! The wise old cardinal was not offended and the incident is included in his *Life* by Georges Goyau.

of secular purposes—a glance at the long list of items under "St. Louis" in the *Encyclopaedia Britannica* will amaze you— St. Louis' performance as a Crusader in Africa was a lamentable failure. Upon his death the sultan is said to have agreed to pay the Christians the cost of the expedition if they would go away quietly. The amount was "ten mule loads of silver." They then sailed for Europe.

Instead of being converted the people of Tunisia were inspired with a greatly increased dislike for Christianity. Previously there had been in Tunisia and other parts of the West a certain easy tolerance, spotted with occasional violence. Tunis had its Christian traders. There had even been a Christian archbishop in what was left of Carthage. The Dominicans had premises at Tunis, the Franciscans had some following at Fez. Marrakesh had a Christian church (see page 316). Gafsa, Edrisi states, was speaking Latin in the twelfth century. There is continuous mention of the use of Christian soldiers by Moslem rulers.

St. Louis' attack roused fanaticism. At the sacred city of Kairouan Christians were henceforth forbidden. Jews too. From the days of St. Louis until 1881 when the French took over Tunisia the rule was that persons of both religions were forbidden to pass the night inside the city. Many Jews are said to have become Moslem, but to have worn Islam on the surface only, still—even after six centuries—observing the Jewish Sabbath. I have found no indication of how Kairouan's Christian population reacted to the ruling.

Another result of the Crusade was a renewed effort—still not completely successful—to demolish Carthage whose ruined walls had served as an improvised fortress for Louis' army.

*   *   *

TODAY A CATHEDRAL MARKS THE PLACE OF ST. LOUIS' MARTYRDOM. Its building was rushed through for its symbolic value when Tunisia became a French protectorate. Ten bishops and the resident general of France attended its inauguration on Ascension Day, 1890. The great colonial cardinal, Lavigerie, is buried there. Frenchmen had at last carried out a part of St. Louis' ambition. But wiser Frenchmen than he, who did not see it as a duty "to exterminate all enemies of their faith," and who made no move to interfere with Tunisia's worshiping in her own age-old fashion

PART THREE

The Crescent Shines in the Open

AFTERNOON IN AFRICA

THE LATTER MEDIEVAL CENTURIES WERE TO NORTH AFRICA THE glowing afternoon of a glorious day; to Europe the dawning hours that followed a long and lugubrious night.

What we persist in calling the "middle" ages, although the prolongation of the ensuing Modern Ages of history, so called, have caused the middle to lose its place, both with respect to a stage of development and with respect to time, were the grandest period for North Africa as a whole. In Europe they were a passage toward which we look back, rightly or wrongly, as a sodden gap between classical culture and modern civilization, as something like a dull wait between trains in the railway station of time. Just when Europe was dragging herself out of the "awkward age," North Africa slipped back. The great turning point of history, Gautier says, was to us the Renaissance: to us, new life; to the Moslem world, death agony.

DOOR AJAR

UPON THESE LATTER MEDIEVAL CENTURIES IN AFRICA WE BEGIN TO possess other testimony than the Arabic records which informed us about the start of the Moslem period. To the outside world North Africa was no longer a mystery behind an opaque curtain; the complete privacy of the continent as far as Christian knowl-. edge was concerned was coming to an end. Our Christian testimony was largely supplied by belligerents, for—oddly—Europe's battling upon African soil increased after the Crusades were ended, but illuminating, nonetheless, and had made the late Middle Ages in Africa more familiar to the average person. Therefore I shall sweep more rapidly across these centuries, not giving such detail as I did in the case of the hidden years of early Islam about which most of us knew practically nothing.

ACROSS NORTH AFRICA IN THE LATTER MIDDLE AGES

LET US TRAVEL ACROSS NORTH AFRICA IN THOSE LATTER MEDIEVAL days, that period of culminating Moslem splendor. One thing we will note: a change was coming over the mentality of the West. The religious fever which had so long excited its people had cooled. They were still pious Moslems. But they no longer fought furiously amongst themselves for sectarian differences. They still fought amongst one another, but for motives that were tangible and practical. The romantic hero worship of a holy chief, the fanatical readiness to die for a religious idea were, with a few exceptions, no more.

One reason for the psychological change was that in banding together to fight Christian attacks they had merged their own religious differentiations. Another reason was the increasing influence of the more practical Arab strain—Arabs of the second invasion, and Arab refugees from Spain.

This change makes North African history approach more closely to the conventional historic model of other lands of the day; North Africans were no longer fanatics, but merely greedy, or angry or frightened citizens like other men.

*   *   *

FOUR CAPITALS INFLUENCED—ONE CANNOT SAY CONTROLLED—THE Mediterranean coast: Fez, Tlemcen, Tunis and Cairo. In each of these reigned a long surviving system of rulers, none of whom depended upon any specific religious prestige. These were the Merinides of Fez (see page 319), the oft-deposed and reinstated Abd-el-Wad of Tlemcen, later called Zeinides, the Hafsides of Tunis (see page 317) and Cairo's Mamluks.

TLEMCEN

TLEMCEN, CLOSE TO THE MODERN FRONTIER BETWEEN ALGERIA AND
Morocco, was the capital of a buffer kingdom between the Hafsides
and the Merinides. It was a buffer with prickles. Few cities had
so many adventures as Tlemcen during the years of its prime
historic importance.

Though it now comes for the first time prominently into our
story, Tlemcen was already old. Very old in the opinion of its own
people who boasted that it contained a piece of masonry dating
back to Moses. In the Koran (sura XVIII) there is an account of
how Moses and a companion went journeying to "the confluence of
the two seas," came to a city, found "a wall that was about to fall,"
which the companion repaired, while Moses chided him, " 'If thou
hadst wished, thou mightest have obtained pay for this (work).' "
The city where this happened was locally believed to have been
Tlemcen and the wall in question was pointed out by medieval
residents. Learned Arabic opinion, however, repudiated the claim
on the grounds that Moses never went so far westward. Tlemcen
unquestionably was the site of a Roman town by another name.

The name Tlemcen meant the reunion of two things—that is,
the land and the sea. It was a few miles off the Mediterranean and
on a direct route to the Sahara. A splendid trade position. It
ranked as the third richest city in the West. Traders from Negroland passed that way. Traders from Europe came to its port,
Honein. There were at Tlemcen hotels *(fondouks)* where Genoese
and Venetians lodged and did business; Tlemcen had treaty relations with Aragon; proof of its commercial vitality was the existence of a big Jewish population—these lived in a single street and
obligatorily wore yellow turbans.

From all this trade Tlemcen's sovereign drew great profit. His
ten per cent upon a single ship could touch fifteen thousand
ducats. The Saharan trade was even more valuable. As one of
Tlemcen's kings remarked contentedly, Tlemcen sent into the
Sudan loads of the cheapest local merchandise and got back in
exchange "gold, which all the world obeys." The trade with
Europe pleased him less since this latter was an affair of sending

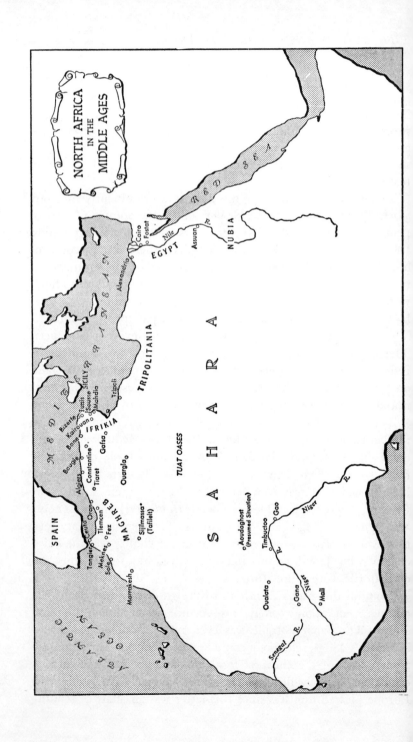

away gold and getting back "objects which wear out easily, or else corrupt the ways of my people."

*   *   *

THE KINGS OF TLEMCEN, OF WHOM THE ABOVE ONE-SIDED TRADER was the fourth, were a dynasty called the Abd-el-Wad. The name meant "Servants of the One and Only God"; they were an old Berber tribe, some of whose warriors had accompanied Sidi Okba on his celebrated expedition to the Atlantic. It was their hero, Yaghmorasen, "a lion whose den none dared to enter, and who never gave up his prey," who made the tribe into an independent nation (1235). His new kingdom, with its capital at Tlemcen, had to withstand attacks by the newborn dynasty, the Hafsides, by the moribund Almohades and by the Merinides, a people traditionally inimical to his tribe. In the encounter with the Almohades Yaghmorasen took a notable item of booty: a treasured copy of the first edition of the Koran, a volume which had been prepared in the year 30 A.H. (650 A.D.), had been preserved reverently in Moslem Spain and been captured and brought to Africa by the Almohades.

"HOW NEAR IS ALLAH'S HELP!"

THE SIEGES OF TLEMCEN ARE FAMOUS. IT WAS IN AN IDEAL PLACE FOR trade on the great East-West Road across the top of Africa, but a poor place for peace and tranquility. The sieges followed at almost incredibly short intervals. The endurance of the civil population must have been stupendous.

In the great eight-year siege started by the Merinides in 1299 they suffered, so contemporary opinion believed, "such ills as never had befallen any population in the world." They ate mice and serpents. Food prices of the usual items of human diet became startling. Today we might not blink—except in envy—at some of the prices, such as a beef for the equivalent of 180 current United States dollars. But considering that a head of lettuce was three dollars, a cat about four-fifty, a rat the equivalent of one-fifty, we suspect that the beef was nonprocurable and was included in the list in purely academic fashion. The list was supplied by a learned sheikh who went through the siege. Bear in mind that the

usual peacetime value of, say, a chicken in that part of the world
then was the equivalent of two current United States cents.

Surrender seemed inevitable. The slave woman, Dad, came to
the king of Tlemcen, grandson of the lion-hearted Yaghmorasen,
and spoke on behalf of the women of the royal harem: "Spare us
the shame of capture by the enemy. Kill us first." The king agreed.
He would hold out three more days. Then, if no miracle came,
the women would have their throats cut "by the Jews and the
Christians" of the city, and he at the head of his men would make
a last fatal sortie.

At that very moment there arrived a messenger from outside the
beleaguered city. The sultan of the Merinide besiegers had been
assassinated, victim of the pique of one of his black eunuchs. The
siege was lifted.

After that the mint of Tlemcen inscribed upon its coins, *"How
near is Allah's help!"* Many put the words upon their house fronts.

But prudent Tlemcen did not depend entirely upon Allah for
their future. The king built up a food and arms reserve. He filled
up great cisterns with melted-down grease. He packed fortresses
full of salt, charcoal and fuel wood. "The ground in the interior
of the city was nothing but a great grain silo." Thirty years later
another Merinide siege found Tlemcen well fed. But Allah withheld help. And the king of the moment was a poor creature
"plunged in voluptuous habits, dissipated, and always drunk,"
according to the *Rawdat en-Nisrin* (The Garden of Wild Roses,
a fourteenth century Merinide history). The king, so this enemy
historian continues, was a weakling who always drooped when he
stood up and was in consequence known as "The Little Flower."
This time Tlemcen's downfall may have been because a local
mason revealed to the enemy the situation of the secret spring
from which water was brought into the city by hidden pipes.

Tlemcen fell temporarily to the hated Merinides, along with
the treasured first edition of the Koran. The Merinides kept the
Koran, but not the city. Members of the Abd-el-Wad family
returned to power and the old series of attacks were resumed.
To be besieged was Tlemcen's natural state, its normal civic condition. I have mentioned but two out of many. Yet Tlemcen
became the most renowned beauty spot in western North Africa
of the day—illuminating as to the nondestructiveness of old-time

wars. It survives now "the architectural jewel of Algeria," can still show us a mosque from the twelfth century, a minaret of the days of Yaghmorasen, and so on.

FEZ

FEZ HAD ACQUIRED A CONJOINT AND BECOME A CAPITAL AGAIN. THE Merinides after defeating the Almohades (see page 319) had not fancied Marrakesh for capital. Beside Fez they founded Fez-Djedid, "New Fez," or "The White City." The horoscope of New Fez was taken with due solemnity and promised brilliantly: "No sultan will die here; no army go forth except to victory!"

These were fine words for a fighting dynasty like the Merinides which presently set itself to try to control all the top of Africa from the Atlantic to Tripoli and beyond. According to the scientific ideas of the time theirs was obligatorily a fighting race: "Morocco is in the Third and Fourth Climates, and the Third Climate is the one in which people shed blood, where hate reigns, and envy and treachery. . . . It is under the influence of Mars. . . . These folk kill a man as easily as a sparrow," wrote a thirteenth century Moslem geographer. Said another Arabic authority, "The Climate where people are the most violent, the wildest, the most full of hate is Morocco."

Whether the reason was the climate or no, it is true that Moroccans were notably warlike, and their habit of boiling over into their neighbors' homelands rose to especial heat during the big days of the Merinides.

     *   *   *

THE APEX OF MERINIDE POWER WAS IN THE MIDDLE PART OF THE fourteenth century under two kings, father and son, Abu'l Hasan and Abu-Inan. The two men did not enjoy the happy destinies promised by the horoscope of New Fez. The father was deposed by his son and died a refugee; the son was deposed by his army and strangled. But such fates were but usual: a throne in medieval North Africa was the most dangerous spot on which a man might sit.

Abu'l Hasan, the father (reigned from 1331 to 1348) wrote at the height of his greatness informing the sultan at Cairo that all the world from the ocean to the near-frontier of Egypt was his. He was known as "the great king of the West." Contemporary mentions of him drip with honeyed flattery in the exuberant Arabic manner. One description: "They report such facts about him as could perfume the breezes and give enhanced flavor to Tasnin" (the exquisitely delicious waters of Paradise). He could also, we are assured, break rocks with his hands.

He made Tunisia his puppet. The local royal family, the Hafsides, subsisted by his grace under an arrangement sealed by the gift of a Tunisian princess to his harem. He conquered the Abd-el-Wad of Tlemcen, took Sijilmassa on the Saharan border, and occupied the Tuat oases far into the desert. He held Gibraltar and other towns in Spain. He installed a system of watchtowers from the Atlantic coasts of Morocco to Algiers against possible Christian attack. He fortified Gibraltar so that "the mountain was ringed with walls like the moon by its halo."

The military value of Gibraltar was fully appreciated. Abu'l Hasan's son carried on the work of fortification. In the palace at Fez could be admired a model of this fort of Islam in all its details: "walls, towers, citadel, gates, arsenal, mosques, munitions, stores and corn granaries, together with the shape of the *Jebel* (hill) itself . . . a fine piece of craftsmanship."

TWO DISASTERS

ABU'L HASAN MANAGED TO HOLD GIBRALTAR, BUT THE GREATER part of the conquests which this greedy Moroccan had heaped on his plate soon slid away. Two specific defeats befell him, renowned in Arabic record as "The Disaster of Tarifa" and "The Disaster of Kairouan."

At Tarifa on the Salado River in 1340, which is one of the famous dates of Spanish history, Christian troops in their fury fought into Abu'l Hasan's very camp and tipped over the royal tent. Abu'l Hasan fled to Africa, mourning the Tunisian wife who had been his especial delight and who had been killed in the melee. The defeat gave Alfonso XI the soubriquet "He-of-the-Salado-River" and was a bitter blow to Moslem pride. The celebrated traveler, Ibn-Batuta, heard about it with dismay in far-off Bagdad where he met an informant from Morocco and cried woefully, "May Allah repair the breach which Islam has suffered!"

The "Disaster of Kairouan" (1348) was very nearly Abu'l Hasan's immediate ruin and gave the hint to his son and successor that the time had come to shove his father off the throne. Again Abu'l Hasan fled.

*   *   *

ONE MORE BRILLIANT MOMENT AWAITED ABU'L HASAN, ALBEIT with a comic touch added. It was the reception of foreign ambassadors at Tunis a few months after the Kairouan disaster. These ambassadors—there were Christians from Spain, Negroes from the Sudan beyond the Sahara—had come bearing rich gifts for the erstwhile triumphant king of Morocco, and on arrival had learned that he was triumphant no longer. At last they made contact with him in a very shaky position in Tunis. Notwithstanding the reception was carried out with due ceremony and it is recorded that the Negro ambassador prostrated himself before the Moroccan king in his native fashion; "one of his suite carried a basketful of dust and whenever the king spoke graciously to him the envoy 'dusted himself'—i.e. threw dust over himself." This method of showing respect for royalty was a regular part of court etiquette in Negroland, persons addressed by the king throwing dust upon their heads and backs, "for all the world," as the traveler, Ibn-Batuta, observed, "like bathers washing themselves with water."

IBN-BATUTA'S PUBLISHER

ABU'L HASAN'S REBEL SON, ABU-INAN, SOUGHT TO RECAPTURE THE ground which his father had lost and was partially successful.

Upon his personality we have a flowery tribute from Ibn-Batuta. The traveler's extreme enthusiasm is comprehensible for it was Abu-Inan who extended to him "the gracious command that he should dictate an account of the cities he had seen on his travels and of the interesting events which he retained in his memory, and of the rulers of countries, learned men and pious saints he had met." It was Abu-Inan who provided the amanuensis-editor and from this royal patronage resulted one of the grandest travel books—perhaps the grandest—of all times. Its title: *A Gift to Those*

Interested in the Curiosities of Cities and in the Marvels along the Way.

In view of this patronage it is no wonder that Ibn-Batuta praised his royal protector in these discriminating terms: "The awe that surrounded him made me forget the King of Irak; his elegance that of the Emperor of India; his politeness that of the King of Yemen; his bravery that of the King of the Turks (meaning Egyptians, I presume); his religious carriage that of the Emperor of Turkestan; his knowledge that of the Emperor of Sumatra."

Yet something was lacking; five years later Abu-Inan was assassinated, strangled by his own vizier. The author of that oddly named history of the Merinides (*The Garden of Wild Roses*) who knew him personally states that "no man in his army had a more opulent beard, nor a better figure" and that he begot 325 children, one of whom succeeded him.

TUNIS

LET US CONSIDER THE TUNIS OF THE LATTER MIDDLE AGES.

Tunis was the doyen of African capitals, already more than two thousand years old and carrying along gallantly her civilized heritage. The city's name, pronounced in the local manner (Too-nis) means "She inspires gentleness." It was the current Moslem opinion that the inhabitants of the region stood apart from the rest of North Africa "by the sweetness of their characters, by their agility of intelligence, good manners and natural amiability."

Tunis had been educated by many foreign contacts, being, as she was, in a splendid trade position. She had been improved by many foreign cultures: Punic, Roman, Christian, Islamic.

Also she benefited by the suave influence of learned Spanish Mohammedan refugees, driven from their homes by the ever-rising Christian pressure. For in the Spain of those days "with every dawn came a new calamity, a day of mourning for Islam, a day of festival for our enemy" (from a pathetic poem recited at the Tunis court by one Abu-abd-Allah-ibn-el-Abbar, a Spanish Moslem imploring sympathy for his coreligionists). Ibn-Khaldoun says, "At Tunis's court one could meet a crowd of Spaniards

(Moslems); some were distinguished poets, others graceful writers, learned savants, noblemen, intrepid warriors—all come to shelter themselves under the royal protection."

Tunis was regarded as a bright spot in the generally darkening Mohammedan sky. Its Hafside rulers had acquired a mighty reputation by their ability to stand off St. Louis' Crusade. In their best days they controlled African territory that was "thirty-five days' march from east to west." The temporarily successful attack of their Moroccan neighbor, just mentioned, did not cripple the Hafsides for long. Their dynasty outlasted the Middle Ages.

WHEN BIZERTE WAS A HUNTING PARK

THE MOST PICTURESQUE AND POWERFUL OF THEIR SULTANS, EL-Mostansir, beautified the city and its environs with many novelties. His hunting park at Bizerte was supposedly unique in the world of its day (mid-thirteenth century). In this region, known in World War II as the strongest position in Tunisia, El-Mostansir walled in a vast section which he stocked with a troop of wild animals. There when the mood seized him he would go with falcons, hunting dogs (slougui) and hunting leopards for a day's sport. The physical well-being of the ladies of the court was not neglected. A private walk, so walled on either side as to insure absolute privacy, led from the palace to the garden, Ras-el-Tabia. Here the harem ladies could go without being exposed to the public eye and protected by eunuch guards. Another and vaster garden, the Abu-Fehr, outside the city had every known tree and flower. In its middle was an artificial lake fed by the help of the colossal old Cathaginian aqueduct. In this lake the sultan's ladies were wont to practice sports: each seated in a tiny boat they would hold races.

*   *   *

ON FESTIVAL DAYS THE TUNIS SCENE WAS GORGEOUS. THE SULTAN'S black guards, called "Guinea-men," led off—lance in hand, silk flags in the wind, each dressed in a white, belted gown, sword at side. The sultan rode in the midst of his own standards of honor, white, red, yellow, green. Each tribal chief had his own banner with its special inscription, such as "There is no God but Allah," or "The power is to Allah." The horseman to the sultan's right was band leader and would give orders to the drummer groups in turn. "Beat, So-and-So!" he would shout, naming the leader of this or that drum corps. And the drums would roar. This is from the description of a fourteenth century observer at Tunis.

The Hafside sultans were, of course, elegant in their apparel. The royal garment for ceremonies was a green-black silk. This silk was allegedly extracted from the sea. Ibn-Said gives an account of this fabric, of whose possible modern counterpart others may know better than I do. Says he, "I have seen how it is collected at Sfax (Tunisia). Divers go into the sea and bring out tubers resembling onions, having hairs on their upper part. These 'onions' burst open, letting out hairs which are combed, spun into thread and woven into cloth. . . . This is what is called in Egypt and Syria 'fish wool.' "

A silken royal costume was a thing of high price. To give an actual idea of its value let me indicate what its cost was in comparison with another article at the same place and time: The most desirable quality of meat was then to be bought in Tunisia at such a figure that twenty thousand pounds of it would cost exactly the same amount as one royal silken ceremony robe!

*   *   *

THERE CAN HAVE BEEN FEW CITIES OF THE LATE MEDIEVAL PERIOD to approach Tunis in sophistication and general worldly experience. Perhaps there are few today. Where would one meet so mixed a crowd of businessmen, sailors, travelers and pilgrims as Tunis saw? Tunis was truly cosmopolitan, treating foreigners of antagonistic religions without ill will, and entertaining Christians from Europe in her *fondouks*. As for its visitors from Negroland—such trade made Tunis' fortune. She was the exchange place where gold, ivory, slaves, spices were traded for the goods of Europe.

*   *   *

IN THE YEAR 1257 TUNIS ENJOYED A RARE SPECTACLE. A KING OF Negroland sent gifts to the sultan. Amongst these gifts was a giraffe, "an animal whose outward characteristics," as Ibn-Khaldoun puts it sedately, "were of the most illmatched." The inhabitants of Tunis ran in a crowd to see it, "so that the plain overflowed with people. They felt a profound astonishment at the sight of a quadruped whose strange form suggested at the same time several animals of different species."

The giraffe was an advertisement as well as a token of inter-royal amity. It was a striking suggestion of the goods which exotic Africa could offer. These exchanges of royal gifts, of which we hear so much picturesque detail in the pages of medieval writers, often included—along with practical objects of local produce—a showpiece to attract public notice. The giraffe in question and the other strange animals of whose long journeys we read were an aid to trade. The whole royal present probably was intended to constitute a sort of traveling trade fair.

DOCILE TRIPOLI

BETWEEN TUNIS AND EGYPT OUR TOUR ACROSS NORTH AFRICA PICKS up but one point of importance, Tripoli, and Tripoli—given that it had been the name of a region of some consequence in classical days and was destined to be again prominent in modern times—was curiously inconspicuous and spineless in the Middle Ages.

Tripoli had no ambition to control her neighbors. She did not crave independence. She was a city of wealth and trade, content to touch her hat to a more vigorous neighbor—usually to Tunis.

Her trade position was excellent. She was near Europe and, of all the North African ports, hers was the best gateway to the Sahara and the lands of the Negroes beyond. Indeed, Tripoli was almost part of the Sahara, being half-circled by "a vast expanse of desert against which the city leans," in the expressive phrase of one of the early explorers, whereas most of the African ports were separated from the Sahara by mountains and forests. Tripoli's port was safe and large, having in mind the size of medieval ships. Her sea trade was so extensive that an old-time Moslem observer said ships rode there at anchor side by side "like horses in a stable." Tripoli was rich and possessed "magnificent houses."

But Tripoli lacked the empire spirit. She never founded a real dynasty in the Middle Ages. She does not figure large in the pages of Arabic writers, and such references as there are to her name concern rather some attack upon her by this or that outsider than any vitality of her own.

When Tripoli in a rare mood of independence did set up temporary local rule it is noted as something unusual. In 1326-27 the people of Tripoli went so far as to appoint a ruler, son of a sheikh of the Thabet family, who for twenty years exercised absolute authority. But "to hide the appearance of power he went about his business and dressed like a trader, walked about on foot in the streets and carried home his own provisions." His son succeeded him and ventured to "adopt the dress and ways of a sovereign." Six years later he fled at one of the several Christian attacks of which Tripoli was victim and, as Ibn-Khaldoun says scornfully, "there was not left in the place a man of heart or courage." After that, persons of the Mekki family of Gabès in south Tunisia took over power for a short time on the strength of having lent Tripoli the ransom money which induced the Christians to go away. A Thabet then put out the mortgagee, and Thabet governorship was resumed, Tripoli, however, recognizing the sultan of Tunis as her overlord and paying tribute.

Ibn-Batuta saw Tripoli at the start of the fourteenth century and, though usually so full of quick enthusiasm, found nothing in the capon city to remark upon. His comments upon his sojourn at Tripoli are almost exclusively personal, concerning an aborted marriage deal of his own and his subsequent wedding to a lady whose father was more reasonable in dowry demands.

One point made by Ibn-Batuta about the Tripoli region is significant. He says that his traveling group was accompanied by "a hundred or more horsemen as well as a detachment of archers out of respect for whom the Arabs kept their distance." This is suggestive. The Arabs of the second invasion had fallen on the country round Tripoli in their first undiminished hordes. The population therefore had been crushed by conquest and broken down by interbreeding; they were no longer the fighting native Berber stock. This goes far to explain Tripoli's supine policy and relative unimportance in late medieval and early modern history.

A fable recorded by a modern Arabic author typifies Tripoli's slackness in those days: A merchant of the town entertained foreign traders. His display of wealth included the crushing of a valuable pearl which he offered those at table to dust over their food in lieu of pepper. But when the melon was served he had to borrow a knife to slice it with from one of the foreigners. "We never carry knives," he explained, "it would be accounted impolite to our guests."

THE MAGNIFICENT MAMLUKS

THIRTY-NINE DAYS' MARCH FROM TRIPOLI WAS EGYPT. THE ROAD traversed a territory then of trifling importance. The days when Cyrene and Barca figured large in history were long past.

Cairo was in those days magnificent under the rulership of its beggars on horseback, its Mamluks, or White-slave sultans, who for nearly three hundred years owned Egypt like a private estate. It was a wild, rowdy period, peppered with assassinations in high places, and pretty well constant alarms in lowly ones. The average life expectation of a Mamluk when he seated himself on Egypt's throne was five and a half years, and any hope of passing on his high office to his offspring was slim. Notwithstanding this disorder and violence Cairo was the greatest Moslem power of its day: strong in the field, conquering both Mongols and Christians, beautiful at home with such development of art and such fine buildings as Egypt had not known since the days of the Ptolemies.[12]

The White-slave Sultans, proud of their origin and carefully maintaining their breed, renewed the slave stock by purchase as death or assassination reduced their numbers, the climate of Egypt being unfavorable to the fertility of these foreigners. It is a puzzling state of things. Even with the somewhat hazy ideas of liberty under which the modern world operates, it seems inconceivable that a man physically owned by an individual master could rise to play a great independent role in history. It is one of those things we must accept uncomprehended.

*   *   *

THE MAMLUKS WHOSE FIRST RULER WAS THE EX-SLAVE GIRL, PEARL-Spray, were started to true greatness by the celebrated sultan, Bibars (1260-77). His career like hers was handicapped. She overcame the almost insuperable obstacle of womanhood. Bibars was not only a humble slave, but was afflicted in youth with a cataract of one eye. He became one of Egypt's greatest rulers. He was one of the numbers of foreigners who dominated and reanimated the country—a fellow member of the group which includes Alexander the Great, the Fatimite conqueror, Moizz, and Saladin.

[12] Stanley Lane-Poole, *The Art of the Saracens in Egypt.*

Bibars came from Kipchak, and as a young slave had been classed as a bad buy on account of his disability, fetching the equivalent of only 240 current United States dollars—regarded as a cheap price for a young fighting man. He rose to be the most powerful Moslem of his day, "the Sultan of Sultans," and as picturesque and romantic a king as Egypt had ever known during the uncountable centuries since the misty days of Mena. He figures in Marco Polo's story of adventures. It is said that his exploits were in part the inspiration for the *Arabian Nights*.

It would be impossible to parallel such a success story as his in all the annals of our own Age of Opportunity.

A GAY AND TREMBLING CITY

Cairo was not only one of the greatest capitals of the latter Middle Ages, but unquestionably the gayest.

On fete days the streets were hung with silk and satin and filled with dancers, jugglers, and the horrible and thrilling performances of dervishes. The court were hard drinkers, gorgeously dressed and great chasers of women. The native Egyptian population was something quite apart from the Mamluks. They went about their business, gaped at their rulers and kept out of their way as much as possible. To Cairo's women the taking of a bath became a major risk. A woman might go away from home a respectable young matron, leaving her cook pots on the fire and her children at play, and eat her next meal as a member of a Mamluk harem, for it was a merry Mamluk habit to raid the public baths and carry off by force the likeliest of the lady bathers.

Mamluk prowess paraded the streets. Cairo saw the caved-in drums of beaten Mongols, and heard bloody tales of the defeat of the Christians at Antioch.

IMPORTATION OF THE ASSASSINS

Egypt's natives saw a yet more striking indication of Mamluk capacity. They saw the domestication of the wildest band of fanatics the world has ever known, the famous Assassins. In vain Saladin had tried to squash the Assassins, as indeed he had every reason to do, they having twice attempted to assassinate him.

The Mongols had greatly weakened them. It was the Mamluk sultan, Bibars, who completed their subjugation and then imported the survivors into Egypt and transformed them into useful citizens, ready to turn their unique talents to Egypt's benefit. An amazing feat.

*   *   *

THE GENERAL OUTLINE OF THE STORY OF THE ASSASSINS, PROBABLY named from hashish, and of their so-called Old Man of the Mountain are well known. I cannot forbear to remind the reader of Marco Polo's account of how the Old Man is supposed to have produced the synthetic Paradise by means of which he fooled his disciples to fanatical heights of foolhardy obedience. Marco Polo was by no means the first to report on the Assassins, whom he does not, by the way, designate by this name. There is an earlier Christian report and a mention by the Jewish traveler, Benjamin of Tudela, who journeyed in 1165-73 and who seems to take a surprising satisfaction in the fact that their band included "four communities of Israel who go forth with them in wartime."

It is, however, Marco Polo who tells of the paradisiacal premises prepared by the Old Man of the Mountain: In a luxurious garden the Old Man caused to be planted every fragrant shrub that could be procured and to be set up palaces ornamented with works in gold and furniture covered with rich silks. Cunningly contrived conduits carried through the garden brooklets of wine, milk, honey and pure water. "The inhabitants of the palaces were elegant and beautiful damsels accomplished in the arts of singing, dancing and especially those of dalliance and amorous allurement."

Likely recruits—youths from twelve to twenty who showed martial disposition—were drugged unawares, introduced into this pleasure park while asleep, and upon awakening found themselves "surrounded by lovely damsels who attracted their regard by the most fascinating caresses, and served them with delectable viands and exquisite wines." Naturally, "This is Heaven!" they said. After four or five days of bliss the youths were redrugged and woke again to everyday life. They were assured that those who died in the service of the band were sure of Paradise everlasting, as per sample. It is no wonder that all fear left them and

that they were ready to take any risk in carrying out the com-
·mands of the Old Man.

Modern and mild-mannered descendants of this sect are stated
by Professor Hitti to number one hundred fifty thousand, living
mostly in India.

THE CROSS TOTTERS IN NUBIA

OF BIBARS' VARIOUS EXPLOITS ONE WAS PLAYED UPON THE AFRICAN
scene, in Nubia.

The kingdom of Nubia, isolated by geography and antagonistic
by religion, was Egypt's poor relation—the place where the black
slaves came from—and was little noticed by Moslem chroniclers.

Nubia in the earlier Mamluk days was still Christian. One is
struck by the pathetic situation of this lost pocket of black
Christianity up the Nile—a group of faithful cut off from contact with their white brethren, following the old beliefs, repeating
words and formulas which—passed down from century to century
—must have become a meaningless jargon, fumbling in the old
sacred gestures, but holding somehow steadfast to Christ despite
everything. In the fourteenth century their faith waned at last
and most of them turned Moslem. Yet two centuries later there
were still some surviving Christians in Nubia who sent a pitiful
appeal to the outside world, please to ship them a priest.

*   *   *

THE GREAT SULTAN, BIBARS, DISLIKED CHRISTIANS VERY MUCH. HE
had been fighting them since his youth. A letter of his has been
preserved in which he gloated over the fact that his armies had
demolished Christian churches at Antioch, that "the crosses were
sawn asunder" and "the Moslems had trod in the Holy of Holies,"
slaughtering monks, priests and deacons "on the altar." Toward
the end of his reign (1275) Bibars turned his attention toward the
Christians up the Nile.

From the Egyptian point of view [13] the attack was successful
and profitable. King Daoud of Nubia was no more. The Church

---

[13] Macrizi's *Es-Selouk* gives an account of the expedition, of which there is
an abstract in John Lewis Burckhardt's *Nubia*, which—though published in
1819—is still a primary source on Nubia.

of Ysous (Jesus) of Dongola was ruined, the golden cross and silver church vessels were taken away and the invaders captured so many Nubians that "after they had killed many and sold great numbers at three dirhems (say fifty-seven United States cents) per head, there still remained 10,000 of them on their hands."

But the Nubians who got away clung to Christianity. At last Moslem pressure became too strong. Further attacks came from Egypt. The Nubian king fled up the Nile, was pursued for a distance of fifteen or eighteen days beyond Dongola, and again great numbers of Nubians were dragged back to Cairo's slave markets. Three years later (1290) another attack by an army of forty thousand was launched with the idea of finally subduing Nubia. The Egyptians proceeded up both banks of the Nile and used a fleet of five hundred ships. The people ran before them. Dongola was found inhabited by only "an old man and an old woman."

The chiefs, officers, bishops and priests then abandoned the Nubian king and went over to the Moslem conqueror. As symbols of the Christian collapse "a dinner was spread in the Church of Ysous." Only a minority stuck by the old faith; Nubia as a whole went Moslem.

*   *   *

IT IS SAD TO HAVE NOTHING BUT BLOOD AND SORROW AND EVENTUAL religious defeat to repeat on historic authority about this marooned Christian group up the Nile. If we but knew, it is certain that there would be much of a happier kind to tell about Nubia during its centuries of Christianity. They were fine people, physically and in character. The beauty of their women was proverbial; they were described by Edrisi as "ravishing" (see page 201 for his lush description of their loveliness). Their men were brave soldiers when carried away in slavery into other lands. They had high moral qualities: there is a tradition that Mohammed said, "He who has not a brother should adopt one from amongst the Nubians" (Yaqout). Obviously therefore Nubia must have known good days.

But Nubia's medieval history has trickled down to us almost exclusively by items of Moslem origin wherein the people as a whole were naturally viewed unsympathetically and without respect—as infidels and dangerous enemies who harried the Egyptian frontier, and as a subject race which continuously slipped away from its subjugation and neglected to send the expected tribute. This tribute, called *Bakt,* was an annual quota of slaves. In addition Egypt expected animal tribute: elephants, giraffes, panthers, etc.

Such testimony gave no notion of the country from within. We must be content to admire the moral courage and spiritual tenacity of the Nubians without knowing much about them.

THE NILE DIVERSION BOGEY

EGYPT HAD ANOTHER AND VERY STRONG REASON FOR HER SUSPICIOUS and unfriendly attitude toward these peoples up the Nile. Egypt had an agonizing horror lest some enemy up the river might stop off the Nile and reduce the land to a desert. This catastrophe was, in their opinion, most to be feared from the remoter Abyssinian region, but Egypt was nervous about all the country to the south, especially as she had then no definite knowledge as to the Nile's source. European exploration did not make this discovery until 1862.

Medieval Arabic geography suggested that the river came from mountains so high that from their peaks one could see both poles. A fourteenth century savant mentioned that these mountains were the home of ferocious creatures, part man, part animal, and were further protected against investigation by the so-called "Lover or Magnet of Men," a rock glowing like silver which dragged men to it and held them there clamped tight until they died but "always gay and joyous." [14]

*   *   *

EGYPT IMAGINED THAT THOSE LIVING UP THE NILE COMMANDED ITS sluices and could at their pleasure submerge Alexandria and the Delta, or withhold the river. When, for instance, the Nile failed in the eleventh century, resulting in a hideous famine (see page 278) the reason assigned was that the people up the river had "let the channel get into a bad state" and a message was sent to the Abyssinians inviting them to repair the Nile and put it back in its proper bed!

[14] From Dimisqi, who died 1326, a résumé of whose Nile theory is given by Ch. de la Roncière in *La Découverte de l'Afrique au moyen age,* Tome II, (Cairo, 1925).

The people of Abyssinia promulgated such fears enthusiastically. They sent envoys to Cairo demanding that certain favors be shown to the Christians living in Egypt or else "the Nile would be held back in such fashion that it would never reach Egypt." This happened in 1325. The Mamluk sultan of the day was brave enough to refuse to be bluffed, but the incident made an impression and it is later reported that Egypt paid annual blackmail to Abyssinia of three thousand gold besants and that one year when the tribute was withheld King Dawit of Abyssinia (1380-1409) "commenced the work of diverting the Nile's course, at which the Egyptians hurriedly sent him presents, notably four pieces of the True Cross."

Fra Mauro's map of Africa (1459) shows Abyssinia's supposedly strong position. The Abyssinians, according to the map's text, could close "the gates by which the Nile went to the Sudan (and Egypt) and . . . the Nile would go to the land of the Negroes (i.e. Central Africa) and not to Egypt." Very easy on paper, though presumably an excessive undertaking for Abyssinian medieval engineers.

As late as the middle of the fifteenth century an ultimatum was addressed to Egypt and it is stated that an attempt might actually have been made had not the king of Abyssinia known that a great number of Christians lived in Egypt who would die of hunger if he stopped the Nile.

This constant nervousness about their precious Nile very naturally made medieval Egyptians antagonistic to those living nearer its sources than themselves. It was probably held strategically necessary that Nubia—though she could not herself stop the Nile at its source—should be subjugated and should be seduced away from the religion of Abyssinia and become a Moslem ally of Egypt.

So we see another reason why Nubia fared badly at Egypt's hands, both actually and in Moslem literature—both by the sword and the pen.

THE LEARNED NEGROES BY
THE NIGER

IN CONTRAST TO NUBIA, THE EASTERN SUDAN BY THE NILE ABOUT which we have so little internal information, the western Sudan by the Niger can show us a fairly ample and very romantic history.

The Negroes of the Niger country were a learned lot. They were Moslems and they wrote in Arabic. The two outstanding locally written Sudanese histories have been mentioned (see page 255). These two volumes are the most interesting Sudanese items as far as the modern reader is concerned. But the Sudan produced many books and possessed many learned men, especially during the sixteenth century when the University of Timbuctoo was a renowned institution to be mentioned with those of Cairo and Fez.

The most famous author of them all was Ahmed Baba (1556-1623), a Saharan born of mixed Negro and Berber stock, who survived a cruel deportation when the Moroccans conquered his homeland. He was dragged away in chains and made to cross the Sahara, thrown from his camel and broke his leg, kept four years in prison—yet he retained enough vigor to make the pilgrimage to Mecca after he was set free. He wrote more than forty learned works.[15]

At his death contemporaries described Ahmed Baba as "the illustration and benediction of his times, the very learned, the unique of this century and the phoenix of his epoch." Which shows that the Sudanese knew how to appreciate their authors! So great was his reputation that when the manuscript of the famous Sudanese history, the *Tarikh es-Soudan,* first came into European hands its authorship was as a matter of course attributed to him. This was a mistake; the *Tarikh es-Soudan* was the work of Es-Sa'di of Timbuctoo, born forty years after Ahmed Baba.

---

[15] Most of these titles are listed in the account of his life which is one of a series of 360 biographies of learned Moslems prepared by Prof. Mohammed ben Cheneb. This work includes mention of several other Negro savants and appears in the *Actes du XIVe Congrès International des Orientalistes* (1905, *IIIe partie*).

Ahmed Baba was but one of the celebrated intellectuals of Negroland. While in captivity he said, "of all my friends in the Sudan it was I who owned the smallest library, yet I possessed 1600 volumes." It was he however who seemed to typify Moslem Negro culture. A curious item about the dark savant is that "the name of Mohammed was written upon his right forearm in white characters formed naturally in the skin." Or, so says the *Tarikh es-Soudan*.

THE LAST DAYS OF GOLDEN GANA

THANKS TO THE HISTORIANS OF NEGROLAND AND OTHER ARABIC sources we know much of what happened in the Sudan by the Niger. Gana, capital of the gold country, fell in the end of the eleventh century to the Almoravides. A century later another set of conquerors came. These were the people oddly named the Soso, about whom there is much argument and very little definite record.

There are today in West Africa members of a tribe of the same name—Soso. I have met some of them in French Guinea, and brought away a souvenir supplied by a Soso acquaintance, namely my note of his way of saying the year Nineteen-thirty-five, date of our meeting, which for the reader's amusement I reproduce: *"Wulu nun keme solo manani nun tongo sakhan nun nani."* Other Sosos live in Sierra Leone. There must be many persons of Soso stock in the United States. Probably none of these modern Sosos is aware of the stir created by a group of that name whose sweep of conquest overran Gana in the early thirteenth century. "They made an impression on the population along the Niger banks comparable to that which the Huns produced in Europe in the days of old." They pushed their conquests to the Atlantic and it has been suggested even that the word "Sudan" derives from their name. This suggestion I repeat with reserve, the usual derivation of Sudan being from *Berr es-Sudan,* "Country of the Blacks."

A CITY KILLED BY ITS CLIMATE

THE SOSO DID NOT HOLD GANA FOR LONG. ANOTHER CONQUEROR came. Gana, an old city now, was suffering hard blows, but still the city of gold clung to life. Ibn-Khaldoun in the following century met a Gana citizen traveling in Egypt (1393). Gana was even visited, if we may believe the report, by a Spanish Franciscan in the neighborhood of 1348.

Another Christian visit is recorded by the celebrated Ramon Lull, one of the earliest of that great company of African missionaries, who was at eighty years of age stoned to death outside the walls of Bougie, Algeria (1315), because of his attacks on the Moslem faith. Lull did not claim to have gone to Gana himself, but mentions it in his report about a journey made by another Christian sent to look into Africa's religious state. In the course of his explorations this investigator—the first white Christian the natives had ever seen, according to Lull—discovered a region where "a dragon was honored by sacrifices and adored as a god." This, being told to the Pope when the investigator returned home, caused His Holiness "great disappointment." During his travels the investigator saw Gana, Lull claims, finding there "princes who were idolators and who worshipped the sun, stars, birds and beasts, they being tall Negroes who obey no law."

Gana evidently survived repeated sacking. But Gana was dying and finally went out of existence. The reason is odd: Gana was killed by her climate, by the inexorable drying up of the city's site, which was upon the Sahara's rim. The climatic change "of which we now possess proofs," in the words of Maurice Delafosse,[16] a great authority upon this part of Africa, produced a

---

[16] Maurice Delafosse in his great work, *Haut-Sénégal-Niger* (1912), said that Gana was destroyed by a conquerer in 1240 (Vol. II, p. 180). Twelve years later he revised this opinion, see his article in the *Bulletin du comité d'études historiques et scientifiques de l'Afrique Occidentale Française* for July-Sept., 1924, where Delafosse says that Gana's disappearance was especially to be attributed to "the progressive drying up of the region of which we now possess proofs."

See also Henri Labouret, *Les Manding*, 1934 (p. 31), and Augustine Bernard, *Afrique septentrionale et occidentale, IIe partie-Sahara*, p. 296 (Tome XI of *Géographie universelle*, 1939).

Compare with p. 15 where I discussed the question of the progressive drying of the Saharan region.

sort of civiç lingering illness. Gana gradually withered and died.

But the posthumous fame of the rich gold capital lived on for centuries. European explorers searched for the city of gold and geographers were quite assured in the early nineteenth century that Gana could be identified with Kano in Nigeria, a mere twelve hundred miles away from the site of Gana's ruins, but irresistibly similar in name!

FOUR GREAT CITIES OF NEGROLAND

So Gana was lost. But the western Niger region had four other fine cities: Timbuctoo, Gao, Oualata and Mali. Of these the first three survive today. But Mali—once the greatest of them all—is no more.

THE FOUNDATION OF TIMBUCTOO

Timbuctoo is relatively young. It was founded, says Es-Sa'di, the author of the *Tarikh es-Soudan,* at the end of the fifth century after the Hegira, which corresponds with the eleventh century in our way of dating. It began as a camp of the Tuareg or Veiled Men of the Sahara (see page 281). Es-Sa'di loved his home town. He calls it "an exquisite city, pure, delicious, illustrious, blessed, luxuriant and full of life." Furthermore he boasts that Timbuctoo was noble in that it had "never been soiled by the worship of idols," which fact is really nothing to brag of, being attributable to the fact that Timbuctoo was founded after the Moslem conversion of the countryside, rather than to any superior religious discernment of its people.

Timbuctoo, he goes on, gradually developed into a trade center; its greatest days did not start till the end of the fifteenth century. Then it became the meeting place for traders from Egypt, from the Libyan Desert, from Fezzan, Ghadames, the Tuat oases, Sijilmassa, Fez, and the Gold Lands.

Timbuctoo, says the *Tarikh el-Fettach,* that other important source on the history of the Sudan, "had (at its zenith) no equal among the cities of the Country of the Blacks for the solidarity of its institutions, its political liberty, the purity of its morals, public security, compassion toward the poor, clemency to foreigners, courtesy to students and men of science, and the amount of help given to this last class." And, by the way, it is a description of which any modern white city might be proud.

Timbuctoo was at "the crossroads of travel," close to the great water route of the Niger and on the Sahara's shores. At Timbuctoo desert caravans met traders' boats—camel met pirogue. Timbuctoo was a double-faced port, a two-way terminus.

In modern times—it is hard to say why—Timbuctoo became to the outside world the most widely talked about city in inner Africa. It has been the subject of uncountable exaggerated yarns, gags and Limericks. Its name is so bandied about that many persons consider it is not that of a real town, but the symbolic designation of the remote and the unattainable. "Going to Timbuctoo," is a saying that conveys the same idea as going to the moon. There is no doubt as to Timbuctoo's remoteness. It was a crossroads for inner Africans, but is a difficult place to approach from the outside, the non-African world. Hundreds died making the attempt in the early days of European exploration. By land or water routes it is still hard to reach, as I found out for myself. And today it is not much of a city.

Perhaps one reason contributing to the renown of Timbuctoo has been its odd name—to our ears. Es-Sa'di says it was called after a slave woman who was sometimes left in charge in the days when it was a Tuareg camp, and that the name meant "Old Woman." Other suggested translations of the word include "She-of-the-Big-Navel." Another explanation is that the name meant the "Well of Buctoo." In all events it sounded comical to Europeans and contributed to advertise the tantalizing town which they were told had roofs of gold and to which for so long no outside travelers could penetrate.

GAO

SOME TWO HUNDRED MILES DOWN THE NIGER FROM TIMBUCTOO IS Gao. Gao, founded about the seventh century, was the capital of the big black empire of the Songhai. It was in a similarly favored trade position to Timbuctoo, and its great days were in the fifteenth and sixteenth centuries. But the place knew a rebirth when it became the terminus of a big North-South Saharan Highway from the railhead in Algeria to the Niger.

Gao comes down in local legends as a place of fairy tales. No city in all North Africa has such a fantastic past. Es-Sa'di boasted that his home town of Timbuctoo had never been soiled by the worship of idols. Gao on the contrary had a dark pagan record, and a lively set of traditions. The attempts of Gao's Negroes—congenitally imaginative and boastful—to explain their origin and rise to greatness under the foreigners who came to organize and inspire them provide quaint stories and a pleasant vision of Negro character. I will offer a few of these legends, the setting of which is sometimes given as Gao and sometimes as Gao's predecessor, a little farther down the Niger (known as Koukiya, or Gounguia).

As a start: It was claimed that it was from this region, noted for its talented sorcerers that the Pharaoh imported the troop of magicians whom he used in a controversy with Moses, and whose ability was so great that, when they and Moses were tested against one another, "Moses conceived a secret fear within him" (Koran, sura XX).

Originally the sovereign of Gao was "a great fish who appeared every day at midmorning and gave audience to the people till midday" (reminiscence here of one branch of their ancestors who were Niger fishermen). The Songhai (Gao people) of old were divided into two groups, says Captain Urvoy in his *Histoire des populations du Soudan central,* the Sorkos, fishermen, and the Gabibis, farmers.

There arrived in the land two foreign young men of Arabic ancestry, on the side of their mother and grandmother respectively, and of Christian heritage as to their fathers. These two were seeking a lost cousin who had run away from his home in Arabia as a little boy and had miraculously got safely to the Niger. The two provided the runaway with a charm by which he was able to kill the great fish and make himself king of the country and first of a dynasty.

Reminiscent, this, of the uncontested fact that the blacks of the Gao region were in the remote past organized by a conquering white tribe, Berber nomads of the desert.

Reminiscent also of something more hazy. The legend insists on the Christian fatherhood of both of the young men who had come hunting for the runaway: they had been born respectively to the Arab woman who first went in search of the boy and had been captured and loved by a Christian, and to the daughter of this union and another desert Christian. It has been suggested that Gao's first foreign white kings were in truth Christians; Delafosse thought so, or at any rate that "they professed a sort of bastardized Christianity."

A variant of the king-fish story explains Gao's past as follows: Certain persons came upon a footprint shaped like that of a man, but three *coudées* long and two across (about a yard and a half by three quarters of a yard), and each toe as big as two hands. Though frightened they tracked the giant and came upon a brown man with "an enormous belly and head, holding in his hand a cane with an iron top," who spoke Arabic, which they did not understand. This person married a local woman "who had a child like her husband in size"! The son grew up to be bilingual, became king of the region and was first of a dynasty.

                    *   *   *

IN CONTRAST TO THE FANCIFUL AND ASSORTED BACKGROUNDS OF THE first king of their dynasty, there comes down a strict and exact list of its members—of the thirteen pagan (or possibly Christian) kings who succeeded its founder and reigned at Gao before its conversion to Mohammedanism. The first was Dia-Alayamau. The first convert to Islam was Dia-Kosoi—the prefix "Dia" having been the opening sound of the explanatory sentence spoken by the first foreigner who came to rule Gao when he said, "I come from Arabia." The word became a title, prefixed to the name of each of his successors.

Before we leave Gao's pleasant legends let me quote one bit more: "When the kings sit down to eat, people beat a drum and Negresses begin to dance, letting their heavy hair fly in the wind, and nobody in the city does any work until the king has done. Then they throw the left-over food into the river and the crowd standing by utter shouts and exclamations to let the people know that the king has finished his dinner."

                    *   *   *

THE STORIES RELATED OR QUOTED ABOVE COME RESPECTIVELY FROM the *Tarikh es-Soudan,* the *Tarikh el-Fettach,* a fragment attributed to Ibn-el-Mokhtar, and the pages of El-Bekri.

Proof of Gao's widespread importance in olden days is to be found in the many variations of its name, as it was understood and rendered by authors and travelers of different races. I have noted eight or nine variations, some beginning with *G,* some with *K.* El-Bekri says the name was a piece of onomatopoeia intended to imitate the roll of drums, the symbol of royalty: *Kao-kao.* In Gao itself I found that the city's name is now pronounced as if spelt *Ghar-oh!* with a scorpionlike lift of the tail.

NAUGHTY OUALATA

OUALATA HAD EVEN MORE NAMES THAN GAO. ITS MOST COMMON alternate was Biro. In addition I have found the place referred to in the pages of medieval geographers by names starting with nine different letters of the alphabet. Furthermore Oualata went often by the sinister nickname of "Serpent's Throat" because of the unhealthiness for which it was famed. Such prodigality of appellations complicate the student's task.

Oualata was on the Sahara's edge where the scrub land meets the sand, where the roads from Negroland met the roads across the desert. Between Gana's downfall and Timbuctoo's rise Oualata was the commercial center through which goods went back and forth from Egypt and Morocco to the Sudan. Its geographic position is dead to the westward of Timbuctoo.

Vestiges still remain of Oualata's old-time beautiful houses whose interiors are embellished with colored arabesques, designs in white upon the violet-pink of the plastered base. Explorer Théodore Monod believes this work was originally done by a guild of woman specialists.

When Oualata was at the height of its prosperity the great traveler, Ibn-Batuta, stayed there for fifty days in 1352, and was profoundly shocked. His account of the place is one long attack on its naughtiness and now, after six hundred years, the scandalized comments of the priggish old traveler make up almost our only information about the place in its days of glory.

The women of Oualata, Ibn-Batuta says, were "of surpassing beauty" and dressed themselves in fine imported Egyptian clothing. But their behavior was amazing and the complaisance of their husbands something he could scarcely believe. The married women of Oualata, contrary to all Mohammedan custom, had "friends"— male friends—and their husbands were "quite impervious to jealousy." Says Ibn-Batuta, "A man will enter his own home and see a friend of his wife alone and talking to her, and without the least emotion or attempt to disturb them he will merely come in and sit down on one side till the man goes." Ibn-Batuta's hair rose, and he commented that at Oualata "no one claims descent from his father," but rather through the maternal line, something which he had observed hitherto only amongst pagans. He has other stories to tell: the Oualata judge, his erstwhile friend, whom he cut dead after a disturbing contretemps when he came in upon the learned gentleman entertaining "a young woman of remarkable beauty" not a member of the judge's family; the Oualata pilgrim who expressed the desire to take along his mistress on the holy journey to Mecca. . . .

Oualata's moral code is the more surprising since it was in no way a matter of general social laxness. Oualata was a pious place then and always, and Ibn-Batuta found its ladies ardently religious. Oualata had been built alongside the ruins of a yet older town which was the center of the Berber tribe that traditionally converted all that part of the Sudan to Islam.

At a later period Oualata was associated with that saintly figure Sidi Ahmed el-Bekkay, known reverentially as "the pole of mystics, the very learned, the director of men, the renewer of principles, the guide to the ways of life" (from the *Tarikh Kounta* annals communicated to the French explorer, Captain Cortier). The peculiar designation "Pole," I will explain, is one which has tremendous value. The Poles were "saintly personages to the number of twenty chosen by Allah to carry the weight of a great part of the evils which but for them would afflict our poor humanity."

The saintly Sidi Ahmed el-Bekkay performed at Oualata miracle similar to that of his ancestor, Sidi Okba, the great Arab conqueror. Sidi Ahmed drove away the lions which plagued Oualata's countryside. In 1504 he was buried near the scene o his great exploit and when exhumed was found to be in perfect preservation with tears running down from his eyes into his beard. From this circumstance came his posthumous title of "el-Bekkay," the Weeper. Concurrently with their saintly importance the Bekkays—for the name stuck—were destined to wield something almost like royal powers (see page 571).

So Oualata, as the above will indicate, was a place of especially high religious tone and it is clear that—in holding the ultra-modern sex notions which shocked Ibn-Batuta—the community was acting not from moral laziness but from conviction.

Later all this changed and Leo Africanus (fifteenth century) reports that Oualata was in such a state of intersexual bashfulness that both the men and the women wore veils and "had no civility between them."

This little study of the sex customs and religious notions of a far land at a remote period is inserted with the idea that from a mosaic of such items we may be helped to an understanding of the Mohammedan psychology of today.

THE GLORY OF MALI

TWENTY-FOUR DAYS' MARCH FROM OUALATA WAS THAT FOURTH city of the Niger region about which I set out to tell. This was Mali, capital of the kingdom of the same name, which at the crest of its prosperity was the most powerful place in the Sudan. Indeed no capital in all North Africa controlled so great an empire. The people of Mali were masters of Timbuctoo and Gao and the rest of an important strip along the Senegal and upper Niger rivers, where terminated most of the Saharan trade. They owned the famous gold mines and the indispensable salt mines. Their empire stretched from the Atlantic far into inner Africa, stretched down into the jungles of savage cannibal land and up into the middle of the Sahara. At the height of Mali's greatness it was claimed that it required a full year to march across Mali-Land. Perhaps this was an exaggeration. So perhaps was the boast, reported by Macrizi, that it would take a man three years to walk around Mali.

*   *   *

MALI'S CAPITAL IN THE GREAT OLD DAYS HAS DISAPPEARED; IT WAS
about eighty miles southwest of the modern city of Bamako. The
village of Niené, shown only on large-scale maps, is near its former
site, and I shall always regret that in ignorance of its historic
associations I once hurried through the Niené neighborhood en
route from Bamako to Kankan.

It is noticeable that so many of the Sudan's great historic towns:
Gana, Gao, Timbuctoo, Oualata and Mali (as well as its modern
capital of Bamako) grew up inside so small an area, inside a triangle whose apex was Gao at the east, and whose other two corners, at Gana and Mali respectively, were a bare seven hundred
miles away, and less than four hundred miles apart. Despite all
the immense available space of Africa in which to build, the men
of old knew this small triangle to be the best. Here centered trade
and history.

*   *   *

MALI'S PEOPLE SURVIVE TODAY AS ONE OF THE MOST IMPORTANT OF
the Negro races. They are known in English as the Mandingos
and with their assimilated tribes they populate a considerable
part of the French and English West African colonies and Liberia.
They are influential out of proportion to their numbers. (There
are 2,793,000 born Mandingos, Henri Labouret states in his book,
Les Manding, 1934) because their language has been adopted
as a second tongue by many other races. A sort of "pidgin Mandingo" is the common language of the regiments called Senegalese. The Mandingo language is one of the "big three" of all
Africa, so far as natives' speech is concerned. The great explorer,
Binger, declared that a man could go from the Cape to Egypt
without an interpreter if he spoke Mandingo, Hausa and Arabic.

The Mandingos' forebears once lived in the semidesert country
of the southwestern Sahara. Two factors drove them from their
home: the drying up of the climate and the introduction of the
camel into North Africa, which transported across the desert
those forceful Berbers who pushed the Malis out. Vaguely we hear
of them in early Arabic geography. They were associated with
mentions of Wangara where gold "grew." Edrisi speaks of a town
of Mali, small and unwalled and perched on a red hill, and tells
how to the west of it lived peoples "who go naked and marry

without dot or ceremony," meaning, I suppose, that love was free. He adds, "No men exist who breed more children."

After centuries of obscurity Mali's rise was sudden and spectacular. In the early part of the thirteenth century there rose a Mali chief who jerked his people into history. We have a full record of Mali's rapid climb to a point which would seem to be the peak of all known Negro accomplishment. Ibn-Khaldoun secured first hand information about Mali's history from the mufti of Gana and from a traveling cadi who had lived in the region. As in so many cases Ibn-Khaldoun is again our best source.

The chief in question was the conqueror of Gana, the celebrated Soun-Diata (or Mari-Diata) the never forgotten and still revered of his people. His name speaks for his bravery. Diata meant Lion. The rest of it meant either "Prince" or "Famished." Delafosse passes on the legend—there are uncountable legends about this hero—that he once plunged his hand into molten iron to prove his courage and worthiness to be supreme leader, pulling it out again unharmed. Another incident of his effort to attain supremacy is not admirable. He is alleged to have killed off, one after another, his eleven brothers inside a year so as to secure his father's heritage.

He was, although a Moslem, a practiced sorcerer. He cured himself by magic means of a paralysis of the legs which had fallen upon him as a youth of seventeen. And his victory over the Sosos, then masters of Gana, was attributed to his preparation of a magic arrow which, when it wounded the Soso king, caused him to become a block of stone along with his horse and his wife and a child who were riding behind him.

In his magic tricks Soun-Diata received aid from his womenfolk. His sister had wormed herself into the affections of the Soso king and "in the course of a night of love got him to reveal the magic secret which led to his ruin." Another tradition makes Soun-Diata's mother reveal the enemy's secret to her son in a deathbed vision. The prominence of feminine aid in the legends of Soun-Diata is notable. The Berbers and Arabs of Africa have very little to say about women. But in Negro Africa women played a more important role. When Ibn-Batuta was at Mali he found that the first wife of the king shared his throne. In Mali the use of face veils was unknown to womankind. "The slave girls and young girls go about in front of everybody naked, without a stitch of clothing on them," Ibn-Batuta says, "even the king's daughters." It was startling, but also indicative of a freer and more natural sex relationship than maintained in the lands of Mediterranean Africa where women were bundled up nonentities in so far as the public was concerned.

*   *   *

Soun-Diata was succeeded by a series of sons and nephews. In 1312 there came to be king of Mali the man I submit was the greatest and most interesting Negro who ever lived.

THE MAN WHO WAS AFRICA

He was Kankan-Musa (1312-37), Mansa (meaning Emperor in the language of his own people) of Mali. The Kankan part of his name was given him either because it was the name of his mother, or the name of the place of his birth. There is today a considerable city of that name in French Guinea.

To the outside world of later medieval days he was more than an individual. *He was Africa.* He figured by name on every map. He became in person the symbol of the mystery and of the fabulous wealth of the unknown continent. He was this during his lifetime. He still held the position nearly two centuries after his death.

We are familiar with the verse of Swift's about how geographers in making maps of Africa were obliged, because of their ignorance of what the continent really was like, to "place elephants for want of towns." Elephants—and Kankan-Musa!

For the information of those who have not happened to see reproductions of medieval African maps, I explain that map makers were wont to use, not prosaic outlines and dots in the staid modern manner, but a splatter of written inscriptions and fantastic figures. From 1339 to 1502 the unmistakable portrait of Mali's great emperor, almost always called by name, "Mousamalli," dominates Africa's maps. Every student and mariner for two centuries was familiar with the figure of Kankan-Musa, accompanied by some such phrase as: "This Negro Seigneur, called Mousamalli (Musa of Mali), is the Lord of the Negroes of Guinea;

he is the richest and noblest king of all the land, so great is the abundance of gold which is collected in his country."

The "Negro Seigneur" whose personality became so familiar to the world at large is placed on the maps like some royal spider in the center of a web of trade routes leading to Mali, the Gold Land. Sometimes he is shown sitting under a tent, sceptered and splendid, sometimes in profile against a background of all Africa. His figure is as big as twenty of the castles which arbitrarily dot the continent. Peculiar animals garnish the scene: camels that seem to have dachshund ancestry, elephants with toes and claws. And almost always the "Negro Seigneur" holds outstretched that famous lump of gold which was the symbol of Mali's wealth.

The lump of gold was not only symbol but actuality. Mali's king imitated the king of Gana, the earlier and now defunct gold capital. Like Gana's king he displayed at his palace a colossal block of unworked gold, intended to show his country's riches and to startle strangers. The size of this gold lump varies in the telling from the equivalent of a modest 167 pounds to "such a weight that twenty men could scarcely move it."

These maps [17] showed the world all it knew of Africa beyond the Mediterranean. Kankan-Musa became a familiar hero to the world. Two maps in which he figured went into especially important hands. That of Benincasa (1482) where Mousamalli is mentioned with the usual reference to his "abundance of gold" inspired Christopher Columbus. It contained certain elements about the Atlantic which, according to Charles de la Roncière, gave Columbus "the sudden confidence" enabling him to persuade the Catholic Kings to give him support. The Vallseccha map (1439) where Mousamalli is described as usual and shown with a gold ball in his hand belonged to the man whose name was given to two continents, Amerigo Vespucci.

[17] Reproductions of many such maps are included as plates illustrating Charles de la Roncière's *La Découverte de l'Afrique au moyen age*, 3 vols. (Cairo, 1925-27). Especially interesting are Dulcert's map (1339); those of Cresques (1375); Viladestes (1413); Vallseccha (1439); Bertran (1482); Benincasa (1482). In the text is a description of a map dated 1502 by Canerio which shows Kankan-Musa, then nearly two centuries dead.

A NEGRO ADVERTISER

SUCH A REPUTATION AS THIS, ENDURING FOR SO LONG AFTER DEATH and spread amongst foreign peoples who were then but vaguely interested in Africa as a whole, cannot have been accidental.

It is true that Kankan-Musa was a very great man, well deserving to be called—as he is sometimes—"The Napoleon of the Desert," well deserving Charles Monteil's summing up that "he was the most considerable person of the Land of the Blacks probably of all times." But Kankan-Musa's fame was due to something besides individual greatness. Kankan-Musa was a wonderful self-advertiser. He made himself and his country known by a piece of personal display which—gossip borne by the tongues of Christian traders, sailors and travelers—made "The Golden Emperor of Africa" famous in Europe.

Mali's riches, able government and brilliant conquests never would have attracted spontaneously the attention of the remote white world, though it is true that Mali was wonderful. Mali contained salt mines and gold mines. It contained the saltless regions where salt was exchangeable for gold "load for load" (see page 249). It contained copper mines to the east and a population in the gold mine section to the west who were eager to buy copper for sixty-six per cent of its weight in gold. Mali was master of the trade centers—Timbuctoo, Gao and others—whence gold could be shipped away.

Its organization and discipline were extraordinary, not to be duplicated in Mediterranean Africa, perhaps not anywhere in the world of the day. Ibn-Batuta visited Mali in the fourteenth century and reported, "There is complete security. Neither traveller nor inhabitant here has anything to fear from robbers or men of violence. They do not confiscate the property of any white man who dies in the country, even if it be uncounted wealth." Ibn-Batuta goes on to explain how such property is protected until the white man's rightful heirs come to claim possession of it. By "white man" Ibn-Batuta means traders from Mediterranean Africa. We have no record that any white European saw Mali in those days.

KANKAN-MUSA'S PILGRIMAGE

IN 1324 EMPEROR KANKAN-MUSA CARRIED OUT AS STRIKING A PEACE-time expedition as had ever been performed by any royal personage since the days of Sheba. He made the Mecca pilgrimage de luxe, a glittering gold procession that almost put Africa's sun to shame, which thrilled Arab and Sudanese chroniclers and drifting to Europe by word of mouth made his name familiar, his wealth proverbial and his fame almost immortal in Europe's geography.

Says the *Tarikh es-Soudan,* the king left home with an immense cortege—sixty thousand men. Before him as he rode marched five hundred slaves each carrying a staff of gold weighing the equivalent of just over seven pounds. Detail in the *Tarikh el-Fettach* mentions eight thousand guards, nine thousand slave workers for well digging, etc., and five hundred women including his royal wife.

His arrangements included a system of transporting live fish and growing vegetables for his nourishment along the Saharan part of his journey, and such organization that in the desert's most arid stretch a swimming pool could be dug, lined with a watertight mixture and filled with water for the royal baths.

These are the records and legends of the Sudan. We might suspect them of being pieces of Negro patriotic exaggeration did we not possess accounts by several nonprejudiced eyewitnesses who observed Kankan-Musa when—the desert crossing accomplished—he marched into Egypt and paused there awhile on his way to Mecca.

The interpreter at Cairo told Ibn-Khaldoun, "King Musa arrived with eighty camel loads of gold dust, each weighing 225 pounds." Another who saw Kankan-Musa says that twelve thousand young slaves clad in brocade and Yemen silks served the king. The author of the *Masalik* actually saw Kankan-Musa and also benefited by the reminiscences of an important person at Cairo's court who became Kankan-Musa's friend and confidant, and of other eyewitnesses of the king's visit.

*   *   *

THE EMPEROR AND HIS SUITE WHILE IN EGYPT, STATES THE MASA-
lik, were so prodigal in their spending, buying Turkish woman
slaves, Abyssinian eunuchs, singing girls, gorgeous clothing and
sacred books, that Cairo was flooded with gold and money was
demoralized on the market.[18]   The Negroes from the western
Sudan were country cousins in Cairo. Local merchants fleeced
them. The noise of their wealth and easy spending filled the
bazaars and was long remembered. Kankan-Musa spent so wildly
and gave such gorgeous presents to his hosts that he had to borrow
money to get home.

*   *   *

I GIVE SPACE TO A PASSAGE IN THE UNFAMILIAR HISTORY OF THE
Sudan just because it is unfamiliar. Black people and white people are at present considering their relations toward one another.
The past is admittedly a key to the understanding of the present.
Black people have ample opportunity to find out about the past
of the whites. But whites have little chance to learn about the
history of the blacks. Indeed, I presume the average well-read
person is unaware that the blacks of Africa possess any history.
Certainly, to inform oneself about it requires special facilities
and research. So it has seemed to me desirable to go into this
novel subject rather than to dwell upon certain other aspects of
North Africa's past with which readers are already familiar, or
about which—should they desire—they can secure information
without too much difficulty.

Let me therefore tell a little more about the unique figure of
Kankan-Musa, a Negro about whom—because of the interest
roused by his prodigal pilgrimage—we chance to possess such
ample contemporary accounts. Kankan-Musa literally and in the
vernacular "put Mali on the map." His pilgrimage—one for Allah,
and two for Mali, in intent, we suspect, though he is described

---

[18] "The year of Kankan-Musa's arrival the gold *mithkal* had not fallen
below 25 drachmes. Then its value went down. It did not go above 22
drachmes—even less. It has remained thus for twelve years since that time
(i.e. Kankan-Musa's presence in Cairo) because of the great quantity of gold
they brought and spent in Egypt." From a contemporary report in the
Masalik. The effect of this Negro spending upon the Cairo exchange became
legendary. Something over half a century later we find Macrizi making
preposterous claims about the fall of Egyptian money during the period.

as a saintly man—was both an education to the emperor and one of the finest pieces of publicity ever undertaken.

Mediterranean Africa had never before seen Negroes displayed with such dignity. There had been pilgrimages of Negro kings before. (Naturally the journey to Mecca was the only motive likely to take a princely black so far from his homeland.) But these previous black royal pilgrimages had been poor affairs which attracted no attention. Macrizi lists those from Mali without comment; one Mali king twenty-five years before Kankan-Musa's time was killed on his return trip from Mecca, indicating a small and feeble retinue. Negro pilgrims as previously observed had been on the whole a shabby lot by the time they reached the Mediterranean, always worn and ragged after the desert crossing, almost always reduced to petty trading and beggary.

CAIRO SEEN BY A NEGRO KING

IN CAIRO KANKAN-MUSA SAW ARCHITECTURE, CIVIC AMENITIES AND splendor for the first time, his route across the desert not having passed via any of the other cities of Mediterranean Africa. Kankan-Musa must have been startled but he kept his head. His personal self-confidence was unshaken and he protested vigorously when invited to bow down before the sultan of Egypt. It seemed to him inconceivable. Kankan-Musa was accustomed to receive the most abject of obeisances—obeisances which to us are laughable, but which were a serious part of the ceremonial of Negro courts. Those approaching the king went through odd calisthenics.

Barefooted they went into the royal presence—penalty of death to him who disobeyed this rule. Then came the so-called "Drum Salute": the beating of an imaginary drum, the body of the subject bent forward over an invisible instrument. Followed the "Dust Ceremony." Pantaloons lifted to mid-thigh, the subject knelt, thumped the ground with his elbows, then listened to the royal words. Before replying he would toss dust upon his head and back. If the king extended special favors, the subject was then expected to roll on the ground from one end of the reception hall to the other, which little journey accomplished, he would by the aid of onlookers be dusted with ashes, "always kept ready for such use at the end of the room," and then he would

repeat the "Drum Salute." The above is from Ibn-Batuta's observations at Mali and from an eyewitness at Kankan-Musa's establishment while he stayed in Cairo. A study of the various methods of saluting Sudanese kings and kinglets according to the local
rigid etiquette is included in Henri Gaden's *Légendes et coutumes
Sénégalaises* (*Revue d'ethnographie,* 1912). A very early Christian
traveler in the Sudan, Ca' Da Mosto (fifteenth century) commented,
"If God, Himself, descended from Heaven I do not think it
would be possible to show Him so great honor and reverence."
An English explorer in the mid-nineteenth century reported that
the "Dust Salute" was used to all rich men by their inferiors.
"The beggars throw dust about in clouds!" he says.

*   *   *

HABITUATED TO SUCH GROVELING PROSTRATIONS AT HOME, KANKAN-
Musa found the idea of himself bowing down to any man intolerable. Protocol became tangled until a tactful man of Kankan-
Musa's suite found a way round the difficulty, whispering a suggestion in Kankan-Musa's ear.

"Right!" cried the Negro emperor. "I do not mind prostrating
myself before Allah." This he did. The Egyptian sultan took the
salute as for himself and protocol was saved!

The two kings were greatly pleased with one another and exchanged gifts. Kankan-Musa was made happy by the present of
"a robe of honor," a complete costume with trappings, in which
figured a garment of gauze veiling ornamented with the images
of animals and trimmed with squirrel fur, castor and gold em-
broidery, a brocade bonnet with gold clasps, a handkerchief
stitched with gold, and so on. Kankan-Musa's gift to the sultan
had elegant simplicitv. It was "numerous camel loads of pure
unworked gold."

*   *   *

THE CAIRO WHICH KANKAN-MUSA SAW HAD A MILLION INHABI-
tants. Such is the statement of a contemporary learned man. Ibn-
Batuta who was in Cairo within a few months of Kankan-Musa
puts it more poetically: "Her throngs surge as the waves of the
sea and can scarce be contained in her, for all her size and capacity." The editor of one of the editions of Ibn-Batuta, H. A. R.
Gibb, instances a passage confirming this and dated half a century later to the effect that such was the housing shortage that

one hundred thousand persons had to sleep outside the city every night.

Cairo, Ibn-Batuta goes on, had twelve thousand water carriers, taking water about the city on camels. This despite the fact that some buildings had their own water supply, as we know from another and yet earlier visitor who reports finding in his hotel hot and cold, running water and flush toilets. There was a system of street watering.

Thirty-six thousand boats plied the Nile for trade. In all probability the postal system initiated by Sultan Bibars some sixty years before was in going operation; this system put Cairo at only four days from Damascus.

MEETING OF TWO PRODIGALS

CAIRO WAS THEN THE SEAT OF ONE OF THE GREATEST OF THE MAMluks, En-Nasir of the three reigns (1293 to 1294; 1299 to 1309; and 1310 to 1341), a grim, little, limping man with a cataract of one eye—immensely competent. His temper had been spoiled by repeated dethronements engineered during his childhood and youth by a series of rebellious and intriguing viceroys and ministers. Austere in his personal life, En-Nasir was prodigal in court display.

As a prodigal he could teach nothing to Kankan-Musa in so far as ephemeral show was concerned. Mammoth feasts where thousands of animals were consumed, a court so wasteful that the equivalent of from six thousand to nine thousand current United States dollars were spent daily on raw material for the table, the careless destruction of valuable fabrics—all this was no shock to the Negro royal spendthrift.

But from the prodigality of En-Nasir, the builder, Kankan-Musa learned much. He learned that Extravagance could mate with Art and bring forth lasting beauty. To the Negro this was a new idea. The buildings of Mali were primitive—houses of sun-dried brick, roofs of osier. Kankan-Musa saw a new vision, a new way to spend his vast wealth. He too could be a patron of architecture.

*   *   *

HIS MAMLUK HOST AND MANY OF HIS PREDECESSORS HAD ERECTED
fine buildings. En-Nasir's own mosque, now a ruin, must have
been a lovely sight with its marble portal filched from the Christian church at Acre. Cairo under the Mamluks plucked flowers for
its architectural bouquet from all the East. There were glowing
Persian tiles, a many-colored castle after a model in Damascus.
There was mosaic made of red porphyry and green stone and
black dorite from the mountains of the Arabian Desert. The
carved woodwork of Cairo, arabesque and geometrical in design,
was, however, a local invention. There was graceful furniture:
lamps of exquisite filigree silver inlay and tables of brass filigree
with inlays of silver. The period where political life was a rowdy
hurly-burly and the populace lived no more easily than so many
fish bubbling in a kettle of fat, was curiously the flowering time
of Moslem art.

THE MEDIEVAL HOSPITALS OF AFRICA

ONE BUILDING OF THE PERIOD OF KANKAN-MUSA'S VISIT WAS ESPE-
cially noteworthy. It was the great hospital. (Medieval Cairo
possessed four in all, of which one was built after the time in
question.) This great hospital was famous, the wonder of travelers.
It had been built and endowed in 1283-84 by En-Nasir's father
who—taken ill at Damascus—had been cured by remedies furnished by the hospital there and in gratitude bestowed a model
hospital on Cairo. Ibn-Batuta said, "No description is adequate
of its beauties." It had, besides rooms for the sick, lecture rooms,
theaters for operations, surgeons' rooms, mortuary, professors'
lodgings, cells for mad patients, and a mosque. It provided musicians to cheer the sick. It contained special segregated wards for
infectious diseases.

Leo Africanus saw the hospital a couple of centuries later. Said
he, "It is so endowed that all the sick no matter what their malady
can stay there with every convenience during their illness, being
visited by doctors and supplied with all their needs until they are
convalescent."

*   *   *

I AM TEMPTED TO TELL OF ANOTHER MEDIEVAL HOSPITAL IN AFRICA, that of Marrakesh in Morocco, also a royal foundation set up by El-Mansur (1184-99). He placed his institution in a park planted with trees and supplied with little canals bringing water alongside each room. All was free, even night and day clothes, summer and winter weight, for the patients, and when cured poor folk received a sum of money to see to their wants until they could again earn their livings. "There was no exclusion. Any stranger who fell sick in Marrakesh was carried there and cared for till well. Every Friday (Moslem prayer day) the sultan rode over on his horse and asked news of each patient." This account is from a contemporary source and is quoted by Millet in his book on the Almohades, who comments, "What a contrast to the *hotels-Dieu* of Christian (medieval) Europe; it would even put to shame the Paris hospital system of today!" Or any other hospital system, we add, in so far as true benevolence of attitude toward the sick is concerned. It is sad to have to mention that the cost of all this kindness came from racial gouging, being the proceeds of a special tax imposed upon the Jews of the city.

*   *   *

CAIRO'S HOSPITAL HAD A SECTION FOR CONTAGIOUS DISEASES. THIS part of the institution was needed, and—had it been as big as all Cairo itself—would sometimes have been inadequate. Cairo's outbreaks were proverbial. "Allah, preserve us from Egypt's *ouabaha* (pestilence)!" had been the camel drivers' prayer for centuries as they crossed the top of Africa from the west. The country had a bad name. Leo Africanus described its air as "hot and noxious." He—a great traveler—considered that there was "no other country more infected, nor where the smallpox was more contagious and more violent." Shakespeare had his word to say in *Antony and Cleopatra* about "the tokened pestilence," referring to the saying that the spots which show out on those infected were "God's tokens" because their appearance was passport to another world. When the Nile failed and did not cover the point which the natives called "The Angels of Death" famine came with pestilence clinging to its tail.

The apex of Egypt's plague horrors occurred a quarter of a century after Kankan-Musa's visit to Cairo. It was what Europe called the Black Death. It afflicted Egypt for some seven years following 1348.

How many died in Cairo nobody knows. It scarcely seems as if it could have been as many as nine hundred thousand, but this is the estimated figure. Ibn-Batuta, the fixed idea of travel in his head, crisscrossed the Near East during Black Death times and despite his foolhardiness escaped to tell how Cairo had twenty-one thousand deaths per day. At Damascus he witnessed something like mass hypnotism used as an infection preventive. It was July, 1348. The viceroy of Damascus ordered everyone to refrain from food for three days. Then "after the dawn prayer (on the fourth day) everyone—men and women, small and large—went out together holding their Korans in their hands. . . . The Jews came with their Book of the Law, and the Christians with their Gospel, all of them with their women and children. The whole concourse, weeping and supplicating . . . made their way to the Mosque of the Footprints (said to be Moses' footprints, much venerated) and there they remained in supplication and invocation until near midday. They then returned to the city and held Friday service, and God lightened their affliction; for the number of deaths in a day at Damascus did not attain 2000, while in Cairo and suburbs it reached 24,000." This is from the H. A. R. Gibb translation. The very old translation by the Rev. Samuel Lee (1829) made from another Arabic version of Ibn-Batuta says "the plague ceased that very day." Some sort of miracle evidently was brought about, public courage restored, a state of resistance established. Also the fasting and consequent keeping away from the crowded and infected market place may have helped.

IMPORTATION OF AN ARCHITECT

EXCITED BY THE BEAUTIFUL AND COMMODIOUS BUILDINGS OF CAIRO, Kankan-Musa set himself the ambition of improving the cities of his own empire. At Mecca he met a Spanish poet-architect, a Moslem by name Ės-Sahali and induced him to accompany the royal party to the Sudan. It proved a long but profitable exile for the architect, who never went back to his native Granada and who received from the grateful monarch as one of his professional fees gold dust to the weight of one hundred twenty pounds, and may have been rewarded with another honorarium of just over three times that amount.

The Spanish architect erected a mosque and palace at Timbuctoo, which was part of Kankan-Musa's empire. At Mali City he constructed a splendid audience hall for the king, solidly built and plastered, a type of edifice quite new to the country. Ibn-Khaldoun described it in the words of a friend of his who had been a protégé of Kankan-Musa's. Says this informant, "Es-Sahali drew upon all his genius. The hall was square with a dome; it was ornamented with arabesques of brilliant color. It was an admirable piece of architecture and the king was charmed." Other reports speak of its windows framed in gold and silver, of the curtains imported from Egypt, of the gorgeous spectacle when the king, under his royal golden umbrella with its gold top, watched the sports and dancing and acrobatics from a raised balcony just without the palace. Slave girls, about a hundred in number, in beautiful robes, with gold and silver balls in their hair, sang and played music by twanging the strings of bows. Musicians played on gold and silver *guimbris* (two-stringed guitars). The king wore a red velvet tunic of European fabric and "a gold skull cap bound with a gold band which had narrow ends shaped like knives more than a span in length."

PALACE NEAR THE NIGER

To this palace near the Niger came an embassy from the sultan, Abu'l Hasan of Morocco, bearing rich gifts. In this palace was held an odd ceremony called "a commemorative banquet," when news came that the sultan of Morocco, a friendly monarch, had died. Ibn-Batuta attended this banquet at which the Koran was read.

In this palace died in 1374 King Diata (Lion) a successor of Kankan-Musa's, the first recorded individual victim of sleeping sickness. He was attacked by what Ibn-Khaldoun's informant called "the lethargy, such being a sickness common in the country and which attacks especially people in high places." Diata suffered two years, finally he could scarcely keep awake for a single minute and succumbed. This fourteenth century account of a disease much discussed in modern times is of interest.

King Diata was a wastrel and during his reign the palace lost a traditional and celebrated ornament. The gold block of Mali was sold to a group of Egyptian merchants for some bit of finery or other which the wastrel coveted.

* * *

So we have made the tour of North Africa from Morocco to Egypt, from the Sudan by the Nile to the Sudan by the Niger, as they were in the last fine days of the Middle Ages.

VISITORS WITH SWORDS

North Africa in the latter Middle Ages was no longer a completely hidden land. Christians came visiting, sword in hand. Europe's strength was increasing, that of North Africa diminishing.

From the time of Roger II of Sicily to that final blow which made all North Africa a suburb of Europe—I mean the twentieth century conquest of the Tripoli region by the Italians—there was a series of European expeditions against Africa. To capture the whole top of the continent was a spotty and fumbling job, full of wasted lives, costly disasters and false starts. But, looking back, it is evident that Africa's days of continental integrity were waning. When and where Africa was observed to be weak an opening was seen. When and where she was strong and rich she roused desire. When and where she misconducted herself she offered a pretext. During the centuries since Roger's day almost every European country has been an attacker, and almost every coastal city has been attacked.

* * *

It was in Morocco that Europe had its earliest definite success. Since it would be impossible to rehearse anything like the whole list of the raids and temporary occupations elsewhere along the coast, we will concentrate on Morocco's experience. What happened in Morocco is particularly interesting because it led indirectly to the alteration of all North Africa's way of life. By these attacks on Morocco and their resultant tragic memories there was roused an appetite for Africa in one of the oddest characters with whom the continent ever came in contact. The influence of this appetite on Africa's destiny was enormous.

THE FIRST PERMANENT CHRISTIAN CONQUEST IN AFRICA

NATURALLY MOROCCO AT THE STRAIT OF GIBRALTAR SEEMED especially suitable to attack from Europe. In the early fifteenth century Ceuta and Tangier were battle centers. Tangier was one of the oldest cities in the world, allegedly named after a sweetheart of Hercules. Ceuta also claimed great antiquity and an association with an actual historic figure—Moses. The Koran (sura XVIII) mentions that Moses on his journey to "the confluence of the two seas" was accompanied by a fish which at a certain point near a rock "took its way to sea." The place in question was supposed to have been Ceuta. The offspring of this holy fish lived on in Ceuta waters and got to be associated by local Moslems not only with Moses, but with Jesus. It was a foot and a half long and was "half a fish"—flesh on one side and merely skin on its bones on the other side. If anyone ventured to eat one of the holy fish it was found to be an aphrodisiac. Such legends have value as suggesting the long-continued life and importance of a town. Ceuta's wealth was such that its tax return came third of all Moroccan cities, those of Fez and of Marrakesh alone were larger.

Ceuta is Christianity's oldest holding in Morocco—in all Africa. It was taken in 1415 and has been in Christian hands ever since, being now Spanish. Tangier, now international—so that when mailing a letter one may shop around for the postage stamps of his fancy—was a Christian holding for two centuries from 1471 under a series of European owners: Portuguese, Spanish, English. The English, who had received the place as part of the dot of Charles II's wife, found that the holding of it was a bloody and unprofitable business and abandoned it to the Moslems again (1684).

The original Christian capture of this section of Morocco was made a possible, though very expensive adventure by the decay of Morocco's home government. The Merinide sultan, Abu Said (1398-1420, died by assassination) sat an unsure throne. The dynasty was on its last legs and was soon to fall (1465). The Chris-

tian world had seen with what relative ease the Castillians had
wiped out Tetuán as a warning to Moroccan pirates, killing half
the population and taking away the other half as slaves. Portugal's
king heard of the anarchy in Morocco and resolved to take Ceuta.
He sailed forth in person, surprised and took the city in 1415.
Ceuta's mysterious holy fish seems to have played its part. The
attacking fleet rode before the frightened town, so numerous that
"if all the trees in Portugal had been cut into planks and all
Portugal's men turned boat builders it seemed as if they could not
in all their lives have constructed such a multitude of vessels!"
(This was the Portuguese boast.) Then, as two of the king's sons
were together upon one ship of a Friday morning "a fish left the
sea, rose in the air and fell upon the bridge." This occurrence
seemed preternatural and a celestial sign to the Portuguese historian, Azurara.

It was Portugal's first African adventure—a triumph. Ceuta's
grand mosque was purified, exorcised with salt and water and
dedicated to the service of Our Lord Jesus Christ. The three
princes were there—"a beautiful sight to see . . . their armor was
brilliant and richly ornamented, at their sides hung their blessed
swords." These were the swords given them by their English
mother for use in the Holy War as she lay dying of the plague a
few days before the expedition's departure. The trumpets blared
across Ceuta, the drums beat, the princes and their father were
happy conquerors.

Morocco was stupefied. It was their first such loss, their first
experience since the birth of Islam of Christian occupation of
their land. They were the untamed horse feeling for the first
time the alien bit. But they could not throw off the invader.

The last of the Merinides came to the throne of a disordered
and angry country while he was still in the cradle. He was Abd
el-Haqq, who grew up feeble and was controlled during most of
his reign by a series of regents of the Wattas family, kinsfolk of
the Merinides. A new ebullition of pious fever excited the people
and just before the sultan was murdered there rose an ephemeral
religious government. Then a change of dynasty with a series of
Wattas sultans in power.

*   *   *

SOME TWENTY YEARS AFTER HER CEUTA SUCCESS PORTUGAL UNWISELY attempted to continue her African adventures. It turned out as miserable a disaster as is to be found in the whole story of the European effort at African conquest. The element of surprise which had helped in the case of Ceuta was lacking. The second expedition had been discussed openly at length in Portugal and bruited round Europe. The Pope had been consulted and sent a somewhat lukewarm and evasive reply, the text of which is given in Ruy de Pina's contemporary chronicle. The other element which had helped Portugal to capture Ceuta still existed—disunion in Morocco, but at rumor of the attack Moroccans were shocked to loyalty. They banded for a Holy War. Fighting men came hurrying from the mountains and from the desert's edge. Tangier, which was the expected point of attack, was ready with bared teeth.

During thirty-seven tragic days in 1437 the Portuguese struggled —twenty-five days to get into Tangier, and twelve in trying to hold it. They had eaten raw horse meat (fuel lacking as well as food) and sucked mud through their teeth for lack of water. Then a truce and peace terms of the most humiliating kind: Portugal to promise to refrain from troubling Morocco for a hundred years, to undertake to give up Ceuta and to leave the king's son as hostage; the Portuguese to be allowed to go home.

Each side claimed that the other violated the truce terms. The Portuguese stuck to Ceuta. The Moroccans held the hostage, Dom Fernando, for years in vile captivity. The Moroccan population in general thought of him as "the King of the Christians." He was deliberately martyrized "so that the Portuguese, on hearing about his sufferings, would hasten to give up Ceuta." Fra Joao Alvares, his secretary and fellow captive, tells the detail of his humiliations and tortures.

Notwithstanding, the Portuguese held firm to Ceuta and the hostage finally died in an old latrine where he had been shut up alone for fifteen months. The Moroccans then hoped to use his corpse as a lever, causing his body to be filled with salt, myrrh and dried bay leaves so as to preserve it as something exchangeable with their enemies. The Moroccans, be it understood, sincerely thought that Portugal had cheated them: "the Christians are traitors and do not give us back Ceuta," the young Moroccan sultan's regent is reported to have said in justifying his treatment of the hostage.

Eventually the body was bought by Portugal, after it had hung naked on the Fez walls, object of popular insults, spat upon and pelted with rocks and rotten oranges. But the Portuguese clung to Ceuta and some years later were able at last to take Tangier.

AFRICA'S SIDE DOOR

HOWEVER EUROPE'S MEDIEVAL ATTACKS ON NORTH AFRICAN Mediterranean ports did not so vitally affect North Africa as did what might be called the crashing of the continent's side door. Africa's whole future was profoundly altered by the opening up of sea routes down her Atlantic coasts and by the ensuing discovery of the sea route to the east.

It was Prince Henry of Portugal (1394-1460), called "Henry the Navigator," who inspired the exploration of Africa's Atlantic coast. Son of an English mother and of the king, Joao I, he was as a youth a member of the Ceuta expedition of conquest and leader of the Tangier fiasco. He was a man—we meet them occasionally in history—over whom Africa had truly cast a spell. He longed to return to Africa, but could not. But he took Africa in his hands and reshaped it. No man, I think and shall try to prove, ever so greatly influenced the continent. In his hard, almost monastic, life of fasting and chastity—he died a virgin—he loved only Africa, and by the intermediary of those he sent out in ships sought to unveil the mysterious continent of his dreams. He sat at home waiting for their reports, eager to gaze at the strange souvenirs they brought back to him, as gradually—urged on by him—they pushed farther and farther down Africa's shores.

*   *   *

NOT SINCE THE TIME OF HANNO, THE CARTHAGINIAN, HAD AFRICA'S Atlantic coast been methodically investigated. No one had ventured beyond Moroccan waters and come back with an intelligible story of what he had seen. The Africa of Europe's geographic theory was perforce a bobtailed continent, cut off short a bit below the Sahara, or at most possessed a purely imaginary tail, small and lean like the state of Florida.

It is true there had been adventures along Africa's coast, both Arabic and Christian. Notable amongst the latter was that of the two Vivaldis who left Genoa in May, 1291, to seek an Atlantic route to India and Grand Tartary and never came back, the only hint to their fate being that another traveler 170 years later claimed to have seen a descendant of the Vivaldi company—presumably wrecked in Guinea. This seems a tall tale, first of a series of similar pretended findings of the descendants of lost African explorers.

Also there is that alleged French venture of the fourteenth century (i.e. nearly a hundred years earlier than Henry the Navigator's effort). The debate as to whether Norman traders then got to the coasts of Negroland has been—to quote a modern French geographer—"a passionate argument still unsettled."

Such episodes as these—the lost Vivaldi expedition and the possible Norman trading ships—did not add to contemporary Europe's knowledge of Africa. Nor did they represent, as did Henry's systematic work, the beginning of the end of Africa's autonomy.

In Henry the Navigator's youth Cape Bojador on the north Sahara was the limit of knowledge. Before he died his sailors had investigated as far as Guinea. A generation after his death Portuguese had doubled the Cape of Good Hope.

WHITE FACES IN AFRICA

HOW DID AFRICANS REACT TO THIS SUDDEN AND STARTLING INTRUSION into their age-old privacy? Except in Mediterranean ports they had practically never seen a European white. The exceptions are negligible: a few dubious cases of European travel in inner Africa, and two recorded instances told of in old manuscripts, now in the Bibliothèque Nationale, and published by Charles de la Roncière, the second of which is ornamented with such genic circumstance as to damage its credibility.

The first case, that of Malfante, is convincing. In 1447 this Genoese traveler made his way to the Tuat oases. In his own words (translated from the Latin in which his narrative was written) "These people have never seen a Christian. . . . Everybody wanted to look at me and cried out amazed, 'This man is a Christian, but he has a face just like our own!' "

The other Christian traveler was by name Anselme d'Isalguier, from Toulouse, who allegedly reached Gao on the Niger in 1405, married a beautiful and rich Negro girl of good family and lived with her there for eight years, then returned to France, bringing with him the fruit—the odd fruit—of his miscegenation. This was a pretty little girl, quite black except for a streak of white upon her forehead and two white fingers on her left hand!

Such were the two—the only two, so far as I know—travelers from Europe who have left personal records of journeys into inner Africa previous to the era of the Portuguese explorations. So there can be no doubt that Henry the Navigator's men created a stir when they visited—progressively growing bolder—first the Saharan shores, then the country at the mouths of the Senegal and the Gambia Rivers, and later the Guinea coast. This last was then the ocean frontier of the Mali Empire. On modern maps the regions visited are known as Mauritania, Senegal (with the two ports, St. Louis and Dakar), Gambia, Portuguese Guinea, and French Guinea. As it continued farther south Portuguese exploration passes beyond the limits of this book.

The astonished natives thought that European ships were huge fish or immense birds. Such is the report of Azurara, author of the first book written by a European about the west coast of Africa. European men were thought to be lepers, or perhaps to be artificially whitened. According to their several tempers natives fled from them in horror, or spat on their fingers and tried to scrub the white off their visitors' hands, or fired poisoned arrows at them and killed them.

POISONED ARROWS

THE POISONED ARROW WAS A HORRID SURPRISE TO PORTUGUESE explorers. In one attack all but two were killed in a group of twenty-two. So—meet another new weapon! Or rather one which was new to its victims though one of the oldest in the usages of war.

The Portuguese' tragic experience cited above occurred on the fringe of the Mali Empire. Another such attack had already been made upon them in the neighborhood of modern Dakar. One risked attack by poisoned arrows anywhere. I pick a few items upon the dread weapon from my scrapbook on African ways and customs:

A twelfth century Arabic text describes poisoned arrows seen in Morocco. They were poisoned with the blood of yellow serpents. Burckhardt in Cairo in 1816 was told by Sudanese pilgrims about the arrows of their homeland: "The smallest scratch causes the body to swell and is inevitably mortal unless counteracted by an antidote known to the natives. This antidote is prepared from a small worm which is dried and reduced to powder. The wound is rubbed with the powder and some of it is eaten. Whenever soldiers go to war they are furnished with a small box of this powder." This last seems a modern touch indeed.

The English explorer, Richardson, just a century ago found poisoned arrows for sale in the markets of Ghat in the central Sahara. A French traveler, Soleillet (1878-79) when in the bush not far from Bamako on the Niger, noted that "each village possesses its own particular poison for which it knows the counter poison." Bragging of the special deadliness of their local poison would therefore have been a part of native war propaganda.

Africans had discovered hideous poisons for arrow and other use. Leo Africanus believed that the Nubians knew of one so violent that one grain of it divided amongst ten men would exterminate them in less than a quarter of an hour, or if given all to one man would cause him to expire instantly. The bark of a tree called *mpungwanyoni* is so venomous that, according to Father Maurice (writing in one of the 1938 issues of the organ of the Société de Géographie) "birds who perch upon it drop dead, whence its name which means 'the killer of birds.'" Some poisons suitable for use with arrows are listed by Desplanges: the *soumpigna*, the *yaima*, etc. He adds, "arrows are often treated by being stuck into a decomposing corpse or into the glands of the black spitting serpent. Also use is made of a certain fly, *macamogo*, which is powdered and proves fatal."

These scraps may console some of us who blame civilization for demoralizing man and causing him to invent nasty ways of killing his fellows. Man has not been demoralized. He was made that way. Primitive man had the same instincts.

AFRICAN SOUVENIRS

IMMENSE COURAGE WAS NEEDED BY THE MEN SENT FORTH BY HENRY the Navigator—no navigator in fact; he stayed at home and scanned the horizon for their return with new knowledge and strange gifts.

We read of a Danish volunteer in his service who was massacred while attempting to buy a live elephant from a vassal of a king of Mali. Henry was itching with curiosity to see an elephant. He had listened to extraordinary stories: how it was so huge that its meat could feed twenty-five hundred people, how its excrement was "as big as the body of a man," and maybe he had heard that the elephant had such prestige that the king of all Mali was called "The Great Elephant" by his jungle subjects. The unfortunate Dane had planned to carry back to his patron the skin and bones of the beast, which alive could scarcely be traveled upon a caravel. Another foreigner in Portugal's service, the Venetian Ca' Da Mosto, was luckier. He procured an elephant and had some of its meat salted to take back to the prince, who presumably ate it.

Henry, though a particularly abstemious man who fasted half of each year and never touched wine, did enjoy the exotic edible and drinkable souvenirs which his emissaries fetched back from Africa. Three times he ate ostrich eggs brought from the Saharan coasts and reaching Portugal perfectly fresh and good. He drank water from the Senegal River, two barrels of which had been carried back to him and felt, Azurara assures us, that even Alexander the Great never had tasted a drink brought to him from so far a distance.

He also received nonedible African souvenirs: There was a living lion which was eventually sent to Ireland as a present to an old servitor of the prince. And there was a gift full of significance: a small quantity of gold powder—the first gold ever to reach Europe by the ocean route.

NEGROES TO PORTUGAL

BUT MORE SIGNIFICANT YET BY FAR WERE THE HUMAN GIFTS OFFERED to Prince Henry—"black gold," so called, though the first important batch of these men and women captives from Africa contained persons of every color from nearly white to deepest black.

Azurara gives a pitiable account of the arrival of such a shipment. He tells of their faces bathed in tears, of their wistful songs in languages none understood, of how they flung themselves to the ground in despair when driven ashore and ranged for Henry's inspection.

Twenty per cent of all African treasure was attributed to the prince personally. So five groups of captives were made up, "each to have similar value. To do this it was necessary to separate the children from their parents, the women from their husbands." Henry rode up "on a big horse" and picked his forty-six assorted Africans. The other four fifths were parceled out and sold from hand to hand so that you might find "a father in Lagos (south Portugal), the mother in Lisbon, and the children in still some other locality." Azurara says that they were otherwise well treated and such as were not Moslems—that is of looser pagan upbringing —"embraced without objection the law of Christ."

*   *   *

THUS SLAVERY'S SEED WAS SOWN—SEED OF THE SLAVERY OF AFRICA'S Negroes on a colossal scale. The African slave trade had previously been a small affair, consisting of the sale of war captives or tribute slaves. The transportation of Negroes across the Sahara had been too troublesome to permit the trade to be exploited in a big way. With the opening of Africa's shores to ships this changed. How easy to exchange some bit of finery, a few gargles of rum for Negroes, and how easy to squash them between the decks of a ship. Gradually there followed all the loathsome horror of the slave trade. Followed indirectly the swift growth of the Americas, the Civil War, the present color problem in the United States. All these things were to follow Henry the Navigator's discovery of a sea route to Africa's coast.

"TALENT DE BIEN FAIRE"

GIVEN THE AWESOME POTENTIALITIES OF HIS ACT WE MARVEL AT Henry's motto: *"Talent de bien faire"* (Talent for doing good). Henry's sailors, Barros says, were accustomed to carve these words on African trees to mark the right of possession to the lands they discovered. Could the natives have understood what the words meant they might have disagreed. To many of those poor blacks the arrival of Europeans would eventually mean removal from their homes to a land where they, in their fear and ignorance, believed "the sun was unknown, there were no trees, no sheep and the women were not like real women." I quote from a French trading official on the coast. Ca' Da Mosto says they were of the opinion that "we live on nothing but human flesh and only buy Negroes so as to devour them."

Yet Henry's motives were of the noblest, his piety of the most elevated. His reason for exploring Africa was to propagate the Christian religion and check Mohammedanism. Also to seek out the so-called "Terrestrial Paradise" and to find possible pockets of Christianity supposed to exist inside Africa.

PRESTER JOHN

EUROPE'S DISCOVERY OF A CHRISTIAN POCKET IN ABYSSINIA CAME after Henry's time and was in a region outside the limits of this book. But let me remind the reader nonetheless of the Prester John story which had medieval Europe by the ears.

First heard of in Asia, the Priest King is said to have been a convert to Christianity in 1007. He lived on in travelers' tales. Marco Polo and others told of him. This Christian potentate supposedly isolated among Asiatic heathen excited the medieval imagination.

Then came rumors of a Prester John living in Africa—the wealthiest ruler on earth, with fifty-two (or seventy-two) under-kings doing his bidding. The stories of his magnificence glowed with details about precious metals and jewels, told of tables made out of gold and amethysts, of a palace of crystal, a scepter cut from a single emerald. Also included mention of a place of wonder where the aged could doze their lives away, as well as a Fountain of Youth.

Christendom was mad to see this mysterious personage and his gorgeous kingdom. The hope of finding him inspired Henry the Navigator's explorers. But his address was wide and indefinite: just "Prester John, Africa." Some of Henry's men heard of him on the west coast, probably putting the words into their Negro informants' mouths.

Finally in Abyssinia on November 19, 1520, Prester John was seen by European eyes in the flesh. His flesh was found to be "the color of a russet apple, not very dark." His setting was disappointing when compared with European expectations expressed as recently as half a century before, which had been to the effect that he would be found seated upon a solid gold throne, set upon a platform of rubies, and that the royal bed would be "made of sapphires, because this stone induces sleep."

He was David (Dawit) II of Abyssinia, a predecessor of the deposed and restored Negus Haile Selassie, victim of Italy's short-lived conquest.

TRADERS' PARADISE

WITH THE PROGRESS OF DISCOVERY AFRICA'S COASTAL TRADE GREW and the nations of Europe joined Portugal in its exploitation. Obviously there could be no maintaining the original papal concession giving away all the new African discoveries to Henry's countrymen, later modified so that Spain should enjoy a slice. The carving up of Africa without Africa's consent as represented in such concessions was to the Christian notion particularly justifiable in the case of the countries of pagan Africa. A tolerant papal attitude was expressed toward the Moslems of the continent, who were to be attacked only if they troubled Christian property or proved to be obstinate. Such a text is given by Ruy de Pina, the fifteenth century Portuguese historian.[19]

African coastal trade could not be preserved as the exclusive privilege of one or two nations. It was too exciting a venture. Too promising of profit. Consider such enticing tales as these: that "thirty-nine basins and two small white saucers were exchanged for three ounces of gold"; that "within one quarter of an hour I took one pound and a quarter of gold"; or that "we made sales for the gold of the country to the quantity of 150 pounds weight."

[19] See collection of Portuguese texts prepared by Virginia de Castro e Almeida, under the general title in the French edition: Les Grands navigateurs et colons portugais du XV et du XVI siècles, Tome II, pp. 38, 39.

These are from the record of Master William Towrson (1555) and that of Thomas Windham (1553) as set down in Hakluyt.

Yet more capable of arousing traders' greed was the report that you could sell ship's bilge water to the natives who believed it had medicinal value and cured toothache. Or the fact that those shells called cowries which were used for money in the Niger region at the rate of four hundred to a ducat, according to Leo Africanus, could be procured in the East for practically nothing (one million two hundred thousand for the value of three current United States dollars, Ibn-Batuta says; four million eight hundred thousand for the value of eight or nine 1840 dollars according to an explorer of that date). The shells could be carried as ballast to Africa's coast and swapped for gold.

The cowry, incidentally, is a pretty white shell about half the size of a lady's little fingernail. It was still in use—along with official currency—when I was in the Sudan. Dr. Oskar Lenz says that its use as money is a very old and widely distributed custom and that shells of this sort have been found in ancient tombs and prehistoric stations in Sweden.

Traders were invigorated when they heard that certain articles classed as luxuries in Europe could be got in Africa for almost nothing, sometimes for actually nothing. Any day a lump of ambergris might be thrown up onto the ship's deck by the waves. There was a celebrated chunk of ambergris that weighed a hundred pounds and sold for the equivalent of seventeen thousand, three hundred and ten current United States dollars.

There was that luxury condiment, the meleguete pepper, long appreciated in Europe and hitherto fetched at great pains from the west coast of Africa across the Sahara to the Mediterranean and thence by ship to Italy, where, so Barros says, "the Italians, not knowing the place of origin of the meleguete and because it was a spice so precious, called it 'Grains of Paradise.'" Now traders in ships could procure it in exchange for bits of cheap European goods (beads and basins, tin pots, common red cloth and so on, as listed by Hakluyt's travelers. The list oddly includes "sleigh bells"!).

"Fourscore tunne" of Grains of Paradise were urged upon a single captain by a native king. Another ship's cargo: "twenty-four tuns of Grains of Paradise and seven hundred elephants' tusks." The Ivory coast still lives on modern maps, but the then more famous "Meleguete Coast," where Columbus is said to have believed that he saw sirens, is a forgotten name.

AN ALTERED CONTINENT

GREAT OPPORTUNITY FOR FOREIGN EXPLOITATION OF AFRICA. GREAT loss to Africa's own traders robbed of the age-old exclusive profits of self-exploitation. The continent's whole trade system was altered, and North Africa was particularly and profoundly affected. No longer was the Sahara the essential highway of commerce, crisscrossed by caravans which alone could bring Africa's gold and Africa's exotic wares to the north. No longer were North Africa's ports the only access to these things. No longer—once the Cape of Good Hope had been doubled—was Egypt (and Egypt's empire in Syria) the fairway to India and the rest of the East. Egypt was nearly ruined.

This is why I suggest that no man ever so greatly influenced Africa as Henry the Navigator. Another might have done what he did. But it was Henry the Navigator who did do it. This wonderful executive and dreamer who fell under Africa's spell began the systematic exploration of Africa's coasts. I do not think it is too much to say that Henry castrated a continent.

GRIEF IN EGYPT

EGYPT WRITHED IN JEALOUS FURY AS EUROPE'S SHIPS BEGAN TO SAIL round Africa to the East. That trade which for centuries had dripped profits all along the way as it passed across her territory dwindled. To Egypt it was tragedy. She tried force, fighting sea battles with the Portuguese. She tried blackmail, threatening the Pope that the holy places in Palestine would be destroyed if the sea trade continued. Of course her efforts were futile. They were the nagging of a discarded sweetheart. Egypt was no longer the indispensable trade route.

Already Egypt had become weak. The years since En-Nasir's glories amazed Kankan-Musa had taken her downhill. The Black Death had been followed by another plague nearly as destructive.

Through sickness and bad government the country's population had diminished to a third. Disorder was such that women dared not appear in the streets, and many a Cairo woman had never been outdoors.

TAMERLANE

ALSO THERE HAD COME THE DEADLY DANGER OF TAMERLANE (Timur-Lang, the lame) who at the end of the fifteenth century made all the world quake with his frightfulness, with his massacres and the monuments built of human heads by which he commemorated his conquests: ninety thousand at Bagdad in a pyramid, twenty thousand at Aleppo "in mounds ten cubits high by twenty in circumference, with all the faces on the outside."

Sultan Barkuk of Egypt defied Tamerlane, held him off and had the desperate courage to execute Tamerlane's ambassador to Egypt. Barkuk was the first vigorous and efficient ruler Egypt had had in forty years and had lately deposed the twelfth of En-Nasir's relatives—mostly children—who had been lifted onto the throne and kicked off again in a jumbled series of uprisings and royal assassinations indicative of a very shaky state of national affairs. Barkuk had founded a new group of Mamluks, the so-called Circassians.

IBN-KHALDOUN ON A ROPE

TAMERLANE WAS GROWING OLD AND THE UNFINISHED BUSINESS OF Egypt irked him. Barkuk had been succeeded by his son Faraj. Faraj set off for Syria to meet the danger. In his entourage was the great historian I have so often quoted in these pages, Ibn-Khaldoun, who for sometime had resided in Egypt, much of the while acting as grand cadi.

Aleppo had become Tamerlane's prey in the manner mentioned above. Ibn-Khaldoun and the royal party arrived at Damascus and the Egyptian troops met Tamerlane with some success. Then, in the frequent Mamluk fashion, there occurred a revolt on the home front and Sultan Faraj in consternation bustled back to Egypt, abandoning Damascus feebly defended.

Ibn-Khaldoun and the other notables decided that their only

course was to approach Tamerlane and try to make terms. The commander of the little Damascus garrison considered this futile, and as it turned out he was right for Tamerlane later broke the agreement and butchered the city in his usual manner.

Ibn-Khaldoun and his associates, the commander having refused to let them go, dropped themselves down from the city wall one night by ropes. The historian was then a venerable person of sixty-eight. Nor was his vigor at that age merely physical. He charmed and fooled Tamerlane. The ferocious conqueror received the deputation with politeness; he admired learned men and "his policy was to attract to his service persons of every country famed for any particular art or science." Another surprising item is the conqueror's own smug claim—this last is passed on by Gibbon—that "I am not a man of blood and God is my witness that in all my wars I have never been the aggressor"!

Ibn-Khaldoun so fascinated old Tamerlane that he did not want to part with him. The wily historian tricked his way out of the lion's jaws. He read aloud to Tamerlane the rough draft of a biography upon himself. Tamerlane was delighted and wanted to see the work completed. Ibn-Khaldoun pretended that nothing would please him better than to enter Tamerlane's service and write his historic works in such fashion as "to assign to yourself (I quote Ibn-Khaldoun's speech to Tamerlane, as set down in a contemporary chronicle) first place among kings, and to give such a recital of your exploits as to make the reader pale." But, Ibn-Khaldoun added, he must be permitted first to go back to Cairo to fetch his manuscripts so the revisions giving Tamerlane pre-eminence could be made. Then he would joyously give the rest of his life to proclaiming Tamerlane's fame, for "Allah be praised, I have found in you someone who shall be my patron forever!"

Tamerlane agreed and let Ibn-Khaldoun depart for Cairo to fetch his manuscripts and his family. Needless to say Tamerlane never saw him again.

* * *

THOUGH DAMASCUS BATHED IN BLOOD, EGYPT ESCAPED. SULTAN Faraj abased himself diplomatically, probably talked about "peace in our time" and was raising a new army when Tamerlane died

(1405). Else Egypt might have seen pyramids of heads dotted amongst the stone pyramids of the Pharaohs.

TURKS

Toward the end of the century Egypt met yet greater danger, that attack upon her whole economy represented by the discovery of the sea route to the East. This last was the greatest misfortune of all her immensely long history. With her foreign trade slipping away and the home government in disorder it was evident that yet another change was due. It was to be a change of masters which would affect not only Egypt but in due time almost all Mediterranean Africa.

*   *   *

If we were to read history without any preliminary notion of how the story would develop, as we read novels, we would expect that the next chapter upon North Africa—the chapter on the sixteenth century—would tell of a Christian capture of the land. Christian Europe's persistent attacks on the Mediterranean and adjacent Atlantic shores of Africa, Christian Europe's pushing open of Africa's side doors to the west and east by sea discoveries would lead one to expect a final Christian triumph. But Providence, the Author of History, shows us a surprise. The next chapter reveals almost all of Mediterranean Africa—obviously ripe for somebody's capture—as falling into the hands not of Christian Europe, but of Moslem Turkey.

*   *   *

"The rise of the Ottoman Empire (that of the Ottoman Turks, named for Othman or Osman, their thirteenth century chief) was one of the major events of history, the significance of which is yet not fully appreciated by those who supply the school histories for western European and American readers" (from *Turkey at the Straits* by James T. Shotwell and Francis Deak, 1941)

By the latter half of the fifteenth century the Turks had taken Constantinople, at which feat of Moslem arms Egypt, little foreseeing her own fate, went wild with joy.

In 1515 after preliminary bickering Turkey made her great drive against Egypt under the sultan, Selim I—"Selim the Grim,"

"Selim the Adamant," called in his lifetime "The Grand Turk." Firm in decision though he was, Selim had some qualms about this inadequately provoked attack on a sister country of Islam. A curious account of his moral turmoil is given in a Moslem source, El-Ayachi's work called the *Rihlat:* [20] Selim consulted his advisers, seeking a pretext. The "subtle Ibn-Kemal-Pasha" helped him out. Selim should inform the sultan of Egypt, he advised, that he desired to cross Egypt en route for Mecca to perform the pilgrimage and that he counted upon the Egyptian sultan to authorize this and to feed his people on their journey. In his suspicious and uneasy mood, the Egyptian sultan would be certain to refuse, prophesied the subtle counselor and "if he acts thus you will have the legitimate right to attack him, for he will have made a hostile act in opposing your pilgrimage."

Selim thought the advice good—a stratagem likely to fool Allah! —and informed Egypt of his proposed holy visit. The Egyptian reply was as hoped: "You will never drink a single mouthful of Nile water unless you come here across a bridge of corpses!" Selim's conscience was satisfied. He attacked.

* * *

THE AUTHOR OF THIS DEFIANT LETTER, THE SULTAN, EL-GHORY, died in battle near Aleppo, Syria, where the Mamluks of Egypt were totally defeated by the Turkish aggressor. He was the last of the Mamluk rulers except the stopgap sultan who held the position for three months.

On January 26, 1517, Selim entered Cairo and drank Nile water to his throat's content. He had his bridge of corpses too— twenty-five thousand Mamluks who lay dead on the field. Thenceforth Egypt was a province of the Turkish Empire.

* * *

IN THIS BRILLIANT VICTORY A NEW WEAPON TURNED THE DAY. THE Turks used firearms. The Mamluk warriors, as Professor Hitti neatly puts it, "clung to the antiquated theory that personal valor is the decisive factor in combat."

[20] The pages dealing with this matter are quoted in El-Oufrani's *Nozhet-elhadi,* trans. Houdas, Publication de l'école des langues orientales vivantes (1889). The *Rihlat* is a seventeenth century work.

PART FOUR

The Crescent Blinks

BARBARY PIRATES

NORTH AFRICA CHANGED PROFOUNDLY WITH THE COMING OF THE Turks. All across Mediterranean Africa, except in Morocco, the Turk became master. All across Mediterranean Africa, except against Egypt, Christian attacks increased. All across Mediterranean Africa, except in Egypt, and down along Morocco's Atlantic coasts as well, piracy came to be North Africa's most extensive and profitable business.

* * *

THE BARBARY PIRATES OR CORSAIRS ARE VERY FAMOUS. ALONG WITH the Punic Wars and the 1942-43 campaign they stand out as the most widely familiar items in all North African history.

But it was not the people of Barbary of the sixteenth century who first taught the world about piracy. Piracy was probably as old as ships. It followed navigation as night the day. To our knowledge Egypt was so plagued by pirates some thirteen hundred years before Christ that she was obliged to institute a marine police service to patrol the Nile Delta. The first pirate to win individual fame seems to have been one Dionysius of Phocaea who, as Herodotus says, "sallied forth out of Sicily" in the fifth century B.C. Carthage, Greece, Rome all practiced piracy without shame. But it was North Africans of the sixteenth century who developed piracy into a national effort and made it the occupation of the best brains and bodies of the land.

The Barbary pirates were the "scourge of Christendom," under whose whip commerce bled for three hundred years. To be cap tured by pirates and sold into slavery was the regular risk of sea travel. People had to expect it. It happened to Cervantes. It happened to St. Vincent de Paul. "Robinson Crusoe's" experiences were based on fact. It is said that in the year 1634, for example, there were twenty-five thousand Christian slaves in Algiers alone. Amongst the twenty-five thousand were certain victims, however, who had not risked the hazards of travel. There was notably a group which had gone to bed in their home in Baltimore, on the southern coast of Ireland, and waked to struggle with Algerian pirate-raiders. More than two hundred, including cradle babies, were dragged back to Algiers.

*　　*　　*

IT IS EASY TO UNDERSTAND WHY NORTH AFRICA TURNED SO ENTHU-siastically to piracy. Her coastal trade had been injured by the increasing use of the sea routes. Her temper had been roused by Christian attacks upon her cities and by the ejection of fellow Moslems from Spain, most of whom came to Africa. Eight centuries before Africans had crossed Gibraltar as conquerors. Now their descendants came back with their tails between their legs. It was a profound shock. While these things were happening African pride was also being humbled by the Turkish invader gradually gobbling control from Egypt to the Moroccan frontier. No wonder that a still active and very angry population took to piracy. Hatred was fed by greed. It was gratifying to be able to injure the Christian enemy and grow rich at the same time.

To be a corsair (from "course," the chase, the hunt), to cut through the waves in a swift galley rowed by Christian galley slaves, the swish of the lash and their shrieks in your ears, the fleeing rich ship falling back toward you—thrilling work for young Moslems. Dangerous too. Many a Moslem pirate was captured and in his turn chained to Christian galley benches to feel the whip cut against his own shoulders. For Christians too practiced piracy.

Some Christian captures were notable. One was Hasan of Granada, who subsequently became the famed geographer and travel writer, Leo Africanus, from whom I have frequently quoted. He was caught by Sicilian pirates, taken to Rome, given to the Pope, became Christian and assumed the Pope's name of Leo. In his book Leo uses such phrases as "the damnable and pernicious Mohammedan sect," "the false prophet, Mohammed," and the

like. This was mere sleek tact on Leo's part, for when he was able
to get away from Rome and go to Tunis he became a Moslem
again. The Christian pirates failed to get that prodigious traveler,
Ibn-Batuta, who in early corsair days twice escaped them, but
had so bad a scare that he records, "I made a vow to fast for two
successive months if Allah would deliver us."

TAKERS OF THE TURBAN

ODDLY ENOUGH MANY OF THE MOST POWERFUL PERSONAGES IN
North Africa and some of the most successful corsair captains were
renegade Christians, men who had been captured, and had chosen
to forswear Christ and turn Moslems. The word, renegade, has a
low and hateful sound, but—if we consider the position without
prejudice and with charity—we must admit that the switch over
was really something like a process of naturalization whereby a
man, usually not of a spiritual type—accepted the customs of the
country in which he was obliged to spend the rest of his life,
and secured, in exchange for harsh slavery, his liberty and a
chance to make his fortune.

There have been many turban takers: It is recorded that in
Spain in the days of the Mohammedan conquest whole sections
of the erstwhile Christian population went over to Islam. They
were known as Muladies, derived from a word meaning "adopted,"
and after a while they made up "the majority of the population
of several cities." To bring the matter closer, we are told that in
the days of the United States-Barbary Wars five Americans from
the captured *Philadelphia* became Mohammedans. A lucky nine
teenth century renegade was the well-known Rais (Captain)
Morat, a Scot, who got to be high admiral in Tripoli and married
into the royal family. Another lucky nineteenth century Scottish
renegade was the so-called Ibrahim Aga who rose to high honors
in Egypt.

In a passage in Hakluyt we read of the assorted reactions of
some men of the ship *Jesus* in the time of Queen Elizabeth. The
young purser, Richard Burges, and one James Smith were invited
"to turn Turks" (i.e. Mohammedans). Both refused. A renegade
young man who was son of a yeoman in the Queen's Guard
essayed to persuade them. Eventually they were told, "By Mo

hammed, you shall be made Turks!" Then their captor, son of the ruler of Tripoli, "called for his men and commanded them to make him (Purser Burges) a Turk, and they did so, and circumcised him. . . . Yet, said he, 'A Christian I was born and so I will remain.' " As for the other brave youth, "He was very strong, for it was as much as eight of the king's son's men could do to hold him, so in the end they circumcised him and made him a Turk."

The English renegade, Joseph Pitts, became celebrated in his day (end of the seventeenth century). Captured as a boy sailor by Algiers pirates, he stood firm to his faith under torture, but finally yielded when his master beat him nearly to death. Pitts' own words: "The more I cried, the more furiously he laid it on, and to stop the noise of my crying would stamp with his feet on my mouth." Pitts eventually got away to resume Christianity and to publish a book about his adventures. During his renegade days he saw Mecca and is regarded as the second Christian in point of time ever to have witnessed the pilgrimage.

*   *   *

CERTAIN RENEGADES, WE ARE ASSURED, SUFFERED MENTAL TORMENTS. One of them—a great corsair leader, familiarly called "The Scurvied"—is said to have endured more pain from soul sickness than from his horrid malady. In secret, they claimed, he practiced remorsefully the forms of his lost faith.

THE FATE OF THE FAITHFUL!

MOST OF THOSE WHO REFUSED "TO TAKE THE TURBAN" FACED A miserable future. Some few escaped or were ransomed. The rest —if young and good looking of either sex—went to a life of shame. If of less beauty but strong the males went to the galleys. "What care we how the wind blows?" cried corsair captains. "We carry the wind in the sinews of our Christians!" Middle-aged women and ordinary men did menial work ashore. Crabbed persons, persons of an especially religious turn, recaptured escapees were tortured with accomplished enthusiasm.

Europe shuddered. There were stories of the peculiarly devilish manner in which certain captured priests were roasted alive. The anchor of a galley would be partially buried in the sand, the priest "fastened thereto by a chain round his middle, but at such distance that he could walk round the stake." Green wood, slow burning, would be fired in a ring built round him eight or nine feet in diameter, his garments having been sprinkled so that his agony would be protracted. The illustrations of a contemporary work show various horrors allegedly inflicted on Christians at Algiers: a man dragged at a horse's tail, one rolled in a barrel lined with nails, one buried alive up to the neck, one pulled apart between four rowboats, a man skinned alive, and so on.

"THE HOOKS"

THE BAB AZOUN "HOOKS," OR CHINGAN, WERE FAMOUS. THE name still survives as that of a bright modern shopping street bordering the Algiers Casbah. In the old days the gate, Bab Azoun, was in a wall situated in the big modern Place de la République; beyond the wall, according to a 1725 map, was rolling country. This wall had on the outside "a number of long large hooks, very sharp." The victim was seated upon the wall just above the hooks and pushed into space, landing haphazardly on a point below, sometimes breaking from one point to another. The length of his sufferings depended upon which part of his body caught. "Happy he who is struck mortally. Some have been known to hang yelling for five or six days by the foot, chin or ribs, or like not vital parts."

"The Hooks" are authentic. There were corpses suspended upon them when in 1830 French troops took the city. So far as some of the treatment of Christians is concerned there may have been exaggeration. The historian, Laugier de Tassy (1725) who resided at Algiers is somewhat less gruesome. Most of our direct information about what happened to Christians is from priestly sources and may have been colored to inflame Christendom to aid in a work of the church, the redemption of captives. Outstandingly we have reports by F. Diego de Haedo, a Benedictine who was in Algiers from 1577 to 1581, and by Pierre Dan, a Redemptionist Father who gave most of his life to the effort to help and try to buy back Christian slaves in Barbary. However there is firsthand nonclerical testimony as to cruelty in a book by J. Morgan, who lived in Algiers for many years prior to 1720. Morgan,

for instance, tells that he himself saw a Christian victim "proces-
sioned" through Algiers streets, his guards calling out, "A stick
for Allah's sake!" and inviting each householder to contribute
fuel with which the wretched exhibit was to be burnt alive.

Morgan gives most of his seven-hundred-page book to startling
and quaint items about the corsairs. I cannot forbear to give a
résumé of the passage in which he tells about what he calls "a
preter-natural vehicle," a sort of submarine. His passage is curious, having in mind that it was written before 1731. It seems,
says Morgan, that the corsairs would not go out in late February,
at a period called Al-Aasoom, because at that time "a galley of
brass ranges the seas under the surface of the waters" and if this
brass galley "sights any vessel at sea the said vessel together with
its whole crew will infallibly perish."

THE HISTORIC DEBUT OF
ALGIERS

WHILE THE CORSAIRS WERE DEVELOPING THEIR PICTURESQUE AND
infamous trade North Africa was the scene as well of some sixty
years of conflict between Christians and Turks. The home population was in the bad fix which comes to weak or disorganized
groups when two powerful enemies choose their country as a
battleground. North Africa was squashed by both and alternately
tricked by each. Her beaches were soggy with blood; her port
cities taken and sacked first by one side, then by the other. Eventually the Turks won.

The brightest battlers of the day fought on African shores and
in African waters: for the Christians Charles V, Don John of
Austria, Doria, the great admiral; and for the Turks strange barbarous figures—inspired admirals and generals who seized kingdoms for their Turkish master and practiced piracy on the side as
a sport and a source of revenue.

Algiers, till now almost ignored by history, was the setting for
the first big Christian-Turkish conflict in Africa. Algiers had risen
from insignificance to be an important pirate center, what Morgan
calls "the dreaded retreat of lawless freebooters . . . a Nest of
Wasps and a Den of Thieves." Its piracy infuriated Spain and in

1509 Spain set up a disciplinary fort on an island commanding the city and only three hundred yards off shore. Piracy was much hampered.

Then came the Barbarossas. First the elder brother of the scarlet beard and the silver false arm—memento of a battle with the Christians at Bougie—and the gorgeous red brocade mantle. An accomplished pirate, he had wormed his way into a deal with the Hafside king of Tunis on the promise of giving him twenty per cent commission on all his pirate takings in exchange for the use of the Tunis port, had made himself master of much of the Algerian countryside, and had become a sort of kinglet. His day was short. Spain sent an army of ten thousand; Barbarossa died fighting with his own good and his one silver arm, and the crimson brocade cloak was taken from his corpse to be the dress of St. Geronimo's image at Cordova, to be known by the pious as *"La Capa de Barvaroxa."*

The younger and greater Barbarossa could not therefore pick up his brother's mantle, as the saying goes, but he did do just what the phrase suggests. First he got himself named as governor of Algeria under the Turkish sultan. Presently he threw the Spanish garrison out of the island fortress which dominated Algiers. Great Charles V, Holy Roman Emperor and King of Spain, brooded over the humiliation. His brooding led to one of the most surprising military exploits North Africa ever saw—a tragic comedy, depending on whether you view it from the side of Charles's followers or through the eyes of Algiers. Algiers laughed about it for centuries.

Charles V set forth to take Algiers with 516 ships, carrying 12,330 sailors and 23,900 soldiers (1541). He began landing near the city and felt very sure of himself. Algiers possessed no adequate defense. Charles V, already master of Tunis, saw himself adding the words "and Emperor of Africa" to his title. He even hoped for victory without a fight and was so confident that his expedition included children and many women—both ladies of the court and girls of the people—in the intention of colonizing after the conquest. Algiers believed that there were 1300 of these hopeful females and that all perished.

The approach of the Christian fleet looked to Algiers "like a mountain advancing on the sea.[21] It seemed as if the sea had spawned men."

THE ALGIERS MIRACLE

Then Allah intervened. Such a storm broke as never these coasts had seen. "You would think the world was going to turn over." It lasted for days. One hundred forty of Charles' ships were lost. Thousands of his men were drowned, or engulfed in mud and destroyed. "The corpses of infidels (Christians is meant; it is a Moslem writing) and their horses filled the space from Dellys to the east to Cherchel on the west (a distance of almost one hundred fifty miles). Only He who caused them to perish could have counted them!" Many were captured. After the fiasco you could have a Christian slave in the market place in exchange for an onion, said sneering Algiers, and the city, triumphant and unscarred, sat radiant upon her hill, "like a betrothed girl at her wedding festival proud of her fine raiment and her jewels."

Locally the cause of the miracle was ardently debated. It was attributed to a variety of saintly and strange personages. Some said that Sidi Abu't Toqa rose from his tomb the night before the storm and prayed for some event to save the city. Others thought that another Moslem holy man practiced a sort of magic, breaking up earthen pots, each breakage a symbol of the simultaneous sinking of a Christian ship. Wide gratitude was felt toward a third, by name Ouali (meaning saint) Dadah, a Turk, who "seized suddenly by a divine inspiration, rushed to the seashore, entered the water up to his belt and excited the waves by mystic words and by whipping up the waters with a stick. The tempest was unchained at his call." Still another claimant, choice of the vulgar, was a poor Negro eunuch, Isouf, a popular sorcerer who prophesied and allegedly procured Algiers' salvation.

No wonder superstition rioted. Algiers had got rid of the invader by what may indeed have been as Sir Harry Johnston says, "the storm that determined the destiny of North Africa." I won-

---

[21] From *Ghazaouat,* an eyewitness account. Several contemporary Algerian impressions of the attack are available to the student in the original text and in French translation in Prof. René Basset's *Documents sur le siège d'Alger en 1541* (Paris and Oran, 1890).

der was there ever any other case in history where weather played
a bigger role.

*   *   *

ALGIERS REMAINED A MOSLEM CITY, MORE OR LESS LOOSELY HELD
by Turkey, and a virtually undisturbed pirate center for nearly
three hundred years thereafter.

TROUBLE IN TUNIS

TUNIS WAS FAR MORE CRUELLY INVOLVED IN THE JAGGED UPS AND
downs of the Christian-Turkish power shuffle than was Algiers.
The poor folk of Tunis grew giddy with the change of rulers.
Four times in forty years the cross replaced the crescent, or vice
versa.

Local rule at Tunis had got feeble and fumbling. The Hafsides
had degenerated since the vigorous days when one of their dynasty
had repulsed St. Louis' Crusade. The dynasty was going down
in a welter of family assassinations. Hassan, when his father's
death left the throne without an occupant, is said to have got
rid of his forty-four elder brothers, killing or blinding them all,
and to have shut away the females and little ones in prison.

Despite this drastic house cleaning, Hassan quivered on his
throne, and was deposed by Barbarossa II. Barbarossa pretended
that he planned to replace Hassan by his eldest brother who had
contrived to escape the holocaust. Actually he wanted Tunis for
Turkey.

Hassan cried out to Charles V for help, and Charles came, not
of course for Hassan's sweet sake, but because he wanted Tunis
for the Christians.

Christian intervention (1535) brought such misery to Tunis as
that section of North Africa had not suffered since the fall of
Punic Carthage. Charles V had promised his soldiers that they
should sack the town. Hassan, resentful because Tunis had been
disloyal to him, was in full agreement. So after the city fell
Charles V let his soldiers do as they liked for three days. Their
likings were primitive. They pillaged everywhere. They raped
every girl they could catch. They fought one another in the streets
for the booty and the women. Tunis was a shambles.

The Spaniard, Marmol, who afterward wrote a long descriptive book of Africa, was one of Charles V's army. He tells how Hassan informed Charles that he need not spare a single inhabitant of Tunis on his account, and how the soldiers methodically killed every civilian they met, "particularly the German soldiers who spared nobody." As of this mention of Germans it must be remembered that Christian fighters from almost everywhere supported Charles' effort. There were seven thousand Germans. The attack on Tunis was looked upon as a sort of Crusade. Charles gave as battle cry the words, "JESUS CHRIST!"

When Tunis fell thousands of Christians who had been pirates' captives and were imprisoned there were freed from what in those days was called "white slavery." Others of the Christian captives were nonchalantly killed in the turmoil by members of the Christian force which had come to deliver them.

Besides the slaughter within the city there perished a piteous mob which had tried to save themselves by running into the open country. "You could see everywhere great piles of women and children, crushed and dead of suffocation and thirst," says Marmol. Hassan himself estimated that more than seventy thousand of his subjects perished in this tragic scramble, whilst uncounted others were deliberately killed in the streets and some forty thousand taken into slavery.

*   *   *

AFTER CHARLES V'S VICTORY TUNIS—WHAT WAS LEFT OF IT—REmained for a while a sort of protectorate of the ungentle Christian. Hassan was put back on his blood-slimed throne. But those who survived among his people hated him. They gave ready credence to the story given out by his son, Hamid, that Hassan, when he went on a trip to Europe to interview his protector, Charles V, had really gone there so as to turn Christian. When Hassan came back to Tunis his son, Hamid, was—thanks to this scandal—in a position to arrest him and "two days later he offered Hassan the choice of death or being blinded, and—since he accepted the latter—caused him to lose his sight by putting a red hot basin in front of his eyes." The basin had come back to roost —how many had not Hassan blinded!

Later a surviving brother of Hassan's took over Tunis and avenged the crime by blinding Hamid's eldest son. Hamid came back to power and destroyed all the leaders of the opposition, throwing some of them to be eaten alive by big watchdogs.

Very naturally Tunis and the country round about was in anarchy, and a generation after the Tunis massacre at the hands of Charles V's "Crusaders," the corsair, Ochiali, was able to turn the city back again under the control of the crescent. This lasted only four years.

Then Charles V's brilliant bastard, Don John of Austria, pounced on Tunis. He was a Moslem hater by inheritance, being the great-grandson of Ferdinand and Isabella. One of his own proud achievements had been the bloody crushing of the Alpuxarras revolt, the last Moslem stand in Spain. He wished to give Tunis a Christian king, and toyed with the notion that this king might be himself. Tunis fell to Don John in 1573, but the city saw no Christian dynasty. The next year corsair Ochiali recaptured it. The crescent had won. From that time Tunisia was vaguely a Turkish dependence for more than three centuries.

THE SKULL TOWER

In addition to the Tunis kaleidoscope and the miraculous saving of Algiers there were somewhat less dramatic conflicts in Tripoli, plus a number of major fights in minor places. Spain had set up garrisons in the effort to stop the use of certain harbors by the pirates. At Bougie, for instance, and at Bône and at Oran. Naturally there was corsair retaliation. As the corsairs grew stronger these little nests of Christians, clinging in isolated groups to an enemy coast, often had a poor time. The Bône garrison became so demoralized in 1540 that they expressed readiness to go Moslem in a bunch. They were starving and their pay long overdue.

Mahdia, formerly called "City Africa" and once believed impregnable, was tossed back and forth from Turks to Christians. The island of Djerba, the land of the lotus, was the setting for a Christian disaster. A Christian force was surprised there by Dragut, that peculiarly ferocious corsair who carried the lash scars of his three years' slavery on Christian galleys. He took great satisfaction in slaughtering eighteen thousand Christians on Djerba's beach and in building a tower of their skulls, which horrid monument remained in place till just a century ago.

Finally the Turks had defeated the Christians all along the coast. The remaining Christian holdings outside Morocco were trifling. Notably Oran and Mers-el-Kebir (scene of the sad conflict between allies when the English and French navies fought on July 3, 1940). Spain clung intermittently to these places until the earthquake of 1790 destroyed Oran and led Spain to evacuate.

MOROCCO MUDDLED THROUGH

MOROCCO WAS OUTSIDE THE TURKISH-CHRISTIAN BATTLE ZONE. THE Turkish occupation of North Africa stopped short at Morocco's frontiers.

She had however Christian invasions in plenty. Her coasts had been grabbed by Portugal and Spain; Portugal held an unbroken strip on the Atlantic; Spain had holdings in the Gibraltar region. Later Morocco was able gradually, town by town, to push her Christian parasites into the sea, except for a few Spanish possessions at the strait. At all times Morocco somehow muddled through, remaining her own master for nearly four centuries after her eastern neighbors had become Turkish adoptees. Her fall from independence is very recent. Morocco had more national vigor than her neighbors. Moroccans had always been famed as violent fighters. And they were still idealists and romantic, capable of hero worship in a religious cause. Such a religious recrudescence, reminiscent of early medieval days, jerked Morocco from the depression and disorder of the sixteenth century.

So it was that, at a period when Morocco's neighbors to the east were Turkey's servants and were—especially Algeria—preoccupied with piracy and blackmail—Morocco shows us big men and big undertakings against a colorful, still medieval background. Morocco was the center of North Africa's nobility and drama.

THE GREAT SULTAN AHMED

CONSIDER THE CAREER OF THE SO-CALLED GOLDEN SULTAN, AHMED, surnamed also El Mansur (The Victorious) of the Sharifian dynasty. (The word *sharif* has no relationship with our sheriff, but means "of noble descent," specifically from Mohammed's daughter and her husband, Ali. A succeeding Sharifian dynasty still reigns in Morocco.)

At the debut of the dynasty enemies claimed that the family did not really spring from the Prophet's stock but were merely members of a tribe called the Benou Sa'ad. The new dynasty was called Sa'adians by the opposition in contempt. It was one of those jeers that misfire. Sa'ad means happiness in Arabic. The population, long misgoverned, clutched at a name of good omen. The sultans themselves were too haughty to use the name, and according to the *Nozhet-Elhadi*, the history of the dynasty by El-Oufrani, nobody dared use the lighthearted name of Sa'adians in their presence.

*   *   *

AHMED, THE GOLDEN AND THE VICTORIOUS, WON THE SECOND PART of his pseudonym on the field of battle (1578). How he got the first of his nicknames we shall tell later.

It was a battle with the Portuguese fought at El-Ksar-el-Kebir (Alcázarquiver on modern maps) near Tangier—a decisive battle in Morocco's history. It was a socially distinguished engagement. In it three kings died: the dethroned king of Morocco, "Black Mohammed," who had gone over to the Portuguese; the actual king, poisoned on the battlefield and his death concealed so that—riding along a corpse in the royal litter—he led a charge; and Dom Sebastao of Portugal. This last was a young fanatic, lusting for Africa as had Henry the Navigator, dying a virgin like Henry, bewitched by Africa's charm. The battle was also an international affair. The Pope sent troops. Small groups of Italians, English, Germans and Spaniards fought beside the Portuguese.

To Portugal it was a major disaster. Our Moroccan historian, El-Oufrani, records what he describes as "a singular and pleasant circumstance" that the Portuguese lost so many men as to cause their bishops "in the fear that the country would be depopulated, to authorize the people to commit adultery so as to augment the births."

*   *   *

STARTING FROM THIS HOUR OF VICTORY, AHMED THE VICTORIOUS, brother of the sultan who led a charge after he was dead, reigned for a quarter of a century. He made Morocco so rich that the nose of the great Turkish sultan was out of joint. He made Morocco so important that Queen Elizabeth, according to Ch. André Julien, considered—though she repudiated—his proposal that he and she should join together to conquer and split up Spain. Moslem opinion was that "the peninsular would have been easy to tear from the hands of the infidel and it would have taken only a short time." [22] A remarkable alteration in European history had it been put to the test and succeeded.

Ahmed inherited an admiration for Elizabeth from his predecessor who entertained her ambassador, Edmund Hogan, "with pastime of ducking with water spaniels and baiting buls with English dogges," and who said to Hogan significantly, "I know what the king of Spaine is, and what the Queene of England and her Realme is" (Hakluyt). It was in Ahmed's reign that a Christian embassy visited Fez with gifts which were "loaded on chariots and carriages—things which caused profound astonishment among the city's inhabitants"—Morocco being then wheelless. Morocco was something like a world power. Presently her sultans would assume this proud title: "Emperor of Africa, Emperor of Morocco, King of Fez, Suz and Gao, Lord of Dra and Guinea, and Great Sharif of Mohammed."

The story of how this title was, more or less, justified is an interesting one.

THE CONQUEST OF TIMBUCTOO

MOROCCO STARED INTO THE SAHARAN EMPTINESS AT HER SOUTHERN frontier and longed to own the gold country which lay at the desert's other side. Specifically Morocco hankered for the rich city of Timbuctoo through which funneled the wealth of Negroland. Morocco's covetousness led to one of the most difficult military expeditions of all time.

* * *

TIMBUCTOO, VASSAL OF MALI IN THE DAYS OF THAT GREAT BLACK emperor, Kankan-Musa, had come up as Mali went down. Timbuctoo was now the pride of another Negro empire, successor to

[22] Quoted from the *Rihlet Ecchiha Ila Liqa Elahbab* by El-Oufrani.

Mali, that of the Songhai of Gao (see page 356). Timbuctoo was, despite a passage of bad government, at the zenith of her prosperity. Local trade profits were almost incredible. An example: A grown slave girl could be had there, Leo Africanus says, in exchange for a yard and a half of the worst quality European cloth. She could be resold in Morocco for the equivalent of at least three hundred sixty current United States dollars, and for as high as four times that amount, if unusually handsome. Timbuctoo brokers who brought buyers and sellers from the north into contact with Negro merchants, interpreted for both parties, and handled the sheltering and warehousing for both, made vast fortunes. Timbuctoo's wealth became a proverb. It was why Timbuctoo got the name of having "roofs of gold."

The scheming greed of Ahmed Mansur was roused. He wanted Timbuctoo and the rest of the western Sudan. He wanted to control Saharan commerce. Trade across the Sahara had diminished, it was true, since the opening of sea routes, but the prospect of controlling it at both ends was still very tempting. Especially valuable and an inalienable source of gain—sea routes or no—was the item of salt. Saharan salt was indispensable to the Sudan's life. Even had traders from Europe brought salt in their ships it would not have suited the Sudanese taste. To the Sudan the old-fashioned article from the great Saharan salt mines, cut into slabs like tombstones and marked in bright colors with a pious phrase or a revered name, was the salt of their cravings, the salt that in their opinion preserved their health.

Ahmed Mansur sent a diplomatic spy across the desert to learn what was the actual military potentiality of the Songhai. The reigning Askia (king) may have suspected the motive behind the Moroccan ambassadorial visit with its superb gifts. But he politely sent back presents in return, including eighty valuable eunuchs.

The Askia came of a clever and bold line. About a century earlier the first Askia, a usurping Negro general, had hitched the title to his dynasty by a piece of inspired impudence. Upon the death of the old king, his master, this general had stolen the throne. At the news of his perfidious act a daughter of the late king cried out in the local language four short words which, run together, were "askia!" and which meant something like, "He can't get away with it!" When her threatening prophecy was repeated to the usurping general he retorted, "Oh yes he can! And her words shall be my title and the dynastic name of my successors."

So had started in 1493 a series of Askias, whose empire in the Sahara, in Middle Africa and on the Niger could probably have matched in geographical extent and in wealth that of any nation of the contemporary world. But weakness had come. The Askia grip was slipping.

Shortly after his spying ambassador had reported his impressions the sultan of Morocco sent an army of twenty thousand toward Timbuctoo. Part way across the desert the larger part of the army perished of hunger and thirst and the rest turned back.

This costly failure seemed to prove that a trans-Saharan military expedition was an impossibility. The Songhai Empire felt itself to be safeguarded by "General Sand." But Ahmed Mansur had clutched a dream and he would not let go. Why should not an army cross the desert? He knew that in the past certain armies had penetrated deep into the Sahara. His own troops had recently driven as far as the Tuat oases. A predecessor of his had led an attack into the desert, of which we have an account written by Marmol, the Spanish captive, who accompanied him. Another Saharan expedition had been carried out very profitably by an Algerian corsair (1552) who actually dragged three cannon into the deep sands, battered down the walls of Touggourt and subdued Ouargla, returning with "fifteen camel loads of gold." None of these efforts however approached in difficulty the plan Ahmed Mansur cherished of sending an army right across the Sahara to conquer the country at the other side.

* * *

Tantalizing news came to him, Songhai seemed ripe for conquest. The country was shaken by revolts. The private morals of its erstwhile wholesome, primitive people were polluted. The *Tarikh es-Soudan* says, "There was not a single one of the things forbidden by Allah which was not done openly. They drank wine, gave themselves to sodomy, and—as for adultery—it had become so usual that the practise seemed to be lawful." Songhai's general morale was also enfeebled, as shown in the fact that the exploitation of the famous Teghazza salt mine was abandoned in favor of a mine nearer into the Sudan at Taodeni.

Sultan Ahmed Mansur sent his ultimatum across the sands. He it had been, he boasted, who had pushed the Christians back and kept Africa a Moslem land. So it was he who deserved to be master of the Sahara as well as of Morocco. Moreover he was of the blood of the Prophet. Who was this Askia? Both the Moroccan historian El-Oufrani and the Sudanese historian, author of the *Tarikh es-Soudan,* give a résumé of Ahmed Mansur's communication. It was evidently a hot document.

It received a hot answer. The Askia then in power replied with written insults, significantly illustrating his meaning by the addition of a bunch of javelins and a pair of leg irons—to wit, we will fight and you will be captured! He declined to give up his claim to the Saharan salt mines, whose profitable and terrible premises were an ancestral holding.

*   *   *

THE TEGHAZZA SALT MINES AND THEIR SUCCESSOR THE MINES AT Taodeni were places of infamy. They stood alone in the desert's cruel heat, that is to say there were no oases near and absolutely no resources. The workers lived in houses made of salt rock of different colors that glittered blindingly. There was no decent water. Ibn-Batuta says with gentility, "We found the water at Teghazza to be injurious." A modern and less modest writer reports baldly the warning issued by the native workers to newcomers at Taodeni. The warning: "A man should have his left hand upon the string of his drawers when he takes his calabash into his right hand to drink our water." The purgative quality of certain Saharan wells is said to be beyond that of any liquid sold by pharmacists.

The workmen were further weakened by the climate. "There blows a wind from the southeast in summer," says Marmol, "which makes them lose their sight and causes a sort of gout at the knees so they become lame."

To these miseries of body was added gnawing anxiety. All food, of course, had to be brought from the Sudan by caravan. The mine locations produced nothing edible but salt. Sometimes the caravan was delayed, sometimes lost en route. Starvation was always a possibility. As food dwindled workmen stared into the desert with their half-blind eyes and trembled. Sometimes a whole gang died a slow death. Then the Sudan had to send a new work gang.

I am reminded of a distressing story whose victim I knew—in fact he made my bed at Bidon V when I crossed the Sahara by the central route a few years back. His name was Ouadidi. He was a black from the Sudan and his work was to remain at Bidon V during the winter auto-coach season to take charge of the camp where twice a month motor cars stopped for the night.

He awaited in the early summer the arrival of the last auto-coach of the season which would take him away from his absolutely lonely camp in a peculiarly bleak desert, more than 500 kilometers from all human, animal or vegetable life of any sort. The coach was delayed that year. Ouadidi's food and water ran short. He began to suspect that he had been forgotten, that there would be no more coaches till next autumn. He watched the horizon until he went mad, and saw a mirage of auto-coaches everywhere, coming, going, rushing across space.

At last, three days late, the coach came. Ouadidi ran out to meet it, threw himself in its road so that it would not rush on across space like the others. He was nearly run over. He scrambled to his feet and began to fondle the great car. He kissed its engine hood. He licked its tires. He stroked it all over like a lover. The driver who told me the incident had tears in his eyes.

But Ouadidi resumed his duties at Bidon V next season. And the Teghazza and Taodeni salt miners willy-nilly went on with their work. Nor did the misery of their lot disturb the Sudanese Askia who controlled the salt trade nor the Moroccan sultan who craved to take it away from him.

* * *

WHILE THE ASKIA, PARTLY FROM CONFIDENCE THAT "GENERAL Sand" would never permit his enemy to reach the Sudan and partly from incompetence, let time slip by without making adequate preparations, Ahmed Mansur planned his trans-Saharan expedition.

He chose for its leader a remarkable person. He was one Jodar (or Djouder), called "Pasha" by courtesy, an ex-Christian from Almeria, Spain, who—fallen into Moslem hands—had become a

renegade. Other ill had also befallen Joder: he was a eunuch.[23]
This little, blue-eyed man led a small picked army, including
many other renegades and Christian soldiers of fortune, over the
terrible desert during five months of agonizing effort (October,
1590 to March, 1591), kept their courage high though perhaps
two thirds died, reached the Niger, defeated the Songhai and
occupied Timbuctoo. The countless hordes of Negroland were
nothing to him. They were in the Sudanese phrase, "his chickens."

FIRST GUNS IN THE SUDAN

TO HAVE GOT AN ARMY ACROSS THE GREAT DESERT IN THOSE PRIMI-
tive days was something of a miracle. It seems something of a
miracle even now when we have trucks and airplanes. The exploits of Free French soldiers who came from the Lake Chad
region to the top of the desert in the winter of 1943 thrilled the
world press. But if the accomplishment of the Moroccan army in
getting to the Niger was marvelous we have to admit that their
victory once they got there was not marvelous at all. It was inevitable. The bunch of javelins sent by the defiant Askia had been
a tragic symbol. Javelins and the like were the Sudan's only
weapons. The Moroccan army had guns. It was the first time
that the sound of firearms had shocked the still air of the Sudan.
The first time that Sudanese soldiers had felt the pang of agony,
seen the gush of blood from their bodies, whilst their enemy stood
at a far distance merely pointing a stick at them.

The Askia made himself a shield of a thousand cows so that the
balls would strike them rather than the royal person. But the
cows liked gunfire no better than did the Askia and his people.
When they heard the fusillade they turned in panic and overran
their masters. Some of the blacks were so stunned by the new
mystery weapon that they squatted down on the sands on their
shields and waited to be killed.

It was as Ahmed Mansur had foreseen when he told his plans
to the assembly of his counsel in Morocco. They disapproved
of the expedition. Ahmed cried, "The Sudan with lances and
swords cannot stand against the new engines of war!"

[23] Dr. Barth, Appendix IX of his *Travels* gives a Spanish source as to the
valeroso eunoco renegado.

Ahmed had captured an empire which, as a court author of the day boasted, "stretched from Nubia to the Atlantic." His empire was a great triangle, one corner of which was Morocco—a triangle mostly made up of sand, it must be admitted. The author adds, "It was immense, the equal of which no person before him had ever possessed." In square mileage this may have been true. But this immense empire was like some great dog with cockleburs which it cannot dislodge from the hair round its throat. Christian forts still clung to Morocco's home coasts.

The gold of Timbuctoo was his. He had become Ahmed the Golden (Ed-Dehbi). Morocco held Timbuctoo for nearly two centuries, albeit somewhat loosely during the latter half of the period. Morocco's gold returns from the conquest were the subject of hyperbole. There were stories of how in one day there arrived thirty mule loads of gold dust, talk of one shipment of 16,065 pounds avoirdupois. "At the gates of the palace 1400 hammers every day beat out gold coins." The palace (this concerns the days of a later sultan, Moulay Ismail) had "massive bolts of pure gold and gold kitchen utensils!"

A WORLD-FAMED LOVER

THE SAHARAN CONQUEST ENTHRALLED THE MOROCCAN PUBLIC AND took on that supernatural quality which when used by a primitive people as a wrapping for some historic incident is proof of great national pride. An English traveler in Morocco in 1721, a century and a quarter after the capture of Timbuctoo, tells how Moroccans had glamorized the story of their desert conquest and also had decided to impute it to a spectacular living figure:

> In the year 1690, before Moulay Ismail was master of the Sahara, there came a woman from that people to him, who—hearing of her coming—went to meet her on horseback at the head of 20,000 men.
>
> She told him the people of the Sahara were desirous to put themselves under his protection, but that he must fight her at lance play, if he had a mind to have her, as at once the pledge of their fidelity and the prize of his victory.
>
> She set him hard at first, but afterwards suffered herself to be

overpowered, was put among the rest of his women and troops were sent to control the Sahara.[24]

This latter-day Amazon, coming from the wide spaces of the Sahara, would have found herself in a rather crowded setting in Moulay Ismail's harem. For Moulay Ismail, who reigned from 1672 to 1727, made himself and his country world famous largely by the immensity of his love life. He maintained a practicing harem of five hundred women of all races and tints. As they aged he retired them. He never aged, so it is said. The number I mention is conservative, some put it in the thousands—three thousand or four thousand. This would not have been fantastic for, according to Windus who visited his court and learned much harem gossip from an English inmate, "he seldom would bestow his favors on one woman more than once."

To some extent Moulay Ismail lived maritally in a showcase. For she who received his caress would immediately thereafter be "carried in a procession round the palace." Nor was everything smooth. Sometimes the women would become troublesome and a batch would have to be put out of the way by a method called "geesing"—a sort of tourniquet round the neck, tightened with a stick. Windus' informant added that "the very excrement and spittle which came from the Emperor were preserved in little boxes by his women who believed that anything which came from him would keep them from distempers."

Among his favorites was an English girl who had turned Moslem, and he scandalized the court of Louis XIV by sending along the formal request that the Princesse de Conti, of royal blood, bar sinister, be shipped to Morocco and added to the number of his wives and sweethearts. The suggestion was refused without thanks. Moulay Ismail was amazed.

Many called him father. In his maturity he could count seven hundred sons "able to mount horse"—i.e. beyond the years of childhood. His girl progeny was not a matter of public knowledge.

*   *   *

THE AMOROUS ENTHUSIASM OF ITS RULER NATURALLY BECAME THE focus for such attention as the world had to give to Morocco. But

[24] *A Journey to Mequinez and the Residence of the Present Emperor . . . for the Redemption of British Captives* in the year 1721 by John Windus (London, 1725).

Moulay Ismail was a great king as well as a notable family man. His largess in love was not the indication of sexual derangement, but of phenomenal general vitality.

Moulay Ismail was an early sultan of the second Sharifian dynasty (also variously called Filali, Hassanian, or Alaouite) which had superseded the first Sharifians (the Sa'adians) in 1649. It originated at Sijilmassa, and is reigning yet. It claims descent from Mohammed via Fatima and Ali, and boasts of an intervening ancestor, the remarkable Moulay Ali. This ancestor was grandfather to Moulay Ismail. He was a mighty hero and a saintly personage, also a physical curio in that "he had no children until he was eighty years old; then he had nine, of whom five were by the same mother (*Nozhet-Elhadi*).

Morocco still thrilled with religious fervor. Her sultans were regarded as sanctified people, were associated with Moulay Idris, the saint-hero of old Fez, whose supposed remains were allegedly dug up intact (1437) and who waked from his six-century-long sleep to address his relative, one of the Sharifian sultans.

To Moroccans Moulay Ismail, whose life seemed so very unsaintly to the Christian world, was a revered figure of great holiness. His genealogy was "a chain of gold." "O Moulay Ismail, O Sun of the World!" cried a contemporary Moroccan poet.

ISMAIL, THE WARRIOR

HIS REIGN SAW MOROCCO GROW STRONG AND TEAR THE CHRISTIAN cockleburs from the national throat. "The stain of the infidel" was wiped out. Among towns taken from the Christians was Mehdia (where United States troops debarked on the first day of the North African campaign of 1942).[25] Tangier shortly afterward was abandoned by the English. Larache was besieged in a bitter struggle (1689). Larache was a bitter memory to Moroccans. Here

[25] Mehdia, now a trifling place, has seen a lot of history. It was founded by Hanno of Carthage, being the first place on the Atlantic coast to take his fancy on his famous Periplus (see p. 67). Hanno called the place Thymiaterion. Mehdia got its present name from the self-styled mahdi, founder of the Almohades. Besides being the scene of Moslem-Christian adventures in which Portuguese, English, Spanish and Dutch were involved, it was a pirate base. Allied forces landed there in November, 1942. Four years later American marines from a near-by base attempted to save Mehdia from a devastating fire (July, 1946).

they had been victims in a fight some half century before of a new Christian weapon in what was called "The Battle of the Spikes." This invention "had four points, one stuck into the ground, the other three stood up in the air and constituted a terrible stratagem which caused great damage to the Moslems, both to their men and their horses." So it was a particular pleasure to El-Oufrani to record that Christian Larache capitulated and "the enemy race was exterminated." Immense quantities of powder were taken and one hundred eighty cannon—twenty-two being of bronze and the rest of iron. One of them was thirty-five feet long and fired a ball weighing thirty-five pounds, a famous piece of the day. The Portuguese were made so uncomfortable at Mazagan that after Moulay Ismail's death they were easily squeezed out of the last Christian hold on the Atlantic Moroccan coast. Ceuta and Melilla remained a pair of humiliating Spanish pimples on Morocco's Moslem cheek.

There were further conquests in the interior. Moulay Ismail's domain was even more extensive, in El-Oufrani's opinion, than that of Ahmed, the conqueror of Timbuctoo. From the jungles beyond the Niger to the Mediterranean, as far eastward as Biskra (south of Constantine, Algeria), the Sahara was his. El-Oufrani sums up his account of Moulay Ismail, the conqueror: "Allah knows in whom to put confidence."

Furthermore Moulay Ismail so competently pacified and policed his own turbulent people that the saying was that a woman could travel unprotected from Oujda (northeastern Morocco) to the far corner of southwestern Morocco at the Oued Noun.

MOULAY ISMAIL, BUILDER WITH MORTAR AND MEN

Moulay Ismail was a mighty builder too. He erected his famous palace at Meknes with such vigorous delight that he worked the pick himself when his convicts and Christian slaves faltered.

It was enormous, a square building each side a mile long with walls twenty-five feet thick. It was made of mortar without stone, pounded down by hand labor. Windus, already quoted, says he was told that thirty thousand men and ten thousand mules worked at one time on the great job. Of the laborers a tenth were Christian captives. They were often victims of Moulay Ismail's whimsical brutality.

> One day passing by a high wall on which Christians were at work and being affronted that they did not keep time in their strokes as he expects they should, he made his guards go up and throw them all off the wall, breaking their legs and arms.
>
> Another time he ordered them to bury a Christian alive and beat him down along with the mortar in the wall.

However, the resultant palace was one of the wonders of North Africa, and was called "the Moroccan Versailles."

Moulay Ismail adored building for its own sake. Sometimes he put up structures just to have them pulled down again. Had they all been left standing it was computed there would have been enough of them to make a solid street from Meknes to Fez, a distance of some thirty-seven miles.

*   *   *

HE WAS EAGER TOO AS A BUILDER OF MEN. HE PERFECTED A SYSTEM by which he was able literally to manufacture vigorous and loyal soldiers. He bred them on a stud farm between Meknes and the coast, mating Negroes from stock imported from the Sudan and instructing them that the production of children was their life-work. When the black babies had grown to puberty they were marched before Moulay Ismail for inspection and the best male specimens put to military training. Thus he procured an army of some one hundred fifty thousand splendid, nonthinking fighters who looked upon him as a sort of god. It was a precious possession to one who sought to rule over an emotional, argumentative nation like the Moroccans. Moulay Ismail's black guard was a pampered lot. An old print shows one of them in his fine uniform and bears the caption that *"almost all these guards wear silk stockings."*

"THE SALLY ROVERS"

IN MOULAY ISMAIL'S DAY THE PIRATE INDUSTRY IN MOROCCO ENtered its best phase—from the Moroccan pirates' point of view. The replacing of galleys by sailing vessels made for efficient piracy

in Atlantic waters. Salé was a sort of incorporated concern paying
a ten per cent royalty to the royal treasury on its piratical takings.
It was there that "Robinson Crusoe" lived as a pirates' captive in
the days of Moulay Ismail's youth. His reign and the few ensuing
years made up the great period of the "Sally Rovers," of which
Gibbon wrote with the indignant pen of a suffering contemporary
(Salé . . . "so infamous at present," said he). Gibbon was born
only ten years after Moulay Ismail's death.

THE STORYBOOK LAND

THOSE WERE ROMANTIC, GORGEOUS AND HORRIBLE DAYS, MARKING
what was at once the zenith of Morocco's magnificence and the
overture to the last act of Morocco's appearance upon the world
stage as an independent power. More than that, they give us our
last view of the medieval way of life as displayed in North Africa.
The Middle Ages were over, but they survived in Africa. Morocco
of the period stood out in a drab world and was described with
mingled delight and disapproval by several Europeans who
actually saw the storybook land of Moulay Ismail.

They tell of Moulay Ismail, a very swarthy, bearded man with a
"beauty mark" alongside his nose. Of his palace with its hundreds
of variotinted ladies and its many locked-up rooms full of gold,
silver and jewels, under the charge of his treasurer, a black
eunuch, who had "a seraglio of his own maintained purely out of
ostentation!"

Other items: Moulay Ismail's bridge of still-warm human
corpses, thrown across a Moroccan river when at his orders all the
prisoners of battle were "killed and woven into a bridge with
rushes for his army to pass over." His menagerie at Meknes where
he fought lions and wolves against dogs. His fashion of showing
his agility, and—horrid as the method was—it must have demanded
astonishing athletic ability and some dangerous practicing simultaneously to leap into the saddle, draw a saber and decapitate the
slave who held the stirrup.

Now a pleasant and quaint scene: At the Meknes palace Moulay
Ismail would ride along the miles of interior verandas "in a small
calash" with a team of pretty women enacting the part of horses.
We see in an old print Moulay Ismail at Marrakesh selling

Christian captives to a rescue mission at so much a head. He on horseback, insolent and bargaining shrewdly—a few impaled Christians exhibited to encourage the rescue mission to pay high. Moulay Ismail at Fez, proudly surveying the trade center of his rich kingdom. Fez with its two hundred caravansaries of fifty to a hundred rooms each, and goods from all the world. Fez smelling of cinnamon and sulfur and benzoin, bright with gaudy silks, soft muslins, quicksilver and little mirrors, and rich with gold dust, ostrich plumes and elephants' tusks. Its streets thronged with foreign faces. Pale men from England and Holland. Dark men from South Europe. Darker men yet from Barbary. And shiny black Negroes from Timbuctoo.

Moulay Ismail making his way to the great open-air festival marking the end of the fast of Ramadan (Mohammedan Lent). Riding well for all his seventy-five years. Behind him were led a group of spare horses should he care to change mounts. Twenty of them, each under "a saddle of beaten gold set with emeralds." Around about him rode the army of his sons, men he had bred from women of every race and tint. Moulay Ismail studying their ranks and finding gaps. Where was Mohammed, the rebel? Ah, dead to be sure! His right hand and left foot cut off at Moulay Ismail's own order. Zidan was dead too. . . . But there were plenty left. Hundreds of them. Plenty to upset the peace after Moulay Ismail's passing.

Moulay Ismail troubled by a novelty—his conscience. Pestered in his old age by nightmares wherein friends and favorites he had wantonly killed came to plague him, getting up often in a mood to seek ease by killing yet more. His court waited every morning in shivers. Would he be cruel or kind? How was he dressed? Yellow was known as his "killing color"!

*　　*　　*

AFTER MOULAY ISMAIL CAME THAT CONFUSION WHICH OFTEN follows when a great king dies after prolonged power. "God save our country from a long, strong reign," was a saying. One of his sons was proclaimed and dethroned six times. One generation saw twelve shifting enthronements.

But Morocco still stood, a nation independent and full of individuality when the rest of Mediterranean Africa had slipped under Turkish thralldom, a country which carried the picturesque and startling atmosphere of the Middle Ages into modern times.

B O O K   F O U R

RETURN OF THE CHRISTIANS:

NAPOLEON TO EISENHOWER

Part One:
MANY COME; NONE REMAINS

Part Two:
FRANCE CONQUERS; AFRICA WATCHES

Part Three:
ENGLAND AND OTHERS IN NORTH AFRICA

Part Four:
THE UNITED STATES AND OTHERS

Many Come; None Remains

SUPINE EUROPE

FROM MOROCCO TO TRIPOLI EUROPEANS WHO HAD SET OFF TO SEA on voyages and been captured by pirates were being held in slavery. Christian women and boys were being forced into degradation. Persons supposed to be rich were being systematically tortured so that their friends at home would, on hearing their plaints, hasten to send generous ransom money.

Europe's reaction to this—or Europe's failure to react—and her actual complacence in the face of such insulting abuses seems puzzling.

Admittedly it would have been difficult to get Europe's nations to pull together in a punitive expedition. But the respectful, even affable attitude of Europe toward the rulers of Morocco, Algeria, Tunisia, and Tripoli is amazing. It proceeded from "sheer cowardice, the terror of a barbarous power supposed to possess boundless resources and unquenchable courage," as Stanley Lane-Poole, an Englishman, has confessed. It proceeded also from a cunning hope held in various quarters that the Barbary pirates, if unchecked, would do more harm to rival nations than to themselves.

Nation by nation Europe paid tribute openly or by way of "presents" to the Barbary States, thinking to get better treatment than their neighbors, thinking that "the scourge of Christendom" would fall upon the backs of other countries whilst they got but the flick of the whip.

The familiar phrase of Benjamin Franklin's explains the attitude of the big maritime powers. Franklin attributed to the merchants of London the saying, "If there were no Algiers (i.e. no pirates) it would be worth England's while to build one." Pirates tended to keep weaker and poorer nations from competing in the carrying trade.

So rich powers made extravagant gifts to the Barbary rulers in a mixture of blackmail and subsidy. It was not a passage of which European history can be ~roud.

*   *   *

BARBARY SAW THE MATTER IN QUITE ANOTHER LIGHT. THEIR PIRACY was proof of vigor and courage. They ruled the sea. Piracy was their glory. They had brought to perfection a practice which was then in usage round all the world. That was what Barbary thought.

Little was done by their victims to suggest to Barbary that a great difference lay between the piracy of a group of outlaws in danger of being hanged if caught, and the organized piracy sponsored by a state with the added infamy of systemized capture and enslavement of crews and passengers. Barbary's rulers were treated not as Captain Kidds, but as honored royal personages: "Right high and mightie King," writes the mayor of London to the dey of Algiers (1584); "Right honorable Lord," writes an English ambassador to the bey of Tripoli, concluding with a wish for "all true felicity and increase of honor" (1585); and William III wrote to a corsair dey that he was his "loving friend"! Elizabeth, as we have indicated, was on pally terms with the emperor of Morocco to whom she wrote, "Right high and mighty Prince." Talleyrand addressed the ruler of Tripoli as "Very illustrious and very magnificent seigneur."

European ambassadors visited Barbary courts. Whatever the critical tone of these gentlemen after they got away from Africa we may be sure they were respectful and flattering while there. In this connection I quote the retrospective spite against Morocco expressed by M. de Saint-Olon:

> *Pour moi, je tiens pis que damnée*
> *Cette nation basanée*
> *Qui n'a jamais logé chez soi*
> *Honneur, sincerité, ni foi.*
> *Ils disent, et puis ils dedisent;*
> *Leurs serments comme verre ils brisent.*

("I hold worse than damned this tawny nation which has never known honor, sincerity, nor good faith. They say a thing and take it back. They break their word like glass.") This verse was written in Saint-Olon's hand in a copy of the first edition of the book he wrote (1694) after an unsuccessful mission in Morocco to try to buy back captives, and is quoted in Roland Lebel's bibliographical study on French authors about Morocco. Some European official representatives in Barbary sincerely admired their hosts. The well-known *Tully Letters,* describing Tripoli at the end of the eighteenth century are full of gushingly sycophantic references to Tripoli's royal family.

*   *   *

TREATIES WERE MADE AND BROKEN AND REMADE AS TO "PEACE AND Commerce"—as for instance between Charles II and "the Most Illustrious Lords of the Famous City and Kingdom of Algiers" (1682); between "the most sacred Majesty George and the most excellent Lords of the most noble City of Tunis" (1716); and in the same year with "the most excellent Lords of Tripoly." A treaty between Moulay Ismail and England repudiated piracy and the right of search (1721). However, Morocco possessed English captives long thereafter.

By implication all this diplomatic work countenanced the practice of piracy and the enslavement of pirates' victims.

PRESENTS FOR ALGIERS

EUROPEAN GIFTS POURED INTO BARBARY. MOULAY ISMAIL HAD seven or eight state coaches—gorgeous, but useless in the then roadless condition of Morocco. Barbary rulers counted on this Christian generosity as children count on Christmas. Naïvely they would say, like the writer quoted in the *Nozhet-Elhadi,* "If we (in Morocco) wanted 50,000 *mithkals* we need only ask the king of Holland or the king of England."

Here are some figures as to Algeria's profits from the various nations of Europe in the first quarter of the nineteenth century:

King of Sicily—annual tribute equal to seventy-two thousand current United States dollars, plus "presents" to the value of sixty thousand more

Tuscany—no tribute; each new consul gave to the value of seventy-five thousand current dollars

Sardinia—also got off with presents at each consular shifting. (It is to be imagined that this arrangement, which was common, led to frequent Algerian requests for consular replacements)

Portugal—same as Sicily

England—gave "presents" (even after the activity of Lord Exmouth in 1816)

Austria—by special mediation of Turkey gave nothing

France—exempt by treaty, but gave "presents" just the same

Sweden, Denmark—annual tribute paid in terms of naval munitions equal in value to twelve thousand dollars, plus a "present" of ten thousand dollars at each treaty renewal.

These figures are given in the French edition of Dr. Shaw's *Travels.* Dr. Shaw was English consular chaplain at Algiers in the early seventeenth century who published his observations on the Barbary States. Almost a century later a French edition, brought up to date by a well-informed geographer, was issued in Paris. The editor goes on. "We are informed that at the actual moment (this would be just before 1830) there is more treasure accumulated in Algiers than in any other city in the world and that the sums amassed in the coffers of the dey come to 40,000,000 piastres." This would work out at sixty million dollars today.

*   *   *

IT WAS WITH SHOCKED SURPRISE THAT BARBARY EXPERIENCED THE occasional European attempts at punition. Three times in the reign of Louis XIV Algiers was bombarded. This led to no lasting reformation. It did however produce a distressing incident from the French point of view. The vicar apostolic—French acting consul—who for half a lifetime had lived in Barbary working among Christian captives was blown from the cannon's mouth in reprisal. At the same period the French tried to attack Tripoli without success and Sir Robert Mansell conducted what the old-time historian calls a "miscarriage" against Algiers. Spragg at Bougie, however, was more fortunate and sank several Barbary ships. In the next century there was a spate of attacks: the Danes (1770) a failure; three Spanish attempts, one led by O'Reilly

(1775) and two by Barcello (1783-84)—all three failures—while the Venetians failed to take Sfax in Tunisia.

These and other European attempts to stop Barbary piracy were sporadic and ineffectual. Even the big attack of Lord Exmouth (1816) aided by the Dutch, though it did great damage at Algiers, did not stop piracy. Nor did the United States effort of which I shall speak presently.

MARTYRED CONSULS

THROUGHOUT THIS CURIOUS PASSAGE OF HISTORY THE MOST PITIABLE persons of all were the consuls sent to Barbary by the nations of Europe. Really these men seem to have been, all considered, worse off than the Christian captives.

Physically they were in danger—especially when any Christian power attacked: I have mentioned the priestly consul who was blown from the cannon's mouth. They were liable to be put in irons or set to work with the slaves if tribute was delayed. They were at all times distressingly humiliated. A consul when presenting himself to the dey of Algiers "had to take off his shoes and reverently kiss the ruffian's hand," according to Mr. Lane-Poole. In 1740 a French consul refused, was threatened with instant death, and gave in. A few years later an English ambassador at the dey's court managed to do his kissing by proxy: the officers in his suite kissed for him.

The most painful element in the consular life, however, must have been its mental torture. When a prize ship, a captured European vessel, was towed into harbor by the pirates, cannons cracked in rejoicing, cracked all day long if it was a rich prize. The consul studied its flag and might recognize his own with a pang. At each arrival all the consuls proceeded to the presence of the dey to note what members of his own nation might be amongst the ship's company—all now, of course, slaves. Then at the slave market consuls watched erstwhile honorable compatriots put through their paces—sullen, frightened men, modest women, trembling girls, and boys likely to find vicious masters.

To be a consul was a horrid occupation. One, Consul Cartwright, described his work as "the next step to the infernal regions." It is to be wondered that men could be found to accept

the consular office. No doubt there were opportunities for gain.
Consuls in early days were for the most part businessmen. "The
English consul," writes Laugier de Tassy, who was in Algiers in
the early eighteenth century, "is the only merchant of this nation
and makes the best profit. He sells powder, balls, bullets, grenades,
hatchets, anchors, cordage and other war and marine material,
and the dey in recognition gives him exclusive export rights to
oil, grain and other products."

The English consul to Algiers (1580) was the very first Englishman to be consul anywhere. (The English consul at Alexandria
was appointed almost simultaneously.) His name was Master John
Tipton. Hakluyt gives his letter of official appointment, making
him also consul for Tunis and Tripoli; one of Hakluyt's other
items reports how in 1586 an English traveler was entertained by
him at Algiers: "I lay with, M. Typton, Consull of the English
nation, who used me mostly kindly, and at his own charge."
Another English consul at Algiers was the famed and pathetic
explorer, Bruce, who subsequently made in all sincerity the
jubilant claim that he had discovered the Nile source, when he
had not.

BARBARY'S NEW VICTIM

AT THE VERY END OF THE EIGHTEENTH CENTURY BARBARY MADE
contact with a new contributor, the young republic of America.
America took the Barbary grievance seriously. To the United
States the Barbary Wars stand as a chapter in her history, whereas
Europe's various attempts to deal with Barbary were of a hap-
hazard and casual sort. Europe made slap-and-away attacks.
America, when eventually her temper was roused, made a sober
and prolonged—though not successful—effort to reform Barbary.

DEYS

IT WAS IN THE TIME OF THE GOOD DEY, MOHAMMED BEN-OSMAN
of Algiers that Barbary recruited this new member to her group
of tribute payers—the far-off land of America whose ships, previous
to the Revolution, had come under the lump protection money

disbursed by England. After American independence the four Barbary states saw a chance to benefit by enrolling a new national victim. Algiers, as the most important of the group—piratically speaking—promptly nudged the American elbow by capturing a pair of vessels belonging to the new republic.

* * *

ALGIERS ITSELF WAS ALSO IN THOSE DAYS A SORT OF REPUBLIC—AN odd sort—governed by a dey, a generalissimo, elected by the military group called the Janissaries. Turkey clung to the notion that Algeria was a province of her empire. This was almost a fiction. Algiers was practically independent, but saw no reason for waking Turkey from its dream and showed a respectful mien to those who were master in name only. To themselves Algiers was "The Sultan City." The military caste elected their ruler and got rid of him at will. The job was a dangerous one. The typical Algiers dey was described as "a despot without liberty, a king of slaves, and a slave to his subjects." Of the thirty deys who succeeded one another, during the whole of the eighteenth century plus a short margin at each end, fourteen took over power from assassinated predecessors.

* * *

THE GOOD DEY, MOHAMMED BEN-OSMAN OF THE AMERICAN Revolutionary period, was an exception. He reigned a long while and was beloved: "By Allah, he is a saint, our Dey!" runs the refrain of a Janissaries' song of the day.[1] It was under his leadership that Algiers beat off the Danish and Spanish attacks already mentioned. Algiers' soldiers sang, "We offered our breast to the ball; we are covered with vermilion blood, for the love of (the dey) Mohammed, the Elected, the Glory of the Universe!"

* * *

A SUCCESSOR OF THIS POPULAR HERO RULED ALGIERS WHEN IN 1793 the Algerian pirates suddenly became dissatisfied with their new American tributary and seized ten American merchantmen. The American consul and other Americans saw the dey. One of the group, William Eaton, wrote in his journal of February 22, 1799,

---

[1] By Serferli-Oglu, song written in colloquial Turkish in about 1784, conserved in the Bibliothèque Nationale of Algiers, translated into French with editorial notes by J. Deny, and included in *Mélanges René Basset*, II (Paris, 1925) a publication of the Institut des hautes études marocaines.

an account of how they went to the dey's palace and "ascended a winding maze of five flights of stairs to a narrow dark entry leading to a constricted apartment of 12 by 8 feet, the private audience room. There we took off our shoes and entering the cave (for so it seemed) . . . were shown to a huge shaggy beast sitting on his rump upon a low bench with his hind legs gathered up like a tailor or a bear." The consul, Eaton recounts with disgust, had to kiss the paw of this personage and "we all followed his example."

Next year Algiers was visited by an American frigate, the *George Washington,* which had come to deliver United States tribute payment. These tribute payments were considerable. For instance in 1798 they had consisted of twenty-six barrels of silver dollars. The dey, Mustafa, saw an opportune occasion to squeeze a little extra service from the *George Washington.* He ordered its captain to transport an Algerian mission to Constantinople. The dey's opinion was that all who paid him tribute were his servants. If the American captain, who was anchored under the guns of Algiers, should venture to refuse, the dey's piratical navy would fall on American shipping. The *George Washington* yielded and loaded upon her astonished decks not only the Algerian mission to the number of one hundred persons, but also a number of Negro women and children, four horses, one hundred fifty sheep, twenty-five horned cattle, four lions, four tigers, four antelopes, twelve parrots and a lot of valuable gifts and finery.

Nor was the *George Washington's* humiliation at an end. At Constantinople the port officer informed them that his government had never heard of such a nation as the United States (this happened in 1800), while Turkish authority subsequently aggravated the insult by remarking patronizingly that this unfamiliar nation must be some sort of obscure little cousin of their own, since its flag—like theirs—showed heavenly bodies. Turkey's crimson flag had a gold crescent moon in the middle; that of the United States then showed fifteen big stars.

It is interesting to note that it was another ship bearing Washington's name which avenged the Algerian abuse of the unhappy *George Washington,* plus other affronts, sixteen years later.

"TO THE SHORES OF TRIPOLI"

THE BARBARY STATES, HAVING DEVELOPED AMERICA INTO A GENER-
ous new source of income, became jealous of one another's American tribute and "presents."

Tripoli was the most jealous of them all. In May, 1801, Tripoli's
pasha declared war on the United States and cut down the consul's
flagpole—the usual gesture in the Barbary States to mark rupture
of diplomatic relations. It was in and about Tripoli that the
excitement of the United States-Barbary Wars concentrated. At
Tripoli occurred the capture of the *Philadelphia*. Tripoli saw the
Philadelphia's company dragged through the streets to prison.
Tripoli saw Decatur's exploit (called by Nelson "the most daring
act of the ages") when the captured *Philadelphia* was by a courageous trick burned in the harbor. Tripoli grinned at the fiasco of
the American fire ship which had sneaked into her port "pregnant
with concealed magazines of death" and blown up without doing
Tripoli any damage at all. And Tripoli experienced interference
with her home government by the intrigue of an American,
backed by an American attack on one of her provincial cities.

* * *

THESE THINGS AND OTHER MATTERS INVOLVING TRIPOLI ARE AMPLY
known to American history and celebrated in American song and
story. The Marines' hymn reminds us of "the shores of Tripoli."
The invention of the famous saying, "Millions for defense, but not
one cent for tribute," is often, though incorrectly associated with
the United States-Tripoli dealings. We read George Washington's
strikingly broad-minded comment on the treaty with Tripoli, that
"the government of the United States is not in any sense founded
upon the Christian religion."

* * *

TRIPOLI WAS THE UNITED STATES' FIRST EXOTIC ADVENTURE. HERE
is the background against which it was played:

Tripoli—for so long the least vital of the Barbary countries—had
become vigorous. This would seem to have been due entirely to
one individual, by name Hamet Coromali, who lifted Tripoli
from the position of a Turkish province. (Tripoli through the
centuries had almost always been *somebody's* province, see page

343.) Hamet the Great, as he got to be called, made Tripoli an independent nation. Under the Coromali dynasty Tripoli was master of important holdings in the Sahara and enjoyed a better reputation in Europe than her neighbors in Barbary. Tripoli tried to make an honest living, cut piracy to a small place in her economy, and made peace with the countries of Europe.

It was Hamet the Great's fourth lineal descendant who ruled in the days of the United States-Barbary Wars. He was Yusuf Coromali, a powerful person who climbed to the throne across his deposed relatives.

We possess a most delightful account of his debut and rise in a book usually known as the *Tully Letters*. It is a peculiar book in that its authoress modestly concealed her identity behind that of her brother-in-law. He was Richard Tully, British consul at Tripoli, she his anonymous sister-in-law. As a letter writer this unknown lady was a marvel and her book is the accepted source on Tripoli of her period and on the earlier days of the Coromali dynasty.[2]

THE DYNASTY OF HAMET THE GREAT

HAMET WAS A WILY AND FEARLESS PERSON. AT THE TIME WHEN HE grabbed power he was pasha on behalf of Turkey which had long held the country in subjection. "He contrived without any disturbance to clear Tripoli of all the Turkish soldiers." This is how he did it: "At his palace he gave a superb entertainment and invited all the chiefs of the Turks to partake of it. Three hundred of these unfortunate victims were strangled one by one as they entered the *skiffar*, or hall. This *skiffar* was very long with small dark rooms or deep recesses on each side, in which a hidden guard was placed. These guards assassinated the Turks as they passed, quickly conveying the bodies into these recesses out of sight, so that the next Turk saw nothing extraordinary going on and met his fate unsuspectingly. Next day the rest of the Turks were found murdered . . . only a few straggling Turks remained to tell the

---

[2] *Narrative of a Ten Years' Residence in Tripoli in Africa from the Original Correspondence in the Possession of the Family of the late Richard Tully Esq.* (1817) second edition. The letters cover 369 quarto pages and date from 1783 to 1793, to which added material carries the narrative to 1795.

dreadful tale. Great presents were sent by the pasha (Hamet the Great) to Constantinople to appease the Grand Signior and in a day or two no one dared to talk of the Turkish garrison which had been totally annihilated. Having in this dreadful manner freed himself and his family of the Turkish yoke and having succeeded in keeping the Grand Signior in humor, he caused Tripoli to remain entirely under a Moorish (meaning local) government."

*   *   *

THE GREAT GRANDSON OF THIS VERY DEFINITE GENTLEMAN WAS Yusuf, America's opponent. Opponent also to the author of the *Tully Letters* and of the consul, her relative. Yusuf's machinations set aside his father and eldest brother—the latter he personally murdered—and drove away another elder brother. His violence and trickery provoked Turkish intervention which failed to dislodge him. The result of all this was that Consul Tully and his sprightly sister-in-law found themselves obliged to leave Tripoli, where the consular family had been pets both of the royal persons Yusuf had deposed and of the population as a whole. On "our parting evening (August 22, 1793) writes the lady, "people were continually coming to express their regret in the strongest terms on the consul's leaving the country. Many of every rank met us yesterday in the street and wiped the tears from their eyes as they passed him. The whole of last night Yusuf kept up a constant firing upon the town." Her last word is to mention her sympathy for the Tripolitans under Yusuf's rule, being of opinion that power would "but aggravate his crimes."

As a matter of fact Yusuf reigned long and efficiently and England was presently friendly with him. The reason behind his declaration of war on America is obscure.

TRIPOLI SCENE

THE TRIPOLI WHICH AMERICANS OBSERVED AS FIGHTERS, AS PRISoners and as peace negotiators when war was over was a picturesque spot. The *Tully Letters* are full of oriental splendor, unexpected glimpses of sophistication and gentility, and pictures of hideous misery and cruelty. Incidentally the author mentions one of the court officials as speaking English perfectly and as giving English toasts when a guest at the consulate "like any Christian."

A few of her impressions: Here to the sound of the royal *nuba* (band of music) rides the bey (elder brother of Yusuf and later his victim) "resplendent with gold and jewels. He wore a crescent chiefly of diamonds in his turban, a dark purple and gold shawl the two ends of which were embroidered in gold nearly a yard deep. His upper vest was pale yellow satin lined with ermine and ornamented with silver, and his undervest was of green and gold tissue. Gold trappings in the shape of a drop necklace nearly covered his horse's chest. His saddle which he had received from the Emperor of Morocco was studded with rubies, emeralds and other precious stones." The Yusuf of America's day no doubt equaled this gorgeous fellow.

Here we see the curious plague precautions: The consular home (like other European houses) was ordered locked, all keys kept by the consul personally. "No business is now transacted but with a blaze of straw kept burning between the person admitted and the one he is speaking to." The rooms fumigated with bran, camphor, myrrh and aloes. Once a day the consul permitted the opening of the street door in his presence and provisions were brought in and placed in vessels, with vinegar and water for the meat, water with the vegetables. Cold bread and salt in bars and sugar loaf were considered safe. Even the tradesman's bill had to be "smoked on the end of a long stick" before it could be studied by the housekeeper. Wise precautions, for "eight people in the last seven days who were employed as providers for the house have taken the plague and died." Symptoms were "a sort of stupor which immediately increases to madness and violent swellings and excruciating pains, in a few hours terminated by death." All this about a decade before men and officers of the *Philadelphia* were confined in Tripoli's awful prison. There was another plague about a decade after the United States' adventures in Tripoli.

DERNA

AGAINST THIS COMPLETELY UNFAMILIAR BACKGROUND AMERICA ventured to play a deep diplomatic game, and did not come off badly. The intrigue was instigated by the brave and eccentric Eaton who led the celebrated march on Derna. The story is a familiar one in American history. Whittier wrote a poem about it.

Since the North African campaign in World War II attracted notice to this part of the world one or more novels and some historical studies have dealt with Eaton's exploit. An English Saharan traveler of note, Francis Rennell Rodd, had previously written Eaton's biography with special emphasis on his Tripolitan adventure. Less familiar is a native reaction as revealed in the legend of Hadigia, maiden of a regional tribe. Hadigia married a shipwrecked Christian and mothered a son who went away and "came back with five war ships and conquered Derna." I have supposed that this legend associates in a distorted fashion with the amazing arrival of Eaton and the United States Marines. It is recorded in a little Egyptian book by Colonel de Dumreicher Bey.

* * *

EATON, IT WILL BE REMEMBERED, MADE CONTACT WITH THE DEPOSED and disgruntled brother of Yusuf of Tripoli, named Hamet, and, using Hamet's wrongs as a pretext, undertook that expedition against Derna which helped to scare Yusuf into making peace with America. Brother Hamet bore the same name as Hamet the Great, but was a totally different character, deserving to be called Hamet the Little. Having been worsted by Yusuf he wandered about, a melancholy *soi-disant* king in exile. One hears of him at Tunis, at Malta, in Egypt. It was around this ineffectual person that Eaton weaved his plans, hoping to put Hamet the Little on the Tripoli throne and to see America treated in reward as the favored friend of Tripoli. It was a most outlandish fancy carried out with superb energy under great geographical and other difficulties.

The leading of a group of assorted soldiers of fortune from Egypt to Derna across some five hundred miles of semidesert was a triumph of grit and generalship. Eaton's route has been traced in detail by Mr. Rodd. Places he passed coincide with or are near to spots about which we heard much in World War II days: Marsa Matruh, Sidi Barrani, Tobruk, Bomba.

* * *

HAMET WAS NOT THE MAN TO SHARE SUCH AN EFFORT. AT DERNA, a lovely little oasis near the Egyptian border and about three weeks' march from Tripoli, there was not the hoped-for enthusiastic rush to welcome him and support his cause. Derna was of uncertain mind about Hamet. There was fighting in the course of which Eaton fortified a place on the heights, the American fort. Its ruins were still there at the last account.

Eaton had got partial control of Derna and Hamet had won a certain local following when word came suddenly that a peace had been made between Yusuf and the United States. This made any notion of re-enthroning Hamet absurd. It was a horrid and humiliating moment for Eaton, a dangerous one for Hamet and his friends. Many a throat was slit at Yusuf's order. Poor, deluded Hamet resumed his wanderings and eventually received a pension of two hundred dollars a month from the American government. In 1809 we have news of him at Malta in a report of Burckhardt's. He then got another chance to govern Derna and was again driven away from there by Yusuf.

America's first experiment in African kingmaking had been dubious: admittedly she picked the wrong king. Nor does it seem an altogether gracious episode in the history of the United States.

Consider these two "scraps of paper." The first is from a fourteen article convention between Hamet and Eaton, February 23, 1805. The second is from "The Treaty of Peace and Amity" between the United States and Tripoli signed by Yusuf and the consul general of Barbary, June 4, 1805. *Number One:* "the Government of the United States shall use their utmost exertions . . . to reestablish the said Hamet Pasha in possession of his sovereignty of Tripoli." *Number Two* (the Peace and Amity Treaty) containing this, "Americans will endeavor to persuade Hamet to withdraw . . . and his family will be restored to him," and an additional "secret article" says, "The Pasha (meaning Yusuf) believes that his brother Hamet, should his wife and children be immediately restored to him, would renew hostilities against him. Therefore the Pasha is allowed four years within which to deliver up his brother's family." Poor Little Hamet.

The United States was evidently cognizant of the shabby elements in the business. A few years afterward (1822) S. Putnam Waldo in his *Life and Character of Stephen Decatur* mentions Hamet in a manner conveying contrition, saying with regard to America's interference in his life, "Fortunate indeed had it been for him if he had remained in safety and continued in obscurity."

*   *   *

UNDER THE TREATY OF PEACE AND AMITY WITH YUSUF THE PAY-
ment of tribute to Tripoli was discontinued. But the United
States had to give sixty thousand dollars to redeem the *Philadelphia* prisoners. The price first demanded had been seven times as
much, but Yusuf was dismayed by the United States' vigorous
attack. The French diplomatic representative at Tripoli, who had
been continuously sympathetic toward the unfortunate men,
helped arrange the deal.

GREEDY TUNIS

OF THE FOUR BARBARY STATES TUNIS IS THE LEAST·PROMINENT IN
America's Barbary Wars. Of course Tunis, like the others, wished
to milk this new contributor and when she suspected her share
was smaller than theirs she made rumbling noises.

Tunis, like Algiers and Tripoli, was at that time virtually
independent of Turkey. She was ruled by a series of hereditary
beys, sprung from a Christian who had "taken the turban." This
dynasty endures into modern times. In the days of the Barbary
Wars Tunis ranked as pirate power number two, less competent
than Algiers, more so than Tripoli. At one time she threatened
war on the United States. Her blackmail imposed on America was
a "gift" of forty cannon and ten thousand stands of arms. She had
previously had twenty-eight cannon, ten thousand balls and a lot
of powder.

The exaction of war material was a usual thing. This material
would probably be used eventually against the donor. It seemed
cruel and degrading and recalls in its perversity a practice of which
I have read—this being a ruling which obliged a man condemned
to be bastinadoed to pay a fixed sum to the official appointed to
beat him. It must have disgusted Barbary's tributaries to have to
supply Barbary with the materials of piracy.

MOROCCO AND AMERICA

MOROCCO SAW A MORE DIGNIFIED AND IMPRESSIVE ASPECT OF THE
United States. The *Philadelphia*, so soon to be jeered at as
Tripoli's victim, encountered at sea a Boston brig which had been

captured by a Moroccan ship and grabbed the captor. The United
States fleet forthwith proceeded to Tangier to speak severely to
the sultan who had a notion to declare war against America.

On October 10, 1803, at ten o'clock in the morning the American commodore with two midshipmen and another American
marched through Tangier to interview the sultan. It was a tick-
lish adventure and we can imagine that Midshipman Ralph Izard,
whose account of the visit survives in a letter written to his mother
the next day, was well aware of the danger his little party ran in
leaving their ship and approaching a belligerently inclined Barbary monarch in his lair. Midshipman Ralph, however, contents
himself with telling his mother of his surprise at the informality
of the meeting. "We were introduced to His Majesty with very
little ceremony. I had connected with the idea of the Emperor of
Morocco something grand, but what was my disappointment at
seeing a small man wrapped in a woolen *haik,* or cloak, sitting on
the steps of an old castle in the middle of the street, surrounded
by a guard of very ill looking blacks with their arms covered with
cloth to prevent them rusting. We stood before the Emperor with
our caps in hand and the conversation was carried on by means
of an interpreter." (From *Naval Documents Related to the United
States Wars with the Barbary Powers,* Vol. III.)

As a result of the commodore's visit and of the sultan's sight
of the United States ships the old American-Moroccan treaty was
reaffirmed, and the little party of four Americans dined with Consul Simpson at Tangier.

The venerable consul was a celebrated character. Probably he
was then *doyen* of American consuls. President Washington had
appointed him; he resided in Morocco almost steadily until his
death in 1820, a very influential figure and "a most benevolent
friend of Christian slaves and American seamen." His name re-
curs in early American books of travel and shipwreck. Like many
another consul, Mr. Simpson complained of the lowness of his
salary (see memo to the State Department, October 15, 1803). He
also was aggrieved because he heard "so seldom from the Department of State."

*   *   *

AN ODD THING ABOUT THE AMERICAN COMMODORE'S PLUCKY VISIT
to Tangier is the slightness of impression it seems to have made

on the Moroccan public. We happen to possess the account of a European's sojourn in Tangier at the very same moment. It is that of the Spanish traveler who used the pseudonym of "Ali Bey." The Spaniard knew the sultan personally and confirms our midshipman's story as to the simplicity of his person and plainness of his entourage. But as to any suggestion of the local excitement one might have expected "Ali Bey" is silent. Not a word about the commodore's visit. Evidently Tangier was unmoved, unaware of potentialities. This is the reaction of an impartial observer on the spot. It contrasts disappointingly with some of the American history book versions which present a scene of tense drama suggesting the possibility of tremendous conflict.

Tangier would have been in no state to play a part in any tremendous conflict. Her fortifications were impressive when seen from afar but "Ali Bey" reports the gun carriages were "so badly made . . . they would not stand the fire of the enemy for a quarter of an hour," describing them as made of wood and planks and painted black. There was little military discipline. The batteries were left without guard most of the day and all night, everyone going home to bed. Of this slipshod situation the Americans were not fully aware, their information being, "the fort above the town and the batteries in front appear formidable, but it is said they are in bad condition as to their guns" (memo dated three weeks before the commodore's visit).

MOROCCO WAS SLIPPING

MOROCCO HAD BY THEN SLIPPED FROM HER PRIDE OF THE DAYS OF Moulay Ismail. Morocco had lost Timbuctoo the Golden, and recently had been deprived of even a part of her own home territory by an Algerian attack. The sultan whom our midshipman observed sitting on the old castle steps at Tangier was Moulay Slimane, the great-grandson of the forceful and amorous Ismail. Slimane's father had been on treaty terms with the United States and was a benign person who died at eighty-one. For about a year between this old man and Slimane, Morocco had suffered under a despot of the old school, one of those demented demons which African dynasties produced at intervals. He was Slimane's elder brother, Yezid, victim of a suspect hunting accident after he had

piled up spectacular villainy all across the top of Africa. As crown
prince en route for the Mecca pilgrimage he came under the horrified notice of the authoress of the *Tully Letters*. She tells how
the fiendish fellow delighted in inventing novel punishments for
his servants and women. One invention, devised while Yezid was
at Tripoli: four thousand bastinadoes followed by the forced
swallowing of a quantity of sand! Yezid detested Christians, fired
at their horses' heels if he met them while riding and at Algiers
sent a ball through the brim of a Christian's hat. At the outset
of his brief reign Yezid suspected that his late father's first minister
was pro-Christian and too friendly with the Spaniards, so he executed the man and "caused his head to be placed on the Spanish
consular house and his hand nailed to the door, to the dreadful
annoyance of the family!" (It is still the Tully authoress who
writes.)

*   *   *

SLIMANE, YEZID'S BROTHER, HAD BEEN SULTAN FOR ELEVEN YEARS
when the American commodore visited him—a man of quite different nature, as can be the case in Mohammedan lands where a
man has sons by many mothers. It is disconcerting to note, by
the way, that the monster Yezid was the child of a Christian
woman—English or Irish.

Morocco was in an ungainly state of transition. The wild
grandeur of medieval barbarism was merging awkwardly with the
glimmerings of modern notions and the beginnings of tolerance.

Slimane was of a progressive type, desiring to promote Moroccan trade with the outside world. Easy relations were hampered
by the fact that European envoys to Morocco were "men almost
wholly unacquainted with the manners and customs and religious
prejudices of the people and ignorant of their language," in the
complaint of James Grey Jackson, a sixteen-year English resident
in Morocco during the reigns of Slimane and his two predecessors.
Absurd contretemps sometimes occurred. A letter of Slimane's
to the king of England, requiring a reply, remained in London
untranslatable for months. A "treaty of peace and amity" in Arabic, not completely understood by the English consul, was entrusted to a Spanish student, "who instead of giving an accurate
translation, sent one—it was reported—to Madrid and kept the

paper a month, so that the whole treaty was known at Madrid before it was known in London."

Sometimes in the trade relations with Europeans there would be ridiculous and distressing incidents of barbarism, as when a certain European merchant was accused of having injured a native in the course of a row about damages caused by one of his dogs. The native—a woman—claimed she had lost two teeth and blamed the merchant. Being international, the affair was brought before Slimane and the sultan could not stand out against the crowd's fury and was compelled to issue with regret an order that the European merchant should lose two of his teeth in retaliation.

So Mr. Layton, "chief partner in a house of considerable capital and respectability," had two of his teeth pulled out then and there in Sultan Slimane's presence, procuring however the favor that "back teeth be taken in lieu of front teeth."

* * *

THE COMMERCE OF MOROCCO WITH AMERICA WAS IMPEDED FOR two years, Mr. Jackson reports, "by a dispute between that country and the Emperor." When resumed it became a good business for the United States. "Vessels from Salem, Boston and other parts of America, with East and West India produce," came to Mogador (the Moroccan port then given over to Christian trade) and the agents of the American merchants "are enabled to undersell us all in East and West India goods." Morocco sold olive oil, hides, almonds, wax, gums, silver and gold. Also lemons and oranges. "The oranges of Tetuán are the finest in the world," says Jackson, "and are sold per thousand for eight *drahims*" (about a dollar and a quarter in current United States money).

* * *

MOROCCO FOUR YEARS BEFORE THE AMERICAN VISIT HAD BEEN afflicted with a horrifying outburst of plague (1799-1800). Slimane had it twice—thus refuting the idea that a person may have it but once in a lifetime. Whole households were wiped away. The old governor of Mogador lost all but one wife—wives, children, concubines, slaves—all perished. When smitten, one had the sensation that two musket balls had been fired, one into each thigh, or as if a long needle had been repeatedly thrust into the groin. Followed vomiting and the appearance of buboes. Some victims had their bodies covered with small black spots similar to grains of gunpowder. Cures were various: a native doctor treating a certain patient "applied to the swellings the testicles of a ram, cut in half whilst the vital warmth was still in them . . . daily applied for thirty days." The patient recovered.

Jackson's cook was smitten while making bread in Jackson's kitchen, died next day "in such a deplorable state that his feet were putrefied." Mr. Jackson was not startled. "Fear," he reflects, "has an extraordinary effect in disposing the body to receive infection." His sole precaution was to set up a wide table between the dining room and the kitchen, whereupon his food was placed, which he removed himself, thus avoiding inhaling the breath of his servants. The same precaution in his office and counting-house. Also he "received money through vinegar."

Inside a few months one third of the population had died, Mr. Jackson heard. Villages lay empty for the hand of pillagers. Flocks ran about free for anyone to take them. Provisions were cheap and labor excessively high.

Thus it was a chastened and changed country which Americans visited in the days of the Barbary Wars.

AMERICA RAMPANT—DECATUR

IN 1815-16 THE UNITED STATES, HAVING EMERGED FROM THE 1812 War with England, felt strong enough to chastise Barbary. Algiers had been taking advantage of the American preoccupation, had seized United States merchant vessels, demanded and received increased blackmail. For Algiers the month of June, 1815, was the gloomy time of reckoning. Decatur had taken the flagship of the Algerian navy and had appeared off Algiers with an ultimatum: no more tribute, all American slaves (captives from seized ships) to be freed, certain indemnity payments or. . . . In vain the dey attempted to squirm. Some hours later he signed.

Tunis and Tripoli also crawled.

America's vigor and thoroughness must have puzzled Barbary, so long accustomed to the routine of treaty and tribute; broken treaties and halfhearted punitive efforts; and repeat. To discontinue tribute permanently and definitely seemed positively unnatural. America had, in a way, paid Barbary a compliment, not treating the piratical states as bad boys, but fighting them seriously. America *did* take Barbary seriously—feeling that an abuse needed correcting—and proved it in an odd fashion by keeping the name alive, long after it was forgotten in Africa, in the celebrated Barbary Coast in San Francisco.[3]

* * *

ALGIERS GOT ITS WIND BACK AND IN THE SPRING FOLLOWING THE black June of 1815 the dey wrote to the president suggesting that it would be agreeable to him if the Decatur treaty were dropped and good old-fashioned tribute arrangements resumed. The dey had badly chosen his moment. For, while his proposition was on the water, there arrived at Algiers a British-Dutch fleet which bombed Algiers and left the city's defenses in such bad shape that another United States expedition had only to appear in order to quiet the dey's recrudescent greed. In this expedition figured the *Washington,* thus avenging its namesake which an Algiers dey had commandeered for vile uses sixteen years before.

To Barbary all this was a sickening blow. Public opinion was indignant. The dey was deposed and assassinated. Piracy, however, went on. America's Mediterranean fleet guarded American commerce. Europe continued to pay tribute and give "presents." Morocco clung to piratical ways well into modern days. One of Spain's reasons for the 1859 war against Morocco was piracy. At Algiers Christian captives were worse treated than ever during the early years of the nineteenth century.

Piracy was the life and pride of the citizens of Barbary. It was their ancestral means of earning a livelihood. Any consideration of the distress and damage caused to others—and you have to admit that these others were their traditional enemies—did not stop them. Strange psychology, yes. But what nation amongst us in the barbarous world of today can dare throw the first stone at the memory of the Barbary States?

[3] "The identity of the nomenclatorial genius who first bestowed the savage but glamorous designation upon San Francisco's underworld has not been preserved . . ." writes the author of *The Barbary Coast.* Mr. Herbert goes on to say that the name came into general use in the 1860's.

NAPOLEON IN EGYPT

NAPOLEON BONAPARTE, LORD CROMER REMINDS US, DECLARED, "Egypt is the most important country in the world."

Napoleon's invasion of Egypt coincided with the period of the United States-Barbary Wars. These last, we have admitted, made a very trifling dent in local sentiment. The news of Napoleon's capture and brief holding of Egypt not only profoundly affected Egypt, but rang across all Africa.

In far-off Sierra Leone they knew of it. A French explorer could tell a yarn about having been born in Cairo and carried off in infancy to France by one of Napoleon's troops and could be sure that common Negroes who listened possessed the preliminary familiarity with the subject to understand what he was talking about.[4]

The peculiar and romantic behavior of Napoleon while in Egypt and his subsequent grandeur and power thrilled Africa's imagination. He was the *Sultan Kebir* (the Great King). Across all Barbary his Egyptian exploit and his personality were famous. *Bonobarto,* they called him, and—so Lyon, the explorer, reported —they believed that he had an income of two hundred thousand dollars (Spanish dollars) *an hour,* and sat upon a throne of pure gold.

THE INERADICABLE MAMLUKS

EGYPT, WHEN NAPOLEON'S FLEET AND THIRTY THOUSAND MEN suddenly arrived off Alexandria (1798), played a small part in world affairs. Ever since the Turkish conquest (see page 393) Egypt had dozed along with occasional nightmares, allegedly a Turkish province, though in fact reverting more and more to the same old Egypt which the Turks had captured—the Egypt of the Mamluks.

Mamluks were hard to eradicate. Egypt is said to have accepted the Turkish conquest almost with satisfaction, hoping it would mean the end of the slave sultans. But the Mamluks survived,

[4] "During my sojourn in Freetown . . . I told certain Mandingos that I was born in Egypt of Mohammedan parents and brought to France very

continued to import new slave stock to keep up their numbers, and presently reappeared in power. Ali Bey, surnamed "Ali the Great," even called himself sultan for a very brief while starting in 1771.

They were the same swaggering lot of old—good fighters and bad men. In vain Turkey sent pashas (governors) to keep them in check. The Mamluk beys reduced their gubernatorial control to a cipher. An anecdote of the day: The pasha calls a meeting of the divan (council) and communicates the commands of the Porte. "The few who had bothered to attend, as soon as the reading is finished, answer as usual, '*Es mana wa taana*' (We have heard and we obey). On leaving the castle the general voice is, '*Es man wa awsina*' (We have heard and shall disobey)."

A new pasha arrived in 1796—a Pasha of Three Tails; a very fine ceremony at his arrival included a band of music and a display of the tails. The two most important beys did not deign to attend. Soon the pasha demanded the tribute, greatly in arrears. The two big beys dodged the subject and suggested to the pasha that he take the matter up with the younger beys, which he did. "The latter replied that if the pasha sought for money all their treasure was buried in Kara-Maiden, the place where the troops exercised and where encounters between opposing parties frequently took place (the riot ground, so to speak) and that the pasha had only to meet them there. . . ."

These two typical anecdotes of rebellious Mamluk days are told by a youth from Oxford who went adventuring in Egypt and in the Sudan beyond, just before Napoleon's invasion, and who recorded his observations in an excellent book. His name was W. G. Browne.

EGYPT HAD CHANGED

EGYPT HAD CHANGED SINCE THE FINE DAYS WHEN ALEXANDRIA WAS the famed "Market of Two Worlds."

Alexandria, when Napoleon landed on a near-by beach, had

young by French who formed part of the army that went to Egypt, had been brought to Africa by my master and set free. I added that I wanted to go back to Egypt to rejoin my family and regain my Moslem faith." Pp. 217-18 *Journal d'un voyage à Temboctou,* Tome I, by René Caillié (Paris, 1830).

become a scrawny city that could not fill up its old-time walls. The uninhabited spaces of the shrunken town were used for vegetable gardens and for sheltering flocks at night and as garbage dumps. There were everywhere the ruins of superfluous dwellings and heaps of rubbish which the poor dug and sifted in search of coins or valuable debris.

Cairo was not so shabby, but its old gorgeousness had gone and its population diminished. It then sheltered less than three hundred thousand people. No longer the highway to the East, Cairo dealt almost exclusively in African and Arabian goods. The trade of eastern Africa brought black slaves and exotic stuff. From Arabia came coffee—no longer the Arabian monopoly which it had been in the previous century, but still a much-sought item. Egypt's commercial fleet, maintained in the Red Sea, was trifling and its seamanship deplorable. Some European ships—French and English—plied the Red Sea in the interests of the coffee trade. Cairo's European traders were a much-reduced lot since the grand old times before the discovery of the Cape of Good Hope route to India. For example, England's affairs were of so little importance that they were handled on the side by the Venetian consul, and France had only three commercial establishments.

Cairo's European colony congregated on a street parallel to the old cross-town canal, El-Khalig, where water ran in the high Nile period and which was something like a prolonged dung pit and refuse ground for the rest of the year. Browne says, "the stench of it was supposed to operate in producing the pestilence."

When the plague raged the members of the European group would throw bridges across the streets from one roof top to another and so avoid dangerous contacts. According to an Englishwoman who was in Cairo in the late eighteenth century they preferred to visit one another by this route at all times, for Europeans walking in the streets were often insulted. The general situation of Christian residents was described as "very, very humiliating, ignominious, and distressing" by Ledyard, the American (1788).

It was, commercially speaking, the lowest point in Egypt's career. The organized land route across the country which preceded the cutting of the Suez Canal had not yet been developed,

Egypt's usefulness as a shuttle between the Mediterranean and the East was negligible.

But in one respect Egypt was unchanged from the days of her grandeur. Such wealth as there was still remained in the hands of the few. There was the same tragic gap between the way of life of the common native Egyptian and that of his foreign rulers.

A workman got the equivalent of eight cents a day.

A Mamluk who rose to the official rank of bey—of such there were twenty-four—gouged out of the country an income of from three hundred to one thousand "purses" annually. The most rapacious and active of them all, Murad Bey, secured up to two thousand "purses." This storybook fashion of counting money was then employed for large sums. A "purse" had a specific but fluctuating value. At one time it had equaled seven hundred fifty current United States dollars. It eventually fell to be worth one hundred eighty-seven. In the day when Murad was one of the two top beys and when Napoleon appeared in Egypt a "purse" was equal to three hundred seventy-five current dollars. Two thousand of them was a large salary for one man to take out of a small country.

Murad Bey's wife was wont to urge against extortion. She was a noted local character, Fatima, daughter of Ali the Great who had been for a little while sultan. She used to tell all the beys, "Do not pillage the people; they were always spared by my father." This tribute to Great Ali was presumably based merely on filial piety. Gentleness to helpless people was not in the Mamluk creed.

The poor lived wretchedly. "The villages are the most miserable assemblages of poor little mud huts," wrote the American, Ledyard, in describing the country between Alexandria and Cairo, "flung close together without any kind of order, full of dust, lice, flies, bed-bugs and fleas and all the curses of Moses. People poorly clad, the youths naked. In some respects they are infinitely below any savages I ever saw."

In contrast the learned classes fared well under Mamluk patronage. Here, for example, was the happy life of one Ez-Zabidy, traveler and author and a protégé of one of the beys, who undertook his support and provided him with "the richest vestments and the handsomest horses." In his latter years this author resided in a mausoleum erected for his departed wife, a place rich with rugs and tapestries, where he received the intelligentsia of the day (1782)—poets and pious men—serving them *couscous,* coffee and sherbets. He became so prosperous that "he refused the presents offered him by the great ones of Cairo."

Such tangible appreciation of learning was an honor to the Mamluk beys, since their own education in those days was often quite neglected. Murad Bey—though he could earn the equivalent of seven hundred fifty thousand dollars a year—could neither read nor write.

NAPOLEON AND THE MAMLUKS

ON JULY 1, 1798, NAPOLEON'S TROOPS LANDED ON THE SHORES near Alexandria and easily took the city and rushed south. Three weeks later they won the famous Battle of the Pyramids alongside Cairo.

The story runs that Napoleon exhorted his men to special valor by pointing to the near-by pyramids and crying, "Forty centuries are watching you!" His soldiers, when they confronted their enemies, must have felt that they were watching a reincarnation of the Middle Ages. The Mamluk warrior under Egypt's summer blaze was a startling creature: crimson, immensely wide pantaloons, red slippers, a green cap wreathed with a turban, an open helmet and ancient ring armor of interwoven links of steel, a saber, a pair of horse pistols and a *dubbus,* or battle-ax. Their mounts were superb Arab horses. Their riding also was superb and their saber work splendid to see. Of battle maneuvers they were quite ignorant.

The survivors of this spectacular army fled to Upper Egypt, led by Murad Bey. One of Napoleon's generals chased them as far as Assuan. The other top bey of the moment, Ibrahim, burned his Cairo palace and also fled.

The people of Cairo could only hope for that occurrence which allegedly had saved other oriental cities from their enemies in the past: a miraculous dazzling of the attackers' eyes "so that they could not find the place though constantly roving around it." (This bit of fantastic optimism was communicated to the explorer Horneman in all seriousness, he being actually inside Cairo at the time Napoleon arrived.) No such miracle occurring, Cairo next day at dawn sent a message of submission to Napoleon who entered the city on July 25 and set up his headquarters in a bey's palace, occupying the site where now stands Shepheard's Hotel.

Six days afterward the people of the village of Abukir near Alexandria saw the annihilation of the French fleet by Nelson which left Napoleon in the position of a "Robinson Crusoe" conqueror. He could say, "I am monarch of all I survey," but he was cut off from the world.

A FRENCHMAN WHO READ THE KORAN

NAPOLEON'S FIRST WORDS TO THE PEOPLE OF EGYPT WERE THAT HE had come as a friend of Moslems to combat the Mamluks and make Egyptians happy. This, of course, was propaganda. Of the many reasons assigned by various historians for the French invasion of Egypt the one cited by Napoleon—that he came to make the common Egyptian happy—is the least convincing of all. Some more reasonable motives: The ripening of France's long-cherished ambition to capture Egypt, an ambition dating from the days of Louis XIV. Combined with this a plan to reopen the old route through Egypt to India. A nascent French longing for an African colony. A desire to injure, and divert the forces of the English enemy. Napoleon's romantic craving for a big Oriental adventure. And perhaps a wish on the part of enemies at home to deport the young Napoleon Bonaparte from the capital.

But Egypt heard the newcomer's announcement with relief and Napoleon's good will toward their religion was a glad surprise. It was North Africa's first experience of a Christian who was tolerant. Napoleon was not only tolerant but extravagantly friendly to Islam.

He gave his soldiers orders to respect mosques and saw to it that pilgrims traveling across Egypt to and from Mecca were made welcome. He even let it be known that he toyed with the idea of going over to Islam himself. He declared that he was *Muslimmun Muwahhidun* (a Unitarian Moslem). He studied his appearance in Oriental garb and changed back to trousers, seeing himself too short to wear draperies with dignity. He was content to see one of his generals, Menou, become an out-and-out convert

to Mohammedanism, marrying a Mohammedan woman and signing his name "Abdallah Menou." Napoleon himself announced
that he would build a mosque, the finest in the world. He took
the leading part in the Moslem fete of Ramadan and the traditional Nile festival.

Partly all this was from policy. It is said that Napoleon had
conceived the grandiose project of becoming "the Emperor-Caliph
of the whole Orient." This I quote from a Mohammedan source.
It seems a far-flung notion. But it is true that Napoleon's original
hope had been to avoid trouble with Turkey and to consolidate
relations with the whole Moslem world of Africa and Asia.

Partly, however, Napoleon's pre-Mohammedanism was sincere.
The Orient had roused his imagination. In an article in the
Quarterly Review of 1815, naturally anti-Napoleon in sentiment,
I find this: "The turn of his mind was oriental; the vast prospects
of Asia suited his vague and wild propensities." Then Napoleon
himself is quoted as having said, " 'There has been nothing to do
in Europe these two hundred years. It is only in the East that
anything great is to be done.' "

Napoleon dreamed of the East, loved Egypt for its own sake,
and read the Koran for pleasure.

*   *   *

ONE THING IS INDISPUTABLE: NAPOLEON'S RESPECTFUL ATTITUDE
toward the Mohammedan religion and culture became a special
French habit of mind and has greased the way for French colonization in North Africa. It was not only far more courteous but far
more constructive than the previous Christian point of view. To
insult a man's religion is not a method of winning his collaboration. From this error the French have been relatively free and
we may assume it has been because of the example set by the
romantic young Napoleon in France's first colonial African adventure.

EGYPT WAS DUBIOUS

THE PEOPLE OF EGYPT OBSERVED THE NOVEL PSYCHOLOGY OF THEIR
latest foreign conqueror with mixed sentiments. At first Napoleon's interest in their faith plus his undertaking to shove away
the Mamluks delighted them. On the day of the Nile festival

about a month after the French entered Cairo the population was in an intoxication of joy. They exchanged felicitations with one another. But the realism of French occupation was not so nice: sanitary measures that offended old customs, the public selling of wine for the soldiers, new tax regulations, the taking of a census and so on. The defeat of the French navy had wiped some of the shine off the new masters. The Mamluk beys from their hiding places sent agents to sneer and to criticize. Egyptian opinion was affected by Turkey's attitude. Turkey put no confidence in Napoleon's statement that he had no ill intentions toward their position as Egypt's overlord and declared war on France. There was an insurrection in Cairo, quelled in a fortnight.

European ways were not their ways. They did not think as Europe expected them to. Their reactions were unpredictable. An example: The French sent up a primitive balloon, believing this extraordinary thing would impress Cairo with a notion of their greatness. Cairo's comment was (the passage is from an Arabic author of the day, quoted by Professor Gautier) "The French have built a monster which rises in the sky with the intention of reaching up to and insulting Allah. But it only rose a little distance and fell back, ridiculously impotent!" The comment is not without its wisdom today.

*   *   *

THE FRENCH OCCUPATION LASTED ONLY THREE YEARS (1798-1801). But Napoleon's visit led to two things which profoundly affected Egypt, neither of them perhaps for Egypt's benefit.

One: The cutting of the Suez Canal which endowed Egypt with a tremendously valuable piece of world property which Egypt had not the strength to take care of, thus retarding Egypt's hopes for independence. The canal was a project of Napoleon's, a project fostered by France after his day against England's violent opposition. Of course a canal to the Red Sea was one of the oldest engineering jobs in history. (It will be recalled that Queen Hatshepsut's expedition used such a route to go to Punt.) A modern canal might have been cut anyhow. But the fact remains that Napoleon was the godfather of the plan and de Lesseps and other Frenchmen, its sponsors.

Two: The development of archaeology with the consequent invasion of Egypt by students in masses and tourists in hordes—

something of a doubtful benefit to a country's morale. Napoleon brought a body of scientists with him. The resultant study gave the world its first serious information about Egypt's antique wonders. So Napoleon was also the godfather of Egyptian archaeology and it was he who beckoned into the land the hundreds of thousands of foreign visitors who have taught Egyptians to scream, "Bakshish!"

A VISIT TO SUEZ

THE INFLUENCE OF NAPOLEON'S OCCUPATION WILL ENDURE AS LONG as there are ships on the sea. It may have been the most important thing that ever happened in Egypt.

He started for Suez the day before Christmas, 1798, with his experts and intent on studying a canal project. Suez was a poor little village whence at low tide one could wade across to the other side of the Suez Gulf. Some Bible students have picked this as the place of the Israelites' flight and the Pharaoh's disaster. Napoleon made the crossing and, not being a tall man, nearly got drowned when the tide came rushing in, and had to be carried ashore on a native's shoulders.

Napoleon put his experts to work at their calculations and himself prophesied that one day boats would pass along that way. To foresee that upward of thirty-six millions of tons of shipping would go by that route annually (figures for 1947, the canal's best year to date) was beyond his dreams.

Another feature of the Suez scene brought up an element also beyond the imagination of his day. Browne who was at Suez two years before Napoleon's visit mentions it, saying, "A rock on the African side of the Gulf furnishes *petroleum* (Browne's italics, indicating it was to him an unfamiliar word) which is brought to Suez and esteemed a cure for bruises, etc."!

THE "DIGGERS'" GODFATHER

NAPOLEON WAS NOT ONLY GODFATHER TO EGYPTOLOGY, IT WAS ONE of his men who made the study possible. This man found the now famous Rosetta Stone (see page 11) which was to lead to the deciphering of the hieroglyphs and the unfolding of Egypt's history. The stone was found near Rosetta at one of the mouths of the Nile. At the French capitulation the English claimed this potential treasure which had been thrown down in the mud in the hope that it would pass unnoticed. It must have been heartbreaking to the scientists of Napoleon's party to realize the greatness of their loss when the ugly stone, containing the code to History's tremendous mystery, was snatched from them.

The most brilliant of France's young savants had joined the expedition; it had been to them "a craze . . . like that which seized our forefathers at the time of the Crusades." These enthusiasts fell on Egypt and its ancient monuments like a band of learned wolves. Some years afterward there appeared one of the results of their studies, the well-known *Déscription de l'Egypte,* into the editing of which Jomard had put the work of eighteen years, and when you see the *Déscription* you do not wonder. It contains amongst its assorted and many volumes certain of the biggest books I have ever handled—books published for an ampler age when libraries were spacious. The pages of the several major volumes of illustrative matter measure twenty-seven inches by forty-two. There are also numerous volumes about half that size and nine volumes of reading matter. Editor Jomard was known as "the incarnation of geography" and whimsically it was said of him that he had "married Egypt."

One of Napoleon's first acts after taking Cairo had been to establish his stable of savants in one of the ex-bey's palaces and to give them the group name of the "Institut d'Egypte." They held their meetings in what had been the great hall of the harem, studying according to their several bents the future development and the past secrets of the country. Napoleon—sneers the English publication of 1815 already quoted, the *Quarterly Review*—adored antiquity, symbol of the immortality his vanity craved. Shrewdly too he used the mysterious antiquities that surrounded his army as an inspiration to his troops. He engraved the names of forty who fell in the battle for Alexandria on Pompey's Pillar. He called on the pyramids to witness French bravery.

RETURN OF THE PILGRIMS

TOWNS AND VILLAGES ALL OVER BARBARY HAD BEEN SHAKEN WITH anguish when word came that "the Franks" had seized Egypt. Husbands, sons and fathers absent on the Mecca pilgrimage were given up as lost, for how would they get across Egypt again? Horneman, the explorer, who traveled with a pilgrims' caravan in September, 1798 (two months after the French occupation started), tells of the pathetic joy of the home folk along the route when they saw their dear ones arriving safe after all.

The returning pilgrims had a surprising story to tell of how, instead of massacring them, the Franks had pushed them benevolently along their way. This had been wise policy on the part of the French. With Nelson's victory they were blockaded in Egypt. Obviously the good will of other North African countries would be precious. Across the top of Africa might pass communications from Europe, now cut off by the all-sea route.

Napoleon made a deal with the Tripolitan sheikh who commanded the pilgrim caravan from his country. The deal was cemented by the gift of a watch with a chain enriched with diamonds, and he was promised nobler recompense if he kept his part of the bargain. The sheikh undertook to carry various communications to Tripoli and to get them there in thirty days or less.

One of these messages was to the pasha of Tripoli, our old friend, Yusuf Coromali, who declared war on America, to the effect that Napoleon was a friend of his people and his religion. "Tell him that tomorrow we celebrate here in Cairo the fete of Mohammed with the greatest pomp. The Tripoli pilgrims' caravan is leaving. I have protected them and they have nothing but praise for us."

Another communication was for the French consul at Tripoli asking him to send all available newspapers by desert courier so that Napoleon would be aware of what was happening in the outside world from which he was cut off.

The French forces' isolation was distressing. All sorts of methods of communicating were suggested. The home government was invited to try no less than six different routes, making six copies of each dispatch in cipher, and joining to each a set of newspapers. The final result of all this was delay and disappointment.

ADVENTURES OF TWO LETTERS

TAKE, FOR INSTANCE, THE ADVENTURES OF NAPOLEON'S LETTER TO the Tripoli consul entrusted to the sheikh who got the watch, and of the consul's letter in reply.

The sheikh left Cairo on August 21, promising to deliver the letter within thirty, and perhaps within twenty days. It was October 24 before the consul saw it. (These dates and other details I have from Charles-Roux's carefully documented study of this phase of Napoleon's Egyptian expedition: *Bonaparte à la Tripolitaine*, published by the Académie des Sciences Coloniales, 1929.) The pious sheikh had a rambling list of excuses about a camel drowned in the Nile, another which fell sick, and about enemies skulking round the caravan so that he dared not send a swift messenger ahead of the main body.

The consul promptly got together the material Napoleon craved —printed newspapers and written abstracts of news—and having discussed the problem with Yusuf Coromali, arrived at what seemed a sure plan for putting the matter into Napoleon's hands. The material was enclosed in a little case. This Yusuf Coromali undertook to ship toward Egypt. For prudence's sake the little case was sent in the care of Yusuf's uncle, then believed to be either in Cairo or Alexandria, and was sent via the bey of Benghazi (part way along the route to Egypt). The bey would know just where Yusuf's uncle was at the moment and would push the case forward. Thus no one along the route would suspect the case contained anything but an exchange between Yusuf and his uncle, and no one would tamper with it.

It was a seemingly ideal manner of safeguarding Napoleon's news. The trouble was that the uncle, while the little case was on the road, had left Egypt for Rhodes. The bey of Benghazi, knowing this, thought it best to put the little case away in a secure place and await further instructions. It was not until the beginning of February that the Tripoli consul heard what had happened.

Thus over five months had passed and Napoleon was still waiting for his newspapers from Tripoli! The consul made another try. But I have carried the story far enough.

*   *   *

NAPOLEON'S MEN PINED FOR NEWS OF THEIR FAMILIES. SOME STORIES have it that it was during this almost newsless period that Napoleon first learned of Josephine's infidelity.

An exasperating communication must have been the much-delayed dispatch which reached Napoleon when things were going very ill with his campaign. It had been sent in better days and, after four months, one copy of the four sent reached his hands with the bright suggestion that he might now march on India, or take Constantinople!

NAPOLEON AND THE WEST

PRESENTLY ALL BARBARY EXCEPT MOROCCO DECLARED ITSELF IN A state of war with France. Turkey had cajoled and threatened the States in turn. Tripoli had held out to the last. Tripoli had been petted by France as adjacent to Egypt and especially likely to be of use to the marooned French army. At one time during the troubled period Yusuf Coromali and his court received gifts from France the itemized list of which takes up more than a printed page: jewelry, furniture, watches, chinaware, and "a great clock containing no representation of the human figure" (this would have been offensive to Moslem ideas). Yusuf thought so much of France during this petting time that he once condescended to go to tea at the consular house with his suite.

Nonetheless Tripoli was obliged to declare herself at war with France for a while, though Yusuf dodged the Turkish command that he should put himself at the head of an army and go attack Napoleon in Egypt—a formidable march and a hazardous campaign to propose to poor Yusuf. Tripoli was threatened by the English fleet and went into war against her will, soon making it up with France.

Tunis and Algiers—less petted by France—slipped into war more readily. French residents were mishandled. Some remained forty or fifty days in chains (Algiers, Bône). Others were jammed into a single building to the number of 125 (Tunis) and their property confiscated.

The Barbary powers passed worried years. The French-English-Turkish dispute in Egypt held nothing but trouble for them.

In the beginning they feared that if France was fully successful in Egypt there might follow a French attack upon themselves. There was a rumor at one time that a French army was being made ready to invade Tripolitania.

On the other hand Barbary feared that, if France failed in Egypt, she might fall back upon them in her withdrawal.

When France capitulated and England occupied Egypt Barbary was again alarmed.

Another matter for uneasiness: now that Turkey was again titular master in Egypt Turkey might, they feared, seek in her pride to discipline them for past insubordination and might push pasha, bey and dey off their respective thrones.

*   *   *

EVEN MOROCCO WAS NERVOUS, ALTHOUGH FAR FROM THE EGYPTIAN scene and immune from Turkish intimate pressure since she had never acknowledged Turkish titular control.

There was a rumor that Napoleon not only planned to conquer Morocco, but that he was actually secretly in the country, spying out the land. He was, rumor said, passing by the name of "Ali Bey." This "Ali Bey" whose account of Tangier at the moment of the American commodore's visit has been quoted, was in truth a Spanish traveler who had assumed a native pseudonym for convenience. The fantastic notion that he was Napoleon was built up by his prodigal spending and sumptuous way of life. He tipped extravagantly, giving more munificent gratuities than the emperor of Morocco himself.

Indignant and confused Morocco no longer spoke of Napoleon as Bonaparte, but "denominated him merely 'Parte': they would not add *Bona* as the word signifies 'good' in the *lingua franca* of Barbary" and Napoleon, supposedly plotting against their independence was regarded as "a devil incarnate." This bit of Moroccan reaction to Napoleon I find in an obscure "Fragment," included in a book of Jackson's, a contemporary resident in Morocco.

Such fears were not foolish, though the notion that Napoleon was amongst them in the flesh was outlandish. After his Egyptian defeat he still hankered for Africa and at one time ordered a plan to be drawn for an attack on Barbary, which plan afterward was useful in the expedition which gave Algeria to France a generation later.[5] Napoleon himself did not however undertake personally any further African adventures.

*   *   *

GIVEN THE GENERAL DISTRUST OF NAPOLEON ALL OVER BARBARY it was no wonder that Barbary frowned at the French attempt to send reinforcements cross-country to Egypt.

On June 23, 1801, a French squadron appeared off Derna, some five hundred miles off the Egyptian border. These ships carried four thousand soldiers. The optimistic plan was to put them ashore and march them overland to aid their countrymen in difficulty by the Nile. It was a very wild notion. It is true that Eaton, the inspired and perhaps unbalanced American, was able to make the same appalling march in the reverse direction, but Eaton's band were mostly local people, used to the desert. To dream of pushing four thousand Europeans across these wastes in midsummer was seeming madness.

From his ship the French general in charge addressed a letter to the bey of Derna explaining that he had come on the order of "The Great and Invincible Bonaparte" and that he proposed to go ashore and proceed along his way in all friendliness, giving no vexation to anyone in the Derna neighborhood and paying "cash on the nail in good gold money" for supplies and camel rent.

Derna's bey had his own ideas about permitting four thousand foreign soldiers to invade his territory. When a preliminary party of a few hundred rowed toward the shore, waving flags as token of peace and good will, Derna's best marksmen were bustling about upon the beach, shouting and beating a big drum. As soon as the small boats came within range they were targets for Derna's fire. In view of this hostile reception, the French general saw that there was no hope of a swift rush across country to Egypt and withdrew.

---

[5] "In 1808 his Minister of Marine, acting on his order, asked the Service of Archives of the Foreign Ministry to get up a 'documentation' on the Barbary States." Next year a reconnaissance by Col. Boutin helped the consul-general, Dubois-Thainville. "He brought back a very carefully studied plan for a debarcation at Sidi Ferruch and an expedition against Algiers." Charles-Roux, *Napoleon et la Tripolitaine*, p. 180.

Had the French chosen to fight a running battle over the sands to the Nile they would have found on arrival that they had made a futile sacrifice, for—all unknown to the army of reinforcements —Cairo had capitulated almost the same day that the squadron reached Derna. A few weeks later the French occupation of Egypt was officially over.

* * *

THE FRENCH WERE IN EGYPT ONLY THREE YEARS, BUT THE SIGNIFI-cance and the influence of their occupation were enduring. Not oñly did the French teach Egypt new ways of working and think-ing; far more vital to the destiny of Egypt and all Africa was the fact that Europeans had come and conquered and occupied the land. It was the beginning of that absorption of all Africa which was one of Europe's important activities in the hundred years to come.

* * *

AFRICA, "TIERCE PARTIE DU MONDE," ONE THIRD OF THE WORLD, AS Leo Africanus called it, had been a continent often invaded, often conquered in spots, but retaining a sort of integrity. Only under Rome had Africa been exploited in the modern sense, and then only in part. Presently would start among the nations of Europe a greedy race, known at the time as "The Scramble for Africa."

The Koran says, "The earth is God's: to such of his servants as He pleaseth doth He give it as a heritage" (sura VII). The taking over of Africa by Christian Europe was Africa's inescapable destiny. Exploration of her mysteries, conquest of her lands, ex-ploitation of her resources, control of her strategic points—all the developments which gradually turned Africa's whole original population from their former varied status into the lump we indiscriminately call "natives"—it was inevitable.

Africa was, in the Koran's phrase, Europe's heritage. Whether Africa has attained her final phase as a continent of colonies and protectorates the future will tell.

ENGLISH REPULSE IN EGYPT

A SHORT AND VERY GRIM CHAPTER IN THE STORY OF THE ENGLISH IN Egypt was written in 1807, six years after the collapse of the Napoleonic expedition and four years after the English withdrawal from Egypt, where they had been co-victors with the Turks.

This 1807 chapter was a disaster stained with the horridest of attendant circumstances. The English had attempted to come back. No sooner had they landed than misfortune started: bloody ambush at Rosetta, defeat a month later which eventuated in the surrender of the forces engaged and complete abandonment of the venture. The whole sad business had lasted six months. Some hundreds of English prisoners were marched through Cairo between a hedge of English heads, mounted on stakes.

One escapee from the British forces, a Highlander, fled with Mamluk protectors some two thousand miles up the Nile and then, alone and unhelped, made his way back to Cairo in safety. His story—if we had it in detail—would give us a thrillingly true notion of this tumultuous period in Egypt's history. But the nameless Highlander, so far as I know, never recorded his adventures. (Burckhardt mentions him briefly in his *Nubia*.) Another who escaped and who never told his story was the Scot, "Ibrahim Aga," who promptly and enthusiastically turned Mohammedan, became the devoted and very competent servitor of his new masters, held the highest of offices and at one time was actually governor of the very holy city of Medina.

LAST OF THE MAMLUKS

THE MAMLUKS WERE WRITHING IN THEIR LAST AGONY. RETRIBU-tion had caught up with them.

When the Napoleonic expedition withdrew the Mamluks came galloping back from their hide-outs, hoping to resume their old wild tyranny.

They had met an antagonist as ruthless and a good deal cleverer than they were. It was the renowned Mehemet Ali. (For the reader's convenience I retain the old-fashioned and distinctive spelling of his first name.) Mehemet Ali, an Albanian of modest origin, had been a member of the Turkish army which fought against France. In the days of his greatness he ruled an empire and set Europe by the ears. He grew strong enough to secure a hereditary claim to the governorship of Egypt, thus founding the dynasty of the khedives, forerunners to the present Egyptian kings.

Mehemet Ali made fools of the Mamluks. Sometimes he would

bargain to co-operate with them, as in 1807 when he induced some of them to help him eject the English. Sometimes he rounded on them. He trapped them to walk into his parlor in great groups to be massacred—not once, nor twice, but three times (1805, 1811, 1812). In the third massacre it was Mehemet Ali's son who enacted the part of spider. The survivors of the second massacre had run toward the south and, just beyond Luxor, some four hundred of them were so incredibly silly as to be victimized again by a variation of the old trick. Mehemet Ali's son, who was chasing them, approached their hiding place in the hills. There the Mamluk group, "cut off from all the comforts and luxuries of Egypt to which they had been accustomed," were foolish enough—despite what had happened to their mates the year before—to accept the invitation of Mehemet Ali's son to come down to his camp and talk things over with a view to being permitted to return to Cairo. On the way they were overcome and stripped of their clothes and armor, and arrived naked for the slaughter.

It is curious to observe how erstwhile ferocious fighters fall sometimes in their decline into a sort of second childhood. History shows many such cases. None odder than that of the Mamluks who had tyrannized over Egypt for nearly six centuries.

Southward across Nubia to Dongola what was left of them—less than five hundred—ran before the son of Mehemet Ali, by name Ibrahim. Their plight was pitiable. Mehemet Ali, not caring to sent troops any farther, put a strangle hold upon them by prohibiting the sending of gunpowder to the south. What we call a black market supplied a trickle of ammunition to the Mamluks in Dongola. To procure six dozen cartridges it was necessary to give a slave. They were isolated among semisavages. They had no money left and the fleshpots of the Egypt they had exploited and rooked through the centuries called to them. The fever of the southland, prevalent in summertime, killed off many. "Unable to bear the heat in their thick woolen dresses which they continued to wear," writes Burckhardt who passed near their retreat in 1814, "they constructed a number of rafts on board of which they passed the whole of the summer under awnings of mats kept continually wet by their slaves." Certain of them vowed that they would not cut their hair or beards until they returned to their former state of life in Cairo. They must have been as peculiar and melancholy a set of refugees as ever the world has seen.

*   *   *

SUCH WAS THE FINISH OF THE MAMLUKS. LITERALLY THE FINISH. There are believed to be no recognizable descendants of them in Egypt today. At no time, even when safe and powerful, had the Mamluk been a successful family man.

Possibly the Egyptian climate was unfavorable to the fertility of these foreigners from cooler lands. It is sometimes suggested that European families who have settled in Egypt die out in the second and third generation. There is an old wives' tale that Egyptian women never conceive to Europeans. Furthermore it is possible that the general violence and rowdy uncertainty of Mamluk life did not inspire the usual oriental desire for a large family. Browne observed they seldom had children: "of eighteen beys whose history I particularly knew only two had any children living."

GLIMPSES OF THE EASTERN SUDAN

THE COUNTRY UP THE NILE TO WHICH THE MAMLUKS FLED HAD had no contacts with Egypt for a long while. Between the days of Mamluk greatness when expeditions of conquest had driven up the Nile (see page 348) and the day when the draggletailed Mamluks came there as refugees, the Sudan had not been interfered with.

This up-Nile region, which has had so many different names through the ages, had by then taken on something like the pattern now designated as the Egyptian Sudan, and included several sections to be found on present-day maps, amongst them Dongola, Sennar, Kordofan and Darfur.

Dongola was alongside the main Nile stream (the White Nile) with two Dongola cities (old and new sites) both on the river. Sennar was a triangle between the White Nile and the Blue Nile and took in at its top corner the site of modern Khartoum. Kordofan was across the Nile to the westward. Darfur adjoined Kordofan yet farther west.

These sections had been in part Christian. Christianity had

disappeared and the population were *soi-disant* Mohammedans. But to judge by the observations of early travelers they did not, as a whole, take much notice of the sterner side of Islam's discipline. Viewed as a mass, they drank deep, lived a full and unrestricted love life, scrapped amongst themselves and piled up very little detailed history. They were not men of culture and high piety like the Sudanese of the West. As a whole they did not cherish their national and tribal traditions. They have no *tarikhs* to offer us, nor did they have any intellectual centers like Timbuctoo.

We gain our only idea of the eastern Sudan's way of life, during the centuries when Egypt left it alone, through European travelers who ventured up the Nile and got home to tell their story: amongst these, Bruce, the Scot; the Frenchman, Dr. Poncet; Browne, our young English friend; and the Swiss, Burckhardt.

Burckhardt tells us that, if one traveled up the Nile from about the Third Cataract to Sennar, he would pass by twenty-five different little kingdoms.

* * *

ON SENNAR WE HAVE THE REPORT OF DR. PONCET, WHO WAS THERE just before 1700, along with a cleric who wept at the realization that these people were once Christians and fell away merely for lack of priests to maintain their faith. Sennar City in the state of Sennar was a place of one hundred thousand. The king's residence had carpeted floors and a courtyard paved with a sort of delft tiling. You could buy a hen for a penny at Sennar! The government was semirepublican; when a king died the great council picked a successor from among the royal children. Then—presumably to keep the peace—they killed all the rest.

Bruce saw Sennar about seventy years later and reported that the kingdom was managed by the vizier, the king being a mere shadow. Bruce was called in to act as medical adviser to the king's forty wives, whose thoroughgoing fashion of presenting their persons for his examination made the Scot nervous, he fearing the king might at any moment appear.

At about that time the ambitious vizier decided to take over Kordofan on the opposite side of the Nile. Local tradition represents him as proceeding in a quite modern manner by sowing disunion amongst Kordofan's tribes and then stepping in to

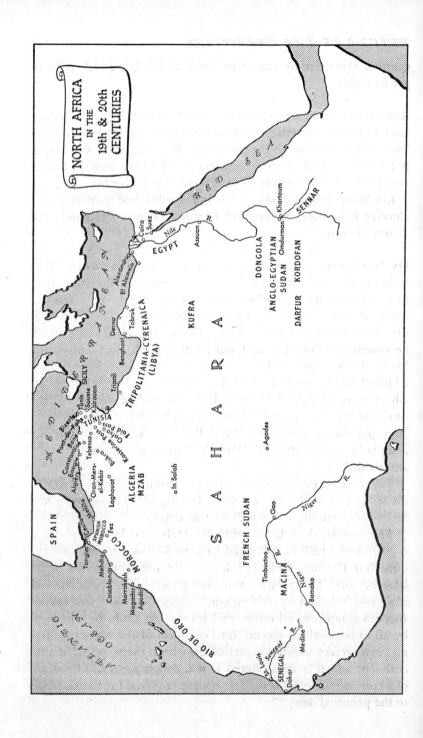

NORTH AFRICA
IN THE
19th & 20th
CENTURIES

conquer them one by one under pretext of helping each tribe to get its rights.

* * *

KORDOFAN WAS ON A LOWER STAGE OF DEVELOPMENT. JUST A MERRY land where sex morals played so little part that its people were "not only indifferent to the amours of their daughters and sisters, but even attached to their seducers," and where *merissa* flowed very freely. *Merissa* was one of the names for native beer.

Kordofan was unlucky in being sandwiched between two cleverer neighbors, Sennar and Darfur, and was alternately the victim of each.

* * *

ON DARFUR WE HAVE FULL AND PICTURESQUE INFORMATION. THIS is due to the misfortunes of the young adventurer, Browne, who—first of Europeans to see the country—went there in 1793 and was detained there virtually a captive for nearly three years. This was due to an embarrassing contretemps soon after his arrival, which he describes: "One day, as I was reading in the hut, one of the house slaves, a girl of fifteen, came to the door, when—from a whim of the moment—I seized the cloth that was round her waist which dropped and left her naked. Chance so determined that the owner of the slave passed." A hullabaloo followed: an infidel had damaged the property of a True Believer. Such alone was the complaint against Browne. Darfur's abstract moral code was not affronted.

Browne was impoverished by heavy reparations and he became the subject of dangerous notoriety. During his enforced long stay he had opportunity to study Darfur in detail.

The country had been definitely Mohammedan for about a century and a half, he estimated from traditions communicated to him. But Darfur's Mohammedanism did not seem to be of an irksome sort. The people even maintained a few pensioned-off idols and indulged in old-fashioned human sacrifice on occasion. Incest was not a social crime, and love scenes could be witnessed by all as one walked abroad, for "the form of the houses secures no great secrecy to what is carried on within them, yet what concealment which is thus offered is not always sought. The shade of a tree or long grass is the sole temple required for the sacrifices to the primeval deity."

Dancing, "both grave and lascivious," was Darfur's joy. Slaves even danced in their leg irons. As for drink: "a company often sits from sunrise to sunset drinking and conversing till a single man sometimes carries off two gallons of the liquor called *bouza.*"

All this gaiety did not prevent a certain commercial efficiency. Caravans went regularly to Egypt or Tunis and back. Exports were slaves and exotic animal products—ivory, rhinoceros horns, hippopotamus teeth, and whips made of hippopotamus hide, ostrich feathers, parakeets and monkeys.

*　　*　　*

DARFUR'S IDYLLIC LIFE WAS NOT DESTINED TO ENDURE. AN AMBItious reformer came to power—the usurping sultan, Abd-er-Rahman, with whom Browne had so much trouble at the time of his little indiscretion. Abd-er-Rahman was a stern man who had only a scant two hundred wives, the predecessor whose children he had despoiled having possessed a thousand and had been so uxorious that he would take five hundred along with him when he went on a journey!

Abd-er-Rahman introduced a shocking novelty: the prohibition of strong drink, issuing an order (March, 1795) punishing its use by death in the case of males, and compulsory head shaving, if females. All houses were to be searched and the utensils for making *merissa* and *bouza* destroyed. The ways were prickly with bits of broken-up earthen jars, but the well-to-do managed to go on drinking. The sultan was hated.

Later the serpent of evil knowledge whispered into the sultan's ear. He heard rumors about guns. He had never seen a gun, but conceived the idea that, if he had such weapons, he could conquer straight across country and secure Sennar and its reputed gold mines. He sent an emissary to Cairo which resulted in the dispatch toward Darfur of four little brass cannon, six-pounders. This was after Browne managed to get away from Darfur and he did not know whether the little cannon ever got there. Subsequent events suggest that they did not.

CONQUESTS UP THE NILE

DARFUR'S DREAM OF A FAR-FLUNG SUDANESE EMPIRE WAS REALIZED and exceeded by another, by Mehemet Ali of Egypt.

In the early 1820's he sent three of his family—two sons and a son-in-law—into the Sudan with troops. The venture was a military success, but tragic in its eventual results.

The son-in-law, known by the name of his function as "The Defterdar" (treasurer general) went west of the Nile. The army which opposed him was quaintly ill assorted. Darfur's cavalry wore armor—pointed steel helmets and coats of mail. Their horses wore plates of copper on their heads and were gay with ostrich plumes. Darfur's associates, the men of Kordofan, were naked except for a loin scarf. The women of Kordofan mingled with their men, singing war songs and dancing. Many women fought and died in the battle.

The cavalry put The Defterdar's horsemen to flight. But The Defterdar had artillery and musketeers with whom he attacked Kordofan's naked soldiers. These had never heard the thunder of guns. Their bravery in the face of this appalling novelty was glorious. Although many fell, dead and mutilated, the rest rushed forward and cut down the artillery men at the big guns. "They obtained a brief possession of them and, had they known how to turn them on the flying enemy, the day might have been theirs. The fire of the infantry brought them down in ranks and at last they were obliged to retire and abandon the captured guns. The wounded placed their fingers in their wounds, wondering how they could have been made, so ignorant were they of the effect of firearms." (This is from a local account of the battle which was communicated to Petherick a generation later.)

* * *

AGAIN NEW WEAPONS HAD MADE HUMAN COURAGE FUTILE. THE same through the ages ever since first a man discovered he could cup his hand round a stone and injure his amazed enemy by jerking it through the air. The Hyksos horse-drawn chariots vanquished the Egyptians. It is proof of the happy isolation of the eastern Sudan that firearms, which had crushed the western Sudan over two hundred years earlier, did not reach Kordofan until the nineteenth century.

Meanwhile the two sons of Mehemet Ali fought to the east of the Nile.

Khartoum was then founded, as capital for the projected Egyptian-owned Sudan of Mehemet Ali's dream. Its name meant "elephant's trunk" from the odd-shaped peninsula which pokes between the White Nile and the Blue. It was a magnificent situation for practical purposes and a romantic site as well, being the place of the reluctant mating of two great rivers. For some distance after their junction the waters refuse to mingle. The old Arabic fable was that their waters furiously combated one another for nearly a day's journey. A medieval investigator took water from the White Nile and poured it into the dark waters of the Blue Nile where "it fell like milk and it was an hour before the waters mixed."

*   *   *

SHENDI, A LITTLE TO THE NORTH OF KHARTOUM, WAS PRESENTLY the scene of a terrible drama. Ismail, the younger son, appeared there one night in October, 1822, and ordered the recently deposed kinglet of the place, Sheikh Nimir (The Tiger) to get together for delivery next morning a preposterously large number of horses and cattle as a contribution to the conquerors.

Nimir begged in vain for time, was refused, and then cooked up and executed a courageous but childish scheme. He would murder Ismail and set Shendi free. The leading men of Shendi agreed to co-operate. So the soldiers of the invader were offered *merissa* by every householder and soon made drunkenly unsuspicious. At midnight the people of Shendi set fire to all sides of the flimsy place where the prince slept and burnt him alive. The scared soldiery, coming out of their stupor, fled the town.

*   *   *

THE DEFTERDAR, WHO HAD JUST MOPPED UP THE REGION WEST OF the Nile, came hurrying to avenge his brother-in-law. The manner in which he punished Shendi was something never forgotten. Afterward they said in the Sudan—and they had that monster, The Defterdar, primarily in mind—"Where a Turk has set his foot no grass will grow!" (Egyptians in that region were then called Turks, after their titular masters.) We can well believe that The Defterdar thought of hideous and novel fashions of torturing the population which had murdered his relative. He had always been a man of perverse wit in such matters. An instance (from Petherick): One day at Khartoum there came before him a native woman complaining that one of his soldiers had stolen a jug of milk from her. She pointed out the suspect, who denied the charge. She insisted. He would soon know the truth, declared The Defterdar, and if she had picked the wrong fellow she would lose her head. Then he made an expressive sign with his finger and the soldier was thrown to the ground and his stomach slashed open. The old woman had been right! The Defterdar smiled and tossed her a dollar.

His having dollars to toss might puzzle the reader. The Spanish dollar was then current in the region. The natives set greater value to those which bore several strokes after the king's name. Burckhardt says he saw at Shendi "a blacksmith secretly employed in adding a 'I' to the Charles III dollars" and thus adding a sixth to their buying power.

When The Defterdar had finished Shendi was no more. There is another city there now by the same name. Old Shendi had been a pleasant place and prosperous, and one of the largest market towns in the eastern Sudan. Burckhardt spent a month there nine years before its annihilation and speaks of Sheikh Nimir, "The Tiger," as a free trader who extorted no taxes from visiting merchants, which made Shendi a popular caravan center. He was mild in government, the maximum sentence being two or three days in prison or a small fine. There was a good deal of drinking and "no night passed without my hearing the loud songs of some *bouza* meeting." The people were clean and well dressed and the women of easy morals kept off the streets. Our informant adds, "The most fashionable among them fixed the price of her favors at a loaf of sugar." Sugar, by the way, was chewed neat, not mixed into sweetmeats or used in cookery. At Shendi it was accounted an elegant luxury item.

Previously to Nimir, "The Tiger," Shendi had been ruled by a woman, Settina (meaning "Our Lady"). I have wondered whether she may have suggested "She" to Rider Haggard.

THOSE OLD SOFT DAYS

THE DESTRUCTION AND GREAT CRUELTY SUFFERED BY THE SUDAN was a tragedy relatively small compared with the long-continued misery resulting from Mehemet Ali's conquest. Consequent upon his several expeditions into the Upper Nile country—there were subsequent missions sent, notably in 1839-41—was the immense development of the slave trade. A source of supply had been opened, a new door crashed into Negroland. Four centuries before the ships that ventured down Africa's west coast had crashed a similar door on the other side of Africa. Now all Negroland was open and in danger.

*   *   *

THE GROWTH AND CIRCUMSTANCES OF SLAVERY SCANDALIZED THE Christian world. Folk were then sensible to horror. Were I writing this book previous to the 1939-45 war I would feel, if I instanced typical, distressing items about the old slave trade, I would be addressing readers of similar mentality to the sensitive folk of other days. But of late we have forgotten how to shudder. Stories of mass deportations of slave laborers, of the perverse cruelty of concentration camps have become a commonplace to us. If we are to understand the mood of the early nineteenth century, we must make an effort of imagination. Only so can we comprehend the burning desire to interfere in Africa, which shaped in part the continent's history. Try to picture the reaction when, upon ears unfamiliar with such abuses, there fell tales of families torn asunder, villages depopulated, slaves whipped across country like cattle or jammed in the awful stench of the "Middle Passage" on slave ships.

Our forefathers in their innocence of unnatural cruelty, to which we have become hardened, were nauseated at accounts of the manufacture of eunuchs (see page 127) and of the indescribable mutilation of girl slaves.[6] They heard with indignation about the extent of the slave trade, trifling to the millions of such victims in World War II, but running into annual thousands which were to them shocking and disgusting.

*   *   *

MEHEMET ALI'S EXPEDITIONS AND CONQUESTS UP THE NILE OPENED the great South-North Slave Road. The slave trade via this route, with its outlet in the Asiatic market, was more difficult to arrest

---

[6] Browne (published 1799), p. 349, supplies detail on "an artificial impediment . . . with a view to prevent coition." Burckhardt (published 1819), p. 332, "girls in this state are worth more . . . often suffered to remain in this state during the whole of their lives." Titles of both works appear in the Bibliography.

than the transatlantic trade starting from the West Coast. Agitation rose over the situation in the eastern Sudan. Sincere pity and hysteria both played their part. There may even have been some of that calculated playing upon popular indignation which politicians use to justify invasion and occupation of foreign lands.

All in all, Mehemet Ali's southern conquests led indirectly to the occupation of his own country.

It is worth noting that there was nothing accidental about Mehemet Ali's development of the slave business. One of his leading motives in pushing into Africa was to kidnap blacks to be used as soldiers. These Negroes were formed into regiments and, ably trained by a French ex-colonel turned Mohammedan who was known as "Suleiman Pasha," they became the strongest rung in Mehemet Ali's ladder of success. The growth of the slave trade was an outcome of the kidnaping of potential soldiers. As the trade developed Khartoum became a vast slave mart.

THE MIGHT OF MEHEMET ALI

MEHEMET ALI'S ACTIVITIES IN AFRICA MADE EGYPT MASTER OF A wider empire on that continent than she had possessed even under the most venturesome of his predecessors. His African adventures were only part of this turbulent person's lifetime effort. His conquests and campaigns and intrigues outside the continent concern general European history. His rebellion against Turkey's titular authority was like the attack of a blowfly which points out decay. Mehemet Ali showed Turkey's feebleness to the world. Soon the world would learn to call the Turkish sultan "The Sick Man of Europe."

With the nineteenth century we come to a time when Africa is often closely involved with European jealousies and politics. Such things are outside the scope of this book and I shall only hint at them in passing.

The single non-African exploit of Mehemet Ali's which should not be omitted from North Africa's history is his disciplining of the Wahabi. The fighting took place in Arabia, but the sentiment of the dispute affected all Islam and concerns Africa.

At the beginning of the nineteenth century the Mohammedan

world was startled by the sudden rise of a new sect, the Wahabi, named after its teacher, Mohammed-ibn-Abd-Wahab. This teacher had inspired a vigorous disciple who—starting with a band of seven men—built up a mighty force. This disciple was the first of the famous Ibn-Sauds. A scion of the same family rules in Arabia today.

By 1803 the Wahabi had taken Mecca. Furthermore, invigorated by their special dislike to pomp and display at tombs, they had performed what the rest of the Mohammedan world regarded as acts of wicked desecration at Mecca and elsewhere. Their enemies said that the desecration was motivated by greed and that sixty camel loads of costly objects had been torn away from Islam's holy places and confiscated, in the Wahabi process of restoring primitive simplicity.

Mehemet Ali, the most vigorous Mohammedan individual of the day, went to Arabia to interfere. The subduing of the Wahabi was costly in men and took years. The Wahabi fought like furies. At the Battle of Bissel, the culminating Wahabi defeat, groups of their warriors met the Egyptian charge in solid masses, having first chained themselves together. Soon after (1818) their chief, Abdallah—one of the Ibn-Saud family—capitulated, was brought as prisoner to Cairo along with a portion of the jewels his father had removed from Mecca, and was finally beheaded in Turkey by the sultan.

A hundred and thirty years later we see the President of the United States conferring the Legion of Merit on one of the same Saud family, now ruling in Arabia and friend of the Allies in World War II. The Wahabi sect, once regarded as a shocking innovation, now ranks high. Said Ibn-Saud in 1929 at a banquet given to distinguished pilgrims, "We are not the champions of a new way. . . . What Mohammedans need is not novelty but a return to the purity of old time principles." This is reported by Dinet, a French Mohammedan, who was a guest at the banquet.

THE RESTLESS PASHA

THE LIBERATION OF MECCA AND THE OTHER HOLY SPOTS MADE Mehemet Ali's reputation. He was a man of restless ambition, turning the life of his Turkish overlord into a misery. His campaigns in Syria brought him almost into Europe. His armies came close to Constantinople. European powers alternately petted and thwarted him. He never became a recognized king, but did succeed in establishing a hereditary claim to the rulership of Egypt under the vague supervision of Turkey. His line rules in Egypt today.

A less familiar manifestation of Mehemet Ali's itching greed for power was his alleged plan to capture the whole of North Africa right to the Atlantic. Tripoli was in a state of frenzied alarm— quite needless, as it turned out. To launch his scheme Mehemet Ali tried to come to an understanding with France—then in a very bad temper with the dey of Algiers. The understanding he sought was that, for a consideration, he would chastise the dey on France's behalf. Presumably such a deal would have meant the start of Mehemet Ali's great All-Africa empire. But the deal was balked.

He was a planner of peacetime activities as well as of campaigns for conquest. Not only did he reorganize Egypt's army on European lines, fortify Alexandria and Cairo, and set about endowing Egypt with a fleet. He also started to remake Egypt on the lines of a civilized European land.

His most far-reaching accomplishment was the development of cotton in Egypt. The Sudan had been raising cotton and its women spinning in their traditional fashion "with a small spindle made of a thin piece of reed placed in a broken bit of earthenware with a hole in the centre to contain the spindle." Mehemet Ali saw the possibilities, and under the management of a Frenchman Egypt's cotton helped make Mehemet Ali rich.

Within a decade of taking charge of the country he doubled its revenue. Also, in the heartless manner common to previous Egyptian rulers, he extorted immense sums from the people for himself. His annual income was said by Burckhardt to be from two and a half to three million pounds sterling.

He was very eager to find coal somewhere in his possessions and employed a French searcher and a Welsh engineer in the hunt. To the latter, Petherick, he explained that he longed for coal so as to be able to make guns and steam engines and "to feel myself independent of England." He was scarce in the saddle as Egypt's ruler when he set up a musket factory. He possessed a gunpowder manufactory run by an Italian. Also a distillery of rum operated by an Englishman.

He is said to have foreseen England's role in Egypt. "England," he remarked, "will take Egypt some day as her share of the Ottoman Empire." Incidentally an offer was made by the czar, Nicholas I, to England a decade before the Crimean War, that England should take Egypt (and Crete) with his blessing, provided he got certain privileges elsewhere. The offer was declined. Sir Harry Johnston says this refusal was a blunder and that England has "been the poorer for it by many millions of money and many brave men."

HE COLLECTED FOREIGNERS

MEHEMET ALI HAD A CATHOLIC TASTE IN FOREIGNERS, LIKED THE French best, but surrounded himself by persons of all nations. A Frenchman was instructor to his fleet. A Frenchman turned Mohammedan, as I have mentioned, trained his black troops, and a Scottish Mohammedan held high office. His engineer-in-chief was a Belgian. Assorted foreigners accompanied his Sudanese expeditions. He was on the lookout for talent. One can read how he sent for bright young men who attracted his notice, as, for instance, Lyon, the explorer, who received and refused an offer to quit his English employment and come work for Egypt with "a most generous allowance." Egypt saw men from all Europe, and men of all sorts: idealists like the Saint-Simonian group of French socialists, practical artisans, and sober men of science. Also a horde of adventurers: it was a paradise for the bright young crooks of the day.

He established schools to teach foreign languages and learning to Egyptian boys, and sent a band of youths to Paris to study. He showed periodical publishers a point when, having decided to start a newspaper and having discovered that it was unlikely to have enough subscribers, he made subscribing to it compulsory upon all government employees earning above a certain salary.

EGYPTIAN HOSPITALITY

THE MATTER OF THE MUCH DISCUSSED SUEZ CANAL PUZZLED Mehemet Ali. The project which so deeply interested Napoleon was urged upon Mehemet Ali by the French. The Saint-Simonians, an idealistic band—fifteen of whom died in Egypt of plague and other ills while striving to push their cherished plan—saw the canal not as a mere commercial venture, but as "The Union of Two Seas," which would bring the Mohammedan and the Christian world together in a beautiful friendship.

Mehemet Ali was more worldly wise and saw the canal as a potential troublemaker. England was against the canal. Turkey also. Perhaps he saw little benefit in it even for Egypt. Professor Gautier suggests he may have thought it would be a mistake for Egypt voluntarily to take on a burden as embarrassing and frictional as the Bosphorus. He preferred another Napoleonic plan, the Nile barrage at the Delta, and startled a good many sober folk by suggesting that the Pyramids be torn down to get suitable stone.

As a substitute for the canal an overland route was developed from the Mediterranean to the Red Sea. Travelers left one ship at Alexandria, proceeded via a minor canal, and via the Nile to Cairo, from Cairo took two-wheeled, four-horse vans to Suez, and there connected with another ship. This route, it is said, brought fifteen thousand persons across Egypt every year, a profitable and educational stream, probably superior in value to the country to what a canal would have been.

Christian Europeans began to be treated with more kindness. Mehemet Ali wanted it so, and also they were observed to be paying guests. European women were still in danger of being stoned if they appeared abroad with unveiled faces, and European men—if they met an Egyptian high official in the streets—were expected to dismount and salute him with the right hand across the heart. Occasionally a Christian would be spat upon. But it was a great change from the wild old days of the latter Mamluks when a Christian, passing before some especially holy building, was liable to be seized and circumcised. Even in the early days of Mehemet Ali's governorship Cairo's streets were a terror to travelers. An Italian, Belzoni, though in Egypt as Mehemet Ali's employee, was shot at in the street by a petty officer. Belzoni's comment was that some Cairo folk "would murder a European with as much indifference as they would kill an insect."

*   *   *

BELZONI, INCIDENTALLY, WAS ONE OF MEHEMET ALI'S MOST EX-traordinary foreign employees and was a spectacular character in his day. He was a man of six foot seven with an English wife, big in proportion. The two had been performers in street shows in London. He went to Egypt to install a water system in the gardens of the seraglio and, though quite uncultured, subsequently became a "digger" of some repute, shipping home antique Egyptian wonders for display in London at the old Egyptian Hall in Picadilly. His final phase was an attempt to discover the unknown but tantalizing city of Timbuctoo. He perished of sickness (1823) in a native village of Africa's west coast. Curiously he died close to one of the mouths of the Niger River, for whose outlet explorers were then searching. He did not know that he had almost found it. Quite a career.

*   *   *

BELZONI TELLS AN APPALLING ANECDOTE OF DANGEROUS CAIRO before Mehemet Ali's reforms: "A charming young lady of sixteen years of age," he writes, "daughter of the Chevalier Boety, now consul-general of Sweden, went out of her house in company with her mother, sister and some other ladies to go to the baths. They formed a cavalcade on asses and had not proceeded far from their door when they met a soldier who took a pistol from his belt and with the greatest coolness fired and killed the young lady." Belzoni adds with quaintly expressed sarcasm, "This is quite enough surely to invite young European ladies to the country."

Mehemet Ali caused the murderer to be executed. Within a few years European travelers were commenting upon "the perfect security" of the country.

JUNE 9, 1788

ONE JUNE EVENING IN 1788 SOMETHING HAD HAPPENED IN A LONDON tavern which had profoundly affected Africa.

The age-old curiosity about the mysteries within the Dark

Continent had come suddenly to a boil and a group of Englishmen had banded together to subsidize investigation. They named their enterprise, The Association for Promoting the Discovery of the Interior Parts of Africa, and usually referred to it as The African Association. So a private, nonmilitary, nonpolitical and non-commercial effort to explore Africa repeated the attempt of the Nasamonian youths after more than two thousand years. The difference was however that the Nasamonians did their own exploring (see page 132) while the members of the African Association hired young men to do it for them. Their association was the forerunner of geographic societies, which did not concentrate exclusively on Africa, of which the Paris society was the first. The African Association lived for some forty years and then merged with the Royal Geographical Society of London. America set up a geographical society in 1852.

The members of the African Association each agreed to subscribe five guineas a year for three years to finance exploration. Their prospectus declared that Africa's interior "is still but a wide extended blank, on which the geographer, on the authority of Leo Africanus and Edrisi, has traced with a hesitating hand a few names of unexplored rivers and of uncertain nations," and that "almost the whole of Africa is unvisited and unknown." By the investment of about seventy-five dollars each this group of imaginative persons bought the splendid and romantic privilege of financing the unveiling—or the attempted unveiling—of the African mystery.

Their work and the work of their successors and imitators has gradually mapped Africa. Explorers were the pioneers. Commerce and conquest followed. Therefore it seems to me that the evening of June 9th, 1788, was a very important date in African history.

NILE AND NIGER

TO GEOGRAPHERS THE MYSTERIES TO BE FIRST ATTACKED CONCERNED the two great rivers, Nile and Niger. Where did the Nile come from? Where did the Niger go to? To the ordinary European of the day, the man in the street, the mystery of Timbuctoo with its "roofs of gold" was even more tantalizing.

Much was already known about the upper reaches of the Nile.

The various missions of Mehemet Ali were presently to find out more. The precise location of its source was not certain until 1862.

The Niger was far more intriguing. When the African Association started, the river was nothing but a name. "The course of the Niger, the places of its rise and termination and even its existence as a separate stream are still undetermined," complained the association.

AN ADVENTURER FROM CONNECTICUT

THE ASSOCIATION'S FIRST EMISSARY DID NOTHING TO ENDANGER Africa's privacy. He was the first and one of the many victims to the cause of privately organized African exploration. He was the American, John Ledyard, seemingly just the man for the job, and it is distressing to have to record his death before he made even a step into the unknown. His mission was to go to Cairo, up the Nile to Sennar and then strike across the African continent to the Atlantic, investigating the Niger en route. When the African Association invited him to tackle this stupendous journey quite alone, he accepted enthusiastically. When they asked him when he would be ready to start, he replied, "Tomorrow morning!"

America never bred a more whole-souled adventurer. Born a Connecticut Yankee (the Nile was not a mite more impressive than the Connecticut River, he maintained), he attended Dartmouth for a time, contemplated becoming a minister, went to sea instead and was a member of Captain Cook's great Third Voyage. He was a friend of Jefferson's in Paris and once entered into an adventurous business deal with Paul Jones. His life had been full of hazardous travel and hardship. If the extravagantly far-flung mission entrusted to him could have been performed by anyone it seems as if Ledyard should have been that man. But he was reckless in all things. In Cairo on the eve of departure into the unknown he felt bilious and made a truly weird experiment in self-doctoring. He took "a powerful dose of acid of vitriol, and the sudden uneasiness and burning pain which followed this incautious draught"—I am quoting from the Association's records —"impelled him to seek relief in the violent action of the strongest Tartar emetic." It was Ledyard's last adventure.

He is said to have been a wild but polite person with a streak of gentleness and a great deal of charm. "I have always remarked," he wrote, "that women in all countries are civil, obliging, tender and humane, and that they do not hesitate like men to perform a generous action. To women, whether civilized or savage, I never addressed myself in the language of decency and friendship without receiving a decent and friendly answer."

Ledyard's life by Jared Sparks was published in 1828. The *Quarterly Review* of July-October, 1828, has a puzzled but appreciative article about this odd American cousin who died in England's service. The *Proceedings* of the African Association (1790) tells of the Association's dealings with him and describes. him as one "formed by Nature for achievements of hardihood and peril."

FIRST VIEW OF THE NIGER

OTHER LOSSES AND ABORTED JOURNEYS FOLLOWED. THEN THE brilliant exploit of Mungo Park who actually saw the Niger (1796), thus proving that it did exist "as a separate stream." He did not find out where it went to. The motto for his second, tragic expedition: "If I do not succeed . . . I shall at least die in the Niger," proved but too true.

Almost simultaneously with Park's first expedition a German employee of the Association, Horneman, vanished. This earnest and vigorous young man, whose boast was that he knew sickness only as the name of something which happened to other people, and who prepared himself by Arabic and Koranic study and by causing himself to be circumcised, was in Cairo awaiting departure for inner Africa when Napoleon surprised Egypt. This did not stop Horneman. He saw the conqueror, explained his project and won Napoleon's support. He then set off on a preliminary journey and got as far as Fezzan, hitherto unknown to European travelers. There he sickened with fever, proving himself human after all, and turned back. Presently he made a fresh start, sure that he would clean up the Niger mystery and see Timbuctoo. That was the end of Horneman. Uncertain reports and rumors came through. Some said he had died in mid-Africa. Some that he had settled in a land beyond the Niger and become a local holy man. A generation after his disappearance another explorer met a man

in the African interior who claimed to be Horneman's son. He
called himself Musa ben-Yusuf (the son of Yusuf, which was
Horneman's Moslem alias) and was a person of noticeably superior
intelligence. Perhaps Horneman fell in love with Africa, "went
native," and forgot his sponsors in England. Perhaps he was
detained a prisoner. Perhaps he perished. The Association waited
for him patiently but in vain.

The Swiss, Burckhardt, whose remarks on Egypt and Nubia I
have sometimes quoted, was another of their young men. Burckhardt trained so long and carefully for the great adventure of
exploring inner Africa that he became inhibited. He became like
the well-known centipede in the ditch. He spent over eight years
in Cairo and the Near East and Nubia in various studies and
practices. His accounts of Mecca and Nubia are famous. "In the
intervals of his studies he exercised himself by long journeys on
foot bareheaded in the heat of the sun, sleeping upon the ground,
and living upon vegetables and water." His letters to England
were full of requests for more money to complete his apprentice-
ship and of requests for indulgence at his delay in making a start.
He died at Cairo, babbling on his deathbed of his hopes to get to
Timbuctoo and the countries of the Niger.

TWO COMMON LITTLE RUNTS

SOME THIRTY YEARS HAD PASSED SINCE THE JUNE EVENING OF 1788,
and the Niger still rolled its mysterious course, no one knew
where, and Timbuctoo was still a mere tantalizing name.

It is curious that the actual discovery of where the Niger went,
and what Timbuctoo was really like—which explorations had been
attempted by so many upstanding and learned men—should both
eventually have been performed by common little runts: one an
ex-servant of another explorer (English), the other a poor little
ignorant, French free-lance adventurer.

Lander found the Niger's mouth in 1830. It was comprehensible
that it had been hard to find. It was not to be expected that a
river would run for twenty-six hundred miles over an almost
complete circle, so that source and mouth were only some eleven
hundred miles apart.

The course of the Niger was a burning question previous to

Lander's discovery. Perhaps no geographical problem was ever so much discussed. It seems today to have been a rather futile excitement. But geography's big mysteries are now all solved and it is hard to understand the mood of other days. Some of us, however, remember the fuss when the North Pole was reached, something of even less potential value than the course of the Niger to the ordinary person.

About the Niger there were several theories which now seem silly indeed. Probably the most widely held was that the Niger and the Nile were the same river, the Niger running into the Nile somewhere in the Tropic Zone. A few of the many other theories: that the Niger was the upper part of the Congo River; that it evaporated in the desert; that it flowed into Lake Chad and was lost.

* * *

LANDER, WHO FOUND OUT THE TRUTH, THAT THE NIGER EMPTIED into the Gulf of Guinea, had been Clapperton's servant on his second and fatal expedition. Clapperton on his earlier expedition had been a member of the first European party to report a trans-Saharan crossing. They had discovered Lake Chad and christened it Lake Waterloo, a name which—had it stuck—would have been very displeasing to the present masters of the region, the French.

Lander, when he traveled as Clapperton's servant in the African wilds, was called by the natives "The Little Christian" (*Nasara Currami*). He had been a "gentleman's gentleman" since he was eleven years old, a remarkable little man, who declared, "There was a charm in the very sound of 'Africa' that always made my heart flutter on hearing it mentioned." No valet in soul was he!

Clapperton died in his arms. Lander got back to England to tell the story and shortly thereafter (1830) left again for Africa, this time his own master on a government mission to find out where the Niger went. His instructions from Downing Street show how complete was still the Niger mystery. Lander was told to follow the river, that—if it emptied into Lake Chad—he was to go home via Fezzan and Tripoli, and—if it led him to the Atlantic —he should return by ship.

The payment offered does not seem to accord with the importance and danger of the hunt: as an advance, his outfit and two hundred dollars cash; plus "if absolutely necessary, a further sum not exceeding three hundred dollars. He was promised five hundred dollars as a prize if he brought the Niger's mouth home in his pocket. But Lander, the queer little servant whose heart fluttered at the very word, "Africa," was paid in more exalted coin than mere money. He followed the Niger to the Atlantic. The Niger mystery was solved.

*   *   *

CAILLIÉ, THE OTHER COMMON LITTLE MAN WHO SUCCEEDED WHERE imposing figures had failed or perished, got to Timbuctoo in 1828, starting his journey from the Guinea coast and returning with his report via the Sahara and Tangier, thus performing the longest journey over new ground yet accomplished by an African explorer. It was a journey of terrible difficulty, still hard going as I can testify myself, having followed his route rather closely in preparing myself to write the first account of Caillié ever to appear in English.

The sum laid out in financing Lander seems skinny. Nothing at all was laid out on Caillié. He discovered Timbuctoo at his own expense, using money he had saved up for his dream. He was a man with an *idée fixe*—to discover Timbuctoo. He was frail of physique. He contracted scurvy and a painful disease of the feet, but he tramped on and on, never faltering, never forgetting the role of an Egyptian Mohammedan which he had assumed. He and Lander carried big wills in little bodies.

*   *   *

THE QUESTION OF THE DISCOVERY OF TIMBUCTOO IS COMPLICATED. The dictionary definition of discover: to find and bring to the knowledge of the world, fits only Caillié who gave the world its first real story about a place made famous by Arab fantasy and vague native tales. But Caillié was not a clear-cut discoverer in the sense that he was the first European to visit Timbuctoo. Other Europeans had seen the city. There were many renegades in the Moroccan army of conquest: A Florentine trader is known to have been there in the fifteenth century. A French captive named Imbert was taken there from Morocco by his master in the seventeenth century. None of these persons supplied the world with any information. On the other hand, an American oddity—either a crook or a victim of delusions—supplied a vast amount of absurd detail about Timbuctoo without having been there at all. His book, *The Narrative of Robert Adams, a Sailor who was wrecked on the western coast of Africa in the year 1810, was detained three years in Slavery by the Arabs of the Great Desert, and resided several months in the City of Timbuctoo,* was published in London in 1816. The book fooled some of the wise men of the day, was intentionally issued in matching format to that telling Mungo Park's immortal story of lone adventure, but evidently did not convince the public as a whole, for the Timbuctoo search went on.

In addition to these European glimpses and alleged glimpses of the mysterious town there is a possibility that certain Portuguese emissaries managed to reach Timbuctoo at the end of the fifteenth century. This nation, however, was then so secretive about its discoveries, classing them as so much national wealth, not to be shared, that—even if they did get there—the world would have been no wiser.

But the performance which outstandingly caused discussion as to the Timbuctoo discovery was the arrival there and death near by of Laing, a Scottish explorer, almost two years before Caillié got there. Laing's papers were lost; his exploit had not advanced the world's knowledge of the mysterious town, except to emphasize that it was a fanatical and dangerous place. But English bitterness was great and there were charges that Caillié had employed Laing's lost papers' in preparing his day-by-day journal of the route. A foolish charge, since—even if Caillié had wanted to do so, and even if he had been able to get hold of the Laing papers—they would have been of no more use to him than a guidebook of Egypt would be to a person seeking to fake up a story of travel in Russia. Laing's route and Caillié's coincided only at Timbuctoo and the near vicinity.

THE LONG WAY TO TIMBUCTOO

CAILLIÉ'S ROUTE WAS FROM THE ATLANTIC TO THE UPPER NIGER, and downstream to Timbuctoo. Laing started from Tripoli on the Mediterranean and got to Timbuctoo by crossing the desert.

Tripoli was then a favored jumping-off place for explorers. The rest of Barbary was impossibly inimical to Christian travelers. The people of Tripoli were "better disposed to Christians than in any other part of Africa," in the opinion of Colonel Warrington, English consul and long-time resident in Tripoli. Tripoli could supply explorers with credentials for use along the road since she exercised something like a general chaperonage over the adjacent desert and even over parts of the Sudan. The sultan of Bornu, near Lake Chad, had been a hostage at Tripoli; the king of Wadai, farther to the east in mid-Africa, had been a slave there and had procured his freedom through Warrington's influence. Fezzan, the oasis group in the near Sahara, was a dependency of Tripoli—its ruler was called "sultan" at home, but shrank to the rank of mere governor when he visited his overlord.

At Tripoli Laing married the daughter of Consul Warrington and two days later plunged into the unknown, never to see his bride again.

He proceeded to Ghadames, so far as I know the first European to see the old desert city since Roman days. We have no detailed account of what he saw there, the first European report of Ghadames being that of Richardson's who was there twenty years later.

The local people, Richardson says, claimed that their city was very, very old, that it was founded four thousand years before by Nimrod and Abraham. For once African tradition, so inclined to brag of the antiquity of its home town, was modest. It is possible that Ghadames was a station of what is called Capsian culture in prehistoric days. It is certain that a bas-relief found there is characteristically early Egyptian.

Sidi Okba was at Ghadames on his triumphant rush through Africa. The emperor, Kankan-Musa, rested there on his glittering pilgrimage. Ghadames was a much-frequented junction point in the north Sahara, peopled by the shrewd, careful and well to do. Even its date palm garden was walled. It had houses five stories high and its streets had been covered against the great heat and were like tunnels. Traders and pilgrims from all Africa sojourned at Ghadames and six different languages were in current use.

*   *   *

LAING'S VISIT WAS REMEMBERED BY A LOCAL SILVERSMITH FOR THE reason, Richardson tells us, that he carried with him thirty-six bottles of wine, grave indiscretion in a Moslem country. Laing, throughout his expedition, was insistently Christian, a credit to his religious sentiments, but not tactful.

Another who remembered Laing and spoke of him to the explorer, Duveyrier, after an even longer interval, was the Sheikh Othman. (I will not trouble the reader with the Sheikh's full name which is three printed lines in length.) Sheikh Othman could repeat after thirty-three years a few English words which Laing had taught him as a young man when he guided the Christian to In Salah. This native, by the way, was the first person of the Tuareg race ever to see Paris (1862).

THE FORBIDDEN CITY OF IN SALAH

BUT FOR OTHMAN'S FRIENDSHIP LAING COULD NEVER HAVE GOT TO the next stop along his route. To push into In Salah—though the world did not then know this—was even more of a feat than to enter Timbuctoo. In Salah was ferociously anti-Christian. It was not until the eve of this century that it yielded to the French.

Laing was the only avowed Christian who had ever, previous to its capture, seen In Salah's insides and lived, if we except a shadowy individual, known as Iks-linglezi (Hicks, the Englishman). Army interpreter Martin, an indefatigable searcher of native archives, has dug out a local record, where there is mention of "Iks's" presence as a trader back in 1631. "Iks" seems uncertain and hardly counts. The great German explorer, Rohlfs, did see In Salah during its inviolable period (1864) but he traveled as a pseudo-Moslem. Sheikh Othman, Laing's old friend who had seen a lot of Christians in Paris, pierced his disguise, but let him go away unharmed. To pretend to be a Mohammedan was not easy. Rohlfs at one point of his travels was seized and examined to see if he were circumcised. On another occasion he roused suspicion because corns and cramped toes showed he had been a shoe wearer.

In Salah was fanatically independent. Its proud chief in the days of Laing said, "The Heavens are Allah's, but the earth belongs to me!" One may, at the price of rough going, visit In Salah in normal times today. I did so in 1939.

It was in caravan days at the world's navel. As a bird flies it was at equal distance from Timbuctoo, Tangier, Tripoli, Algiers and the Atlantic coast at Mogador. It controlled the inner desert and dominated what is called the green strip of the Tuat—not

truly a strip, but rather a line of green island strung across the
bleak desert. At In Salah itself it sometimes has not rained for
twenty-five years. The average is said to be a rain every decade.
It is, to my notion, a far stranger place than Timbuctoo. It is the
very essence of the Sahara's weirdness and loneliness and silence.

*   *   *

FROM IN SALAH LAING WENT TO TIMBUCTOO. ON THE ROAD HE WAS
attacked and injured almost fatally. On his route away from Timbuctoo he was murdered. His papers were lost and all the information gained from his courage and sufferings is contained in the
few personal letters he had succeeded in dispatching along the
way.

*   *   *

CAILLIÉ'S ACCOUNT OF TIMBUCTOO WAS A DISAPPOINTMENT TO A
greedy world. No roofs of gold. No promise of great plunder such
as had given the Moroccan sultan who conquered it in the old
days the name of "The Golden." Timbuctoo was still a great
caravan center, a trade gate between Sahara and Negroland,
but Caillié's report suggested that you had to work to make money
there just as everywhere else.

The gold of the Sudan, the gold of ancient Gana, has indeed
proved of little value. The region where, according to Arabic
geography, gold grew "like carrots" has given small returns and
compares badly with the modern gold finds of California, Australia, Alaska, etc., of whose richness—to be fair to them—medieval writers had no conception.

Caillié did not know how unimportant were the Sudan gold
fields and favored a scheme of establishing a fortified post domi-
nating the gold country, so that it might be exported despite the
natives' enmity. There was even advanced by some persons a crazy
proposal to dig a great canal so as to facilitate the gold trade.
People hoped to get enough gold out of the Sudan to pay off
Europe's national debts!

*   *   *

GRADUALLY AND WITH FORMIDABLE HARDSHIP INNER AFRICA WAS
investigated, its mysteries unveiled. Many brave men suffered
and many died. I have mentioned only a few of those first heroes
who dived into its completely blank spaces. "We trust there will
be an end of the sacrifice," cried the *Quarterly Review* in 1828,

adding, Africa has been "the grave of Europeans." Humane words to which adventurous men gave no heed. They were devoted patriots, scouts for the army of European occupation. After a while exploration would be succeeded by exploitation.

THEY HATED EXPLORERS

INSTINCTIVELY THE NATIVE POPULATION RECOGNIZED THE POTENTIAL danger to their independence and hated explorers. In addition they shrank from them as a set of what they considered distasteful maniacs.

These aliens in ways, religion and dress who courted peril and hardship in the end "to write down the country" (the native phrase for notemaking along the route) were a hateful puzzle. "What do you come for? Only to walk and make a book!" was the substance of their taunt. "Have you no rivers in your own country?" they demanded of Mungo Park when he kept asking his way to the Niger.

Even when explorers learned to be careful not to write their notes in public nor to ask too many questions, they could not pass through the country without arousing excited interest. "The Sahara," said Duveyrier, "is a house made of glass." Gossip raced across its sands. They say—it seems incredible—that while Lenz, the Austrian who was the fourth explorer to see Timbuctoo (first: Englishman, Laing; second: Frenchman, Caillié; third: German, Barth) was still in Morocco making his plans, his project was fully known in Timbuctoo.

The oddest coincidences happened. Caillié was shown—and had to pretend to view with indifference—the compass of the dead Laing at a spot over a thousand miles from where Laing had been murdered. Lander, when in a small town on the west coast, gave his shirt to be washed and got back one marked "Thomas Park." It had been entrusted to the washwoman by Mungo Park's son, in Africa searching for his lost father. The son died of tropic sickness before his laundry was ready.

*   *   *

WE HAVE READ MUCH OF WHAT EXPLORERS THOUGHT OF AFRICA. We have seldom considered what Africa thought about its explorers.

The more primitive of Africa's coastal population decided that white men lived exclusively on ships and had no dry land homes at all. "Do you sow barley on the decks?" they asked soberly. Relatively sophisticated natives who had been converted to Mohammedanism, disapproved of Christians who "drink wine, eat pig, embrace dogs and wear their shoes to church."

During Victoria's reign British explorers met sneers everywhere. They were ruled by a sultana—shameful! It was rumored that Victoria's sending of explorers into Africa argued a desire on her part to come there to live. "She is now in Tripoli," Richardson was assured when traveling in the Sahara, "and proposes to come to live at Ghat and has offered to buy half the town." Ghat was then a peculiarly shabby place of dirty sundried brick houses, which possessed only one large building. A mid-Saharan sultan, En-Nour of Air, expressed the gallant wish to send Victoria a present. He suggested the gift should be a *mehari*—a racing camel! The offer was not accepted.

*　　*　　*

THE VERY APPEARANCE OF EXPLORERS WAS AN AFFRONT TO AFRICA. They wore their usual European clothes. To the Moslem eye, as yet unfamiliar with such revealing dress, this costume was indecent. "A man with no other clothing than a piece of linen tied round his middle would excite less criticism," said Jackson, a European wise in the ideas of the country. Trousers, which outlined the crotch of male legs, were accounted a deliberate insult to public modesty. Many a man, all unaware, died for his trousers' sake. There was much in Christian behavior that shocked the Moslem code. Such unwitting offenses pointed up the natives' general distrust of the exploration of their country. The sound of guns echoed in every explorer's footsteps. The conqueror was coming nearer.

France Conquers; Africa Watches

DUBIOUS ROLE OF A FLY-SWATTER

ON JULY 4, 1830, THE FRENCH CAPTURED THE CITY OF ALGIERS.
It was the first definitive move in the Christian absorption of
North Africa and was by far the most important of them all—
French, Spanish, English or Italian—in its consequences. France's
capture of Algiers led, by a series of conquests and diplomatic
actions, to her gaining control of all the western section of Mediterranean Africa (Algeria, Tunisia, most of Morocco), of almost
the whole of the western side of the Sahara, and of the whole
western side of Negroland to the desert's south, plus much of
Equatorial Africa. So sweeping was the French success that the
term "North Africa" is often used with the special meaning of the
French holdings, just as "America" is often applied to the United
States alone.

The French attack on Algiers was popularly attributed to the
familiar incident of the fly-swatter, called fan by courtesy. The
dey, Hussein, of Algiers had a dispute in the spring of 1827 with
the French consul and struck him with the handle of his fly-
switch—a fancy article trimmed with peacock plumes. The incident was much advertised.

But it would be naïve to believe that such an important move
was motivated merely to avenge an affront committed in an interview without witnesses against one of the consuls at Algiers—a
group often humiliated—and against a man who individually was
neither a tactful diplomat, nor a man of good repute. It would

be almost equally naïve to attribute the move to the complex financial dispute in which France and the dey were involved, along with a certain powerful local Jewish group.

The French attack was part of the inevitable development of history. We have seen that it had been planned back in the time of Napoleon (see page 457). The Barbary States were too close to Europe, too troublesome and too far behind the civilization of the day to continue unmolested. They were that ramshackle building in a block of modern houses—inevitably destined to be remodeled.

The Barbary States sensed their danger and were believed to have a secret defense alliance. When the time came Algeria's western neighbor, Morocco, helped vigorously. Her eastern neighbor, Tunisia, was scrupulously neutral.

Following the fly-swatter incident, France's plans were no secret. She blockaded Algiers. England opposed the projected attack; a punitive expedition so readily turns into a permanent occupation. The argument between England and France on various phases of the African situation was a chapter of the nineteenth century and early twentieth century "Scramble for Africa." Before the fly-swatter affair came up England's eye had already swept hungrily across all the top of Africa. An English "Plan for the Conquest of Algiers" had been unofficially outlined more than ten years before the French attack. Also a scheme for putting the whole Sahara under English influence. I have before me the "Prospectus of a plan for forming a North African or Sudan Company," dated 1819, shares one hundred pounds each, whose object was "to lay open the whole interior regions of North Africa to British enterprise." Tripoli seemed for a time to be almost in England's mouth. There were published expressions of an English wish to take Tunis and Tangier. Eventually England reluctantly accepted the distasteful French conquest of the Algiers region as a *fait accompli*. And, with the passing of the years, France's undisputed occupation of almost the whole western side of North Africa became part of an amicable diplomatic bargain between the two nations.

THE SWIFT CAPTURE OF ALGIERS—THE TEDIOUS CONQUEST OF ALGERIA

THE CITY OF ALGIERS FELL SWIFTLY TO THE FRENCH. ONLY TWENTY days passed between their landing at near-by Sidi Ferruch, erstwhile home of Ferruch, a saintly Mohammedan hermit, and their capture of the capital. Dey Hussein was told that he might remove his reputedly vast personal treasure and go in safety. He departed for Italy, later visited France and died in Egypt, continuously protesting that he had not got away with his full bag of personal wealth and begging France for a pension. His concurrent intrigues against France were troublesome.

On the other hand the conquest of the country about the capital to which the name, Algeria, was given after the French came, took a hard and long effort. The name of Algeria has been elastic. It now encompasses regions Dey Hussein never heard of, in fact on today's map Algeria comes near to being the largest country of all Africa. Fighting between France and the native population lasted for a generation in coastal Algeria; in the back country it went on into modern days.

*   *   *

NO MILITARY ADVENTURE IN HISTORY PRESENTS RECORDS SO FULL of romantic, humorous and queer incidents. In fact no military adventure records so much of everything. The literature of the Algerian conquest is immense. It was the first time that modern Europeans had gone in numbers to any exotic country near home. They noted down their impressions for an eager audience, recorded them with enthusiastic facility, French wit and sympathy, and sense of fun. It seems to me that the reader will be better served if I repeat a few typical items from contemporary reminiscence than by a recapitulation of the military events of a long-drawn-out conquest. The expedition was a real journey of exploration. They fought with their eyes open.

*   *   *

A GRIEVANCE INFINITELY MORE EXCITING THAN THE FLY-SWATTER incident confronted them as they entered Algiers. On the gate called Bab Azoun, always a favorite repository for hideous souvenirs, they saw two hundred Frenchmen's heads, some nailed to the

wall, others hanging to "The Hooks." These included the heads
of members of the crews of two blockading ships which had been
wrecked on the Algerian coast a few months before. Part of these
crews had been killed at once, part driven to the city of Algiers—
victims all along the way of insult and cruelty. Even women and
children howled at them and pelted them. Of another blockade
ship lost on the coast only one sailor survived. "He was dragged
to town as a trophy, compelled to carry in each hand the head of
a dead shipmate, which—all bloody and mutilated—the population
forced him to kiss over and over, as he staggered along."

A few survivors of the blockade ships rushed forward to meet
the French army as it entered Algiers. It was a moment of great
emotion.

In all there were only 122 Christian captives in the city, where
once there had been thousands of such unfortunates. Nor was
Algiers in other respects the great place it had been at the zenith
of piracy days. Famines and epidemics had killed off large numbers. The population when the French came was only about
30,000. But, even in its decadence, Algiers was a rich prize. The
casbah was stuffed with gold money, lingots of gold, precious
stones and other valuable objects—pirates' treasure all. Its value
is said to have been equivalent to 16,000,000 current United
States dollars.

*   *   *

THE WHITE FLAG OF OLD FRANCE WITH ITS FLEUR DE LYS FLUTTERED
above the casbah and other public buildings for a little over one
month. Then word reached Algiers that there was a new government at home. It was a most curious situation. French soldiers
had been dying with the brave words, "For Country and King!"
all unaware that news was on the sea that the king for whom
they were making the supreme sacrifice was now a quite different
personage, that Charles X had been replaced by Louis-Philippe.

The white flag had to come down. Tricolors were improvised.
The army made itself provisionally little flags from "a bit of a
shirt sewn to a scrap of a coat and a fragment from a trousers."

*   *   *

THE ALTERED BACKGROUND AT HOME, THE EXOTIC NOVELTY OF THE
African scene gave the French a feeling that they floated in a
sort of fairy tale. The first native male they captured was such a

curio in his draperies that they almost squashed him to death in an effort to get close and examine him. Native women were tantalizing in their veils and voluminous bundles of wrapping. Orders against flirting with these females, who showed no aspect of humanity except their big dark eyes, were very strict with harsh penalties.

Presently a realistic commander imported from France some feminine society for the army—these women being modestly described as laundresses on the ships' manifests.

One of these women had a picturesque career. She married an Arab of importance, turned Mohammedan, lived among his people and gave herself out to be also a person of high degree—"the daughter of the sultan of France," no less! She got to be regarded with great reverence and ventured to boast that she would not only put her husband on the throne in Algiers, but would make him ruler of France. All the world, she prophesied, would one day be Moslems. No soldier of the army had a more spirited set of adventures than this whore.

*   *   *

THE SOLDIERS LAUGHED THEMSELVES SICK AT THE FIRST SIGHT OF camels, then not familiar to the untraveled by pictures, circuses and so on, as today. The camel's lank, seemingly deformed shape, disdainful and solemn facial expression "like a grumpy dowager with her lorgnette"—its slow and mincing walk, were irresistibly funny to boys from the French countryside.

You did not have to go far from the city in those days to see other and wilder beasts. Lions, chitas, leopards and so on were in the brush country. Lions, allegedly pets, were sometimes led through the Algiers streets; probably you could have bought a young lion any day on the quayside. The former Christian slave prison in the Bab Azoun section had the name of the Quarter of the Lions. Even ostriches could be admired by soldiers who went on missions into the back country. The people of the day called them "plumed camels," seeing a resemblance in general build and demeanor between the two animals. As for farm creatures—you could buy a sheep for a franc and a half, and a young ox for six or eight francs!

*   *   *

THE OTHER SIDE OF THE PICTURE: A BAD CLIMATE (GIVEN THE HY-gienic conditions then maintaining), deplorable medical care, epidemics. In Algiers three thousand sick at one time. Ferocious, cunning foes who fought the Christian invader like demons. Except for a few coastal towns, there was for years really no conquest. French forces could communicate with one another only by sea.

Oran to the west of Algiers (a cholera nest) was French, having given up simultaneously with the Algiers occupation—a city of checkered vicissitudes: once Spanish, abandoned by Spain, taken back again and definitely given up as a bad job after it had been wrecked by an earthquake. When the French acquired Oran it had shrunk to a miserable village, mostly inhabited by Jews. Under French control it was to become one of the important coastal cities of the Mediterranean. Alongside Oran was Mers-el-Kebir, whose name, of course, means Great-Port and which thoroughly merits to be so called. It had been famous as a safe harbor since the twelfth century. "I do not think," said Leo Africanus, "there is in all the world another port so ample." (Leo had no opportunity to see Sydney and Rio!) "It can easily receive several hundred ships. The Venetians (traders) bring their galleys here when the sea is angry." We remember its name with sorrow for it was at Mers-el-Kebir that the English and French fleets came to blows in one of the most painful episodes of World War II (July 3, 1940)—an episode which caused the British Prime Minister to sob when he announced it to the House of Commons.

* * *

ANOTHER EARLY FRENCH CAPTURE, AND ANOTHER PEST SPOT WAS Bône. But Bône kicked itself free, massacred the garrison and had to be retaken. Four hundred yards outside the city was enemy land. The same with Bougie, where the French were practically prisoners.

CONSTANTINE'S RECORD

THE TRAGEDY AND TRIUMPH AT CONSTANTINE WERE TYPICAL OF THE French struggle in those early days. The old city was ruled by a fierce Christian hater, the Bey Ahmed. Perched upon an inaccessible rock, it was the ideal natural fortress. It threw the French back with cruel losses at the first attack, and did not yield till seven years after the conquest of the city of Algiers.

Constantine was our advanced command post in the hard struggle of the winter of 1943. It is not often that an army installs itself on a site which has been pretty continuously an important stronghold for some twenty-five hundred years, and which has the record of having been in the successive possession of Phoenicians, Numidian pagans, early Christians, Jews, Mohammedans and French Christians. Constantine was a headquarters to take pride in. The Phoenicians founded it. Its original name, Cirta, presumably meant merely "The City." It was there that Massinissa stored his many wives, children and savage dogs just before the last Punic War. As early as 303 it contained a "house where the Christians assemble," to quote the old document, which must have been one of the earliest Christian churches in Africa. The name of the city became Constantine after the great emperor. "The Cahena," supposedly a Jewess (see page 189) was there. Then the Mohammedans came.

The common natives deformed the name to Cucutin and were puzzled by its historic remains. They were of the opinion that certain groups of statuary were relics of the teachers and students of a college, "turned into stone for their vices." I do not know what explanation they invented for the bas-relief on the old bridge showing a woman with two elephants and wearing a single loose garment which she lifted provocatively in front with a lewd backward glance at the city.

Learned Moslems called the place Cosantina-el-Hawa (Constantine-in-the-Air) and stated that its towers were so high that the famed regional storks could not get to them without great effort. The city was approachable only from the west by a bridge at so dizzy a height that "the water at the bottom of the ravine has the aspect of a little star." In the days before the French at last crushed the frenzied defense of Bey Ahmed it was reported that one of the city's proud possessions, kept in the casbah, was the rib of a giant, the bone being "too large to have come from any terrestrial animal, even an elephant." In Constantine Eisenhower lodged. All in all, quite a civic history.

"THE MOUTH OF THE SAHARA"

THE COLLAPSE OF THE NATIVE DEFENSE OF CONSTANTINE OPENED
the way toward the desert. As the troops passed from the bleak
steppes through the gorge which is called in Arabic *Foum es
Sahara* (The Mouth of the Sahara) at El-Kantara the thrilled
bandsmen without orders broke into a blare of music, a spon-
taneous tribute to as sudden a scenic contrast as the earth can
offer. The breath-taking suddenness of it is more striking to a
traveler on the foot road (as I noted) than on the railway.

On they went southward to Biskra, "Queen of the Date Country," a prosperous place since the days of the Romans, which
claims that its name comes from a word meaning "sweet." It was
not sweet to the French soldiers in those days. Their garrison
was wiped out by native resisters.

Biskra became familiar to American troops, and is known—
in a somewhat fanciful fashion—to countless United States persons
who have seen the cinema versions of *The Garden of Allah.*
Biskra was early destined to popularity. It was a winter resort
back in the old diligence days. It was—before that—the Montmartre, the Broadway of the desert. An early visitor said, "Biskra
is a pleasure city. The flutes and drums do not rest day or night,
and it has as many *cafés chantants* and dance places as there are
entertainment establishments in any European capital. It therefore goes without saying that its population is largely composed
of young persons of light morals."

It was a surprise to the invading French of a century ago to
find so populous and sophisticated a place in the Sahara, albeit
only on its fringe. The popular impression had been that the
desert was a blank empty no man's land—"a disinherited country
with no humans nor growing things."

LITERATURE OF A CONQUEST

TO THE MEMOIRS AND JOURNALS OF THE EXCEPTIONALLY ARTICULATE
French army, which are now mostly "hard-to-find" books,[7] there

---

[7] Charles Tailliart in his important work, *L'Algérie dans la littérature
française* (Paris, 1925), gives excerpts from many of these military reminiscences, which after the lapse of a century are difficult to find in libraries.

were added, as the years passed, travel sketches by certain world-famous writers. These last possess indirect historic value and may be readily found in any reference library. They include works by Daudet (who was in Algiers, 1861-62); Fromentin, the colorful painter-author, who told of the Sahara's loveliness; Loti (*Au Maroc,* 1890); Dumas (who was in Morocco, Algeria and Tunisia, 1846, see his *Le Veloce*); Maupassant (*Au Soleil, La Vie Errante*).

One especially interesting but less familiar romantic writer on Algeria was the Moslem, Isabelle Eberhardt, whose work was delightful and whose life was black tragedy. In her poverty she did laborer's work in male dress. She perished saving her spahi husband, a native Algerian, from drowning when a sudden storm turned the Oued Sefra, usually an "invisible" river, into a raging torrent.[8]

REACTION OF THE CONQUERED

ALGIERS' OWN REACTION TO THE INVASION IS NOT, AS FAR AS I know, adequately recorded. Dismay at the fall of "The Sultan City" was tempered by the fact that it had been for centuries under alien control. The spirit of Algiers was already broken.

There was the usual sorrowful stream of refugees. Traders scuttled away with their riches. As far as possible the intellectual treasures of the city, its libraries of Arabic manuscripts, were removed to safety. Some of them went to Morocco. Many of the intelligentsia fled.

As a part of the pacification effort it occurred to the French to bring to Algiers a person likely to put the wisdom of Algiers completely in the shade. This was Robert Houdin, the famous conjuror. The claim was that Houdin by his tricks, which made no claim to be miracles, would prove to the people that their own marabouts were mere fakers. Houdin thrilled and amazed the people, but Islam was unshaken. As far as a display of legerdemain was concerned, Houdin would have been hard put to equal the performance of a legendary local expert—an executioner. This

---

[8] See notes on her life in her own book, *Dans l'Ombre chaude d'Islam,* which was recovered from the flood waters and dried out after its author's death in 1904. See also René Louis Doyon's biographical sketch in her volume, *Mes Journaliers,* and Stéphan's *Isabelle Eberhardt ou la Révélation du Sahara.* Her other titles: *Notes de route; Pages d'Islam; Trimadeur.*

Ali Sief at a certain execution whirled his sword round and round the condemned man in flashing circles. "Get on with it and kill me!" cried the man. Ali Sief grinned, took out his snuffbox and held a pinch under the victim's nose. The man sneezed and his head fell off onto the ground. So deftly had Ali Sief done his work that the head had remained in its place and the man hadn't known he was dead! Nor did even a drop of blood show. A public nourished on such yarns as this was hard to startle by the best of French conjuring tricks.

THE ROMANTIC SOLDIERS OF FRANCE

ONE ELEMENT OF THE INVASION WAS PUZZLING AND LAUGHABLE TO the native especially at the beginning. This was the dress originally worn by the invaders. The French army went into their African midsummer expedition in the most unsuitable clothing imaginable. Pictures of the day show, for example, two soldiers, as they stand upon a hill looking down into a sun-drenched city and cry, "*Voilà donc Alger!*" (There is Algiers!) They are swathed as for a campaign in northern Russia—overcoats to mid-calf, collars to their ears, tall, stiff, nonshading hats. A French cavalryman is represented buttoned up to the chin and topped with a hat, practically visorless, as he fights in the July heat before Algiers. There was no notion of dressing the army comfortably to fit the climate.

Presently uniforms were modified: a more flexible, floppy style of military clothing was adopted. Soon Africa became familiar with a romantic set of soldiery: Zouaves, Spahis, the Foreign Legion, Meharistes.

The Zouaves, formed in 1831, got their name from an Algerian tribe whose members had early come over to the French side and joined the army. The Zouaves' dress helped to make them famous. Their characteristic jacket has been imitated in women's fashions off and on ever since. The name Zouave was used by certain groups in the army in the American Civil War.

Spahis was an old name, having the same meaning as sepoys. Turkey employed Spahis for five centuries. The Spahis of the French army were native recruits with French officers. Off duty they stalk the streets and sweep across the sands like oriental noblemen, a sumptuous red burnous (long cloak) flung back dramatically from their shoulders. One of their earliest colonels was the eccentric Creole, Bouscarin, later general, whose quirks made the army laugh. His best performance was the inscription which he caused to be put on an old tomb discovered in the mountains, which he erroneously believed to be that of the great Numidian king. The inscription, "To my pal, Massinissa, from General Bouscarin." An army capable of such lightheartedness under difficulties was bound to win.

The Foreign Legion was organized in 1831 and has been, I should think, the most widely written about fighting group of all times. In the beginning the various nations of the Legion were segregated, each national group operating as a separate unit. The system was altered. The earliest *légionnaires* were a different looking lot also, wearing French infantry dress, very unsuited to Africa: blue coat, red trousers and a high black shako. They fought their first fight near Algiers at Maison Carrée.

The French Saharan Meharistes are a peculiarly colorful organization. Their officers are French, the men, desert fellows. They pacified, and now they police the Sahara. Never did policemen live so austere a life: a man's monthly ration weighs thirty kilograms (sixty-six pounds) consisting of flour, vermicelli, sugar, tea, oil. His allowance of liquid for all purposes—cooking, drinking, washing, if any—is often but four quarts a day.

The Meharistes are the fulfillment of an old dream, dreamed by Napoleon back in 1798. Napoleon's dream was based on misinformation. He believed that *mehara* (fast camels) could do 100 kilometers (sixty-two miles) day in and day out, and naturally regarded this form of cavalry as likely to be of immense value in a day when the horse was the swiftest available transportation known to Europe. Napoleon must have found out his error as to the speed of camels, for he tried camel riding himself. Just before World War II the camel which he used in Egypt was exhibited, stuffed, at the Louvre Museum in Paris. Pictures of him on camel back also survive.

Fantastic stories have been told of the speed of the *mehari*. Leo Africanus contributed his bit, saying that the king of Timbuctoo maintained an express service which could do one hundred miles a day for ten consecutive days. There was a yarn that a certain breed of camels could go in a day the distance ordinary camels took nine days to cover. "One of these camels once came from the Senegal River to the trading establishment of Messrs Cabane and Depres at Mogador in seven days," we are assured—that is right across the Sahara. Another reputedly went from Tripoli to Ghadames in a day. Even as a bird flies this is four hundred miles. These two absurd stories are not native boasting, but the sincere statements of two English nineteenth century travelers.

The apex of camel-lying is included in the travel reminiscences of the Rabbi Petachia of Ratisbon who went to Bagdad in the twelfth century and saw "a flying camel"—not actually a winged animal, but one that went just as fast as the rider could bear. "In one second," said the good rabbi, "the flying camel can gallop a mile."

Reverting to facts, a good average speed for a *mehari* is 28 miles a day. In emergencies tremendous feats have been accomplished. A doctor rode 341 miles in 9 days. Men seeking to rescue comrades in distress made 388 miles in 7 days, and on another occasion did 62 miles in 24 hours. A lone rider, whose performance therefore cannot be checked, claimed to have done 372 miles in 5 days on an attempted rescue mission. Such stunts are harmful, often fatal to the camel, and—unless precautions are taken—shake the rider's bowels dangerously.

The first use of camels by the French army was hesitant and timid. At the moment of the Algerian invasion the general-in-chief was under the impression that camels were a dangerous factor in battle and that his men would meet as tough a test as the Romans did when they first encountered elephants in the days of Pyrrhus. He had an idea that squadrons of furious camels would charge, and no doubt he had read the published report that "camel bites were capable of producing more carnage than gunfire"!

When the soldiers of the invasion actually met the vague, slow-moving camel they were, as I have said, amazed and amused. An attempt was promptly made to use camels for transport work. But the French soldiers were then unaccustomed to the queer ways of the beast. Once, a military anecdote goes, they had piled all the gear of a certain general onto two camels and were driving them to the next camp. Across the wastes came the cry of camels in a nomad bivouac. Off went the two camels in their absurd, jerky gallop, and the general never again saw his belongings.

* * *

IN 1943 AMERICAN SOLDIERS TRIED CAMELS, AND AT THAT TIME there was released a newspaper story of how in the long ago the United States had employed a camel corps to link artillery outposts in the Southwest. About eighty camels were imported from Africa with a native caretaker. Their first expedition covered four hundred miles to California and never lost a camel. The Indians were too astonished to do anything but run away. The Civil War then interrupted the experiment. The camels were dispersed. Some wandered off free into the desert. Some were grabbed for shows.

The Camel Corps of Africa will not, I suppose, survive indefinitely into the truck and airplane age. But its usefulness in the opening up of the Sahara has been splendid.

THE GREAT RESISTER

ONLY ONE NATIVE FIGURE STANDS OUT IMPORTANTLY IN THE EARLY years of the French invasion of Algeria, that of Abd-el-Kader—unless we count as a native the picturesque General Yusuf, who fought on the French side. Yusuf was a national mélange, a double renegade, born in Christian Elba, captive and bey's favorite in Tunis, volunteer with the French, first classed by them as a native soldier, then made a French officer, taking part in almost every big engagement, a fighter nonpareil, and a curio to comrade and foe. His picture in the souvenirs of a contemporary: "Proudly riding on a high native saddle, followed by two Negroes, preceded by a company of Spahis, gun held high, wearing a turban of green cashmere, color of the Prophet, Yusuf looked more like an oriental prince going to fight the French Crusaders than like a member of the French army."

* * *

ABD-EL-KADER WAS ALGERIA'S GREAT RESISTER. HAD IT BEEN IN THE North African character to unite as a block, he could have thrown the French out altogether. As it was, he very nearly did. He was furthermore a man whose name lives because he charmed. Even his enemies, the French, admired him enthusiastically. He was like Saladin in being one of the few Mohammedans of all time of whom the Christians speak well.

Abd-el-Kader was born about twenty-two years before the French came, near Mascara, an inland town in the Oran neighborhood. He had much to capture the loyalty of his fellow Algerians. He came of the blood of Mohammed. His name was one firmly driven into popular affection. Abd-el-Kader-el-Jilani, who lived in the twelfth century, was "Sultan amongst the Saints." *Koubbas* (little chapels) in his honor are sprinkled all across the country. He was the patron of the poor and the blind, known lovingly as Bou-Derbala, "The Ragged Man." Beggars still cry his name and unhappy folk of all stations invoke his help. Soldiers used to beg his favor in battle. ("Algiers has a guardian in Abd-el-Kader!" ran the local war song, referring to the saint and sung a generation before his namesake, the great resister, was born.) The twelfth century saint was moreover the patron of one of the largest and oldest fraternal religious organizations of Algeria, which bears his name and exerts strong general influence.

The resister therefore started with a name that thrilled his countrymen and gave him belief in himself. At Bagdad, as a boy, he saw the tomb of his saint and had a revelation that he would one day be Prince of the True Believers. It was a vision which came true.

Abd-el-Kader must have been the original inspiration of the many sheikh stories which have delighted readers and cinema audiences. He was very handsome, a superb horseman, chivalrous, loftily pious, devoted to the traditions and noble etiquette of his people, and was a man of much learning and taste and a poet. He supplied most of the material for a book, *The Horses of the Sahara*, prepared by Daumas, later a general, who was attached to Abd-el-Kader's court during the period when France attempted to make Abd-el-Kader what we call a collaborationist—France had to do most of the collaborating, incidentally. The book deals, not alone with the Arab steed, but with the pride and customs and poesy of Mohammedan North Africa, and is worth reading, if you can find a copy; it has been translated into English.

Abd-el-Kader was a brilliant and romantic spot in a dun-colored world, and for that alone deserved the generous pension which the French gave him after they had at last defeated him.

* * *

Two years after the capture of the city of Algiers young Abd-el-Kader preached a Holy War and was chosen as the people's leader (1832). On the Macta River, between his capital, Mascara, and Oran, he proved the wisdom of their choice. He surprised and surrounded a French group. It was a burning day in late June. The scene was a frenzy. The French milled about in the marshes, unable to fight clear. "A sort of delirium came over the soldiers. Men half naked, their arms lost, threw themselves on the Arabs screaming with laughter. Others, blinded by gun smoke, fell into the river and attempted to swim away in its few inch depths. Others fell to the ground crazed by the sun and you could hear them singing." The last survivors chanted the "Marseillaise." It was rout complete.

France heard the story with horror. It was great news for native Algeria.

THE "SMALA"

Another piece of luck for Abd-el-Kader. He negotiated an agreement with the French by whose terms he got himself recognized as sultan of most of western and central Algeria. It was a diplomatic triumph for the young leader. He gained a respite in which to plan bigger things. As might have been expected, France and Abd-el-Kader resumed their fight.

Now Fortune frowned on him. He lost Mascara, his capital, and set up a sort of ambulating headquarters, for which the native name is smala. This he could do without loss of dignity. It was a nomad country and a fixed residence did not possess the sacred value it holds in our minds.

Noble natives were accustomed to travel the land with all their followers, family and possessions. It was a wonderful sight to see, a quite different sight from the shabby migrations one may glimpse in North Africa today. Here are a few sentences from Fromentin's impressions of "a little nomad city on the move," as he observed it not long after the era of Abd-el-Kader. The great resister's smala must have presented much the same aspect.

Fromentin tells that the warriors led the procession on their
fine horses, standard blowing in the wind. Then came the musicians, "riding in two ranks, each with his bridle hooked in his
arm, some striking with a martial air upon little square frames
covered with leather, others playing upon tambourines, others
blowing long bagpipes. After that came the camels carrying
atatiches (this word means palanquins on camel back for Moslem
ladies to travel in privately). The camels were big lean animals
with lustrous almost white skins and walking, as the Arabs say,
'with the noble step of the ostrich.' They had black satin scarves
around their necks and silver rings on their front legs. The
atatiches were great baskets covered over with cloth and with a
flat bottom spread with cushions and carpets, whose ends hung
down like curtains on the two flanks of the camel, giving the effect
of daises on promenade.

"Picture an assortment of every sort of precious stuff: lemon
colored damask striped with black satin, with arabesques of gold
on the black stripes, and silver flowers on the lemon background;
another outfit in scarlet silk, barred with two bands of olive color;
another orange, alongside violet; rose pink, mingled with blues—
blues tender as cold greens; then cushions, half cherry and half
emerald. Carpets of soberer tints: crimson, purple, garnet. All
this married with that taste natural to the oriental—the only col-
orist in the world." (This, remember, was the writing of a painter-
author.)

Fromentin goes on, "One saw nothing of the lady travellers in
those sumptuous cradles, but a Negro, who held to the drapery of
each, from time to time lifted his head and exchanged words with
a voice which spoke to him through the tapestries."

After the *atatiches* came the pack animals with the tents, furniture, kitchen utensils of each family, and accompanied by the
poorer women, children and servants. "There were chests, big
bundles in yellow and brown striped wrappings, *couscous* platters,
copper basins, arms tied up in parcels, black water skins, live
chickens hung by their feet . . . 150 pack camels." Except for
the harem of the chief's family, the women traveled on foot and
unveiled. Then came the flocks, spare camels, mares with foal.
The nomad city took an hour to pass.

Said Abd-el-Kader, himself, writing of such a spectacle: "Thou wouldst have said that a field of anemones were bedecking themselves in their richest colors."

       *   *   *

To track down Abd-el-Kader's *smala,* his traveling capital, believed to be made up of twenty thousand persons, became the mission of the French army. One May morning in 1843 a French group commanded by the Duke d'Aumale, son of the king of France, surprised the *smala* halted alongside a watering place. The Spahis with picturesque General Yusuf closed in around the caravan. The French were in smaller force, but they caught the caravan in disorder.

Abd-el-Kader's *smala* was no more. Many died fighting. Many were captured. The gaudy booty was so immense as to be an embarrassment. Abd-el-Kader escaped disaster, being that day absent from the *smala,* fighting elsewhere. He had lost treasure, family, friends, records, prestige—everything except the courage to fight the Holy War to the end.

SHORT WAR IN MOROCCO

Abd-el-Kader fled to Morocco and called upon the sultan to help him throw the infidel out of Africa. There followed a short and dramatic war between Morocco and France, which might have led to France's occupation of the country but for the disapproval of England.

The war was just one battle in length. On the River Isly, at a place one can see from the window of the train going from Morocco into Algeria, General Bugeaud defeated a force of three times as many Moroccans under the sultan's son. Again the picturesque General Yusuf played his part.

It was so decisive a French victory that the sultan—also scared by the bombardments of Tangier and Mogador—asked for peace, and that General Bugeaud changed his name to Duke d'Isly (after the river of the battle scene). The sultan agreed to give no more help to Abd-el-Kader and to intern him if he could catch him. But this he could not do.

BLACK DAYS OF THE CONQUEST

THE GREAT RESISTER WAS NOT THROUGH. HE COULD STILL FIGHT and still could and did win. He could still put the city of Algiers in a state of jitters and produce a situation so alarming that the French commander had to arm the military convicts in the prisons. The two dramas of Sidi-Brahim were still to come.

A year after the Isly battle his horsemen surprised and cut to pieces at Sidi-Brahim (near the Algerian-Moroccan frontier) a French force of a few hundreds. The survivors were shockingly misused, a blot on Abd-el-Kader's chivalry. But the war had got into a desperate, all-out stage.

French prisoners were massacred in a group in cold blood after a hideous march across country, during which they were obliged to suffer piteous indignities. Abd-el-Kader wished to prove to his disintegrating partisans that he had won a big victory. "He had decapitated the Sidi-Brahim dead and wanted to preserve and display their heads. He compelled the French prisoners to take them at each riverside along the way to wash them and rub them with honey so that they would last till the journey's end"! As I say, the war was in its final, desperate stage. The other side, the French side, admit to black cruelty and the destruction of native property. There was the scandal of the fired grotto where hundreds of natives, some of them children, were smoked to death in a cave.

There were provocations for French cruelty. A Frenchman wrote: "We turned the course of a stream and buried our dead, then let the stream run back in its channel, thinking thus to save our comrades' corpses from the profanation of the enemy." Useless precaution. That night the French heard "drum beating, roaring and shouting," and saw that the natives had recovered the bodies, stamped on them, profaned and outrageously mutilated them. Another French fighter, Colonel Pein, says in his memoirs, "I have seen women mutilate the wounded, bodies cut up while still alive, stomachs slashed open, feet and limbs amputated."

*　　*　　*

FOR ABD-EL-KADER THE SECOND DRAMA OF SIDI-BRAHIM WAS THE end of the fight. On December 23, 1847, it was there that he surrendered. He could do no more. He had resisted for fifteen years.

LAST DAYS OF ABD-EL-KADER

TO HIS DISMAY ABD-EL-KADER WAS TAKEN TO FRANCE AS A PRISONER instead of being permitted to go as a free exile to the Orient. After four years, and upon giving his oath never again to interfere in Algeria, he was allowed his liberty, and eventually, and characteristically, played a noble part when he protected his erstwhile enemies, the Christians, against a native uprising at Damascus.

He died possessed of the Grand Cross of the Legion of Honor —odd gift and odd acceptance for a bitter foe—and of a princely pension from France, equivalent to twenty thousand gold standard dollars a year.

It was the French who, though they defeated him, gave him the chance to fame. Had the dey gone on ruling at Algiers he would have remained the obscure son of a minor provincial leader. As it was his reputation lives a century after his career as resister ended. Proudly the guides show you his luxurious prison in the chateau of Henry of Navarre at Pau.[9]

At Damascus he was a notable figure. Burton, then consul there, met him in 1871—"an old man living in retirement with five wives." Mrs. Burton says he wore "a lovely cashmere robe like a dressing gown and a necklace of large emeralds." He lived to be about eighty years old.

*   *   *

THERE HAS BEEN CONSIDERABLE FUSS, AND CRITICISM OF FRANCE because Abd-el-Kader was not immediately allowed to go to the Orient as he had been led to expect when he surrendered. This criticism is wrongheaded. It was the colonists of Algeria whose

[9] Translated from the *Guide Bleu:* "Apartment of Abd-el-Kader: 1st room (called the Louis XIV) former bedroom of Abd-el-Kader during his captivity in 1848, Flemish tapestry of 16th century, bed hangings embroidered for Louis XIV at Saint-Cyr under the direction of Mme. de Maintenon. In the 2nd room, former bed chamber of the wives of Abd-el-Kader, beautiful tapestries of Flemish subjects, statues of François I and of Henry IV in *biscuit de Sèvres.* In the 3rd room, fine Flemish tapestries showing the history of Psyche, a Louis XIII chest."

roars of alarm obliged the government to keep Abd-el-Kader under control until his influence was deemed abated. The colonists had every right to roar, and the government every right to listen to them and to set aside the ultrachivalrous military undertaking given impulsively in the excitement of victory. To the city of Algiers only a few months before Abd-el-Kader had been a figure of terror. His troops in earlier days had massacred colonists across the countryside. It would have been ludicrous to have permitted him to proceed immediately to a relatively near-by Moslem country to plot, and perhaps to contrive to return to the old fighting ground.

HARD BIRTH OF A COLONY

ALGERIA WAS THE HARDEST JOB WHICH ANY COLONISTS HAVE EVER tackled. The climate, until the ground had been cleared and drained, produced conditions that were deadly; it was a far different country from the delightful Algeria of today. There was no subservient native labor available at first, as would have been the case in more primitive parts of the world, where conquered races are readily cajoled or forced to work for their conquerors. The colonist had to do all the heavy work himself. Moreover the indigenous population round about was persistently belligerent— as in the case of the American Indian—and was far more dangerous, being no simple savage, but almost as well equipped and almost as clever as the newcomer. One or two of these difficulties have been met in other places where Europeans went colonizing, but it seems to me that it was only in Algeria that colonists met all three at the start: unwholesome climate, no labor, the opposition of well-armed, intelligent natives.

The Algerian colonist suffered in addition a form of mental torture. There was constant debate at home as to giving up the Algerian venture altogether. There was for the colonist the constant, haunting fear that he might be told any day that all his effort had been wasted.

The early colonists in Algeria had to be iron men and iron women and iron children.

*   *   *

THE WORK OF TAMING ALGERIA TO BE A HOME FOR EUROPEANS began in the Mitija, the coastal strip alongside the city of Algiers. It was then a sort of jungle: "a marsh of thick, tangled and impenetrable bush, gigantic grass tufts, prickly shrubs, dwarf palms, growing in a soggy ground into which one sank at every step." It was ideal country for untamed vegetation, and deadly for humans. Its stagnant pools were breeding grounds for fever. One fifth to one third of the colonists died annually. The general opinion was that it would never be made habitable.

Today the Mitija produces wine, oranges, cereals, plants for the perfume industry, fancy vegetables, and tobacco.

But how hard it was: In the old days a local paper printed a cartoon showing two men, one, fat and well dressed with a bagful of money; the other, skinny and ragged. The caption read, "I HAVE JUST COME FROM CALIFORNIA," and "I AM FROM AFRICA."

*   *   *

IN 1860 NAPOLEON III AND EUGÉNIE INSPECTED THE COLONY, EVIdently with some approval. The emperor later made his oft-quoted statement, "Algeria is at once an Arab kingdom, a European colony, and a French camp." By the 1880's Algeria had become "a colony *de luxe*," in the words of an English observer. "The railways are as good as the best in France. The roads are unsurpassed." In 1830 when the French arrived there had not been a real road in the country, nor were any needed, for there was not a single carriage, even in the capital. To the native mind a carriage was an object grossly cruel to a horse: Europe might be, they admitted, a paradise for women, but it was a *jehennem* (hell) for horses. Fancy the noble steed dragging a wagon!

*   *   *

SO GRADUALLY, WITH PAIN AND WITH EVENTUAL SUCCESS, ALGERIA was yet again conquered and occupied by an alien race. The first phase of the Christian conquest of North Africa was accomplished.

*   *   *

CONQUEST IS TRAGIC. BUT IT IS EVIDENTLY PART OF NATURE'S system by which she moves races about the earth and mixes blood and customs. It would be especially sentimental to weep over the Christian conquest of North Africa. To be conquered and reconquered has been North Africa's destiny.

In the Arabic phrase, *mektoub*, "it was written"—written by the geography of Mediterranean Africa which makes organized resistance to a strong attack almost impossible. A ribbon of green is backed by high mountains, then by a vast desert stretching into Negroland. The population is split into groups whose ways of life and whose interests are completely different each from the other. They say that in Algiers alone there were ten languages spoken when the French first came.

One thing only these diverse groups share—the Mohammedan religion. That is a great deal. But, when the Christians came in force, it was not enough. *Mektoub.*

"MOSKOO"

THE TAKING OF ALGERIA HAD NOT PROVED SUCH AN EASY OR SUCH an immediately profitable job as to tempt imitation, and the nations of Europe were for that and other reasons slow in attempting further African undertakings.

The tangled state of Europe itself left little energy for exotic adventures. The Crimean War came along only a few years after the completion of the first phase of the Algerian conquest. France and England were the allies of Turkey against Russia. Turkey still conserved a titular control over Tunisia, Tripolitania and Egypt, and was in religious affiliation with Morocco. It would have been uncouth to help Turkey against Russia with one hand and to despoil her of her African holdings with the other.

The Crimean War and Turkey's previous contests with Russia created a prodigious stir in native Africa. Africans seemed to sense and fear that great unknown force of Russia which has so often made the world nervous. A few instances of Africa's uneasiness will be interesting.

At the end of the eighteenth century Africans had been whispering about "The Yellow King" (the czar) and his plan to destroy all Mohammedan power. Four thousand fighting men went from Alexandria alone to fight Russia in one of the several Turkish-Russian wars. A Mamluk bey tore down the ancient building called St. Louis' Tower and used the material to build a big fortress near Damietta to keep the expected Russian invasion out of Egypt.

"Moskoo"—Africa's usual name for Russia as a whole—got the reputation of being something terrible and immense. Explorers in the deep Sahara report hearing "Moskoo" mentioned with awe. To say that some place was "as large as Moskoo" had become a catchword.

The Crimean War was regarded as a Holy War, the Moslem equivalent of a Crusade. The ordinary North African ignored the English and French participation or discounted it. Said a Tunisian officer who had taken part in the struggle, "The sultan called in his vassals (meaning England and France!) only in order to save as far as possible shedding the blood of the Faithful." This in a conversation overheard by Nachtigal in Tunisia. Up-Nile native gossip ran in exactly the same fashion. In the Near East Burton heard that "the sultan had ordered the czar to become a Moslem. The czar sued for peace, but the sultan cried, 'No, by Allah!' The sultan is expected to dispose of Moskoo in a short time, after which he will turn his victorious armies against all idolaters, beginning with the English."

Africa's nervousness about Russia continued after the Crimean War. There were stories that "Moskoo" was seeking to push into North Africa by the back gate, worming into Abyssinia on the pretext that the form of Christianity practiced there should link Abyssinia to the Russian Greek church. Some of Russia's missionaries were said to carry guns as well as prayer books.

ISOLATED TRIPOLI

Turkey had heard the tolling of the bell when Algeria was captured by France. But Turkey affected to be deaf. It was years before she would admit officially that France was in possession. Mathuisieulx wrote in 1901, "Would one believe that our occupation of Algeria is not yet diplomatically accepted by the Sublime Porte!" This peculiar attitude showed Turkey's alarm and distress. Turkey had once owned the whole Mediterranean part of Africa except Morocco. Now the empire was melting away, Algeria was lost. Egypt under Mehemet Ali had won quasi independence. Tunisia, though under Turkish titular authority, was an open friend of France.

Something had to be done. Turkey went into Tripoli with a strong fist and clutched Tripoli in so tight a grip that, during the rest of the nineteenth century, the country was practically squeezed off from the outside world. Thus Tripoli was preserved to Islam, and we see an odd situation: the country which had always been the feeblest of the five states of Mediterranean Africa held out the longest against Christian occupation.

Tripoli herself had invited the Turks to resume firm control of the country. The sons of the local ruler, old Yusuf Coromali, America's one-time antagonist, were fighting one another in typical Coromali style. The people of Tripoli appealed to the sultan to restore order. The sultan's men came and conquered quickly. Tripoli became again a Turkish province. This happened in 1835.

Having got the Turk back the people hated him. But Tripoli was ever a spineless place and sulked ineffectually. There were minor revolts in the hilly back country. A certain mountain torrent ran a bloody stream. Villages in ruins were mementos of Turkish ferocity. An uprising was attempted at a moment when the Tripolitans believed their masters had their hands full in the Crimea. It was a failure. Tripoli then settled down to the Turkish yoke and was ruled by a series of governors. They made it one of the most isolated countries of the day. The sultan of Turkey forbade all visitors. A visitor was a spy, he considered; and a spy was an incipient conqueror. As time passed it became harder and harder for foreigners to get into the country. A few travelers saw the port of Tripoli. The interior lived in a sort of national *purdah*.

The old times when Tripoli was a favored jumping-off place for explorers of inner Africa were no more. Permission to penetrate inland was given with the greatest reluctance. Tripolitans rarely saw any Europeans except the consuls and a sizable Maltese colony, which latter were not regarded by the natives as true Europeans, but classed as a sort of anomaly: "Arabs varnished with Christianity."

Our knowledge about Tripoli in the second half of the nineteenth century and start of the twentieth is sparse. A few explorers succeeded in passing through the country: the Englishman, Richardson (1845 and 1850); the Germans, Barth (1850 and 1855) and Nachtigal (1869); the Dutch explorer, Miss Tinne (1869) [10]; the Frenchman, Duveyrier (1861), the Frenchman, Monteil (1892) and a few others. In 1901 a Frenchman, Mathuisieulx, managed with great pains to get permission to perform a short inland excursion and wrote an admirable book, crowned by the French Academy: hidden Tripoli was news then—only a few hours' sail from Europe and yet so remote and mysterious. A Tunisian Mohammedan, the Sheikh Otsmane, also performed a trans-Tripolitan journey (1896) and recorded his impressions in a book.

*   *   *

FROM THE RECORDS OF THESE TRAVELERS A PICTURE OF THE Tripolitan scene—Middle Ages in our own times—can be pieced together.

The population was a crazy quilt—men of all colors: white, beige, brown, black, so that the variety of human types which a free port might enjoy was hers despite her isolation. There were Arabs, Berbers, Turks, Jews (one quarter of Tripoli city was Jewish), Maltese, Negroes and Kouloughlis. The last was a name given to the offspring of Turks mating with Tripolitan women. They gave themselves airs on the strength of that part of their blood which came from the ruling class. The natives detested them. The Negroes were slaves who had been, or whose forebears had been, dragged across the Sahara. The slave trade died a slow death at Tripoli, although allegedly forbidden. There was a Sudanese village outside the city with round-topped straw huts like those to which these poor people had been accustomed in their far-off homeland.

Naturally Tripoli was far behind the times. The city had no banks; the country had no railways, nor tramways. Tripoli possessed however one two-wheeled cab in 1869. The governors were

---

[10] Alexine Tinne was brutally murdered by certain Tuareg—on the confines of Tripoli's desert territory a few months later. She was the first female explorer of Africa and, at the time of her death, had the project of crossing the Sahara—a feat, by the way, which no European woman ever accomplished until the days of the automobile. She was young, beautiful, very rich and of a noble family. Her extraordinary and romantic story deserves to be more familiar. Some items about her appear in my bibliography. One, especially curious, is M. Djebari's brochure, published in Tunis in 1895, in which he attempts to show that Miss Tinne was not killed, but kidnaped and forced to marry a desert native, by whom she had two children. This is probably not true.

wont to brag to their rare foreign visitors of grandiose visionary
plans for modern improvements, and did get as far as installing
gas street lamps. A foreign book, even as impersonal as a dictionary, was liable to seizure by the customs.

The population had strange ways and strange notions. Duveyrier
observed the hideous spectacle of an execution. The son of the
murdered man did the executing personally, clumsily beavering
the murderer's head off. The widows of the murdered man were
present in their best clothes "and drank the blood of the executed
man."

Local superstitions were curious: Saffron, a regional crop so
important as to have given its name to the town of Zaafran (we
more usually call it Sirte; the Allies occupied it on Christmas day,
1942) would scarcely grow at all since the hated Turks had come.
"In former times, they said (I am quoting from Barth), several
stems usually shot forth from the same root, whereas now scarcely
a single sample can be found with more than one stalk—a natural
consequence of the contamination or pollution (*nejes*) of the
Turks."

In contrast to this, let us consider Sheikh Otsmane's report on
the enticing food situation at Benghazi in 1896: a pound of meat,
twenty-five centimes (then equaling five cents); pigeons a dime a
pair; a fat hen, fifteen cents. The sheikh lived well, with meat
twice a day, for twenty cents daily. He adds that you could buy a
donkey for the equivalent of sixty cents. These bargains in living
would have reconciled such persons as visited Benghazi to the
absence of post office or telegraph service.

ALL EYES ON TRIPOLI

TRIPOLI WAS IN A SPLENDID POSITION FOR TRADE. IT WAS THE
Mediterranean gateway to the Chad basin across the desert. But
the country operated at a loss. To Turkey the province was a
costly piece of prestige. Turkey had to send money every year to
pay its expenses. The country's total trade, export and import,
did not come to the equivalent of seven million current United
States dollars, according to French consular reports.

To Europe the mysterious land shut up tight as a clam was felt,
however, to possess great potential value. The wise German, Barth,

insisted, "The importance of Tripoli must not be underrated, for it may long remain the most available port from which a steady communication with many parts of the continent can be kept up." Barth was addressing the English public; he was a mercenary explorer, a German hired by England. England had considered the idea of taking over Tripoli previous to the Turkish reconquest, and it is to be suspected that she continued to consider the idea from time to time during the Turkish rule.

The oddest stories of English aggression were believed locally. In 1896 Benghazi still kept vigilant guard over certain near-by ruins because thirty years before two English vessels were said to have come pretending to be sponge fishers and to have sent men ashore to search and pillage these ruins, removing "silver vases, statuary and jewels . . . including the statue of an ancient king in pure gold," all of which they allegedly crammed into their ships and then "swiftly sailed back to London."

In 1901 a story was current that the English had actually occupied clandestinely the fine Bay of Bomba in eastern Tripolitania and had prepared a coal depot there and had camped sailors on the beach. Their motive for this supposed secret occupation was to be on hand to forestall any other European attempt to take over the country.

Italy on her side suspected that France had designs on Tripoli. The Italian press warned its readers that French officers were traveling there incognito, preparatory to a *coup de main*. Sneeringly the *Giornale de Sicilia* referred to "these pseudo-tourists, kodak in hand" and reported that the native population greatly feared a French invasion. A very fanciful story, since all tourists were rigorously barred.

Italy was naturally a likely suspect herself. Italian was the only Christian language used by the natives. Italian newspapers were the only European periodicals ever read by Tripoli's literate class. Italy was said to be spending considerable money on a local school with teachers sent over from Italy.

EXTRAVAGANT TUNISIA

TUNISIA, TRIPOLI'S NEIGHBOR, MET THE CHRISTIAN MENACE IN quite a different fashion, though the result in the end was destined to be the same: Christian occupation.

Husain, the bey, sent a message of congratulation to the French general who conquered the city of Algiers; he so detested the dey that he rejoiced to see his humiliation, even at the risk of having a Christian power on his frontier. A proof of Tunisian good will to France is to be seen in the permission presently granted for the construction of a chapel to St. Louis. To authorize the honoring of an old enemy and a nonbeliever was indeed broad minded.

Turkey noted all this with alarm and made an attempt to reconquer Tunisia; Turkish troops sneaked into the country by the back desert route, but the invasion was a failure. So Tunisia's beys remained in control and showed themselves intrigued by European novelties—too greatly intrigued for their own good, as it turned out.

England as well as France, and later Italy as well, flirted with Tunisia. London's Crystal Palace showed "a conspicuous and pleasing" display of Tunisian products and industry in 1851 and maintained an exceptionally slick representative at the Tunisian court. Indeed at one time it even looked as if England might "extend British protection to the bey," to quote the suave phrase. This did not eventuate.

During the period when Europe was courting Tunisia the country was encouraged to borrow large sums of money to pay for its modernization, until there came a day when she discovered, like the weak and extravagant heroines of old-fashioned drama, that she was hopelessly compromised and the puppet of her creditors. Nachtigal, the German explorer, stayed at Tunis to recover from consumption from 1862 to 1868, part of the time being the bey's physician, and tells of the decay of her economy. One example of her folly: Tunis bought "canon by the hundreds" for the equipment of the country's single and sole frigate.

Then Nature reproved her extravagance by sending a long drought. Crops failed. There was a famine. In 1866 cholera. In 1867-68 typhus. Starvation. Nachtigal says that in remote places "they went so far as to kill children and eat them." The agricultural system broke down completely. It is said that only a tenth of the farm land was kept up. Only the debts grew and grew!

* * *

THE BEYS COULD NOT STRUGGLE AGAINST FINANCIAL CHAOS. THEY were politely described as a debonair lot. It probably seemed futile to be sober with such a national income, and such a national debt. One of them, Mohammed Bey, shut himself away from the bill collectors with twelve hundred ladies and died of too much loving.

SLAVES OUT OF A JOB

POOR TROUBLED TUNISIA PERFORMED ONE ACT OF MODERNIZATION which was praiseworthy. In 1846 the bey Ahmed abolished slavery. Yet even this humane action harmed the country's industry and economy in many ways. Furthermore provincial places which handled the incoming slave supply lost a big revenue and complained bitterly. Even the slaves themselves did not at first appreciate the change.

In Algeria where emancipation was proclaimed immediately after the conquest it was thought necessary to emancipate gradually over a period of two years. But the delay did not prevent great loss to incoming slave caravans which had brought strings of slaves from Negroland in good faith only to have their human stock in trade confiscated and turned loose on arrival. The eventual result was the ruin of trans-Saharan commerce.

The slaves were profoundly puzzled by the idea of freedom. They were scared by the prospect of having to handle the responsibility of their own lives as free individuals, and even ashamed not to belong to anybody. Some scuttled off secretly to offer themselves for sale in Tunisia where a black market in Negroes still existed.

This black market was comprehensible. People had been accustomed since time immemorial, since the days of Carthage, and probably before, to the affectionate, devoted and frolicsome Negro servant. The new law was a shock. There was naturally no way to keep up the Negro domestic staff save through slavery; no Negroes, of course, came crossing the Sahara at their own initiative to offer their services.

When Nachtigal bade farewell to the bey of Tunis before starting his exploration into inner Africa—this was some twenty years after the emancipation—the bey said with wistful playfulness, "If you can, bring me back some little niggers!"

In Morocco slavery endured long after the neighboring Barbary States had abolished the practice. In 1923, when I first visited Fez, I spoke with a woman in early middle life who stated that she had worked as a slave in a big local household.

RESENTFUL MOROCCO

Morocco's resentment to the Christian threat had been prompt and vigorous. She made war against France as Abd-el-Kader's ally, as has been mentioned.

Very soon thereafter Morocco had another war to fight against another Christian power, Spain. But this conflict does not really enter into the pattern of the European effort to absorb North Africa. It was rather another act of a long family quarrel. Spain and Morocco had been scrapping for over a thousand years. They were very close together geographically and had swapped populations back and forth. Gibraltar had been just an outsize river between twin lands, both Moslem, which alternately attacked and conquered one another's shores. Back in Roman days there had been a time when part of Morocco was classed administratively with Spain.

In 1859 Spain declared war on Morocco. In 1893-94 there was further trouble. Both times Spain won the war but lost the peace in so far as any important territorial gain in Morocco was concerned. Spain's Moroccan holdings remained small.

A COUNTRY WITHOUT A FRIEND

Morocco's national ideal at this time was to live in a world of her own. She dealt with Europe officially only through the peephole of Tangier. No Christian consul or ambassador was allowed at the sultan's court. They all remained at Tangier and communicated with the central government via the Tangier governor. Algeria alone—being Mohammedan, albeit under Christian management—was allowed a consul at Fez (obligatorily a Moslem).

In the rustic phrase, Morocco, sensing Christian danger to North Africa, sought to crawl into a hole and pull the hole in after her. It is a state of mind learnedly named "xenophobia," a hatred of foreigners. It was based on an instinct for national and religious self-preservation. Of course, it could not last. The sultan, Moulay Hassan, saw himself obliged to import foreign experts to reorganize his army so that he could hold his empire. Six French officers came to instruct his troops in artillery. Italian aid was brought in to help install an arms factory at Fez.

These things were a double wedge driven into Morocco's closed door, not only introducing foreigners but also rousing the jealousy of other European nations. This jealousy was a potential threat. But still the door did not open. Aside from the Spaniards in their small region by Ceuta, and aside from the consuls at Tangier, the few other Europeans were restricted to trading places at certain ports. No sane European would have dreamed of trying to live in the interior. At Casablanca the European colony in 1894 came to 150 persons. They could not safely leave the city even to get a breath of air and a bit of exercise on the beach. In 1883 when Foucauld (later the martyred Saharan hermit, Père de Foucauld) undertook to explore inner Morocco it was so dangerous for Christians that he had to assume the character of a Jew. In explaining why Christians in Morocco were in "peril of their lives," he said, "This is not religious fanaticism . . . to them a European who travels in their country can be but an emissary sent to study it in view of an invasion; he is a spy."

So Morocco, a biscuit toss from Europe, was as a whole more mysterious than central Africa.

* * *

AT MOULAY HASSAN'S DEATH THE NEW BOY SULTAN, OF WHOM I shall speak again, won himself the name of the "Sultan Mahboul" (the Mad King). He took up with foreign ways and undignified foreign amusements. The common people were disgusted. They were angry at the proposed telegraph installation and the proposed railway. The telegraph lines and railway workshops were sabotaged. Wheels were the devil's invention. They say that the first wagons at Fez were stoned.

But foreign novelties were intriguing. Foreign loans were tempting. Morocco went the regular path of backward nations—alternately indignant with the teasing outside world, alternately accepting favors that compromised. However, during the whole of the nineteenth century she was able, except for a trifling aggrandizement of the old Spanish Ceuta territory, to keep her country intact and independent.

EGYPT'S OPEN DOOR

EGYPT MARCHED MEANTIME ALONG THE SAME ROAD AS HER NEIGHbors toward the inevitable Christian master. But Egypt marched in quite another measure, quite out of step with the rest.

Egypt was full of foreigners. At a time when Algeria knew only soldiers and struggling colonists, when Tunisia was desolate and Tripoli and Morocco fanatically hidden away, Egypt was a tourist resort and a home of worldly gaiety.

Cairo had its opera season, and the "Khedive's Ball" was "the culminating event of the winter festivities and as brilliant a function as oriental splendor and cosmopolitan fashion could compass." This enthusiastic description is from the pen of an old lady, Miss Mabel Caillard, who spent a lifetime in Egypt from the days of the Khedive Ismail to the eve of World War II.

Cook's, the travel people, were already transporting foreigners along the Nile to stare at the antiquities. Egypt had become aware of the potential value of her monuments, which the Mohammedan world till then had regarded as idolatrous trash, pillaged for building materials, or torn ruthlessly apart in treasure hunts. Egypt's newly roused interest in her marvelous past was shown in the fact that the corvée, forced labor system, was applied to the work of excavation undertaken by Mariette, the first director of the Cairo Museum.

* * *

EGYPT WAS FASCINATED BY EUROPEAN LUXURIES, GADGETS AND improvements. Mehemet Ali had started the Europeanization of the country; his immediate successor was reactionary, but short lived. Then came a period when Egypt emulated the drunken sailor, and spent hand over fist. Mehemet Ali had been a little abashed at his novel improvements and, so they say, preferred to sleep on a rug on the floor beside his imported four-poster bed. Later Egyptian rulers had no such inhibitions. They practiced and combined all the extravagances of the Orient and of the West. They spent crazily.

Some items of Egyptian royal lavishness became notorious. There was Said's toilet set: toothbrush, comb and hairbrush, which cost the Egyptian taxpayer the equivalent of fourteen thousand dollars. It would be interesting to see that toothbrush. It was Said who gave permission for the construction of the Suez Canal. His dearest toy was the railroad connecting Cairo and Alexandria, and his greatest delight was to order out special trains. In connection with special trains the United States consul in Cairo had an amazing experience. Mr. Thayer was invited to a reception at Alexandria given by Ismail at his accession on the death of Said. Consul Thayer did not receive his invitation till late and had no opportunity to send for his gala clothes which were in Cairo. Ismail heard about this and commanded a special train to be sent to fetch what the consul needed to make a good showing at the party. Mr. Thayer records in his diary his mixed sentiments of horror at the extravagance and pride at being probably the only man of his day (1863) whose clothes ever traveled in lone glory in a specially ordered train.[11]

THE SUEZ FESTIVAL

THE PEAK OF EGYPT'S SPECTACULAR PRODIGALITY WAS THE FESTIVAL which celebrated the opening of the Suez Canal (1869). To this came an emperor (Austrian), an empress (French), a crown prince (German), the Prince of Wales, an Italian prince and others of high degree. Eugénie led the procession through the canal on her yacht and the rest followed—as was right enough, the enterprise having been one which France initiated and pushed through while others disapproved. Incidentally, it was during her journey to see the Suez opened that Eugénie received from the sultan of Turkey a dress which allegedly had cost the equivalent of six hundred thousand current United States dollars!

[11] Mr. William Thayer's hitherto unpublished diary is quoted in Gordon Waterfield's *Lucie Duff Gordon* (London, 1937).

Verdi's *Aïda* was composed especially for the great celebration at Cairo which followed. In the crowd scenes three thousand players took part. No need to hire Negro supers and to fake properties; genuine Sudanese carried real antique statues from the Cairo Museum. The costumes were gorgeous; the stage jewelry, Paris-made copies of authentic ancient pieces.

After the performance at a gentlemen's supper six of the most beautiful girls of the ballet troupe were borne to table on gold platters "with a mere garnishment of custard."

Ismail had picked up prodigality where his predecessor, Said, laid it down. Said had been happy with a several-thousand-dollar toothbrush; Ismail ran an opera season of ninety performances every year with high-class imported artists, and fetched over the Coquelins, Jane Hading and other big stage figures to play before him.

DEBTS

ALL THIS COST IMMENSELY. NEITHER EXCESSIVE TAXATION OF A downtrodden people, nor the increased cotton profits during the United States Civil War, when the value of Egyptian cotton went up to five times its previous value, could begin to pay Ismail's bills.

Ismail began to borrow abroad. He borrowed wildly. The country's debt rose from fifteen million dollars to something like five hundred million.

"THEY ALWAYS LOSE"

ISMAIL'S INSOUCIANT BORROWINGS, HIS LUXURIOUS MODERN CAPITAL, and his gorgeous way of life made him a famous personage. This was his delight. To "the band of brigands" in office life in Egypt was very profitable. To the hundreds of adventurers and scabby financiers who exploited the country Egypt was a delight. To the ordinary laborer and farmer Egypt was hell on earth. A Frenchman said long ago, "Whoever wins a civil war in Egypt, the Egyptian common people always lose." It was equally true of that period of modernization of their country.

Cairo was a beautiful show place, or part of it was. Penetrate into the poor quarters and up country and there was desolation.

The taxes were cruel. A system—then regarded as very shocking—of collecting taxes in advance was introduced. "People are terribly beaten to get next year's taxes out of them," wrote Lady Duff Gordon, who is said to have been the only European living then in the remote country districts. Again, "The courbash has been going on my neighbors' backs and feet all the morning."

The courbash was the traditional and accredited aid to Egyptian government, regularly used by the police. It was made in up-Nile countries from the skin of the hippopotamus, the skin being cut in narrow strips when freshly taken from the dead beast. These strips, five or six feet long and tapering to a point, were rolled up so that the edges united to form a sort of pipe, tied fast and dried in the sun. They were rubbed with butter to make them pliable and their artful manufacture was a profitable and gruesome Sudanese industry. They were an old invention, already familiar in the days of El-Bekri (eleventh century) who knew them as *ceryafa*. They were obligatorily an exclusively African article for in colder climates—even in the Near East—they became brittle, cracked and lost their elasticity.

As a help in tax collecting the courbash was most effective. When persons of Egypt's common class first went to Europe it is said that "the novelty of not being beaten (by the street police) was quite intoxicating."

THE CORVÉE

THE NOTORIOUS CORVÉE MADE THE PEOPLE MISERABLE AND INSECURE. For the making of the Suez Canal twenty thousand fresh laborers had to be found each month. The laborers had to feed themselves; their families starved.

And all for an end which brought them embarrassment rather than profit. In latter years the canal was something which stiffened Egypt's pride, yet impeded her hopes of independence. Egypt obviously was not strong enough to guarantee the protection without outside help of so vital a piece of world property. The canal reduced the income of the common Egyptian. Travelers on ships sailed through their land without spending the money which in the days of the land shuttle had enriched the inhabitants. Egypt's plain man was by-passed by an enterprise to which he had given his sweat and his blood. Presently Ismail, hard pressed, sold his canal shares to England, so the enterprise also by-passed the ruler.

TELEGRAM TO ISMAIL

ISMAIL IN HIS GLORY HAD GOT HIS OFFICIAL TITLE CHANGED FROM viceroy to khedive. (Contrary to the usual parlance, the rulers of Egypt of Mehemet Ali's family line did not acquire the name of khedive till 1867; the word means prince or sovereign.) Ismail had enjoyed the thrill of showing his titular master, the sultan of Turkey, his first railway train, when he came on a visit to Cairo. He had been received by Queen Victoria and by the Pope, and had been the honored host of most of the great folk of his time.

Suddenly one June morning in 1879 he received a, telegram from the sultan of Turkey addressed to "The Ex-Khedive." It parallels the miner's ungainly fashion of breaking the news of a fellow workman's fatal accident: "Does the Widow So-and-So live here?" Pushed by the Great Powers the sultan had deposed Ismail. Ismail with three hundred of his best ladies sailed away from the country he had so gorgeously and improvidently decorated and improved and so cruelly despoiled and mismanaged to finish his days virtually a prisoner near Constantinople.

A so-called Dual Control (English and French) had been introduced tentatively and was now reintroduced. There were mutterings of "Egypt for the Egyptians!" It was a cry that History was not yet ready to hear. Egypt was instead to become a Christian puppet. Or shall we say pupil? Egypt had made it amply clear that she was not as yet able to rule herself. Men who submit to the corvée cannot aspire overnight to independence. It is a long road from the courbash to the voting booth.

WAITING FOR DESTINY

THUS IN THEIR VARIOUS WAYS THE STATES OF MEDITERRANEAN Africa—Tripoli, Tunisia, Morocco and Egypt—faced the menace of Christian domination during the years that followed the conquest of Algeria by France. Let us leave them suspended on the brink of their inevitable destiny. Let us glance at what was happening to the rest of North Africa during this same critical period.

Europe was driving wedges into the interior of the continent, penetrating and pacifying the Sahara and Sudan. To tell the story in detail would be impossible here; I can but pick out a few typical items in widely distributed places. From these the reader may get a notion of the whole process which was to end in the European control of all inner Africa. It is a passage of history not generally familiar and may therefore be of special interest.

WHY THE SAHARA WAS TEMPTING

WITH THE ALGERIAN CONQUEST A WAY TO THE MIDDLE AND WESTERN Sahara was opened to Christian occupation. This occupation was naturally to be French since they controlled the gateway. This obvious thought was diplomatically confirmed by the convention of 1890 wherein was included the statement that the desert below France's Mediterranean holdings was recognized by England as falling under the French "sphere of influence." (This somewhat comical phrase—considering the difficulty of "influencing" savage or barbarous peoples—had lately been added to diplomacy's vocabulary at the Berlin Conference of 1884.)

* * *

FRANCE HAD GONE INTO THE SAHARA EVEN BEFORE THE ALGERIAN conquest was consolidated.

This had not been for the sake of the Sahara's beautiful eyes. The Sahara was not desirable in itself. There was, indeed, no doubt that a British statesman was justified in his sneer, after the 1890 conference had split a line through Africa, "We have only given the Gallic Cock some sand to scratch!" And there was no arguing against the jeers of some of the French home folk who—opposing Saharan expansion—declared that the whole of the Saharan trade was not as valuable as the business done by a big town French grocery store!

The reason why it seemed necessary to pacify the Sahara was that this wild stretch of country at the back door endangered Algeria. It was a refuge and a conspiring place for the colony's native enemies. It had to be policed. Such was the inescapable "law of expansion which obliges every civilized nation when in contact with backward peoples to push forward constantly to insure the protection of the territory already acquired"—the endless chain of colonial aggrandisement.

The pacification of the Sahara was also important because it was regarded as a potential route to the Sudan and the west coast of Africa. This visionary idea took hold of the European imagination.

So, for the first time since the Romans went to mysterious Agisymba, European troops attempted to penetrate into the Great Desert.

RESISTERS AND COLLABORATIONISTS IN THE DESERT

THE PEOPLE OF THE SAHARA AS A WHOLE REACTED AS MIGHT HAVE been expected. The desert, to the outside world, seems a weird and terrible place, but the Saharan adored it. Its vast spaces, its freedom, its constant challenge to courage, its opportunities for the pillage of caravans and for the sudden attack of oases—crack and grab and away!—all this made up a very attractive scheme of life for wild, brave and lazy men, who had never known the amenities of green fields and running brooks.

A few Saharans, it was true, favored the Christian intrusion, realizing that it was an irresistible movement and hoping that they might benefit by the newcomers. Such as these ignored the sultan of Morocco's exhortation that the people of the Sahara should refuse all commercial contacts with the Christians, should "seize their goods . . . and be like a single hand against foreign enterprise."

The rest of the desert's people resisted fiercely, fighting and dying to try to keep the Sahara for the Saharans. There were curious personages amongst these desert resisters.

"*THE MAN WITH THE TOPKNOT*"

THE ODDEST FIGURE OF THEM ALL WAS "BOU-CHOUCHA," A REFUGEE from South Algeria, whose nickname meant "The Man with the Topknot." He had started life as a wandering minstrel or singing pimp, who celebrated the charms of dancing girls. Then he joined the French Spahis and deserted. Presently he set up as a religious figure, a sort of mahdi, and gathered behind him discontents from Algeria and from many of the oases. He now boasted of supernatural powers, claiming to be impervious to gunshot. He would let people fire at him point-blank, having secretly in advance removed the shot and replaced a pellet of wool.

But he was brave in battle: "Alone, head bare with his topknot in the wind, he rode straight at the French troops, receiving no wound, though two horses were shot under him."

Finally "Bou-Choucha" was captured and shot in the early 1870's. For this life story of a curious patriot about whom there is little general record, I am indebted to the notes of an old-time official interpreter, Jean Galtier, discovered by that indefatigable searcher of Saharan archives, Martin.

"*THE CHERIF*"

HE WHO WAS USUALLY CALLED "THE CHERIF" WAS A RESISTER MUCH more generally familiar. You can find his name, Mohammed-ben-Abd-Allah, in the *Encyclopaedia Britannica*.

"The Cherif" started his Holy War activities at the very old and important Saharan town of Ouargla (see page 247). Ouargla was then a semi-republic with a sultan who was a mere showpiece, despite his expensive ancestry. The local tradition was that the first of the line of Ouargla's sultans had been imported from Morocco at great cost, the sultan of Morocco having been prevailed upon to ship a suitable prince into the remote desert by the offer of his weight in gold dust. (From hearsay information about Ouargla collected by General Daumas before Christians ever went there.) But Ouargla's sultans were no longer of much account. The last to hold office bred a son and heir whom the arriving French described as being "a hair's breadth from an idiot."

"The Cherif," a very shrewd old man, worked up a following. The substance of his preaching was, "I am the great cherif from the south, sent by the Prophet. The French are not so numerous as it is said. They are not so strong as they seem. Follow me and we will have an easy win!"

Some he won by persuasion. Others by threats. He got to be known by that title sometimes given to the inspired leader. He was *"Moul-es-Saa,"* or "The Master of the Hour."

THE BATTLE OF LAGHOUAT

THE CENTER OF HIS ACTIVITY BECAME LAGHOUAT, A PLACE OF SOME consequence on the desert's shores directly south of Algiers. Its population was renowned for bravery back in the days of Ibn-Khaldoun. Their fighting spirit was phenomenal; no outsider could master Laghouat. The Arabs tried it in vain. The dey of Algiers had managed to get a yearly tribute of seven Negroes from Laghouat, but only in exchange for permission to buy grain in Algeria. Within the city the same spirit of belligerency prevailed; Laghouat was divided into two parties, separated by a wall and each with its own government. Sometimes they shot at one another. When such feuds occur in an oasis with sand and rock all around, there is no moving away, people have to stay on and snarl. Laghouat's two groups snarled at one another, they say, for three hundred years.

In the early part of the nineteenth century one party finally defeated the other, and in 1844 the French received a message from the chief of the winning side, expressing a wish to make friends with "the French sultan." After that Laghouat became a dependency of France.

"The Cherif" drove the pro-French chief away and occupied the place. To the French it seemed to have unique value as the gateway into the Sahara and the whole southland beyond. They came in force, and Laghouat, with its record of ferocity and internal discord, became the scene of one of the most murderous little battles of African history (1852). It had been prophesied. A local saint had said a century before, "You will devour one another like lions forced to live in the same cage, until one day the Christians come—those tamers of lions—to conquer you all and muzzle you!"

Laghouat's sandy streets were a sponge of blood. Her wells were stuffed with corpses. A French general was killed. France recaptured Laghouat and "The Cherif" fled to Ouargla, a couple of hundred miles deeper into the desert.

SI-HAMZA, COLLABORATIONIST

SI-HAMZA, FRIEND OF FRANCE, THEN TOOK UP THE TASK OF disciplining "The Cherif."

Si-Hamza was no ranting upstart like "The Cherif," but a Mohammedan religious dignitary and a political personage of high standing, who had decided to join the winning side.

Near Ouargla he defeated "The Cherif." But the old man was undaunted. He still made converts to his Holy War, still believed he could throw the Christians out of the Sahara. At Tougourt he had his final lesson (1854).

France had pushed a little way—such a little way—into the sands. Two years later, near the scene of "The Cherif's" defeat, France sank the first modern-style artesian well ever pierced into the Saharan sands.

GEOGRAPHERS' NEW
PLAYTHING

THE SAHARA HAD BECOME THE GEOGRAPHERS' NEW PLAYTHING AND problem. What could be done with this enormous and almost useless stretch of the world, of which they were just beginning to get some notion? There was promptly a suggestion that it ought to be flooded and put to work at agriculture. Another suggestion was that parts of the Sahara be turned into an inland lake. To show the wide interest that was taken in such schemes I mention that an official French bibliography gives sixty-four titles dealing exclusively with the subject, to which list my own reading can add a dozen or so other items in the shape of incidental discussions and comments.

Roudaire, a military man, was the active partisan of the inland lake. De Lesseps, of Suez fame, also fancied it and is said to have thought that the cost would be about the same as that of digging the canal. It was proposed to make a lagoon about as big as Lake Ontario.

Another and very fantastic plan was that put forward by one Donald Mackenzie who conceived the idea of inducing the Atlantic Ocean to come in and romp across the Sahara as far as El-Djouf in the Southwest. El-Djouf is a depression, sometimes called "The Belly of the Desert." The plan in question would have meant flooding a district of some one hundred thousand square kilometers. Mackenzie who dreamed this ambitious dream had founded an informal British colony at Cape Juby on the Atlantic desert coast, then described as "a patch of land which occupies the peculiar position of being British, and yet is not recognized as such by Great Britain." Now it is part of the Spanish Río de Oro. The vast desert background irked Mackenzie and he had the godlike notion of transforming it. The curious thing is that his plan, though pronounced by one of his countrymen to be "an ignorant scheme," was much discussed at the time.

But the Sahara remained its old arid self.

The future should show a Sahara taught to work for the space it occupies in a crowded world. Our knowledge of the Saharan problem has immensely increased since the early days when travelers reported seeing broken ships' masts sticking up out of the sands or lying prone there and therefore believed they had found proof that the Sahara had recently been a navigable sea. What they saw were petrified tree fragments. We are told, it is true, that the Sahara was once submerged. But this was long before there were sailboats or men to sail them.

"THE MAN WITH THE TURBAN"

RETURN TO THE SAHARA'S RESISTERS—THE SAHARA BREEDS GLOOMY thoughts and violent behavior; emotions are easily roused to fever. Resentment is bitter. So the Sahara's sparse population was hard to subdue in any lasting fashion. In the time of Si-Hamza, the friend of France, it had looked as if it might be relatively easy. Si-Hamza was ambitious. He hoped that, as France's protégé, he would control the whole desert as far as the Niger. So, as France's propagandist, he preached friendliness. But after his death his tribe, the Ouled Sidi Cheikh and various members of his family had other ideas and made trouble.

Africans were easily roused by cunning talk emphasizing religious antagonism. We decry this as fanaticism, but up to that time there had been in the African experience little to suggest that the coming of Christians would be anything but destructive and humiliating. Benevolent, helpful, health-improving Christian behavior were things only to be observed within the last century by the North African native.

Especially proficient in fomenting religious prejudice was "The Man with the Turban" (Bou Amama), whose real name was Mohammed ben-Arbi. He founded a fraternal organization inside whose frame he preached revolt, announcing "The moment of deliverance is near!" His followers massacred European workers in the esparto (alfa) country of south Algeria. He was a continuing worry to France, withdrawing into the deeper desert after a defeat to gather a renewed band of enthusiasts. He was a viper under the rock, and much admired by the Moroccan sultan, who used to send him messages of encouragement.

MZAB

DURING HIS MOST ACTIVE PERIOD "THE MAN WITH THE TURBAN" had asked and had received supplies and arms from the people of the Mzab, who live in seven little cities deep in the northern belt of the Sahara. This aid he received despite the fact that the Mzab was under French protection and alleged domination by virtue of an agreement made some thirty years before.

The earlier resister, "The Cherif," had scared one of the seven cities by a terrible mauling: he had cut down two thousand of its date palm trees, the ultimate of war's cruelties from the Saharan viewpoint. Thus frightened, the Mzab had permitted him to use their country as a hiding place.

The Mzab having become a tool for France's enemies and being in a strategic situation, France decided that the vague protection arrangement must be replaced by definite military occupation. This was in 1882. In so doing France adopted as odd a community as exists on earth.

*   *   *

THE MZAB CONSISTS OF FIVE LITTLE CITIES IN A CLUMP, SOME FOUR
hundred miles south of Algiers, and two others standing apart
from the five. The most important and best known is Ghardaïa.
I know them all and was in negotiation to establish my winter
home in the Mzab when World War II arrested my project.

The Mzab is unique on earth as the strange home of a strange
people. (For the origins of the Mzabites, Mohammedans of a
nonorthodox sect, the ultrastrict Abadites, see pages 220 to 224.)
No place is more typical of the Sahara's fascinating ugliness. No
people are more typical of the crankishness which the Sahara
fosters.

Before its inhabitants, who had been in turn driven from their
two previous homes, Tiaret and Ouargla, came there to live, there
was no natural oasis in the Mzab. The country was like the inside
of an immense earthen pot, dry as a bone. The so-called Mzab
River runs wet only on rare occasions. Between 1728 and 1882
there were just twelve big rains. A single moderate rainfall may,
with luck, occur every third or fourth winter. To dig down to
water level—to what the natives call "The Sea under the Ground"
—it was necessary to excavate by hand wells of sixty or a hundred
or sometimes of three hundred feet deep. In 1939 they were again
attempting to improve the Mzab by sinking artesian wells; a
South Dakota man was bossing the work.

                    *   *   *

TO THE MZABITES OF OLD THE CHARM OF THE PLACE LAY IN ITS
very awfulness. They believed that they would be let alone to
live in their own peculiar way because nobody on earth would be
perverse enough to invade their desolate country. They adopted
what they called "The Secret Way." Since the year 1011, when the
first city of the Mzab was founded, they have kept themselves
apart from the world—a body of religious eccentrics, intensely
pious, intensely austere, intensely solemn, and very competent in
trade.

By isolation, inbreeding and their special way of life, the Mzabites have developed a racial type. "They have become," writes
Professor Gautier, "a distinct biological species. . . . It is a case
where the subordination of the physical to the moral appears with
astonishing clearness." In other words, they have been able, by
centuries of striving, to keep apart from the world, to build their

bodies into a special shape and coloration. Originally Berber, a brunette people, the Mzabites have acquired a particularly white skin. (On this see Professor Seligman's *Races of Africa.*) Their cheeks are of ivory whiteness, faintly rosy. Their legs are usually short and ungainly. Once observed, you would know a man of the Mzab anywhere.

As for their women, nobody ever observes them. I never saw one. The Mzabite woman lives in complete seclusion. If ever she leaves her home she is wrapped in such heavy woolen bundling that she can scarcely walk. Should she meet a man, she must turn and face the nearest house wall and wait till he has passed by. A Frenchwoman who has lived alongside Ghardaïa for twenty years told me that she once, because of a very unusual circumstance, had the extraordinary experience of seeing a Mzabite woman unveiled. She was fragile, pale and beautiful.

*   *   *

IN THE MORAL CODE OF THE MZAB EVERYTHING JOYOUS IS FORBIDDEN: music, dancing, wine, tobacco, all amusements. No Mzabite female has ever been authorized to travel away from the country. For a thousand years, mother to daughter to granddaughter, they have been desert prisoners. The men at times have left on trading expeditions or to earn money by working in more prosperous lands. They have had to, or starve. For the Mzab was too desolate to support itself; the animals—camels and donkeys—used to drag water buckets up from the deep wells ate almost as much as the gardens could produce. Yet the Mzabites—it is hard to believe— became very rich. Back in 1882 when the French first came, a square yard of ground in this glum country sold at the equivalent of fifteen current dollars. The Mzab had become a great caravan junction. The Mzabites had become the Sahara's bankers and jobbers. They had a gift for business. One Mzabite, the saying went, was as good as two Jews. They paid a subsidy to near-by fighting tribes to leave their caravans alone and to act as their mercenaries to protect the Mzab from attack. Time spent in war was time wasted, they thought.

Old Mzabite writings recall with pride the name of one of themselves, Sheikh-Abu-Yakuk-Yusuf, traveler and author, who first led their people into the trans-Saharan slave trade which made the country's fortunes. Leo Africanus tells of the wealth of the Mzab.

Their business reputation was spotless, and their honesty passed into proverbs. "They were the sworn enemies of lying; they would die of hunger alongside goods (food supplies) entrusted to them. If a Mzabite says to you, 'God be with you,' sleep easy; he will watch over you."

"KANOUNS"

IT WOULD BE WRONG TO LEAVE THE MZAB WITHOUT GIVING A FEW passages from their *kanouns,* a word derived from the Greek (our canons, laws) and which somehow drifted into use among Mohammedans. In the case of the Mzabites, the word is applied only to a list of punishments for social breaches.

Here are a few items from the *kanouns* of the various little Mzabite cities:

> Any individual who is convicted of addressing a word in the street to a woman, fined 25 reals (about 18 current United States dollars) and banished for two years—until he has seen the sea (Ghardaïa)
>
> He who is convicted of having drunk fermented liquor, same fine and to receive 80 blows (Ghardaïa)
>
> One convicted of using fermented drink or eating pork or human flesh or other filth may be punished up to 500 blows (El-Ateuf)
>
> Rejoicings with music or divers games or the use of henna on the occasion of weddings, births or circumcisions forbidden—penalty fine of five reals and temporary religious excommunication (Melika)
>
> All instruments of music forbidden them. Who uses them—up to 20 blows (El-Ateuf)
>
> Use of lewd language in public, if not carrying the implication of adultery or fornication, 20 blows. If carrying such implication, as many as 40 (El-Ateuf)

*   *   *

AS MIGHT BE EXPECTED THE RULING ON SEX MATTERS WAS ESPEcially savage. No man might marry a non-Mzabite girl—punishment: leave the Mzab forever. A woman attempting to quit the conjugal home with another man to be "beaten indefinitely." The bastinado to be applied by her father, brother or nearest relative, who was authorized furthermore to imprison her at his discretion. What could imprisonment have meant to a woman who was a prisoner already? I have read that delinquent women were let down into a little dark cell with a single opening in the top and fed by scraps thrown down to them.

There was a formal etiquette for beatings. A woman should be bastinadoed upon the shoulders, entirely covered by her veil. Beforehand another woman should inspect her to make sure she did not wear a heavy garment capable of softening the blows. "To prevent a woman exposing her person in struggling she shall be obliged to sit in a big basket coming up to arm level, or be put in a big bag, tied under the armpits. To avoid the sight of physical accidents, which pain or fear might produce in a woman, water shall be sprinkled beforehand in the basket or bag and upon the adjacent ground. A pregnant woman never to be bastinadoed; she shall receive her punishment after the accouchement."

The above is from a brochure on the *kanouns* of the Mzab by Professor Marcel Morand of the Law School of Algiers, and from a similar work by Motylinski, military interpreter at the Mzab. The history and customs of the Mzab have been industriously studied—their oddities being naturally of great interest to students, and there is a considerable literature on the subject.[12] It has seemed worth while for me to give a little space to this curious small state—a medieval community preserved in full running order

[12] A few of the best items are:

Daumas, *Le Sahara algérien*, pp. 52 to 71 (Paris, 1845).
Commandant Robin, *Le Mzab et son annexation à la France* (Algiers, 1884).
Dr. Charles Amat, *Le Mzab et les Mzabites* (Paris, 1888).
Emile Masqueray, *Chronique d'Abou Zakaria* (Algiers, 1879).
Marcel Morand, *Les Kanouns du Mzab* (Algiers, 1903).
E. Zeys, *Legislation mzabite* (Algiers, 1886).
A. de C. Motylinski, *Guerara depuis sa fondation* (Guerara is one of the Mzab's seven cities) Algiers, 1885.
Marcel Mercier, *La Civilisation urbaine du Mzab* (Algiers, 1932).
Curiously enough the justly renowned *Cambridge Medieval History* contains a veritable cat's cradle of errors about the Mzab (Vol. II, p. 378, by Prof. Becker of the Colonial Institute of Hamburg) wherein the Mzab is represented as a principality existing prior to 800 (the first Mzabite city was not founded till 1011) and its "prince" as being the man who established the Aghlabite dynasty (see p. 227 of this book). Prof. Becker presumably confused "Mzab" with "Zab," the latter being an old-time name for the Tunisian section of coastal Africa, and also confused the name of the dynasty, "Aghlabite," with the name of the religious sect, "Abadite," to which the Mzabites belong. The German professor's is a fine case of double malapropism.

into our own times in its desert setting, like those frogs which, we are told, survive for countless years embedded in rock.

*   *   *

WITHIN JUST TWELVE MONTHS OF THE FRENCH OCCUPATION, THE Mzab was connected with both the North and the South by good French-made roads. Perhaps after a while these preternaturally solemn people forgot the original French affront of marching through their leading city with drums playing. At the time this simple act represented mental cruelty of the most painful type.

TUAREG

THE FRENCH CAME INTO CONTACT WITH ANOTHER VERY PECULIAR people in the Sahara—the Tuareg. From the outward and visible point of view they were even queerer than the Mzabites: their men always wore veils, their women showed their faces to the world.

The Tuareg were of the same general family as the Almoravides of old who conquered Morocco and Spain in the eleventh and twelfth centuries (see page 282).

The Tuareg lived across the middle and southern part of the Sahara, lived there as nomads. Moving was easy. A Tuareg's home was of the smallest, a leather tent no bigger than an umbrella. A well-to-do Tuareg family could carry everything it possessed upon the back of a single camel. But, notwithstanding his simplicity of life, the Tuareg was no common savage. He—among all the peoples of North Africa—had his own written language. All the rest used Arabic script. His etiquette was complex. His women were held in high honor and treated with chivalrous gallantry. His children were well behaved. I speak of the Tuareg in the past tense, since—though still existent—he has lost much of his old prestige, and with it, some of his old-time punctilio. He has forgotten how to read his Tifinagh inscriptions. I hope he still maintains his romantic *ahal* (courts of love in the medieval mode) where men and maidens sang and recited verses.

*   *   *

AT FIRST THE TUAREG WERE RELATIVELY TOLERANT OF THE FRENCH newcomers. They were Mohammedans, but by no means an ultra-pious lot, and were not subject to Holy War excitement against Christians. Indeed, there seems to have been in the remote past some Christian element in the Tuareg's own background. A very distinct cross is the motif of all their ornamental designs. The dagger worn with a bracelet on the left arm has a grip in the form of a cross; a cross often appears on their tent supports and on the bow of their camel saddles. The Tuareg has retained, without knowing why, the symbol of a faith which he once presumably followed. Barth tells that in his day—a century ago—they were known by the Arabs as "the Christians of the desert." In all events Tuareg sentiment toward the invader was not inflamed by fanaticism.

* * *

SI-HAMZA, THE FRIEND OF FRANCE ALREADY MENTIONED, WAS AN excellent propagandist and convinced the Tuareg that they would best serve their own interests by welcoming the newcomers. It was he who persuaded Sheikh Othman to visit the French in Algiers. Othman subsequently went to Paris, saw the emperor and brought back objects that were a complete novelty in his homeland: shovels and picks and pulleys to aid in getting water up from desert wells.

An understanding between France and the Veiled Men to the end of mutual friendship and trade was summed up in a treaty in 1862. The odd and lively Tuareg fascinated Europeans. Years before the explorer, Horneman, had said that, "if cultivated and enlightened, their natural abilities would render them perhaps one of the greatest nations upon earth." In 1864 Duveyrier who had lived amongst them published their high praise: "lying, domestic theft, abuse of confidence are unknown amongst the Tuareg" . . . "the gallantry of the Tuareg is proverbial." . . . "No European traveller has ever been victim of an act of brutality or fanaticism either in Tuareg territory or at the hands of the Tuareg." [13]

* * *

BUT THE ILL-ASSORTED RACES, CHRISTIAN FRENCH AND VEILED DESERT barbarians, were not friends for long. The Tuareg found that

[13] *Les Tuareg du nord* (Paris, 1864). The literature in French about the Tuareg is fairly extensive; in English it is sparse. An interesting work is *People of the Veil* by Francis Rennell Rodd (London, 1926).

French control was detrimental. Pillage of caravans was their traditional and honored racial industry, as well as their adored sport and amusement. Farming or any work was a disgusting disgrace—a Tuareg proverb: "Dishonor enters a home along with the plough." With the French coming the *razzia* (an armed expedition to capture flocks and supplies) and the pillage of travelers were frowned upon. Furthermore opportunity for pillage was reduced, since France was trying to abolish slavery in Mediterranean Africa so that the transporting of slaves—mainstay of the Saharan caravan business—was cut down. The Tuareg, in short, were bitterly disappointed in their new friends.

In 1881 occurred an incident symptomatic of Tuareg dissatisfaction, and one which shook France's illusions about the chivalrous Tuareg. A French mission was massacred in most cruel circumstances.

It is true that there had been isolated unpleasant incidents before. I have mentioned the murder of Miss Tinne (see footnote, p. 513). But in her case there were extenuations. She had stepped unwittingly into the middle of a Tuareg family row. Her elaborate traveling outfit intolerably roused greed; in their inexperience they imagined that her metal water cases—they knew only skin bags for this purpose—were stuffed with gold. Despite her beauty and generosity, as an unwed woman traveling alone, she was distrusted as a curio. She was even thought to be something a little satanic. At Murzuk, close to where she was killed, the most absurd rumors had circulated about her, "the most credited being that the big dog, pet of the Dutch lady, was in reality a man bewitched who could take on his human form only in the darkness of the night." It is Nachtigal, who was there at the time, who records this nonsense.

THE TRANS-SAHARAN RAILWAY

THE 1881 MASSACRE OF THE FRENCH MISSION WAS NO ISOLATED crime against an imprudent and puzzling individual. It was the planned destruction of an important official group, involving the deaths of many native troops and of ten Frenchmen, one of whom was Colonel Flatters of melancholy memory.

The mission of which Flatters was leader was seeking to trace the route for the proposed Trans-Saharan Railway, about which the world has now been talking for about a century. Such a railway was a notion advanced at first as a fantasy, almost a joke. But the always lively French seized on the idea. It is said that the first sober reference to it to appear in print was made by Hanotaux in 1860: "Who knows," he wrote, "but that one day steam will join Algiers to Timbuctoo and put the tropics within six days of Paris?"

Ever since, except during the period of revulsion following the Flatters disaster, the Trans-Saharan Railway, later retitled the Trans-African with hopes of connecting the Mediterranean with the railways of the Congo and of South Africa, has been the subject of voluminous writings and extended debates.

Where would it start from at the Mediterranean end? From Morocco? Or Algeria? Or Tunisia? Or even from Tripoli? And what would be its arrival point at the other side of the desert? Near the Atlantic? On the Niger? Or on Lake Chad? . . . Politics, personal interests and whims came into the discussions. Strategic considerations played a very prominent part.

But still the railroad across the Sahara is a dream. The farthest point served in the desert is Colomb-Béchar. The line is laid as far as Abadla, fifty kilometers beyond. From Colomb-Béchar one may travel by autobus to the Niger and beyond.

When I made the journey I did not see a human being outside our own party between the finish of the oasis system of the North and a point half a day's ride from the Niger. The Sahara is not in itself capable of producing business for a railroad. Recognition of this, plus uncertainties as to the best route, have delayed the enterprise until the age of the airplane.

*   *   *

DURING WORLD WAR II WE HEARD A GREAT DEAL ABOUT THE GERman effort to push through the construction of a trans-Saharan line or lines. Pearson and Allen (October 16, 1941) carried an item to the effect that a railroad from Casablanca to Dakar was "almost finished." *Life* in November, 1941, had an important illustrated article about another, quite different, German-sponsored trans-Saharan rail line, departing from the Mediterranean and leading to the Niger. The *Life* article reported Hitler's plan to use such a railway as a help in his conquest of America, since it "would bring heavy supplies to the Dakar air-base." For this fortunately aborted plan the Germans intended using, as one link, the existing line to Colomb-Béchar, mentioned above, and as another link, the existing Bamako-to-Dakar line. The space between links was immense, and it appeared a most tedious fashion of transporting heavy supplies.

Being familiar with the terrain, I was encouraged when I read about the German plan in the depressing days of 1941, seeming to see in the scheme indication of such inherent folly as must make her lose the war. Even it seemed that Germany herself must already have sensed inevitable defeat and be seeking to deceive the world and her own self by this much-boasted and extravagant effort.

*   *   *

THE TRANS-SAHARAN RAILWAY IN THE EARLY DAYS OF THE DISCUSsions seemed to Europeans to be the most romantic project imaginable.

To the native Saharans it was detestable. How conduct a *razzia* against a train? There would be no more caravans to pillage after the trains came. The train seemed a mysterious monster of doom.

We read that when the first train of Kitchener's Desert Railway in the up-Nile region roared its way across their country, the local natives thought it a living creature and "hastened to touch its oily and dusty tender, believing it to possess magical powers, and some of them declared that its touch had cured their ailments." The more intelligent and dignified Tuareg would have met the locomotive in a quite different mood. But he probably would have been frightened. The Tuareg is an exceptionally superstitious person, peopling his desert with fantastic creatures: goblins, spirits and sorcerers. *Tammekhelout* is the witch; at night she "milks the dugs of the moon" and fabricates a brew that turns folk mad. *Taner'out* is the beast, round as a ball and big as an ox, which squirts boiling water out of its mouth onto lone travelers, and eats the cooked victim. The apparition of a locomotive belching smoke across the emptiness would have been a terrifying horror.

FLATTERS . . . "FALEZLEZ"

THE SAVAGERY OF THE FLATTERS MASSACRE PROVES THE DEPTHS OF Tuareg bitterness toward Christian intrusion, for the Tuareg as a rule has the reputation of being a gallant fighter, not given to cruelty.

On the 18th of February, 1881, Colonel Flatters and his party —ten Europeans and seventy-eight native troops—were in a peculiarly desolate part of the Saharan high mountains, near a spot usually called Bir-el-Garama, and about a thousand miles due south of Bône, Algeria, as the crow flies. It was in the weird, wild Hoggar country, a place of unearthly quality, like our notions of a landscape upon the moon. Flatters was studying a possible route for the Trans-Saharan Railway. He had the indiscretion to split his forces.

Suddenly a troop of Tuareg appeared on galloping *mehara* and massacred one group: Colonel Flatters, himself, and several of his officers. (There is an alternate story that Flatters was captured and lived for years with the Tuareg—probably not true.) Another group was attacked, another Frenchman killed. Then another. Under a French lieutenant the rest of the mission was encamped at three hours' march away. These men—four of them French— attempted to get back to civilization. Their guides had deserted to the Tuareg, had probably been partisans of theirs all along. Food was short. There were not enough camels. They ate grass and were almost without water. Some men died of hunger or thirst. They could not keep in formation as they staggered along and again they were attacked and pillaged, and some taken prisoners. They began to realize that the Tuareg were playing with them, cat-and-mouse fashion. But the survivors marched on. The heat was intense.

Twenty miserable days after the original ambush and murder of the leader, Flatters, the Tuareg who hovered around them offered them the present of a few pounds of dates. The famished men—except for a few lucky ones who were absent when the gift was made—fell on the dates with avidity.

Of the whole wretched business this was the most ghastly and the most dramatic episode. The dates had been treated with *falezlez*, a regional plant which can kill a horse or a man, and one of whose properties, when not fatal, is to produce temporary madness. There, surrounded by their enemies, this handful of French officers and their soldiers, who had gone ambitiously into the Sahara to plan the line for a railroad, went mad in a body. Some ran about and screamed. Some dashed off into the desert. It was a heart-rending scene.

Now they were attacked again. Though weak from the poison they fought with splendid courage. Just one Frenchman was left. With him survived thirty-three native troops. The march continued. They had now only four camels, and, one by one, these were killed and eaten. Then despair. Then cannibalism. Finally the French sergeant, already near death, was killed for food.

A few native soldiers survived to tell the story.

*   *   *

NEWS WENT OUT ACROSS THE SAHARA THAT "A SMALL FORCE OF Tuareg had defeated a whole French regiment"! Anyhow it was a mighty triumph for the Veiled Men. To them the results were most satisfactory. French public opinion was so disturbed by the disaster that attempts to push into the deep Sahara were almost completely arrested for years to follow.

TIT

THE TUAREG WERE AMAZED THAT THERE WAS NO RETALIATION. IT IS an African saying that a woman must not weep for her assassinated menfolk till they are avenged. Yet France made no effort at vengeance. A Tuareg proverb: *"Imidranen teffart n amelroun"* [14] (Argument—after an affront—marks the coward.) But the French, they well knew, were no cowards. The Tuareg were puzzled and apprehensive.

They saw France's strength increase. France forgot the first revulsion following the disaster, and occupied the leading oases. The Tuat was conquered. Even In Salah, so long impregnable (see

---

[14] Tuareg proverb noted by Père de Foucauld, long-time missionary among these people. See *Textes Tuareg en prose,* edited after Foucauld's death by René Basset (Algiers, 1922).

page 485) gave up (December, 1899). Other Tuareg far to the south by the Niger were vanquished. But the group responsible for the Flatters massacre went unpunished for some twenty years.

Then occurred the Battle of Tit. The word means "Eye," used in the poetic sense—the earth's eyes are springs. There was water at Tit. It was in the same general region as the scene of the massacre and nowadays one who is riding into the heart of the Tuareg mountains at Tamanrasset crosses the battleground. Tit for the Tuareg was a decisive defeat. The best of their warriors fell. The Tuareg lament afterwards, "blood covered us like a mantle . . . but we did not hide in the rocks." After they had licked their wounds, something like friendly relations developed again between the French and the Veiled Men.

But with the pacification the joy is out of their lives. The Tuareg are bored like animals in a zoo. As Professor Gautier puts it, now that they are protected and policed by France they have become like a section of humanity in a museum. They no longer feel themselves to have a *raison d'être*. Sometimes, it is said, a group of Tuareg will go out on a mock *razzia*—warriors in their panoply rushing off in a band on camel back, shouting brave defiance mid the exhortations of the women, as in the days of old. All just as it used to be—except there is no motive for the raid, and after a while they have only to rush back again to the camp. It is all pathetic make-believe—a "vegetarian lamb chop."

This is not to say that the one-time terrors of the Sahara have been completely reformed. There are occasional grave incidents, and it has sometimes seemed to me that desert-wise persons in my company showed uneasiness if, before the dawn hours, our car broke down in Tuareg country. The Trans-Saharan Motor Rally of 1930 was warned to expect a big *razzia*. None eventuated.

*   *   *

THE TUAREG CAN BOAST THAT THEY STOPPED THE PROJECT OF THE Trans-Saharan Railway. It was not until the winter of 1922-23 that the first non-camel borne crossing of the Sahara was performed. A fleet of caterpillar cars traveled from Touggourt to Timbuctoo (Haardt-Audoin-Dubreuil Mission).

Two sections of Christian-held Africa thus were joined. The road was opened from the Mediterranean to the Niger.

ST. LOUIS

THE ROAD FROM THE ATLANTIC TO THE NIGER HAD BEEN OPENED
long since. At first its point of entry had been St. Louis on the
ocean just above the mouth of the Senegal River; later it became
Dakar, over 150 miles to the south at the very tip of the bulge of
Africa.

St. Louis was settled in the first half of the seventeenth century
by Normandy traders. It became the biggest settlement on the
African western coast beyond the desert. Its history was a dizzy
chapter. The proprietorship of the city, and the adjacent country
as it was pacified, kept changing hands. Between the middle of the
eighteenth century and the opening years of the nineteenth the
colony had passed seven times from France to England and back
again—average of a change of ownership every eight years. After
the downfall of Napoleon, St. Louis was permanently French.

As capital of Senegal, St. Louis became the focal spot of the
French colonial effort on the Atlantic coast of Africa.

To the native, St. Louis became a wonder spot, reputed to be
immensely rich and beautified with all sorts of white man's gadgets
and novelties. Moors of the desert and Negroes up the Senegal
Valley never called St. Louis anything but "The City" (N'Dar).
There was no need to particularize. St. Louis had no rivals.

To its European population St. Louis seemed hellish. The climate of Senegal, they grimly boasted, was the hottest on earth.
The whining mosquito fed on their thick European blood. Fever
shook them. Epidemics blazed. Up to eighty per cent of the Europeans who came to Senegal in those old days never got home. One
year twenty-one of the colony's total of thirty doctors died of
yellow fever. There was not adequate water in the city and in the
dry season they had to send tank ships up the Senegal River beyond the line where it was salt from the Atlantic. In those early
days they had no mosquito nets and men after nightfall wore Ku-
Klux Klan hoods and slept in gloves.

But, like all colonists, they had great expectations. Africa's
repute was golden. And to the boy that is in every colonist,
the country offered a thousand thrilling sights and adventures.

The great desert lay beyond the town; the tropic river rolled its way from mysterious lands, bringing pirogues loaded with flamboyant savages and strange products. A little way into the back country they could see hippos and elephants and crocodiles; and trees, each big enough to cover the population of a village. In St. Louis itself were the lovely *signares,* mulattresses of rare charm who consoled lonely Europeans.

PICTURE BY LOTI

FOR A PICTURE OF ST. LOUIS' EXOTIC FASCINATION AND TRAGIC LONEliness, its torrid heat and hectic viciousness, one may read Pierre Loti's *Roman d'un Spahi.* Loti tells how French soldiers burned their young lives out in bacchanalian extravagance, how of an evening beautiful half-caste girls, white as Spaniards, with chestnut hair, and blue eyes of a Creole languor, trailed gorgeous Paris dresses across the Place du Gouvernement, and how the young Spahi's rapacious little black sweetheart smelt of musk under her muslin *boubou* and tempted him to his ruin—"a savorous fruit of the Sudan" was the girl, "quick ripened by the tropic spring, swelled with intoxicating juice, full of unhealthy voluptuousness, feverish, unknown."

* * *

ONE MIGHT ASK HIMSELF WHY ST. LOUIS WAS CHOSEN TO BECOME the chief place for European exploitation along the west coast of Africa, when St. Louis was afflicted with so many disadvantages. The answer would be that every other place on the neighboring coast was as bad, and that St. Louis possessed one great advantage. St. Louis was at the mouth of the Senegal River, a thousand-mile roadway into Africa. St. Louis was regarded as the eventual port for Timbuctoo, if and when Timbuctoo could be approached by European traders. Furthermore St. Louis had a site which in the old days of short-range naval guns was easy to defend.

THE RIVER ROAD

THE SENEGAL RIVER LED TOWARD THE GOLD COUNTRY—EVENTUALLY to be a disillusionment. And the Senegal passed alongside what proved to be of more practical value: the gum country. To its shores the tawny, shaggy Moors of the Sahara brought each year the so-called Arabic gum for which European traders clamored.

From January to July the trading places along the river were like so many tumultuous fairs: Moors arguing and quarreling for more and more "pieces of guinea" in exchange for the gum of the acacia tree which Nature supplied them without other effort than that of collection. A native could collect six pounds a day. A "piece of guinea" could be had in exchange for thirty pounds or more, varying with the crop. The money value of a "piece of guinea" (about seventeen and a half yards of blue cloth) was something over nine current dollars. Guinea cloth was the money of the country. What the Moors did not require for their clothing could be swapped for luxuries: glass beads for the women, gunpowder, tobacco, etc.

To the Moors the gum trade was a bonanza. They had no idea why the Europeans wanted this, to their notion, useless stuff, and inferred from the traders' eagerness to buy that gum must be something indispensable to European life. They thought they had all Europe's welfare in their hands. Their arrogance and rapacity became immense. It was necessary for traders to bribe and cajole them with presents and free entertainment. When the trade season was over and when the mosquito season opened in all its terrors, the Moors withdrew to live an idle life till the next crop was ready for collecting.

They were, of course, nomads, and were of a mixture of bloods: part Berber, part Arab, part Negro. They were Moslems of an excessive and gloomy piety and their family life showed many oddities. Their women, for instance, did never a stroke of work of any sort at all, except an occasional bit of stitching of their husband's primitive blue guinea clothing. Each man had but one wife. She ate before he did, and he served her meals to her. Even the nursing of her offspring was usually spared to her. As for the unmarried girl, her sole occupation was to sprawl about in her jewelry and await her marriage day, striving always to get a little fatter (see page 28 for an account of the forcible feeding of desert Moorish girls).

MAURITANIA

THE ANTIQUE NAME OF MAURITANIA WHICH ONCE APPLIED TO Morocco and part of Algeria, has been attributed to the territory which these peculiar and fiercely independent people occupy at the rate of one half of a person to every square kilometer. France occupied Mauritania in 1904.

The coastal patch north of Cape Blanco had already been claimed by Spain. The patch is called Río de Oro, from the alleged River of Gold, when in medieval days natives used to bring their gold dust there to trade it with European ships. No spot was ever more incorrectly named, there being no gold near by, and it not being a river, but a bay.

The Río de Oro colony includes, in addition to the mythical River of Gold of which medieval Europe prattled, one of the most noted sites in North Africa from the native point of view. This is Seguiet-el-Hamra (The Red Canal), a sacred Moslem region whence holy men, originally refugees from Mohammedan Spain after the Christian conquest, went out as missionaries across the continent as far as the Egyptian border, making the name Seguiet-el-Hamra something mysterious and revered.

NECESSITY THE MOTHER OF DAKAR

THE SENEGAL RIVER ROAD WAS THE SOLE WAY INLAND. WHEN THE river was full, navigation was open to large, swift boats; in the dry season it was a tedious matter of poling and towing. But, fast or slow, the Senegal was the only practical route into that part of deep Africa. Cross-country journeys were not attempted except by adventurers and explorers. So St. Louis, key point on a key communication road, maintained its importance despite what might have been thought a fatal handicap. This was that St. Louis had no harbor on the ocean. Only small ships could approach.

The sand bar which ran in front of the city shifted every day; at no time could sizable ships come inshore. Sometimes even tenders could not use the port for days or weeks and merchandise had to wait for discharge, while passengers and mails could be landed only by means of native canoes which invariably tipped over several times during the rough journey.

As the size of ships and the quantity of trade increased, St. Louis' position became ridiculously difficult.

So Dakar, now one of the great ports and one of the greatest strategic bases in the world, came into existence—not one of those love children among the world's cities, built up because people liked to live there, but conceived in cold blood to supply a need. It had been an insignificant native village. In 1857 France occupied the site. It was to serve as a port for St. Louis, distant over 150 miles away, and about ten years later the first ships arrived at Dakar. But its growth was slow. In the early 1880's it was still almost uninhabited. Travelers for St. Louis disembarked and went on their way, or vice versa.

The business of getting from Dakar to St. Louis was distressingly difficult. Little boats usually carried passengers and mails— a twenty-four-hour journey. Sometimes weather made this impossible. Then folk had to ride on camel back—a three days' trip—or on a mule or horse, if one could be hired. It was urged that a railway should be built between St. Louis and its port. This was done.

Then—after all this effort to give St. Louis a port—the bell tolled for St. Louis. Dakar took St. Louis' place. Surprise to many at the time, though it seems as if everybody would have foreseen that trade and travel would not continue to pass into Africa via St. Louis just for old time's sake.

Today Dakar is connected with the Niger by railway and is the capital of all the colonies which France groups under the name of French West Africa (Afrique Occidentale Française) some of which belong geographically in the territory covered by this book. We heard aplenty about Dakar as a potential danger to America during World War II.

My own memory picture of Dakar—just before that war—is peanuts. The piles of peanuts on the quayside seemed as tall as houses. For it has been the vulgar little peanut which has made the fortune of the country.

PEANUTS

SUCH HAD BEEN THE DREAM OF ONE OF THE EARLY FRENCH GOV-
ernors. "The peanut," he declared in 1847, "could save this colony!" Peanuts were not indigenous; they had been brought to
Africa's coasts from Peru by slave traders in the seventeenth century. The little new nut pleased the African natives who took to
growing it round their huts. Early European explorers comment
on the peanut as if it were to them a complete novelty. It was
scarcely known then to botany. "A species of shell fruit called
Sudan almonds," wrote an English traveler in 1848, and his pub-
lisher considered an explanatory footnote was required to inform
the reader that "the taste of the fruit is not disagreeable" and
that "many of the shells are double, very soft and easily broken."
French travelers called them ground pistachio nuts.

In 1849 after various attempts to develop the peanut trade
with France, a shipment of one hundred fifty thousand pounds
was exported from Senegal for oil making. The peanut gained
rapid friends. Three years later one trading company handled
over two million pounds of the nut, as against two and a half
million of Arabic gum, and—alas for the golden hopes of old!—
only two hundred forty-five grams of gold.

Raising peanuts for profit delighted Africa's natives. It was an
easy crop and the native a lazy fellow. He brought his peanuts to
the trading post, received cash—nice silver five-franc pieces, which
he called *gourdes*—swapped them for guinea cloth, American
tobacco, gunpowder, sugar, also a little jewelry for his wives. Then
home to loaf till more peanuts were ripe.

* * *

BUT THE COMING OF THE EUROPEANS HAD ANOTHER ASPECT. THE
natives were well content to have the Europeans come trading,
but they did not want Europeans encroaching on their territory.
Yet it was inevitable that encroachment and conquest should follow the opening up of trade. It was a part of that "law of expansion which obliges civilized nations . . . to push forward" when
in contact with "backward peoples." So gradually trading posts
were moved inland and forts established as necessary for their
protection.

THREE DARK HITLERS

OFTEN ONE READS WITH A CERTAIN REGRET OF THE CONQUEST OF
primitive populations by civilized nations. In the case of the
French conquest of the Sudan there is no need for such senti-
mental sorrow. The natives during the nineteenth century had
got themselves into such a desolate mess that a foreign conqueror
was a savior. Indeed one might say that France entered the Sudan,
as it happened, like a nurse who comes to bind up wounds and
tidy up the premises after some awesome family fracas.

During the whole of the nineteenth century the people of the
western Sudan and certain adjacent Negro lands were victims of
a series of what we might call dusky Hitlers, who rushed back and
forth conquering, who pillaged, enslaved and depopulated the
countryside, and were in turn conquered by the next dusky Hitler.
Much of this wild work was done within the limits of North
Africa.

Three names of conquerors stand out: that of the great Fula
emperor, that of El-Hadj Omar, that of Samory.

FULAS

THE BOILING UP OF FULA AMBITION WAS ONE OF THE BIG EVENTS
of African history. It happened rather suddenly about the start of
the nineteenth century. A sober historian calls it "the prodigious
push of a race"; another historian's phrase, "an historic earthquake." Fula expansion was as startling as the puffing up of a
child's balloon.

A mysterious and strange race are these Fulas. (I use the simplest
form of their name; alternates are Fulani, Fulbe, Fellata, Poul,
Peul, Pholleys, etc., derivation from a word, *Pul,* meaning reddish
or light brown.)

They are, as the name indicates, not Negroes. They do not
resemble Negroes either in skin color or in shape of features.
They are of a coppery tint and are noticeably handsome. The
praises of Fula women have been sung from the days of the first
explorers. Their charm for men was an old proverb back in the
slave days: "If you bring a young Fula girl into your home as a

slave she will soon be the mistress of the house." For myself, having seen many Fulas, I would add that you would have to hunt the world to find in any young girl such a combination of prettiness, coquettishness, soft modesty, and calm social confidence, based on the universal acceptance of the fact that she belongs to a race of especial charm.

Where the Fulas came from has been much discussed. The prevailing opinion now is that they originated in northeastern Africa, but all sorts of theories have been advanced, including that they were Jews from Syria, that they were gypsies, that they came from the Orient—even from Anam—that they were displaced Egyptians. One truly fantastic theory was that the Fulas sprang from certain Roman legions made up of Gallic soldiers who got lost in the desert. Another just as fantastic makes the whole race descend from Sidi Okba, the Arab conqueror (see page 177). All this theorizing to explain their origin indicates how different Fulas appear to be from the rest of the Africans.

COPPER-SKINNED PROPHET

THESE STRANGE FULAS BECAME POLITICALLY PROMINENT IN THE early nineteenth century. Their great leader was Othman dan Fodio, whose personal activities were carried out in lands of mid-Africa beyond the territory of this book. Our business lies with a protégé of his who set up a Fula empire and turned everything topsy-turvy along a belt stretching across the upper and middle Niger from about 1815 to 1844.

It will be no surprise to anyone who has followed thus far with me the history of North Africa to hear that this man used religion as a prop and a vehicle for his ambitions. He, like so many other prominent North Africans, was a prophet, miracle worker, fanatic, reformer and *soi-disant* descendant from Mohammed.

His name—and this makes the tracing of his career difficult— is complex and variously given, though his identity and life story are perfectly definite and authenticated. Sometimes he is spoken of as Mohammed Lobbo; sometimes as Mohammed Cissé; sometimes the second name of Boubou figures. Sometimes he is called by the given name of Ahmed, Amat, Ahmadou. Frequently his name is prefixed by the title Cheikou or *Sekou* (Venerable, from the Arabic word sheikh) which title was confusingly misunderstood as "Ségou" by some Europeans of the day, Ségou being the name of an important Sudanese city. This last rendered the tracing of his career a little harder. I shall refer to him as Cheikou Ahmadou.

Cheikou Ahmadou was a self-made man, a brave and pious Mohammedan from a little hamlet near the Niger, whose activities as a religious leader roused the suspicions of the lord of the district.

The district was the kingdom whose capital was Ségou (referred to above) on the Niger. Its king was one Da, a Bambara Negro. Those who have read their Mungo Park will remember how the Scottish explorer was turned back at Ségou on his intrepid lone journey into Africa by Ségou's king, whose name is quaintly given as Mansong by the Scot. (Ma-N-Son, in Labouret's Chronology of the Kingdom of Ségou.) "Mansong" sent Mungo Park a bag of five thousand cowrie shells, equivalent to one pound sterling, enough in those days of cheap living to feed the Scot and his horse for fifty days!—and ordered Park to go back instantly to where he came from. "Mansong" did not like interference. Neither did Da, his successor. Da distrusted the ranting Cheikou Ahmadou. The more so since Da's people, the Bambara, were complacently and contentedly pagan and had no desire at all to turn to the rigors and exactions of Mohammedanism. Da gave orders to suppress Cheikou Ahmadou.

Da's people had a fighting and independent past. At his capital of Ségou, slaves had risen the century before, dethroned a king and put one of their own number in his place—and with good reason, for there is a tradition that Ségou had used their group with horrible cruelty and that its "walls rose on the corpses of 60,000 murdered slaves." But Da's people could not stop Cheikou Ahmadou.

"GLORY-BE-TO-GOD!"

CHEIKOU AHMADOU PROCLAIMED A HOLY WAR AND CARVED AWAY a part of Da's kingdom. Presently Cheikou Ahmadou was master of the great city of Jenné and of famous Timbuctoo. Neither of these suited him as capital however. He founded a royal residence of his own which he called Hamdallahi, a contraction of the Arabic words which mean, "Glory-be-to-God!"

Now Cheikou Ahmadou assumed the lofty title of Commander of the Faithful, and uttered high claims on his own behalf. These included, it goes without saying, a boast that he was of noble descent: an ancestor of his had married a great-granddaughter of Mohammed.

A far more daring piece of propaganda was his alleged falsifying of the *Tarikh el-Fettach*, the famous and revered local history (see page 255), to make the work purport to contain a prophecy supposedly uttered three hundred years before and foretelling that one Ahmadou would rise to be the great ruler of the Sudan. It is suggested that Cheikou Ahmadou's publicity department rounded up and destroyed all the authentic copies of the book that they could lay their hands on so that the trick could not be brought home to them by comparison of the original and the doctored texts.

Ahmadou was himself a prophet—perhaps too competent and outspoken for the good of his successors. In about 1838 he received a visit at the city of Glory-be-to-God from a private person of some religious pretensions, a native of Senegal, who was returning from Mecca. "You will," said Cheikou Ahmadou to the man from Mecca, "be one day a great prince, *but you will perish miserably!*"

The man from Mecca was to become the great El-Hadj Omar, destined to disrupt all the countryside. The final sentence of the prophecy must have infuriated the then embryonic conqueror. All in all it came true as Cheikou Ahmadou foretold. One thing which he did not include in his tactless prophecy was that the man from Mecca, before he perished miserably, would be the ruin of Cheikou Ahmadou's own descendants and of Cheikou Ahmadou's own empire.

Cheikou Ahmadou's empire—its limits are not entirely clear—included the Niger valley all along that part of the river's course which rises in a hump culminating at Timbuctoo. It took in the very fertile region, Macina, which—crisscrossed by lakes and streams—is called "a veritable interior river delta, another Egypt." This region is being developed scientifically under French supervision today and it is prophesied that it will be "the granary of North Africa."

There is no need to point out that, while Cheikou Ahmadou was hammering out his empire, the region was often a waste of burnt fields, strewn with corpses.

BLACK PROPHET

EL-HADJ OMAR WAS ANOTHER WHO DRAGGED HIMSELF FROM NOTH-ing to be an emperor and who—again it can be no surprise to the reader—used religion as an instrument for conquest. He was destined to possess such an empire as made the holdings of Cheikou Ahmadou look very small. He was destined to cause the French immense trouble, trouble so great that the very existence of their colony was endangered. He was destined to have it said of him, "Never was a Negro so powerful," although this claim I would maintain belongs rightfully to the medieval Negro, Kankan-Musa (see pages 364 to 374).

Omar, as his name El-Hadj indicates, made the Mecca pilgrimage. This and other travels occupied his early life. He did not become an important political figure until he was in the late fifties.

But from early youth he possessed an extraordinary belief in himself and an extraordinary capacity for impressing people. Omar was a personality. Here is Omar at twenty-eight: In the lower Senegal region not far from St. Louis he built up a legend about himself. The legend was no less than that he, Omar, was a reincarnation of Jesus—not the Son of God of the Christian faith, but Jesus, the Prophet, of the Mohammedans, who is not dead, but in Heaven, another having been crucified in his place. Omar did not say in so many words, "I am Jesus," but he spoke frequently to his pious friends to the effect that Jesus would come back secretly in the form of a Negro, unknown to the world at large. This is from the reminiscences about Omar's youth collected by Soleillet, the explorer, who lived for a time at the court of Omar's son.

When Omar later on returned from Mecca, a mature and legend-hung figure, his followers remembered and many thought of him as Omar-Jesus, or classed him even with Mohammed.

He was a miracle worker, of course. He was an alleged calmer of angry seas; he could throw the army of his enemies into sleep so that they were harmless; he could cause a high wall to rise round him in time of danger.

The greatest miracle, as claimed by his adorers, was his own physique. El-Hadj Omar—a man of great beauty with "perfect hands and feet"—never appeared to be more than thirty years old. No one ever saw him blow his nose or spit. These splendid nasal and throat conditions he passed on, by the way, to all his sons. Neither did he sweat, nor ever feel the cold. He seemed never to tire when marching, and could sit motionless in one position indefinitely. He could go as long as it suited him without food or drink. He was never seen to use a weapon; though he would often lead his army into battle he was never wounded.

It is no wonder that, when El-Hadj Omar's luck ran out and he disappeared, presumably a suicide, there were those who believed that he had entered miraculously into the rocky side of a hill, been transported to Mecca, and might one day return.

*   *   *

DURING HIS TRAVELS AND GRADUAL MATURING THIS MAN SAW MOST of the Moslem Africa of his day. He visited inner Africa down the Niger. Famous Bello—son of the Fula conqueror, Othman dan Fodio, who set Cheikou Ahmadou on the way to success—was delighted with Omar and showed admiration in the Oriental manner by giving him two wives. El-Hadj Omar's dealings with women, we are told, were very extensive, as would be natural in the case of a vigorous and uninhibited African. An oddity was that he never passed a night with a woman, limiting his sojourn near her to the love act; and that he never returned if she became pregnant. He declared that his love life was motivated solely by a wish to produce more and better Mohammedans.

He visited Ségou, capital of Bambara Negroes. These people were mostly anti-Mohammedan pagans. Omar preached against idolatry and exhorted the population to put aside their *gris-gris*, lucky charms, and images. King Tiefolo of Ségou put Omar in chains, but presently set him free.

In the clever and vengeful brain of the black prophet as he proceeded toward his Senegalese home there developed a plan which he later carried out triumphantly. He would toss out both of the Niger dynasties; he would make himself king of both cities where he had been insulted: of Hamdallahi (Glory-be-to-God) where he had heard a detestable prophecy, and of Ségou where he had worn irons. He carried out his plans.

*　　*　　*

STILL ANOTHER OF OMAR'S TRAVEL CONTACTS BROUGHT HIM MUCH prestige. He had made friends while at Mecca with one of the great Tidjani fraternity of Mediterranean Africa, and upon his return home he gave himself out to be the official representative of the fraternity in the Sudan.

It was an anomaly that the bitterest of all of France's antagonists in the Senegal-Sudan section should have chosen to affiliate himself with a religious group whose policy was notable pro-French. At the time of the conquest of Algeria, the chief of the Tidjani fraternity put out a statement that, "It is God who gave Algeria and its dependent provinces to the French." Duveyrier, the French explorer, who quotes this statement, was an honorary member of the fraternity, though, of course, Christian. He tells that the fraternity's members believe it was the prayers of their chief which caused the city of Algiers to fall to the French. Later the Tidjani fraternity proved its friendly sentiment toward France by welcoming enthusiastically the French wife—a Catholic woman —whom their chief had met and married and who became, on his death, the wife of his successor in office.[15] This unusual woman was something like the temporal head of the order and something like a saint in the eyes of its members.

All in all, it was a queer affiliation for El-Hadj Omar to have made. Possibly, having a pretty taste in miracles, Omar was fascinated by the traditions of the Tidjani fraternity. Its founder, Sidi Ahmed-et-Tidjani (end of the eighteenth century), having been affronted by the dey of Algiers, visited him by night and turned him into a woman, leaving him thus until "he" promised in future to treat the brothers of the order properly. The succeeding Tidjani chief was able in the course of a desert battle to cause "the date palms to shoot out projectiles, bullets, balls and fusees"!

The power of the Tidjani fraternity was great in all Mediterranean Africa and spread into the desert, into Egypt and to the Sudan and Senegal. The influence and wealth of such fraternities

[15] *Aurélie Tidjani, "Princesse des Sables,"* Marthe Bassenne, préface de Louis Bertrand, Plon, Paris, 1925

—the Tidjani was but one of several; I have mentioned that of
Abd-el-Kader's namesake (see page 502)—was enormous. Nearly
everyone was affiliated with one order or another; Algeria's Mohammedans are said to have contributed to the upkeep of their
various fraternities sums totaling one half what they paid in government taxes. The importance of religion in North Africa cannot be exaggerated and must be kept in mind today.

A TWO-PRONGED HOLY WAR

IN 1854 EL-HADJ OMAR WAS FIFTY-SEVEN YEARS OLD, THOUGH TO
his admirers he still "appeared to be no more than thirty." He
was ready for his great effort—a very great effort indeed, a two-
pronged Holy War, directed against the age-old pleasant idolatry
of the pagans, and against the rising power of French Christians.

He began by attempting to make a deal with the French. He
invited the governor of Senegal to supply him with munitions
and cannon to help him subdue the idolaters. France would have
none of it. He changed his policy. He had become a big force,
aided by his carefully prepared personal build-up, and by his
Tidjani affiliations, and backed by what had grown into a veritable army, made up partly of Tucouleurs like himself, partly
of Mohammedans of other black races. (The Tucouleur—or Tu-
kolor—Negroes lived near the Senegal River and took their name
from the medieval country of Tekrour, mentioned on page 288
of this book.) All worshiped him as an almost supernatural figure.
He preached against paganism and simultaneously shouted his
intention to push the French into the sea. "The Whites," he said,
"are only merchants. Let them bring their goods in their boats
and pay me tribute. . . . I am ready to live in peace with them.
But I will not have them setting up establishments on shore, nor
sending armed ships up the Senegal!"

THE MULATTO OF MEDINE

AT MEDINE, SIX HUNDRED MILES UP THE SENEGAL RIVER FROM ST.
Louis, a new French fortified post had just been established when
El-Hadj Omar, sweeping across the country with his army, passed
that way. It was in the spring of 1857. Medine had a defense force

contemptibly small in the eyes of El-Hadj Omar. It would, he thought, be an excellent move to wipe out the little fort with a swish of his army's big black paw. Had he succeeded it would have altered the history of that part of the country considerably. He would then presumably have tackled the other French posts farther down the river, and "the possession of the colony as a whole would have been compromised, and European influence destroyed." But El-Hadj Omar did not succeed.

The defense of Medine is celebrated. Paul Holle, a St. Louis-born mulatto, commanded the fort. He had with him eight or ten white men and about fifty blacks. Alongside the fort was encamped a large band of native refugees who had fled before the cruel hordes of El-Hadj Omar. El-Hadj Omar had an army variously estimated at fifteen thousand or twenty-three thousand. They were very self-confident. El-Hadj Omar waited, ready to make his solemn entry into the post. He had assured his soldiers that the French cannon could not wound a True Believer. Even when, charging in their masses, they proved this untrue and fell by hundreds, they did not flinch. El-Hadj Omar might have blundered about the cannon, but he was their "Father." They were fanatical and very brave.

Then he laid siege to the fort and the adjoining refugee camp. The siege lasted three months. The beleaguered people were cut off from the river, so even water lacked. Food, after a while, was just peanuts—raw peanuts, for there was no wood to roast them. Powder got short. Paul Holle dared not admit this fact to the chief of the native refugees, and when asked to pass out supplies would say, "We have killed enough of the enemy. We will produce a pestilence. I will give out powder at the next attack."

Paul Holle, the mulatto hero, had written above the gate of the fortress these words: "Long live Jesus! Long live the Emperor! Win or die for God and the Emperor!" He had decided to blow up the fort with the last of his precious powder rather than surrender. Then, one midsummer day, when food remained for only one more distribution, they heard far-off cannon, ran to the walls of the fort, saw in the distance French uniforms. It was the great Faidherbe come to the rescue. Medine was saved.

El-Hadj Omar had lost the first round to a determined half-breed and to that famed French colonial figure, the "Chief with the Four Eyes" (*Lamdo diom guitte naii*)—Faidherbe wore glasses.

El-Hadj Omar saved face by announcing to his followers that the attack upon the Whites at Medine had been merely incidental and that his main mission was to subdue the black pagans of the interior; he would let the "White Kafirs" go for the present.

* * *

THE FRENCH WERE VERY PROUD OF PAUL HOLLE, THE VALIANT mulatto. They set up a monument to him at Medine, stating that he "covered himself with glory." He was but one of the colony's distinguished half-breeds. The esteemed and efficient Colonel Brière de l'Isle, governor of Senegal, was "a mulatto, tall and of military mien." The great Faidherbe, creator of Senegal colony, the George Washington of French West Africa, married a Negress *à la mode du pays* (that is for the time of his residence in Africa) and had a beloved mulatto son who took his name and became an officer in the Senegalese *Tirailleurs*. The generous words of a French student are worth repeating, to the effect that it is "a cruel and unjust legend"—a sort of old wives' tale—to attribute weedy characteristics, special weaknesses or defects to half-breeds, who so often have given proof of outstanding intellectual and physical vigor.

* * *

THREE DAYS AFTER THE CONCLUSION OF THE MEDINE SIEGE SAW the debut of the most familiar item in all Senegalese affairs, from the outside world's point of view. On July 21, 1857, the Senegalese *Tirailleurs* came into existence. These upstanding black soldiers, the renowned "Senegalese," helped in the desperately needed pacification of their own disordered homeland. They had the ability to stand the climate and a knowledge of native ways and geography. At the end of their period of service they were civilized men, competent to teach their fellows. Their bravery and devotion to France have become a byword.

BLOODY PREACHER

EL-HADJ OMAR FORGOT HIS DISAPPOINTMENT AT MEDINE. ONE point of his two-pronged Holy War was snapped off; he concentrated on jabbing deeper into pagan country. He drove on with his thousands, preaching and plundering. Thousands upon thou-

sands of women and children followed his army, mile-long lines
of donkeys and pack oxen. As the Holy War swept forward, El-
Hadj Omar's people massacred natives, stole food, ravaged villages.
Behind his horde he left a semi-desert.

His cruelty was infamous. He professed gruesome solicitude for
"The Chickens of my Father," meaning the vultures, which in
that climate were instantly waiting to fall on a new-killed corpse.
"We must feed the Chickens of my Father!" he would say, when
commanding a massacre, and it is reported that he once remarked
with grisly whimsicality, "They have no food!" pointing to the
sky, and caused an innocent bystander to be slain on the spot.

When rations were short for his soldiers he ordered that their
women should be driven away so as to get rid of useless mouths.
It is estimated that there were then almost one hundred thousand
of these poor creatures. Some of their menfolk deserted. To do so
was suicide in this devastated country, so far from their homelands.

El-Hadj Omar's reincarnation of Jesus was a shocking travesty.
But on he went and his empire grew. Pagans came to Islam or
perished. He was to become master from near Medine to Timbuctoo. Idols and pagan *gris-gris* were crushed in masses. Two
years after the Medine disappointment he took the rich city of
Ségou on the Niger where he had once worn chains. Painstak-
ingly his troops destroyed some imported ornamental clocks which
had belonged to Ségou's king, since these, they maintained, were
idols or pagan fetishes of some sort. He also took Hamdallahi
(The City of Glory-be-to-God). Thus he had wiped out two big
native dynasties—one Bambaran, one Fula. The grandson of
Cheikou Ahmadou, who had prophesied El-Hadj Omar's "miserable end" years before, he caused to be beheaded.

Then the "miserable end" came. Revolt broke out; among the
Moslems he conquered there was anti-Tidjani feeling. El-Hadj
Omar gave Ségou to one of his sons and stood siege himself in
Hamdallahi. The final scene of his life is mysterious. He escaped
from the encircled city to the hills. There, according to one version, he and several of his sons sat on a keg of gunpowder and
blew themselves up. According to another version, he was smoked
out of a cave and cut to pieces, fragments of his body thrown

far and near. But some of his fanatical admirers would not admit his death at all.

Something over eight years had passed since El-Hadj Omar started his march of conquest into the Sudan. Few men had done so much harm in so short a time. Few men enjoyed power that was at once so great and so brief.

CONNECTING "THE ROADS THAT WALK"

MEDINE OF THE HEROIC SIEGE REMAINED FRANCE'S DEEPEST POST up the Senegal River. But France cherished a plan to connect by a series of strong places the two "roads that walk," the Senegal and Niger rivers, and thus to open a way into the heart of the Sudan. The plan was partly an inevitable step in the law of expansion; partly it resulted from international jealousy. A Frenchman of the day wrote that his country ought to push toward the Niger and penetrate into "the mysterious Sudan" so as "to dispute with England for the products of Africa toward which England's energetic policy is driving at fast speed by exploration, by trade, and by military occupation." It was "the Scramble for Africa."

France's plan to join the Senegal to the Niger by a protected route was a grandiose project, and one very hard to carry out. Certain of the hardships it entailed anyone would have foreseen: deadly climate and resultant sickness; attacks by angry natives and wild animals. Lions, hippos, elephants were a commonplace. "One day a giraffe marched alongside the column, then broke through the ranks, knocking over soldiers and putting the pack animals in disorder." Insect and serpent perils were multitudinous: "spitting snakes whose saliva shot forth in a squirt of poison, monster spiders, scorpions of the most venomous kind." Termites might eat a man's uniform overnight.

Such things as these were to be expected in that country. So also the food difficulty, since there existed practically nothing that a white man could eat, and transport was so hard—conditions which led presently to the use of little traveling vegetable gardens along the march—wagons full of earth where radishes and salads grew to furnish "refreshments" as M. Meniaud writes in his important book, *Les Pionniers du Soudan, 1879-1894.*

But there were other awkward elements involved which you or I might not have anticipated. One was that in the rainy season, starting in April, operations had to be held up. Yet satisfactory river transportation was limited to the season of high water. These two facts required close figuring and cut down every operational year to half. Another inconvenience was that in the dry season of midwinter natives burned off high grass and brush. This, swept forward by the harmattan, the wild winter wind, became a prairie fire, led on by troops of terrified beasts: gazelles, wild pigs, panthers. . . .

*   *   *

THE TELEGRAPH WENT THROUGH, THOUGH SOMETIMES THE GREAT storms of the rainy season tore away ground and poles, and sometimes the greater beasts nonchalantly carried away the wires on their necks and foreheads and jerked the poles up by the roots. In 1885 they could communicate telegraphically from the Niger to Paris. After that there came to every military post, where till then the French newspapers—if any—were three months old, a daily cabled news bulletin from home—twenty-five words, no more! —telling the greatest event of the day. The railroad came later, reaching the Niger in 1904.

Native Africa's reactions to all this were mixed. Some chiefs, back in the days of El-Hadj Omar's tyranny, had sent messages begging France to come and help. Some remained furious enemies. One wrote to the advancing French commander thus: "To the Uncircumcised, Son of the Uncircumcised, Colonel Desbordes, May Allah confound and destroy thy people. There is none more wicked, more treacherous, worse than thou. Thou sayest thou wishest only to make a commercial road. It is false and contrary to good sense and reason. Thy desire is to destroy the country and make war on the True Believers. Thou wilt be the last!"

Sometimes in all friendliness natives put odd problems to the invader. Archinard, another hero of the penetration, received as a gift of appreciation two little black girls of six or seven, one for himself and one for Desbordes. Tact required acceptance, but it was arranged to park the little ones indefinitely with their mothers, instead of employing them as brides, and two dolls with open-and-shut eyes were imported for them from Paris.

Speaking generally, the natives, even if unfriendly, did not oppose an effective resistance. They could not. In many cases they had only bows and arrows (poisoned, it is true), lances and knives to fight with. Those who possessed firearms had old-fashioned guns that had been got originally on the coast in exchange for slaves, had passed from hand to hand and were now likely to be more dangerous to the user than to his enemy. El-Hadj Omar had once been the proud owner of four cannon—probably just showpieces for him—which the French had abandoned on an expedition.

* * *

BAMAKO ON THE NIGER WAS OCCUPIED BY THE FRENCH IN 1883. It is now the capital of French Sudan. Then it was the capital of a little independent state of twenty villages of pagans who had known better days. Bamako was in an excellent position for trade at the falls of the Niger and until El-Hadj Omar tore through the country had been rich. It dealt in desert salt from the Sahara to the northward; in European goods from Timbuctoo, via the Niger, or brought from Senegal or even from Sierra Leone to the far southeast. Its storehouses then held everything the Negro heart desired from guns and gunpowder to tea, sugar, salt, perfumes, beads and aphrodisiacs. There were establishments where caravaners were entertained while they did their trading. Bamako, in short, had been a little cousin to Timbuctoo. El-Hadj Omar and his successor temporarily ruined Bamako by cutting the trade routes, and, when the French arrived, it contained a depressed little population of barely a thousand persons living among the ruins of empty houses. They did not oppose French occupation.

France had had her eye on Bamako for a long time. As much as fifty-four years before, the French had named Bamako's "Resident" or consul, in the person of René Caillié, the explorer (see page 482), and even paid him a provisional salary, pending the time when it would be possible for him to get to Bamako and take up his duties. René Caillié had brought back a very enticing hearsay account of Bamako. Mungo Park had actually been there and reported on its riches and advantageous situation.

And now, after Europe's long period of covetousness, Bamako

had been occupied by the Christians, and no longer belonged to the Bambara. What instinctive foresight there was in the natives' fear of explorers! Between "writing the country" and taking it over was but a step, though in the case of Bamako it had been a very long step. But Bamako benefited by the change. Its few glum hundreds in their deserted city saw a handsome modern town rise upon the ruins and poverty to which El-Hadj Omar had reduced the place. I conserve the picture of a wealthy Bamako Negro, gorgeous in a blue silk mantle, sweeping proudly into his seat in the outdoor moving-picture theater alongside the railway hotel to watch, and probably marvel at a French drawing-room comedy, based on a love triangle. It seemed a symbol of Bamako's altered destiny.

*   *   *

THE SENEGAL AND THE NIGER HAD BEEN JOINED; THE GRANDIOSE plan carried through. The door into the Sudan stood ajar. It had been a long effort. In Dakar today there is a fine building, the "Cathedral of Remembrance," so called, where there is what is known as a "symbolic ossuary" dedicated to those French who died on African soil "for the cause of civilization." It is something to wonder about.

SAMORY

SCARCELY HAD BAMAKO CHANGED HANDS FROM THE BAMBARA pagans to the French Christians than it was furiously attacked by the wildest character of the three native Hitlers of whom I set out to tell. We have seen the other two, Cheikou Ahmadou and El-Hadj Omar, hack their way across the land. Now came Samory.

Samory was a Mandingo, that is of the same great race as the medieval emperor, Kankan-Musa. His talents as a warrior were such that he nearly drove the French out of the Sudan.

To me, however, the most striking thing about Samory is that he was not a holy man. This fact makes him nearly unique amongst all the figures who rose to importance in Moslem Africa for more than a thousand years. For a man to acquire a following and lead conquering armies in Moslem Africa without a religious slogan, without claims to be associated with sacred personalities, was as remarkable a performance as it would be to conduct a great modern war without inspiring references to patriotism, Fatherland, Our Country, etc. Samory was a satanic person, one of the cruelest and most cold-blooded men that ever lived. But he must have been an extraordinary leader and organizer to have been able to triumph without the traditional prop.

He was born pagan, became perfunctorily Mohammedan for political reasons and for the same motive called himself Commander of the Faithful. He is said to have reverted to open paganism at times and the only one of the Mohammedan rules on which he insisted was temperance.

He proclaimed the death penalty for anyone who drank *dolo*. *Dolo* is the name of a variety of Sudanese native beer, frankly adored by the pagan section of the population and often drunk on the sly by Moslems. It is made from millet, is rather bitterish, foamy and of a dark brown color. It was not for any pious reason, however, that Samory forbade *dolo*. It was purely because, so he said, "The drunken man is more likely to revolt," and because brewing wasted his grain resources, needed for war.

*   *   *

SAMORY FOLLOWED THE COMMON NORTH AFRICAN PATTERN IN that he was a self-made man. The reader will have noticed how many of the continent's great men were humbly born. Samory's father was a poor pagan peddler of kola nuts, the treasured delicacy, medicine and aphrodisiac of Africa. His mother was the heroine and inspiration of Samory's life. The story—fabulous perhaps—was that he served seven years, seven months and seven days to redeem her from slavery.

He was a tactician, a diplomat and an organizer. He was absolutely pitiless and trained his *sofas* to be, in this respect, each a little Samory. He turned a great stretch of Africa into a "Land of Corpses," and is said to have reduced its two million population to about two hundred eighty thousand. His method, having built up a gang, was to attack village after village, offering the people the choice of submission or slavery. Whichever way they decided Samory won.

If they would not submit he used them like money: as slaves they could be exchanged locally for horses (one horse cost from four to twelve captives). Or for gold, silver or ivory, which he shipped to Sierra Leone, the English colony on the coast, to buy rapid-fire guns (two, three or four slaves covered the price of a gun). Thus he became the only opponent France met in the Sudan who possessed arms as good as their own.

If a village did submit he took the best men away for his army. Thus he built up his redoubtable *sofas.* The word is from *So* and *Fa,* meaning respectively "horse" and "father" and was originally applied to grooms, but was in Samory's army used for all soldiers. He dressed them in a rust-colored uniform with leather boots and a vest, conical hat with a straw plume on top. Soon each new *sofa* became his faithful adherent and took satisfaction in helping to do to other villages what had been done to his own.

Samory's cunning was boundless. He cajoled the French, held them off with insincere treaty promises till it suited him to fight, perfected a system of falling back before them and devastating the country as he went that made pursuit very difficult. That, to put this system into effect, he must ravage the country and reduce its people to starvation meant nothing to him. He was the spend-thrift conqueror, for whom there is no tomorrow. He shrewdly took advantage of the English-French rivalry, played the two off against one another and got arms and some petting from the English. When it suited him he was smooth as silk with the French. Salutations which he described as "sweeter than honey and sugar" he sent to the French negotiator coming to arrange a new treaty, and signed lightheartedly, took the offered compli-mentary gifts, and broke his word.

Eventually after a pursuit across a land of horror where corpses crawling with worms choked the forest paths and the ground underfoot in low-lying sections was a churned mud of dismem-bered bodies, the French caught Samory (1898). The diary of Gouraud, who was Samory's captor, contains almost unbelievable passages: "At night we were attacked by corpse worms . . . corpses everywhere in every degree of putrefaction . . . the bare feet of our native soldiers poisoned . . . it was the kingdom of death and horror" (from Gouraud's *Au Soudan*). Again he tells of a stretch 115 miles across where not one village was left standing—"everything had been destroyed and burnt by Samory; there remained alive only two or three people hiding in the ruins."

The main part of Samory's devilish career was played to the

tropic side of North Africa. But at and near Bamako he jeopardized the French effort during some years, and his wars against, and conspiracies with other local rulers soaked the Niger valley in blood.

Despite his salutations "sweeter than honey and sugar," his desire was to throw the whites back into the Atlantic and he was sincere only at such times as when he sent a message to his *sofas* moving toward Bamako that he wanted "some Whites for his women to play with" and especially "the head of a colonel"!

CHARNEL HOUSE

IF EVER A STRETCH OF COUNTRY NEEDED NEW MANAGEMENT IT WAS the Sudanese and adjacent country which the French occupied during the days of Samory's misdeeds. He and other tyrants had turned a once-pleasant place into a few starving oases in the midst of a huge charnel house.

In 1890 the French under Archinard took Ségou away from the heritors of El-Hadj Omar, who thirty years before had taken it from the original Bambara. Ségou, when the French came, put up a very poor fight. The men of El-Hadj Omar's family had all bolted, leaving behind a plentiful collection of royal ladies, and one brave lad, Omar's twelve-year-old grandson, who would not abandon his mother. This lad, a potential danger as a figure to rally round—a sort of black Aiglon—was shipped to France by his conqueror for education. He never forgot the gallant French commander who had captured Ségou and sent him to France, and a pathetic story is told of how the little exiled Negro prince, lost once in Paris streets, rushed along the boulevard Montmartre screaming, "Archinard! Archinard! Archinard!"

Ségou from which a desperate resistance had been expected fell without firing a shot. Only the fortified royal residence was temporarily impregnable, not because it desired to resist, but because the royal females who had been shut up there when the royal males ran away could not get the great iron-wood door open. Archinard sent a man up a tree to peer over the wall, told the women to keep at a distance and blew the door to pieces.

Ségou's treasure, like its courage, did not live up to expectation.

Native reports had set this treasure at the equivalent of twelve million current United States dollars. It is a saying that you must cut all figures reported by Sudanese Negroes down to only ten per cent to get the truth. The eventual count of the Ségou treasure came to even less than that. There were many, many women, but none of them with "breastplates of gold," as had been rumored.

But the fall of Ségou, its easy fall, impressed Negroland from the Atlantic to Central Africa. The posthumous prestige of El-Hadj Omar, the alleged reincarnation of Jesus, and that of the most powerful of his sons, Ahmadou Cheikou, was broken.

"THE BLACK FOX"

Ahmadou Cheikou, son of El-Hadj Omar and ruler of Ségou, made his fellow Africans and the French a great deal of trouble for some thirty years. (He is not to be confused with the Fula conqueror who wore the same name in reverse, Cheikou Ahmadou, described a few pages back.)

Ahmadou Cheikou's most familiar exploit was his retention for two years as prisoners of a pair of Frenchmen sent on a mission to him. These two and another, Soleillet, the explorer, were the only white men who ever saw him. His comically insolent message to the two members of the French mission whom he held so long awaiting his pleasure: "When the French and English carry their tribute to Stamboul, the sultan of Turkey makes them wait all day, sometimes longer, with their loads on their heads"!

Soleillet's experiences with Ahmadou Cheikou were, however, satisfactory. He brought away amusing anecdotes of the Negro king, as, for instance, his report that Ahmadou Cheikou was very partial to the white folk's magazines, and especially liked fashion plates in color, favoring those which represented Parisian ladies in ball dress. His must have been a purely sartorial appreciation. The exposure of a woman's form in ball dress would have meant nothing to a Negro king, many of whose female subjects went about their business next to naked, and who himself possessed uncountable wives and concubines.

He was surnamed "The Black Fox"—a name which speaks for itself—and was also a warrior of prowess. He was especially proud to have beaten the ancient proverb that no king may cross the

Niger twice as a conqueror. He boasted, "Me, I am the King of Kings; I have conquered the Niger, I can cross it as often as I like!" When his power was on the decline his defiance of Archinard just before Ségou fell was still fiery. The French, he sneered, were "only merchants, not fit to hold the land!" His last recorded public utterance was, however, "If you ask my advice, don't fight the French. You'll be beaten." He died in relative obscurity in 1898.

A PASSAGE OF HIDDEN HISTORY

THE STUDY OF NINETEENTH CENTURY HISTORY ON THE SOUTHERN borders of North Africa is complicated by the multitude of "Ahmadous," who are presented for our confusion. The Fula conqueror, Cheikou Ahmadou was succeeded by his son Ahmadou Cheikou (1844-52). Then came his grandson, Ahmadou-Ahmadou (1852-62) killed by El-Hadj Omar. There followed "The Black Fox," Ahmadou Cheikou, whose career I have just sketched. There was still another similarly named local celebrity—an Ahmadou Cheikou who preached a Holy War and attempted to march against St. Louis, being defeated in 1875.

Apropos of the study of nineteenth century Senegalese and Sudanese history, there exist ample data for the student. Travelers reported on the country from Atlantic to Niger, in some cases as far inland as Timbuctoo and beyond—Caillié, Barth, Soleillet, Lenz, Binger and others. And there exist many military and administrative records. But this material—Barth excepted—is not in ordinary libraries, especially outside France, so English-speaking readers have little available information. I find, as an example of how completely this patch of history is ignored, that the *Encyclopaedia Britannica* gives less than thirty lines in all to the powerful African personages who raged across country during that hundred years, and of whose wild exploits I have given a hint, and that these lines are tucked away here and there in various articles dealing with phases of European conquest. Nothing from Africa's own point of view.

It has seemed to me worth while to dwell a little upon this unfamiliar period. The turbulent nineteenth century history of this section of Africa has an especial interest for Americans. Often we say in our ignorance that the Negro American is unfortunate in that his ancestors were removed forcibly from Africa to work in slavery in the New World. We picture the interruption of peaceful idyllic lives in primitive villages. It is interesting and consoling to see proof that, whatever may have been the troubles which Negroes met when they were removed to America, they and their progeny avoided troubles far more tragic in their homelands. It was a time of bloody starvation, as—wave upon wave—conquerors stamped across the country.

TIMBUCTOO—"WE ARE WOMEN!"

TIMBUCTOO WAS THE BULL'S-EYE OF THE SUDAN. FRANCE OCCUPIED the city in the winter of 1893-94.

Timbuctoo had passed through experiences that were outstandingly vertiginous even at a time and in a land that was a whirlpool of shifting conquests. A very old man at Timbuctoo—and there were many such, for the people of the town had the reputation of exceptional longevity—could have told an almost incredible story of shifting rule in his city. One race after another mastered and remastered Timbuctoo: Bambara, Fulas, Tuareg, Tucouleurs (during a tentative, short and bloody occupation) and now Frenchmen.

Our old man, in his lifetime of say some seventy-odd years, would have bowed down before masters of all the human colors there are, except yellow: sooty black Negroes, bronze Fulas, tawny Tuareg, and at last white Frenchmen.

Along with this he would have known the social—if not always strongly political—control of the half-breed people called the Armas, the descendants of Morocco's conquering troops of the sixteenth century, some of whom were European renegades. Although they had been intermarrying with local women during the years, the Armas still retained something of the North in their features. The name, Armas, was from a word which meant sharpshooter and had been given to them because they brought gunfire for the first time into the western Sudan. For years after the Moroccan conquest the Armas lorded it at Timbuctoo, even after Morocco no longer had any control there. Blood tells. Just three centuries after the Moroccan conquest the Armas had still such prestige that the French chose two of their number to be local mayors of the city's two sections.

Another foreign element which our old man would have seen in high authority during his seventy-odd years' observation of Timbuctoo's tangled history would have been the Arab family of El Bekkay, religious aristocrats, claiming descent from Sidi Okba (see page 177 and page 361). They had great power in Timbuctoo, casting their influence alternately with or against the Tuareg.

And always our old man would have suffered from the Tuareg. Whether they were admittedly in power or not, they teased and oppressed Timbuctoo. They controlled all the roads into the city. They terrorized its trade and could strangle its supplies. They walked the streets with threatening arrogance.

The Tuareg of the Timbuctoo region—though they lived in a country which it would have been relatively easy to exploit honestly, in comparison with the bleak Saharan mountain lands of their brothers of whom I have already spoken—saw no reason at all to alter the racial habit of living off other people's work. They blackmailed Timbuctoo pitilessly. Timbuctoo residents went about in rags and let their houses go to pieces because the slightest aspect of prosperity attracted a Tuareg gangster raid. Timbuctoo even learned to grind corn silently instead of crushing it noisily in a mortar.

You cannot blame the Tuareg. It was his ancestral habit to pillage people, the only work he knew. He was the fox who raids a farmyard, the wolf who attacks the flock. He had contempt for those who could not protect themselves. He was made that way, a sort of parasite pointing up the weaknesses in his fellowmen. In Timbuctoo he found the ideal prey.

Timbuctoo was a famed trade center, a religious and intellectual center, but politically as flabby as a jelly. Its own people admitted this. In a message sent to the French just before the occupation, one of their notables said, "We are women. We do not fight." They were much divided among themselves. Some had long since asked French protection; a delegate had gone to Paris in 1885 to

implore French help against the Tuareg. As the French came
nearer, they received the visits of envoys from Timbuctoo; at the
same time another faction in this disordered city was sending an
embassy to the sultan of Morocco "imploring his intervention
against the French."

One reason for Timbuctoo's lack of civic guts is that reason that
can make cowards of us all. Timbuctoo had no food of its own.
The town was in a delightful situation for trade, but in an
execrable position in so far as its larder was concerned. It produced absolutely nothing. All food, with the exception of a trickle
of grain from remote Saharan oases, had to come via the Niger.
Incoming supplies could be arrested by an army controlling the
river. Furthermore Timbuctoo was some miles inland from its
river port and even an insignificant gang of bandits could cut the
road from the port to the town. At a place called with infinite
Negro pathos "Nobody-Hears-You" (*Our-Oumaira*)—too far from
either the city or the port to get help—caravans from the Niger
were consistently butchered and pillaged.

*   *   *

A NEW AND COMPETENT CONQUEROR CAME AS A WELCOME RELIEF,
albeit the welcome was preceded by a cunning and bloody Tuareg
trapping of a French column, where eleven European officers, two
non-commissioned officers and sixty-four native troops were killed
(January 15, 1894) in the environs of Timbuctoo, and by the
deaths of two French officers and eighteen of their men at
"Nobody-Hears-You" on December 28, 1893. Both these disasters
are attributed in whole or in part to an overhasty push into
Timbuctoo, which was seized by a too-zealous officer with insufficient forces, and relieved by another officer whose expedition
had been frowned upon and countermanded too late.[16]

"France will never take Timbuctoo," declared Barth thirty
years before. It was one of the great German's few mistakes. On
February 12, 1894, the officer who was later to be General (Papa)
Joffre of World War I, entered the city. Gao, seat of the old-time
Songhai Empire, was taken by France four years later.

The occupation of Timbuctoo was a bitter blow to the Tuareg

[16] Meniaud, *Les Pionniers du Sudan, II,* pp. 494 to 498; Georges Tuaillon,
L'Afrique occidentale française, p. 138; Charles Lavauzelle, *Editeurs militaires*
(Paris, 1935).

of the Niger region, a companion blow to that which fell upon the mid-Saharan Tuareg at the battle of Tit (see page 543).

To the western Sudan as a whole it meant the start of a new life. The taking of Timbuctoo was a turning point. After generations of anarchy "peace and prosperity could be reborn little by little in regions which had been desolated by massacre, fire and ruin."

PART THREE

England and Others in North Africa

THE "MAHDI"

THE LAST OF THE GREAT NATIVE CONQUERORS ROSE IN THE EASTERN Sudan by the Nile. He was Mohammed-Ahmed-ibn-Seyyid-Abdallah. But he is always spoken of as "The Mahdi." He is to most of us the best-known mahdi of them all. In fact the man in the street regards him as the only mahdi that ever existed.

Mahdi, I remind the reader, means one divinely directed, and is the name which has been given to a series of Mohammedan religious leaders who have come up during the centuries and whose followers have thought to recognize in each the true Messiah sent to point out the path to virtue and triumph. North Africa has seen many mahdis.

But never was a mahdi as spectacular as Mohammed-Ahmed of the Nile, a mulatto born at an uncertain date just before the middle of the nineteenth century, who became undisputed and undisputable ruler of an estimated two million square miles of Africa.

The passage of North African history of which the Mahdi was the hero is familiar to us. The drama's focal point was at Khartoum, where during the 1880's and 1890's the Mahdi and his successor, usually known as the Khalifa, opposed two prominent Englishmen: the pathetic figure, Gordon, and the grim and forceful Kitchener.

The Mahdi was called by us a fanatic, his followers, the Dervishes (name meaning a mendicant monk) were called dupes. He was, in short, a dictator. He got to power, as dictators do, because his fellows were miserable and instinctively reached for a strong man to drag them out of their trouble. He seemed the superman who might untangle them from oppression and save them from their own weakness. He rose through religion. From ear to ear among the primitive people up the Nile went whispers of a new saintly personage. He gained the reputation for mystic piety, and sent out religious exhortations. He formed a band of devotees who looked to him for salvation and leadership.

OPENING FOR A DICTATOR

FOR THIS TO HAPPEN IT REQUIRES THE COMBINATION OF ONE fascinating big man and many very unhappy little ones. When the Mahdi, Mohammed-Ahmed, was growing up in the eastern Sudan there were unhappy little men uncountable. The country was disgustingly mismanaged by the Egyptian overlords. Taxation was cruel and unjust. In the hinterland the menace of slavery darkened every village.

Almost it seems as if every individual in the eastern Sudan must have been either associated in some way with the selling of slaves, or else a potential slave himself. It was estimated that there were fifteen thousand professional slave traders. Egyptian officials were indirectly connected with the trade and took profit from it. Native chiefs cold-bloodedly aided in the capture of the populations of neighboring villages. Little black communities went to sleep, a group of free men, women and children, woke to flames and gunshot, to the murder of such men as resisted, and the capture of the nonresisters, the women and the little ones. It was all done in a calculated, businesslike fashion, without the excuse of inter-tribal wars. It was as lacking in sentiment as the business of a fisherman.

Slave handling was not only the main occupation of the region; it got to be pretty well the sole occupation. Other business was stagnant. To expect people to go into any other activity was "as unreasonable as to expect Esquimaux to grow melons," in the picturesque phrase of Schweinfurth, the Russo-German explorer who traveled the slave region in the 1860's and 1870's. The supply —at first—seemed inexhaustible. The demand was brisk. Egypt, Arabia, Persia and Asiatic Turkey were good customers. A slave sold at or near Khartoum for six times his original cost. By the time he reached his final destination the gross profit upon him must have been colossal. The whole country was a slave shop. Sailing up the Nile Schweinfurth "perceived countless masses of black spots standing out against the bright colored sand. They were all slaves!" Gordon estimated that seven eighths of the population of the eastern Sudan were slaves. Doughty in *Arabia Deserta* tells of an African whom he met in Arabia who had been marched for six months barefoot as a child slave—twelve hundred miles across Africa to the Red Sea—and who remembered coming *every night* to a station of the slave drivers.

Inspired by European horror, attempts were made to stop the trade. Pressure was put upon the khedives. An agreement for its suppression was entered into between Egypt and Great Britain. Sir Samuel Baker, and later Gordon went into the Sudan on official missions to strive to put the trade down. Consuls from Europe and even a Copt—representing the United States—kept watch at Khartoum. But it was like the old prohibition situation in America. It was very difficult to suppress the slave trade. Too many people made money out of it.

So, helpless fury grew among the people of the eastern Sudan. There was a dumb impotent hatred for the government under which life was so miserable. They cursed the "Turkos," such being the Sudan's name for Egyptian and other foreigners—including Christian Europeans—who came into the country.

* * *

THE SUDDENNESS OF THE MAHDI'S RISE TO POWER PROVES HOW miserable the Sudan was, how ready to listen to a whisper of hope. He needed no long period of personal advertising like other religious dictators of North Africa (El-Hadj Omar, for instance). He was the boy wonder, quickly sold to a public eager for a helper. At twelve he knew the whole Koran by heart, they say. At about thirty-three, that is in 1881, he began to conquer. At the probable age of thirty-seven he controlled some two million square miles. He was laid to his rest a few months later in a tomb said to have been the tallest building in the eastern Sudan—it was eighty-five feet in height—in the construction of which tomb had been used material from the Christian church of Khartoum, which his army had recently captured and razed. Then a pilgrimage to his tomb was declared to be obligatory on all True Believers, supplanting the pilgrimage to Mecca. It was an amazingly swift career.

He and his advisers were clever men. They had succeeded in balancing opposing points of view—that of the proletariat, the potential slaves; and that of the capitalists, the traders. It must have required neat work to make such promises to these two groups as would weld them into an army. Some of the traders were as powerful as kinglets, and had previously been bitterly offended by Egypt's professed policy to suppress the trade.

The Mahdi announced that his people would conquer the world—first wrest the eastern Sudan away from Egypt, then take over Egypt itself, and proceed to overthrow Turkey and convert or kill all who stood in their way, be they Christians, or Mohammedans of what he classed as heretical sects, or pagans. He taught his followers to swear an oath never to put on a new garment until they had driven the "Turkos" out of the Sudan, and in later years, after the "Turkos" had been ejected and the Mahdi had died, the army of his successor still retained a decoration of patches upon their good new uniforms as a symbol.

From the start the Mahdi was victorious. For him, war news was always good news. I will not go into the detail of the battles won in 1881-84; it is a passage of history about which there is ample available information. The most striking item in the monotonous list of the Mahdi's victories is the destruction of the big expedition led by Hicks, where practically every one of ten thousand perished (November, 1883). All the country as far as the Equator was his, except for a ribbon along the Nile near Khartoum where shivering Egyptian garrisons still held. He looked toward Egypt. In Palestine, Syria and Arabia his name was on men's tongues as an inspiration to independence. At Damascus there were posters in the streets denouncing the Turks. The excitement in Egypt can easily be imagined.

*   *   *

IT WAS A COINCIDENCE WHICH MUST HAVE BEEN REMARKED BY THE learned members of the Mohammedan public at the time that just one thousand years by the Moslem calendar had passed since a former mahdi had initiated the invasion of Egypt. The first Fatimite expedition was in 913 A.D. (equivalent to 301 by the

Mohammedan calendar). The Sudanese Mahdi won his greatest victories in 1883 (1301 A.H.).

The Sudanese Mahdi, like the Fatimite and like all mahdis, claimed descent from Ali and Fatima. Thus again Africans were dying, as they had so often died through the centuries, because of Ali. This was to be the most gigantic and terrible score yet sacrificed in connection with the Ali tradition. In addition to the thousands of Egyptians and English who perished in the Mahdist wars, it is claimed that seven million Sudanese were wiped out.

CRISIS IN EGYPT

IN EGYPT THERE WAS HIDDEN SYMPATHY FOR THE MAHDI. THEY felt that what he had done they too might do. An English resident in Egypt wrote, "The Egyptians are secretly in two minds as to whether they ought not to prefer a prophet of Islam—even a false prophet—to the Christian English, whose tentative domination is not a thing that can be understood, but rests on Mr. Gladstone's promises of withdrawal to be put into effect at the earliest moment." I quote from Mabel Caillard's *A Lifetime in Egypt, 1876-1935.*

Egypt was passing through a crisis. Another of the long chain of foreigners had come to control her country. The English occupation had just started.

The English move had ruined the dreams of the fellah (native born peasant) who had risen to be dictator under the name of "Arabi," with the self-chosen epithet, "The Egyptian," whose motto was "Egypt for the Egyptians," and whose followers decried the khedivial boast, "Egypt is no longer in Africa; it is a part of Europe!" Arabi had led his revolt, massacred a hundred or more Europeans, given orders for the destruction of the Suez Canal, and had produced just the reverse of what he hoped for. Instead of driving out the Christian Europeans, his revolt had beckoned them in. They came in force. His defeat at the Battle of Tel-el-Kebir (1882) was immediately followed by English occupation. England came in to restore order and protect foreign investments in Egypt. In those good old days, loans to foreign countries were taken very seriously by creditor nations.

*   *   *

THE EGYPTIAN CRISIS AND THE REBELLION AGAINST EGYPTIAN authority in the Sudan occurred at the same time. We are told that there is no proof that there was any connection between the two. This seems silly; no proof is needed. Common sense shows us that a shrewd Sudanese leader saw and profited by his chance; and that his successes had their repercussions in Egypt.

As Miss Caillard suggests in speaking of the period of the Mahdi's debut, and, as has been amply clear through ensuing years, the English occupation was especially galling to Egyptians because of the uncertainty of its probable duration.

Beyond this—that is to say, as to the rights and wrongs of this controversial subject—I can add no comment. It was a chapter in the inevitable partitioning up of Africa at that moment when Africa was weak and Europe was strong.

GORDON

AS THE MAHDI'S LIST OF VICTORIES SWELLED, EGYPT TUTORED BY England, decided to abandon the Sudan—what there was left of it to abandon. General Gordon was chosen to supervise the evacuation of the garrisons still in the country, notably that of Khartoum. Given the Mahdi's strength and the distance and character of the country, it would seem that evacuation would have been impossible to any general. Gordon, so brave, so eccentric, was in all events the wrong choice, and the episode is one of the tragic fiascoes of British history.

"Chinese" Gordon was very popular in England. His appointment delighted the public who seemed to expect him to wave his wand and perform wizardry. Literally he was sent with little more than a wand—merely one white officer; no soldiers, no supplies, no arms. Yet, so beloved was he and such confidence did the Sudan have in him, that women kissed his feet and believed that they were saved when he reached Khartoum, then in a panic of fear about the Mahdi, whose cruelty and devastation of captured cities was but too well known.

At Khartoum Gordon departed from his instructions. "If Egypt is to be kept quiet," he wired to his government, "the Mahdi must be smashed up." Gordon's respect for the Mahdi had increased, now that he was on the spot. He still sneered at the Mahdi as a trickster who "put pepper under his finger nails so as to cry in public," but he had found out that the Mahdi was not what he had imagined—the mere tool of one of the great slave bosses. So Gordon's aim became, not the evacuation of the garrisons, but the Mahdi's "smashing." He defended Khartoum for nearly a year with great military skill, hoping for a relief expedition.

He was a man abnormally sure of the rightness of his own opinions and fond of power. He had said, after his return from the up-Nile country on an earlier mission, "Not a man could lift his hand without my leave throughout the whole extent of the Sudan." An odd remark from one quite sane. Many people who watched Gordon called him mad. Certainly one sees unbalanced judgment in one of his acts when at Khartoum. He sent a telegraphed request to "transmit an appeal to British and American millionaires to give me £300,000 to engage Turkish troops from the sultan and send them here. That would settle the Sudan and the Mahdi forever."

It was evident that he felt sure he knew better than the government did, that he had come to the decision that the Sudan ought not to be evacuated after all. It appears that, in disobeying his instructions, he hoped to do just what he did succeed in doing—that is, compel the government to come into the Sudan with a big force to save him personally, and thus incidentally into a territory they had decided to abandon. He counted on his personal popularity, felt that his country would not dare stand by and let him perish. He was right. But his star blinked. Help came just one day too late!

The fault for the whole sad and expensive business lay with those who chose for such a mission a man who was known as "the sport of impulse" and who was self-opinionated in the extreme, one who was too dear to the sentimental public to be sacrificed. A big expedition had to be sent to relieve Gordon and one or two other Europeans (one was the Austrian consul—the French consul and even Gordon's own officer had already quit Khartoum) plus the remnants of a native force, and a largely disaffected native population.

As the expedition—which, since it had to be sent, really should have been sent more promptly—approached Khartoum, its commander carrying a letter demanding Gordon's resignation, presumably as prelude to his censure, Khartoum fell, and Gordon died. The expedition turned back.

Gordon's death scene thrills us and horrified his countrymen. Just before sunrise on January 26, 1885, the Mahdi's men seized Khartoum and rushed the Residence. Gordon, white haired from anxiety and wearing his white uniform, stood in front of his office. One of the Mahdists speared him, others leapt forward to slash him with their swords. They cut off his head and sent it to the Mahdi. They dragged his body down into the garden "where many came to plunge their spears into it." As for his head, "It was fixed between the branches of a tree and all who passed threw stones at it." A pitiful end for "one of the bravest heroes England ever produced."

HIDDEN EMPIRE

AGAIN THE MAHDI HAD TRIUMPHED. THE SUDAN WAS ALL HIS NOW, a black secret land to do what he liked with. A historian of those secret years, writing in 1893, said, "Since that day (when Gordon was killed) the Sudan has been closed to all civilizing influences. Now and then a tale reaches the outside world of what has been going on in the years that have passed since Gordon's death; and the escape of one of the Austrian priests and two of the nuns have enabled us to learn a little regarding the terrible fate of Khartoum." Few holy men and women, by the way, even amongst Africa's notoriously adventurous missionaries, ever had such an experience as that of Father Ohrwalder and the two nuns who were for some ten years captives of the Mahdists and escaped to bring the world its first authentic news of what was going on in the Mahdists' hidden empire.[17]

The Mahdists' empire, under the original Mahdi and under his successor, known as the Khalifa, was immense in mileage, but its population had dwindled. Lord Cromer and others estimated that the inhabitants had totaled eight and a half or nine millions in

[17] Another nun, Sister Teresa Grigolini, did not get away and was rescued after the Battle of Omdurman (1898). She had been, G. W. Stevens says in his *With Kitchener to Khartum*, "forcibly married to a Greek."

pre-Mahdi days. It is estimated that of this total, three and a half
millions were swept away by famine and resultant sickness—the
Mahdist soldiery robbed farmers of their grain reserve and cattle
and presently every strong man was obligatorily a soldier, so that
there were no farmers left. Another three and a half millions were
estimated to have died in fighting either with the Egyptians and
the English, or amongst themselves. It all seems incredible. Captured cities were inevitably destroyed. Every enemy they caught
was slaughtered or maimed. Stores and crops were wantonly
burned up. There remained nothing but desolation. The country
lapsed into a desert.

Revolt against the Mahdist regime seemed impossible. Rebellions were crushed with ferocious competence. Listen to the
experience of one little town which tried for freedom, Metemma,
a short distance down the Nile from Khartoum: The revolt failed;
the Mahdists massacred two thousand men, women and children
outright, and then drew the rest up in a line. The first was
beheaded, the second lost the right hand, the third both feet,
and so on in rotation. The chief of the rebels received special
torturing.

The Mahdi himself died a few months after the fall of Gordon.
The cause is variously reported: possibly he died of smallpox
which raged the land, possibly of poison, possibly of heart disease
or other illness resulting from too much high living. Success had
swept away his original puritanical ideas. He put aside his old-
time single coarse garment for a wardrobe of perfumed silk. The
escaped Austrian priest's story is full of lascivious details about
the ex-anchorite's debauchery. The Mahdi would lie upon a
splendid carpet, his head on a pillow of gold brocade, while as
many as thirty women would attend upon him, fanning him with
ostrich plumes, stroking his hands and feet while he dozed. Some
of his harem were little girls of only eight years.

To his successor, the Khalifa, a life of "swinish sensuality" is
attributed. But his dissipation—possibly rumor from the hidden
empire exaggerated the horrid details a bit—did not halt his
military ambition nor destroy his efficiency. His black flag waved,
his special trumpet—the *onbya*, made from an elephant's tusk—
bellowed across the Sudan and to the gates of Egypt, as he
launched expedition after expedition. His plan was the conquest

of Egypt, a mission bequeathed to him by the Mahdi. The Mahdists sang a song whose refrain was "To Cairo!"

The climax of the "To Cairo!" effort was the Battle of Toski (near the famous site of antiquity, Abu Simbel) in 1889. The Mahdists lost. It was a startling defeat; the song lost its popularity. Close to that antique monument which records Ramses II's victories over the Hittites (see page 33) was placed a marble tablet in English and Arabic commemorating the victory of English and Egyptian troops which had saved Egypt from the Mahdists.

ITALY WAS IN TROUBLE

THE MAIN MOTIVE BEHIND THE DRIVE TO SMASH MAHDISM WHICH England made eleven years after Gordon's death seems truly funny to us today. It was to help Italy which was in trouble with Abyssinia! It is odd to compare this attitude with the antagonism roused about forty years later by Italy's Abyssinian ventures, about which a shrewd French observer, Professor Gautier, wrote in 1939 before the final word had been said, "The Italian conquest of Abyssinia has been a test of strength not between Italy and Abyssinia, but between Italy and England."

On March 1, 1896, Italy had been crushingly defeated by Abyssinia at Adowa, losing three quarters of her force of about thirteen thousand to an enemy horde of nearly a hundred thousand. The Mahdists saw their chance, and England saw that—if the Italians were further weakened—there was danger of a Mahdist come-back against Egypt. An expedition under Kitchener was launched against the Sudan.

KITCHENER

THE KITCHENER EXPEDITION WAS LAUNCHED WITH SUCH SUDDENNESS as to remind one of the much-quoted surprise scene at "Belgium's capital." "On Saturday afternoon, the 14th of March" (1896), runs a soldier's account, based upon diaries, "visitors were assembled on Shepheard's veranda. The military band was playing the latest airs, the British subalterns were basking in the smiles of cosmopolitan beauty and 'all went merry as a marriage bell' when suddenly a startling rumor spread from mouth to mouth." Kitchener had received a cablegram from London to proceed up the Nile at once and commence operations against the Mahdists.

On Sunday, September 4, 1898, Gordon had a belated funeral service, Kitchener's army having won the decisive Battle of Omdurman and marched into the ruins of Khartoum. Kitchener and his staff stood "almost on the very spot where Gordon fell. The Sirdar (Commander in chief, Kitchener) raised his hand, out flew the Union Jack and the Egyptian flag." Bands played the English and Egyptian national airs, and Gordon's favorite hymn, "Abide with Me."

Kitchener's victory had been well and slowly prepared. Its opening phases were observed by Conan Doyle, then a war correspondent. Kitchener had taken his time, moving forward with his railway, the construction of which is said to have beaten all previous records for the laying of a military railroad. Nearly six hundred miles were put down across waterless desert. The Khalifa got away, but was subsequently overtaken and killed in battle. Mahdism was destroyed, "smashed" at last.

By coincidence—there was no possible connection—two widely separated final manifestations of native violence and devastation in the Sudan were suppressed at almost the same moment, and after durations of almost equal length: Mahdism in the eastern Sudan and Samory's turbulent career in the western Sudan were arrested by the English and the French respectively in the same month of September, 1898. The Mahdi and Samory had become important factors at almost the same moment, in the early 1880's.

CONDOMINIUM

A few months after the destruction of Mahdism an arrangement was made between England and Egypt for the joint rule of the eastern Sudan, the Anglo-Egyptian Sudan. The arrangement was called the condominium.

After World War I Egypt took to publicizing bitterly the attitude she had held for a long time: that the condominium contained no *con*, no part for the other partner, Egypt, in the domination of the Sudan. Egypt had only the satisfaction which some authors have when their novels are arranged for the screen:

Egypt's name appeared, in second place, on the Sudanese map. And even that wistful satisfaction was diluted by the fact that on many maps (that, for instance, of the National Geographic Society) the Anglo-Egyptian Sudan is outlined, not in the tint attributed to Egypt, nor in a noncommittal color, but in Britain's traditional red.

This situation has been painful to Egypt because the Sudan is her close neighbor, and—so Egyptian propaganda claims—her vassal since antiquity. This latter reason is open to challenge; history shows Egyptian control over the Sudan to have been a very spotty picture.

Still another reason why Egypt craves the management of the Sudan is so that she may protect the upper reaches of the Nile. The possible theft of Egypt's indispensable river by an enemy upstream is an old bogey.

The eastern Sudan itself, we can safely assume, would like to see both of its prenames discontinued and to be neither Anglo, nor Egyptian. This brings up the great question, which each must answer according to his judgment: Should retarded peoples be held to loyalty to their tutor nations after they have become less retarded through effort, expense and danger undertaken by the tutor? And when may a retarded nation be held to have "grown up"? It is another aspect of the problem of parent and child. It is a question that springs up all over North Africa.

FASHODA INCIDENT

IN THE INTERIM BETWEEN THE CRUSHING OF MAHDISM AND THE signing of the condominium there occurred one of those "incidents" several of which, in connection with Africa, have upset the world's nerves. This was the celebrated Fashoda Incident. It was one of the most delicate and dangerous episodes in the touchy Scramble for Africa, and though Fashoda is far south of the territory dealt with in this book, its "Incident" concerns our subject. "We came so near to war with France," writes Sir Harry Johnston in his autobiography, "that preparations had to be made." He was then English consul at Tunis. He and M. Millet, the French . resident general of what had become a French protectorate, came to a regretful understanding in case war should break. France, Johnston says, had decided to abandon eastern Tunisia as non-defensible. During the excitement the native Tunisians clamored for independence, "and looked eagerly to Great Britain to secure it if France was worsted." Just how that part of it would have worked out is a question. Fortunately the danger was averted, peace maintained.

What had happened to produce the Fashoda incident is this: France, which since the days of Faidherbe had flirted with the notion of putting a tricolor across Africa, by means of a band of French posts from the Atlantic to the Red Sea, and which had observed that the eastern Sudan was in anarchy, had thought the moment opportune to claim a position on the upper Nile.

Fashoda was the position chosen and Marchand was sent with a party to occupy the place. He started in the spring of 1896, crossed Africa's middle, reached Fashoda in July, 1898—that is a couple of months before Kitchener's victory at Omdurman—and ran up the French flag. Word of this reached Kitchener less than a week after he took Khartoum.

Any person of imagination must sympathize with both parties directly concerned in the incident: with Kitchener who had driven through an enterprise and conquered his foes, and who in his hour of victory met an unexpected snag which threatened to mar his hard-won triumph; with Marchand who had struggled for two years across wild country, reached the Nile after painful difficulties, occupied Fashoda as ordered, and now was in danger of ejection by superior force. There was no conflict. Diplomacy took charge and wisely avoided war. Marchand was ordered by France to withdraw.

Never was there greater disparity between the object of a dispute and the important interests involved. Fashoda was a peculiarly horrid place, once used as a deportation spot for Egyptian convicts. Few survived the climate. It was described as "Man's Hell; Mosquitoes' Paradise." Against mosquito attacks the local natives used a complete bodily make-up of ashes which turned their bodies gray or rust colored, "like red devils," according to whether they were poor people who painted themselves with wood ash, or the owners of cattle who could run to ash made from cow dung.

Fashoda had been abandoned by Egypt at the rise of the Mahdists. Previous to the Mahdists Egypt had only been there in occupation for sixteen years. Its natives would have been amazed to know what a stir their ill-favored burg was producing in far lands. The awkward incident produced by France's attempted grab and by England's reaction was officially buried when the name of Fashoda was altered to Kodok.

THE SCRAMBLE

THE SCRAMBLE FOR AFRICA WAS RARELY MOTIVATED, HOWEVER, BY Africa's charms or potential profits. Nor was Africa's strategic importance so manifest in preaviation times. The Scramble probably was not even motivated by a desire to civilize and improve backward peoples, though this was often the reason cited. I quote the lofty sentiment expressed by a citizen of one of the nations which sought African territory—you could parallel such bathos amongst any of the seekers, I daresay: "We wish," said the Englishman, Major Gray, "to extend empire through the enlightened agency of moral sway, of civilized institutions and Christian regulations, and convey to the hapless, the neglected, the enslaved the highest blessings which can dignify, improve and adorn man."

In the inner councils of nations it is probable that the desire to get possession of sections of North Africa was frankly based on the sentiment of that well-known animal, the dog in the manger.

There is no doubt moreover that the manger was in a mess. All North Africa was in disorder. Mediterranean Africa was flabby. There was deplorable anarchy all across the Sudan. A change of proprietorship was inevitable.

With Europe's arguments and near wars and diplomatic bargainings about North Africa this book is not concerned, except as regard their eventual repercussions in Africa.

TUNISIA'S FALL

ONE SUCH REPERCUSSION WAS THE ENTRY OF FRANCE INTO TUNISIA, which followed a train of diplomatic complications. It is odd that Tunisia, scene of one of Germany's great humiliations in World

War II, should have been the special object of one of Bismarck's malicious maneuvers. Germany deliberately used Tunisia as a tempting scrap for other nations to snatch at. Bismarck, we are told, chuckled when Tunisia became the source of ill will between France and Italy. In the course of the Berlin Congress which was, in Professor Shotwell's words, "the starting point of a new wave of colonial expansion by foreshadowing the impending partition of North Africa," Bismarck encouraged France's hankering for Tunisia. All this was some sixty-five years before the period in World War II when Germany's efforts to hold Tunisia for herself made daily headlines.

*   *   *

IN 1881 FRANCE OCCUPIED TUNISIA. THE COUNTRY WAS FEEBLE AND unhappy and in financial disarray, as I have indicated (see pages 516 to 518). The capture of Tunisia was an efficient rather than a dashing or romantic job. A tribe on the Tunisian-Algerian frontier had been misbehaving. This constituted a grievance and justified a punitive expedition. Diplomatically the moment was ripe. Italy might hop into Tunisia first. A French force, coming from Algeria, crossed the boundary. French ships appeared in Tunisian waters. The bey of Tunis was invited to think quickly, did so and accepted the unavoidable. Tunisia was a French protectorate.

Since 1830 when Algiers fell it had obviously been Tunisia's inescapable destiny to be taken over by some European power. Tunisia had fluttered and twisted this half century in the trap of circumstance. She had been weak and extravagant and let herself be badly governed. It is only remarkable that she staved off European domination so long.

Turkey, Tunisia's titular and slack overlord, made vague attempts to interfere with the French occupation, and, failing, took the ostrich attitude and pretended it had not happened, declining for many years to recognize the actual facts diplomatically.

As for the Tunisian population, after it was too late, they reared to indignant action, rebelled against the French and against the spineless bey who had submitted so readily and began a Holy War against the invaders. It came as a surprise to the French, who after the original and instant collapse had expected no resistance. There was some bitter fighting.

MOROCCO'S TURN

MOROCCO IN HER TURN WENT DOWN BEFORE EUROPE, BUT SHE WENT down in a prolonged display of fireworks. It was no overnight acceptance of her fate as at Tunis.

The final years of Morocco's independence were studded with "incidents" that excited the outside world, one of which was a sort of false overture for World War I.

"RAISULI DEAD, OR . . ."

THE FIRST OF THESE "INCIDENTS" WAS SEMICOMICAL IN CHARACTER, in that it gave origin to the flamboyant gag so familiar in the United States at the start of the century, "Raisuli dead or Perdicaris alive!" Mr. Perdicaris was an elderly American of Greek descent who had lived half of his life at Tangier. He was kidnaped away from his "luxurious country seat, 'Aidonia'" by Raisuli. Raisuli was one of the leading rebels of a decade when Morocco suffered on all sides from revolts, the attacks of pretenders and the contests of rival royal claimants. Raisuli—it was his *nom de guerre*—was a person claiming noble lineage, to descend from Mohammed, and to be of the family of the Idrisites, founders of Fez. He was, and with just cause, offended by the misgovernment of Morocco, and also offended—justly or unjustly —by the intrusion of Christian Europeans into his country's affairs.

His Holy War was unintentionally helped along by America. The threats of the United States demanding Mr. Perdicaris in good state or the scalp of Raisuli were backed by United States ships in Tangier harbor. Raisuli commented, "Now the sultan will be compelled to accede to my demands." In effect, Raisuli sold his American captive to the frightened Moroccan government for seventy thousand dollars plus very important privileges.

Subsequent naughtiness of Raisuli's toward foreigners brought French and Spanish squadrons to Tangier. These things, given the touchy state of Morocco's foreign relationships, were dangerous to general peace. The kidnaping of foreigners was Raisuli's specialty. Another whom he captured was the romantic Caid

Maclean. After seven months Raisuli sold this English captive for an even better figure than he received for his American prisoner—twenty thousand pounds. Raisuli's practices and Morocco's inability to discipline him gave the country a bad name across the world, though Raisuli was probably only seeking to finance a movement which he believed would save his country. Even Mr. Perdicaris described him as a genuine patriot.

CAID MACLEAN

CAID MACLEAN, THE TWENTY-THOUSAND-POUND CAPTIVE, WAS ONE of those figures about whom musical comedies are constructed. Being an English agent at a time of great Anglo-French rivalry in Morocco, he and the French were antagonistic. Thus we have quite conflicting accounts of this romantic person, according to whether we read of him in English or French records. One thing cannot be denied: Caid Maclean was the sultan's evil genius. He lost Abd-el-Aziz his throne. He hastened the fall of Moroccan independence. And all by introducing the young ruler to a few European diversions, such as football.

His detractors represent Maclean as a deserter from the Gibraltar garrison who set up as a trader at Tangier, became infantry instructor, then favorite of the young sultan, director of the royal "Amusement Gallery" and the sultan's athletic coach, teaching him boxing, football and even leapfrog. The English viewed him as a valuable agent, having great influence in Morocco. To the sultan's subjects his athletic training of their ruler seemed shocking vulgarity. Abd-el-Aziz got the contemptuous nickname of the "Sultan Mahboul" (The Mad). His European innovations offended many, but his personal behavior—football and so on— was the ultimate scandal.

The sultan, we must remember, was not only ruler, but the religious head of the country. In fact, to quote M. Martin, "to the inhabitants of Morocco their sultan is the caliph, the successor of the Prophet, whose authority extends by rights over all True Believers wherever they may live." To them he is the spiritual head of all Islam. Therefore a supremely holy personage. As well might pope or archbishop jump and kick up his legs in public as such a one as he. Caid Maclean's well-intended attempt to encourage Moroccan-English friendship by bringing the spirit of the playing fields of Eton to Morocco's palace did his pupil great damage.

THE "ROGUI"

THREE OTHER IMPORTANT REVOLTS BESIDES THAT OF RAISULI operated concurrently. The most important of all the rebels was "The Man on the She Ass" (Bou-Hamara), a supposedly saintly figure who proclaimed himself sultan under the name of Moulay-Mohammed-ould-Moulay-Hassan, thereby thieving the name of one of the reigning sultan's brothers. The pretender's career was dramatic and horrifying. In a nutshell it gives us a notion of the wild barbaric character of Morocco which—only a few miles from Europe—startled the prim continent of the very early 1900's. Europe did not then know its own capacity for barbarism!

"The Man on the She Ass" or *rogui* (local word for a pretender) built his popularity upon the unpopularity of the authentic sultan. The *rogui* nearly took Fez. In 1909 he was defeated and captured. His leading supporters were then punished in old-fashioned style. Some had the right hand cut off, or the left foot. The *rogui* himself was put into a cage—you can still see that cage in the Fez Museum—which was carried across country on camel back for people to jeer at. Then he was tortured slowly in the notion of getting him to give up the whereabouts of his treasure. The Consular Corps at Fez protested. The sultan then got rid of the family enemy by means not quite clear: Some say the *rogui* was burnt alive, others that he was fed to a lion.

SEVERAL SULTANS

MOROCCO—AS AN INDEPENDENT STATE WAS WRITHING IN HER DEATH agony. She died from within. In addition to several rebel chiefs and two pretender sultans, she knew two rival royal sultans, simultaneously attempting to rule. They were the already mentioned Abd-el-Aziz, called "The Mad," and Hafiz, often called "Shitan" (Satan).

Abd-el-Aziz had originally secured the throne by a trick, he being the youngest of the former sultan's sons. The trick was not altogether his fault; he was barely fourteen. An ambitious official concealed the death of the old sultan, caused him to appear to review his troops from a litter after he was a corpse, and pretended that the "sick" sultan—then many hours dead—had given orders that his young son Abd-el-Aziz should be his successor. The eldest son was imprisoned and eventually was seen no more, the presumption being that he had absorbed what is picturesquely called "bad coffee" in that part of the world.

Abd-el-Aziz was a good-natured youth, easily led to silly personal behavior and wild spending. His English-learned athleticism, his bicycles which he even taught his women to ride, his toy railway in the palace grounds, his billiard table brought on camel back to Fez from the coast, his harem in ostrich-plumed hats and ruffled silk dresses—Paris style—all these things disgusted Morocco. Also cost a lot of money.

Brother Hafiz was a person of another type, a conservative Moslem of the old style, learned in religion and a hater of foreign ways. Cruel too: it was his idea to feed the *rogui* to the flames or the lion.

Successively, and for a time simultaneously, these two ruled, or attempted to rule Morocco. The fraternal wars and intrigues lasted over half a dozen years.

*   *   *

THESE TWO SULTANS GAVE US OUR LAST VIEW OF THE PERSONAL rulership—the medievally personal rulership—of a North African state under an absolute despot. It is an interesting picture: the one, a childishly curious barbarian clutching at civilization's least valuable trinkets; the other, the old-style barbarian hating all "Christian trash." Both destined to fall before Europe's superior cleverness.

In other days Morocco could have wrestled through this disorder and maintained her integrity. North African countries had survived such rebellions and family rows in the past. But in the past there had been no European interference, or what there was had been frankly belligerent. Now the jealous and intriguing nations of Europe were on the spot, helping one local party or the other, lending money here and there, seeking to assure such an outcome as would protect their investments. Morocco was no longer secret. She was a fish bowl, and a fish bowl into which in-trusive fingers poked and prodded.

THE 1904 BARGAIN

1904 WAS A YEAR OF DESTINY TO NORTH AFRICA. A BARGAIN WAS made in the spring of that year between England and France with respect to Egypt and Morocco. France agreed not to obstruct Great Britain in Egypt "by asking that a limit be fixed for the British occupation or in any other manner." England agreed not to inter-fere henceforth with French action in Morocco.

Ever since England had gone into Egypt in 1882 and defeated the leader of the "Egypt for the Egyptians" movement, Egypt had been fuming and the outside world, especially France, had been nagging and sneering because England's self-styled "temporary occupation" was prolonged. "What is France doing to bring the British occupation of Egypt to an end?" stormed Deputy Mil-lerand after fourteen years had passed. The ministerial reply was "evasive," according to press reports.

In Morocco, France, which felt herself especially suited to step in since she was already established alongside in Algeria, had been hampered by England's rivalry.

After the Anglo-French 1904 bargain there had been optimists in each nation who could dream ambitiously without fear of obstruction from the other. France's optimists foresaw a wide French empire in the west corner of North Africa—Tunis to the Atlantic, Mediterranean to the Niger and beyond. There may have been high romantic patriots in England who saw a vision of an English empire including the Grandmother of Nations, of an eventual English Augustus on the Nile. Meanwhile Lord Cromer, so haughty that the English in Egypt privately called him "The Lord Almighty," and proud, pompous and gorgeous Lord Kitchener, with his gold plate dinner service, were satisfactory harbingers.

In those days a strong Europe could dream splendid dreams. And could implement her dreams with expensive practical and benevolent effort. Egypt and Morocco have received uncountable material benefits from England and France. We must remember this when—as happens sometimes these days—we are told that the 1904 agreement was a callous exchange. We also must remember that in Morocco in 1904, as in Egypt when the English first moved in, the local situation was deplorable, and foreign interference from some nation or other a certainty.

"NO PLACE IN THE SUN"

GERMANY AFTER A PERIOD OF COGITATION BECAME ANGRY AT THE Anglo-French deal in so far as it concerned Morocco, although at the time it was made she had seemed contented. Germany had been a latecomer in the North African Scramble, inclined to view North Africa condescendingly. Bismarck waggled Tunisia in a patronizing way before the greedy eyes of Italy and France, as has been mentioned, and maintained that Germany had no political interest in Morocco. All this changed in the early twentieth century. And we have seen it change yet more drastically with a Hitlerian Germany which announced that Africa was an integral part of Europe.

Germany's late entry into the North African Scramble seems curious in view of the interest taken in the continent by individual German explorers. Germans in the nineteenth century did perhaps the most brilliant work of all the nations in African investigation. The wonder man, Barth, was a German, although his modest expenses were footed by England. (The whole cost of his extraordinary journey was sixteen hundred pounds, of which Barth himself paid two hundred.) Rohlfs was German. So was Nachtigal. Schweinfurth, though born in Russia, was of German parentage, education and affiliations. Schweinfurth had the distinction of telling the world something definite about two races which had been a puzzle since antiquity: the "Men with Tails," so supposed—the Niam-Niam—and the African pygmies, told of by Homer and famed in yet earlier times as the dancing dwarfs which Egypt imported. Schweinfurth actually brought a pygmy alive almost all the way home from Equatorial Africa, but his four-foot, seven-inch light brown Akka, named Nsewue, died near Egypt from overeating.

Nor had the work of Germany's explorers been at all times

purely scientific and nonpolitical. Rohlfs tried to get Zanzibar
for Germany in 1885. Nachtigal's great journey was motivated by
a political mission. He was entrusted with German gifts sent by
King William, later emperor, to the sultan of Bornu, and performed the early part of his travels with "a great crimson velvet
throne with richly gilded legs, life-sized portrait of King William,
Queen Augusta and the Crown-Prince, and a harmonium" all
strapped to camels' backs.

Later Nachtigal acted as German agent on the west coast. In
1884 he appeared with the war boats, *Moewe* and *Elisabeth* off
the shores of what is now French Guinea, offering presents from
the emperor to the Negro chiefs, but did not—in view of France's
position—succeed in his propositions to set up a German protectorate. His behavior gave great offense to France—"incorrect,"
it was called (Arcin, *Histoire de la Guinée Française*). Also to England, one of whose historians (Robert Brown, *The Story of Africa
and its Explorers*) describes Nachtigal as a truculent official, attempting to make treaties with black kings who had only the
faintest idea what it was all about when they signed their cross,
and did not know that the German flags he gave them were "any
more sacred than any other piece of particolored clout." These
sneers show British bitterness about the Nachtigal effort.

As a matter of fact, treaty making in those days in Negro Africa
was often a farce, whatever European nations were involved. Consider this passage from Sir Harry Johnston's autobiography, in
which he tells of his experiences when he was "concluding treaties
to confirm British influence" in the 1880's:

> I extracted a Treaty Form from my despatch box and three or four
> persons of prominence (or so they seemed) crowded into the canoe
> to make crosses on it with my ink; but the proceedings were alto-
> gether too boisterous for serious treaty-making. . . . After the
> crosses had been splodged on the Treaty-Form and I had made my
> present of cloth and beads . . . we resumed paddling.

Another comical story of the lengths to which international
rivalry went in Africa is told by General Gouraud. Just before
the Convention of 1898 and when the so-called "Struggle for Influence" was almost fantastic along the middle Niger, two little
parties, one French, one English, met at a point of minor value

which each wanted. The method was to mark localities claimed with a flag. While the two officers were politely discussing which really had got there first, a Senegalese *Tirailleur* swarmed up a tree, unnoticed, and attached the tricolor to one of its branches, then slipped down to his officer's side and whispered, "Me climbed up quick. Flag is up top!" It was such an absurd, yet touching, bit of loyalty on the part of the Negro soldier that the English officer could only laugh and yield the point. The Convention of 1898 stopped such nonsense.

THE TANGIER INCIDENT

IN VIEW OF GERMANY'S ACTIVITY IN TROPICAL AFRICA, WHERE HER holdings just before World War I had an extent of more than a million square miles with a population of over fourteen millions, her early indifference to Mediterranean Africa is puzzling. She had considered Morocco—all Mediterranean Africa, indeed— to have, for herself, a nonpolitical, a merely economic interest.

But suddenly, a while after the 1904 Franco-English deal had been made, Germany altered her stand. The next year there occurred the well-known Tangier Incident. The Kaiser on board the imperial yacht arrived at Tangier and made a discourse to the sultan's uncle who had come to welcome the visitor. Said the Kaiser, "I send greetings to the sultan in his quality of an independent sovereign," and he continued by expressing the hope that Morocco would go on as a country without international preferences and "without annexations" and stated that he considered the sultan "an absolutely free sovereign." Finally he warned the sultan against "reforms"—i.e. French innovations.

The natural effect of this pat on the back and this warning was to give the sultan self-confidence and make him uppish in his dealings with France. The German consul at Casablanca declared enthusiastically to his Moroccan friends, "Our two sultans are brothers!"

A year after the Kaiser's visit to Tangier came the international Algeciras Conference, a discussion of Morocco's position and future. This was something of a blow to France. Her agreement with England about Morocco and Egypt looked rather like a one-sided exchange.

CASABLANCA

INSIDE MOROCCO WAS TURMOIL. THE RIVAL SULTANS, THE PRETENDER and various rebel leaders were then fighting across the land. There was intense hatred of Christians. At Casablanca there was a massacre of European workmen who were operating a miniature railway in connection with port improvements. The little railway had especially riled the population who thought it a noisy affront on the part of the Infidels toward the near-by tomb of a holy man.

There followed pillage of the homes of Moroccans friendly to Europeans and of European establishments from which their owners had fled either to the consulates or aboard ships in the harbor. There were then only about three hundred Europeans living in Casablanca; now it is an almost purely European town in aspect, and a very important one.

A French naval vessel came promptly, landed a few men who were opposed, and subsequently bombarded the town, as did also a Spanish ship. Further French forces came. Soldiers were put ashore in force. It was the beginning of the conquest of Morocco.

It marked also the birth of Casablanca as one of the world's big cities. Casablanca till then had not played a very important role. Its medieval name was Anfa, said to be because aniseed, local name *anfa,* grew in the neighborhood. Edrisi gives it only passing mention. It was the Portuguese who christened it Casablanca, which Morocco adapted to Dar Beida. It had been grudgingly attributed as a port of entry for European trade (see page 519). Now "Casa" has nearly two hundred times as many Europeans as it possessed that day in 1907 when its ill-considered attack on the miniature railway workers provoked great events.

ANOTHER INCIDENT

IT WAS THEN THAT THE WORRIED PEOPLE OF MOROCCO CHANGED leaders. Adb-el-Aziz, "The Mad," has been thought to be selling the country to the Christians. Hafiz "Satan" hated foreigners. Section by section Morocco went over to Hafiz and in 1908 he was definitely proclaimed sultan. But disorder continued. Hafiz proved a disappointment. This erstwhile pious man took to drinking forbidden liquor, and was charged with the use of morphine. A new *rogui* (pretender) arose and was proclaimed sultan in the provinces.

Fez was besieged by rebels, and inside the city there was a demand that Hafiz should in his turn give place to another brother, Zein. Sultan Hafiz, whose "plank" had been a detestation of foreigners, was obliged to beg French help, and to thank the French general who came to save him. Fez was even hung with flags in honor of the Infidels!

There followed another incident with Germany. It was that which occurred at Agadir on the Atlantic coast of South Morocco when the German vessel, *Panther,* appeared to "protect German interests," that is to stake out a claim to part of coastal Morocco and to balk the French occupation which looked to be imminent.

*   *   *

A GREAT WAR SEEMED VERY CLOSE AT THAT MOMENT (SUMMER, 1911)—almost unavoidable. But it was averted by various diplomacies and by feeding a hunk of Central Africa into the German maw. So Agadir, which had passed through many hands during the ages, remained a part of the sultan's shaky empire.

To forswear Agadir and the adjoining territory was something of a loss to Germany. Agadir was a site of potential value. From Hanno, the Carthaginian hero of the Periplus, to the Kaiser, Agadir's importance had been appreciated. Its present name, Agadir, was given to it by the Phoenicians and meant "a fortified place for storing grain." In between Hanno's time and the Kaiser's the place had answered to many other names, a sure indication that a series of different peoples had in turn recognized the value of its situation. It was presumably the same as the Roman Portus Risader; it was sometimes called Founti; Leo Africanus wrote of it as Guerguessem; the Portuguese called it Santa Cruz. It was also known by the nickname of Bab Sudan, gateway to the Sudan (via the desert). Long before the *Panther's* threatening visit to its harbor there had been a plan advanced for England to buy Agadir for an annual stipend and thus "command the whole commerce of the Sudan at the expense of Tunis, Tripoli, Algiers and Egypt." It was one of the few promising harbors on an inhospitable coast.

Germany can be presumed to have given up her claim reluctantly and with the idea of trying again soon in another fashion.

THE FRENCH PROTECTORATE

THE FRENCH PROTECTORATE WHICH GERMANY HAD SOUGHT TO impede followed (1912). In vain did Hafiz snarl when the treaty was presented.

The grand vizier who had been in Europe spoke: He had seen the Christians, their military strength, their industrial organization. He had seen the eminent position taken by France, which had been able to make a bargain for England's withdrawal from the Morocco race, to gain the German consent to French aims, and the Italian renunciation, and which could afford to ignore Spanish hesitations in the matter. (Spain's small holdings in Morocco were not directly affected, of course, by the proposed protectorate, but Spain was slow in giving approval.) "The other tribes of Christians," added the grand vizier, "were indifferent to what happened in Morocco." [18]

So the great Sharifian seal was put upon the treaty.

Some weeks later Hafiz abdicated. They say his last official act was to smash in pathetic fury the royal umbrella, symbol of his lost power. Still another brother from this providentially prolific family became sultan. He was Yusuf, a docile and biddable prince.

REBIRTH OF LIBYA

EXCEPT FOR THE TRIPOLI REGION AND SOME INSIGNIFICANT SCRAPS of the hidden interior, all Africa from the Mediterranean to the Niger, and from the Red Sea to the Atlantic was under or hovering on the verge of Christian dominion.

Tripoli dangled on the limb. It was a Turkish possession, but Turkey was then feeble. Some European nation would get Tripoli and would get it soon. Italy reached for her gun.

There had been an understanding between Italy, France and England that this should be Italy's share when the time came. It was now suspected that Germany, after her disappointment in

[18] A. G. P. Martin, *Quatre siècles d'histoire marocaine* (Paris, 1923).

Morocco, might leap into Tripoli. Italy therefore not only reached for her gun, but fired it off with a suddenness that surprised the world. Italy declared war upon Turkey and instantly invaded Africa. Less than two months later (November, 1911) she was able to announce that Tripolitania and Cyrenaica were "definitely and irrevocably put under the complete and absolute sovereignty of Italy."

The reason given for the attack on Turkish territory was very shadowy. So shadowy that great play had to be made of a grievance about a sixteen-year-old Italian maiden, Giulia Franzoni, who was "fraudulently abducted from her family of honest laborers employed by the Ottoman railroad works of Adana (Turkey), seized, converted by force to the Moslem faith and married by violence to a Mohammedan." This incident, though deplorable, did not seem to the outside world an adequate cause for war.

But Giulia's unlucky and sordid romance launched far, far more ships than did that of Helen of Troy, if we include—as we reasonably may do—the whole sequence of events involved with Italy's African adventures from 1911 through to the end of World War II.

The unprovoked and unexpected attack on the Tripoli coasts vaguely shocked the Christian world. But nothing was done about it by the nations of Europe. Egypt's sympathy would have been translated into action but for England's strong hand. Algerians and Tunisians sent money to their Tripolitan coreligionists. Some Tunisians wanted to join the fight. But Tripoli slid with docility from one yoke to another, from the Turkish overlord to the control of Italy. Tripoli had rarely shown independence of spirit. A year after the invasion it was—or then seemed to be—all over. Turkey formally renounced Tripoli. Soon Italy had pushed deep into the Sahara to Ghadames and Fezzan.

The new Italian colony was called Libya. The name by which all Africa except Egypt had been known in remote days had come back to the map.

*   *   *

WITH THIS THE CHRISTIAN CONQUEST OF NORTH AFRICA WAS COMplete. The movement begun in 1830 when France took Algiers had been concluded. Church bells were free to ring across all the land.

SUBMISSIVE COLONIES AND
GOOD WOMEN

TO THE OUTSIDE WORLD, NOT ASSOCIATED WITH ITS MANAGEMENT, A colony is really interesting only twice in its career: at the moment of its conquest and at the moment when it breaks away. A submissive colony or one whose revolts come to nothing is like a good woman—it has no history of consequence to outsiders.

It would be undesirable for me to try to tell of the various manifestations of loyalty and of dissatisfaction across North Africa after it became a place of colonies and protectorates.

It would be equally undesirable to indicate the many splendid things done to improve what used to be barbarous and semibarbarous lands. North Africa has been reformed and modernized by Frenchmen, Englishmen, Spaniards and for a little while by Italians. To us it has seemed an admirable, often a noble accomplishment.

North Africans themselves have watched with mingled sentiments the efforts of these outsiders who knew so much and were so able and ready to change traditional African ways. Some of those who approved the changes had demanded, "But, if we had been left alone, who is to say that we might not have modernized our lands by ourselves?" Some natives of wide vision watched Europe's work with joy, and co-operated. France seems to have been particularly happy in her dealings with the native mentality, as I can testify, having seen almost every important locality in French North Africa from the Mediterranean to the Niger. But even the French relationship with Africa has several ugly patches to show.

*   *   *

FROM THE VARIOUS REACTIONS AGAINST EUROPE'S INTERFERENCE I shall choose two examples as typical and tell of them in some detail. They involve all four of the European nations who have come into North Africa, and represent the two classes of opposition Europe has met and will meet in North African management: the religious agitation, and the agitation caused by a brilliant individual. Though neither revolt was successful, both were concerned with names which have lately become again news. The two examples I have chosen are the resistance of the Senussi and the Riff revolt under Abd-el-Krim.

SENUSSI

BEFORE WORLD WAR II ALMOST NOBODY OUTSIDE AFRICA HAD heard of the Senussi. Suddenly their name became familiar to newspaper readers. Those of us who knew of them of old were surprised to see how the Senussi had changed their face. They had been regarded always as fanatical enemies. All at once they were transformed into splendid patriots. Now they were on Our Side!

The Senussi were not, as some hurriedly got up newspaper accounts would have it, "a tribe." No more than Freemasons or Christian Scientists are a tribe. The Senussi organization is made up of many races and skin tints—several millions of them. It is a religious organization powerful across all North Africa and elsewhere, which went into politics and eventually into war. During World War I the Senussi were opponents of the Allies. During World War II they were our very useful friends. They claim to the rulership of all Libya. Their directorship is a hereditary office, descending through the family of the organization's founder.

The founder [19] was Sayed-Mohammed-ibn-Ali-el-Senussi (1787-1859), an Algerian who saw and bitterly resented the French occupation of his country. He claimed, it need hardly be said, descent from Mohammed; he was a very learned person by Mohammedan standards, and a born leader of men. A prominent part of his teaching was the detestation of all Christians, Jews,

---

[19] The earliest firsthand account of the Senussi is Duveyrier's, from information acquired in the early 1860's. The *Acadèmie des Sciences* published a fuller account in 1884. I particularly like, however, a biography of the founder by Cheikh Mohammed-ben-Otsmane-el-Hachaichi, from information collected in 1896 (*Voyage au pays des Senoussi*). See also Appendix B of Rosita Forbes's *The Secret of the Sahara: Kufra,* and the work of her associate in exploration, the Egyptian, Hussanein Bey, author of *The Lost Oases.* Hussanein is especially qualified to tell about the Senussi, having visited their headquarters twice and having dealt with them when secretary to a European mission that made a treaty with the Senussi shortly after World War I.

or even of those who were under foreign domination or influence. Our sort of civilization was to him a crime.

Seeking air that had never been and did not then seem likely to be polluted by the Europeans he founded communities for his followers near the frontier between Cyreñaica and Egypt. But presently the Senussi moved farther from the distasteful proximity of the Turks, a hatred of whom was also part of their tenets, and went to Jaghbub in the desert. The new site was a wretched place, having only one well of bitter water, and soil so hard that in order to dig more wells it was necessary to blast with dynamite. Hard work made the place habitable. In 1894 the son and successor of the founder, Sidi Mohammed-el-Mahdi, moved the Senussi center yet farther into the wilderness to the mysterious and impenetrable oasis of Kufra.

The Senussi fraternity grew rapidly; it had more authority than the Turkish overlords; its membership spread across all Mediterranean Africa and as far as Lake Chad, also to places outside Africa. The order was very rich. Its members contributed two and a half per cent of their *capital* every year.

Such prodigal contributions prove that the members found the organization was of very great practical value to them. The Senussi tamed the eastern Sahara and developed a new trans-Saharan caravan route passing through Kufra. Senussi members secured virtual monopoly of the slave trade, which could no longer use other routes because of the French. Another valuable line of Senussi business was arms importation from Europe for the hinterland of Africa. Caravans of colossal proportions passed through Kufra. "A man could walk for half a day from one end of a caravan to the other!" was the reminiscent boast made in the hearing of Hussanein Bey.

KUFRA

As a capital for an organization which desired no dealings with foreigners Kufra was ideal. It was one of the most isolated habitable places on earth. Kufra is an oasis group lying some three hundred miles in every direction from any inhabited place. It is seven days from the nearest well. Any attempted approach by undesirables could be immediately checked by Senussi guards.

The explorer, Rohlfs, got there, but was so mishandled as only to increase Kufra's reputation as unattainable. During the days of the Senussi dominion no other Europeans saw Kufra except two European prisoners dragged there after battle, and later Rosita Forbes.

At Kufra the Senussi chief sat in the center of his web and directed the native policy of a vast territory. The life of the chief and his staff is like something out of *Atlantide* or a Rider Haggard romance. Kufra had been turned into a hidden wonderland. "My day began with the arrival of an immense bowl of roses"— gift from a local notable, writes Hussanein Bey. Rosita Forbes, as a Senussi guest at Kufra, sat down before a meal of "twelve dishes of lamb cooked in different rich sauces and a score of poached eggs on silver plates with fifteen vegetables."

A Tunisian Moslem, Sheikh Otsmane-el-Hachaichi, gives a charming picture of life in the inner Senussi circle: the brothers, so called, beautifully appareled in silks from India and cloth from Tunis, their bodies perfumed with the essences of flowers and their clothing scented with amber. They consulted him on a delicate point. They had received some cologne from Tunis and hesitated to use it, though tempted—it being a foreign product. The Sheikh reassured them, saying many good Moslems in his country regarded cologne as "pure."

The Senussi library was notable—more than eight thousand books. "They do not print in the whole world," says the sheikh naïvely, "a single book but that these savants seek to procure it!" Some of the brothers knew by heart twenty thousand verses of poetry!

*   *   *

ALTHOUGH THE DETAILS I HAVE CITED DO NOT BEAR IT OUT, THE original teachings of Senussism had included puritan simplicity. Wine, coffee, tobacco were forbidden. It was rumored, but it is hard to believe, that if a man's sleeve but smelt of stale smoke, his hand would be cut off. One stimulant only was permitted—tea. The good sheikh sets down a long poem in praise of tea which he heard recited at an evening reunion. Part of it:

> Drink tea without fear; its use is permitted, and none can blame you,

> Tea opens the door to the two best desires which nature
> has given to man: loving and eating.
> It holds back for lovers the moment of supreme voluptuous-
> ness, a delay full of delights. . . .

The joy of love was not a thing disapproved by the Senussi
puritans. When they were originally instructed to renounce the
world and forgo luxury in ornamentation, exception was made in
favor of the womenfolk since "such things augment their seduc-
tiveness."

RIVAL MAHDIS

SOMEWHAT LAUGHABLE TO THE NON-MOSLEM WORLD WAS THE
jealousy between the second and greatest Senussi leader, whose
given name was "Mahdi" and whom some regarded as a mahdi,
and his contemporary, the turbulent Mahdi of the eastern Sudan.
The eastern Sudanese Mahdi, the slayer of Gordon, sought to
profit by the renown of the Senussi chief and favored a partner-
ship of some sort between the two leaders who both hated Christians. The Senussi, head of a long-established sect, indignantly
refused any connection with his upstart Sudanese namesake and
snubbed all proposals. The Senussi El-Mahdi, incidentally, was
a white man, and so beautiful that he was surnamed "The Moon";
his rival in the Sudan was brown. Both groups attributed miracles
galore to their leaders. In this the Senussi had definitely the better of it, making the succinct but splendid claim that upon the
day of the death of their founder both sun and moon had an
eclipse.

THE SENUSSI AND THE CHRISTIANS

SENUSSI INFLUENCE AND PROSPERITY WERE GRAVELY THREATENED
by the coming of the Christians: the French push into the central
Sahara and central Sudan, the Italians into Tripolitania. The
latter was particularly disastrous—it menaced the outlet for slaves
and the incoming of arms.

The Senussi reacted vigorously from the start. It is believed
that they instigated the massacre of the Flatters Mission (see page
541), thus arresting the proposed Trans-Saharan Railway.

When the Italians set up their colony of Libya (Tripolitania-Cyrenaica) the Senussi laid low and watched their chance. It came with the outbreak of World War I. The Senussi became allies of the Germans and Turks, although to them the Turks were detestable, and the Senussi founder had cursed them in what was to him terrible language: "O Allah, see to it that whatever lands the Turks may occupy upon this earth shall be taken away from them by the Christians!" Germany gave help: money, arms, military advice.

The Senussi head was then a man of bellicose type. Under his leadership the Senussi engineered upheavals in the Sahara, Sudan and the Egyptian desert which troubled Italians, French and English during World War I.

The opening move was to chase the Italians out of the advanced posts in the Sahara which they had occupied in the first flush of their conquest of Tripolitania. The terrified Italian garrisons ran across the desert to the French for protection, leaving their arms behind them. This last was a joyous circumstance to the native resistance movement. The lost Italian arms were subsequently turned against the French and against such feeble efforts as Italy was henceforth disposed to make in Africa during World War I. For the time being Italy bade the larger part of her colony good-by and reduced her holdings to a few coastal points.

Continuing their policy the Senussi promoted such bitter fighting against the French as endangered French control of the whole mid-desert and required the use of troops needed on the European front. As a main instrument the Senussi used the Tuareg, those veiled wildcats of the desert. The Tuareg took little interest in the Senussi doctrines—the Tuareg not being greatly pious—but were easily inspired to fight the European intruders at a moment when Europe was preoccupied.

In December, 1916, occurred that dramatic and shocking episode, the killing of Père de Foucauld, the aged hermit and missionary among the Tuareg. To the French and to Catholics in general this seemed the wicked murder of a saintly old man who had given his latter years to the good of the Sahara's natives. But the Tuareg band which assassinated him viewed Père de Foucauld as a French agent and an enemy, and considered that his home was a little fortress and a storage place for arms.

At the exact same time came Tuareg trouble in the Agades region, also fomented by the Senussi. Had the Agades revolt succeeded it might not only have lost the French their holdings in the central Sahara and middle Niger country, but might also, in the opinion of Francis Rennell Rodd, have lost Northern Nigeria to the English. The siege of Agades lasted three months and resulted in a French win.

AGADES—MANNA TO SALT

AGADES, WHICH HAS NOT UNTIL NOW COME INTO MY PAGES, LIES IN the desert about eight hundred miles dead to the east of Timbuctoo. Its importance is relatively recent. The older Arabic geographers do not mention it, but in the sixteenth century Leo Africanus speaks of it in a curious connection. "Alongside Agades," says Leo, "falls manna which the inhabitants go out and collect of a morning in little baskets and bring in and sell fresh in the town." This seems to be the true manna of the Bible (Exodus 16:16 and following) which had to be picked fresh every day. Leo does not tell whether the Agades manna would keep good over the Day of Rest.

In our own times a more familiar food item has made the fortune of Agades. It is salt. Agades became the center for the salt traffic from the central Saharan salt mines, a great caravan place. Twenty thousand laden camels passed that way each year. In the first decade of this century Agades was occupied by the French.

World War I gave the opportunity and the Senussi gave encouragement to a revolt in 1916-17. The sultan of Agades, supposedly a French puppet, in combination with Tuareg—who had been incited by the Senussi and who were aided by arms abandoned by the Italians—rose against the French, making an unsuccessful attempt to bite the same hand that had raised him to the throne.

SENUSSI—A MAJOR ANXIETY

SIMULTANEOUSLY WITH THE DISORDERS WHICH THEY PROVOKED IN Italian Libya and in the French Sahara, the Senussi attacked the English in Egypt and associated themselves with revolts in the eastern Sudan. The then commander of the English military forces in Egypt stated that the Senussi peril was at the moment his "principal source of anxiety."

EGYPT IN WORLD WAR I

TO BE A MAJOR ANXIETY IN EGYPT AT THAT MOMENT WAS AN AC-complishment indeed. Egypt had never before in her long history seen such multitudinous and assorted troubles as she did during World War I—thrusts from without and tremors within. Her position was peculiarly awkward. There was war between the nation which was her actual master and the nation which was her titular suzerain and her religious associate.

The Turkish sovereignty was abruptly declared terminated. An English protectorate was openly avowed; the anti-English khedive deposed. A new ruler was appointed under a new title —Egypt had a sultan again after four centuries almost to a year (1517 to 1914). The romantic title was to endure only eight years. By the way, it is odd that during just over half a century (1867-1922) Egypt's rulers—all members of the family of Mehemet Ali, who himself wore the title pasha—operated under four different titles: vali, khedive, sultan and king.

Egypt made two attempts inside a few months to assassinate her new sultan. The population was suspicious, dissatisfied and disloyal. It watched the arrival of wounded from Gallipoli with a grin and destroyed railway stations and telegraph lines to show hatred of Christian innovations. Turkish attacks threatened to destroy the Suez Canal. There was an uprising in the eastern Sudan and an invasion aimed at Khartoum.

SENUSSI—FALL AND RISE

THE BELLICOSE SENUSSI LEADER ENJOYED A MOMENT OF GORGEOUS dreams. If his attack upon western Egypt succeeded he would— so his German mentors led him to hope—be ruler of all Egypt. But his attacks did not succeed. His German-trained Arab general was captured and he himself fled, first into the desert and then on a German submarine to Constantinople.

A new Senussi chief was appointed, the same Idris who became a prominent personage in World War II. Having judiciously greased the Senussi palm, England and Italy made a joint friendly agreement with Idris in 1917, and after the war was over Idris actually visited the king of Italy. Then came a quarrel. Italy had recommenced her effort in Tripolitania, so humiliatingly interrupted during World War I, and Italy saw that her colony was not big enough to hold both herself and the Senussi. So Italy tried to destroy the Senussi. In Derna's mosque, for instance, was read the announcement: "Orders have been received from the Italian government that all mention of the Senussi must cease. No one will be allowed to practise the religious observances of this sect."

Kufra, Italy saw, must be wiped out. A massive and grandiose expedition was dispatched—a very big fire to cook a very small bird. Kufra had only some five hundred men under arms; Italy sent seven thousand camels, thousands of camel attendants, three hundred trucks, a squadron of armored cars, twenty airplanes and three thousand or more soldiers. Kufra gave up in two hours.

Senussism seemed a dying cause. Then World War II; Senussism came back. Senussi influence was still valuable. At the call of Senussi leaders men from the Italian colony escaped into Egypt to help the British. There was a promise that, when the war was won, Senussi power would be restored. At his temporary home in Cairo Idris received newspaper correspondents. The Senussi had played their cards well.

Whatever may be their future, their story is of interest. The powerful career of the Senussi is typical of the—to us—abnormally important role held by religion in North Africa.

ABD-EL-KRIM

THE NAME OF ABD-EL-KRIM—WHICH MEANS "SERVANT OF THE Generous (God)"—is familiar to us. In the winter of 1946-47 newspapers spoke about him. He was to be allowed to return from a twenty years' exile at Réunion. Franco of Spain bitterly opposed the benevolent idea. As it turned out, Franco was right. In the summer of 1947 Abd-el-Krim, en route back from Réunion, escaped and sought refuge in Mohammedan territory, in

Egypt. His escapade made page-wide headlines in Paris. His supporters maintained that President Roosevelt had given Abd-el-
Krim courage by his alleged promise that, after World War II,
Morocco would be helped toward independence. In Morocco
there had been set up a "Franklin Roosevelt Club," whose members were old-time Abd-el-Krim partisans.

By all this we were reminded of Abd-el-Krim's leadership in the
Riff War, a very serious business in the 1920's.

The Riffian rebel leader was not one of those fanatical religious
types of which the history of North Africa shows so many and
which puzzle Christians who take religion with more apathy.
Abd-el-Krim's psychology was similar to our own. His motive
was ambition plus patriotism. He was first inflamed by a personal affront.

Abd-el-Krim viewed religion in the modern Christian manner,
with easy tolerance. As a young man he had so little repugnance to
Unbelievers that he went to work for the Spaniards in Melilla,
being employed in the Service of Native Affairs.

There it was that Spanish General Sylvestre treated this educated young Moroccan, son of the caid of a Riffian tribe, with brutality. Abd-el-Krim did not forget. The general had cause to
remember in sorrow. Alongside Melilla a few years later (1921)
the ex-office employee defeated his former employer in one of the
most painful defeats ever inflicted on a European army by a
native North African force. Spain lost in that disaster twenty thousand men, one hundred twenty cannon and uncountable other
items of war material, also four million pesetas in money given
to Abd-el-Krim for the ransom of prisoners. Spanish Morocco was
reduced to a coastal fringe.

The Riffians were drunk with success. Their country—a little
place in the high hills to the eastward of the Strait of Gibraltar
—had shown all Morocco, all North Africa, a point in how to deal
with intruding Europeans. Always ferociously independent, notable as pirates in the days of old, the high-spirited Riffians saw
themselves ejecting the Spaniards altogether, ejecting all the
Europeans. Abd-el-Krim's fame spread; in the Near East his
fancy portrait was shown, hacking the Christians of North Africa
to pieces. As head of the so-called Riff Republic he was not offended if addressed as sultan. He toyed with the notion of con-

quering Morocco and supplanting the actual sultan, whom Abd-el-Krim described as a squashy French puppet.

So had a great destructive impulse come out of a small seed: a personal injury inflicted on an ambitious, proud and vengeful man. It seemed typical of the Spanish adventure in Morocco which had in the past been often unlucky. Costly expeditions in the nineteenth century had gained but small rewards. Spanish Morocco remained scrawny and awkward, a difficult colonial child to raise. At one time the situation had been so unpropitious that a German financial group proposed to rent the Spanish zone, exploit its mines, and pacify or organize it—according to information reported by M. Maurois in his life of Marshal Lyautey. Just before World War I, however, Spain's holdings had increased. In 1910 it was worth while for King Alfonso to pay a visit to the little Spanish colony in Morocco. During World War I the Spanish zone was helpful to the Germans.

World War I caught the French protectorate in Morocco with one foot off the ground, so to speak. The protectorate was a new thing, two years old and opposed by much of the population. There had been a peculiarly bloody second revolt at Fez. With World War I the French needs in Europe demanded the withdrawal of many troops. Lyautey, with brilliance and infinite pains, set out to swing Morocco along on a shoelace. His method: to maintain outward appearances unaltered, no retirements from positions that had been captured, the keeping up of "the apparent contour of the occupation" while emptying the inside; the French army was to be "like a sucked egg behind its shell" (Lyautey's words).

Lyautey succeeded in holding France's new protectorate through the war years despite German propaganda which included gushing references to the Kaiser as "the servant of Allah" and descriptions of him as "El-Hadj (the Mecca pilgrim) William." Thus Lyautey won a marshal's baton though far from the war's principal front. A town, Port Lyautey, was named for him. Then came the Abd-el-Krim emergency.

In 1924 Abd-el-Krim, having humiliated one set of Christians, turned toward the French. This was no barbarian, fighting in medieval style. Abd-el-Krim had arms captured from Spain and imported from Europe. He made war in the European manner of the day; laid out telephone lines, built bridges. He had the aid of an able German deserter from the Foreign Legion, Klems, whom the Riffians called "The German Chief." A clever soldier who organized their army.

Rich Fez trembled as Abd-el-Krim approached, but his attack failed. Abd-el-Krim had to surrender. His final defeat was the work of Marshal Pétain. In 1947 while the disgraced marshal sat in his island prison off the coast of France, Abd-el-Krim was allowed to leave his island exile and a villa was prepared for his reception on the Côte d'Azur. But Abd-el-Krim slipped away to Egypt.

* * *

JUST AS THE SENUSSI TYPIFY NORTH AFRICA'S EXTRAORDINARY PRE-occupation with religion, Abd-el-Krim typifies the more normal, world-wide, national longing for independence. Both these elements combine to make up North Africa's unrest.

PART FOUR

The United States and Others

WORLD WAR II

WORLD WAR II MADE THE WORLD ACQUAINTED. TO THE FAR CORNERS
of the earth went news of African localities never before mentioned. Service men and women from almost every belligerent
country came to Africa.

We got to know Africa and Africa got to know us. There were
few North Africans who did not see with their own eyes some
phase of the conflict. World War II went everywhere.

On the Red Sea, up and down the Atlantic coast, in Senegal and
in the Sahara, as well, of course, as all along the Mediterranean,
Africans watched Christians killing one another. Though North
Africa's native population took little part in the fighting, World
War II will probably turn out to have been the most important
event in forming Africa's destiny since the Roman conquest in the
days of Cleopatra. World War II was the conclusion of history's
prelude in Africa.

It was characteristic of Africa's history, always peculiarly dominated by geography, that the last great drama should have been
set along the great East-West Road from Egypt to the Atlantic,
along that strip between the Mediterranean and the desert.

* * *

NORTH AFRICA'S FIRST IMPORTANT EXPERIENCE OF THE WAR (EXCEPT
for the naval tragedy at Mers-el-Kebir, Oran) was at the Egyptian
frontier. In the autumn of the war's second year Italy, a latecomer
in the struggle, began a massive attack. The frontier between
Libya and Egypt was to be the scene of six separate advances and

retreats: Axis forward and Allies backward, then vice versa, then repeat. It was a sort of macabre square dance on the sands.

The population upon whose territory the maneuvering took place remained as far as possible spectators. Speaking generally, the natives of Cyrenaica and Tripolitania, who made up Italy's colony of Libya, had little sympathy with Italy's effort. And Egypt, though helpless to keep her lands from being involved, announced formally her refusal to enter the war, thereby indicating how she felt toward the British effort. It was as if the fight were conducted in a requisitioned hall, whose owner was indifferent to the outcome. A most peculiar situation. The hall was badly damaged: Alexandria, Cairo, the Suez region, Tripoli, Benghazi and so on were badly bombed and rebombed. At one time Alexandria was only sixty miles from the battlefront.

THE OLD ROAD

THEN IN NOVEMBER, 1942, THERE STARTED ALMOST DAY FOR DAY two great marches into North Africa. One from the west, from landing places in Morocco and Algeria. One from the east.

*   *   *

THE MARCH FROM THE EAST TRAVELED ONE OF THE OLDEST ROADS ever trod by man. Its sand had been crushed by invaders, migrants, Jewish refugees, and Mecca pilgrims. If emotion could leave some trace in the atmosphere, that route would quiver beyond all roads on earth with remembered bravado, greed, terror and religious exaltation. From the days of the First Dynasty Libyans, we are told, went this way to ravage Egypt. Darius' Persians went over this road at the call of Cyrene's cruel queen mother. Over part of this road traveled Herodotus, Father of History, and first of journalism's great foreign correspondents. So too did Alexander, Cato, Sidi Okba and the conquering Arabs, the Fatimite on his way to take over Egypt and found Cairo, the Negro emperor with his golden escort, and a million other pious black pilgrims from the western Sudan—even our own eccentric kingmaker, General Eaton, rode this way.

Now an Italian army fled across this road—an army whose Duce only a short time before had been so sure of victory that he had shipped over a white charger to carry him triumphantly into Alexandria. (It is, by the way, odd that the two equine celebrities of World War II were both white!) A German army was fleeing too under the bitterly disappointed Rommel, who had trained his Afrika Korps in an artificial hothouse in Germany and who also had been very certain of victory.

A sober little British general was chasing them. With Montgomery went Sherman tanks from the United States.

It was one of the longest retreats in history. Too long. "Desert Fox" Rommel was able to get across the Mareth line into Tunisia with the remnants of his men. Those fifteen hundred miles were strewn with the skeletons of valuable war machinery and the bodies of the dead, marked with the ruins of native villages and of recently modernized towns. Great was the destruction of brand new and costly Italian colonial effort.[20] What happened, I wonder, to the eighteen hundred concrete houses built for eighteen hundred peasant families shipped out of Genoa to the new colony only four years before (October, 1938) at a cost to Italy of twenty million dollars? What happened to the eighteen hundred portraits of Mussolini with which these houses were embellished?

It had been a pathetically short dream of African empire. The reconquest of Libya after the Italian fiasco of World War I had not been completed until 1932. The conquest of Abyssinia—"stupefying" to the world, to use Professor Gautier's word—followed four years later. Italy had visions of capturing Tunis and Suez, and of absorbing Egypt. Now, as Montgomery's armament roared westward, it was all forgotten. A dark posterior sat again on Abyssinia's throne, and lucky were the Libyan colonists who had managed to get back to the motherland empty handed.

FRENCH FIGHT IN THE DESERT

To many of the pursuing army the sands were new. Some imagined that they were in something like the Sahara's depths. But the really deep Saharan exploits of World War II were exclusively a French campaign, in so far as the Allies were concerned.

[20] On colonial Italian effort see Jean Despois, *La Colonisation Italienne en Libye* (Paris, 1935).

Up from Lake Chad, Free French came across the Sahara, a total distance of more than three thousand miles, given the scouting operations and evolutions of the combat, to take Kufra, the old-time Senussi capital, Fezzan, the big and important oasis group, and age-old Ghadames away from the Italians and to join Montgomery. Their entry into Tripoli, the meeting place, in their battered trucks, the hurrahs of the British, crying, "Here are the Free French!" their own emotion at seeing again the Mediterranean whose waves washed the shores of their enslaved homeland, their amazement at being again hemmed in by city streets after years of roaming the wide desert tracking down the Italian foe—it all makes one of the most dramatic moments of the war.

Already another group of Free French had made high lights in the war, holding through sixteen days of hell to the post of Bir Hakeim on the Egyptian border until the region round them became "an ossuary of tanks," and delaying the Axis plans (May 26 to June 10, 1942). Their stand was called "a second Verdun." [21] The French were perhaps more bitter than any of the fighters in World War II's African campaigns—furious and hurt at heart, a little handful trying to carry a quivering flame.

But all those soldiers, allies and enemies alike, knew mental torture new to the warrior. War had gone into each homeland— a new element of horror. Win or lose in battle, a man might find at the finish that his country was but a shell and a ruin.

The old East-West Road had never in its thousands of years served such fighters as these, fighters whose task was so hard and whose hate was so bitter, fighters whose mental torment was so great.

THE NEW ROAD

AT THE SAME MOMENT ANOTHER ARMY THRUST INTO AFRICA FROM the west. It used a new road. No invader of North Africa had ever before pushed in deeply from the Moroccan and Algerian

---

[21] Felix de Grand'Combe, *Bir Hakeim,* 1945. On the Saharan operations which ousted the Italians from Kufra, Fezzan, etc., see Gen. Ingold, *L'Epopée Leclerc au Sahara,* préface du Gen. de Gaulle (Paris, 1945) and *Les Operations sahariennes du Tchad,* text of a speech made before the Société de Geographie, Oct. 21, 1945, by Gen. Ingold and published by the society.

coasts. In two respects the army from the west differed from that which came along the Old Road. Its soldiers suffered only the normal, age-old tribulations of warriors. *Their* homeland—I speak of the Americans—was unscarred and they could hope to go back and find it as they left it. But their route was infinitely more complex. Theirs was no straight and relatively simple drive. They made their way in a veritable maze, weaving over mountains and through gorges.

As landing places, or as scenes of combat, or as stopping-off places of one sort and another, nearly every town in Morocco, Algeria and Tunisia and most of the country between towns, was trod over by American boots and American tires. Reports told us at home of Americans in localities never before heard of outside Africa. Old Phoenician Mehdia of Hanno's Periplus came into the world press as one of the first landing places. Fedala too, which till then had been an unimportant little industrial port and bathing beach. Now it became the theme of a soldiers' song about "Stella, the Belle of Fedala," a young woman who was always hungry.

In Tunisia the campaign brought sudden fame to a quantity of unknown spots. I think I must have been one of the few persons, except Tunisians themselves, who had ever been to many of these villages sprinkled across interior hills. I feel confident that no other American slept at Pont du Fahs, say, before the army came—which I did, and also passed through Kasserine, all unsuspecting the tragedy and triumphs its near-by pass would soon be showing to the young men of my nation.

Kasserine must once have been a place of consequence. Under its ancient name of Cillium it was the scene of a military disaster in the days of Solomon, the eunuch general. In the near-by forests he was killed and his army totally lost—all this fourteen centuries before that grim February of 1943. In the Middle Ages it got the pretentious name of Kasserine, meaning Two Castles.

Medjez-el-Bab (Ford of the Gate) was a little better known than some of the World War II combat sites. Faid Pass, where happened what the war commentators described as "one of the only two major breaks through American lines during the war," was so insignificant that it does not figure on a large-scale civilian prewar map of Tunisia, where the small country is shown on the scale of eighteen miles to an inch. It is in the midst of hills in south central Tunisia.

THE MEETING PLACE

JUST FOUR MONTHS AFTER THE DAY WHEN ALLIED LANDINGS IN North Africa had been reported, soldiers who had crossed Morocco, Algeria and Tunisia met soldiers who had come from Egypt, across Cyrenaica and Tripolitania (Libya). The meeting place was again a spot of no previous consequence: Jebel Chemsi ("Sun Hill"), near a secondary road from Gafsa toward the Mediterranean. It was April 7, 1943. A few weeks later it was over.

THE THREE CONFERENCES

THE SWEEP OF ALLIED VICTORY IS SHOWN BY THE CHOICE OF PLACES for the African conferences. There were three.

The first, held two months after the invasion, was at the Atlantic port of Casablanca. Its distinguished members, including Roosevelt and Churchill, dared rest only their toes on a still-unconquered Africa. It was called by the President of the United States, "The Unconditional Surrender Conference" (January 14 to 24, 1943). Its period coincided with the start of black days in Tunisia for the Allies. At first the invasion had worn a rosy aspect. Morocco and Algeria were ours. We entered Tunisia. We were within ten miles of the city of Tunis. Rommel was falling back. Then came disappointments and reverses. Rommel had succeeded in getting the main body of his men over the frontier out of Tripolitania into Tunisia. Those sinister little places in Tunisia began to figure in grim headlines.

Ten months later (November 22 to 26, 1943), the Axis being a forgotten menace, the two leaders and others were free to meet at the opposite side of the continent, near Cairo, at Mena House, named after Egypt's traditional first king.

A third conference, a United States affair—Eisenhower and Roosevelt—was held at Carthage, Tunisia, in December, 1943.

Anywhere in Africa had become a safe place for valuable personages. The sites of the three *C* conferences took us back through time: Casa, modern; Cairo, medieval; Carthage, antique. They gave a certain additional grandeur to the African campaign.

The Allies had won a continent. Axis prattle of a united Europe-Africa was stilled. Axis losses, in this search for "A Place in the Sun" had been enormous. Churchill announced that only 638 men escaped from the debacle in Tunisia. Africa too had suffered badly, especially Tunisia. Tunis' water front was a complete desolation from bombing; other cities were crippled. Farms were destroyed. In one region 800 out of a total of 3000 were gravely damaged.[22] Struggling French colonists lost the work of a lifetime.

Tunisia also lost its bey, Sidi Moncef, who would not or who could not collaborate when Roosevelt sent him a kind letter of invitation, and who was after the victory deposed and exiled to France.

VICTORY PARADE AT TUNIS

A FEW DAYS LATER TUNIS, A CITY THEN NOT FAR FROM BEING THREE thousand years old and one of the most venerable operating capitals in the world today (far older than Rome; not so old as Athens), saw something new. Tunis was the setting for the Allied Victory Parade, reviewed by Eisenhower. In itself it was a glorious sight. In its implications it was tremendous.

American men and women of the army. British troops. Fighting Frenchmen with General Leclerc. Black Senegalese. Tawny Moroccans. And those almost human tanks which had fought so well. The streets were deep with crushed flower petals. Planes roared. Bands blared. Bagpipes shrilled. It was the Allies' first big victory celebration and—so an optimistic war correspondent wrote from Tunis that day—it "foreshadows others to come: Rome, Berlin, Tokyo." He predicted well. Victory in Africa was the beginning of the end of the Second Great War.

[22] For the Tunisian campaign as viewed by local eyes, see *La Guerre en Tunisie* by Comdt. Audouin-Dubreuil (Paris, 1945). After the victory the author spent a year roaming the battlegrounds, interrogating victims and local fighters and old colonists, reduced to living in caves and huts alongside the ruins of their erstwhile farms.

PRELUDE'S END

With that victory parade which Eisenhower reviewed let me bring Africa's prelude to an end.

World War II profoundly affected the world's attitude toward Africa. It also profoundly affected Africa's attitude toward the world. We found out that Africa, once coveted largely from diplomatic jealousy and just in case it might turn out to be of real value, had become—with the debut of long-distance flying—a continent strategically indispensable. Africa, on her side, made the invigorating discovery that the outside world, the European and American world, had desperate need of her.

Also she learned something else. The realization of her own value came to her coincidentally with a great surprise. In World War II Africa saw, displayed right under her nose, proof of the human feebleness and folly of those who had set themselves up as her tutors and masters, of those whom Moslem Africa—classing them together as "the Christians"—had viewed as supermen in the practical things of the world. Africa, lazily perhaps, had let herself depend on Europe, disgruntled at the loss of independence, but resting and avoiding responsibility—as often she had done before—by submitting to foreign leadership. Suddenly she saw this foreign leadership disintegrate. The immediate impression was a startling disillusionment and a flare of nationalism. Africa has seen the humiliation of the overlords on the battlefield; she has heard of postwar sorrow and disorder in the Europe of which she once stood in awe. No longer can Africa make the wistful remark with a sting in its tail: "You Christians know everything—except Allah!" Africa suspects that the gap between herself and the rest of the world may not be so wide after all.

North Africa's future is peculiarly problematical at a moment when all our futures seem clouded. Has Africa come to yet another turning point in her long, tortuous history? I have no prophecy to offer, nor—in the long life of continents—could any personal prophecy hope to ripen to its fruition while still it was remembered. Prophecy is the prerogative of prophets. *The* Prophet to hundreds of millions foretold Africa's eventual destiny, so tradition has it, in the words: "The Holy War, having ceased everywhere, will recommence in Africa (in the section we now call Tunisia) and tribes from all parts of the world will gather there." Another, and a queer, old prophecy was communicated to me recently. It is to the effect that Moslems will again rule Africa; then will come calamities; there will be the irruption of a ravaging race of savages. These are wild men whom Doul Karnein (Alexander the Great) imprisoned underground beneath a great iron cover, which at last has rotted away. This horde will "drink up all the lakes and rivers, eat all the food and make Africa one vast desert. Then Jesus will come and massacre the wild men. But soon Jesus will die at Mecca; the human race will cease to reproduce; the end of the world will come!" The Algerian student who dug this fragment from an old manuscript comments, "Ponder this fable wisely, and you may find wisdom."

*   *   *

FANTASY ASIDE, AFRICA IS INDEED THE CONTINENT UNGUESSABLE. We can divine something of the spasmodic strugglings of the two old continents, Asia and Europe, can foresee the continued impetuous, the turbulent vigor, of the young Americas and Australia. But Africa's spirit is neither young nor old and her possibilities are unpredictable. For all the burden of her long past and despite her recent generations of comparative lethargy, she is by no means sitting in slippered ease in the afternoon of her life. Rather she seems to be unjaded by the mighty adventures through which she has passed, to be relaxed and resting, fresh and juvenile, and capable of meeting a new destiny, to be—in the pretty phrase of the Orient—"perpetually a virgin." Africa is a land where there are many elements of especial uncertainty. To mention but one of them: the redemption of the Sahara could change everything.

Africa can afford to measure time generously for her past is tremendous and she seems ageless like a star. Her history may be only just starting and greatness may come to her again, so that she will be once more the world's bull's-eye, as in the days of the Pharaohs.

* * *

AFRICA'S CONTINUED PLACE IN HISTORY IS A STRANGE THING, FOR SHE is not a tame and pleasant stage for great events. Hers is no comfortable place of meadows and rivers, of green pastures dotted with cattle, of cool streams rich with fish; even a field of grain has been the occasional rare gift only in certain favored sections, or the reward of harsh labor. Her good lands, such as they are by Nature's gift, have framed a terrible desert, as the niggardly flesh surrounds the outsize pit of some wild fruit.

Perhaps in Africa's very awfulness has lain her attraction, the challenge which brought vigorous men and great deeds. Certain it is that to the scrawny dugs of this haggard land the dramas of history have clung—litter after litter—for seven thousand or more years.

Flick once again through the pageant of her past, see her romance and her wonder:

See the Pharaohs—thirty dynasties of them—poised in power by the Nile for thousands of years, perhaps through fifty centuries. See the sleek, slim Egyptian queens of antiquity, golden skinned, with long perfumed fingers and graceful lean bodies.

See the merchant princes of Carthage, rich and dour, tossing their own little ones to the flames to save their hides; Greeks in their brazen armor; light, neat chariots bounding over the sands; sturdy Roman soldiers clanking along indestructible Roman roads.

The magnificent Ptolemies: helpless child Ptolemies wiped out like flies; obese, old, ribald Ptolemies; a procession of wicked Cleopatras climbing one after another to the throne across a carpet of corpses. Arab warriors streaming across a continent on fleet, sinewy steeds; despots crouching behind locked palace doors, trembling at nightmares of the assassin's knife.

Fanatics and charlatans and sincere saints leading Moslems by millions to their deaths for some quibble of religious differentiation; the lost Christians up the Nile clinging pathetically to the faith of their forefathers; slaves dancing in the oases to the crash of the foot-long iron castanets that are called *keghrakeb*.

See the dark kings by the Niger, proud as lions; and the white kings that some call Jews, who reigned at golden Gana and tied their horses to a hitching post of solid gold. The little figure of Napoleon, the "Sultan el-Kebir," riding high on a camel beside the pyramids. Moroccan sultans and Egyptian khedives enthralled and seduced by costly foreign toys and trinkets.

Colonists burning with hopes of Africa's riches, shaking with fever; explorers perishing of thirst madness, dying with the bloated wounds of poisoned arrows; Frenchmen weeping at the sight of French heads hanging like butcher's meat on the hooks of the Bab Azoun.

And—this is prelude's final passage—see in South Tunisia, where once they hunted elephants for Hannibal's attack on Rome, American and German tanks that shake the ground; see American troops meet British at Sun Hill near Gafsa, which was a settlement for primitive man before History began.

ASHEVILLE, NORTH CAROLINA   PAU, FRANCE
1942   1948

APPENDIX

A NOTE ON READINGS ABOUT NORTH AFRICA

A FULL BIBLIOGRAPHY ON ALL THE SECTIONS OF NORTH AFRICA IN all languages from the dawn of history till now would, I estimate, take up a great many volumes.

Even a complete list of my own readings would be unwieldy.

There follows a selected bibliography in which I have listed items chosen from the various phases and categories of the literature touching the subject. The lists given attempt to be typical rather than even remotely exhaustive, and contain a few of the best examples of works from many languages and periods plus certain interesting rarities and oddities.

The titles are divided as follows:

I—Ancient authors and works
II—Arabic and Jewish writers and works, mostly medieval
III—Books originally written in European languages (English, French, German, Italian, Spanish, Portuguese, Dutch)
IV—Special articles in journals, learned publications, brochures, general reference books, etc.

In addition to works indispensable to the student I have included many travelers' records, from classical days to our own, for nothing is so valuable as the report of the man who was actually there. Also included are a few descriptive works of repute—such as Fromentin and Masqueray—which build up the picture, and even three novels: Demaison's French Academy prize-winning story of the conquest of Timbuctoo by Morocco, Academician

Loti's half-autobiographical tale of St. Louis de Sénégal when France was subduing the country in the 19th century, and a curious romance by Lucca, dating from 1737. The last I include because its fantastic representation of the Sahara and Sudan shows how abysmal was Europe's ignorance of inner Africa. For the same reason I list—by the soulless process of alphabetical arrangement it appears before all the rest in its group—one of the several hoax books on Africa, the widely read narrative of Robert Adams which fooled the public something over a century ago.

I. ANCIENT AUTHORS AND WORKS

Athenaeus, *The Deipnosophists*
Caesar's "Commentaries," supplementary books attributed to Hirtius
    on the Alexandrian and African wars
Curtius, *The History of Alexander the Great*
Dio Cassius
Diodorus Sicilus
Herodotus
Josephus
Justin
Pliny, *Natural History*
Plutarch's *Lives*
Polybius
Procopius, *De Bello Vandalico*
Sallust, *Jugurthan War*
Strabo's *Geography*
Virgil, *Aeneid*
        and
Old Testament: Exodus, Judges, Kings

II. ARABIC AND JEWISH WRITERS AND WORKS, MOSTLY MEDIEVAL

(Pursuant of my general plan for simplification I have thought it undesirable to encumber this list with the immensely long, full Arabic names of authors and complex titles)

Abou Zakaria (see Masqueray in List III)
Benjamin of Tudela

Edrisi
El-Bekri
Eldad the Danite
El-Oufrani
En-Noweiri
Es-Sa'di (author of the *Tarikh es-Soudan*)
Ibn-'Abd-el-Hakem
Ibn-el-Ahmar
Ibn-el-Athir
Ibn-Batuta
Ibn-Fadl-Allah-al-Omari
Ibn-Khaldoun
Ibn-Khordadbeh
Ibn-Said
Leo Africanus
Macrizi
Mahmoud Kati (author of the *Tarikh el-Fettach*)
Masudi
Mohammed-ben-Otsmane-el-Hachaichi
and
The Koran

III. WORKS WRITTEN IN EUROPEAN LANGUAGES

(English, French, German, Italian, Spanish, Portuguese, Dutch)

Adams, Robert, *Narrative of Robert Adams a sailor who was wrecked off the coast of Africa . . . and resided several months in Timbuctoo* (London, 1816).

Alford, Lt. S. L., and Sword, Lt. W. Dennistoun, *The Egyptian Soudan, its Loss and Recovery* (London, 1898).

"Ali Bey," *Travels in Morocco, Tripoli, Cyprus, Egypt,* etc. (Philadelphia, 1816).

Allen, Gardner W., *Our Navy and the Barbary Corsairs* (Boston, 1905).

Alvares, Fra João, *Chronique du Saint-Infant Dom Fernando . . . qui mourut au pays des Maures* (15th cen. Portuguese, trans. into French), edited by Virginia Castro y Almeida (Paris, 1934).

Amat, Charles, *Le Mzab et les Mzabites* (Paris, 1888).

Arcin, Andre, *Histoire de la Guinée Française* (Paris, 1911).

Audouin-Dubreuil, *La Guerre en Tunisie, 1942-43* (Paris, 1945).

Azurara, Gomes Eannes de, *Chroniques* (15th cen.).

Baikie, James, *The Amarna Age* (New York, 1929).

Egyptian Antiquities in the Nile Valley (New York, 1932).

A History of Egypt . . . to the end of the XVIIIth Dynasty (New York, 1929).

Bainville, Jacques, *Bonaparte en Egypte* (Paris, 1936).

Barros, Joao de, *Asie* (16th cen. Portuguese).

Barth, Henry, *Travels and Discoveries in North and Central Africa, 1849-55* (London, 1857).

Bassenne, Marthe, *Aurélie Tedjani* (Paris, 1925).

Bates, Oric, *The Eastern Libyans* (London, 1914).

Bazin, René, *Charles de Foucauld* (Paris, 1921).

Beazley, C. Raymond, *The Dawn of Modern Geography* (London, 1897, 1901, 1906).

Beechey, Capt. F. W., *Proceedings of the Expedition to explore the North Coast of Africa from Tripoli eastward in 1821-2* (London, 1828).

Bérard, Victor, *Les Phéniciens et l'Odyssée* (Paris, 1902-3).

Bernard, F., *Deux Missions françaises chez les Tuareg* (Algiers, 1896).

Beslier, G. G., *Le Sénégal* (Paris, 1935).

Bevan, Edwyn, *A History of Egypt under the Ptolemaic Dynasty* (London, 1927).

Binger, Capt. L. G., *Du Niger au Golfe de Guinée* (Paris, 1892).

Bissuel, Capt. H., *Les Touareg de l'Ouest* (Algiers, 1888).

Bobichon, Henri, *Mission Marchand* (Paris, 1937).

Bordeaux, Henry, *Henry de Bournazel* (Paris, 1935).

Boulger, Demetrius C., *The Life of Gordon* (London, 1896).

Breasted, James Henry, *A History of Egypt from the earliest times to the Persian conquest* (New York, 1912).

Brown, Robert, *The Story of Africa and its Explorers* (London, 1892-94.)

Browne, W. G., *Travels in Africa, Egypt . . . 1792-98* (London, 1799).

Budge, E. A. Wallis, *A Short History of the Egyptian People* (London, 1923).

Bunbury, E. H., *A History of Ancient Geography among the Greeks and Romans from the earliest ages to the fall of the Roman Empire* (London, 1879).

Burckhardt, John Lewis, *Travels in Nubia* (contains appendices giving excerpts from Macrizi, Ibn-Selim-el-Assouani. . . . London, 1819).

Burton, Sir Richard, *Personal Narrative of a Pilgrimage to . . . Meccah* (memorial edition, London, 1893).

Ca' Da Mosto, Alvise de, *Relation des voyages à la côte occidentale d'Afrique 1455-57* (Venetian travelers record first issued in 1507, trans. into Old French) ed. Ch. Shefer (Paris, 1895).

Caillard, Mabel, *A Lifetime in Egypt, 1876-1935* (London, 1935).

Caillat, J., *Le Voyage d'Alphonse Daudet en Algérie, 1861-62* (Algiers, 1924).

Caillié, René, *Journal d'un voyage à Temboctou* (Paris, 1830).

The Cambridge Ancient History (London, 1923-1939).

The Cambridge Medieval History (London, 1911 and following).

Certeux, A., and Carnot, E. Henry, *Contributions au Folk-lore des Arabes: Algérie Traditionnelle* (Paris-Algiers, 1884).

Channing, Edward, *The Jeffersonian System* (Chapter on the Tripolitan War), New York, 1906.

Charles-Roux, F., *Bonaparte et la Tripolitaine* (Paris, 1929).

Charléty, S., *Enfantin* (Paris, 1930).

Cobern, Camden H., *The New Archaeological Discoveries and their Bearing upon the New Testament* (7th ed., New York, 1924).

Cortier, Capt. Maurice, *Mission Cortier, 1908-9-10* (Paris, 1914).

Cromer, The Earl of, *Modern Egypt* (New York, 1916).

Daumas, Lt. Col. (later General), *Le Sahara Algérien* (Paris, 1845).

Le Grand desert (Paris, 1848).

The Horses of the Sahara (trans. by Hutton, London, 1863).

Delafosse, Maurice, *Haut-Sénégal-Niger* (Paris, 1912).

Les Nègres (Paris, 1927).

L'Ame Nègre (Paris, 1922).

Demaison, André, *Le Pacha de Tombouctou* (a novel—see introductory note above) Paris, 1927.

Denham, Major, *Voyages et découvertes . . . 1822-23-24* (Denham's story of the first Clapperton expedition, trans. from English) 1826.

Desplanges, Lt. Louis, *Le Plateau Central Nigérien* (Paris, 1907).

Despois, Jean, *La Colonisation Italienne en Libye* (Paris, 1935).

Dinet, E. (El-Hadj Nacir ed Dine), *Le pèlerinage à la maison sacrée d'Allah* (Paris, 1930).

Dubois, Felix, *Tombouctou la mystérieuse* (Paris, 1897).

Notre beau Niger (Paris, 1911).

Dubois-Yakouba, *Industries et principales professions des habitants . . . de Tombouctou* (Paris, 1921).

Durand, J. P. L., *A Voyage to Senegal* (London, 1806).

Duveyrier, Henri, *Les Touareg du Nord* (Paris, 1864).

Journal de route (Paris, 1905).

Ellis, A. B., *The Tshi-Speaking Peoples of the Gold Coast* (London, 1887).

West African Sketches (London, 1881).

Eydoux, Henri-Paul, *L'Exploration du Sahara* (Paris, 1838).

Faris, Nabih Amin, *The Arab Heritage* (Princeton, 1944).

Faure, Claude, *Histoire de la presqu'île du Cap Vert et des origines de Dakar* (Paris, 1914).

Flamand, M. G.–B. M., *La Position géographique d'In Salah* (Paris, 1913).

Forbes, Rosita, *The Secret of the Sahara: Kufra* (London, republished, 1937).

Foucauld, Vicomte Ch. de (later Père de Foucauld), *Reconnaissance au Maroc* (Paris 1888, reissued 1939).

Père de, and Motylinski, A. de C., *Textes Touareg en prose* (Algiers, 1922).

Fromentin, Eugène, *Un Eté dans le Sahara* (Paris, 1856).

Une Année dans le Sahel (Paris, 1858).

Gautier, E. F., *Le Passé de l'Afrique du Nord, les siècles obscurs* (revised edition, Paris, 1937).

La Conquête du Sahara (revised edition, Paris, 1935).

Moeurs et coutumes des Musulmanes (Paris, 1931).

Le Sahara (Paris, 1928).

L'Afrique Noire Occidentale (Paris, 1935).

L'Afrique Blanche (Paris, 1939).

Gibbon, Edward, *The History of the Decline and Fall of the Roman Empire* (London, 1776-1788).

Goes, Damiao de, *Chronique du Prince Dom Jao* (16th cen. Portuguese, trans. into French), edited by Virginia de Castro y Almeida (Paris, 1938).

Gorce, Pierre de la, *La Conquête de l'Algérie* (Paris, 1934).

Goyau, Georges, *Le Cardinal Lavigerie* (Paris, 1925).

Gouraud, Gen., *Souvenirs . . . au Soudan* (Paris, 1939).

Grey, Major William, *Travels . . . from the River Gambia to the River Niger* (London, 1825).

Gsell, Stéphane, *Histoire ancienne de l'Afrique du Nord* (eight vols., Paris, 1913 and following).

Hérodote (Algiers, 1915).

Haardt, Georges Marie, and Audouin-Dubreuil, L., *La Première traversée du Sahara en automobile* (Paris, 1923).

Hakluyt's *Voyages.*

Hardy, Georges, *La Mise en valeur du Sénégal de 1817 à 1854* (Paris, 1921).

Hitti, Philip K., *History of the Arabs* (London, 1937).

Hourst, Lt., *La Mission Hourst* (Paris, 1898).

Hussanein Bey, *The Lost Oases* (New York, 1925).

Ingold, Gen., *L'Epopée Leclerc au Sahara, 1940-43* (Paris, 1945).

Jackson, James Grey, *An account of the Empire of Marocco* (London, 1809).

An account of Timbuctoo with notes, etc. (London, 1820).

Jobson, Richard, *The Golden Trade* (1623, reissued Teignmooth, Devonshire, 1904).

Joffre, Gen., *My March to Timbuctoo* (London, 1915).

Johnston, Sir Harry H., *A History of the Colonization of Africa by Alien Races* (Cambridge, reissued 1913).

The Nile Quest (London, 1903).

Julien, Ch. André, *Histoire de l'Afrique du Nord, Tunisie, Algérie, Maroc* (Paris, 1931).

Labouret, Henri, *Les Manding et leur langue* (Paris, 1934).

Histoire des noirs d'Afrique (Paris, 1946).

Lander, Richard, *Records of Capt. Clapperton's Last Expedition* (London, 1830).

Lander, Richard, and Lander, John, *Journal of an Expedition to explore . . . the Termination of the Niger* (London, 1832).

Lane-Poole, Stanley, *The Barbary Corsairs* (London, 1890).

A History of Egypt in the Middle Ages (London, 1901).

The Art of the Saracens (London, 1886).

Cairo (London, 1898).

Lebel, A. Roland, *L'Afrique Occidentale Française dans la Littérature Française* (Paris, 1925).

Les Voyageurs Français au Maroc (Paris, 1936).

Leca, N., *Les Pêcheurs de Guet N'Dar* (Paris, 1935).

Lemprière, William, *A Tour from Gibraltar to Tangier, Sallee*, etc. (London, 1793).

Lenz, Oskar, *Timbouctou* (from the German), Paris, 1886.

Leyden, John, *Historical Account of Discoveries and Travels in Africa* (Edinburgh, 1817).

Loti, Pierre, *Le Roman d'un Spahi* (Paris, 1881).

Lucca, Gaudention di, *Memoirs* (a novel, see introductory note above), London, 1737.

Lugard, Lady, *A Tropical Dependency* (London, 1905).

Lyon, Capt. G. F., *A Narrative of Travels in Northern Africa, 1818-19-20* (London, 1821).

MacOrlan, Pierre, *La Légion Etrangère* (Paris, 1933).

Mahaffy, J. P., *A History of Egypt under the Ptolemaic Dynasty* (London, 1899).

Major, Richard Henry, *The Life of Prince Henry of Portugal, surnamed The Navigator* (London, 1868).

Margoliouth, D. S., *Mohammed and the Rise of Islam* (3rd ed., New York, 1905).

Marmol, *L'Afrique de Marmol* (first publ. 1599, trans. into French) Paris, 1667.

Martin, A. G. P., *Quatre siècles d'histoire Marocaine* (Paris, 1923).

Maspero, Gaston, *The Dawn of Civilization* (trans. from French), New York, 1922.

Masqueray, Emile, *Chronique d'Abou Zakaria* (Algiers, 1879).
    Souvenirs et visions d'Afrique (Algiers, 1914).

Mathuisieulx, A. de, *A Travers la Tripolitaine* (4th ed., Paris, 1913).

Maurois, André, *Lyautey* (Paris, 1931).

Meniaud, Jacques, *Les Pionniers du Soudan* (Paris, 1931).

Mercier, Ernest, *La Condition de la femme musulmane dans l'Afrique septentrionale* (Algiers, 1895).

Mercier, Marcel, *La Civilisation urbaine au Mzab* (Algiers, 1932).

Mézières, A. Bonnel de, *Le Major A. Gordon Laing* (*Tombouctou, 1826,* Paris, 1912).

Millet, René, *Les Almohades* (Paris, 1923).

Milne, J. Grafton, *A History of Egypt under Roman Rule* (London, 1898).

Mollien, G., *Voyages . . . aux sources du Sénégal en 1818* (Paris, 1820).

Monod, Theodore, *Meharées, explorations au vrai Sahara* (Paris, 1937).

Monteil, Lt. Col. P. L., *De St.-Louis à Tripoli* (Paris, 1894).

Morgan, J., *A Complete History of Algiers* (London, 1731).

Nachtigal, Gustave, *Sahara et Soudan* (trans. from German), Paris, 1881.

Naval Documents, United States Wars with the Barbary Powers, Vol. III (covering Sept. 1803-March 1804) Washington, D. C.

Park, Mungo, *The Travels of* . . . (reissued London, 1922), see Proceedings of African Association for original publication.

Pein, Col. M. Th., *Lettres familières sur l'Algérie* (Algiers, 1893).

Petrie, W. M. Flinders, *A History of Egypt from the Earliest Times,* 3 vols. (London, 1884-1901).
    The Making of Egypt (New York, 1939).
    Seventy Years in Archeology (London, 1931).

Petherick, John, *Egypt, the Sudan* . . . (Edinburgh, 1861).

Petherick, Mr. and Mrs., *Travels in Central Africa and Explorations of the Nile Tributaries* (London, 1869).

Pina, Ruy de, *Chroniques du Roi Dom Duarte*, edited by Virginia de Castro y Almeida (15th cen. Portuguese), Paris, 1934.

Pococke, *Travels in Egypt* (London, 1745).

Pottier, René, *Un Prince Saharien méconnu: Duveyrier* (Paris, 1938).

Poulet, Georges, *Les Maures* (Paris, 1904).

Puigaudeau, Odette, *Pieds nus à travers la Mauretanie* (Paris, 1936).

Richardson, James, *Travels in the Great Desert of Sahara* (London, 1848).

Robin, Comdt., *Le Mzab et son annexation à la France* (Algiers, 1884).

Rodd, Francis Rennell, *People of the Veil* (London, 1926).

General William Eaton: The Failure of an Idea (New York, 1932).

Roncière, Charles de la, *La Découverte de l'Afrique au moyen âge* (Cairo, 1925, 1927, 3 vols.).

Rostovtzeff, M., *A History of the Ancient World* (Oxford, 1930).

Saulnier, Eugène, *La Compagnie de Galam au Sénégal* (Paris, 1921).

Schonfield, Hugh J., *The Suez Canal* (London, 1938).

Schweinfurth, Georg, *The Heart of Africa* (London, 1874).

Seligman, C. G., *Races of Africa* (reissued London, 1930).

Shakespeare, William, *Antony and Cleopatra*

Shaw, Thomas, *Travels and Observations relating to Barbary* (London, 1738, trans. into French, edited by Maccarthy, 1830).

Shotwell, James T., and Deak, Francis, *Turkey and the Straits* (New York, 1941).

Slouschz, Nahum, *Travels in North Africa* (Philadelphia, 1927).

Soleillet, Paul, *Voyage à Ségou* (Paris, 1887).

Sparks, Jared, *The Library of American Biography*, Vol. IX, containing life of William Eaton (New York, 1844).

Speke, John Hanning, *Journal of the Discovery of the Source of the Nile* (reissued, London, 1922).

Stevens, G. W., *With Kitchener to Khartum* (London, 1899).

Sutherland, Wm., *Alexandrine Tinne een haagsch meisje . . . in Noord Afrika—Haar Leven en Reizen* (Amsterdam, 1935).

Tailliart, Charles, *L'Algérie dans la littérature française* (Paris, 1925).

Talbot, P. Amaury, *In the Shadow of the Bush* (London, 1912).

Tassy, Laugier de, *Histoire du royaume d'Alger* (Amsterdam, 1725).

Tauxier, Louis, *Moeurs et histoire des Peuls* (Paris, 1937).

Trotter, J. K., *The Niger Sources* (London, 1816).

Tuaillon, Georges, *L'Afrique Occidentale Française, par l'Atlantique ou par le Sahara?* (Paris, 1936).

Tully, *Narrative of a Ten Years' Residence in Tripoli in Africa from the original correspondence in the possession of the family of the late Richard Tully* (London, 1816).

Urvoy, Capt. Y., *Histoire des Populations du Soudan Central* (Paris, 1936).

Vecchi, Paolo de, *Italy's Civilizing Mission in Africa* (Florence, 1912).

Vuillot, P., *L'Exploration du Sahara* (Paris, 1895).

Wakefield, Gordon, *Lucie Duff Gordon . . . in Egypt* (London, 1937).

Waldo, S. Putnam, *The Life and Character of Stephen Decatur* (Middletown, Conn., 1822).

Weigall, Arthur, *A History of the Pharaohs* (New York, 1925-27).

Williams, Joseph J., *Hebrewisms of West Africa, from Nile to Niger with the Jews* (New York, 1930).

Windus, John, *A Journey to Mequinez and the Residence of the Present Emperor of Fez . . . for the redemption of British Captives* (London, 1725).

Winlock, H. E., *The Excavations at Deir el Behri,* 1911-31 (New York, 1942).

Wright, William, *Palmyra and Zenobia* (New York, 1895).

Young, George, *Egypt* (London, 1927).

Zeys, E., *Legislation Mozabite* (Algiers, 1886).

IV. SPECIAL ARTICLES IN JOURNALS, LEARNED PUBLICATIONS, BROCHURES, GENERAL REFERENCE BOOKS, ETC.

Gaudefroy-Demombynes, "Une lettre de Saladin au Calife Almohade" —in *Mélanges René Basset,* Tome III (1925), publ. through L'Institut des hautes études marocaines.

Levi-Provençal E., "Fragments inédits d'une chronique anonyme du début des Almohades (ditto, see item above).

Marcais, Georges, "Notes sur les Ribats en Berbérie" (ditto, see item above).

Motylinski, A. de C., "Chroniques d'Ibn-Saghir sur les imams rostemides de Tahert," included in Actes de XIVe Congres international des orientalistes (Algiers, 1905), Part III.

"Expédition de Pedro de Navarre et de Garcia de Tolède contre Djerba (1510) d'après des Sources Abadhites" (ditto, see item above).

Tinne, John A., "Geographical Notes of an Expedition in Central Africa by Three Dutch Ladies" (Liverpool, 1864).

Bulletin du Comité de l'Afrique française, 1905 (on German kaiser at Tangier).

Bulletin du Comité d'Etudes Historiques et Scientifiques de l'A.O.F., Publ. at Gorée, Sénégal and Paris, issues for 1921, 1923, 1929 (items on Mali by Vidal, on Gana and Mali by Delafosse, and a book-length account of Mali by Ch. Monteil).

Bulletin de la Société de Géographie, Paris, 1826, 1827, 1829, 1830 (items on Laing and Caillié, and the discoveries along the Niger), issue for 1870 (Nachtigal on the death of Miss Tinne).

Journal of the Royal Geographical Society, London, 1832 and 1844 (items on the Niger or Quorra, as then known, and Linant about the White Nile, and on Tripoli).

Outre-Mer, Paris, 1932 (G. Vieillard on Peuls).

Proceedings of the Association for Promoting the Discovery of the Interior Parts of Africa, I and II, London, 1790 through 1802 (items on Ledyard, abstract of Mungo Park's expedition, Horneman, 1797-98).

Quarterly Review, 1815-16 (sober review of the hoax book by Robert Adams).

1821 (review of Balzoni in Egypt).

1823 (on Clapperton and others, on Belzoni).

1825 (further on Clapperton; discussion. Are Niger and Nile the same?)

1828 (review of Ledyard's biography, items on Laing, Clapperton).

1829 (Niger discussions).

1830 (attack on Caillié).

Revue des Deux Mondes, 1938 (Nanteuil, René Caillié).

Revue Militaire de l'A.O.F., Dakar, 1932 (Capt. Péfontan, "Les Arma").

Revue de Paris, 1894 (Comdt. Monteil, "Tombouctou et les Touareg").

Société de Géographie d'Alger et de l'Afrique du Nord, 1905 (Lt. Charlet, "Les Palmiers du Mzab").

Tour de Monde, 1871 (Zarcher and Margolle on Miss Tinne).

Les Territoires du Sud de l'Algérie, 4 parts, Algiers, 1922-23 (Part III is composed of a 320-page bibliography).

BROCHURES

Augieras, Capt., *Sahara Occidental* (Paris, 1919).

La Pénétration du Sahara Occidental (Paris, 1923).

Barbet, Charles, *La Femme Musulmane en Algérie* (Algiers, 1903).

Basset, René, *Documents Musulmans, le siège d'Alger en 1541* (Paris-Oran, 1890).

Cortier, Capt. M., *Reconnaissance Ouallen-Achourat* (Paris, 1913).

Djebari, M., *Les Survivants de la mission Flatters* (Tunis, 1895).

Gayet, Al., *Itinéraire des expéditions de Jean de Brienne et de Saint Louis en Egypte* (Cairo-Paris, 1900).

Guerhard, Paul, "Les Peulh du Fouta Diallon" (from *Revue des études ethnographiques*) Paris, 1909.

Le Barbier, Louis, *L'or dans la valée du Sénégal* (Paris, 1910).

Levi-Provençal, E., *La Fondation de Fès* (Paris, 1939).

Margoliouth, D. S., *The Last Days of Fatimah* (Mélanges Hartwig Derenbourg), Paris, 1909.

Morand, Marcel, *Les Kanouns du Mzab* (Algiers, 1903).

Motylinski, A. de C., *Notes historiques sur le Mzab, Guerara* (Algiers, 1886).

Rohlfs, Gerhard, *Le Tafilelt* (*Comité du Maroc*), Paris, 1910.

Rosetta Stone, *Report of the Committee appointed by the Philomathean Society of the University of Pennsylvania* (1859).

Schirmer, Henri, *Pourquoi Flatters et ses compagnons sont morts* (Paris, 1896).

REFERENCE BOOKS

Géographie Universelle, Tome XI, *Sahara-Afrique Occidentale,* ed. Augustin Bernard (Paris, 1939).

Dictionary of American History, ed. James Truslow Adams (New York, 1940).

The Universal Jewish Encyclopaedia, ed. Isaac Landman (New York, 1942).

The Jewish Encyclopaedia, ed. Isidore Singer (New York, 1901).

A Dictionary of the Bible, ed. James Hastings (New York, 1905, 1916).

Encyclopaedia Britannica, 3rd edition, 11th edition, 1945 edition.

A New Standard Bible Dictionary, ed. M. W. Jacobus (New York, 1936).

INDEX

INDEX